The Changing Organization

The Changing Organization provides a multi-disciplinary approach for studying the management of change under conditions of complexity. Single-discipline approaches frequently miss essential elements that reduce the possibility of seeing coherence within a multi-agency organizational setting. Using a cybernetic 'living system' approach, Guo, Yolles, Fink, and Iles offer a new agency paradigm designed to model, diagnose, and analyse complex real-world situations. Its capacity to anticipate patterns of agency behaviour provides useful means by which the origin of crises can be understood and resolutions reflected upon. Scholars and graduate students in fields as diverse as management, politics, anthropology, and psychology will find numerous applications for this book when considering socio-political and organizational change. It offers an invaluable guide for consultants who may wish to apply advanced techniques of contextual analysis to real-world situations.

KAIJUN GUO is Director of Strategy and Associate Chairman at the Baoshang Bank in China. He has a doctorate in Management from Liverpool John Moores University and post-graduate teaching experience. He also has Asian responsibility for the Centre for the Creation of Coherent Change and Knowledge, based at Liverpool John Moores University.

MAURICE YOLLES is Professor Emeritus in Management Systems at Liverpool John Moores University, and has main interests in social cybernetics. He heads the Centre for the Creation of Coherent Change and Knowledge. Within this context, he has also been involved in and is responsible for a number of international research and development projects in Europe and Asia. He has published three other research books, with another currently in preparation, as well as innumerable academic papers in peer reviewed journals. He is also the Coeditor of the *Journal of Organizational Transformation and Social Change*, with Paul Iles

GERHARD FINK is a retired Jean Monnet Professor. During 2002–2009, he was the Director of the doctoral programmes at Vienna University of Economics and Business, Austria; and the Director of the Research Institute for European Affairs during 1997–2003. His current research interests are in cybernetic agency theory, normative personality, organizational culture, and cultural change in Europe. He has about 290 publications to his credit. He was editor and guest editor of numerous journals; among others, in 2005 he was guest editor of the *Academy of Management Executive*, and in 2011 he was guest editor of *Cross Cultural Management: An International Journal*.

PAUL ILES is a retired Professor of Leadership and HRM from Glasgow School for Business and Society, Glasgow Caledonian University. Previous appointments have been at Salford, Leeds Metropolitan, Teesside, Liverpool John Moores, and the Open universities. He is a chartered psychologist, Associate Fellow of the British Psychological Society, and Chartered Fellow of the CIPD. He has a particular interest in leadership development, international HRM and talent management, publishing many articles on these issues in leading refereed journals. Paul has designed and delivered leadership and change programmes in the public, private, and voluntary sectors, and worked on applied research programmes with the Learning and Skills Council, British Council, and Standards Board for England.

The Changing Organization
Agency Theory in a Cross-Cultural Context

Kaijun Guo
Director, Baoshang Bank, Beijing
Maurice Yolles
Liverpool John Moores University
Gerhard Fink
Vienna University of Economics and Business
Paul Iles
Glasgow Caledonian University

CAMBRIDGE UNIVERSITY PRESS

CAMBRIDGE
UNIVERSITY PRESS

University Printing House, Cambridge CB2 8BS, United Kingdom

Cambridge University Press is part of the University of Cambridge.

It furthers the University's mission by disseminating knowledge in the pursuit of education, learning, and research at the highest international levels of excellence.

www.cambridge.org
Information on this title: www.cambridge.org/9781107146808

© Cambridge University Press 2016

This publication is in copyright. Subject to statutory exception and to the provisions of relevant collective licensing agreements, no reproduction of any part may take place without the written permission of Cambridge University Press.

First published 2016

A catalogue record for this publication is available from the British Library.

Library of Congress Cataloguing-in-Publication Data
Names: Guo, Kaijun, author. | Yolles, Maurice, author. | Iles, Paul, author. | Fink, Gerhard, author.
Title: The changing organization : agency theory in a cross-cultural context / Kaijun Guo, Director, Baushang Bank, Beijing, Maurice Yolles, Liverpool John Moores University, Gerhard Fink, Vienna University of Economics and Business, Paul Iles, Glasgow Caledonian University.
Description: 1 Edition. | New York : Cambridge University Press, 2016. | Includes bibliographical references and index.
Identifiers: LCCN 2016016757| ISBN 9781107146808 (Hardback) | ISBN 9781316600917 (Paperback)
Subjects: LCSH: Organizational change. | Organization.
Classification: LCC HD58.8 .G856 2016 | DDC 305.3/501–dc23 LC record available at https://lccn.loc.gov/2016016757

ISBN 978-1-107-14680-8 Hardback

Cambridge University Press has no responsibility for the persistence or accuracy of URLs for external or third-party Internet Web sites referred to in this publication and does not guarantee that any content on such Web sites is, or will remain, accurate or appropriate.

Contents

List of Figures	*page* viii
List of Tables	xi
Preface	xiii
Introduction	1

Part I The Agency — 19

1 The Cultural Agency — 21
   1.1 Introduction — 21
   1.2 The Configuration Approach and the Socio-Cognitive Approach — 26
   1.3 Viable Living Systems and Cultural Agency — 31

2 The Instrumental and Strategic Agencies — 41
   2.1 Introduction — 41
   2.2 Two Views on Strategic Management — 43
   2.3 The Knowledge Management Paradigm — 48
   2.4 Complexity and Viable Systems — 54
   2.5 The Strategic Agency — 59
   2.6 Agency Pathology — 75
   2.7 Social Responsibility and Practice — 76

3 Agency Personality — 83
   3.1 Agency Minds — 83
   3.2 From Minds to Personalities — 88
   3.3 Agency Trait Theory and Maruyama Mindscapes — 94
   3.4 Intelligences and Efficacy Agency — 104

4 The Intelligent Agency — 111
   4.1 Introduction — 111
   4.2 Theories of Intelligence — 114
   4.3 Organizational Intelligences — 120
   4.4 Agency Process Intelligences and Efficacy — 125
   4.5 Knowledge Strategy Agency Case — 132

5 Agency Traits and Types — 138
   5.1 Introduction — 138

	5.2	Traits, Enantiomers, and Agency Type	143
	5.3	Individualism and Collectivism	160
	5.4	Some Thoughts	172
6	**Agency Consciousness**	174
	6.1	Introduction	174
	6.2	Undecidability and Generic System Hierarchies	174
	6.3	Substructure Modelling	177
	6.4	Illustration of Superstructure Modelling	188
	6.5	Internalization as Knowledge Migration	191
	6.6	Generic System Hierarchy Generator	194
	6.7	The Case of Negotiation and Agency Internalization	196

Part II Agency Change 203

7	**Joint Alliances**	205
	7.1	Introduction	205
	7.2	International Alliances in Central and Eastern Europe	207
	7.3	Knowledge Management and Knowledge Transfer in a Cross-Cultural Context	210
	7.4	Viable Knowledge Creation and Learning in International Alliances	213
	7.5	Modelling Alliances	217
	7.6	Application of the Model to a Case Study of the Czech Academic Link Project (CZALP)	225
		The CZALP Project Phase 1	226
		The CZALP Project Phase 2	227
	7.7	Outcome	230
8	**Agency Dynamics**	231
	8.1	Introduction	231
	8.2	Kuhn, Piaget: From Paradigm Crisis to Transformation	233
	8.3	Understanding Paradigms	235
	8.4	Paradigms under Change	239
	8.5	Transformation of Paradigms	242
	8.6	Agency Life-Cycle	246
	8.7	Baoshang Bank Case Study	252
	8.8	Conclusion	261

Part III Agency as Society 263

9	**The Sociological and Political Agencies**	265
	9.1	Introduction	265
	9.2	The Sociological Approach	265
	9.3	Parsons	267
	9.4	Luhmann	272
	9.5	Habermas	280
	9.6	Agency and Socio-Cultural Processes	286
	9.7	The Political Agency	289
	9.8	Luhmann, Habermas, Agency, and Practice	296

Contents

10	**The Economic Agency**	**303**
	10.1 Introduction	303
	10.2 Economics and Policy	305
	10.3 Macroeconomic Modelling	308
	10.4 Economic Agency	315
	10.5 Traits, Policy, and Macroeconomics	321
	10.6 Case Situation: The 2007/2008 European Recession and Mindscapes	326
	10.7 Observations	331
11	**The Financial Agency, Society and Corruption**	**333**
	11.1 Introduction	333
	11.2 The Chinese Context	336
	11.3 The Chinese Banking Industry	339
	11.4 Finance and the Evolution in Chinese Banking	341
	11.5 The Impact of Shadow Banking	343
	11.6 Understanding Agency Issues and Corruption	349
	11.7 Society, Development and Corruption	366
Bibliography		371
Index		434

Figures

1.1	Model of organizational culture connecting internal and external environments	*page* 27
1.2	Model of a sociocultural agency	28
1.3	Socio-cognitive trait model of the agency connecting normative personality with social and cultural systems	32
1.4	Relationship between the ego, superego, unconscious mental states and preconscious disposition in an agency personality	39
2.1	Dynamic relationship between the operative and figurative systems of the instrumental agency and its environment	42
2.2	Connection between resources and competitive advantage	44
2.3	Six forces model as an extension of the five forces Porter model	46
2.4	Model of the resource based approach to business strategy	47
2.5	Relationship between the knowledge and strategic gap through visualization	51
2.6	The Relationship between knowledge and sustainable competitive advantage	52
2.7	Semantic map showing the outline concept of the Strategic Viable System Model, with implicit connections between management and operations	58
2.8	Cybernetic map for the Strategic VSM	59
2.9	The VSM migrated into the strategic agency	63
2.10	Distinction between the system schemas and their orientations in the strategic agency	70
2.11	Reactions to fluctuation affecting an organization showing control action through anticipation, where knowledge processes are inferred	72
2.12	Influence diagram exploring the epistemological nature of an autonomous agent with inferred cognitive system	73
2.13	Possible relationship between learning, knowledge and intelligent agencies	75
2.14	Transverse psychological model of the collective showing type O and F pathologies	76

List of Figures

2.15	Representation of the strategic (noumenal) agency adopting attributes of VSM	81
3.1	Normative personality as a cognitive system with figurative and operative intelligences, seated in the noumenal domain of the plural agency	90
3.2	Socio-cognitive trait model of the agency connecting normative personality with social and cultural systems; Boje's personality traits here are technical-interest power, self-relational ethics, and knowledge disposition	100
5.1	Illustration of personality temperament trait for a 'personal political' space showing trait enantiomers, with social collective terms shown in brackets	148
5.2	Distribution of strategic economic agency (normative personality) meta-types in a three-dimensional trait space, each displaying its cultural and social trait natures	162
6.1	Agency with a single cognitive metasystem, which controls its operative system, showing potential generic pathologies as bars across operative intelligence (including feedback)	177
6.2	Core concept for the Cultural Agency	180
6.3	The Cognitive Agency with a knowledge creating cognitive system and instrumental figurative system, illustrating generic pathologies	181
6.4	The Affective Agency indicating the role of emotions in the agency, and their connection with the cognitive agency	182
6.5	The Defining Plural Agency, with new generic autogenetesis (self-defining), showing generic triple-loop learning (with generic pathologies) and feedback.	184
6.6	Learning theory terminology permits seeing the Defining Agency as a Cultural or Socio-Cultural Agency	185
6.7	Cultural Agency involving a Collective 'Personality' using superstructure modelling in the Cultural Agency substructure, I's indicating intelligences with possible generic pathologies	190
6.8	Recursive simplex generator for an nth order simplex model through the generation of (n+1) higher order generic constructs in an implied autopoietic hierarchy	194
6.9	Illustration of levels of consciousness from an action context to the living system and onwards, where the dotted area indicates living system occupation	195
7.1	Knowledge migration between two agencies, one operating as a source and the other as a sink via knowledge intermediaries	214
7.2	Development and performance in alliances, including CZALP	216

7.3	Relationship between types of worldview and behaviour	218
7.4	An operative suprasystem of agencies in an alliance and a decision making imperatives metasystem of one partner	219
7.5	Relationship between the parent agencies entering an alliance, and the resulting child agency	223
8.1	Cycle of paradigmatic change, and the relationship between four modes of science	242
8.2	Corporate body embedded in an ambient national culture	251
8.3	Adaptation of the corporate life-cycle (assumption: ambient culture is in normal phase of stability)	256
9.1	An interpretation of Parsons General Theory of Action Model	268
9.2	The frame of reference enabling a rational speech act	286
9.3	A representation of the cultural agency interacting in a social environment	288
9.4	Basic systems model for political policy making	292
9.5	Model of socioeconomic development deriving from political arguments of Huntington (1968)	293
9.6	Agency model that relates to political development	295
11.1	Impact of change on China	337
11.2	Interrelating attributes of organizations and impact of World Trade Organization (WTO)	338
11.3	Typical relationship between Chinese banks and larger sector shadow banks	345
11.4	The national (Chinese) politico-economic agency	350
11.5	Type F and O pathologies	356
11.6	Interpretation of Piaget's notion of the relationship between subject and object	357
11.7	Interactive relationship between distinct images of objects, each interaction susceptible to (type L1 or L2) lateral pathologies that interfere with the deductive reasoning processes that affect perspective coordination	357
11.8	The Strategic Agency expressed in terms of the interaction between Ideology (Legitimacy, Opportunity) and Ethics.	360
11.9	The nature of opportunity in a politico-economic agency	362
11.10	Deeper notion of legitimacy with possible pathological breaks	363

Tables

1.1	Consciousness defined in terms of three psychic domains	page 38
2.1	Proposed attributes for sustainable competitive advantage	53
2.2	Types of capability	56
2.3	Description of VSM model	57
2.4	Examples of weaknesses seen through the lens of VSM functions	60
2.5	Identifying the strategic aspects of VSM with agency	65
2.6	Distinction between learning, knowledge, and intelligent organizations	74
2.7	Types of ontological pathology, and possible associative relationships between type combinations	77
3.1	Maruyama's core epistemic types with connected Boje traits	102
4.1	The non-conscious dispositions of habitus	115
4.2	Gardner's (1983, 1993) classes of competence intelligence	116
4.3	Organizational competence intelligence, catalyzed from Gardner's classifications	117
4.4	Nature of cybernetic intelligence in organizations	121
4.5	Migrating conceptualizations of knowledge strategy to the cultural agency	134
5.1	Trait variables and their enantiomers for personal political temperament in MBTI trait space, and its equivalent social trait space	145
5.2	Cultural agency traits, strategic economic agency traits and social agency traits, and their possible polar orientations	151
5.3	Summary of the traits and their bi-polar enantiomers for an agency	156
5.4	Nature of the Maruyama mindscapes	161
6.1	Literature support for paradigm shifts of different agency intelligences	187
6.2	Characteristics of paradigms	192
7.1	Example Alliance situations and their cognitive attributes as viable systems	229

8.1	Explanation of the options for paradigmatic change	243
8.2	Sources of firm growth and evolving crises	247
8.3	Causes of insolvency – information collected in Austria and Germany	250
8.4	The phases of the corporate cycle	257
8.5	Illustration of the connection between the first two phases of the corporate life-cycle and its dynamic development process	258
9.1	Types of autonomous system in Luhmann's theory	273
9.2	Communication is a synthesis of three elements	275
9.3	Concepts associated with meaning in social systems	276
9.4	Equivalence between Shannon and Weaver's and Lynn's models of communication	278
9.5	Types of rationality in Habermas' theory of communicative action	281
9.6	Habermas' three worlds model of communications	285
10.1	Illustration of economic intelligence to figurative trait value options	323
11.1	Nature of the terms and coupling relationships in Figure 11.5	361
11.2	Variables to fight corruption, illustrations/explanations deriving from Anderson and Grey (2006)	367

Preface

This book is a research monograph concerned with social collectives and change. It presents a theoretical and practical framework capable of improving our understanding of the nature and processes involved in socials (i.e. social collectives/organizations/systems) and our capacity to anticipate their patterns of behaviour. It is an output of the loosely structured international Organizational Orientation, Coherence and Trajectory (OCT) project (www.octresearch.net) centred at Warwick University in the UK. It arose as the result of a selected collection of peer-reviewed research papers that have been assembled, reformulated, and integrated into a coherent theme, put together to service the developmental needs of a fast-growing Chinese commercial bank needing to ensure that its distributed branches recognize some of the issues relating to rapid growth through start-up branches or joint alliances.

The theme is about the plural agency – a *learning* viable organized social collective that might be an enterprise, a nation state, or a civilization. Agencies pass through change, and the issues that this promotes arise where, for instance, a corporate body engages in a merger or acquisition, thereby creating a cultural schism over its new self, or when a social moves through immanent processes to embrace a plural value system, cleaving cultural coherence. In either case, a culture may become unstable, and when this occurs the agency may find that a coherent set of values becomes incoherent, and single values may become collectively or individually confused, *and* the instrumental norms that populate its cognitions and behaviours lose meaning, becoming semantically vacuous. For an agency to regain cultural stability it requires a coherent value system and set of meaningful instrumental norms to emerge. Zetterberg (1997), commenting on the distinction between values and norms, suggests that values are associated with actualization and the emergence of spontaneous order, while norms are associated with compliance. Order from values occurs with a shift back to *cultural stability*, while compliance occurs with *instrumental stability* when cognitive and behavioural norms facilitate order. Models can be useful to explain how long regaining stability might take. Strang & Meyer (1993) suggest diffusion models for this. By diffusion we mean the socially mediated spread of a coherent set of values and semantic norms within a population. Young (2009) distinguishes between types of diffusion: contagion, social influence, social learning, and inertia. Inertia is likely to be most relevant to the spread of core values, since people tend to find it quite difficult to replace one set of core values with another. The time it takes for an agency to regain stability will be dependent on its conditions, like population mass. For Yolles, Fink, & Frieden (2012) this is a metaphor for *resistance to change*. While early inertial models of society have been unable to represent the dynamic nature of its culture (Pickering, 1987), more modern treatments (e.g. Yolles, Fink, & Frieden, 2012) can provide explanation for inertial dynamic processes and hence explain change through social momentum (e.g. Green & Griffith, 2002; Ching & Yu, 2010) from instability to stability.

Using systems concepts, a plural agency is populated by sub-agencies, some of which may be plural (e.g. groups) and some singular (individuals). Agency is also viable having *cybernetic* processes of control and communication, as it develops and maintains itself, with qualities of adaptability, survival, and (more or less) coherence, particularly in relation to successful strategic processes and a capacity for efficacious performance. As a modern meta-framework approach, it avoids the problems of mainstream social science with a paradigmatic framework whose conceptual walls advocates often have difficulty in breaching (Alvesson & Willmott, 1996; Jeffcutt, 2004; Koot, 2004; Suddaby, Hardy, & Huy, 2008; Suddaby & Huy, 2009). While such partitioning may well assist in creating greater theoretical depth, it loses the perspectives needed to relate disciplines and their points of interaction. This is implicitly supported by Yoon (2010) who points out (citing Almond & Verba 1963; Barry, 1978; Patemann, 1980; Almond 1980; Inglehart, 1990 & 1997; Harrison and Huntington 2001) that economic, social, political, and cultural processes are all intimately connected, and to consider one without the other creates explanatory deficiency.

This text offers a dynamic cultural theory that couples with advances in agency theory. The agency may be modelled to have representative variables, called *traits*. These are influenced by its instrumental norms, creating formative orientations that influence collective cognitions and patterns of behaviour, immanent dynamics, and interaction with complex environments. The trait orientations are influenced by a cultural trait, which creates a field of attraction with particular cognitive pathways that predetermine strategic approaches and behavioural potential.

Understanding change in an agency requires the support of suitable theory. Traditional systemic frameworks used to model the nature and function of systems have limitations, while more recent complex adaptive systems theory draws on broader principles that involve uncertainty and emergence within and across dynamic contexts (Amagoh, 2008). Such systems are not just concerned with objects, but are populated by people who communicate, may be conflictual, respond to management processes, and may or may not conform to the cultural norms that contribute to organizational coherence. The approach taken in this text is to create a *meta-framework*. This can deliver specific *context-dependent* frameworks such that, with purpose and intention, systemic detail and evidence of complexity result. The nature of the meta-framework is that it adopts a high level of conceptualization. As a result, complexity tends to become less relevant (Glassman, 1973).

We have said agency theory is a meta-framework. This consists of a *living system* substructure, with detailed theory added in as a superstructure. Its substructure is formulated as a super-system representing human agency, composed of systems that are ontologically distinct but interactively coupled. The systems are autonomous, generalized, and information rich. There are various agency models. The strategic agency represents a 'living personality' with an information-based cognitive system that strategically influences decision-making. In the cultural agency, *culture* drives agency norms and orientates agency traits. It has *cognition* that drives processes of individual and collective thought that together with emotion deliver action. *Context* derives from what may be identified as a set of environments in relation to the agency's immanent dynamics. A consequence of change in culture, cognition, and context is that the agency must adapt to maintain viability. Agency substructure, influenced by superstructure, creates behavioural *anticipation*. Anticipation is not prediction (Rosen, 1985; Schwarz, 2001; Leydesdorff & Dubois, 2004; Collier, 2006). Predictions are theoretical expectations often using system models to identify future states from structural properties (Rosen, 1985), while anticipation arises when the structure itself enables dynamic projections to the future to facilitate potential behaviour. Yolles & Fink (2015) offer an illustration of the differences: human agency uses strategic management models that interpret an environment from an examination of behavioural perturbations, while anticipation involves strategic and operative networks of processes that dynamically condition the way that the agency behaviourally responds to environmental perturbations.

Agency is a substructural *living system* enriched with superstructure. Living system theory (Vancouver, 1996: 165):

[first, should] provide a framework for describing the micro (i.e. human), macro (i.e. social organizations), and meso (i.e. interaction between the two) levels of the field without relying on reductionism or reification. The more parsimoniously it can do this, the better (Bacharach, 1989; Whetten, 1989). Second, it should provide a model of the major processes of dynamic interaction between individuals, situations, and behaviour to address the major phenomenon of the field like behaviour, cognition, and affect (Bandura,1986). Finally, it should provide researchers with research ideas (Whetten, 1989).

Vancouver continues by saying that living systems theory entails the proposition that living systems can maintain regularity despite irregularity in their environments. This regularity is accomplished by comparing current or anticipated states with internally represented desired states and converting any difference into actions that will enable the maintenance of small differences. He further notes that in living systems theory influences emerge from evolutionary and biological to sociological and economic processes. To capture such attributes, agency theory as presented here adopts the concept of autopoiesis, which Mingers (1995, 2001) notes refers to systems that are *self-producing* or *self-constructing,* and this is indicative of certain properties of *living* as opposed to *non-living* entities. This modelling approach has been enlarged, notes Mingers, to encompass cognition and language, leading to what is known as second-order cybernetics. Schwarz (1997) developed a more comprehensive general theory of living systems in which autopoiesis constitutes one part, the other being autogenesis or *self-creation*. Yolles (1999, 2006) has elaborated this into a knowledge-based theory that has its seat in the theory of anticipation. In this book we show that living systems theory can also be set within the context of learning, as represented by Piaget (1950), where autogenesis and autopoiesis are represented through forms of process intelligence.

It has been said that this text originated from the servicing needs of a rapidly growing distributed Chinese bank. It began its life as a series of lectures that derived from published papers in academic journals. Selected papers have been reworked and integrated with new material in order to create a streamed monograph. The bank's cultural diversity occurs since its origins derive from culturally diverse regions of China. Each branch constitutes a semi-autonomous organization that is expected to contribute to corporate coherence and as such is required to conform to national corporate goals. However, issues of goal adherence may arise where common understandings of goal meanings differ across the culturally diverse regions. That the corporate culture is distributed enables a plurality of normative differences to result, and while this can create corporate opportunity, it can also create corporate fissures. Corporate culture is the 'glue' that holds organizations together by providing cohesiveness and coherence among the parts (Schneider, 1988). Corporate growth is the result of ambitious intention. Corporate development is like having a plurality of cross-regional corporate projects, each a culturally distinct semi-autonomous branch running sub-project teams, where 'coordination and communication among the players is paramount for an efficient and effective outcome' (Evaristo et al., 2004: 177), and where 'culture, in itself, is a multidimensional factor, all affecting the performance of distributed projects in different ways' (ibid.: 184).

Introduction

Processes of organizational and societal change are complex. This can be demonstrated quite easily by considering the development of the Western economic recession, which provides lessons of how change processes can impact organizational behaviour. We shall take a little time to explore this.

The Case in Hand

In 2008 and 2009 the world economy experienced its worst ever financial crisis, the apparent onset of which came in 2007, and was triggered by the relaxation of the constraints on its financial institutions and their responsibility in managing debt. The major impact came initially in the United States through the development of unsecured lending that led in due course to the collapse in the sub-prime market (composed of people with questionable credit ratings who sought to secure home loans), resulting in uncountable corporate failures and financial disasters. A consequence has been the deepest recession since the 1930s (Dolphin & Nash, 2011).

The crisis resulted from a combination of complex factors that drew on the relationship between smaller-scale microeconomics and larger-scale macroeconomics (Dopfer, Foster & Potts; 2004; Goldspink & Kay, 2004; Gibson, 2008). The problematic microeconomic factors included high-risk lending by financial institutions, regulatory failures, inflated credit ratings, and high-risk and poor quality financial products designed and sold by some investment banks (Lavin & Coburn, 2011).

The crisis was aggravated by its shadow banking system, which embraces unregulated financial activities, because since it operates through rational expectation during stability it is welfare improving, but otherwise is vulnerable to crises and liquidity dry-ups when investors ignore risks (Crotty & Epstein, 2008; Gennaioli, Shleifer & Vishny, 2013; Sanches, 2014). Despite this, it is attractive to the individualists of this world who led policy formulation. As a result, US policy deregulated the provision of credit during the period 2002–2008, allowing high-risk lending and borrowing practices. Substantial changes were made to the banking industry that resulted in the relaxation of the rules under which banks operated, and the encouragement of risk-taking. In the United States in 1994 a novel relaxation was created by Congress to explicitly authorize interstate banking, permitting federally chartered banks to open branches nationwide more easily than before. Perhaps relatively harmless on its own, in addition more deregulation occurred in 1999 with the repeal of the Glass-Steagall Act of 1933. This had required that organizations concerned with investment (banks, investment banks, securities firms, and insurance companies) should operate separately, and the repeal allowed them to openly merge operations (Levin & Coburn, 2011). Developing further on such deregulatory macroeconomic policies, in 2002 the US Treasury Department along with other federal bank regulatory agencies altered the way capital reserves were calculated for banks – effectively allowing them to hold less capital in their reserves than if the individual mortgages were held directly on the banks' books. More, than two years later the U.S. Securities and Exchange Commission (SEC) relaxed the capital requirements for large broker-dealers, allowing them to grow even larger, often with borrowed funds. Having let the deregulatory genie out of the bottle only then to discover its malevolence, in 2005 SEC attempted to assert more control over the growing hedge fund industry by unsuccessfully requiring certain hedge funds to register with the agency, an attempt that was overturned in a federal Court of Appeals opinion in 2006.

This tendency towards unbounded deregulation has not been a problem for the United States alone. Countries of the European Union were also pursuing policies of deregulation that broadly paralleled those of the United States over the last score years. This resulted in the development of competitive forces and political shifts that appeared to be towards the right (Eichacker, 2012), but which are better seen as moves towards *Individualism* (Limerick & Cunnington, 1993) with political right tendencies. Individualism has its own particular properties that are often associated with the political right, but could also be embraced by the political left. This conceptual shift offers opportunity to create a more macroscopic perspective on the crisis. Individualism is the doctrine that all social phenomena (their structure and potential to change) are in principle explicable only in terms of individuals – for instance, their properties, goals, and beliefs (Oyserman, 2002). In contrast, *Collectivism* is its polar opposite, and relates to people coming together collectively to act unitarily through normative processes in order to satisfy some commonly agreed and understood purpose or interest. Agencies that adopt varieties of Individualism or Collectivism have realities that are differently framed, maintaining distinct ontological and epistemic boundaries. These constitute frames of view which create barriers to the development of coherent communications. In political regimes that embrace Individualism, political policy making is guided by its principles that support the freedoms of the individual above the collective, and the obverse for Collectivism. Individualism and Collectivism are strategic orientations that are dynamically interactive polar opposites which are responsible for creation of fundamental policy provision vectors that determine the character of a society. Following Triandis (1988), Ball (2001) undertakes a study that indicates that Individualism and Collectivism will both influence the course of economic development, while economic growth, in a way that is dependent on its initial conditions, and changes in economic structure will alter the orientation of the society towards one of these strategic orientations. How this occurs is of particular interest. Allik & Realo (2004: 46) note Hofstede's (2001) demonstration that wealth creates Individualism (not that Individualism creates wealth). This is supported by Inglehart & Oyserman (2004: 37), who note that 'Individualism is not a static individual-level psychological attribute but is closely linked with processes of socioeconomic development.' However, for Veenhoven (1999: 4) there is not a one-to-one relationship between economic development and Individualism, since 'Individualization is not adequately measured by economic development,' and that interestingly '...individualization is detrimental to the quality-of-life' (Veenhoven, 1999: 13). None of these studies actually *equate* economic development with Individualism. Indeed, there seems to be evidence contrary to this, when Triandis, Bontempo, Villareal, Asai & Lucca (1988: 328) tell us that *both* Collectivism and Individualism may be associated with low economic development. This suggests that it is not Individualism or Collectivism per se that are related to economic development, but rather shifts from one of these cultural conditions (Sorokin, 1937–42) to the other. This is supported by Leung et al. (2005: 362) who note that Inglehart and Baker (2000) 'showed that..... economic development was associated with shifts away from traditional norms and values towards values that are increasingly rational, tolerant, trusting, and participatory'. Whatever constitutes such 'rational, tolerant, trusting, and participatory' behaviour is, presumably, a function of the dominantly prevailing cultural condition of an agency. So, if it is the case that the relationship between Individualism/Collectivism and economic development centres on the shift from one to the other, the question must be raised as to what is happening when this occurs. Well, one response is that Individualism/Collectivism are not only cultural conditions, but are also politically strategic orientations that are responsible for distinct alternative policy pathways, so that whichever strategic orientation comes to power, a shift in policy framework is to be expected which will in turn interact with economic development. Now if we assume that economic development (when it occurs) is responsive to continuity in policy orientation, then it is likely to suffer when a policy framework shifts. This is implicitly supported by Lent (2009), who explains, through the exploration of Perez (2002) in evolutionary economics, that a policy framework is important and its shifts can be related to economic crashes. While the context of Lent's and Perez's studies relate the rise of new technology, the relationship between policy framework and economic development still stands.

Thus, it seems to be a conclusion that the rise of a renewed Western political culture of Individualism, probably around about three decades ago, with its attendant policy shifts towards deregulation, can be seen as being ultimately responsible for the economic crisis of 2007/8. This implies that it is not deregulation that is responsible for the recession as such, but rather the fundamental policy shift to deregulation that developed more or less over the last score years. If this is so then it is likely to be because the financial organizations that were participant in deregulatory dynamics had not obtained any ideological or ethical appreciations that would enable them to grasp the consequences of their actions towards excessive unbridled greed, having not developed any meaningful norms of self-control in this respect. There is another facet to this argument. Following Sorokin (1962), the rise of either Individualism or Collectivism is tied to particular cultural orientations which likely change cyclically in relation to each other. When a cultural orientation is unstable, shifts in strategic orientation can more easily occur. Where a cultural redirection is sufficiently strong, policy orientations may be dramatically shifted, thereby resulting in an impact on economic development and implying the likelihood of another recession. At this juncture, it may be worth noting that Individualism/Collectivism may be seen as approximations to collective social mind sets, and as such it is not surprising that they are not easy to distinguish as an explicit part of a sociocultural dynamic.Let us move from a macroscopic reflection to one that is more microscopic. The 2007/8 economic crisis provides an illustration of the dramatic situations that can arise when the idealistic deregulatory trails of Individualism and partisan patterns of macroeconomic policy develop in a previously more Collectivist society. This leads to unbridled microeconomic dynamics that highlight policy failure. Such policy sets the scene for a crisis that involved: (1) conflicts of interest in regulatory bodies, (2) inadequate control processes (e.g. the failure of regulators, the credit rating agencies, and the market itself) and no control of financial excesses, and ultimately, (3) the use of the wrong models to guide control processes (Levin & Coburn, 2011).

A vivid illustration of the problem of conflict of interest in regulatory bodies was provided by the Enron Scandal (Teather, 2002). Enron was a US energy, commodities, and services company that employed 20,000 people. The scandal occurred in 2001, and concerned the falsely reported financial condition that constituted accounting fraud, with the passive assistance of its auditors. This was undertaken systematically and was creatively planned. The demised company has now become an exemplar for wilful corporate fraud and corruption.

This type of problem also arises in industries within which organizations are required to self-regulate, as has been the case in the news industry, which has been exposed to have issues connected with criminal behaviour and corruption (Marsden, 2012; Parliamentary Report, 2012), and the banking industry, where there is often a benchmark of cosiness, and where a *nod and a wink* are seen to be sufficient controls (Parliamentary Commission, 2012). For Ferguson (2010), the conflicts of interest referred to in this case are also reflective of the development of corrupt practices, which imply issues of ideological and ethical drift. An argument to support such a view can be made quite easily by looking for recent evidence of corrupt banking practices, not so difficult to find if one considers the remark by the UK Member of Parliament Steve Collins, who publically in 2012 referred to the banking industry as a sewer of dishonesty. As illustration, Barclays bank was fined £290m in June 2012 by the Financial Services Authority in the UK and the Commodity Futures Trading Commission and Department of Justice in the United States. It seems that for four years (2005–2009) Barclays lied about the interest rate it had to pay to borrow, to make the bank look more secure during the financial crisis and, sometimes working with traders at other banks, to make a profit. As a consequence of its unethical behaviour, Barclays lost its Chairman, Chief Executive Officer, and Chief Operations Officer, forced to resign from office for corrupt practice in relation to Libor by public pressure and the UK and US authorities. Libor is the London InterBank Offered Rate, the average interest rate estimated by leading banks in London that they would be charged if borrowing from other banks. Libor is determined by a daily poll carried out on behalf of the British Bankers' Association that asks banks to estimate how much it would cost to borrow from each other for different periods and in different currencies.

Beyond Libor, Stibor (Sweden's main interbank rate), Sibor (the leading rate in Singapore), and Tibor (the rate in Japan) have been among other rates facing fresh scrutiny because, like Libor, they are based on banks' estimated borrowing costs rather than real trades. In some cases these rates may be easier to rig than Libor, as fewer banks contribute to their calculation (Vaughan & Finch, 2012). Regulators and industry groups have been interested in determining whether other benchmark rates have been manipulated similarly. Thus: Sweden's central bank, the Japanese Bankers Association, the Monetary Authority of Singapore, and South Korea's Fair Trade Commission all announced probes into how their domestic rates are set; traders at Deutsche Bank, HSBC Holdings Plc (HSBA), Societe Generale SA, and Credit Agricole SA have been under investigation for interest rate manipulation. Yet more, Citigroup Inc. and UBS AG were also ordered to suspend some operations in Japan in December 2011 after the Financial Services Agency found their employees attempted to influence Tibor to a 'favourable level' for derivatives trading. Citigroup was banned from any trading for two weeks – tied to Libor and Tibor, as was UBS, which received a one-week suspension. While interest rate fixing seems to be an easy target for banks, it is not the only area of possible corrupt practice. JPMorgan Chase, the largest US bank, was being investigated for energy-market manipulation (Klimasinska & Kopecki, 2012), while the US-based HSBC bank was accused of drug money laundering (Reuters, 2013). Bankia too, a leading Spanish Bank, was being investigated for practices of fraud, embezzlement, and stock price manipulation. Among those accused of being involved was Rodrigo Rato, the bank's former chairman and the International Monetary Fund's managing director from 2004 to 2007 (Minder, 2012). Suggestions have been made that the banking system appears to operate as a cabal.

Reflections on the Crisis

The case of the crisis provided above offers some indication of the complexity of social environments and how what appear to be simple if accumulating policy change can have dramatic impacts on organizational and social dynamics. There is some validity, therefore, in examining aspects of the case to enable considerations to be made in relation to the theme of this book.

A number of problems were identified earlier in the case study. These included conflicts of interest, the wrong model which decomposes into a question of agency and a structural issue, and issues of control.

Conflicts of interest in regulative bodies (as well as those that they regulate) require regulative control processes to avoid the development of corrupt practices. A conflict of interest is:

> ...a set of conditions in which professional judgment concerning a primary [professional role] interest...tends to be unduly influenced by a secondary interest (such as financial gain). The primary interest is determined by the professional duties... the secondary interest is usually not illegitimate in itself, and indeed it may even be a necessary and desirable part of professional practice. Only its relative weight in professional decisions is problematic. The aim is not to eliminate or necessarily to reduce financial gain or other secondary interests (such as preference for family and friends or the desire for prestige and power). It is rather to prevent these secondary factors from dominating or appearing to dominate the relevant primary interest in the making of professional decisions...It is also a mistake to treat conflicts of interest as just another kind of choice between competing values, as occurs with ethical dilemmas involving...[for instance, issues of economic, social or cultural profiteering, or of] confidentiality.... To do so dilutes the concept of a conflict of interest and encourages the attitude that conflicts are so pervasive that they cannot be avoided. In ethical dilemmas, both of the competing interests have a presumptive claim to priority, and the problem is in deciding which to choose. In the case of financial conflicts of interest, only one of the interests has a claim to priority, and the problem is to ensure that the other interest does not dominate. This asymmetry between interests is a distinctive characteristic of conflicts of interest (Thompson, 1993: 573).

It is thus apparent that conflicts of interest need to be addressed within a strategic environment through an appropriate regulatory framework. To identify such a framework, there is a need to obtain an improved understanding of the nature of conflicts of interest, and a clearer formulation of standards that could respond to the problems that this presents. Such an improved understanding can be provided by exploring the boundary issues that distinguish between primary and secondary interest, as provided, for instance, by Ulrich (1983) in his methodology referred to as *Critical Systems Heuristics* (CSH). CSH has been defined as a framework for reflective professional practice that is organized around the central tool of boundary critique (Ulrich & Reynolds, 2010). From the principles espoused in CSH, one can impute (from Ulrich, 2005: 4) that boundary critique attributes relating to conflicts of interests and their oft-associated corrupt tendencies can be addressed by:

1. *Identifying* the sources of selectivity that condition a conflict of interest by surfacing underpinning boundary judgements.
2. *Examining* these boundary judgements regarding their practical and ethical implications and the differences they make to the way a situation in question may be perceived by others.
3. *Finding options* for determining the reference system that conditions a potential conflict of interest, by giving alternative answers to some of the boundary questions, since such a referencing enables an appreciation of selectivity.
4. *Consulting with relevant others for mutual understanding* regarding different reference systems and an approach towards the coordination of distinct perspectives.
5. *Where necessary challenging* alternative perspective through the emancipatory use of boundary critique.

In relation to the comment that the 'wrong model' was being used by regulators, reference is being made to the specific financial models. These relate to the following financial issues: the lack of use of relevant mortgage performance data; unclear and subjective criteria used to produce ratings; failure to apply updated rating models to existing rated transactions; and a failure to provide adequate staffing to perform rating and surveillance services, despite record revenues. However, the comment relating to the wrong model could as well refer to the general model of the organization, which if incorrectly adopted by an organization can lead to failing business practices. This latter situation is reflected in an inability of main stream organizational theory to predict problem issues or crises (Alvesson & Willmott, 1996; Clark, 2000).

The 'wrong model' problem does not only refer to the 'business model' of an organization that reflects expected inputs and outputs. Rather, it is a ubiquitous one affecting all forms of inquiry, analysis, and diagnosis, and it often occurs when the context of what one is exploring is not commonly well-defined or understood. This suggests a need to appreciate how models are created and how they can be made relevant to contexts. One of the core features of model building is ontology. This has two dimensions of philosophical question: one of *agency* and one of *structure*. We shall briefly consider each of these in turn.

The agency question refers to whether people have free will and whether they are wholly responsible for their own actions, or whether life is predetermined in some way (Hatch & Cunliffe, 2006). This draws on the philosophical arguments of whether what one sees may be subjectivist or objectivist or some place between them. Subjectivists occur at one end of the reality continuum in their belief that something exists only when you experience and give it meaning, while objectivists believe that reality exists independently of those who live in it. Subjectivists argue that people experience realities in different ways because individuals and groups have their own assumptions, beliefs, and perceptions that lead them to do so. Objectivists argue that people react to what is happening around them in predictable ways because their behaviour is part of the material world in which they live and it is determined by causes. However, also associated with the agency question is whether an agency is (more or less) autonomous, often associated with the ability of an individual or group to (among other things) create their own realities – and in so doing reflect their behaviours on epistemic elements that result in the pursuit of their own goals, respond to a changing environment through adaptation, and self-organize.

The structural issue embraces the philosophical study of the kinds of entities that exist in reality and their relationships (Floridi, 2003), which should provide clear, coherent, and well-worked accounts of the basic structures to be found in reality (Lowe, 2006). This can be expressed through ontology, which refers to a category of being, and to its related general or formal relationships that can be identified (Spear, 2006). Here, set within an information context, these relationships affect the way in which information is or may be organized. In the case that there is a plural set of categories of being, an entity has an ontologically plural nature with ontologically distinct components. Where these components are in some way connected, their interconnecting manifolds determine the way in which that ontological information is recognized. The structural issue for an entity with a plural ontological nature then relates to the relationships that define it, and the way in which information is organized and manifested across its ontological dimensions.

This explanation takes the structural dimension to be one of ontology. It is core to the development of theory, and from a pragmatic perspective this needs to be sound. Soundness in turn calls on theory coherence. Coherent theories are logically interconnected sets of propositions, built on a set of basic concepts that can weave together to form paradigms, though not all theories have developed paradigms. Where the theories are related to limited contexts and arise from particular narrow perspectives of inquiry, then the nature of the propositions and the interconnections between them can be classified as idiosyncratic. Such theories thus have an internal structure differentiated through the creation of universals and their sets of particulars.

In contrast, paradigms form for sufficiently broad contexts that arise from wider perspectives and where support is offered by populations of inquirers. So paradigms are social phenomena as much as theory ones. When theory builders attach themselves to a given paradigm their capacity to create variations from the base structures becomes increasingly limited as the paradigm develops. With this, committed paradigm holders exclude other structures and reject alternative paradigms. Where the contexts are limited the capacity of the theory to represent broad aspects of reality is bounded, and so a paradigm may not form. In contrast, where theory is created that supports generic principles for open themed contexts, then meta-theory develops which may form into a meta-paradigm.

This situation can be related to organization theory. It is a discipline that can be identified through three theoretical and practical components (Hatch & Cunliffe, 2006). These are *organizational structure and environment, management and purposive behaviour*, and *organizational change and dynamics*. There has been a failure of organization theory to develop a coherent horizon of theory (McAuley, Duberley & Johnson, 2007), with extreme fragmentation and no agreement concerning the underlying theoretical dimensions or methodological approach to be employed. This failure has not given rise to new meta-paradigms capable of formulating new ideas (Clegg et al., 2006). One can surmise the reason for this. Organization theory is passing through a dynamic process of change, and has hit a mode of reconstruction that some might refer to as its chaotic ante-narrative stage of development (Boje, 2011). An outcome of this can result in one of three options: a return to traditional intellectual orthodoxy (Clegg et al. 2006), the development of a new meta-paradigm, or the demise of organization theory due to its irrelevance.

The problem of control, and by association the communications processes that are crucial to it, is another central issue: and this is the natural domain of cybernetics. So, one way of satisfying the needs for modelling control processes is through the creation of a cybernetic meta-framework capable of representing a theory of meaning through the construction of meta-theory (Oakley, 2004), an idea that we shall return to in due course. Meta-theory provides the capacity to connect knowledge-related models that might normally not be associated with one another. For the purposes of control and communications, probably the most useful meta-theory is one of cybernetic agency. This approach is normally interdisciplinary and through a cybernetic perspective it is concerned with the control and communication features of coherently controlled (systemic) structures and their regulation that are essential to all social contexts. It is also normally concerned with agency 'circular causality', i.e. action by an agency in an environment that in turn draws consequences to itself from the environment. This process occurs through information feedback, which in turn can affect the way the system then behaves: that is its dynamics. This cybernetic frame of reference can be formulated to create a general 'living system' meta-model that if culture based, can draw on a variety of particular context-sensitive models.

Such an approach would necessarily be bedded on a complete understanding of the nature of communications, as has been developed within previous sociological work concerning the normative nature of organizations, composed as they are of collectives of individuals working together according to some purposes that influence both individual and collective behaviours. The sociological work referred to is driven towards an understanding of how social groups form and maintain themselves. It connects psychology of the individual with social psychology of the collective. It also involves the concept of life-world originally proposed by Husserl (1950), and after Habermas (1987) is taken as a mental meeting place where a group of worldview holders participate in structured communications according to some cognitive interest or purpose that can result in plans and decisions. It is a place where autonomous agencies maintain their proprietary local worldviews, and communicate with intention over a theme. The communications are structured to enable coherent participation of the worldview holders. This enables them to make sense of the acts of communication that occur in relation to other acts. The communication occurs through the transmission of meaningful symbols that enables the possibility of meanings to be embraced by worldview holders, and occurs through both information and knowledge migration. Information migration arises through the principle of hermeneutics (Heidegger, 1978; Baecker 2001, p. 66): the philosophy and methodology of text interpretation describing how information is communicated between agencies. Luhmann (1995) (as explained by Seidl, 2004) adopts the hermeneutics principle within the context of his communication theory of social (living) systems. Here, information around a theme is manifested in one worldview from others, and meanings then arise. To understand how this occurs requires the idea of knowledge migration. The information that is contained in messages is knowledge laden, i.e. its frame of reference is worldview knowledge belonging to an autonomous agency through which understanding and meaning develop. While the migration of information results in the accumulation of related thematic information, under certain conditions knowledge can then emerge. It is this emergence that is meant by the term knowledge migration, a potentially complex dynamic process that is susceptible to uncertainty, and that may or may not result in the

Introduction

development of new or renewed understanding and meaning. It is therefore through knowledge migration across agencies (interacting purposefully over a theme in a lifeworld) that a potential is offered for the formation of collective agreements. Since such agreements require common meanings, where worldviews significantly differ in their knowledge about a theme, agreements are potentially unstable.

Now, worldviews are cultural entities, and in the context of an organizational agency with a dominant culture, a dominant collective worldview will normally develop (though there are caveats to this that engage with issues of complexity). In larger organizations with a number of autonomous divisions the dominant culture typically oversees a set of subcultures that are associated with each division – where each thus maintains its own collective worldview. For complex information, the meaning differences across the migration can become elaborated across these subcultures.

The development of such collective worldviews is a reflection of lifeworld. This is not the private world of a given viewer or of any other viewer, or even of more than one viewer added together. Rather it is the world of common experience of those viewers who together define a semantic communications suprasystem (Schutz and Luckmann, 1974). In the lifeworld there exist boundary conditions that derive from tacit knowledge that comes from the sedimentation of experiences. These form the limits within which subjective experiences are arranged in certain structures. Subjectively, they can be experienced as transcendences of the everyday world.

This notion of lifeworld derives from what Durkheim has called the 'conscious collective' as seen from the internal perspective of members. Lifeworld holds patterns of meaning for the social community as a whole (Habermas, 1987). It is a transcendental site where speakers and hearers meet for intersubjective affairs like dealing with validity claims, settling disagreements, and achieving agreements. The lifeworld appears as a reservoir of elements that are taken-for-granted, are unspoken convictions, and that lead to interpretation through cooperative processes. Single elements are mobilized as consensual knowledge when they are relevant to a situation. The lifeworld is defined as a culturally transmitted linguistically organized stock of interpretative patterns. It has relevant structures that are interconnections of meaning holding between a given communicated utterance, the immediate context, and a horizon of meanings that are implied within communications but not stated. Lifeworld is goal orientated, and is connected with the cognitive interests and aims of at least one participant. It circumscribes a platform of relevance for thematizable elements of the situation. Fundamentally, lifeworld is associated with culturally transmitted background knowledge. Communicative actors are always moving within the horizon of their lifeworld to which they belong as interpreters and speakers. That which can be mastered and identified as a structured problem is restricted to an action situation of what remains encompassed within the horizon of a lifeworld – however blurred these may be. Every step we take beyond a horizon of a given situation opens up access to a further complex of meaning.

Parsons (1950) had an interest in the social, for which he developed a theory of action. His modelling ontology involved three autonomous systems referred to as culture, society, and personality. His interest lay in the 'societal community', which is seen by Habermas (1987: 139) to refer to the lifeworld of a social group. This forms the core of 'society' –understood as the structural component that determines the status of group members in relation to their legitimately ordered interpersonal relations. Culture and personality are represented only as functional supplements of the 'societal community', and culture supplies society with values that can be institutionalized. Socialized individuals contribute motivations that are appropriate to normed expectations.

Habermas (1987) developed his theory of Communicative Action within the context of the lifeworld. The structural ontology adopted distinguished between three interconnected autonomous worlds: the *internal* and *external* worlds of individuals, and their *social* world. He used this basis to develop a theory of communication that explained the semantic processes that enable collective social agreements to be made. Each world is distinct, is bounded away from the others, and maintains its own autonomous epistemic content. It is from this that all organizational processes derive in which meaning and consensual behaviour has significance. Luhmann (1995) is another sociological theorist who developed an alternative theory of social development through communication. It distinguishes ontologically between living, psychic, and social subsystems that together establish the basis for a 'living system' theory of society through communication. The three systems are each autonomous and are interconnected through a mutual structural coupling. The connection between psychic and social systems creates meaning, and their structural coupling implies that they coevolve. Here, communication is core, and the living system is largely concerned with emergent processes of communication, where socially all else follows since the social is dependent for its existence upon communication. Habermas (1987: 155) notes that Luhmann's theory of society can also be presented in terms of the lifeworld, but it is a background phenomenon which operates through organized interactions, not directly connected to action situations of society.

Like that of Habermas, Luhmann's theory of society concerns its communicative nature, but through the use of its cybernetic principles. This is appropriate since cybernetics is the science of control and communications. However, like many cybernetic approaches, Luhmann's work is not directed towards social dynamics or strategy, and has little interest in examining the pathologies or conditions of social ill-health that can arise. In contrast, Beer's (1979) theory of the strategic organizational agency is capable of identification, analysis, and diagnosis of pathologies. It is also susceptible to Habermas' comment applied to Luhmann's theory that it has an underlying (if inferred use of the) lifeworld concept. Beer's Viable Systems Model, as he refers to it, operates through five generic epistemic functions referred to as *System 1–5*. They are mutually interactive, acting together as a filter between the environment and an organizational agency's management hierarchy, and they connect management processes and their communications channels. The filter attenuates (reduces the importance of) some data while simultaneously amplifying other data. The filtered data is converted into information that is relevant to different levels of management. An auxiliary auditing function ensures that the correct data is being collated. The 'living system' approach Beer adopts in his organizational modelling is reflected in the interconnections between the generic functions. These are distributed across two interconnected ontological structures. One of these structures is referred to as a behavioural system, and the other its related cognitive metasystem. The system and metasystem are connected as a systemic couple through which communication occurs, and which represents the organization as an autonomous agency. In any complex organization there are normally a nested set of such autonomous agencies, and an example is an autonomous university having the nested autonomous set of faculties, itself having a nested autonomous set of departments.

This approach, while useful within its own strategic contexts of complex organizations with diagnosable pathologies, does not address the myriad of situations beyond strategy that arise in complex situations. This includes culture, which is important. This is because changes in culture have the capacity to change everything else in their social system (Costanza, Wainger, Folke & Miler, 1993). As though in refection of this, Dauber, Fink and Yolles (2012) explain that there has been an increased interest in using culture as a fulcrum through which different theories can be explained. Prevailing theories of management and organizations are not able to fully capture organizational dynamics or change and their adherent complexity (Smith and Lewis, 2011). As a solution to this, the creation of appropriate organization theory can be developed through a configuration approach (Meyer, Tsui & Hinings, 1993). This essentially adopts existing theories that conceptually interlock as building block units, and which together are capable of creating a meaningful assembly and avoiding paradigm incommensurability. This latter attribute occurs where the theoretical blocks are connected across distinct paradigms by ensuring no propositional or construct contradictions occur (Guba & Lincoln, 1994). Theory or meta-theory can be formulated from a multidimensional constellation of distinct characteristics that may commonly occur together. They typically include numerous dimensions of concept, environments, industries, technologies, strategies, structures, cultures, ideologies, groups, members, processes, practices, beliefs, and outcomes that have been said to cluster into configurations, archetypes, or gestalts. As such, a configuration model of organizational culture accounts for the multidimensionality and complexity of organizations that arises from a multidisciplinary approach. Coming from this direction, Dauber, Fink and Yolles (2012) create a rationale for the assembly of theoretical elements that arise from a variety of sources, and since these elements come together as a collection of concepts, meta-theory results.

This rationale naturally extends to the culturally based cybernetic agency meta-theory that we adopt, and is a reflection of the ideas of Bandura (2006). Here, agency may refer to an individual or collective, and explains the socio-cognitive aspects of self-organization and change, and the efficacy of migratory connections between its structural components. A collective agency may behave independently from the individual agencies that compose it because the normative anchors for social behaviour may be different from the anchors of individual agent behaviour. In the meta-theory we develop here the agency is culturally centred, and when involving culture in the social it is important to recognize the involvement of lifeworld at least as a backcloth, and the related communicative processes that are associated with it. Lifeworld establishes a valid entry into the broader cybernetic world of autonomous behaviour in complex change situations, where decision-making, information, and knowledge processes are central – as are the capacities to create processes of diagnosis for agencies with pathologies. This backcloth arises in particular with Habermas' distinction between the *internal*, *external*, and *social* worlds, and provides a basis for explanations about why an agency may differentiate its behaviour in each of the *private*, *personal*, and *public* contexts that it experiences. An illustration is indicated by Ackbar, Abbot & Bakan (2005: 2): Sir Mark Moody-Stuart was chairman of Royal Dutch Shell and representative of his organization. He debated *privately* (in the corporate external world of Shell Nigeria) with activists about the need to pursue human rights. *Personally* (in the corporate internal world), the company was seen as responsible for the violation of human rights by creating one of the world's worst centres of pollution. He seems not to have made any *public* (social world) statements on the issue.

While agency theory implicitly assumes the lifeworld, its explicit meta-theory arises from concrete 'living system' concepts as originated by Schwarz (1998), developed for the social context by Yolles (2006), and summarized by Yolles, Fink and Dauber (2011), rather than through configuration as described by Dauber, Fink and Yolles (2012). In this, migration occurs across ontologically structured parts of the agency, and the quality of the migratory process is an indicator of agency intelligence. As such an agency may be operating more or less intelligently as a function of the efficacy with which migration occurs. So, variations in the degree of efficacy can produce variations in agency intelligence. Since efficacy is seen as a function of migration, it is therefore dependent on the relative relationship between the meaning-potential that can be assigned to migrated information by individuals and groups which populate the structure where it arises and the structure to which it is migrated. The degree of convergence between these meanings will be a function of agency coherence (Guo, Yolles & Iles, 2009).

Structure of the Book

To explain the plural agency, this book is structured into eleven chapters, and divided into three parts. Part I is concerned with the nature of agency and consists of six chapters. Chapter 1 acts as an overview of a number of attributes of this book, as well as explaining the basis and attributes of the cultural agency. Chapter 2 is concerned with the instrumental agency, as well as the strategic agency. While the two are intimately connected, the strategic agency is considered more fully due to the extensive literature on strategy. In exploring the strategic agency, it creates connections with the more traditional strategic approaches found in the literature. As part of this it explores the way in which strategy is a reflection and driver of the way that an organization sees itself in relation to the competitive environment in which it likely tries to operate sustainably. It also takes the view that for organizations to viably survive they need to be adaptable, especially under conditions of complexity. They in addition need to seek continuous improvement and change to meet the needs of changing environments, and as part of this recognize and deal with impermanence and chaos in a competitive environment. The chapter also explores strategy in terms of corporate social responsibility, and how this can contribute to an organization's reputation and hence success. Chapter 3 is concerned with agency personality. We also introduce the concept of the normative personality, which is explored in some detail, especially with respect to its trait nature, where a set of normative traits that are deemed to exist can be used to anticipate an organization's patterns of behaviour given a known context. Chapter 4 explores intelligence associated with agency. It discusses various theories of intelligence, like the concept of habitus, multiple intelligences, and knowledge-based intelligence. These are then related to agency theory. Since personality is part of these theories, it is appropriate to recognize that agency theory also operates through personality. A plural agency has a normative personality which arises through normative cultural anchors. Finally, we examine a knowledge strategy case study within the context of the intelligent agency, and relate it to other ideas about intelligence including habitus and the theory of multiple intelligences. In Chapter 5 agency types are explored more deeply. Connections are also made to ideas about individualism and collectivism. The next chapter of this part of the book is

Chapter 6, concerned with agency consciousness. This is a topic that is rarely considered within texts related to organizational studies, but it links importantly with organizational learning, which is a well-established topic in the literature. The chapter examines the nature of the plural agency in terms of how it makes sense of its environment, and the process of internalization that it pursues in this regard. It explores internalization within the context of the generic system hierarchy that constitutes agency. It also indicates how agencies create processes of visualization that enable them to create higher orders of consciousness that can be applied to agency contexts. Overall, it represents consciousness as a complex attribute of the mind that can develop levels, has a participatory role for perception, has influences from its non-conscious attributes, and operates through a bounded capacity for information.

Part II has two chapters, and is concerned with agency dynamics. Agency change can be initiated by exogenous impulses from (arising from outside the agency) or immanently (from with the agency itself). Outside impulse for change emerges from cultural and political pressure (legitimacy changes) and from performance feedback imperatives. Immanent change comes from value or interest divergences or conflicts within the social system. In both instances the impulses for change are subject to the dialectic process that in the Chinese Taoist philosophy may be described through what may be called yin-yang processes. It begins with Chapter 7 on joint alliances, which constitute a major force for change, especially cultural change. In particular, we adopt a broadly human resource perspective, exploring the nature of joint alliances, and the issues that may arise during this process. The coupling of two or more agencies into a joint alliance from two 'parent' agencies results in a 'child' that is neither one nor the other parent, but draws on attributes of both. Finally in this chapter, we introduce a practical example of the development of an alliance in a cross-cultural context between two universities across Europe. Chapter 8 is concerned with agency dynamics, but through the lens of changes in their dominant paradigms that represent the nature of an agency. The general dynamic change processes that they pass through are then explained for conditions of complexity. The dynamics of immanent change are also explored. The dynamic modelling process also explores corporate life-cycles, and explains how each phase in the life-cycle passes through complex processes of change. The arguments centre on paradigms and paradigm change, and it is explained how these are culture based. It follows with a short case study on a Chinese bank.

The third part of the book has three chapters and concerns agency as society, but this does not mean that it is not also relevant to organizations, which can be seen as micro-societies. Fundamentally, the view is taken that all socials with an anchoring culture, no matter what size, have three other dimensions that are important to them, socio-political, economic, and financial. Chapter 9 is concerned with the social political agency. It provides a background to previous systemically oriented approaches to the social, including Parsons, Luhmann, and Habermas. Luhmann and Habermas take communication to be a central tenet of their theories, and so some brief consideration has also been given to semiotics: the study of signs and symbols and their use or interpretation as elements of communicative action. It is then explained how the work of the authors referred to can be migrated into cultural agency theory. Following this, the political dimension of agency is introduced by first briefly noting the approaches that are relevant to politics, and comparing two of these. Practical illustration is provided of how Luhmann's and Habermas' ideas can be applied. In Chapter 10 we consider the economic agency, exploring briefly the background to macroeconomic development. As part of this we introduce mindscape theory, intended to represent the agency personality and indicate its orientation, thereby creating expectations for its patterns of behaviour. Finally, in Chapter 11, we follow the lead of the introduction to this book that explains the Western recession caused by the banking industry, and we explore the banking situation in China, including its unregulated shadow banking sector. As part of this we show some parallels between the two systems, explaining how China could follow the West into recession. This possibility is clear when it is realised that the Chinese financial industry has maintained a number of pathologies that have emerged as corrupt practices. This has created an impediment to economic development and is a cause for macroeconomic instability (Wei, 2001). As such there is some incentive to explore and model corruption, and examine some of its attributes.

This book makes a specific contribution to the existing literature. We offer a cultural agency metatheory that is susceptible to particular forms of modelling, but which operates through cultural, strategic, and operative dimensions that are perceived as distinct but interactive. The assembly of these components has particular certain cybernetic attributes of control and communication that reduce the need to validate models. The assembly also has the capacity to relatively easily create particular models that can service contextual needs, and in many cases idiosyncratic penchants. Unlike most approaches that adopt a cultural orientation, the theory adopted here embraces both complexity and dynamic processes.

The book is not just a theoretical excursion into agency; it also explores a number of relevant and appropriate case situations. In Chapter 2 there is a case on corporate social responsibility, seen as part of the strategic agency. In Chapter 6 we consider the case of negotiation in terms of agency internalization and how agency consciousness is raised in the negotiation process. In Chapter 7 we consider the case of a joint alliance between two European Universities, one based in the UK, and the other in the then newly developing region of Central and Eastern Europe after the demise of the Soviet Union in the 1990s and onward. While the case may be almost a generation old, the principles raised are still very current. In Chapter 8 we introduce a study on a significant Chinese bank, indicating the problems that it encounters due to its fast pattern of growth and disparate geographical and cultural locations. The distinctions between them are illustrated through the development of a technique that arises from agency theory, which broadly examines the frames of reference of distinct cultural groups through a dynamic explorative technique. In Chapter 9 we consider the connection between different socio-political perspectives and show how these may be linked in pragmatic terms. In Chapter 10 we use mindscapes theory to illustrate how it may be possible to anticipate patterns of behaviour as Europe approaches its economic recession. Finally, Chapter 11 may be seen overall as a case study of the financial, economic development of China, and the nature of corrupt practices that occur there.

It has been said previously that the horizon of organizational theory has hit a chaotic mode, thus leaving uncertainty among theoreticians about the trajectory for future research, and a potential for conflict between paradigms. The modelling approach adopted in this book can be related to the configuration approach adopted by Dauber, Fink and Yolles (2012). It will therefore be of interest as a supporting text for academics, more advanced students of organizational studies, as well as strategic management, general management, organizational behaviour, and human resource management courses. Elements of this work are also relevant to political science, especially where a system of sociological approach is adopted. In addition, it would be appropriate for practitioners and policy makers interested in organizational change, societal change, and the modelling of impacts of policy or regulation. There are no texts that are comparable with this text at present. In addition, it might be of interest to organizational theoreticians, and consultants who are interested in understanding organizational processes.

Part I

The Agency

1 The Cultural Agency

1.1 Introduction

Looking around the literature, it may be realized that there is not just one agency theory. After Bandura (1986), we shall refer to three classes of agency: (1) mercantile agency, (2) emergent interactive agency, and (3) autonomous agency:

The Mercantile Agency is an internal instrumentality through which external influences operate mechanistically on action. Internal agency events are a reflection of the impact of external environments from which causal attributes are ignored, and the self-system is simply a repository and conduit for environmental forces. This type of agency is consistent, for example, with contractual theory (Eisenhardt, 2000) and economic theory (Spence, 1975), where the agency operates through self-interest and bounded rationality, embraces risk and outcome uncertainty, and agency hierarchies exist that correspond more or less to behaviour-based contracts. This is in contrast to the markets that agencies operate in, which correspond to outcome-based contracts.

The Emergent Interactive Agency defines Bandura's (1986) view of agencies. Agencies are emergent and interactive, and apply perspectives of social cognition, making causal contributions to their own motivations and actions using 'reciprocal causation.' This adopts attributes of self-regulation, control, action, cognition, affect, and other personal, environmental and interactive factors. Yoon (2011) notes that this agency has the capacity to exercise control over the nature and quality of its life, and in doing so operates with the core features of intentionality, forethought, self-reactiveness and self-reflectiveness.

The Autonomous Agency is able to embrace the concepts of both the mercantile agency and the emergent interactive agency. An autonomous agency is self-directed, operating in, and being influenced by, interactive environments. It may additionally have its own immanent dynamics that impact on the way it interacts. It is also proactive, self-organizing and self-regulating, participative in creating its own behaviour, and contributes to its life circumstances through cognitive and cultural functionality.

This book is concerned with autonomous agencies which here are broadly structured social living systems that learn and have consciousness. Such agencies are here defined using a meta-theory constituted as a *substructure* constructed through a *generic system hierarchy*. The substructure houses *superstructure*, composed of testable propositions that conceptually *enrich* substructure, and which may be migrated from other commensurable theories. The substructure also has various dynamic properties that include autonomy, a capacity to learn, and a potential for viability and hence adaptability. Agency also implicitly embraces inherent dynamic superstructural attributes that arise from socio-cognitive theory, including: collective identity, cognition, emotion, personality; purpose and intention; and self-reference, self-awareness, self-reflection, self-regulation, and self-organization/

This chapter provides a general introduction to many of the concepts that underpin agency and more specifically cultural agency. Cultural agency theory creates anchors of viability through its stable culture. It arose because of the need to address complexity and to better understand the nature of organizations and their behaviours. Its development rests upon a theoretical construct, cybernetics. Cybernetics is concerned with control and communications, as adopted here is explained through concepts adapted from Schwarz (1995), with influences from Beer (1975). Setting Schwarzian concepts of cybernetics within a knowledge context has provided the basis for a general theory (Knowledge Cybernetics: Yolles, 2006). It is a cross-disciplinary paradigm that encourages the careful migration of theory from other paradigms. Taking a leaf out of the cross-disciplinary approach by Kets de Vries (1991), broadening its scope to include cross-disciplinary concepts of psychology and social psychology enables new theoretical insights to arise, allowing us to introduce and explain the nature and functioning of the plural agency mind and personality.

Cross-disciplinary research can be compared with technology convergence (Papadakis, 2007). It can establish conceptually deep interactions between disciplines, leading to new conceptual syntheses not accessible to single disciplines (Haapasaari, Kulmala & Kuikka, 2012). It can be unattractive to significant single discipline academic journals, since articles directed there often do not conform to known terminologies or satisfy their citation expectations. Cross-disciplinary is sometimes addressed when academics (perhaps non-consciously) borrow from other fields without citation, and thus invent new terminology. A possible example might be Nonaka & Takeuchi's (1995) theory of dynamic innovation which is directly relatable to Piaget's (1950) learning theory. The orientation towards single paradigms results in an overall fragmentation across fields, and this occurs when, for instance, an academically attractive concept is consciously borrowed from one field and applied in another. Thus for instance, the concept of *constructivism* (also usually attributed to Piaget) leads Taber (2006) to note that the literature is not coherent about its nature, with its conceptualizations becoming rarefied away from its original context and meaning.

More frequently in single discipline approaches one finds a lack of research novelty and conceptual dead ends. Thus for instance, there is an increasing awareness of theoretical limitations in the field of organization theory. This is illustrated by the numerous scandals that have in general caught organizational theorists by surprise, for instance by the infamous 'Enron's meta-theatre' in which the corporation set up a sequence of companies to move money around fraudulently, with the implicit assistance of its auditors. There is no theory that is able to adequately identify such misconduct, leading therefore to a renewed interest in organizational theory and its capacity to discover, diagnose or predict such behaviour (Boje, 2002; Greve et al., 2010). Organizations develop misconduct through the rise and maintenance of pathologies (Samuel, 2010: 159). Organizational theory is in general unable to create any degree of coherence in the field due to the plurality of its unconnected and unrelated models (Scherer, 1998; Suddaby et al., 1998). A core problem is that organizations are complex, and comprehensive models seem inaccessible to current approaches (Suddaby et al., 2008). More, there is 'a growing disaffection with the existing set of theories that dominate the study of organizations and organizational behaviour' (Suddaby & Huy. 2009: 1).

A seemingly promising route to connecting distinct organizational theories comes from the field of organizational culture. This describes the psychology, attitudes, experiences, beliefs and values of an organization, concerns the norms that are shared by people and groups, and the controls that relate to how they interact with each other in and beyond their organization (Hill & Jones, 2001). A demonstration of the utility of this approach comes from Dauber et al. (2012) with the creation of a coherent model that arises from the synergy of a number of organizational modelling approaches. One approach that may be classified as part of this, because of its concern with the psychology of organizations, comes from Weick (1969 & 1995). It adopts a *corporate personality* metaphor used to model organizations so as to make them seem 'compact, intelligible and understood' (Cornelisson et al., 2008). This metaphor is well known (e.g. Olins 1978; Davenport et al. 1997; Barley 2007; Gindis 2009), particularly in the area of Identity Theory as part of Strategic Management and Marketing (e.g. Taylor 2000; He and Balmer 2007). In an attempt to understand organizational pathologies, Kets de Vries (1991) explores organizational personality by reflecting on psychological tendencies such as corporate neurosis, guilt, collective psychological defences that reduce pain through denial and cover-up, and unproductive power processes. Further to this approach, Godkin & Allcorn (2009) explain that organizational learning pathologies can result in dysfunctions like institutional narcissism. The relationship between specific pathologies and organizational dysfunction has also been explored. James et al. (1996) show that dysfunction arises when pathologies block possibilities for learning and for change. The organizational personality we have referred to may also be seen as a *normative* personality, where a coherent organization with a stable culture maintains a set of affective-cognitive norms that define the way things are done in the organization and anchors that personality.

The role of culture in organizational conduct and misconduct allows one to recognize that cultural and behavioural norms are of central importance, as will be discussed in more depth when considering socio-political attributes of the agency in Chapter 9. More, the cultural environment is closely linked to organizational patterns of noncompliance with the normative constructs that define legitimate conduct (Shover & Bryant 1993; Hochstetler & Copes 2001) and also indicate the rise of pathologies. Corporate misconduct turns to criminal conduct when legitimate corporate norms come into conflict with the ambient norms defined within a corporation's host culture and from which a legal framework arises to which member corporations should conform. Criminal conduct is permitted when corporate norms are eroded and expedient illegitimate practices become acceptable (Vaughan, 1983: 61). It is through an organization's culture and structure that opportunities are provided for organizational actors to engage in good conduct or in misconduct, though conditions must arise such that awareness of opportunities for misconduct (including crime) enables it to be incorporated into an organization's patterns of behaviour (Coleman 1987: 409). Piquero (2002), referring to work undertaken by Gottfredson & Hirschi (1990) on crime and other risk-taking behaviours, notes its connection with what is called a *trait* of low levels of self-control.

Our interest in this book is to show that *agency theory* is a profitable approach for organizational theorists who wish to better understand and therefore anticipate corporate conduct and misconduct, and the pathologies that cause the latter. It is useful to appreciate the nature and complexity of cross-cultural environments that relate, for instance, to the creation of joint alliances (Chapter 7) and agency capacities to respond to them, for example through cultural intelligence. This notion of cultural intelligence, which became widely known through Earley (2002) and Earley & Ang (2003), is significantly concerned with processes of cultural adaptation (Earley & Mosakowski, 2004; Ang, Van Dyne & Koh, 2006) in cross-cultural contexts that manifest potential or actual conflicts. According to Yolles & Fink (2015c: 320), citing Bogilovic et al. (2014), 'there is an inverse relationship between cultural intelligence and collective creativity. Cultural intelligence is a biased measure which gives too much weight to agency adaptation.' So what is creativity? For Saninno & Ellis (2013) creativity has been primarily seen as the quality of an innovative individual or of a novel outcome, but is an integral aspect of learning that enables and promotes the exercise of learners' agency. It also has an integral connection with performance (Sawyer, 1998). So, it may be said that *creative learning* generates novelty, for instance with the appearance of new knowledge. In contrast, *adaptive learning* results in new patterns of behaviour (Hofstede, 1981: 26). Their distinction principally lies in their membership of different ontological domains (which define some entity belonging to it in terms of a set of generic characteristics): creative learning is existential in nature in that it is related to self-referential identity (Yolles, 1999). In contrast, adaptive learning is phenomenal, relating to structure and consequent behaviour. We have referred to both creativity and collective creativity: their distinction is that the former is an individual attribute while the latter is a social or plural one, but this distinction is eliminated through the concept of cultural agency since plural agency operates through cultural norms. Collective creativity, for Fischer (2001), is a cross-cultural attribute of plural agencies in which learning through multiple knowledge systems is of fundamental importance. This suggests that there is an issue with cultural intelligence due to its adaptation bias, which is not implied by the broader Piagetian (1950) related concept of cultural figurative intelligence that is a feature of our agency theory (Chapter 6). Where cultural intelligence can be measured (as a cultural quotient: CQ), a high score indicates capability in cultural adaptation within an agency, while a low scores suggests greater capability in collective creativity and learning. A principle adhered to within this book is that extreme conditions have the property of ignoring some sociocultural needs, often resulting in inequitable and therefore reduced performance in social environments. As a result, a balance between creativity and adaptability would usually be desirable since it provides improved opportunity for unbiased analysis in resolving (in this case, cultural) issues. Having said this, ultimately contextual and situational factors may demand alternative conditions to balance, for instance where severely socio-political or physically constrained environments limit choice options.

Agency is here taken to be a plurality of sub-agencies that might be individuals of groups. It has a plural personality that goes beyond metaphor. Further in this book we use the term *agency* for a social system (notably an organization) that is capable of developing strategies and putting selected espoused strategies into effect, that is, to realize them operatively. Since we are dealing with agencies as social systems, we also have to take into account that social systems may consist of sub-systems, which ultimately consist of individual personalities. Potential coherent action of a group of individuals (a sub-group of an organization) can be modelled with the embedded concept of normative personality. Then, a *normative personality* is nested into a larger social system which defines the affective-cognitive nature of agency.

To generate theory for the plural agency two approaches are possible that might meet in the middle. The first arises as a *configuration* of models that together contribute to a particular outcome, and the second from *socio-cognitive theory*. Configurations may come from organization theory, psychology, management, anthropology, sociology, or indeed any of the numerous disciplinary fields that exist. Socio-cognitive theory arises from a reformulation of living system conceptualizations, this latter originally arising from Schwarz (1994). Whatever approach is chosen, there is always a conceptual goal to be sought that exists at some undefined or undeclared horizon. Thus, outcomes are not arbitrary or accidental.

1.2 The Configuration Approach and the Socio-Cognitive Approach

For the ***configuration approach***, Dauber et al. (2012) were interested in the dispersed classes of organizational theory contextualized through organizational culture studies. Drawing on ideas within the field of organizational culture, two modelling categories are identified: (1) a dimensions approach (e.g. Hofstede et al., 1990; Sagiv & Schwartz, 2007), and (2) interrelated structure approach (e.g. Allaire & Firsirotu, 1984; Schein, 1985; Hatch, 1993; Homburg & Pflesser, 2000). Linking such approaches with Hatch & Cunliffe (2006) and defining the relationship between strategy, structure, and operations through a variety of works (e.g. Child, 1972; Chandler, 1973; Argyris, 1977; Galbraith and Nathanson, 1978; Schein, 1985; Fredrickson, 1986; Dodgson, 1993; Amburgey & Dacin, 1994; Harris & Ruefli, 2000; Whittington, 2001), a new culturally based model for the organization is created and presented as Figure 1.1, adapted from Dauber (2012).

Here a number of terms are used that might usefully be highlighted. The model shows feed-forward processes that include guidance, externalization, and patterns of behaviour. The term externalization is inspired by Nonaka & Takeuchi (1995). Organizational culture impacts on strategy, structure, and operations. Patterns of behaviour arise from structures and within them constitute the norms that provide what is acceptable – and what is not. Operations are instances of behavioural conduct that are hence both facilitated and constrained by structure. Considering feedback processes starting from operations, performance assessment makes demands on structure to ameliorate or amplify the morphology of the organization. The notions of single and double loop learning arise from Argyris (1977). S*ingle-loop learning* refers to processes of instrumentally detecting errors and adjusting existing strategies to meet new requirements as might be dictated by the needs of organizational adaptation and response. *Double-loop learning* refers to a deeper process of learning that relates to the internalization of knowledge and value adjustment, and is more connected with the demands of change on organizational culture. The two interactive environments shown are referred

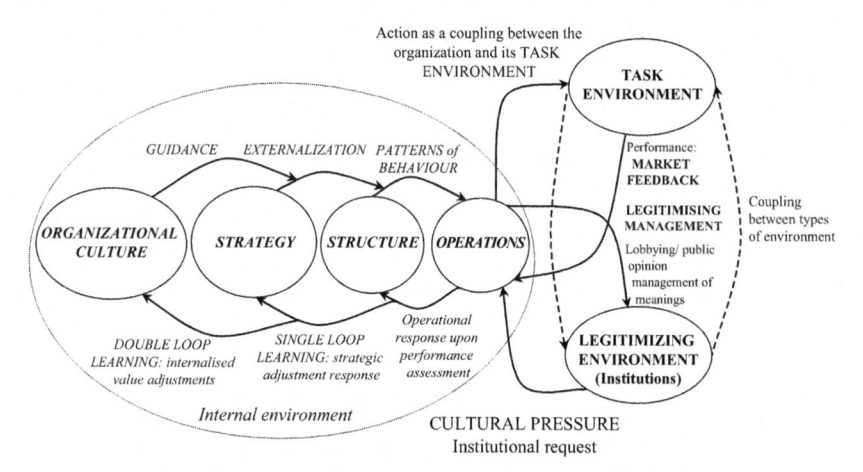

Figure 1.1 Model of organizational culture connecting internal and external environments (adapted from Dauber et al., 2012)

to as *task* and *legitimizing*, and both are structurally coupled to the system of operations – thus having structure – determined/determining engagement and a common history of interaction (Maturana & Varela, 1987). The task environment constitutes what the organization offers and delivers as its services. The legitimizing environment gives legitimacy to the conduct and goals and activities of the organization. The organization may also try to influence the legitimizing process (Anderson & Gray, 2006).

Figure 1.1 may be related to socio-cognitive theory, where an organization has a 'mind' that operates as a complex system (Bandura 1999; Cervone et al. 2004). Socio-cognitive variables develop through socio-cultural experiences. They distinguish between cognitive capacities that contribute to personality functioning, an attribute that is also expressible in the collective organization. This includes skills, competencies, knowledge structures that have been derived from experienced real life situations, self-reflective processes that enable people to develop beliefs about themselves within social contexts, and self-regulatory processes where people formulate goals, standards, and motivations toward identifiable outcomes (Bandura 1986, 1999; Williams 1992). Performance involves the evaluation of directed behaviour and is related to the interaction between the behaviours, which are embedded in personality structures expressed as systems, and the social environmental factors with which it is coupled. Each of the personality systems have schemas that constitute their functional-strategic structures, and traits which take on a regulatory function. The personality is embedded in agency that also has a cultural and operative system. All these systems are ontologically distinct with

28   The Agency

```
                    EXTERNALISATION through a
GUIDANCE through a network    network of processes that
of principles (from paradigms)  constitute operative intelligence
  that constitutes figurative                                          Artifacts
         intelligence                       BEHAVIOUR from            Environment
                                         reflection of intentions
```

- *Cognitive system* **CULTURE** as part of a cognitive base (Belief system & patterns of knowledge) Cognitive intentions Self-reference ***Underlying Assumptions***
- *Figurative system* **STRATEGIC ORGANISING** *as part of its figurative base* Decision imperatives & attitudes Cognitive purposes Self-regulation ***Espoused Values***
- Operative System **STRUCTURE** as part of its pragmatic base. Cognitive interest *Self-organization* **Operative Management**
- *Agency* **OPERATIONS** *Efficacious directed action with social consequence (reaction).*

INTERNALISATION through operative intelligence feedback to cognitive base, paradigms, culture and viable patterns of knowledge:

COMBINATION through a network of information processes that induce ADAPTATION and RESPONSE

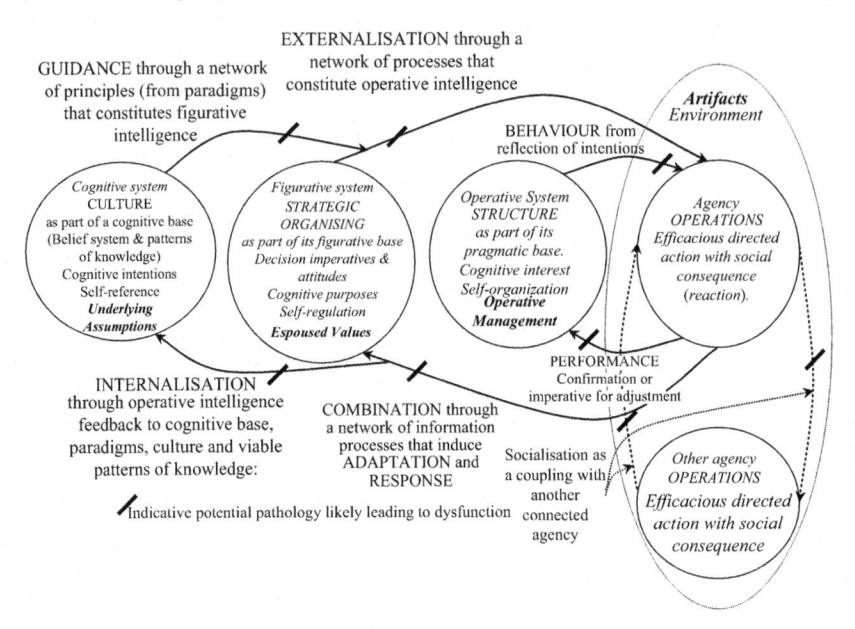

PERFORMANCE Confirmation or imperative for adjustment

Socialisation as a coupling with another connected agency

Other agency **OPERATIONS** *Efficacious directed action with social consequence*

Indicative potential pathology likely leading to dysfunction

Figure 1.2 Model of a sociocultural agency

different generic characteristics and functions. Agency has cultural, conceptual, figurative, operative, and event orientations. They are all connected indirectly through a set of process intelligences – constituted as a network of processes that migrate semantic goods like information and knowledge between the systems that each trait dominates.

In Figure 1.2 we present an agency model, formulated through three distinct *cognitive, figurative, and operative* systems. Each system sits in a distinct generic domain: an ontologically distinct space that has a *class* of identifiable properties. The cognitive system sits in an 'existential' domain, so called because it has thematic relevance that defines the constituents of experience (i.e. the observing, encountering, or undergoing of things). The figurative system sits in a 'noumenal' domain, so called because it has interpretative relevance that creates direction through the selection of relevant aspects of experience. The operative system sits in a 'phenomenal' domain, so called because it has structural relevance (connected with action, the meaning of which is determined by context) that constitutes an origin for experience. Each of the domain-based systems have related functional characteristics and epistemic content. They are connected through intelligences (see Chapter 4, Agency Intelligences): *figurative intelligence* (a form of autogenesis: Schwarz, 1997), which provides its core relational explanations of reality, and *operative intelligence* (a form of autopoiesis: Maturana and Varela, 1987; Schwarz,

1997), which provides its capacity to evidence the figurative base of figurative schemas (espoused strategies like goal options or intended images that define self, called self-schemas) which are deemed useful for practice. Normative agents with poor figurative intelligence do not maintain good representation in their figurative or cognitive bases. Those with poor operative intelligence cannot adequately manifest elements of their figurative base pragmatically, so that they have limited capacity to realize strategic models. In Figure 1.2, possible deficiencies are indicated by the bars lying across the connecting process intelligence loops and illustrate possible pathologies that might arise in the organization (Yolles, 2008).

In the *cognitive system* there exists a collective *cognitive base* that constitutes the 'truths' that form both its *epistemic base* (scientific beliefs that form patterns of analytic knowledge) and its *cultural base* (cultural beliefs that arise as normative standards of conduct), where both are connected with assumptions, beliefs, and trusted propositions that arise within cultural development; the cognitive base may be seen as the result of cybernetic interaction (Maturana and Varela, 1987: 75) between the patterns of cultural and analytic knowledge, and these affect each other through their history of mutual influence, where cognitive intention plays a metasystemic role and creates a cultural orientation for the agency (Yang et al., 2009). Self-reference is essential and establishes an agency identity (Hannah et al., 2008 & 2010). The underlying assumptions (Schein, 1985) contribute to organizational knowledge, where false knowledge when embedded into the culture results in myth.

In the *figurative system* of Figure 1.2 there is a *figurative base* of schemas that is composed of entities and their relationships that have been construed through the sedimentation of information-rich conceptual models (from its cognitive base), with connection to cognitive purpose. It is the home of figurative elements like ideological and ethical structures that contribute to the political and moral functioning of the agency. This figurative part of the agency is also its *strategic part* from which follows the regulation of information flows, decision-making, and patterns of behaviour, the 'internal allocation of tasks, decisions, rules, and procedures for appraisal and reward, selected for the best pursuit of [...] [a] strategy' (Caves, 1980: 64). *Cognitive purposes* (Habermas, 1970) are linked to information, and determine purposeful behaviour (Espejo et al., 1996). This is also the domain of attitudes, manifested from beliefs to create an 'enduring organization of beliefs' (an ideology) around an object or situation predisposing an agency to respond to situations in some preferential manner (Rokeach, 1968). Values are culturally defined (Williams et al., 1993), and when espoused enable the distinction between observable and unobservable elements of culture (Schein, 1985).

The operative system of the agency is its structural component from which behaviour emanates within an environment which becomes populated by artifacts – objects created by agencies, often with assigned cultural significance (Schein, 1985). It is in the operative system where organizational structure is maintained. Here there is a pragmatic base that is constituted by and facilitated through normative modes of practice that respond to standards of validity that constitute evidence, with connections to cognitive interest that are used for acquiring knowledge (Habermas, 1970). Self-organization is important to the survival of an agency, enabling it to create its own order (Kauffman, 1993). It is also the domain of operative management, epistemologically distinguishable from operative processes (Beer, 1975).

In Figure 1.2, it is shown how an agency develops patterns of behaviour through knowledge flows. The network of processes of externalization, combination, and internalization (c.f. Nonaka & Takeuchi, 1995), which respond to the interest in how organizations express, connect, share, and incorporate knowledge, are also important to the organizational processes. As in Figure 1.1, they are constituted as the transitive (across system/domain) process intelligences. These processes provide feedback that is able to constrain or amplify the systemic attributes indicated in Figure 1.2. The process of socialization, through which explicit knowledge can be socially spread, occurs as a lateral (within domain) interactive coupling between at least two agencies, which have a common history of interaction beyond the boundaries of the personality.

Thus, the model in Figure 1.2 has feed-forward processes that are constituted as process intelligences. Through figurative intelligence, organizational culture guides strategy, and indirectly influences structure and operations. Through operative intelligence, externalization processes influence structure and operations. Operations are instances of behavioural conduct that are hence both facilitated and constrained by structure. The transitive coupling between the distinct domains is cybernetic in nature, with feed-forward and feedback loops, where the feed-forward processes represent action orientation, and the feedback processes represent possible adjustment-oriented processes. Starting from the operations system and considering feedback processes, performance assessment creates demands on structure to ameliorate or amplify the morphology of the organization. Information assessment processes induce adaptation and response, for example, through 'combination' of new information with already available information new knowledge might be created and espoused values might be modified. 'Internalisation' indicates that new knowledge is fully internalized into the belief system and the underlying assumptions (for combination and internalization see also Nonaka & Takeuchi, 1995).

The *phenomenal domain* (i.e. the domain of observable phenomena) of the agency embraces an organization's operative system, which is shown to be connected laterally as an interactive coupling with other agents (i.e. other organizations) in an environment, and with which it has a history of interaction from which arises performance.

In the models in Figures 1.1 and 1.2 we find:

1) a set of interconnected domains, that is, culture, strategy, structure, and operations,
2) a set of feed-forward processes, which are directed towards emergent patterns of behaviour and action,
3) a set of feedback processes, which are responsible for information collection, information assessment, adaptation, and learning.

The deficiency of these models is that they do not address the issues that emerge from the alternate perspectives of action and learning orientation. A specific normative personality may focus solely on strategy and action deployment, and another solely on information collection and adaptation to an environment. As indicated by the bars in Figure 1.2, in these two examples either the lower-part feedback processes or the upper-part action-directed feed-forward processes or both are suppressed.

In Figure 1.2, we referred to cognitive, figurative, and operative systems. These in effect house a set of formative traits for the agency (see Chapter 5, Traits and Types). We also have to note that the model in Figure 1.2 is constrained in another aspect. In Figure 1.2 we have a 'Legitimizing Environment (Institutions)' as a second environment, which by and large can be seen as a representation of a wider 'cultural environment' into which an agency is embedded and from which emanate institutions. However, from that cultural environment less visible forms of cultural influences also emanate through numerous petty acts. Thus, we present Figure 1.3 where a normative personality is embedded into a larger social whole (a larger agency), which provides the cultural environment for the normative personality. We shall return to this figure shortly.

1.3   Viable Living Systems and Cultural Agency

Agency theory has its basis in cybernetic living systems theory of Maturana and Varela (1980), biologists who were interested in what distinguishes living systems from not living systems. They came to the recognition that living systems operate through a network of processes called autopoiesis, or self-production. Since then, various extended texts have been written to explore the nature of autopoiesis (e.g. Mingers, 1995). Its development has also come together with the idea that there are 'orders' of cybernetics. Each order represents a means by which the complexity that is perceived to occur in reality can be reduced: the higher the order the greater the improvement in

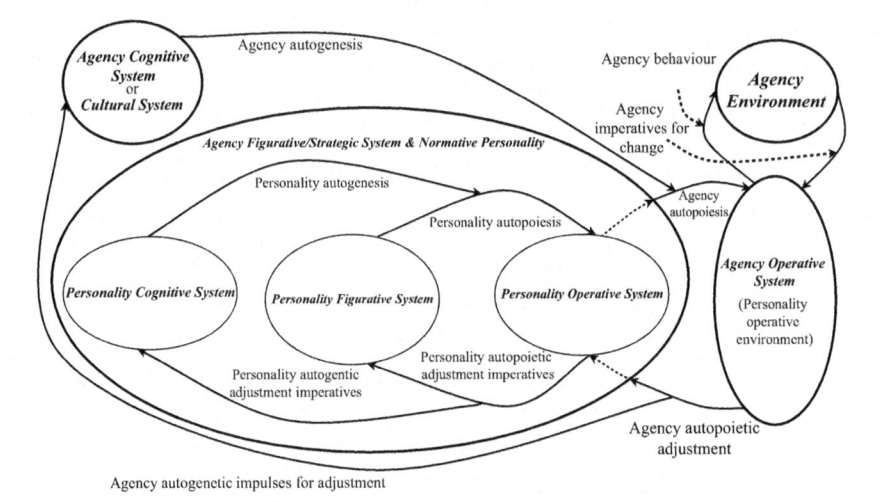

Figure 1.3 Socio-cognitive trait model of the agency connecting normative personality with social and cultural systems

explaining complexity. Autopoiesis is a concept that stimulated some, like von Glasersfeld (1984), to explore what has now been called second order cybernetics. Unfortunately, there has been a gap in the movement towards the development of a general theory of cybernetic orders theory (see Yolles & Fink, 2015a, 2015b, 2015c). The result is that many of the concepts and ideas implied by autopoiesis have been subsumed into second order cybernetics, which has become a catch-all for anything that does not constitute first order cybernetics – simply represented as operative systems in interaction. This is not, in general, recognized by those cybernetic advocates who are only aware of the management cybernetics paradigm.

Underpinning both cybernetic order and agency, *viable living systems theory* is the significant insight of Eric Schwarz (1994 & 1997) who, like others of his time, recognizes that the concept of autopoiesis is fundamental for creating viable and durable systems. The idea of viability comes out of the cybernetic tradition. It means that a system can survive even under considerable perturbation because it can take avoiding action; can acclimatize; can accommodate; and can adapt (Beer, 1989). This capacity for durability also implies other attributes like self-organization, self-reflection, and self-reference. According to Beer (2002), it can also be taken as a capacity for self-sustainability – however, there is confusion and controversy in the literature about the nature and meaning of sustainability (Yolles & Fink, 2014), and for our purposes the term is unnecessary.

The Cultural Agency

The cultural agency is a viable system that arises directly from the viable living systems formulations of Schwarz, transposed into a knowledge-based organizational context (Yolles, 2006). The development of the configuration approach explained earlier would not have been possible without cultural agency theory as an objective at its theoretical horizon.

Schwarz' theoretical conceptualization provides a foundation for holistic living system agency theory. Through extension and elaboration it also leads to a general theory of higher cybernetic orders (Chapter 6). The idea of higher order cybernetics has its basis in second order cybernetics, which arises with Stafford Beer's Management Cybernetics paradigm (Beer 1959 & 1968; Malik, 2002; Rosenhead, 2006). While some important principles of Management Cybernetics also act as a basis for agency theory, the latter should be seen as a different paradigm due to its centring on the Schwarz construct of viability. As a result, the nature of the metasystem in Beer's approach where autopoiesis is implicit to the modelling process is distinct from Schwarz' where autopoiesis is an explicit structural component. Thus it would not be surprising if higher orders of cybernetics are expressed differently in the two paradigms, which is the case.

Beer (1980), unlike Maturana, believed that living systems theory could be applied to both biological and social systems. Luhmann (1986) created a theory that demonstrated this by centring on human communications. While the theory is powerful, if seemingly impracticable, in Chapter 10 we show how it can be transformed to work as a method with practical issue resolution capacity. The book by Mingers (1995) on self-producing (or autopoietic) systems offers a rather complex explanation of the systemic meaning of living. Eric Schwarz' (1994 & 1997) little known theory is much simpler and more powerful, having some coincidental synergy with Piaget's (1950) theory of learning. For Schwarz, a living system involves learning requiring an extension to autopoiesis through a set of higher order processes called autogenesis. Schwarz' theory offers a great deal of theoretical promise, as yet undeveloped, that is capable of embracing Beer's work, even if in different terms. Set within a different context, it is also able to create rich explanations, as shown in Chapter 2. Its distinction from Beer's conceptualization lies in part in his view of the metasystem, different from that of agency theory. The former adopts a general metasystem as an inherent horizon of meanings. Thus, for instance, cultural values are implied, but not represented explicitly. In contrast agency theory demands explicit reference that offers the promise of a richer modelling process.

In Chapter 2 we introduce the instrumental agency. This is really a regulatory pre-living system involving an explicit form of autopoiesis, but it is devoid of other *implied* attributes of higher order cybernetics that arise in management cybernetics. It is pre-living since it responds to its environment instrumentally, but is not capable of creating new knowledge and hence not capable of learning. *Autopoiesis* is equivalent to what Piaget (1950) had called *operative intelligence*, and embraces instrumental learning. A system is instrumental when it operatively manifests its strategically pursued goals or aims. It learns instrumentally when strategic models that facilitate behaviour are modified by experience, where antecedents and consequences are related. This is distinct from cognitive learning where knowledge is developed through experience and accumulated or adjusted. Extending the cybernetic order brings in the concept of a higher order network of processes that Schwarz called autogenesis, and which is equivalent to Piaget's concept of figurative intelligence through which new knowledge can be created.

Agencies conform to the viable living system structure conceptualized by Schwarz. They are not only instrumental, but can generate novelty and are conscious. Agency is represented by a meta-structure defined through a *substructure* constructed through a generic system hierarchy (Chapter 6, Consciousness and Cybernetic Orders). The substructure maintains the properties of a viable living system, though it also adopts a superstructure composed of testable propositions that elaborate on the agency nature, properties, and capabilities. This conceptualization also connects generic system hierarchies with the cognitive processes of internalization that are essential to social learning (Vygotsky, 1978; Wertsch, 1979), and self-reflection. We say social learning – different from personal learning. While personal learning is constituted through the creation of new idiosyncratic knowledge, social learning is knowledge that has been socially validated. The substructure has dynamic properties like autonomy, viability, and adaptability. Agency also implicitly embraces inherent dynamic superstructural attributes that arise from socio-cognitive theory, including collective identity, cognition, emotion, personality; purpose and intention; and self-reference, self-awareness, self-reflection, self-regulation, and self-organization.

Agency internalization transcends what can be observed in its environment. It can be connected with *self-reflection*: a capacity to exercise introspection and a willingness to learn more about the fundamental nature, purpose, and essence of what is observed and internalized (Tu, Chou, & Lee, 2013). Self-reflection is in turn connected with critical reasoning and indeed theorizing about it. For Brown (2000), critical reasoning does not require understanding since people can know what they think about a given thing even if they do not completely understand the concepts associated with it. These are called second order judgements: they enable a judgement about an entity to be made only through the thoughts about it, rather than through critically reasoned explicit evidence. Second order judgements are self-verifying and thus taken to be true (Burge, 1988: 658). Brown further notes that the ability of an agency to perceive the rational relations between their attitudes towards an entity is determined *misunderstanding* and *agnosticism*, where in the latter case they recognize their lack of understanding. While misunderstanding may result in inappropriate pragmatic use of a concept, agnosticism is not likely to. Incomplete understanding, he tells us, undermines the ability to engage in critical reasoning, often occurring because the rational relations between the properties that constitute it are unknown or uncertain. An agency can use reflection to evaluate attitudes and decisions, thereby improving rationality and coherence. However, having a full understanding of a concept does not involve the ability to make a correct conceptual analysis. This is because there may always be a plurality of conceptual analyses possible, and because it is not always necessary for a correct conceptual analysis to be expressed explicitly where there is no need to articulate it.

Self-negotiation is another attribute of the agency related to self-reflection. It may be conceived as an internal dialogue that enables an agency to explore its own existing knowledge and subsequently revise its own output. It is a process that manifests itself externally in self-repair (Han & Ji, 2008), and can also result in self-regulation (Tu, Chou, & Lee, 2013). In Chapter 3 we shall discuss Agency Personality and argue that it has a mind which, through its internal landscape, maintains orientations that define personality. Self-reflection offers a base for thinking about directions of change that may or may not influence personality, and which might be explored through self-negotiation, the outcome being implemented through strategic self-regulation (Chapter 2, Instrumental and Strategic Agency) and resulting in agency self-organization. This implies that agency moves from a more passive to a more dynamic basis for self as it moves through self-negotiation. Agency dynamics are discussed in general terms in Chapter 8 (Agency Dynamics).

We have referred to the feature of agency called viability. This is important from the proposition by Beer (1959), which states that *every viable system contains and is contained in a viable system*. This has immediate consequences for agency theory, enabling Beer's proposition to be extended so that *every viable living system contains and is contained in a viable living system*. The significance of this proposition is that it permits agencies to be modelled recursively according to context (Yolles & Fink, 2015a). In a sense then, agency represents a theory of contexts. There is an easy example of this in the cultural agency of Figure 1.3. Here, one is able to recursively set an agency model into the strategic agency system, thereby delivering personality itself seen as a viable living personality system.

There is a clear distinction between agency and its personality. Agency is a living social system that viably exists in a physical environment towards which it is open to interactions. The characteristics of such a living system are explained by Schwarz (1997) and reformulated within a knowledge context by Yolles (2006). They have a network of (autopoietic) processes that manifests noumenal domain cognitive properties to a phenomenal domain operative system. This noumen is not Kant's noumenal epistemological horizon that is unknown and unknowable, but rather an agency-relative virtual ideate (figurative schema) that within a cultural agency is represented by cognitively defined structures (Yolles, 2006). Later we shall extend this discussion to affective or emotional structures. In contrast to cognitive structures, phenomenal domain entities are reality-based structures that result in action. The generic relationship between noumenal and phenomenal-based systems is referred to as an *instrumental agency* since (cybernetic) feed-forward and feedback instrumental control of the system is maintained by the cognitive system. Agency also has a cultural dimension that facilitates learning and is part of the existential domain having generic characteristics relating to self-referential identity. In the cultural agency existential attributes are constituted as knowledge, while in the strategic agency they are constituted through cognitive schemas that are formulated through (cognitive and affective) attitudes and information. This living system cultural agency is recursively sensitive to contexts. *Thus, every living viable system has within it a living viable system defined in relation to appropriate contexts.* The functional characteristics and epistemic content of these recursive living systems is determined by this context. This is illustrated in Figure 1.3, where the personality is a living viable system that deals with different types of information and constitutes the strategic component of the cultural agency. The noumenal context of the personality is that it deals with cognitive processes like thinking, and is the seat of consciousness.

In Figure 1.3 we also show that the agency operative system interacts with its environment(s). This is a structured system; this structure both facilitates and constrains behaviour. This behaviour is projected into the agencies environment. Behaviour may be seen to occur within both political and sociobiological contexts. Political contexts explore the development and application of power that results in behaviour, while sociological ones examine the social behaviour and its impetus in social terms. These are discussed at some length in Chapter 9 (Social Political Agency), especially by examining some of the more relevant sociological theories and how they relate to agency. Its environment is also susceptible to economic processes, as discussed in Chapter 10 (The Economic Agency). But both are also connected to the more micro-level financial system that agency discovers in its environment; this is discussed in Chapter 11 (The Financial Agency).

As we see in Table 1.1 and in Figures 1.2 and 1.3, depending on the paradigm from which different terminologies arise, there is a systematic link between different terms. We identify these closely related terms:

- The cognitive/cultural system is part of the existential domain (relating to self-referential identity). In the agency cultural system it houses knowledge structures and knowledge from which context-sensitive information can be delivered to personality. The cognitive personality system houses the unconscious and preconscious, and (cognitive and affective) attitudes and information result in structured cognitive schemas.
- The figurative/strategic system is part of the noumenal domain (relating to relativistic ideates). In the agency figurative system this houses consciousness, influenced by the personality subconscious and unconscious. The personality figurative system houses the subconscious, and its structures are represented by figurative schemas that may include goals, ideologies, ethics, and self-image.
- The operative system, which includes organizational structure and operations, is part of the phenomenal domain (related to phenomenal objects and action). In the agency operative system this houses operative structures that deliver real-world behaviour, and normally reflects conscious decisions that arise from the personality. In the personality the operative system is connected to the conscious, and structured operative schemas that can be used in decision-making.

These terms have arisen as a way of explaining the distinction in the generic characteristics of each of the sub-systems of a living system, though it should not be believed that the terms existential, noumenal, and phenomenal are immediately related to their original conceptualizations in the literature.

In a social context the plural agency cognitive system is defined by its culture, that is, the pattern of beliefs, values, and knowledge from which arise noumenal and phenomenal norms. Noumenal norms determine agency standards concerning collective cognitive processes, while phenomenal norms determine standards for behavioural possibilities. These are manifested to the agency's cognitive figurative system through agency autogenesis, resulting in context-sensitive cognitive information that is differentiated in different parts of that system.

The Agency Figurative System, that is, the Strategic System of Figure 1.3, can be explored in psychological terms even though the cultural agency is a plural entity (Yolles, 2006). Until now there has been no coherent framework for consciousness (Koch, 2009) from which a suitable theory can arise, and that can explain the nature of the mind–body relationship. However, here we do deliver such a framework from which a theory of consciousness arises, which incidentally coincides with a new general theory of cybernetic orders. In Chapter 6 we explain these relationships, also showing that consciousness as such is a consequence of three 'living system' personality attributes that couple together the psychic attributes of conscious, subconscious, and unconscious. These are connected with the ego and superego (Freud, 1962), as explained in Table 1.1. The term preconscious as used in Table 1.1 arises with the work of

Table 1.1 *Consciousness defined in terms of three psychic domains*

System	Psyche	Explanation
Existential personality cognitive system	Unconscious/ Preconscious	This involves collective unconsciousness mental states. In the plural actor it is seen as initially heredity (from unitary actors) and some would consider that it operates through symbolic archetypes. It is manifested from culture and functions through the uncoordinated instinctual impulsive shorter term trends of the minds that compose the collective and unconscious drives that can become the cause of cultural conflicts. There is also longer term preconscious mental disposition expressed through attitudes that are related to knowledge and emotion. Dispositions anchor the personality and together with states structure cognitive schemas.
Noumenal personality figurative system	Subconscious	Part of the mind that stores memories and desires, structured as figurative schemas. Associated with the superego, which functions as a consciousness controller, using moral and critical processes.
Phenomenal personality operative system	Conscious	Agency phenomenal awareness. It can be known by others only if they believe expressed introspections and/or by inferring it from the actor's behaviour that arises from operative schemas. It is associated with the ego, which resides in the structures that ultimately determine behaviour.

Wollheim (1999), and the collective unconscious (these days often called the autonomous or objective psyche) is adapted from Jung (1936).

The idea that plural agencies have conscious ego is not new. Every corporation has its own 'life' and its own ego that can compete directly against real people and demand equal treatment under the law (Lasn & Liacas, 2000). Corporate ego-centred consciousness takes on the attitude of 'we versus they', wherein 'we' are on the side of justice, truth, and the good, while 'they' are the exact opposite (Habito, 1999). The subconscious holds or manifests awareness into a form that can be related to phenomenal experiences. For Priddy (1999) it is a subliminal awareness system that is trained through experience. The unconscious is deemed to be inaccessible to the agency, though it is still

The Cultural Agency 39

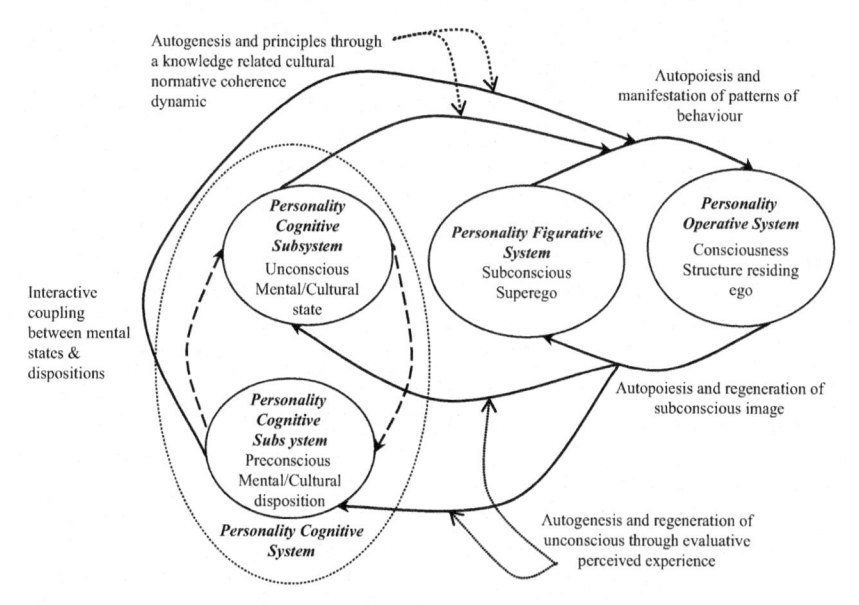

Figure 1.4 Relationship between the ego, superego, unconscious mental states and preconscious disposition in an agency personality

important to consciousness. The plural psyche responds to context-related information from patterns of cultural knowledge. This is underpinned by a belief system that is related to perceived experience, is evaluative and thus related to subjective attributes, and prescriptive relating for instance to conduct (Rokeach, 1968: 113). The relationship between the unconscious, preconscious, subconscious, and conscious is shown in Figure 1.4.

In the cultural agency figurative system a superstructure can be constructed that arises from psychology. The personality has a cognitive/affective landscape that creates psychic orientations that define its nature. These include mental states and dispositions, traits, and emotions. Figure 1.4 distinguishes between mental state and disposition. Referring to Davis (2000), these can be differentiated as follows:

- Mental state consists of impulses, perceptions and instincts, conceptual imaginings, and drives, is context sensitive, being transient, relatively brief, and can reoccur frequently to give the impression of continuity maintenance.
- Mental disposition consists of patterns of information that arise from beliefs, knowledge, and values, and maintain memories, abilities, phobias, and obsessions. These have longer duration and history, and operate as a personality anchor that stabilizes it.

Both mental states and dispositions are causally related: mental state being able to instantiate, terminate, reinforce, and attenuate mental disposition. For Wollheim (1999: cited in Davis, 2000) subjectivity may be only associated with mental states, while mental dispositions can only be indirectly experienced through the mental states in which they are manifest. An example of the relationship between states and dispositions is indicated by the nature of emotions. Emotions are mental dispositions that while not being consciously experienced influence mental states by initiating feelings that can be experienced. As such, emotional control has become an area of interest (Gross, 2008).

Internal conflict may develop when mental states and preconscious dispositions do not maintain an effective interactive coupling, that is, they lose their interactivity. In this case the mental state and its instinctual drives, impulses, tendencies, trends of the mind, motivating force, and hidden desires and wishes may find itself in conflict with the preconscious knowledge, external filtering, migrating knowledge, or emotions.

The idea of the non-conscious mind has been used by Bourdieu (1984) in his inquiry into the coordinated development of regular patterns of knowledge, and by Lewicki et al. (1992) in their exploration of the acquisition of information related to the subconscious. It involves the unconscious and the subconscious. Like the unconscious, the non-conscious mind of the unitary agency consists of knowledge and mental processes that are not currently in consciousness (Baars, 1997). It has content and process that can be arranged on a continuum, according to how easily retrievable they are into primary and secondary (or reflective) consciousness.

Agency manifests cultural and cognitive attributes to the agency operative system, thereby creating potential for behaviour that is facilitated and/or constrained by its operative structure. This is explained through something called living system anticipation. Rosen's (1985) form of anticipation is really nothing other than a strategic schema (i.e. a cognitive/mental model) that may influence the system's structure and that can be applied for a given context. Dubois (2000) developed on this to argue that there is another form of anticipation that arises from the very properties of the living system itself – through its very substructure, for which autopoiesis constitutes a significant component. In fact it is through the substructure as well as through appropriate superstructural elements that anticipation is facilitated.

The particular superstructure that is being referred to is migrated from theories in psychology, and is represented through the formative traits of an agency. Each formative trait is such that it dominates a particular system of the agency, which it controls. These traits contribute to the definition of the agency personality, together with emotions and other attributes.

2 The Instrumental and Strategic Agencies

2.1 Introduction

The *instrumental agency* is really a misnomer in that it is not formally a living system like other agency forms. Rather it is a strategic regulatory couple composed of ontologically distinct operative and strategic systemic parts, connected together through a network of processes called autopoiesis. The nature of the operative system is that it involves a phenomenal structure that facilitates physical action in its behavioural environment. The nature of the strategic system is that it involves a cognitive structure, like theory or goals, which facilitates options manifested in the operative system through autopoiesis. While it is from the operative system that agency behaviour emanates, its figurative system is of utmost importance, especially because of its regulatory functions. So while interest lies briefly in the operative component of the instrumental agency, greater interest lies in the strategic agency, particularly with its important connection with management theory.

Operative systems are organized structures of an agency that facilitate or constrain its behaviours in given contextual environments that, when supported by other attributes, can survive viably. They do this by adapting to changes in contextual environment, thereby reorganizing their structures. The term 'variety' arises because of the idea that complex environments are constantly in change and as a consequence generate conditions that continually test an autonomous self-organizing system. The ability of the system to survive depends on its ability to create the requisite variety (Ashby, 1964) that equally responds to the variety it experiences from the environment.

The operative system is connected with the agency's figurative (or strategic) system and is populated with schemas that create potentials for behaviour. There is a dynamic relationship between these parts of the agency, which we illustrate in Figure 2.1. This extends the operative system and explains the action/responsive couple between the operative system and its strategic regulator. Sometimes in such modelling (e.g. Beer, 1979), the figurative system is replaced by a more all-embracing metasystem, in which higher orders of agency are subsumed, but we shall return to this in Chapter 6.

Figure 2.1

The Instrumental Agency Couple

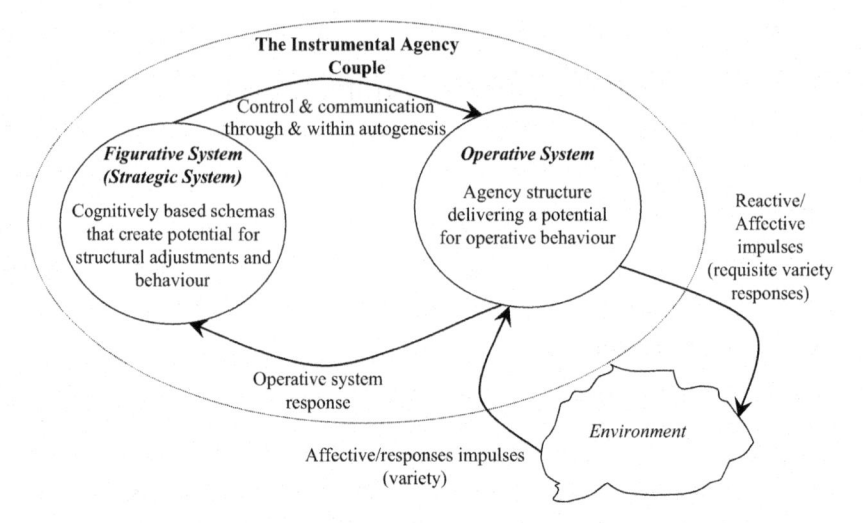

- **Figurative System (Strategic System)**: Cognitively based schemas that create potential for structural adjustments and behaviour
- **Operative System**: Agency structure delivering a potential for operative behaviour
- Control & communication through & within autogenesis
- Operative system response
- Reactive/Affective impulses (requisite variety responses)
- Affective/responses impulses (variety)
- Environment

Figure 2.1 Dynamic relationship between the operative and figurative systems of the instrumental agency and its environment

The instrumental agency couple therefore constitutes an extension to the operative system that involves a higher function. There is also an interactive coupling between the system and its environment, which enables the development of a shared past and future history. This coupling enables environmental variety to be channelled and recognized, unless it is a novel variety, when the agency cannot recognize it without new knowledge. While such new knowledge is not instrumentally possible, what is possible is agency response to known environmental impulses, or the usually inadequate use of known variety to unknown environmental variety. Matching agency responsive variety to environmental variety is called requisite variety (Ashby, 1956). In other words, when a variety of independent affective problem situations arise the system must deal with each of them in an appropriate way.

An instrumental agency cannot be viable, since it has no stability anchor and is not capable of recognizing or creating novelty, and novelty is needed during unanticipated change. For Argyris (1976), the viability of an agency would lie in its ability to respond to unanticipated environmental changes. Further, the instrumental agency cannot be viable because it is not a self-dependent autonomous social collective that has the capacity to respond to changes initiated by the environment or by its own internal dynamic processes, primarily since these processes are limited in their scope and generative ability. The survival of viable systems is deemed to be dependent on their capacity to introduce changes to their structure (which will impact on their behaviour), whether or not the changes have been foreseen. As such, an instrumental agency should not be seen as being autonomous. While the instrumental agency has a capacity for regulation, organization, self-production (autopoiesis), and cognition, its capacity for adaptation is limited. In other words, autopoiesis on its own is not sufficient to define a living system, unless learning is informally inferred.

Where instrumental systems have inferred existential attributes, like culture, they can have implied viability. This would, transposing an argument of Schwarz (1997), require that they can pass through processes of emergence and evolution towards further complexity. This occurs through the development of patterns:

- of self-organization that accommodate phenomenal change through morphogenesis and new forms of complexity;
- for long-term evolution that support autonomy;
- that lead to systems functioning viably through their capacity to create variety and indeed requisite variety.

Curiously, many members of a complex agency do not recognize the nature or importance of the constraints or facilitations under which they operate, and that have been imposed by ideological-ethical and socio-political agency structures. Nor do they appreciate what the significance of this is for agency viability. That applies equally, for instance, to government agencies, corporations, factories, and universities alike.

The operative system with its organizational structure is important to the agency not only because of its organizational structure (which facilitates and constrains agency behaviour) but also because it is a phenomenal system that is visible to other agencies that operate in the same phenomenal space. Thus, for example, other agencies in a phenomenal environment only see a given agency through its structures and actions, being unable to see its cognitive aspects unless as a reflection of its behaviour.

We have noted that the figurative system is of fundamental importance to the agency, since it strategically conducts the operative system. However, here we will explore beyond the capacity of the instrumental agency by incorporating knowledge and knowledge processes. This enables us to move from more traditional strategic approaches to knowledge-based ones (see below).

2.2 Two Views on Strategic Management

Today, there are two basic models that deal with the notion of business strategy and the perceived need to maximize returns that arises out of sustainable strategic (e.g. competitive) advantage: Michael Porter's (1980, 1985) view on **market-based strategy** and the contrasting **resource-based**

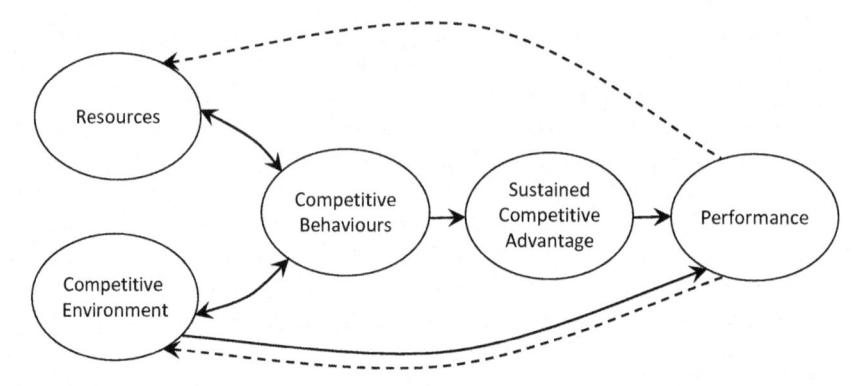

Figure 2.2 Connection between resources and competitive advantage (adapted from Bridoux, 2004)

view by J.B. Barney (1991). However, both are devoid of explicit knowledge processes, and thus constitute instrumentalities.

Bridoux (2004) recognizes that firms compete for resources and may use their resources to compete. The relationship between resources and competitive advantage that results in enhanced performance is illustrated in Figure 2.2. However, to better understand each of these approaches, it is worth their being examined in slightly more detail, especially if either approach can be adopted. Later, we shall elaborate on this model, explaining that knowledge must necessarily also be a component.

Competitive Environment Market-Based View

Many agencies are concerned with ensuring that they maintain strategic advantage and therefore ensure healthy returns, and creating 'healthy' returns is therefore tied to a competitive commercial landscape. This notion supposes that there is a competitive marketplace in which the opportunity landscape is flat; so that, for instance, the maintenance and improvement of the agency's competitive position in the market is possible.

Traditional market-oriented strategy theory sits on the work of Porter (1980, 1985), whose strategic model outlines the primary forces that determine agency competitiveness: the bargaining power of *customers*, the bargaining power of *suppliers*, the threat of new *entrants*, and the threat of substitute products – which combine together to create a level of competitive *rivalry* in an industry. This model argues that to develop effective agency strategies there must be an understanding of and reaction to those external forces, and it is this that will determine the agency's level of competitiveness. This orientation towards the external environment does little to address the capability of an organization to develop its own internal processes. Without this, an agency is likely to be incapable of adequately recognizing the nature of the external environment, let alone creating a sustainable strategic advantage. There was some argument about whether these primary forces were an adequate representation of an agency's competitive environment because theory required a set of 'ideal' conditions:

(a) There is certainty in a market, so that participants can plan for the expected behaviour of others.
(b) Buyers, competitors, and suppliers are assumed to be unrelated and do not interact or collude.
(c) The source of value is structural advantage that creates barriers to entry.
(d) The basis for competitive market strategies is rationality, so that returns can be maximized.

In support of this notion, Sheth & Sisodia (2002) are interested in markets that are largely free of regulatory constraints and entry barriers. Examples are restrictive patent rights or government-controlled capacity licences. In such markets they propose that the market evolves into two types of competitor that result in the contouring of the market place: (1) generalists, who are driven by volume, who compete across a range of products and markets, and for whom financial performance improves with gains in market share; and (2) specialists, who tend to be margin-driven, where financial performance deteriorates as they increase their share of the broad market. However, these propositions, arising as they do from neo-classical forms of game theory (von Neumann and Morgenstern, 1947), are unrealistic. More realistic from the 1950s is Nash (1996), who illustrated that, in a competitive environment, individuals who operate as cooperative groups survive better than those who operate non-cooperatively. This was used by Brandenburger & Nalebuff (1996), who introduced a cooperative component into Porter's five forces model by adding a sixth force, the *complementors*, to help explain the basis for the development of strategic alliances in a competitive environment. This is shown in Figure 2.3, which has all six forces. Porter's five forces are essentially: (i) possible entrance of competitors, indicating the problems of, and barriers to, market entry, (ii) threat of substitutes, indicating the problems of and barriers to product or service substitution and price adjustment, (iii) power of buyers, indicating the strength of position buyers have in a market, and exploring the option of volume transactions, (iv) power of suppliers, and what potential competitor suppliers may enter the market, (v) rivalry in the market, indicating if there is already strong competition and what their characteristics might be.

When an agency sustains returns that exceed the average for its industry, it is said to possess a *competitive advantage* over its rivals in the given marketplace. Indeed, a business strategy goal is to achieve a sustainable competitive

Possible Entrants
Needs characteristics: proprietary products/service; access to resource inputs and product/service distribution; cost advantages; knowledge of government policy and capital requirement; use of economy of scale and brand identity.

Complementors
Needs characteristics: formation of strategic alliances; buyers, competitors and suppliers interact and collude; structural advantage developed

Competitive market

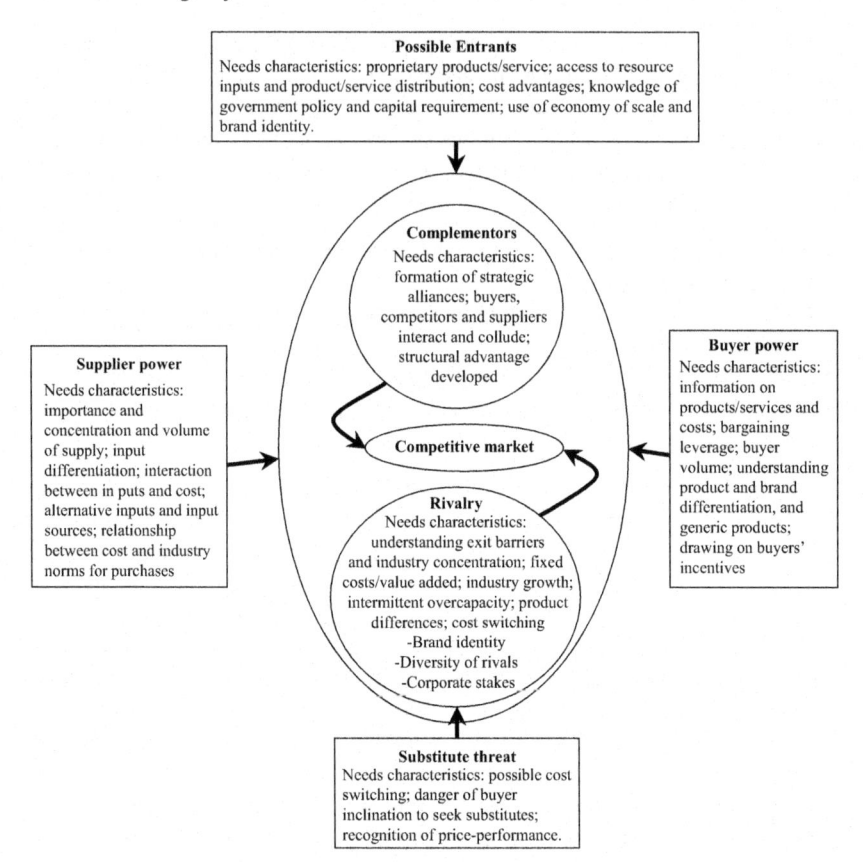

Rivalry
Needs characteristics: understanding exit barriers and industry concentration; fixed costs/value added; industry growth; intermittent overcapacity; product differences; cost switching
-Brand identity
-Diversity of rivals
-Corporate stakes

Supplier power
Needs characteristics: importance and concentration and volume of supply; input differentiation; interaction between inputs and cost; alternative inputs and input sources; relationship between cost and industry norms for purchases

Buyer power
Needs characteristics: information on products/services and costs; bargaining leverage; buyer volume; understanding product and brand differentiation, and generic products; drawing on buyers' incentives

Substitute threat
Needs characteristics: possible cost switching; danger of buyer inclination to seek substitutes; recognition of price-performance.

Figure 2.3 Six forces model as an extension of the five forces Porter model

advantage. Porter (1985) defined two types of competitive advantage: cost advantage and differentiation advantage. Cost advantage occurs when an agency can deliver the same benefits as competitors but at a lower cost, while differentiation advantage occurs when benefits are delivered that exceed those of competing products. These types of advantage are known as *positional advantages* because they can describe an agency's industrial position as a leader in either cost or differentiation.

Resource-Based View

Porter's view can be considered as an extension of the *resource dependence view* (Pfeffer & Salancik, 1978), that is, that ultimately all resources of an organization result from its environment. In contrast, Barney (1991) and others

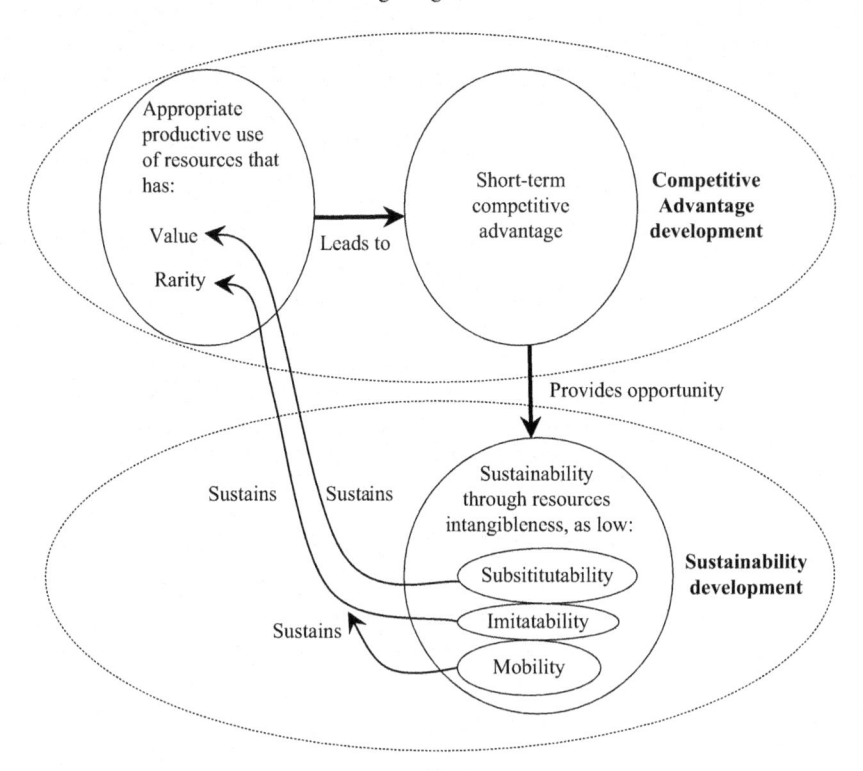

Figure 2.4 Model of the resource based approach to business strategy (adapted from Wade & Hulland, 2004)

(Mahoney and Pandian, 1992; Priem and Butler, 2001) shifted the emphasis to resources internal to the organization of which it disposes directly. These resources are inputs into its production process, and competitive advantage may occur where these resources are rare, valuable, and hard to imitate. Thus, they cannot be easily supplied on external markets.

A representation, adapted from Wade and Hulland (2004), is shown in Figure 2.4. This argues that agencies possess resources that are inputs into its production process, and competitive advantage may occur where these resources are rare and valuable, implying that others do not have access. The model has three 'capital' inputs: physical, human, and agency. The use of these resources is determined by characteristics inside the company, which can permit it to achieve both competitive advantage and a sustainable superior performance – usually expressed in terms of relatively high levels of return on investment. Sustainability is enabled by making the agency responsive to rapidly changing market conditions by maintaining the development of existing resources and capabilities, and creating new ones. One aspect of the resources and capabilities in a globalized accessible world is knowledge, which is deemed to be the most important value-creating asset.

The resource-based view centres on the idea of economic rent or Economic Value Added (EVA): that the agency earns beyond cost of the capital employed in their business, and EVA is used as a measure of competitive advantage. The objective of a company is to increase its economic rent, a consequence of which is an expected increase in return. The agency operates as a collection of assets/capabilities – providing a capacity for a set of resources to effectively perform activity tasks.

The collection of assets/capabilities is said to be 'intangible' (Figure 2.4) if it is to contribute to sustainable competitive advantage. For this to occur it needs to be distinctive, having attributes which competitors are unable to reproduce. A capability might also be proprietary, thus making it agency unique.

2.3 The Knowledge Management Paradigm

The inclusion of knowledge processes to the instrumental agency is technically an inference that extends it from information-based instrumentality to a knowledge-based autonomous living system with implied learning capabilities. Here we shall explore knowledge processes by extending the instrumental agency inferentially in this way, first by discussing knowledge within the context of strategy.

In more recent years it has been realized that in exploring business strategy, the use of economic theory and its notions of price and utility value may be inadequate. This is in particular because the approach still centres on the creation of a framework arising from game-theoretic arguments, in which the agency is seen as a set of utilities that can be optimised and are more orientated towards efficiencies than effectiveness. A bankrupting organization may be both efficient and ineffective. Zack (1999) tells us that few executives are able to express the connection between their agency's intellectual resources and capabilities, and its competitive strategy. This is not surprising, since most of the theory about this is rather fuzzy. The knowledge management paradigm, however, provides an entry into the exploration of corporate effectiveness. Further, the economic/utility theory that underpins current work on strategy proposes that the individual profile of a given agency is unimportant in respect of returns (Connor, 1991). Zack (1999) notes that, consistent with Nash's theory on cooperative games, the overall pattern of relationships among agencies in an industry is of importance. If the industry as a whole, he tells us, is properly structured so that there are sufficient barriers/impediments to competition, then all firms should realize excess returns. Even with the development of the resource-based view of strategy, the internal environment of the agency is still not sufficiently considered, and very often managers know little about intellectual resources of an organization.

According to Furlong (2005), competitive advantage is often related to the core competencies of the agency. Core competencies are those capabilities that are critical to a business achieving competitive advantage, and these are frequently based on *tacit knowledge*. The modern notion of tacit knowledge, attributed to Polanyi (1997), is intangible, unexpressed, non-codified, unstructured, delivers 'know-how' through experience, is difficult to recognize and manage, is connected with understanding, and is difficult to transmit. In contrast, explicit knowledge is expressed and codified, and can be transmitted between individuals but not necessarily understood. With effort some knowledge believed to be tacit can be transformed into explicit knowledge. This body of knowledge is the organization's implicit knowledge (Frappaolo, 2008).

For Furlong there are two factors that have significant influence on the ability of an agency to achieve sustainable competitive advantage. These are: (i) *structure and configuration*, and (ii) *agency culture*. These are inherently linked to corporate paradigms and politics which influence strategic capability, and this is ultimately a reflection of the internal environment. Analysing strategic capability is critical for two reasons. First it determines whether an agency's resources and competencies fit the environment; and second it identifies new opportunities to stretch and exploit an agency's unique and rare competencies in hard to imitate ways, by creating new market directions, or both (Johnson and Scholes, 1999).

The importance of the role of culture cannot be over-rated. Culture is a harbour for knowledge through which meanings are generated. It is these meanings that create understanding for a workforce and create product or service outputs that are consistent with the perceived needs of business strategy. So, rather than simply talking of business strategy, one might be as well to refer to an effective knowledge management (KM) strategy. For Furlong (2005, §6.1) an 'effective KM strategy is one that creates competitive power by robustly linking core competencies, depends on management's ability to develop a work environment that fosters learning, knowledge creation, knowledge sharing and the use/re-use of agency and personal knowledge. Furthermore, management must ensure that the application of knowledge is used in the pursuit of new business and is congruent with corporate goals.'

Zack (1999) notes that today knowledge is considered to be the most strategically important resource, while its acquisition through learning is essential for an agency's strategic capability. However, as he informs us, many of the initiatives being undertaken to develop and exploit agency knowledge are not connected in any way to its business strategy. More, knowledge management initiatives tend to be expressed within the context of information systems projects. The paradox appears to be that while managers tend to intuitively believe that strategic advantage can come from knowing more than competitors, they are not able to explicitly articulate the link between knowledge and strategy.

It has already been said here that few executives can identify a connection between their agency's intellectual resources and capabilities, and its competitive strategy. More than this, however, they have no developed strategic models to assist the creation of linkage between knowledge-oriented processes, technologies, and business strategy, and they have no idea of how to adjust strategic action related to knowledge. Zack refers to the model he develops as *knowledge strategy*. As an entry to this he argues that knowledge can create a sustainable advantage because:

(1) Knowledge is context-specific,
(2) Tacit knowledge
    a. is embedded in complex organizational routines,
    b. has been created from experience,
    c. tends to be unique and difficult to imitate.

Unlike the resources discussed within economic/utility theory, tacit knowledge is not seen as a disposable utility easily traded or optimised. While tacit knowledge is always unique to an individual, relatable knowledge can be acquired by competitors, but this requires that their personnel engage in similar experiences and socialization. If this is possible, then it can be time-consuming and not just a function of investment.

Sustainability of a knowledge advantage comes (for Zack) from knowing more about some things than competitors, combined with the time constraints faced by competitors in acquiring similar knowledge, regardless of how much they invest to catch up. While disposable resources are consumed as they are used, they provide decreasing returns over time. However, knowledge provides *increasing* returns, as it is used as it grows and develops, creating increased value in a self-reinforcing cycle. If an organization can identify areas where its knowledge leads the competition, and if that unique knowledge can be applied profitably in the marketplace, it can represent a powerful and sustainable competitive advantage.

Within this context, agencies need to engage in learning, building up tacit knowledge in their workforce to provide a current or future competitive advantage. However, for an agency to be aware of its knowledge distribution it needs to develop and maintain a context map of its knowledge resources, categorizing and benchmarking it to provide a potential for resource access (Wallis & Wright, 2015). Too few agencies are aware of their own knowledge and where it lies, and they are continually striving to re-invent it within other contexts. A knowledge map can be used to prioritize and focus learning

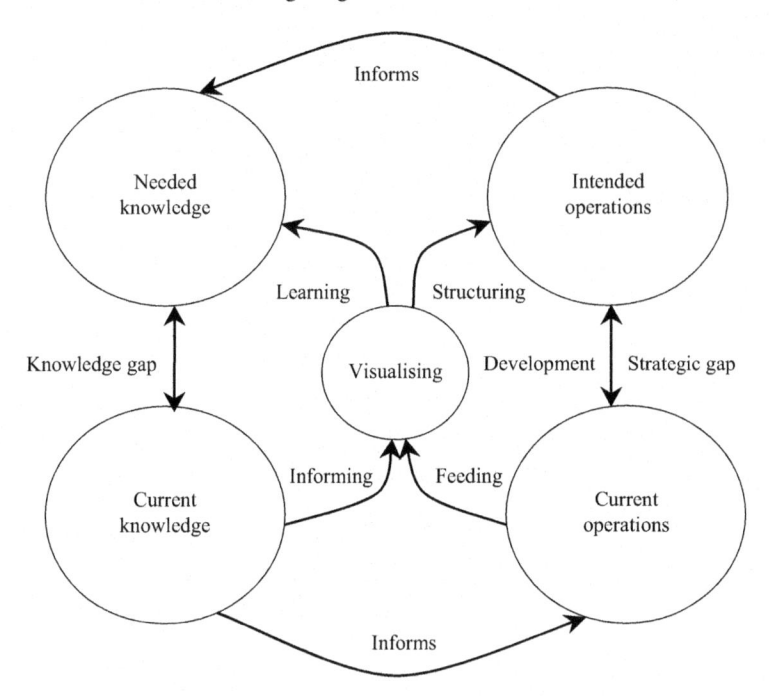

Figure 2.5 Relationship between the knowledge and strategic gap through visualization (developed from Zack, 1999)

experiences, thereby creating greater leverage for its learning efforts. Thus agencies can combine their learning experiences into a 'critical learning mass' around particular strategic areas of knowledge.

To explicate the link between strategy and knowledge, an organization must articulate its strategic intent (Hamel and Prahalad, 1989), identify the knowledge required to execute its intended strategy, and compare that to its actual knowledge, revealing its strategic knowledge gaps. This is illustrated in Figure 2.5, adapted from Zack (1999). However, a need unrecognized by Zack is that knowledge gaps and strategic gaps can only be filled through processes of visualization that enable learning by creating new tacit knowledge and structuring to create appropriate operations.

How then is tacit knowledge able to contribute to the formation of sustainable competitive advantage? This is explained by Johannessen et al. (2000), who have considered the relationship between knowledge and competitive advantage. An adaptation of their considerations is given in Figure 2.6, explained in Table 2.1. For them, sustainable competitive advantage requires the development of individual and corporate knowledge, this being able to

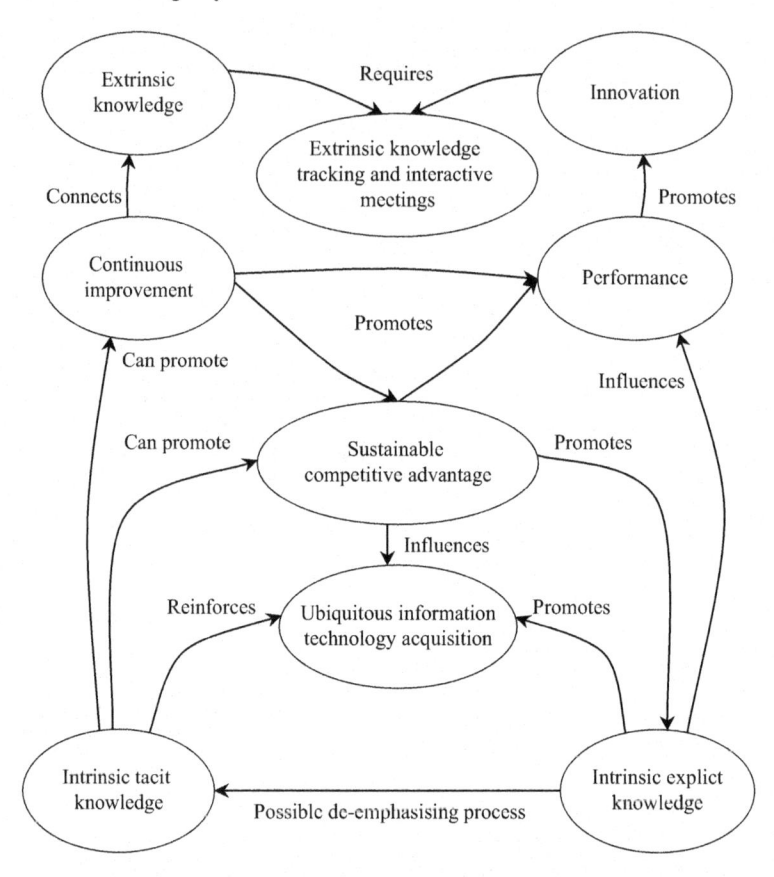

Figure 2.6 The relationship between knowledge and sustainable competitive advantage

drive innovation, create continuous improvement, and develop competence. Intrinsic tacit knowledge may promote sustainable competitive advantage where those who have that knowledge are trusted, and the nature and use of that knowledge can be expressed if not yet made explicit. There is another classification of knowledge: primary and secondary. Primary knowledge is that knowledge that has been created first hand through tacit experience, but it may also have an explicit expression by passing through an implicit knowledge stage. It is acquired as a direct process for the individual and is filtered through worldview. A holder of this primary knowledge may also express it explicitly, however, for purposes that may include personal reflection. Secondary knowledge is knowledge that has been carried from one individual to another. The acquisition of secondary knowledge is indirect, being filtered not only through

Table 2.1 *Proposed attributes for sustainable competitive advantage (based on Johannessen et al., 2000)*

Attribute	Proposition
Tacit knowledge	A toning down of the intrinsic tacit knowledge may lead to devastating consequences for agency ability to create and maintain a sustainable competitive advantage.
Total corporate knowledge	An agency knowledge base involves both tacit and explicit knowledge, and they are both intrinsic and extrinsic. An over-emphasis on explicit knowledge, especially by IT investments, may result in loss of agency competitive edge. Over-emphasis on primary knowledge may have the same outcome, as tacit knowledge development does not enhance the potential for innovation. Secondary knowledge development does not normally offer the necessary speed in information gathering required to maintain competitive edge. Hence, in order to achieve sustainable competitive advantage, companies need to emphasize the total knowledge base of the company, i.e. the explicit and tacit knowledge, both internally and externally.
Innovation	To maintain sustainable competitive advantage, agencies need to focus on innovation processes intrinsically, benefiting from the creative potential inherent among its staff. This is achieved through an interest in the total knowledge process.
Continuous improvement	To maintain competitive edge, agencies need both a sense of stability and continuity, and an awareness of the potential for intrinsic continuous improvement of existing products and services. Primary knowledge is crucial in the success of continuous improvement. Emphasizing total knowledge base promotes this.
Intrinsic knowledge development	Knowledge development occurs through interactive and reflective learning. Successful innovation and processes of continuous improvement connect with the process of organization knowledge development.
Core competence	Develop complementary intrinsic agency relations through mediation for learning (e.g. mentoring and apprenticeships), trust, and positive attitudes as might develop through teambuilding approaches. Effective systems for agency knowledge development presuppose a focus on core competence delivering effective performance.

two worldviews – the knowledge creator and receiver through communication. In complex situations secondary knowledge may act as a catalyst for invention. The extrinsic knowledge shown in Figure 2.6 may also be understood as extrinsic implicit knowledge.

The context for the Johannessen et al. (2000) study is that within complexity many agencies attempt to perform better by using information technology (IT). This relates not only to management information systems, but also to knowledge-based systems. However, while knowledge development has both a tacit and explicit dimension, the technology tends to be limited to the transfer of explicit knowledge; as a consequence, tacit knowledge, whether implicit or not, may become relegated despite its strategic importance. This can lead to knowledge mismanagement.

2.4   Complexity and Viable Systems

There has been a transition in strategic processes that began with the use of economic utility theory that was interested in optimising attributes of the agency relevant to competitive advantage. Such a simplistic approach did not recognize the role of either explicit or tacit knowledge. More importantly, it did not recognize that the internal condition of an organization is more important that its search for competitive advantage and that profitability is a consequence of the capacity of the corporate agency to function effectively and maintain its viability within complexity. Here we shall move to considering these attributes of the agency.

The notion of complexity operates under a variety of related paradigms, but for our purposes it is sufficient to distinguish between two of these. One is sometimes referred to as complexity theory and extends from the work of authors like Stewart (1989) and Kaufmann (1993). The other approach is sometimes referred to as management cybernetics that arose in the 1940s (Rosenblueth et al., 1943) and developed by Beer (1979). Both are interested in complex systems, but the terminologies are distinct, suggesting different paradigms (unless terms have an unlikely linear correspondence). Both approaches have been influenced by the ideas of complexity, explored for instance, by Prigogine (1989) and Nicolis and Prigogine (1989).

Brodbeck (2002) explains that complexity theory has its origins in the natural sciences (Santosus, 1998; Pascale, 1999), and in particular systems science derives from thinking in biology. It holds that in complex systems there is hidden order to behaviour and its development. However, it has few applications to management (Rosenhead, 2001).

Like traditional theory, complexity theory also concerns itself with processes (Lewin, 1999) and how these influence employee behaviour. Complexity theorists see agencies systemically, taking a holistic, organic, and nonlinear approach (Santosus, 1998; Anderson, 1999). It enables markets to be seen as an evolutionary co-evolving systemic environment (Berreby, 1998). Indeed, Berreby advocates that if left to function independently, systems self-organize, bringing about order without apparent cost. As we shall see later, there is a cost, and this is to make sure that the agencies operate viably, limiting the pathologies that they build into themselves.

Within this paradigm, actors are seen as agents that interact with each other in different ways. The environmental system is self-organizing and adaptive if the agents change their actions due to their interactions – hence, self-organizing.

Where these interactions are somehow influenced, the dynamic of the system changes and behaviour and performance alters.

This framework can be applied to business strategy. Consider agencies that seek to improve their business position in a contoured competitive market place. Following Sherman and Schultz (1998), competitive advantage should be seen as fleeting, can change rapidly, and can turn assets into dead weight.

When discussing the dynamics of agencies seen as systems, there is therefore a clear need to explore their internal environment in more ways than have so far been explored. One approach that is probably best embedded within the generic paradigm of complexity comes from Viable Systems Theory (VST). A viable system is complex and adaptive, and is *able* to maintain a separate existence within the confines of its cultural or other constraints. The nature of viable systems is that they should have at least potential independence in their processes of regulation, agency, production, and cognition. A system is viable if it is self-contained in its ability to survive and can respond to changes whether or not they have been foreseen. It can maintain what was earlier called *requisite variety* (i.e. the variety that a system must have in order to deal with environmental variety, an indicator of complexity), and is able to support adaptability and change while maintaining the stability in its behaviour. The internal nature of an agency is central to the approach, and the pathologies that it maintains stand in the way of effective operations in a complex environment.

This concern with the internal (or endogenous) environment of an agency leads to the improved formulation of some notions, like that of capability within competitive advantage as considered in the resource-based strategic view or the agency. In Table 2.2 the definition adopted has been contextualized for the knowledge management paradigm. That of capability is informed by Argyris & Schön's (1978) *double loop learning*, and the terms *coordination* and *integration* by (Beer, 1979).

Perhaps a main author in the area of viable systems and strategic management is Leonard (1999, 2000) who explores Beer's (1979) notions of the viable system within the context of knowledge management. The Beer model provides a way of exploring social collectives in terms of their structural faults by defining a set of generic systemic functions that can represent all of the features of the collective. There are five of these functions shown in Table 2.3, with communicative relationships as migrated into the systemic map in Figure 2.7. It should be noted that there are two terminologies in use: domain and system. The domain has properties, while the system is housed in a domain with properties but also has functionality. Domains may have subdomains and systems may have subsystems. Figure 2.7 sets an agency model in a noumenal domain with cognitive properties. The systems contained in it represent functionalities and operate through information schemas: integration, coordination, policy, and futures/planning. As can be seen

Table 2.2 *Types of capability*

Capability	Nature
Agency and managerial process	This occurs through three areas: (i) Coordination and integration: Coordination among teams in an organization is essential for organizational success. Interdepartmental coordination and resource sharing to reach a common goal are fundamental to creating 'value'. Integrating resources is essential to the sustainable success of agencies. Agencies that are able to integrate resources can develop synergistic effects of resources coming together. (ii) Agency Learning: This is essential to the success of an agency. It determines how an agency collects, distributes, interprets, and responds to market-based information collection and changes in the environment. These changes in the environment could be customer-based changes, technological developments, legal and government restrictions. Agencies have to develop robust market-sensing and spanning capabilities to effectively collect information. Once they collect information they have embedded this knowledge in the products they produce. (iii) Reconfiguring and transformation: The environment for agencies is constantly changing, and constant reconfiguring and transformation is essential to sustainable competitive advantage. Double loop learning and transformation is essential to producing innovative products. Innovative capacity of an agency determines how it reacts and learns from market information. Strategies are reformulated according to impulses from markets under consideration of available assets, external and internal competitive resources.
Positions	Market positions are assets of an agency. Four types of assets/resources can be identified: (i) Technological, (ii) Financial, (iii) Reputational, (iv) Structural. Available internal and external assets/resources need to be reproduced, reoriented, or expanded in conformity with strategy adjustment to keep or adjust market positions.
Paths	Two can be identified: (i) Path dependencies: at the birth of a company usually accompanied with certain orientations. The progenitor brings certain orientations and attributes that stay with the company for a long time. The path the company takes then determines the development of its competencies. (ii) Technological opportunities: Technology development can determine how an agency can exploit opportunities to form sustainable competitive advantage. Very often we see the advent of several technological factors converging into a capability that forms a sustainable competitive advantage.

Table 2.3 *Description of VSM model (Yolles, 1999)*

Function		Nature of Generic Systemic Function
S1	Operations	System 1: This is concerned with the system in focus ('the system') and its behaviour. 'Operations' provides a representation of what the system does and produces; it is usually broken down into functional units and interacts with the environment through futures/planning. It is the system that is itself the subject of control. S1 interacts with the environment directly and through S4. There may be a number of perspectives from which to see S1, and it may be seen from more than one by an organization. For instance, S1 could be seen in terms of product line, technology used, location, cycle time of products, customers, distribution channels, etc.
S2	Coordination	System 2: Since coordination is connected with feedback, this implies the need for effective control that S2 can be associated with. It concerns aspects of culture and is interested in limited synergy across divisions of an organization. It tries to harmonize the culture and structure of the enterprise whilst also trying to reduce chaos and introduce order. It amplifies the control capability to try to induce self-regulation into its behaviour, which is in the implementation of operations. It can be seen as predominantly anti-oscillatory. It implements non-executive decisions like schedules, personnel and accounting policies, and other areas governed by (legal and other) protocol. The aspect of culture it addresses is that of house style rather than the values/identity questions of S5.
S3	Integration/ control	System 3: This function is concerned with effective regulation of the dynamic internal to the organization. Integration/control is in charge of the functional units of the system. It controls and monitors what is going on. It is responsible for the implementation of policies, resource allocation, and the control and monitoring of the implementation activities. It determines information needs. It is involved in synergy-related tasks.
S3*	Audit	System 3*: Investigation, evaluation, and validation of information flow between S1 and S3, noting that the link to S1 occurs only to pick up the information deficit associated with S3.
S4	Future/ planning	System 4: This function is important to the identity of the organization. Futures/planning involves issues of development and strategic planning. It observes the organization from both an internal (resource based) and external (market based) view. It does this by gathering information from the environment and from the system itself. It does all the future-orientated tasks: research and development, training (except the orientation and maintaining skills at System 2), recruitment, public relations, and market research. Consistent with the information-gathering activities, it is also connected with the creation of knowledge.
S5	Policy	System 5: This is concerned with the establishment and maintenance of a coherent context for the processes of the organization. It relates to what the organization sets out to do. It defines the direction of the organization and strategy implementation. It requires an accurate overview that represents the various dimensions of activity. Policy provides the systematic capability to choose from the different problem situations or opportunities thrown up by the environment as emphasized with the market-based view. It is concerned with identity and cohesion. It balances the present and future and internal (resource based) with external (market based) perspectives.

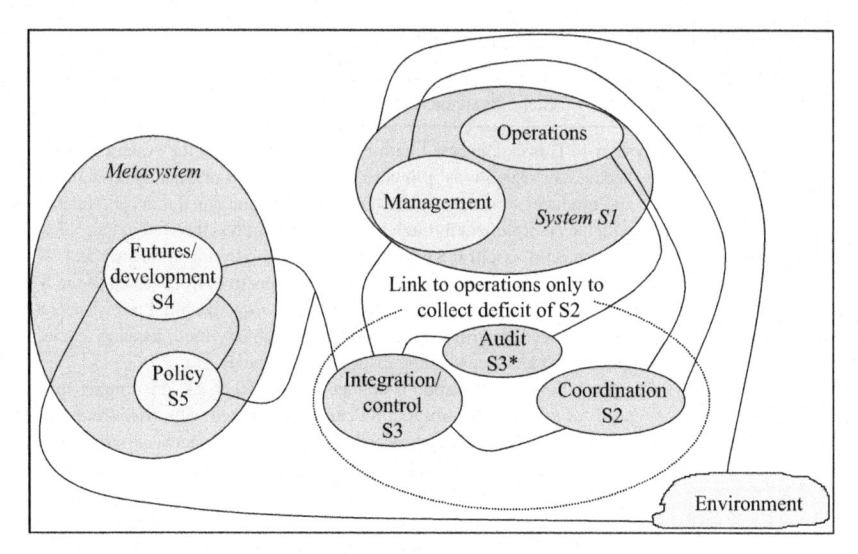

Figure 2.7 Semantic map showing the outline concept of the Strategic Viable System Model, with implicit connections between management and operations (Yolles, 1999)

from Figure 2.8, Beer's VSM was originally set into a cybernetic map in which *integration* is part of the metasystem, though *coordination* was apparently not ontologically located. This anomaly only occurs because we are examining Beer's approach from a different paradigm that can only be understood through a process of migration, that is, using a rationale that explains how material from one paradigm is mapped to another.

Leonard (1999a) explores Beer's model in terms of the strategic processes of the agency. She explains that management adds value to the transactions between operations and its environment of customers. Operations attempts to match the complex variety of its customers with products and services they find useful. It makes offers and modifies them based on market response. Management (as a generic activity) tries to guide and improve the effectiveness of this exchange. There is more variety in the environment than operations needs to know, and more variety in operations than management needs to address. Efficient operations and managers develop skills to acquire only that information needed, while remaining alert to signs of change and inherent instability. In addition, there is a need for customer knowledge that contributes to improving the speed to market of new or modified products. This constitutes, for Leonard (1999), a major competitive advantage. Such needs include general knowledge based on demographics, markets and preferences, and specific confidential information about product or service customer acquisition history and problems.

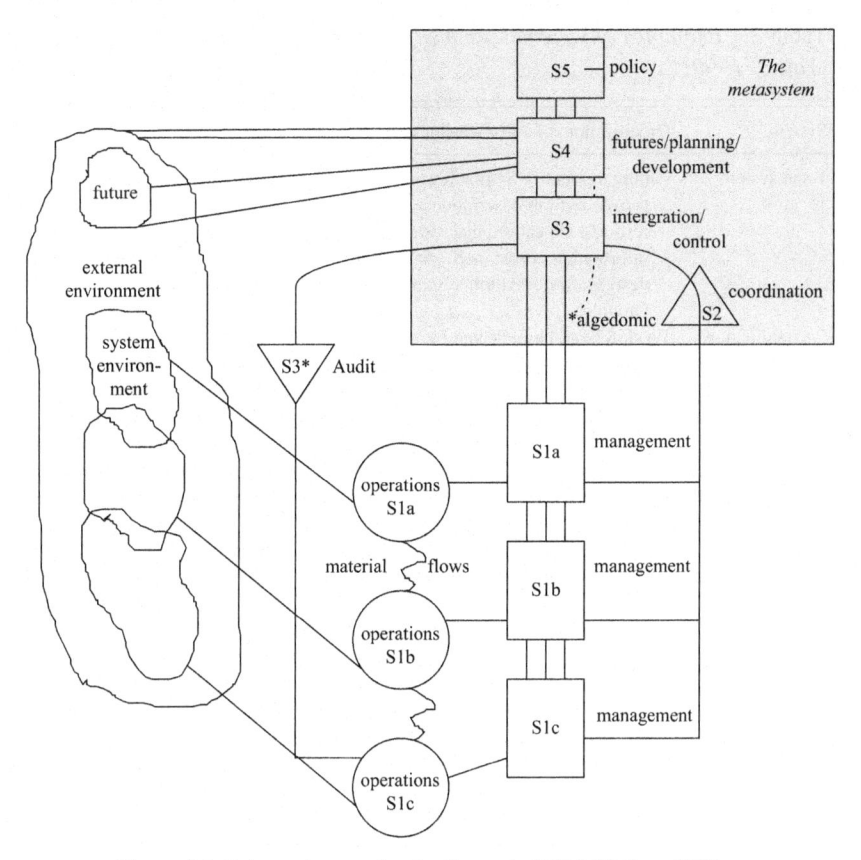

Figure 2.8 Cybernetic map for the Strategic VSM (Yolles, 1999)

The VSM is used to identify organizational faults/weaknesses, and the approach draws on an examination of the organization through the functional lens of Table 2.3. As a practical illustration of its utility, an illustration of the weaknesses that it can find is given in Table 2.4.

2.5 The Strategic Agency

Modelling VSM within the Strategic Agency

Strategic management to a large extent drives the way that an agency sees itself in relation to the environment in which it operates. This environment is one in which other agencies also operate and likely mutually interact in

Table 2.4 *Examples of weaknesses seen through the lens of VSM functions (Yolles, 1999)*

System	Organizational Faults/Weakness
1–the system	Failure to identify S1 manifests itself by such symptoms as: mismatch between formalized job description and actual skill requirements; inoperative resource allocation; inaccurate planning criteria; inappropriate assessment of information needs; ineffective specification of criteria of performance; faulty design of information systems through inaccurate identification of key variables.
2–coordination	Weak S2 can be indicated by: problems of queuing and log-jams, whether in production, service to clients, distribution, or information dissemination; oscillations and violent fluctuations; inconsistent responses to customer queries; unhappy workforce due to uncoordinated wage policy; fortress mentality – 'us versus them'; uncoordinated regulation leading to confusion and mistakes; lagged or inconsistent performance appraisal standards.
3–Integration/ control	Ineffective S3 can be represented by: over-involvement of top management in low level tasks; lack of mechanisms in place to permit sporadic audits of operations; failure to appreciate, trust, and build on self-organizing potential of an enterprise; over reliance on rules and interference; demands between autonomy and cohesion generate conflict; alienation and resentment because of interference from more senior management.
4–Futures/ development	Ineffective S4 can be seen as: policies take little account of external threats and opportunities; over-reliance on short-term issues of control and performance; the efficient dinosaur; little market research; limited encouragement of novelty; reluctance to consider structural changes.
5–policy	Ineffective S5 can cause: use of unrealistic criteria in forming policy; policy directives out of step with expectations of workforce; policy emerges in isolation; over-reliance on either external and long term, or internal and short-term issues; failure to take effective action in response to alerts and alarms; hazy or incompatible notions of core purpose of organization from different perspectives in it; inconsistent guidelines for such things as quality, effectiveness, leadership, team, responsibility.

connection with not only their outputs and inputs, but also in relation to ancillary attributes. If the agency is a commercial organization operating in a socio-Darwinian notion of a competitive market place, then the outputs will be its products or services, and ancillary attributes may be cooperative agreements. This notion of the competitive environment to a large extent centres on the capacity of the agency to be viable in its market while at the same time maximizing, or rather optimising, its returns/profits. So, a conceptual link develops between return optimisation and viability. A positive link between profit maximization and excellence was assumed by Peters and Waterman (1982) in their book *In Search of Excellence*, where they identified a number of companies that were generally considered to be managerially excellent because of their particular managerial characteristics and high profitability. For them, the tenet of 'excellence' was the ability of an agency to maintain a lead in profitability and product improvements over its competitors. Interestingly, within five years two-thirds of these companies could no longer be regarded as excellent. Not surprisingly, this experience led Peters to reconsider his understanding of the nature of excellence. In his next book, *Thriving on Chaos,* Peters admits that 'there are no excellent companies' (Peters, 1987: 3), and recants the notion of excellence: 'don't believe in excellence – only in constant improvement and constant change. That is, excellent agencies of tomorrow will cherish impermanence – and thrive on chaos.' This emergent view does not deviate much from Larry Greiner's (1972, 1998) observations that managers tend to cling too long to an initially successful business model, concluding that the success of yesterday is at the roots of the crisis tomorrow.

Constant improvement, change, impermanence, crisis, and chaos are all features of complexity. So how can agencies embrace complexity in relation to a competitive environment? To explore this, we shall first examine the development of the market-based and resource-based view of corporate strategies. Then we shall make entry to the knowledge management and the viable systems paradigms. This can be coupled with agency theory to illustrate the full complexity of the real nature of strategic advantage, where a particular characteristic or way of doing things may result in more *success*, howsoever success might be measured. In a competitive environment, for instance as depicted for a short-term market economy, success may be related to competitive advantage. However, other ways are possible, too: One way is to create an extrinsic measure of the economic good, where, for instance, one seeks higher levels of accumulation of the economic good, or higher levels in growth in the accumulation of that good. However, in complex situations where there may be a variety of goods the existence of which may be short lived, a more appropriate way may be to seek measures that reflect an agency's ability to survive crises, that is, to improve its viability, and there may be a variety of ways to characterize the components that contribute to this. For instance, in an environment in which Corporate Social Responsibility (CSR) is important, an agency's capacity to position itself on a measurement scale in comparison to others may contribute to its viability, especially where CSR has become fashionable or where it is tied to other attributes of strategic advantage. Another internally directed approach for an agency may be to recognize and diagnose its pathologies, since organizational health creates viability and improved performance.

Eric Schwarz (1997) developed his own representation of the Viable System. Schwarz proposed a generic ontological model that is essentially consistent with Beer's approach, but further developed his ontology and formally addressed the emergence and possible evolution of agencies towards complexity and autonomy. In particular, it relates to self-organizing systems that are far from equilibrium and can refer to any domain of system (e.g. biological, social, or cognitive). From these beginnings, Schwarz explained that all systems become viable when they develop patterns that lead to self-organization through morphogenesis and complexity, with long-term evolution towards autonomy.

Developing on these ideas (e.g. Yolles, 1999; Yolles & Dubois, 2001; Yolles, 2003; Yolles & Guo, 2003) an epistemological approach arose that was designed to specifically address social collectives (Yolles, 2005 & 2006). It is principally concerned with the development of agents like autonomous social collectives that survive through knowledge and knowledge processes in relation to behaviour and thought. The theory is constructed as metaphor, but this does not diminish its significance (Ho and Fox, 1988; Brown, 2003). In a later development (through the integration of principles identified by Bandura, 1986), this became known as agency, and when culture is one of its substructural systems it is referred to as cultural agency.

The basis of cultural agency is that it maintains an ontology shown in Figure 1.3. The three domains of agency (excluding personality) are analytically distinct classifications of *being*, and they each have properties that are knowledge related. The nature of autopoiesis and autogenesis is of particular interest in agency. The two together constitute a necessary and sufficient indicator of autonomy, the former being introduced into the literature conceptually by Maturana and Varela (1979), and the latter by the significant ideas of Schwarz (1997). Here autopoiesis is a term that can now be simply seen as a network of processes that enables noumenal activity to become manifested phenomenally, and in autonomous systems this is conditioned by genesis – a network of principles that creates a second order form of autopoiesis that guides autopoietic processes. Autopoiesis may be thought of as a process belonging to operative management, a term coined by Schwaninger (2001), and autogenesis as a process of strategic management.

There is some synergy between the agency model and the VSM, the two being connected through Figure 2.9. In this figure we do not attempt to present the whole of the VSM but rather its strategic component that resides in agency personality. Here *coordination* and *integration* are placed as goals in the figurative system, both actively seeking to facilitate agency coherence that underpins ideology. They do this through the creation of information-based schemas that identify for the agency their modes of operation. They may be coupled together (dashed lines), thereby creating mutual influences. These goals are manifested to the operative system by autopoiesis (operative intelligence) that establishes means by which coordination and integration may

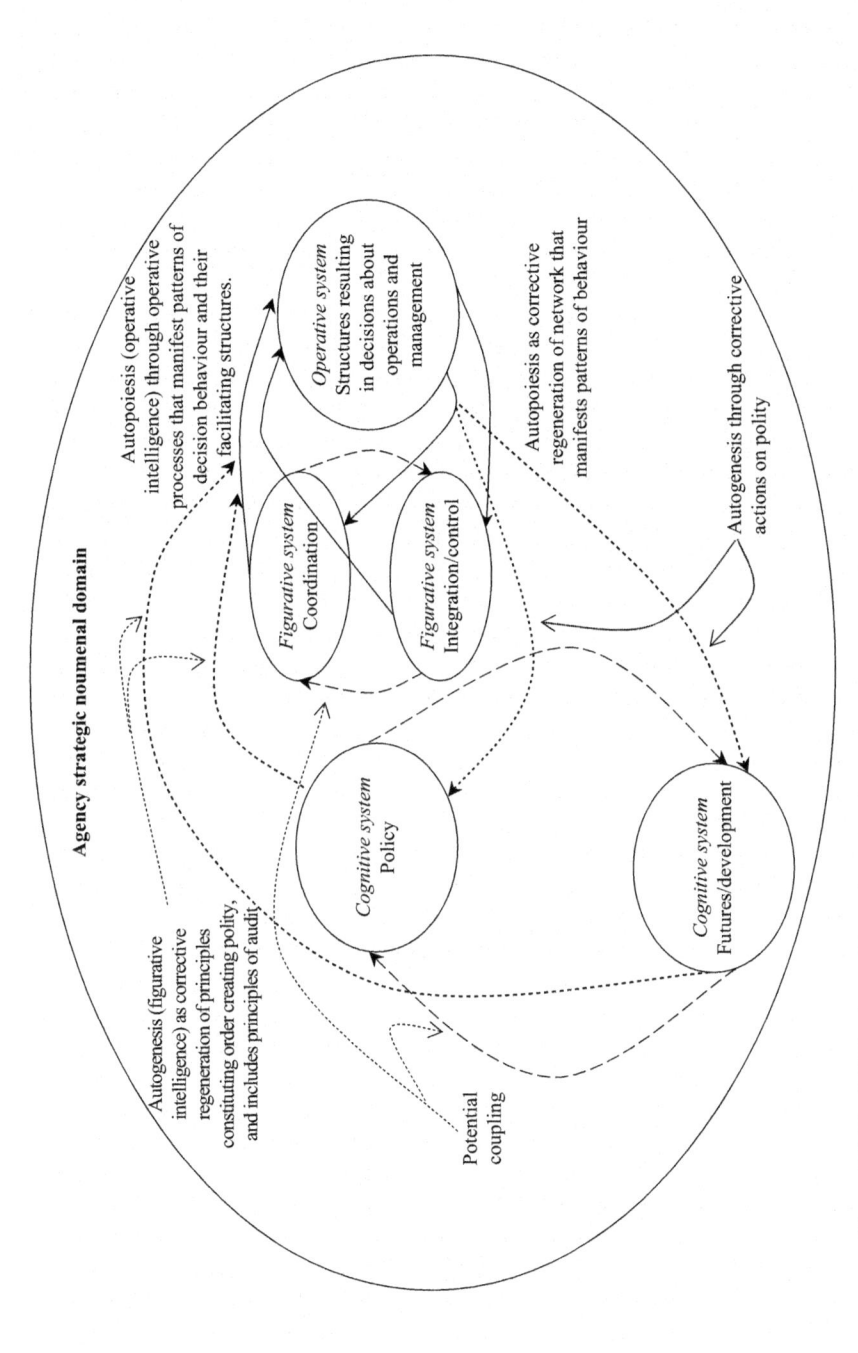

Figure 2.9 The VSM migrated into the strategic agency

occur, and this will be represented in the operative schema. Similarly, *policy* and *development/futures* are placed in the cognitive system, being an outcome of longer term dispositional and shorter term state conditions, and together deliver a structure defined by its cognitive schemas. These define their dispositional structure through patterns of information and attitude, and maintain situational information through state structure. It is through autogenesis (figurative intelligence) that this is manifested as figurative schemas. *Audit* is set as part of autogenesis, since it establishes strategic principles that enable agency monitoring.

Coordination and integration are not just disembodied functions: they are operative functions that are performed by subsidiary living systems, so that any coupling between them can be deemed to be structural, thereby having shared past and future histories. The same applies to policy and futures/development. In the VSM, coupling can occur at a variety of levels internally to the organization, as well as between different organizations. It highlights that autopoiesis is not just a single process of self-production. It is a process that in VSM has at least two meta-structural derivatives, one from coordination and one from integration/control. Even where they are coupled, conflicts may still emerge in the autopoietic processes, and this will affect autogenesis. It must also be noted that since VSM is concerned with faults, the nature of the faults that can occur between policy and futures/development and between coordination and integration/control are ontologically different from those that occur across the transverse domains and must be treated differently. This is because the process of autopoiesis occurs through a transverse ontological coupling that is very different in nature from the lateral ontological coupling that occurs with structural coupling.

The coupling between policy and futures/development arises when each of these systemic functions mutually influences each other in their previous and evolutionary history. Policy requires collective dispositional knowledge that is broadly underpinned by cultural beliefs, attitudes, and values (Yolles, 2006), while futures/development occurs through the harnessing of the innovative and motivational processes. There is similarly a structural coupling between coordination and integration, the two being informational in nature and affecting how each develop.

Figure 2.9 should not be seen as an alternative representation of the VSM but rather an alternative exploration of its strategic features, as explained in Table 2.5. If we add the agency operative system to the model in Figure 2.9, an explicit instrumental agency results that is concerned with operative regulation. However, in VSM culture and identity are attributes that are discussed but not explicitly represented as part of the formal modelling process in Figure 2.8. This suggests that culture *inherently* underpins VSM, as discussed earlier in this chapter, a notion to be revisited in Chapter 6.

Table 2.5 *Identifying the strategic aspects of VSM with agency*

Personality Function	Nature of Generic Systemic
Cognitive system Future/ planning Policy	These functions are a structural outcome of dispositional and state attitudes and information. Dispositional conditions establish an anchor for the strategic agency and are reflected in long-term policy and planning and recognition of the future as a reflection of vision and mission. State conditions establish shorter term planning and are reflective of situational information relating internally and externally to the agency. Identity is also a feature of these functions. These constitute a precondition for espoused strategy that, through the use intelligences, will become manifested as strategic options relating to objectives, goals, and self-schemas.
Figurative system Coordination Integration/ control	Coordination and integration/control appear as figurative schema-espoused strategic aims, underpinned by an ideology of agency coherence, and are responsive to inputs from culture. The schemas are accompanied by a strategic mode of behaviour constituting a self-schema and a set of objectives/goals that result from the manifestation of the cognitive schemas. The figurative schemas are themselves manifested through operative intelligence as operative schemas that establish decision-making imperatives, including means by which coordination and integration, among other elements, can be achieved.
Intelligence Audit	This function is seen to be part of figurative intelligence, adopting principles of policy and futures/development and manifesting them to other parts of the strategic personality.
Operative system Operative decisions	When figurative schemas are manifested to the operative system through operative intelligence, they become operative schema strategy imperatives that offer modes of operation, intended to reflect on decision-making. These decisions have an impact on the agency operative systems where action is taken.

Understanding the Strategic Agency

Figure 2.9 is a recursive model. In agency modelling, recursion is feasible due to a proposition adapted from Beer (1979) that *any viable living system has viable living systems within it.* This representation will enable us to make an entry into exploring the agency and managerial processes in strategic management and allow us to consider at least some aspects of competitive advantage. Table 2.2 explored assets/capabilities within the context of competitive advantage, and these aspects of capability can now be seen in terms of the noumenal activities enabling goals to be formulated and 'value' created. Other factors could now also be considered within this context, namely agency learning and reconfiguration and transformation. These can be considered through the use of two other diagrams. We shall return to other aspects of the nature of capabilities shortly. To enable us to do this we shall explore some other concepts from knowledge cybernetics.

The strategic agency consists of three domains that together represent a general information-supported strategic capacity for the cultural agency, where each domain constitutes ontological distinctions with its own epistemic nature that is a reflection of their properties. When expressed as systems, this not only embraces the domain properties, but also their functionality. Together the three systems have a hierarchical agency in which the functionality of one system is at a higher order than the others. Thus, for instance, the cognitive system has overall cognitive-orienting control in the agency, and the figurative system plays an instrumental role that has orienting control for the figurative schemas to be manifested operatively in decision processes. The operative system maintains structures that, within a strategic context, are concerned with decision-making. The connective relationship between these systems in the hierarchy is said to be transitive.

Each system maintains both strategic information and functionality. The information satisfies functional needs, and so its natures are different. In order to generalize, we shall refer to types and knowledge and information not simply as resources, as suggested earlier, but as *semantic-goods*. We can call it a *good* because it may be seen as an intangible but transferable object or service that can also be sold or bought for a non-negative price where a market for it exists. It also has a *service utility* which facilitates meaning. Semantic-goods may be seen as creating inputs to the production of lifeworld processes, that is, communications. Two types of commonly known semantic-goods already referred to are tacit and explicit knowledge. Other examples come from an adaptation from Marshal (1995) and Paris et al. (1998), who were interested in how strategic decision-making processes in the military occur. They distinguished between three types of strategic information: *identification, elaboration*, and *execution*. These types of information are different, and when used in agency theory, any (transitive) communication between the three strategic domains of the agency occurs through a living system network of processes that facilitate *semantic-good* migration. This is different from *lateral* direct communication that occurs *within* a single domain. Thus in Figure 2.9, policy and futures/development can meaningfully exchange information directly since they both exist in the same existential domain, but communication between the figurative and operative systems is transitive, requiring migration to enable meaning to be created in the target system.

The functionality referred to above ultimately relates to strategic decision-making – since this is the concern of the operative system in the strategic agency. This functionality can be posited from Bonnet (1985) and Sloman (1984) both of whom have discussed decision-making processes within the context of artificial intelligence. Both strategic functionality and semantic-good, which are reflected in Figure 2.9, are summarized below:

The Cognitive System: This maintains selected context-sensitive *identification information* manifested from the cultural system. It facilitates ***cognitive schemas*** (like policy and futures/development) that arise from mental dispositions and states in the agency personality. This is connected with the creation of patterns of recognition related to existential *cognitive interest* which can be related to a given context. In complex situations agencies respond to a large number of events that sometimes unfold rapidly and often unexpectedly. Time constraints may be tight, and there may be an urgent need to identify aspects of a situational context that need to be prioritized. Identification is definitive in that it holds normative characteristics that influence the plural agency overall. It relates to situation awareness (from which arise cognitive interests), needed to inform controls that may in due course be applied repeatedly in tactical settings. Effective identification involves recognizing a context by focusing on the particular configuration of features that are present in it. Identification information occurs as patterns that construct attitudes through a field of influence that vectors the orientation of the agency. This is reflected in cognitive schemas that either implicitly or explicitly promote strategic 'attitude' represented by, for instance, policy and futures/development initiatives. This information embraces the following functionalities:

(1) *Inference,* which identifies likely consequences of experience. It is a deductive feature that has importance for understanding the nature of situations, as well as creating an anticipatory capacity for the future. The deductive feature enables a process of reasoning in which a conclusion follows from a set of determined premises that are conceptually connected. Inference is the ability to apply collected strategic information to a relevant situation and from which conclusions may be drawn.
(2) *Semantic transposability,* which relates to content and enables a meaning to be transformed from one area of activity to another related one. It is the ability to transform meaning from one area of activity to another. It is more general than being related to a particular category of event. It is also underpinned by context-related information extracted from knowledge and knowledge processes. For example, information about the psychology of human beings can be applied to their contextual behaviour – in different types of human situation. Semantic transformation can involve the use of insight and understanding coupled with regulation. To illustrate semantic transformation, we note that the same principles of human psychology can be applied in marketing situations to improve market penetration of goods, as in the National American Space Agency to develop safer human systems during space flight.

(3) *Self-referencing,* which enables a position or identity to be recognized. It is through referential position that one can differentiate oneself from an environment. Strategic identity enables this differentiation to occur in different ways. For instance, the same object or individual can be referred to in different ways, as when the name of a person is replaced by the personal pronoun 'I'. This capacity enables people to be social and differentiate between distinct groups while referring to them in different ways.
(4) *Self-awareness,* which includes the ability to reflect on and ultimately communicate about at least some of one's own internal processes and explain ones actions, decisions, or conclusions. Self-awareness is the ability to be aware of one's own internal cognitive processes, thereby providing rational or inferential explanations about the processes or behaviours that one is engaged in. It may also be a prerequisite for self-consciousness, defined (Yolles, 1999) as the ability to interact with descriptions of self. These characteristics can be consolidated into a variety of capabilities, like the ability to generalize, resolve anomalies, learn from experience, deal with situations under conditions of uncertainty, and be able to improve future performance. They can also be represented in terms of other capabilities, like adaptation.

The Figurative System: This maintains selected *elaboration information* that is influenced by manifestations from the cultural system and the strategic cognitive system. It is connected with the development of figurative schemas relating to a particular figurative *purpose* determined by situational context. Agencies need to elaborate their understanding and interpretation of the context and the development of regulations specified as the *figurative schemas*. These schemas can be understood as espoused strategic options, from which operative system-imperative strategy options arise. In so doing they call on experience that is manifested from the cognitive system to assist in schema maintenance or the creation of new context-related schemas. Some of the elaboration may be related to critical thinking skills (Cohen, Freeman, & Thompson, 1997) and some to case-based reasoning (Kolodner, 1993). Elaboration enables the summarization of experiences. It facilitates the creation of figurative schemas, where the espoused strategies will include coordination and integration in relation to situational contexts. Effective elaboration enables reliable and acceptable hypotheses to be formulated with regard to the operative purposes for the context. Elaboration creates personal agency information (like ideological, ethical, and self) figurative schemas that are tied to posited policy and futures/strategic development, and it anticipates operative processes of decision-making. The functionality of this system is concerned with rational response, identified through figurative schemas that respond to demands, which require action for a specific situation, that action being consistent with a response that is considered normal to the situation it is responding to. Rationality is therefore a relative thing, and may depend upon what different individuals perceive is normal behaviour. It is also a group thing, because what is construed as normal must be normatively agreed by a sufficiently large peer group. *Rationality* is manifested from the existential domain that, within the context of the VSM, underpins perspectives and activities of coordination and integration/control processes. In other words, these two noumenal attributes of coordination and integration/control are more fundamental figurative schemas that define this part of the strategic agency. Policy and futures (strategy development) formulated in the cognitive system are manifested here as figurative schemas, that is, espoused strategies. Another attribute of the agency is affect/emotion, and while this can be very important in the identification of which components of figurative schemas to activate, the investigation of affective functionality is rather more extensive than is appropriate to this chapter. Having said this, one of the attributes of affect that resides in this system is feelings, which act to condition decisions.

The Operative System involves *execution information*. Execution information provides direction for structuring through decision role specifications and related operative activities, and any decision related rules that may be required to guide operative processes. It is concerned with the development of phenomenal structures (like decision-making role assignment) and processes. It centres on the nature of operative decision-making from elaboration information and rationality, and figurative identification schemas like ethical or ideological policy outlines, which conform to espoused strategies. It includes a distribution of forms of information and its structuring through ***operative schemas*** that create decision-making imperatives that specifically relate to internal and external environments emanating originally from personality states, perhaps including operative activities. Arising from personality dispositions, one might find longer term decision structuring, like decision role specifications (e.g. role assignments), and any decision rules that may be required to guide such operative processes, like knowledge about internal operative resources of the agency. These schemas facilitate *operative intention*, embracing *a decision-making structure* and *actions* resulting from decisions. These decisions are applied within the cultural agency, which is capable of taking material actions. Under change, the strategic agency embraces morphogenic transposability, concerned with development of structured forms of decision-making that are related to strategic self-organization.

We have referred to the strategic agency in terms of its schemas. These generate orientations that together with the types of information it holds influence their functionality, as indicated in Figure 2.10. This embraces the previous considerations of Table 2.5 explaining how VSM can be seen in

Strategic Noumenal Domain

Operative System
Operative schemas (like decision rules), phenomenal execution, Operative intention

Figurative System
Figurative schemas (like goals), noumenal elaboration, Espoused strategy, Figurative purposes

Cognitive System
Cognitive schemas (like policy & futures/development), existential identification, Cognitive interest

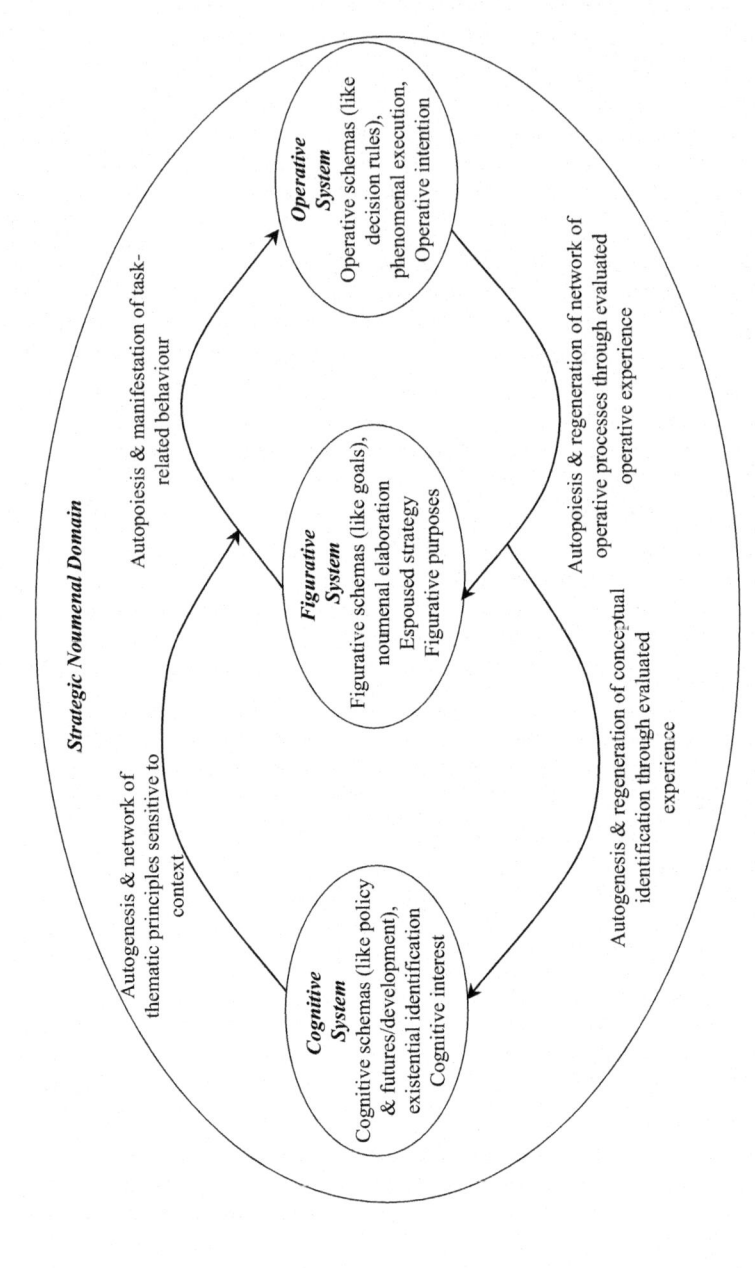

Autopoiesis & manifestation of task-related behaviour

Autopoiesis & regeneration of network of operative processes through evaluated operative experience

Autogenesis & network of thematic principles sensitive to context

Autogenesis & regeneration of conceptual identification through evaluated experience

Figure 2.10 Distinction between the system schemas and their orientations in the strategic agency

terms of agency. Here cognitive and other strategic systems have structures represented through schemas that arise originally from dispositions and states of the personality. Policy and futures/development operates with conceptual identification and cognitive interest. The figurative system develops figurative schemas that are tied in with situational context and point to specific classes of potential behaviour, and embrace elaboration and figurative purpose. The operative system has operative schemas like decision rules that point to the way in which decision-making can be facilitated, and it does this with structural execution and operative intention.

Agencies have expectations, as illustrated by their future planning (Yolles and Dubois, 2001). These derive from the figurative system due to the images of phenomenal reality that they hold there. Expectations are also susceptible to perturbation due to the environment, its interpretation, or to internal pathologies. Intelligent agencies attempt to address these fluctuations where they are not consistent with expectation. They can do this through self-moderation of behaviour by strengthening the appearance of existing structural constraints and cognitive interests, thus appealing to individuals to undertake their own moderation. Self-moderation when formally instituted occurs because of the ability for an autonomous community to undertake self-organization. However, autonomy is not feasible in an instrumental agency, since it is incapable of learning through the creation of new knowledge. Where knowledge processes are inferred, the instrumental agency becomes an *implied* autonomous living system with inferred self-reference and self-identity.

The distinction between self-moderation and self-organization is that the latter in effect shifts the focus of behavioural adjustment from the organization to the lower focus of the behaving groups or individuals that make it up. The organization can also undertake self-regulating[1] adjustments itself. Mostly, we think of self-regulatory control as the ability to manipulate the processes that result in behaviour so that it can be constrained. We note that unregulated fluctuation can indirectly impact on the organization by unintended regeneration of the logical networks that act as the basis of the images that formulate its figurative reality. An example is the formation or development of myth, a form of false knowledge.[2] When these images are held together through false knowledge, then they may be unreliable in the creation of expectation – wrong and misleading strategies will be espoused. It is through this that contradictions arise that can engender inappropriate phenomenal responses by an agency that are pathological and perturb viability. It is when a figurative image becomes structurally

---

[1] Self-regulation is also known as homeostasis, and it occurs through negative feedback so that an organization's outputs are maintained within predetermined bounds.

[2] This links to some theory by Eric Schwarz (Yolles, 1999) on viable systems.

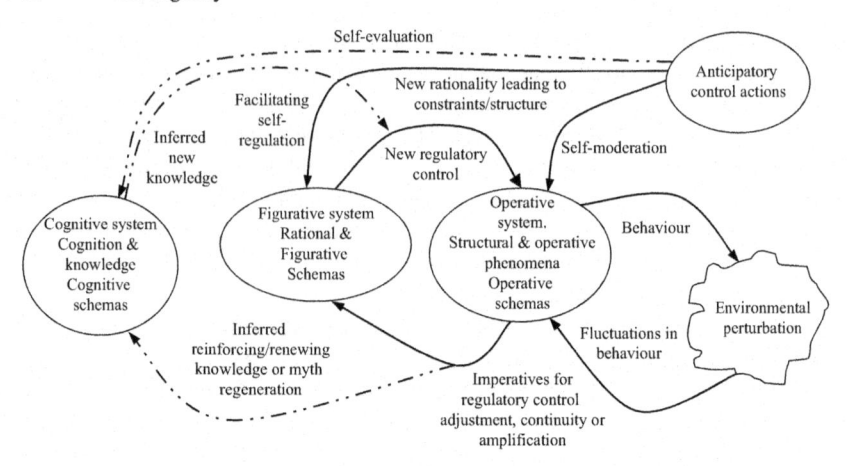

Figure 2.11 Reactions to fluctuation affecting an organization showing control action through anticipation, where knowledge processes are inferred

implemented that its expectations become anticipations. Thus, anticipation changes with self-organization. Another option for an organization is to self-examine its cognition through self-reference, a form of self-reflection. This can result in the development of its own paradigm and thus the production of a new pattern of knowledge, from which incidentally come criteria for self-regulation. As a result, structural constraints may be eased, or, more seriously, new structures may be introduced with their own new constraints. This is because patterns of knowledge condition the interconnection between rational figurative organizing and behavioural phenomena. Knowledge housekeeping enables the organization to manage myth formation and redefine the logical relationships that determine the rationality of its operations and its ability to organize, leading to new patterns of behaviour (Figure 2.11).

There is another set of attributes to consider in the development of agencies towards their capacity to develop competitive advantage. It must be recognized that they must respond to a complexity of experiences, as illustrated in Figure 2.12, and there must be at least an inferred knowledge system as part of the agency. Here, polity is induced through the three types of schema identified: cognitive, figurative, and operative; overall the model is indicative of the paradigmatic nature of the agency. The model is central to providing an understanding of the nature of agency processes, their responses to change, and their ability to achieve competitive advantage.

In this cultural agency model, the operative system is a structural entity from which behaviour is determined, and who may be in interaction with others in an environment. It entertains epistemological migrations that occur between actors. By this we really refer to knowledge processes that essentially operate

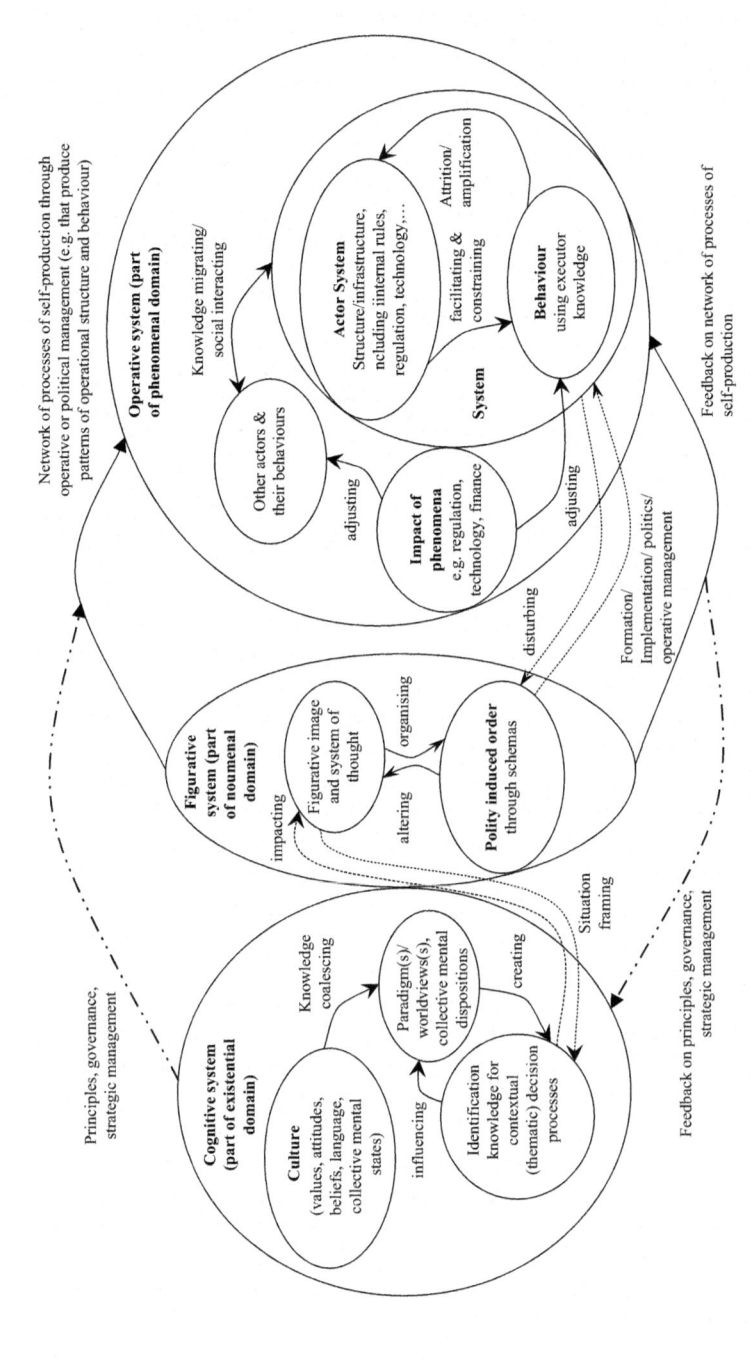

Figure 2.12 Influence diagram exploring the epistemological nature of an autonomous agent with inferred cognitive system

Table 2.6 *Distinction between learning, knowledge, and intelligent organizations*

Type of Organizational Agency	Nature of Organization
Strategic knowledge-intensifying organization	Strategic agencies that extend their knowledge through processes of knowledge intensification. This is a process of learning by acquiring new knowledge, strategically targeted for practical pre-defined benefit.
Learning organization	Learning (according to some strategic vision) through the creation of new knowledge for the benefit of individuals, groups, and the organization as a whole.
Knowledge organization	Conscious awareness of the distribution and development of its tacit and explicit *knowledge* and knowledge *needs*, with the ability to match the two when required.
Intelligent organization	Through its existing implicit processes it is continuously aware of its own condition, and when it requires the use of existing, or the development of new, knowledge.

in the existential domain. By epistemological migrations (dotted lines) we are normally referring to the manifestation of *semantic-goods* between systems.

Finally, the last consideration we need to make is to provide an understanding of the learning agency as an organization and its relationship to knowledge. Four types of organization have been explored by Yolles (2006). These are the strategic knowledge-intensifying agency, the learning agency, the knowledge intensifying agency, and the intelligent agency. Connection between learning agency, the knowledge agency, and the intelligent agency within the context of strategic management has, for instance, been discussed by Stonehouse and Pemberton (1999). These types of agency are briefly defined in Table 2.6, and their possible relationships are indicated in Figure 2.13. Note that in Figure 2.13 the agency model is embedded in the existential domain recursively (one of the properties of agency), indicating that we are essentially referring to knowledge processes associated with each type of agency.

So far we have provided a complex picture of what is actually going on in the agency that enables it to address environmental change and engage in processes that allow it to create at least temporary strategic advantage. We have already discussed the connection between coordination and integration, which couples well with the notion of anticipation. Agency learning involves the creation of new knowledge that can facilitate ways of creating anticipatory processes, these conditioning the agency in respect of its capabilities.

In respect of the other attributes of capability, position is constituted through technological, financial, reputational, and structural assets, all of which were

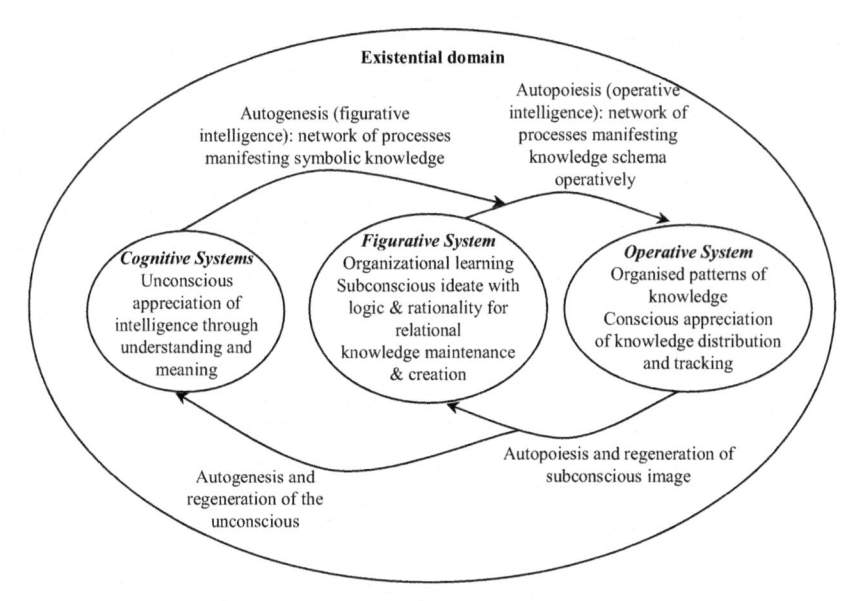

Figure 2.13 Possible relationship between learning, knowledge and intelligent agencies

constituted as part of Figure 2.9. Paths, too, can be explored within this context, though some degree of model elaboration would be required to do so with any usefulness.

2.6   Agency Pathology

The notion of agency pathology (or ill-health) has been used for a variety of situations by a number of people (e.g. Habermas, 1987; Beer, 1979; Howard, 1999; Yolles, 2006), can be applied within the context of ontological relationships, and may be seen to be concerned with the capacity for ontological connections to occur across boundaries. An illustration of a relationship is framed in Figure 2.14. The domains are expressed purely in terms of the (metaphorical) collective psychological condition of an autonomous system, though they can be applied to any of the figures from 2.6 onwards, each creating their own local interpretation from their appropriate context.

The first of the type of pathology that we shall refer to occurs when autopoiesis is blocked, and this can result in dissociative behaviour that has little reference to subconscious images. When this occurs, behaviour may be influenced directly by the unconscious. The second type of pathology that can occur

76   The Agency

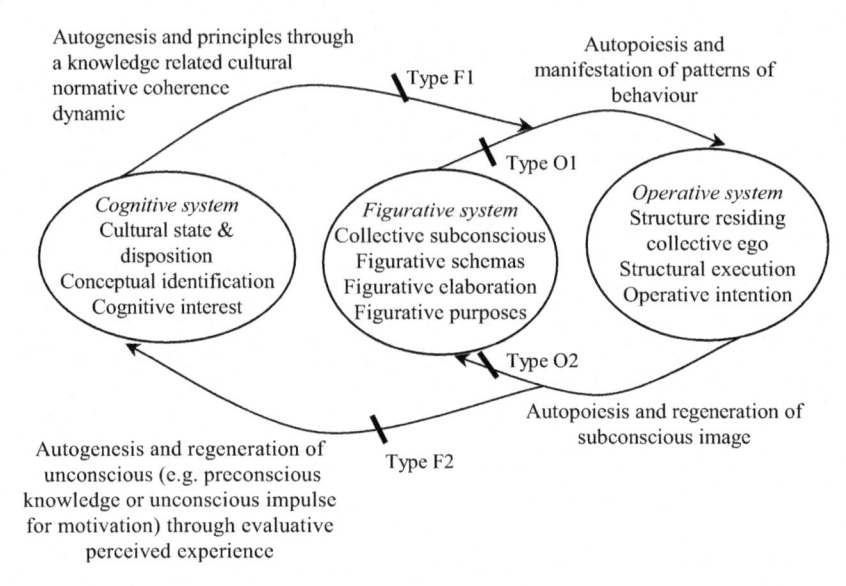

```
Autogenesis and principles through
a knowledge related cultural                    Autopoiesis and
normative coherence            Type F1          manifestation of patterns of
dynamic                                         behaviour

                                    Type O1

    Cognitive system        Figurative system        Operative system
    Cultural state &        Collective subconscious  Structure residing
    disposition             Figurative schemas       collective ego
    Conceptual identification Figurative elaboration Structural execution
    Cognitive interest      Figurative purposes      Operative intention

                                    Type O2
                                                Autopoiesis and regeneration of
Autogenesis and regeneration of                 subconscious image
unconscious (e.g. preconscious    Type F2
knowledge or unconscious impulse
for motivation) through evaluative
perceived experience
```

Figure 2.14 Transverse psychological model of the collective showing type O and F pathologies

is when autogenesis is blocked, so that normative coherence cannot develop within the cultural fabric of the plural actor, in part because learning is not possible. This has major implications for the way in which patterns of behaviour become manifested. Micro-variations to this can occur by defining two forms of each type of ontological pathology, as illustrated in Table 2.7, as types F1, F2, O1, and O3, where F refers to figurative, while O refers to operative. An example of the type O1 problem might be when recurrent patterns of behaviour occur independently of subconscious constraint but responsive to the instinctive or emotional unconscious. In the case of social communities that have cultural instability (where there may be a plurality of shifting norms), this non-coherent and perhaps gratuitous/un-self-regulated behaviour may simply respond to the instinctive or emotional needs of individuals in that community. Later the nature of type F pathologies will be explained. When type O and F pathologies occur together behaviour is purely responsive and determined from structural capacities. Table 2.7 suggests the composite possibilities that can arise with the combination of different ontological pathologies.

2.7   Social Responsibility and Practice

Earlier we noted that CSR could be one strand in evaluating strategic advantage for an agency. Here we shall explore this more fully, not only from a conceptual perspective but also as a practical case example.

Table 2.7 *Types of ontological pathology, and possible associative relationships between type combinations*

Pathology Type	Nature
O1 and O2	Can result in disassociative behaviour that has little reference to figurative schemas. When this occurs, behaviour may be influenced directly. Type O1 relates to phenomenal image projection, while type O2 refers to an ability to have a feedback affect.
F1 and F2	No changes in the normative coherence can develop within the cultural fabric of the plural actor. In type F1 existing knowledge cannot have an impact on the autopoietic loop, while in type F2 learning is not possible. This has major implications for the way in which patterns of behaviour become manifested. An example of the type of pathology might be when patterns of behaviour occur independently of subconscious constraint, but responsive to the instinctive unconscious.

	Associative Type Combinations		
	O1	O2	F2
O2	No figurative projection or feedback isolating strategy and creating direct link to existential domain		
F2	No knowledge development/ learning and no figurative projection. Feedback becomes isolated.	No operative feedback to regenerate figurative projection, and no learning process development.	
F1	No figurative projection, and no possibility of improving viability and coherence through learning.	No regeneration of figurative schemas through experience, and no evaluative process deriving from experience.	No influence of knowledge or knowledge development (i.e. no learning or reflection). Figurative projection cannot develop.

Corporate Social Responsibility as Strategy

Jacobs (2013) *notes that* CSR is also known as 'corporate citizenship', 'sustainable responsible business', and 'corporate social performance'. She notes that the definition of CSR, according to the World Bank, is the commitment of businesses to behave ethically and to contribute to sustainable economic development by working with all relevant stakeholders to improve their lives in ways that are good for business, the sustainable development agenda, and society at large. She tells us that more than half of Fortune Global 250 firms provide regular public statements that specifically refer to CSR. Business decisions and actions can greatly harm people and the environment, and corporations are still under fire for the negative social consequences their business practices may be responsible for. Involvement in CSR is not only of benefit to society, but also to a company's success. Thus, for instance, corporations having CSR policy often have improved relations with the politicians and government regulators who reinforce and track how corporate bodies respond to business standards and regulations. The importance of CSR to corporations is also highlighted by Kinley, Nolan, & Zerial (2007), who note that it has become a common element of corporate board agendas, just as environmental issues were also fashionable a decade or two ago. Transnational corporations (TNCs) represent a particular case for CSR. Their growth during the current period of globalization has been matched by interests in identifying ways of regulating the deleterious impacts on social and human rights standards, since traditional national constraints have no functionality in an international arena. Neither industry-based initiatives (like individual corporate codes) nor multilateral initiatives (like the Global Compact[3]) oblige corporate bodies to honour ethical interests like human rights. Without ethical constraints, corporations tend to misbehave. Unfortunately, as Kinley, Nolan, & Zerial recognize, there are no international standards for ethical behaviour. Rather, there are a plurality of codes of practice and standards that together create an escape path for ethically challenged TNCs.

McWilliams, Siegel, & Wright (2006) explain that CSR is tied to corporate strategy. They understand that CSR occurs when a corporate entity moves beyond compliance, and becomes involved in actions that appear to further some social good. These actions would go further than just corporate interests, as might be required under law. However, they note that beyond the argument of Kinley, Nolan, & Zerial (2007) it is not only a lack codes of practice or standards that are a problem, but even the nature of CSR is troubled with numerous alternative definitions. CSR activities, they tell us, include: the use of social characteristics or features in products and manufacturing processes, for instance, aerosol products with no fluorocarbons; the use of environmentally friendly technologies, while adopting progressive human resource management practices such as promoting employee empowerment; attaining

---

[3] This is a United Nations initiative (www.unglobalcompact.org/abouttheGC/thetenprinciples/index.html) that asks companies to embrace, support, and enact, within their sphere of influence, a set of core values through a set of ten principles.

high levels of environmental performance through recycling and pollution abatement, such as the adoption of an aggressive stance towards reducing emissions; and finally, promotion of the goals of community agencies. Stakeholders also make demands for CSR that vary across nations, regions, and areas of business, with divisional managers being under pressure to increase their commitment to CSR from employees, suppliers, community groups, NGOs, and governments.

Despite these issues, CSR has a strategic role in organizations. Jones et al. (2005) note that in the food industry leading corporate bodies have idiosyncratic approaches to CSR, and there is no commonality in the nature and extent of the reporting process.

Corporate Social Responsibility

CSR recognizes that businesses are an integral part of society and have the potential to make a positive contribution to society. However, the lack of universally agreed definition of CSR makes it a vague and intangible term which is highly subjective. As such it has little meaning.

It is not surprising, therefore, that different agencies have created their own definitions. The Commission for the European Communities (2001) defines CSR as 'a concept whereby companies integrate social and environmental concerns in the business operations and in their interactions with their stakeholders on a voluntary basis'. For the Commission of the European Communities this means not just fulfilling legal responsibilities but also going beyond compliance to embrace wider social, environmental, and economic goals.

According to the Commission for the European Communities (2001) (cited by Jones et al., 2005), CSR has an internal and an external dimension:

- ***Internal***: concerns socially responsible practices within the company. It embraces the management of human resources; health and safety at work; adaptation to change; and the management of environmental impacts and natural resources (like reducing the consumption of resources, polluting emissions, and waste); and human resources (for instance by including diversity within the workforce, responsible recruitment practices, equal pay and career prospects for women, profit sharing schemes, and providing an environment that encourages lifelong learning).
- ***External***: extends beyond the company into the local community and beyond, involving a wide range of external stakeholders. It includes investors and local communities; business partners, suppliers, and consumers; human rights; global environmental concerns; and the provision of products that customers want (whatever this means in the context of marketing) in an

efficient and effective and ethical way. The strong human rights element of CSR extends throughout the supply chain and thus maintains not only a national but also a global extension.

Jones et al. (citing Girod & Bryane, 2003) note that the strategic marketing perspective for CSR is a key tool to create, develop, and sustain differentiated brand names. Its strategic dimension is also clear for both national and supranational governments. Thus the European Community see it as being part of corporate vision.

An indicator that CSR is a part of corporate strategy is that corporations provide significant CSR reports. There are ten leading UK food retailers and all do this; however, they are all distinct in their approach, and all maintain distinct approaches in structuring CSR into the company and reporting on CSR. Thus, for instance, in Tesco a cross-functional team of senior executives provides leadership on CSR. Its main means for communicating policies and performances is its CSR report. In contrast, Sainsbury have a senior corporate executive-led team that coordinates and reports on CSR policy. For Jones et al. (2005), all of these idiosyncratic approaches can be classified according to a clear set of categories: environment, sourcing, employees (i.e. human resources), and customers and communities.

Some provide relatively limited CSR information, while others offer detailed and comprehensive reports. However, they all adopt CSR centrally as part of their corporate business processes. They all conform to the idea that CSR is tied to corporate and stakeholder viability. Operational business imperatives drive CSR. Thus, for instance, CSR reports that embrace environmental issues have a purpose of reducing energy use, waste generation, and hence costs. Similarly, social issues that are concerned with good working environments and conditions, health and safety at work, and training and management development, all contribute to stability, security, and efficiency within the workforce. CSR reports also represent corporate aspirations that may not be fully reflected in daily operations.

Social Responsibility and the Strategic Agency

Functionally, the cognitive system has been able to develop policy through its capacities in inference, semantic transposability, self-referencing, and self-awareness. The figurative system provides rational response through the creation of structures called schemas that respond to demands and needs of a contextual situation. If these situational demands can be described as maintaining a variety of environmental impulses that impinge on the agency, then we can refer to Ashby (1964) and say that the schemas should provide actions that satisfy requisite variety by responding fully to the needs of that variety.

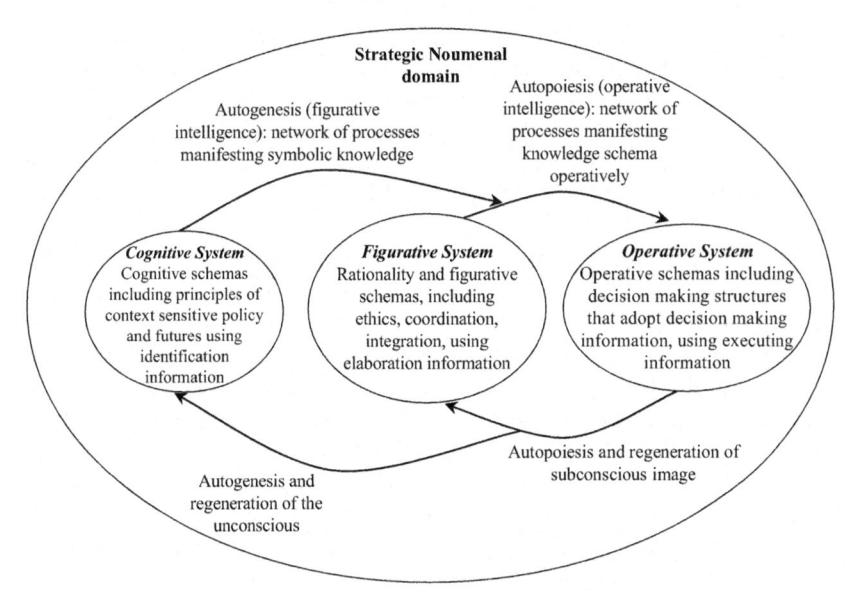

Figure 2.15 Representation of the strategic (noumenal) agency adopting attributes of VSM

The phenomenal domain provides *strategic decision-making structure* that results in decisions, and which will impact on the way in which the cultural agency responds to its environment.

Now, reflecting on the study by Jones et al., it is possible to reframe Figure 2.9 as in Figure 2.15 to explain CSR. We note that a strategic operative system is principally concerned with decision processes that can then facilitate action. In the existential domain we have policy elements that are identified through VSM, but these do not only relate to business processes; in addition, they contain facilitations and constraints that centre on ethical and ideological attributes. CSR is a reflection of both ethical and ideological attributes linked with business needs. These are manifested in the figurative system as actionable policies that may include goals, ethical positions as ideology, as well as self-schemas that represent mode of conduct. In other words, CSR is set up as an actionable plan that may be distributed across various schemas, rather than being represented as an integrated strategy. This results in work having to be undertaken to determine the degree and effectiveness of corporate adherence to CSR principles, where they are adequately defined. The difficulty in the food industry explored by Jones et al. (2005) is that CSR is arbitrarily distributed across these schemas. As such, no matter how impressive a corporate strategic intention may be, a CSR schema is rarely seen. To be convincing and to enable appropriate evaluation of CSR commitment as such, rather than being potentially diluted with other business interests despite accompanying hype, corporate bodies should present an epistemic mapping that shows how their distributed CSR operative schemas coalesce into a single CSR schema that is tied to universal characteristics. However, it would seem that such universal characteristics are still unavailable, since like much of the social sciences uncertainty and theory crises still appear to dominate.

The strategic agency semantic commodity includes distinct forms of information in each domain. In the existential domain we have identification information that is connected with patterns of recognition that are of interest with respect to context. Typically, information will be organized around identifiable features. In the figurative system we have elaboration information which is connected with the development of figurative schemas relating to contextual purpose. As part of this schema there will be regulatory actionable processes that arise from the existential policy formulations. In addition, schemas that are included relate to coordination and integration. In the phenomenal domain there is execution information, concerned with the development of decision-making structures and processes.

The information that each of the systems holds is also a reflection of its intended functionality and nature. This information is manifested from outside the strategic agency. Lateral pathologies may occur when the domains of each agency are in some way functionally corrupted. One reason for this may be that the network of processes that constitute autopoiesis and autogenesis are in some way inefficacious. When this occurs the strategic agency is said to have transitive pathologies. The examination of each of the lateral and transitive pathologies of the ten corporate bodies would likely provide an interesting study.

3   Agency Personality

3.1   Agency Minds

Plural agency is a dynamic conscious entity with a collective mind that has an internal landscape (Davis, 2000) that defines its personality. This landscape may include cognition, affect/emotion, control, trait orientations, states, and dispositions. Personality cognitive structure facilitates decision making, creating a potential for agency behaviour. In this chapter our interest lies in cognitive aspects of personality, though affect/emotion will be briefly considered in Chapter 6. States and dispositions have already been considered (Table 1.1 and Figure 1.4). Discussions of control will be considered under personality traits.

Cultural agency is a social collective of individuals or groups anchored through culture and maintaining cognitive and affective processes through its personality. While individual personality is well explored in the psychological literature, plural agency personality is a relatively new concept that is more in keeping with social psychology. In order to properly explore the plural agency personality, we shall therefore have to adopt and adapt concepts from psychology and apply them to cultural agency, since social psychology does not currently have the required framework.

Social psychology is more commonly defined as the study of the relationship between human mind(s) and social behaviours. It is the psychology of a structured collection of individuals among which has arisen a normative mind, seated in a noumenal domain operating in a way that may be distinct from that of the individuals that make it up. In Chapter 1 we explained that the noumen used here is not that absolute mental region of *Being* described by Kant, but rather a more relative one that exists alongside visions, images, ideas, and patterns of thinking. The normative nature often coincides with fuzzy processes that result from the inability of people to adequately understand each other, due ultimately to the principle of knowledge migration (Yolles, 2006).

More or less coherent social collectives like countries and enterprises are durable and develop behaviour by virtue of the noumenal and existential attributes that they have. The noumen houses a normative collective mind through a personality system which is capable of associative projection (after Piaget, 1977: 20), allowing the coordination of perspectives from others in its social environment, and this can influence its behaviour. Such projection involves two kinds of properties: (a) an interrelation or coordination of viewing points that creates an *object conception*; and (b) the possibility for deductive reasoning through logical processes that enable the determination of relationship consequences. For Piaget (1977: 87), object conception derives from the coordination of the schemes that underlie the activities with objects. This is in contrast to the notion of *objectivity*, which more generally is seen as a derivative of the coordination of perspectives. The capacity of an individual to change the relationship between object and subject through the coordination of perspectives results in an ability to shift roles (or to use the theatre metaphor, change characters).

Both noumenal and behavioural activity are influenced by the collective's existential collective being, often connected with its culture. Behaviour is also normally the result of an explicitly formalized social/role structure, and the two together operate phenomenally.

Noumenal and existential processes are created by a collection of individuals and their empirical psychology. There is thus a broad relationship between the social psychology of collectives and the psychology of the individual. Individual pathologies may not directly affect the plural agency because of normative smoothing, though this can be impaired by its political structures or by inherent agency pathologies.

Individuals have a curious capability of attaching themselves to a collective noumen while being simultaneously able to maintain a psychological distance from it. This is explained by the proposition (Yolles, 1999) that people are able to partition their mind according to context and maintain the partitions separately without contradiction. Indeed there are many illustrations of this when they join groups and operate in a way that is distinct from the way that they would behave as an individual in other groups.

Allport (1924, cited in the Mead Project[1]) thought that the group mind is static and the cause of individual behaviour. Perhaps he was thinking of the ephemeral group whose frame of reference is the individual, and which has not developed a culture or collective mind. Shift the frame of reference to that of the culturally based durable group and we get a very different picture. Here a group mind only properly arises once a group culture has been brought into being. This culture is not static as would be inferred from Allport's view, but is a dynamic thing quite consistent with the idea of the 'Principle of Immanent Change' as proposed by Sorokin (1937), where durable cultures change

---

[1] The Mead Project address is www.brocku.ca/MeadProject/Bernard/Bernard_1924b.html

through their own internal dynamics. As such the group mind and its psychology have characteristics that may well be related to that of the individual, even though there are some fundamental distinctions, including its normative nature, and explicit structures that could not be found in the individual mind.

In modelling the normative mind it is possible to take an ontological and an epistemological approach. The former draws on transitive processes that distinguish between and connect different modes or classes of *Being*, as illustrated for instance by cultural, group mind, and behavioural aspects of a plural agency. The epistemological approach adopts lateral processes of analysis that explore the modes themselves and their contexts. The contexts implicitly coexist and are usually undefined and initially undistinguishable, and during analysis the sets of contexts need to be explicitly related. A coupling of these approaches is sometimes seen in social psychology. This tends to explore complex problem situations and their contexts of the individual and collective mental conditions, and sometimes even in terms of culture. These conditions are actually different modes of *Being* that exist at different ontological levels of examination. Having said this, social psychology uses ontology to explore the relationship between these modes and epistemology to explore the modes themselves.

Psychological approaches have already been applied to social contexts in organizational theory with respect to a collective mind. Thus for instance, Kets de Vries (1991) adopts a Freudian view about dysfunctional and neurotic organizations. We are told that they can develop feelings of guilt, adopt collective psychological defences that reduce pain through denial and cover-up, and operate through processes of power that might be unproductive. However, theory of the social psyche of the collective is less well developed compared to theory of the psyche of the individual.

One of the core features of both a unitary and collective agency attributed with a psyche is its ability to cognitively project. There are two forms of projection that have been defined in the literature for the individual. The first is the Freudian defence process that we will refer to as *attributive projection*. It operates when an agent attributes its unwanted thoughts and feelings to another agent, or the related process when the agent attributes the characteristics of an image it has about a perceived phenomenon, thereby responding to the image not the phenomenon. The second type of projection of greater interest here is *associative projection*, originally defined by Piaget (1977: 20) as a result of his study of child development. Following Priddy's (1999) explanation of this, the mind is active in forming an image of phenomenal reality, rather than simply being a passive receptor. The image is formed through its ability to reason and create perspectives. An agent that has an ability to create *associative projection* therefore also has the capacity to form an image that can be *projected* phenomenally, this image demonstrating recognition of the behaviour of others.

A collective agency with associative projection must also necessarily have a collective psyche that is active in forming collective images through a shared reasoning process, and an ability to create perspectives. The agency has associative projection because it is composed of a set of individual agents that interact in the pursuit of common purposes or interests. These interactions are mediated by cultural structures that create normative anchors that provide a basis for cultural coherence.

The notion of the collective psyche was raised by Jung (1936: 87–110), who argued that an agency can have an inherited unconsciousness. It owes its existence exclusively to the inherited attributes of the individuals that compose the collective. While the individuals may be consciously aware of these attributes, the collective as a whole will not be so aware. So this leads one to recognize that the agency, whether plural or unitary, has both a conscious and unconscious mind. For Wollhein (1999) this relates to mental disposition, but collective mental states may also be envisaged that refer to a plural agency's preconscious mind (Table 1.1).

The collective mind can also be useful in explaining organizational performance. Weik and Roberts (1993) note that organizations (as agency) are not things but processes. Performance occurs in situations that require nearly continuous operational reliability, and the collective mind should be seen as a pattern of 'heedful' interrelations of agency actions. This pattern allows for an agency to behave independently from the individuals that compose it because its normative anchors may be different from the anchors of the individuals that compose it.

Any agency can be seen as being composed of a set of autonomous sub-agencies that construct their actions within a field of interaction resulting in a set of interconnected actions and offering agency properties. One can understand the rise of the agency mind as a result of sub-agency's adopting purposes that become formalized. In this case heedful processes are often the result of purpose/intention, coordination, integration, and hence coherence. For Brown (1961), one can apply a Freudian view, so that individuals as sub-agencies will substitute one and the same object for their 'ego-ideal'. This comes from the idea that people often decide on certain goals very early in their development, and the determinant for this is called the ego-ideal that distracts one from the present – the so-called here and now. In psychology ego-ideal is more or less the conscious ideal of personal excellence and goals towards which an individual strives, deriving from a composite image of the personal characteristics the individual sees as an iconic personality. The result of the use of the ego-goal is that people consequently identify themselves with one another in their ego. Brown (1961: 123) notes that there is a distinction between Freud's view based on patterns of the family, and the social psychologist's view based on the study of work-groups or those that produce things. In addition, adopting the proposition that an agency is a plural collective which can be understood in terms of individual psychology means there is a need for an agency mind that can explain collective actions. The mind perceives phenomena and supplies knowledge that corresponds to a particular viewing point or perspective. In so doing it structures the phenomena into meaningful patterns through the process of projection. Indeed, linking this with the notion of Frieden (1998) that phenomena are themselves created through the interaction between information and cognition, we can align ourselves with the constructivist notion that reality is actually created, but at a non-conscious level. As Priddy tells us, the conscious mind perceives what its other (non-conscious) parts project.

The mind creates images through apperception that is characterized through schemas. Originating with Adler in the eighteenth century (cited in Priddy, 1999), apperception provides a unique self-schema or way of looking at the world, ourselves, and of interpreting experience, and is responsible for subjectivity. It is a process of interpretive observation abstracted from phenomenal experience through interpretation that makes it coherent with other relevant experiences (thus providing context) and gives significance to perception (Priddy, 1999). Apperception eventually delivers images/schemas with processes of internalization (Chapter 6), which have a symbolic cognitive function. Two classes of image can be distinguished: reproductive images that evoke already known events, and anticipatory images that depict events not yet observed (and which become embedded in the structures that facilitate and constrain behaviours). These images are no more adequate in manifesting behaviour than are perceptions. They account for concepts that arise from operative activities and engender operations on the basis of experience. Here the image makes it possible to anticipate the results of cognitive transformations that result in a shift in image which symbolizes knowledge of phenomenal states. The transformations facilitate changes in event apperception and perspective. Transformations involve active anticipations or re-anticipations (through feedback).

In addition to these cognitive attributes, there are also emotional projections that explain strong emotional drives, and are non-conscious and involuntary, motivated by emotions wherein an agency imposes a subjective feeling or a thought on other agencies or situations (Priddy, 1999). For an agency to impose a subjective feeling on another agency or situation is a condition of empathy, usually taken to be an identification through understanding of another's situation, related feelings and motives, or the attribution of one's own feelings. According to Piaget (1977: 132), empathy is knowing what another person feels, or feeling what another feels, or both. Knowing and feeling are indissociable facets of the same event. It is difficult to logically distinguish between genuine empathetic and egocentric projection. Empathy implies a kind of emotional sharing between subject and object that has more than a cognitive explanation. Egocentric projection is distinct from empathy, since the former is *imposed* on what is perceived. Following Priddy (1999), an 'egocentric' agency is unrealized where desires, inclinations, and attachments are more significant to behaviour than other higher interests, and mostly refers to the lower, more selfish aspects of ego (representations of self through a mental self-image/schema constituted as a complex structure of memories and responses).

Feffer (1970) uses the concept of egocentrism as a major explanatory variable in a general theory of schizophrenia. It adopts the notion of decentring (the ability to shift from one focus of examination to another), and is crucial in structuring experience. For Feffer, the inability to decentre is a characteristic of schizophrenic thought disorder. Such agencies lack the ability to formulate communications that reflect an accurate understanding of the information needs of their listeners. This is also a characteristic of plural agencies in which there are competing dominant paradigms. Egocentrism is a polar opposite of perspectivism which together form an egocentric-persepectivistic axis. Egocentrism is applied to the state of recurrent subject–object confusion that operates to confine an individual to a singular and highly personalized point of view, while denying to others the uniqueness of their own vantage. Perspectivism, however, refers to the progressive capacity to differentiate between one's own and others' points of view. It implies the recognition of universality rather than the absence of subjectivity.

Concepts of human psychology can be applied, with appropriate constraints, to any durable autonomous social collective that operates through its noumenal and existential dimensions: that is, when it has a collective mind and a culture.

3.2 From Minds to Personalities

The cognitive structure of agency personality is a determinant for agency behaviour. This applies whether agency is seen as a singular entity (an individual) or a plural one. The distinction, however, is that in the plural agency emotion, states, and dispositions are normative, leading to the idea of the normative personality.

The concept of normative personality has been used within the context of the ambient social *influences* that mould personalities during their formation (Mroczek & Little, 2006). The term thus refers to collective norms that may together coalesce into a unitary cognitive structure such that a collective mind can be inferred, and from which a personality *emerges*. This can be explained as follows. Consider that stable collectives develop a common dominant culture within which shared beliefs develop in relation to the capacity of the collective power to produce desired outcomes. Cultural anchors arise which enable the development of formal and informal norms for patterns of behaviour, modes of conduct and expression, forms of thought, attitudes, and values that are more or less adhered to by its membership. When the norms refer to formal behaviours, and where members of the collective contravene them, they are deemed to be engaging in illegitimate behaviour which, if discovered, may result in formal retribution – the severity of which is determined from the collective's ideological and ethical positioning. This develops with the rise of collective cognitive processes that starts with information inputs, and through decision processes results in orientation to action; and it does this with a sense of the collective mind and self. It is a short step to recognize that the collective mind is associated with normative personality. Where a normative personality is deemed to exist, it does not necessarily mean that individual members of the collective will all conform to all aspects of the normative processes: they may only do so 'more or less'. Where less leads to rarely or never, then there are often processes of penalty or exclusion built into the regulatory mechanisms of an agency for such miscreants. In the remainder of this chapter, when we refer to normative personality we shall mean the development of the collective mind and its *emergent* normative personality. It is related to the notions of cognitive learning theory (e.g. Miller & Dollard, 1941; Piaget, 1950; Miller et al., 1960; Argyris & Schön, 1978; Vygotsky, 1978; Bandura, 1986 & 1988; Nobre, 2003; Argote & Todorova, 2007), where 'learning is seen in terms of the acquisition or reorganization of the cognitive structures through which humans process and store information' (Good and Brophy, 1990: 187). Set within this lies our interest, *cognitive information process theory*, where the collective mind is seen as an information-based system that operates through a normative set of logical mental rules and strategies (e.g. Atkinson & Shiffrin, 1968; Bowlby, 1980; Novak, 1993; Wang, 2007). These rules and strategies may fail when pathologies develop.

In order to understand more about the normative personality we may find some direction from theories of the individual personality. Support for this comes from a number of sources (e.g. Brown, 1961; Weik and Roberts, 1993; Bandura, 1999; Hofstede et al., 2002; Barley, 2007; Gindis, 2009), with agents behaving consistently as 'legal corporate persons', and with a unitary rationality that can be explained. In Figure 3.1 normative personality is taken to be socio-cognitive in nature. Personality assessment differentiates between personality structures and behavioural orientations. The internal structures are assessed through an examination of a system of interacting psychological mechanisms rather than a set of independent variables as in trait approaches. Normative personality traits are essentially contextually sensitive orientations that the personality possesses which conform to unique sets of characteristics. Traits are determinants for patterns of behaviour. The efficacy of personality processes is important. Bandura (1986) defines collective efficacy of the agency as the shared belief that can, as a whole, attain goals and accomplish

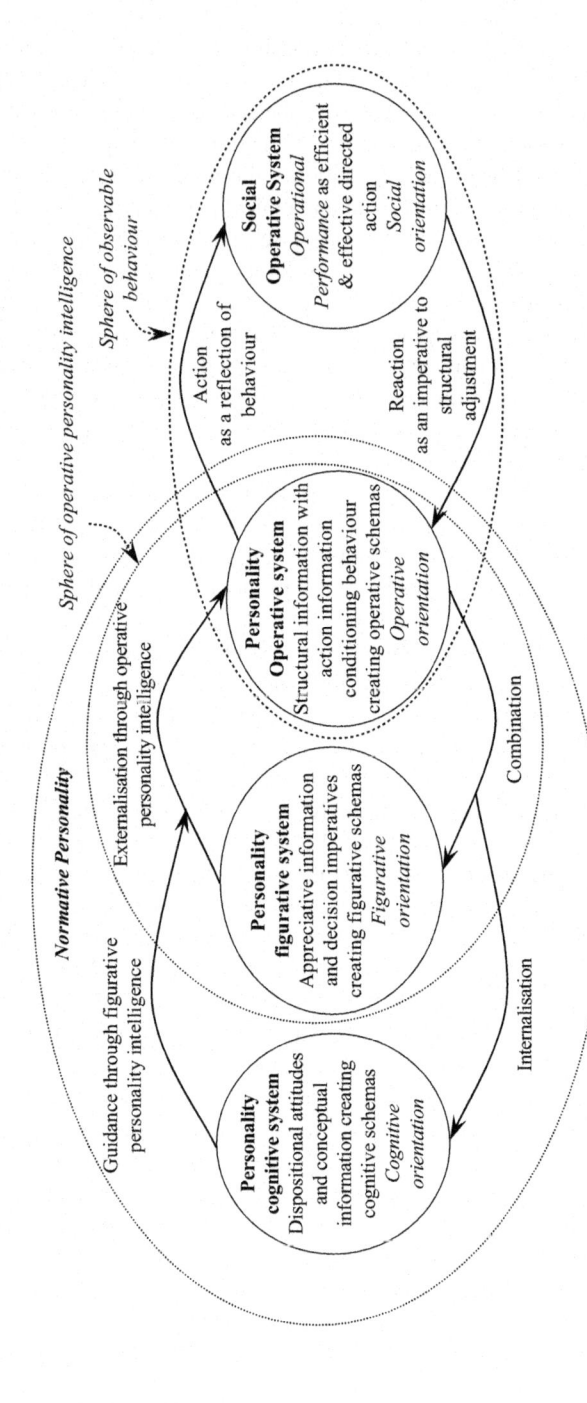

Figure 3.1 Normative personality as a cognitive system with figurative and operative intelligences, seated in the noumenal domain of the plural agency

its desired tasks. It involves a belief or perception that efficacious collective actions are possible in relation to a social need. Problems with the cultural cohesion of an agency may affect its performance through both individual lacks of confidence in individual agencies, and/or perceptual differences in collective efficacy (Bandura, 1995). The efficacy of an agency will also influence its ability to communicate, goal set, and persevere during adversity.

Bandura's (1988, 1994, 1999, 2006) socio-cognitive theory is substantively concerned with personality, though he rarely adopts the term. He has developed the theory through the use of cybernetic information process theory, where organizations may be seen as agents of operative performance. In particular, an agency is seen as having the cognitive capacities of intention, forethought, and the ability to react and to reflect, and it is from these capacities that the *agentic perspective* arises through which adaptation and change in human development occurs. To be an agency is to influence intentionally one's functioning and life circumstances, and personal influence is part of the causal structure. Agencies are self-organizing, proactive, self-regulating, and self-reflecting, adapting, involving autonomous control, and they are participative in creating their own behaviour and contributors to their life circumstances.

The study of personality is directed at orientations or penchants towards certain cognitive attributes and how this may influence agency behaviour. In creating our theory of normative personality, we shall draw on both socio-cognitive and trait theory. In trait theory (McCrae & Costa, 1996; Maruyama, 1988 & 2001), traits are variables that in some way describe personality, but the state values that they take can also indicate personality types (Eysenck, 1957; also cited by Gonsowski [1999] as a Jungian notion), which ultimately control it. McKenna et al. (2002) *note a connection between* personality type and behavioural style that ultimately refers to stable patterns of behaviour. Such patterns are ultimately dependent upon stable personality types (Berens, 2007). This leads to the recognition that traits ultimately take on a personality control function (Van Egeren, 2009). However, it needs to be recognized that the regulative control function, which is unique for each trait, is constituted by distinct frameworks of principles that offer domination and functional governance. Traits have some relevance to organizational conduct (Denison & Mishra, 1995; van Knippenbern et al., 2010) and misconduct (Gottfredson & Hirschi, 1990). While there has been some difficulty in modelling the connection between socio-cognitive and trait theories (Bandura, 1999), some progress has also been made using cybernetic theory (Cervone et al., 2004; Van Egeren, 2009) that we shall build upon.

In socio-cognitive theory the mind operates as a complex system (Bandura 1999; Cervone et al. 2004). Socio-cognitive variables develop through socio-cultural experiences. They distinguish between cognitive capacities that contribute to personality functioning, including skills, competencies, and knowledge structures that have been derived from experienced real-life situations, self-reflective processes that enable people to develop beliefs about themselves within social contexts, and self-regulatory processes where people formulate goals, standards, and motivations towards identifiable outcomes (Bandura 1986, 1999; Williams 1992). Identifiable outcomes can be represented as performance, which involves the evaluation of directed behaviour and is related to the interaction between the behaviours. These are embedded in personality structures expressed in terms of systems, and the social environmental factors with which it is coupled. In each of these personality systems, orientations exist that define a set of schemas that express its functionality and strategic purposes, and traits which take on a regulatory function. They do this through the adoption of regulatory propensities or styles affecting how agencies characteristically pursue their goals. They are seen as ontologically distinct, having different derivative natures. They have cultural, conceptual, figurative, operative, and event orientations. They are all connected indirectly through a set of process intelligences – constituted as a network of processes that migrate semantic-goods like information between the systems that each traits dominates.

Figure 3.1 links closely with the cybernetic model of personality by Yolles et al. (2011), and acts as the basis for normative personality introduced here. It is an agency model formulated through three ontologically distinct systems: the cognitive, figurative, and operative, each of which has distinct epistemic content and characteristics. In the cognitive system there exists a collective *cognitive base* that constitutes the 'truths' that form both its *epistemic base* (scientific beliefs that form patterns of analytic knowledge) and its *cultural base* (cultural beliefs that arise as normative standards of conduct), where both are connected with assumptions, beliefs, and trusted propositions that arise within cultural development; the cognitive base may be seen as the result of cybernetic interaction (Maturana and Varela, 1987: 75) between the patterns of cultural and analytic knowledge, and these affect each other through their history of mutual influence, where cognitive intention plays a metasystemic role and creates a cultural orientation for the agency (Yang et al., 2009). Self-reference is essential and establishes agency identity (Hannah et al., 2008 & 2010). The underlying assumptions (Schein, 1985) contribute to organizational knowledge, where false knowledge when embedded into the culture results in myth.

In Table 1.1 it was indicated that schemas exist across the personality that can be applied to Figure 3.1. These are represented in Figure 3.1, which explains how the three types of schema arise. Cognitive schemas are structures that arise from dispositional attitudes and patterns of information that are themselves manifested from beliefs, knowledge, and values. They involve attitudes and information that define longer term disposition, which anchors the personality in the same way as culture does for agency, and shorter lasting states. State information relates more to situational action that can be manifested as appreciative information. Figurative schemas arise with appreciative information (Vickers, 1965) that defines a somewhat reflective view of a situation and decision imperatives that indicate decision options. Figurative schemas are manifested from cognitive schemas and defined through a *figurative base* composed of entities and their relationships that have been construed through the sedimentation of information-rich conceptual models (from its cognitive base), with connection to cognitive purpose. The figurative system is the home of figurative elements like ideological and ethical structures that contribute to agency political and moral functioning. Operative schemas arise from figurative schemas, and the appreciative information that they carry conditions behaviour through action-related information and decision processes.

The figurative part of the agency, its personality, is also its strategic part from which follows the regulation of information flows, decision-making, and patterns of behaviour, that is, the 'internal allocation of tasks, decisions, rules, and procedures for appraisal and reward, selected for the best pursuit of [...] [a] strategy' (Caves, 1980: 64). Cognitive purposes (Habermas, 1970) are linked to information, and determine purposeful behaviour (Espejo et al., 1997). This is also the domain of attitudes, manifested from beliefs to create an 'enduring organization of beliefs' around an object or situation predisposing an agency to respond to situations in some preferential manner (Rokeach, 1968). Values are culturally defined (Williams et al., 1993), and when espoused enable the distinction between observable and unobservable elements of culture (Schein, 1985). They are also central to an agency's capacity towards the creation of strategic definition, being manifested from its culture and providing a basis for ideology that enables the construction of regulatory constraints that condition the agency in its internal behaviour.

The operative system of the personality is its structural component, from which behaviour emanates within an environment, which becomes populated by *artifacts* – objects created by agencies, often with assigned cultural significance (Schein, 1985). It is in the operative system where organizational structure is maintained. Here there is a *pragmatic base* that is constituted by and facilitated through normative modes of practice that respond to standards of validity that constitute evidence, with connection to cognitive interest that are used for acquiring knowledge (Habermas, 1970). Self-organization is important to the survival of an agency, enabling it to create its own order (Kauffman, 1993). It is also the domain of operative management, epistemologically distinguishable from operative processes (Beer, 1975).

The network of processes of *internalization, externalization,* and *combination* (Nonaka & Takeuchi, 1995), which respond to their interest in how organizations incorporate, express, connect, and share knowledge, are also important to the organizational process. In Figure 3.1 they are constituted as the transitive (across system/domain) process intelligences. These processes provide feedback that is able to constrain or amplify the systemic attributes. The process of socialization, through which explicit knowledge can be socially spread, occurs as a lateral (within domain) structural coupling (Maturana and Varela, 1987: 75), where they have a common history of interaction beyond the personality.

As indicated before, the normative agency has process intelligences consisting of: *figurative intelligence* (a form of autogenesis: Schwarz, 1997) which provides its core relational explanations of reality, and *operative intelligence* (a form of autopoiesis: Schwarz, 1997; Maturana and Varela, 1987) which provides for its capacity to evidence its figurative base. Normative agents with poor figurative intelligence do not maintain good representation in their figurative or cognitive bases. Those with poor operative intelligence cannot adequately manifest elements of their figurative base pragmatically, so that they have limited capacity to evidence models and efficacy is constrained.

In normative personality the term *operative intelligence* refers to the capacity for beliefs, values, attitudes, and knowledge to be assembled in a coherent way to be put into effect. *Operative intelligence* is the efficacy of personality structures that facilitate and condition behaviours from which arise performance. In contrast within the context of personality, *figurative intelligence* is the set of figurative images (including mental models and abstractions) that have solidified to form personality. The intelligence attributes would, in this way, relate to the efficacious manifestations of beliefs, values, and knowledge in the normative agent as personality patterns, including attitudes, which govern how decision imperatives can be addressed and responded to.

3.3 Agency Trait Theory and Maruyama Mindscapes

Bandura's (1986) socio-cognitive theory arises through his notions of social learning, and he recognized that socio-cognitive processes are influenced by memory and emotions, and interact with environmental influences. Behaviour is also seen to be guided by cognitive processes that are connected with traits. Bandura developed a theory of self that explores complex psychological and subjective reality as it impacts on goals and expectations. It points towards strategies that are used to satisfy expectations and accomplish meaningful subjective goals, and it induces the affective representation of the perceived problem (Scott-Murray, 2005). It can be seen as a theory of individual differences (Bandura 1999) that recognizes that processes are connected with personality traits that condition personality processes in some invisible way.

Bandura recognizes that they are descriptive behavioural clusters that tell one little about the determinants and regulative structures governing the behaviours that constitute a particular cluster. In his view, for this there is a need for process theory through which can be explored self-efficacy. Self-efficacy beliefs determine how an agency feels, thinks, motivates itself, and behaves. The beliefs produce diverse effects through the major processes of cognition, motivation, effectiveness, and selection.

In contrast, traits have a unique fundamental regulatory and characterizing function in the personality. A trait is usually seen as a distinguishing feature, characteristic, or quality of a personality style, creating a predisposition for a personality to respond in a particular way to a broad range of situations (Allport, 1961). Traits arise from an interaction between personality and situation (Chapman et al., 2000), resulting, for instance, in the interaction model of personality (Stevens and Rodin, 2001). They are also described as enduring patterns of perceiving, relating to, and thinking about the environment and oneself that are exhibited in a wide range of social and personal contexts; they are also habitual patterns of thought, emotion, and stable clusters of behaviour. Traits operate as continuous dimensions that together may define a personality space, and the trait variables may in theory be subject to small degrees of continuous variation. For Eysenck (1957), the scalar value that a trait variable takes may be classed as a personality type, and there are various manifestations of types in trait theory (Costa and McCrae, 1992; Goldberg, 1993; Heinström, 2003). It may be noted, however, that where there are personality theories that explore types but where no traits are deemed to exist (or vice versa), traits (or types) may be inferred. These traits are not of the form identified by Gottfredson & Hirschi (1990), that is, the lack of self-control. Rather they are what Bandura (1999) calls supertraits, Van Egeren (2009) refers to as global traits, and which play a formative role in the development of personality. Here, we shall refer to these as formative traits.

Earlier, in Figure 3.1, we referred to cognitive, figurative, operative, and social orientations. These in effect define a set of formative traits for the agency. Van Egeren (2009) notes the problem that traits are normally arbitrarily defined. To correct this limitation, it must be recognized that the *characteristics* define the traits and give them meaning, and these are not arbitrary. Where trait names in different schemas are the same, their characteristics can vary. Since the nature of a trait is defined by its characteristic, then this is central to the comparative nature of trait schemas. It is these characteristics that are entailed in the orientations that we have referred to. We take it that a set of normative personality traits are orientations that can arise from core properties that commonly exist in relation to the capacity of a collective agency to survive efficaciously. They also operate to establish stable control patterns that underlie patterns of behaviour through regulatory processes. The modelling process that we undertake here establishes particular systems with named properties, and these can be related to contextual orientations that take up the role of trait. Different traits enable the contextual orientations to operate as control functions through the (type) values that they take, and hence they reflect different characteristics. It is not therefore highly relevant how the names of these traits vary, so long as their characteristics can be related. This has been illustrated by Yolles (2009) and Yolles & Fink (2009), where trait schemas have been set into a characteristics typology and compared.

At this juncture it would be useful to explore options for the development of a trait theory that fits with agency. While a number of candidate theories exist, such as the Myers-Briggs Type Inventory (Myers et al., 1998) and the Five Factor Model (McCrae & Allik, 2002), both require significant discussion about the stable patterns of behaviour that their type values generate, as well as discussion about their lack of theoretical underpinnings. A more direct option comes from *mindscape theory* as considered, for instance, by Shani & Basuray (1988: 5), when they discuss organization culture and its related sociological processes and the social patterns of reasoning behaviour:

In each culture, organizations are profoundly influenced by genotypical blueprints of reasoning methods embedded within that culture. The term 'mindscape' is used taxonomically by Maruyama (1980) to identify the epistemological types that correspond to the four causal metatypes in science theories (especially in the social and biological sciences). According to Maruyama, the corresponding epistemic types, or mindscapes, are intended to mean a 'structure of reasoning, cognition, perceptions, conceptualization, design, planning and decision making that may vary from one individual, profession, culture or social group to another' (Maruyama, 1980: 591).

Hence it is feasible to discuss not only the personality of individuals, but the social personality too. The relationship between the individual and social personality is also considered, when Maruyama (2002: 167; cited by Boje, 2004) notes that 'one of the types becomes powerful for historical or political reasons, and utilizes, ignores or suppresses individuals of other types'.

Given that trait values/types are known for an agency, it is possible to identify the constraints on the potential for behaviour that the agency is capable of, under normal conditions, and it is from this that possible patterns of behaviour can be generated for determinable contexts. Now, mindscapes arise from a type theory that enables behaviours to be anticipated under known contexts (Yolles & Fink, 2009). Types are values taken by traits in a trait space that defines a personality, and such a trait space has been considered by Boje (2004), who identifies three traits: power, ethics, and knowledge. Yolles & Fink (2009) have adapted Boje's trait space, and define the three personality orientation traits that better fit with organizational agencies: technical interest power, social-oriented ethics, and knowledge disposition, which we explore here.

Technical interest power is an *operative orientation* trait that concerns the disciplining of operative knowledge, regulating it through the constraining processes of socialization and division of labour. Following Foucault (1972), it may be noted that agents are not free to say just anything when or where they wish, and certain types of knowledge are forbidden in some social environments. This is connected with recognition of the nature of the socially constructed constraints that are imposed on individuals and a technical ability (Habermas, 1970) to engage with the environment and to establish predictions and regulation, presupposing the existence of a structure that both anticipates and facilitates behaviour. In Boje's (2004) terms, the type values that this trait variable may take relate to the 'will to power' and the 'will to serve'. However, it also relates to the capacity of an operative system to be able to respond to recognized processes of cognitive self-organization (of self-regulative strategy as defined in terms of Figure 3.1). Through this trait variable an agent may be high on autonomy when it might react to the lessons drawn from (or opportunities offered by) environmental impulses, and will follow less the guidance by the cultural system at the societal level. An alternative value for the variable might be embeddedness, where a similar construct can be found in Sagiv and Schwartz (2007). Through this the technical interest power trait can represent a durable and distinct personality orientation that is able to cope with unpredictable futures. Since technical interest power structures appreciative information, with both cognitive and evaluative aspects and enabling adaptation, the personality is enabled to facilitate responses to its social environment and predefine its behavioural penchant towards its operations. Agency efficacy affects social orientation and may contribute to the realizing of an agency's full orientation potential, to engage with the environmental predictions that it regulates, and adjust its own operative processes. In contrast, in-efficacy may result in an agential inadequacy that can impact on its operative intelligence or the recognition of agency adjustment imperatives. This trait can also be connected with strong hierarchy as opposed to loose hierarchy. Agencies with a strong hierarchy have rigid rules that have to be followed. Agencies that score high on this dimension (strong hierarchy) can be considered to be less able to change quickly and rely on strategies elaborated by top management. Moreover, organizations with a strong hierarchy provide stringent rules of behaviour. The opposite is true for organizations with 'loose hierarchies'. As an example, we can expect that public organizations differ severely from private organizations, for example, with respect to level of formalization (Hooijberg & Choi, 2001).

Self-relational ethics is a *figurative orientation* trait that is distinct from the normally defined ethics as the process of determining right and wrong conduct. Boje prefers to adopt the different Foucauldian notion of ethics. Following Coveney (1998), Foucault's ethics are individualized forms of self-regulation (e.g. the work ethic). Ethics are thus connected with the relationships we have with ourselves. Ethics in this sense is connected with the mutual ways in which agents are both regulated by others and regulate themselves, and recognition of this occurs through appreciations. For Murtagh (2008), this notion of ethics provides the opportunity for agents to change their relationship to the symbolic order and provides a means to self-orientate out of socially constructed constraints (e.g. femininity and masculinity). Boje (2004) adopts the type options in this trait variable as pluralistic and monistic. However, this also connects with plural 'harmony' or monistic 'achievement' of appreciations or goals that are systemically created in the figurative system and formulate agency orientation. The orientation may be related to the notions of harmony and mastery by Sagiv and Schwartz (2007). To do this it draws on the figurative appreciations that are available within an agency. The figurative system that hosts this is concerned with driving goal formulation as a process that derives from data collection and involves the careful weighing of arguments as opposed to spontaneous decisions following from the spontaneous desires of the decision makers. Self-relational ethics has an attribute of appreciation that maintains an interconnected set of more or less tacit standards which order and value experience, and determines the way an agent sees and values different situations, and how instrumental judgements are made and action is taken. It facilitates how an agent as a decision maker observes and interprets reality, and establishes decision imperatives about it. As such the trait reflects the regulation of the appreciations and resulting goals of the organization with respect to its intended operations, the potential for social interaction, and the ethical positioning that may occur as a response to opportunities provided or indicated by the social environment. Efficacy between this trait and the technical interest power trait can lead to self-principled agencies with aesthetical, intuitive, or ethical/ideological positioning. It can provide ideological images that may facilitate action. It orientates the agent towards a view of stages of historical development with respect to interaction with the external environment. Inefficacy can lead to corrupt and sociopathic organizations (Yolles, 2009a), or, more broadly, agency misconduct (Greve et al., 2010).

Knowledge disposition is a *cognitive orientation* trait that arises in Boje's theory as the will to knowledge, which is historically constituted and scripted, and rather as in a theatrical production, agencies become characters in a *script system* and become script performers and/or script generators (Boje & Rosile, 2003). Boje identifies two types of scripts for this trait variable: transaction and transformation. The will to knowledge in a transactional scripting involves simple repetition and sameness and facilitates the enactment of an agency's own will regardless of situation. The will to knowledge in transformation scripting is about changing the system through emergence and deviation and concerns the enactment of an agency's will to serve in a given social situation. It involves Maruyama's notion of dialectic of deviation-counteracting and deviation-amplifying in the scripts. Knowledge scripting is part of secondary socialization (e.g. by providing them with socially acceptable values). Through this agents internalize the scripts, as well as the character type expected for agencies in their environment. This script internalization is constituted as a means of formation, and enables an agent to be influenced by knowledge that relates to its social environment. The transactional and transformation types can be directly related with opportunity and change seeking, as opposed to reliance on organizational resources that affect structures and processes that define the agency forms that are related to intentions and behaviours. As an illustration, in the field of strategic management there are two diametrically opposed views: resource-based (Barney, 1991) and market-based (Porter, 1980, 1985). A market-based orientation puts a strong emphasis on functional departments, for example, finance, marketing, etc., while a resource-based orientation puts a strong emphasis on real performance 'in the field' and values market feedback. According to the generic model of organizational culture, agencies following the resource-based view will more strongly rely on 'market feedback', 'performance assessment' and 'single-loop learning'. It is necessary to identify and preserve unique resources within the organization to generate a competitive advantage. In contrast, agencies that follow the market-based view would emphasize 'operationalisation', 'patterns of behaviour', and 'action' as resources that are mobile, substitutable, and not rare. Such a dominance of upper processes (directed from organizational culture to task environment) would imply that agencies seek markets where they best fit in and do not necessarily adjust in order to fit markets (Porter, 1980, 1985). Agencies that score high on this dimension follow rather a market-based view.

    This cognitive orientation trait variable of knowledge disposition might involve the effective realizing of potential, recognizing the nature of an agency's social and political processes and of the constraints imposed by social and political structures. This may occur through self-regulation and either the subordination to hierarchy or liberation away from power and bureaucratic regulations allowing normative rule obedience to be defined at a sub-agency level. This trait affects the operative couple between self-oriented ethics and technical interest power traits through its network of efficacy processes, but it can also be seen in terms of directly affecting the technical interest power trait (Figure 3.2), thereby contributing to cognitive coherence. This is connected with a move towards homeostasis – the human capacity to maintain or restore some physiological or psychological constants despite

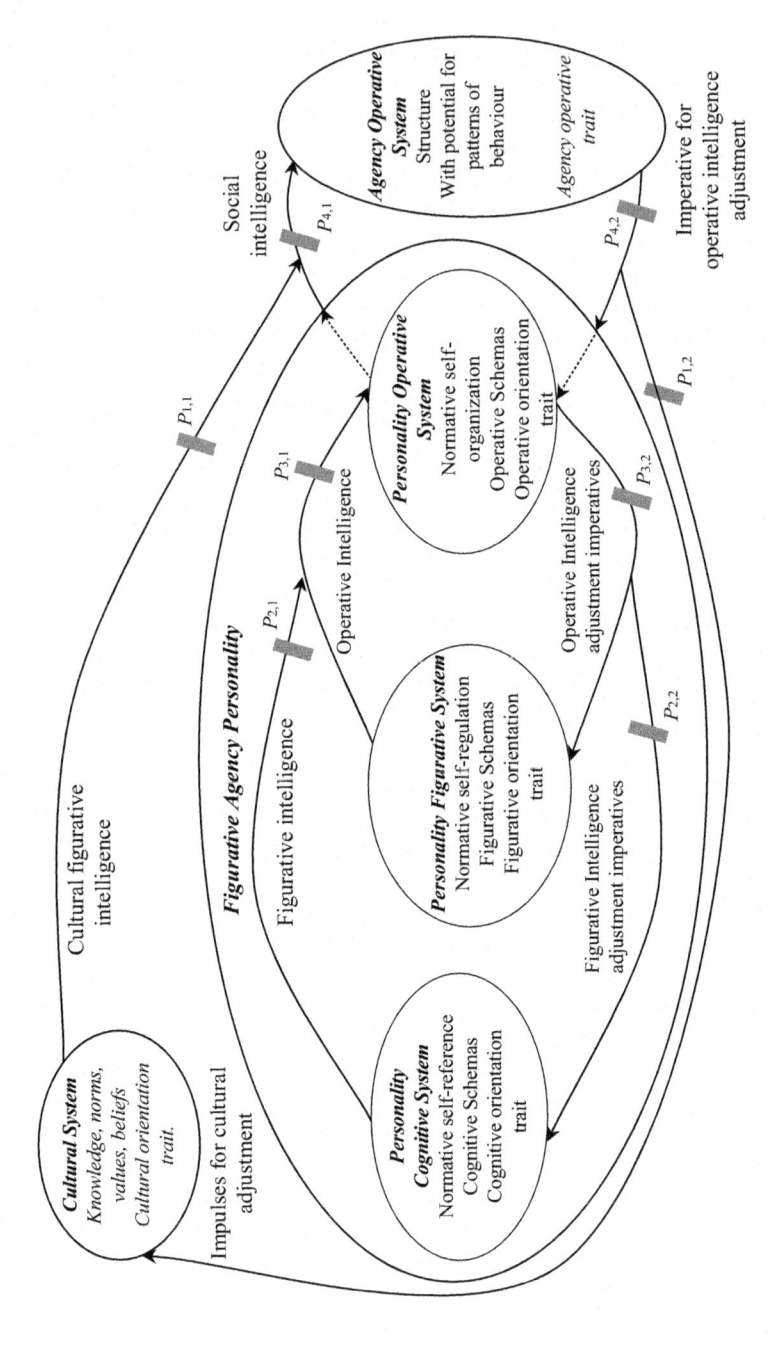

Figure 3.2 Socio-cognitive trait model of the agency connecting normative personality with social and cultural systems; Boje's personality traits here are technical-interest power, self-relational ethics, and knowledge disposition

outside environmental variations (Pasquier et al., 2006). In-efficacy can similarly lead to lack of coherence and cognitive dissidence (Fraser-Mackenzie & Dror, 2009), and this can act as a driver for cognitive state/dispositional dysfunctions (Endler & Summerfield, 1995: 255). So, the cognitive system involves attitudes and emotive impulses that may orientate the agency through its knowledge disposition trait towards *cognitive coherence* or *dissidence*. Knowledge disposition has an impact on unitary and plural fugitive perspectives like strategies, ideology, and morality. It also creates imperatives for the regulation of the patterns of behaviour through intention.

Knowing agency personality types will enable the anticipation of its patterns of behaviour under normal circumstances. The relationship between the stable pattern of types that arises in any agency creates stable patterns of behaviour that drive ones expectations about how an agency is likely to behave in given contexts. Mindscape theory tells us that personalities develop stable states (referred to as H, I, S, and G). These states are dominant agency mindscapes, that 'In a given culture during a given historical period, some type may become powerful and official, and the powerful type may change from period to period.' (Boje, 2004, citing Maruyama, 2001: 65).

Adapting notions from Boje (2004) and Maruyama (2008), Table 3.1 summarizes the patterning relationships between types and mindscape states. States occur as a cluster of types that create stable patterns of behaviour, and while only four states are usually referred to, there may be others. These four states can also be described in terms of the mindscape characteristics: homogenistic, heterogenistic, hierarchical, individualistic, homeostatic, morphogenic, random, interactive. These can also be interrelated, and so can generate a potentially innumerable number of mindscape profiles. The mindscape characteristics have an epistemic nature and arise from styles of attitude. Thus for instance, given that an agency has two cultural opposing groups with distinguishable cultures, Maruyama (1993) attributed conflicts and misunderstandings between their members to differences in value priorities, behavioural patterns, and logical and epistemic structures.

Beyond the three traits we have discussed, two others exist within the agency that must also be mentioned: cultural and social orientation. Cultural orientation is part of the agency, and not the normative personality. It has been explored at some length in Yolles et al. (2008) but arises from the work of Sorokin (1962). It operates not as an information trait, but rather a knowledge trait. The type values that this trait can assume includes sensate orientation, which allows realities to be deemed to exist only if they can be sensorially perceived. Sensate-type members of a culture do not seek or believe in a supersensory reality, and are agnostic towards the world beyond any current sensory capacity of perception. Needs and aims are mainly physical, that is, that which

Table 3.1 Maruyama's core epistemic types with connected Boje traits

Type	H	I	S	G
Keyword characteristics	Hierarchical, homogenist, classificational, competitive, zero-sum, opposition, one truth	Heterogenistic, independent, random, uniquing, negative-sum, separation, subjective	Heterogenistic, interactive, homeostatic (pattern-maintaining), cooperative, positive-sum	Heterogenistic, interactive, morphogenic (pattern-generative), co-generative, positive-sum
Nature	Parts are subordinated to the whole, with subcategories neatly grouped into super-categories. The strongest, or the majority, dominate at the expense of the weak or of any minorities. Belief in existence of the one truth applicable to all (e.g. whether values, policies, problems, priorities, etc.). Logic is deductive and axiomatic demanding sequential reasoning. Cause-effect relations may be deterministic or probabilistic.	Only individuals are real, even when aggregated into society. Emphasis on self-sufficiency, independence and individual values. Design favours the random, the capricious and the unexpected. Scheduling and planning are to be avoided. Non-random events are improbable. Each question has its own answer; there are no universal principles.	Society consists of heterogeneous individuals who interact non-hierarchically to mutual advantage. Mutual dependency. Differences are desirable and contribute to the harmony of the whole. Maintenance of the natural equilibrium. Values are interrelated and cannot be rank-ordered. Avoidance of repetition. Causal loops. Categories not mutually exclusive. Objectivity is less useful than 'cross-subjectivity' or multiple viewpoints. Meaning is context dependent	Heterogeneous individuals interact non-hierarchically for mutual benefit, generating new patterns and harmony. Nature is continually changing requiring allowance for change. Values interact to generate new values and meanings. Values of deliberate (anticipatory) incompleteness. Causal loops. Multiple evolving meanings

Traits		Stable Patterns of Type Values		
Technical interest power	Embeddedness	Autonomy	Embeddedness	Autonomy
Self-relational ethics	Achievement	Achievement	Harmony	Harmony
Knowledge disposition	Transactional	Transactional	Transformational	Transformational

primarily satisfies the sense organs. The epistemic attributes include appreciating the nature of the needs and ends that are to be satisfied, the degree of strength in pursuit of those needs, and the methods of satisfaction. The means of satisfaction occurs not through adaptation or modification of human beings, but through the exploitation of the external world. It is thus practically orientated, with emphasis on human external needs. With perceived reality being dependent upon senses, its operative nature is highlighted in that it views reality through what can be measured and observed rather than reasoned. Cultural orientation may also assume ideationality, which sees reality as non-sensate and nonmaterial. Epistemic needs and ends are mainly spiritual, rather than practicable, and internal rather than external. The method of fulfilment or realization is self-imposed minimization or elimination of most physical needs, to promote the greater development of the human being as a Being. Spiritual needs are thus at the forefront of this disposition's aims rather than human physical needs.

These types act with YinYang bipolar activity (Zhang, 2009 & 2011), where alternate poles in the bipolar arrangement maintain auxiliary functions that interact and can contribute to the emergence of stable intermediate or balanced trait states, creating what Sorokin (1962: vol. 4, 590), in his study of cultural traits, called the Principle of Immanent Change. In this, autonomous agencies with coherent cultures experience cultural change by virtue of its own internal forces and properties. The principle of immanent change means that an agency cannot help changing even if all external conditions are constant. Sorokin (1962: vol. 4, 600–1) tells us that any functional sociocultural system incessantly generates consequences that are not the results of the external factors to the system, but the consequences of the existence of the system and of its activities. As such they are necessarily imputed to it, and this occurs without the benefit of conscious decision. One of the specific forms of this immanent generation of consequences is an incessant change of the system itself, due to its existence and activity. The dynamics of change thus occur naturally as an internal process to the culture. While Sorokin was interested in large-scale cultures which change over long periods of time, those of corporate agencies having small-scale cultures may have an immanent dynamic that changes over small time scales. Due to the intimate relationship between culture and personality, cultural orientation changes must necessarily be reflected through change in attitudes and emotive impulses in the normative personality. Hence it is expected that personality traits will reflect the immanent dynamics of the cultural orientation trait. This is where there is a distinction between the personality of the non-mobile individual who may have little exposure to cultural orientation shifts, and that of the durable agency that will, through immanence, experience its own cultural shifts that may be exacerbated by ambient cultural shifts.

Finally, social orientation operates in a given social environment. This orientation might be seen to exist in a social operative system directed towards action, interaction, and reaction that (re)constitutes the cultural environment in terms of (desired, welcome, undesired, not welcome) activities. So, an agency might put emphasis on action (where its membership is convinced that it will get positive feedback, their product will sell, etc.), or have a more observation orientation and collect (lots of) information before engaging in action. Essentially, therefore, action-oriented arises from an optimistic tendency, while observation-oriented arises from a pessimistic tendency.

As a result of these considerations, a trait model is offered in Figure 3.1 which adopts the same trait logic offered by Yolles (2009) in his exploration of the Myers-Briggs Type Indicator model. We note that Figure 3.2 is an extension of Figure 1.3 with a richer superstructure. The model represents trait systems, with Boje's personality traits for operative orientation being technical-interest power, figurative orientation being self-relational ethics, and cognitive orientation being knowledge disposition. The trait systems are connected by intelligences through which information is manifested, and which are subject to efficacy that controls the emotive impulses that influence the manifestation processes. These intelligences are semantic channels that may be subject to inefficacy or intelligence limitation if expected performance is not achieved, when we say that pathologies $P_{i,j}$ have developed. We may recall that in Chapter 2 $P2,1$ and $P2,2$ were referred to as figurative pathologies F, while $P3,1$ and $P3,2$ as operative pathologies O. However, the current Pi,j symbolism allows for higher order agencies, effectively. The nature of intelligence, efficacy, and pathology will be considered further in the next section.

3.4 Intelligences and Efficacy Agency

The operative intelligence that we have been using is intimately connected with the notion of autopoiesis, defined here as a network of processes that is able to manifest information between trait systems. Coupling Piaget's and Bandura's terminology, operative intelligence has the efficacious capacity of a normative agent to create a cycle of activity that manifests figurative objects as operative objects. In other words, operative intelligence occurs in a personality as the capacity of a network of processes to efficaciously migrate appropriate information content between two analytically distinct traits, in relation to the beliefs that the agent has in this regard. This now leads us to the realization that it is efficacy that factors pathology, a notion we shall return to in due course.

So, limiting operative intelligence can effect a personality in its efficacious migration of any self-relational ethics trait information used as an imperative for the technical interest power trait, and vice versa. The personality cognitive system (which is really a personality metasystem) is connected with this personality operative intelligence by figurative integrative intelligence. This can be thought of as a network of meta-processes or cognitive principles that efficaciously enables and contextualizes operative intelligence. It also connects *identity* with *self-processes*, a notion indirectly supported by Markus and Nurius (1986), who proposed a theory of 'possible selves', which explains how the agent develops a connection between present self, motivation, behaviour, and possible or future self. In addition, it connects with Identity Process Theory (Breakwell, 1986 and 1988; Sullivan, 2000; Twigger-Ross et al., 2003), where the conceptualization of identity is seen to involve four distinct principles of identity (self-esteem, self-efficacy, distinctiveness, and continuity) that together enable the maintenance of a positive self-view.

We have also referred to figurative intelligence. This can be defined as providing precise information about states of reality, and involves any means of representation used to keep in mind the states that intervene between transformations, that is, it involves perception, drawing, mental imagery, language, and imitation. Hence, figurative intelligence will be a reflection of patterns of knowledge, and will exist through figurative imagery and patterns of information. In terms of the paradigm there is a figurative base that is composed of models, which entail structured relationships and both epistemic and informational properties. The capacity of the figurative base to adequately reflect the cognitive base of the paradigm and maintain pragmatic interpretations constitutes its figurative intelligence (Piaget, 1950; Piaget and Inhelder, 1969; Montangero and Maurice-Naville, 1997). The nature of figurative intelligence can be extended beyond Piaget's original notion to include the meta-dynamics arising from a meta-coupling that occurs between the personality metasystem and the personality operative intelligence. It is then responsible for the influence that is created by the network of cognitive principles that define 'I', and result in the agent's own rules of personality production that create impulses for the technical interest power trait. Feedback from the operative intelligence coupled to the technical interest power trait results in its adjustment. In future when referring to figurative intelligence, we shall mean this extended form.

As we show in Figure 3.2, the coupling connections between personality and the social system are referred to as operative social intelligence, and it is the network of operative processes that enables a personality to manifest its decisions from its technical interest power trait to be manifested socially. Indeed, as far as other personalities in the social environment are concerned, the only trait that is visible is that of technical interest power. The coupling between the cultural environment and operative social intelligence (the latter occurring as a migratory dialogue between the personality and the social) occurs through cultural figurative intelligence.

The notion of cultural intelligence connects the knowledge disposition trait with operative intelligence, and in its original meaning is defined as the ability for an agent to successfully adapt to a change in cultural settings attributable to cultural context (Earley and Ang, 2003: 3; Thamas and Inkson, 2009). This definition requires a plurality of cultural beliefs, attitudes, and values, which are in interaction and create a plural figurative base that has some level of cultural conflict within it. However, in the case where there is no such conflict, then cultural intelligence simply reduces to 'the manifestation of the figurative base as patterns of cultural knowledge'. Properly speaking, this is actually figurative cultural intelligence – the capacity to represent the cultural belief system (of values, attitudes, and beliefs) as a coalescence of normative ideological and ethical standards of the culture that ultimately defines what it is that constitutes legitimate modes and means of social behaviour.

Operative intelligence may be seen as the efficacious migration of information between analytically distinct traits of personality; the process channels that the migrations passed through also have an efficacy status. To understand this, consider that, for instance, operative intelligence can be seen in terms the efficacious migration of information between the ontologically distinct traits of the personality of an organization. If efficacy is seen in terms of effectiveness, migratory effectiveness relates to how well information is migrated from the figurative to the operative, and this is likely to be connected with knowledge and understanding. As an illustration of this, for instance, how well does a normative personality manifest its self-relational ethics trait information as technical interest power trait information, or how well is its technical interest power trait information manifested as a set of social events? In contrast, efficiency relates to the capacity of the channels (the network of trait related personality processes or meta-processes) through which the migrations occur (i.e. the efficiency of the interactive network of processes that manifest information between the self-relational ethics and technical interest power traits or the latter as social action). In the latter case, what are the resources that are required to manifest the information as social action, and how can one determine if those resources are available? These resources may be at some level of awareness inherently or intentionally limited. Hence, in any personality, the migratory capacities of each process channel may be more or less efficient, and where inefficiencies occur they result in trait variable assignments. From the variables settling on states we can derive information about preferred personality types.

A normative agency is often interested in a given level of performance that is context specific. Performance is ultimately determined by the efficacy of the migrations of information between trait systems for given personality types. So any normative personality interested in changing preferences will also consistently want (at some preconscious level of awareness) to modify the efficacy by which cognitive information is migrated from one cognitive state to another (e.g. self-relational ethics to technical interest power or vice versa). This clearly has an impact on the degree of interconnection between the traits.

The nature of the model in Figure 3.2 supports the proposition that a normative personality is constituted through its traits, from which stable preference option types arise. We reiterate that while the traits are important, it turns out that the states that they take (which determine personality type) are fundamental to understanding the orientation of the personality (Yolles and Fink, 2009). Ultimately, the personality types that an agent maintains are a reflection of its attitudes, emotive imperatives, and formative perspectivistic information, and it is these that determine what has epistemic value to the personality.

The notion of perspectivistic information is connected with perspective that arises from the ability of an agency to see and respond to an object of attention. For Piaget (1977: 87) the ability to conceive an object derives from the coordination of the schemes that underlie its activities with objects, and its objectivity derives from the coordination of perspectives. The coordination of perspectives originates cognitively through understanding generated from experience. Experience is filtered through and assimilated by available cognitive structures that both change and are changed by potential phenomenological inputs. The knower and the known are inextricably bound up with one another such that the object and the subject are inseparable. The acquisition of knowledge arises from the interaction between the object and the subject. It in particular involves both the operative functions relating to that which can be generalized, as opposed to figurative functions that concern the specific nature of an external event. Piaget further asserts that all cognitions are inherently social. As such there is no distinction between social and non-social situations. The general coordination of actions provides the basis for cognitive structures that are individual as well as interpersonal and social. The capacity of an agency to change the relationship between object and subject through the coordination of perspectives (therefore creating a new frame of reference) results in an ability to shift or assume new roles.

A personality maintains self-reflective, self-regulative, and self-organizational processes. It also has an appreciative system that facilitates the formation of goals, and contributes to behavioural orientations. It has internal cognitive structures that exist as a consequence of conditions that are represented through its traits. Personality assessment can capture (social) psychological tendencies as well as agent determinants of action, and can look towards the exploration of personality coherence and the cognitive structures that it uses to interpret events.

The notion of efficacy applies to the network of processes that constitute the intelligences of the normative personality that determines either preferences or pathologies/dysfunction. In our model, while the traits are concerned with control and the epistemic attributes of a personality (within the metasystem and figurative and operative systems), efficacy is a conditional connector of the ontologically distinct traits systems. *Espoused values* are manifested as preferences from which requisite efficacy arises in the agency. An agency intuits/appreciates what is requisite from an understanding of its environment in relation to the imperatives from its values and attitudes and other emotive imperatives.

It is clear that personality orientations are connected to both intelligences and efficacy, and it is now possible to collect our discussions as a set of proposition appropriate to the normative personality. We have already indicated that personality orientation arises through personality preferences. Also preferences occur in the agency cultural/knowledge metasystem through espoused values, but these are manifested in: (a) the cognitive metasystem of the personality as significant attitudes, preferences, and connected feelings, (b) the figurative system as appreciative schemas, and (c) the operative systems as structural/behavioural imperatives. These manifested preferences determine the set of trait orientations of the personality that together create a personality orientation. Preferences are thus responsible for the nature of a personality, being influenced by both its intelligences and efficacy, and indeed pathologies and dysfunctions. Let us now summarize our postulated propositions.

Intelligence is constituted as a network of first and second order processes that couple two ontologically distinct trait systems. This network of processes manifests information through semantic channels, thereby allowing local meaning to arise from the manifested content in the receiving trait system. **Operative intelligence** is a first order form of autopoiesis that creates an *operative couple* between the figurative and operative systems. It consists of a network of personality processes that manifests significant figurative information operatively, but also it creates improvement imperatives to adjust the figurative system. This network of processes is itself defined by its appreciative schemas and decision imperatives in the figurative system and the improvement adjustment imperatives that arise from the operative system. *Figurative intelligence* is a second order form of autopoiesis (called autogenesis) that projects conceptual information into the operative couple. However, this couple also creates improvement imperatives to adjust the cognitive system, from which figurative intelligence emanates in the first place. This cognitive system is composed of attitudes, feelings, and conceptual information that are harnessed to identify the network of meta-processes that define it, permitting significant conceptual information to be manifested in the operative couple. Intelligences are structured through personality perspectives and preferences.

Personality perspectives arise in the personality meta-system from attitudes, feelings, and conceptual information, and are influenced by the adjustment imperatives carried by figurative intelligence from the operative couple. The perspectives are manifested across the personality through perspectivistic information carried by its intelligences, to be integrated into schemas in the figurative system and structured into the operative system.

Personality preferences define a personality's intended trait orientations, and as a variable this is determined by the type-value that the trait takes. The trait selection of type-value may itself be conditioned in some way by the information carried by the intelligences. The selection of information to be manifested by the intelligences may become uncoupled from the preferences and unrepresentative of the intended perspectives. This causes an *intelligence limitation* that can result in the development of *pathologies* (Figure 3.2) that affect the ability of trait systems to function. This lack of representation occurs because not all of the perspectivistic information is represented. Under such a condition the personality may: (1) have its capacity to conceptualize, schematize, or apply perspectivistic information reduced; (2) have the orientation of its traits perturbed; and (3) be drawn towards un-preferred or unintended conduct that may even 'corrupt' its proprietary strategic ideological or ethical orientations. Perspectives too may become adjusted through pathologic shifts in trait orientations.

Efficacy can refer to the controls of emotional processes that condition what the intelligences do by operating on the manifestations of information that occur between two trait systems, modifying the semantic channelling processes of the intelligences. It does this through the control of emotive impulses. Efficacy status occurs on a strong/weak scale that indicates the degree of efficacy/inefficacy that an agency has. High efficacy status allows impediments to achievement to be seen as surmountable by the improvement of self-regulatory skills and perseverant effort. They can also overcome vulnerability to stress and depression and impact on the choices people make at important decisional points. While rigidly high efficacy status can affect the capacity of an agency to create individual motivations that benefit its performance, low efficacy status can influence an agency's ability to communicate, to develop appreciations, and to set goals and cite tasks. It happens because of the way efficacy conditions the manifestation process and hence drives both local development and the adjustment imperatives for improvement. As such it can affect an agency's feeling, thinking, motivation, behaviour, and performance – including how it perseveres under adversity. Practically, it is the *capability efficacy* that moderates the agency towards operative performance progression and hence achievement, and the adjustment imperatives that indicate the capability of this progression. The notion of capability efficacy assumes that every organization maintains some level of emotive impulse control, which might either dampen or enhance on the emotive impulses. Requisite efficacy occurs when the ability develops to achieve a level of performance through the control of emotive imperatives that are best suited to create preferred achievements. When these preferences are perturbed, then a difference arises between requisite and capability efficacy, resulting in an efficacy distinction (ED) that contributes to the formation of pathologies, indicating the limited capacity of the agency to generate requisite responses to its perceived needs for achievement under perceived environmental circumstances. The EDs of the intelligences shown in Figure 3.2 may result in pathologies. Given combinations of these across the personality may well generate distinct personality dysfunctions. If one considers that dysfunctions arise from standards of diagnosis, then one has to try to find out what pathologies result in which dysfunctions.

Pathologies $P_{i,j}$ (Figure 3.1) that effect both intelligences and efficacy can fall into patterns that create agency dysfunctions. In an ongoing study by Dauber (2010), there is some initial evidence that set patterns of combinations of the pathologies can be associated with identifiable preferences and dysfunctions, thus leading to the possibility of predicting dysfunction. This suggests a need to track the relationships between pathology combinations and dysfunctional agency classifications.

Now, the networks of processes that constitute the intelligences between trait systems are involved in information manifestations. So what manifestations are we referring to? Operative intelligence is concerned with the manifestation of trait information across domains using a network of internal processes, and is an extension of the figurative system. Following arguments from Beer (1975, 1994, 1985, 1989), our generic systems operate through generic functions that may be constituted through formal and/or informal roles which may or may not coincide with departmental structure. So pragmatically, if function A in a collective agent has *appreciative* information directly relating to an intended strategic plan while taking into account the demands of its environmental context, then setting up an operative capacity to allow people in another function B to implement the plan *viably* is a function of the requisite adequacy of the network of processes that manifests that information across the departments: that is, its operative intelligence. If an efficacy deficiency occurs, then a pathology results. In severe circumstances a pathological break can occur and operative intelligence breaks down. So, the efficacy of this normative personality is such that requisite/espoused value preferences demanded by its context cannot be applied as criteria for the manifestation of information between the traits of the collective agent. When this happens in the normative personality, the agent may as a result have a variety of service and/or production distinctions that are unexpected.

4 The Intelligent Agency

4.1 Introduction

Intelligence broadly speaking relates to viability and performance, despite different perspectives distributed across different fields of study and paradigms. Intelligence in individuals/collectives implies individual/collective minds and individual/collective consciousness (Haslam & Baron, 1994; Yolles, 2009b). In social theory there is a consistent endeavour to relate organization and individual theory together, synergizing and harmonizing apparently distinct terms of reference (Bridges, 1992; Boje, 2004). Perhaps more well-known is the work of Kets de Vries (1991) who adopts a Freudian (1962) view of dysfunctional and neurotic organizations. Agencies can develop feelings of guilt, adopt collective psychological defences that reduce pain through denial and cover-up, and operate through processes of power that might be unproductive. Yolles (2008) refers to the collective psyche of a social agency, which behave consistently and have an explainable rationality. The social agency may behave independently from the individuals that compose it because of the cultural normative anchors that constrain social behaviour, which may not be the same as individual idiosyncratic anchors, as illustrated by the literature on *Strategic Groups* (Fiegenbaum & Thomas, 1995) and *Herding* (Welch, 2000; Hirshleifer & Teoh 2003).

If the notion of intelligence is to have broad validity it should be generic and thus needs to be defined in a way that can have relevance across different fields of interest. To do this effectively a meta-framework is required. As indicated in the preface to this book, a meta-framework is capable of reflecting a 'theory of meaning' (Oakley, 2004) through its meta-theory, enabling it to respond to both theory-doctrine and problem-based issues. The interest in cybernetics is that, unlike most other fields from which a *meta-framework* can arise, it is interdisciplinary and concerned with the control and communication features of coherently controlled (systemic) structures and their regulation that are essential to all social contexts. It is in particular concerned with 'circular causality', illustrated by the action of a system in an environment that causes change. That change is manifested in the system through information feedback, which in turn can affect the way the system then behaves. In a meta-framework, theories may be seen as being either oriented towards theory doctrine, or more pragmatic problem-based issues (Jokisch, 2001; Oakley, 2004).

Meta-theory may be seen as having three dimensions: (1) it acts to connect different mid-range theories (Bacharach, 1989); (2) it improves parsimony by accounting for a broader array of phenomena with fewer constructs than was previously possible (Morgan & Hunt, 1994; Tybout, 1995); and (3) it generates new knowledge (Kaplan, 1964) by producing new empirically testable hypotheses. Realist meta-theory is unitary and concerned with principles from which particular theory can develop, as in the case of Bandura's (1986) Social Cognitive Theory. Relativist meta-theory is pluralistic, connecting different relatable theories (e.g. Jackson & Keys, 1984; Jackson, 1991; Adams & Hyon, 2005). Relativist meta-theory building needs principles that can distinguish between paradigmatic differences, similarities, and interrelationships to be comprehended (Gioia & Pitre, 1990). Approaches are required that allow their distinctions to be explored (Parker & McHugh, 1991; Scherer, 1998).

For Oakley (2004) a meta-framework demands a theory of attention, which involves the development of a cognitive semiotic that demands both self and context awareness, and reflection on theory development process. The doctrine of this framework requires cognitive and cultural processes that are subjugated by attention. There may be many alternative meta-theories on which to build a theory of meaning, where one may develop a more successful theory of attention on which to ground a theory of meaning, while simultaneously being attached to a defined context which is in some way problem-driven (Cheng, 2007). The creation of a meta-theory framework thus enables paradigmatic connections that operate on a semantic level, rather than one which is connected with more local paradigmatic propositions. Examples of such frameworks are Management Cybernetics (Beer, 1981), and Complexity Theory (Hemaspaandra & Ogihara, 2002).

If different approaches each embedded in its own paradigms are to be related, then there is also an issue of paradigm incommensurability (Burrell and Morgan, 1979; Feyerabend, 1975). This is explained by Kuhn (1970) when he tells us that different paradigms cannot be legitimately compared or coordinated. This is because paradigms are collectively supported schema with a pragmatic dimension created through cognitive models that involve beliefs, values, meanings, collective cultural and behavioural norms, attitudes, ideology, and define mission. They each develop within their own framework within which they create a conceptual base that maintains theoretical extensions that are logically and analytically distinct (Yolles, 1999). Paradigms may develop within a common context and in a frame of reference that allows them to be conceptually coextensive, but they may still be incommensurable if their concepts cannot be measured on the same scale of values – that is, if they are qualitatively dissimilar. A variety of proposals have arisen to overcome the problem of incommensurability, especially within the context of multi-methodologies (see Midgley, 1995). In principle, paradigm incommensurability is a concept that questions the capacity of an inquirer to relate distinct theories together that have developed autonomously, often within different frames of reference, and within which proprietary propositions result in incommensurable theory. In a particular manifestation of this here, we are interested in relating psychological models of intelligence with social psychological ones. This relates to the idea that notions of individual intelligence are distinct from that of collective intelligence, and potentially delegitimizes any intention of directly relating them. In other words, there is a distinction between empirical individual and normative collective frames of reference that needs to be resolved, and which we shall address in due course.

The recent history of inquiry into intelligence, whether individual or collective, perhaps begins with the psychologist Spearman (1904), who defined general intelligence in reference to mental aptitude tests. Using an empirical approach it was found statistically that people who performed well on one cognitive test tended to perform well on other tests, while those who scored badly on one test tended to score badly on others. He believed that intelligence is therefore a general cognitive ability that could be measured and numerically expressed. The educational psychologist Thurstone (1936) saw intelligence as a collection of different primary mental abilities that included verbal comprehension, reasoning, perceptual speed, numerical ability, word fluency, associative memory, and spatial visualization. The philosopher psychologist Dewey (1937) drew away from such empirically oriented evaluations of intelligence, seeing it as a social phenomenon, and adopting the term collective intelligence that involves interaction and intercommunications. This concept extends to the idea of collective 'emergent intelligence' (Landemore, 2012). The philosopher and sociologist Bourdieu (1971) continued in this vein (Nash, 2012), adopting the concept of habitus – a collection of dispositions that create a tendency to act. In a related vein, Gardner (1983) proposed a meta-theory of 'multiple intelligences' that resulted in context and culturally relative intelligence based on skills and abilities.

An alternative approach came from the child psychologist Piaget (1950), who adopted a process-oriented approach to intelligence that was concerned with the ability of individuals to learn. Intelligence was seen in terms of processing capacity in the individual and collective. Having said this, we note the view of Nash (2005), who explains that habitus has a socio-cultural connection embraced by Vygotsky's (1994) theory of learning. The Vygotsky School adopts the view that learning is also connected with consciousness. Chopra (1991 & 1999) appears to embrace this connecting consciousness with intelligence and self-awareness. Consciousness is seen as cybernetic, operating through information. While Choo (2002) adopts a more limited view of intelligence that arises from the use of information, Chopra explains that the use of information occurs through a self-referral loop, that consciousness influences its own expression in more abstract and unpredictable ways, and in this process consciousness becomes intelligence. So, intelligence is constituted as a very general mental capability that is cybernetic in nature. A pragmatic manifestation of this involves the ability to reason, plan, solve problems, think abstractly, comprehend complex ideas, learn quickly and learn from experience. This notion, arising from Gottfredson (1997), reflects a broader and deeper capability for comprehending one's environment, like 'catching on', 'making sense' of things, or 'figuring out' what can be done. Like the early inquirers, Gottfredson's interest here is the measurability of intelligence in human agencies empirically, rather than the development of a theory of intelligence that can explain through a set of principles and notions its nature and the mechanisms that underpin it. Such a theory would be especially useful for application to the context of organizations where intelligence can be seen in terms of a plural interactive process. Jennings & Wooldridge (1998) are interested in seeing computer systems operating as intelligent agencies, and adopts a cybernetic approach in this. Other approaches that have also developed relate, for instance, to the intelligent organization. This includes Schwaninger (2001), who adopts a management cybernetics perspective and Dealtry (2004), who is interested in strategic intelligence. There are also a variety of other approaches of intelligence, including the consideration of social and cultural intelligence. Some of these approaches will be seen to have relevance to cultural agency theory, like the core theories of Bourdieu, Piaget, and Gardner.

4.2   Theories of Intelligence

Bourdieu (1984) was interested in the nature of intelligence as it developed non-consciously in a social environment, first in child development, but more generally in social agencies. It determines personality, indicating a structure of the mind through its schemas, dispositions, and orientations (Scott & Marshall, 1998). For Bourdieu an agency has 'habitus' (Table 4.1), a set of four dispositions (*inculcation, structure, generative,* and *transposable*) which generate practices, perceptions, and attitudes, and are 'regular' without being consciously coordinated or governed by 'rule'. Inculcation occurs when its extrinsic environment conditions an agency. Such conditioning occurs through the impact of physical, social, and psychological structures that exist for the agency. Structural disposition may be thought of in terms of cultural form, and derives from the preconscious dispositional attributes of the agency that

Table 4.1 *The non-conscious dispositions of habitus (Bourdieu, 1984)*

Disposition	Nature
Inculcation structure	An agency is conditioned extrinsically by its environment. An agency pursues practices, has perceptions, and adopts attitudes that are mental dispositions (not directly amenable to conscious reflection and modification) that are reflected in the social circumstances within which they are acquired.
Generative transposable	A plurality of practices, perceptions, and attitudes are generated. Practices, perceptions and attitudes can be applied from one psychological field for which they were originally acquired to other fields of attention or application.

connects to the culture, responsible for symbols and norms that are applied within logical organizing processes, and the formation of ideology and ethics. Consistent with the ideas of psychology, collective mental dispositions can be seen as a way of expressing wishes of the belief system that may otherwise be seen as incompatible with the collective self. Thus, norms and symbols can be argued to fall into this category since they provide people who belong to a given culture with self-approval for their values and attitudes.

Generative dispositions are indicative of the ability for an intelligent agency to develop a plurality of practices, perceptions, and attitudes. Finally, transposable dispositions enable an agency to apply given practices, perceptions, and attitudes to a variety of fields of attention. These dimensions are generic, and should be adopted into the non-conscious existential domain when we come to developing a more general model. Unlike inculcation, structure Transposition may be thought of as a logical process.

Gardner (1983, 1993) was another author interested in, among other things, the capabilities of children, though some of his work derives from examining normal people whose brains have been injured. This comes after some background work of Guilford (1967; 1977; 1982), who proposed that intelligence is constituted through three dimensions, *operations* that are applied to *contents* that result in *products*. Each of these dimensions has a set of manifestations:

- Operations (cognition, memory, divergent production, convergent production, evaluation)
- Contents (including the symbolic, semantic, behavioural)
- Products (units, classes, relations, systems, transformations, and implications).

Gardner (1993) proposed an alternative, and perhaps more cybernetic, model relating to control, reflection, and existence. In this he defined three classes of intelligence as shown in Table 4.2 and 4.3: object related, object free, and personal. Each type of intelligence can be manifested in its own way, and like

Table 4.2 *Gardner's (1983, 1993) classes of competence intelligence*

Class of Intelligence	Nature of Class
Object related	Controls exerted by the structure and functions of particular objects that relate to an agency
Object free	Occurs through the reflections of object world structures.
Personal intelligence	Relates to the existence of one's own person or the existence of other persons, and involves cultural presentations and interpretations of self. It does this through a process of symbolization, which cultures mobilize for basic information processing capabilities.

Guilford (1982) he identifies a number of these manifestations (e.g. linguistic, logical, spatial, kinesthetics). Object-related intelligence is connected with controls exerted by the structure and functions of particular objects that relate to an agency (in Gardner's case a child). Object-free intelligence occurs through the reflections of structures in the object world. Personal intelligence relates to the existence of one's own person or of other persons, and involves cultural presentations and interpretations of self. It does this through a process of symbolization, which cultures mobilize for basic information processing capabilities.

Gardner's theory can be related to currently developing theory for the social. First, all coherent social communities (those that have developed cultural structures that mediate interactions) can be argued to have three analytically and empirically independent dimensions: culture, structure, and behaviour (Yolles, 1999). Culture is responsible for the development of an organization's paradigm. It exists through a language and a normative belief system that includes beliefs and the nature of normative behaviour or conduct. The belief system of attitudes, values, and beliefs determines structure that, through its process of facilitation and constraint, defines a potential for permissible behaviour. That is, within a given culture certain types of operational behaviour intended to support the purposes or interests of an organization are permitted or expected, and others not.

While facilitation and constraint can occur through the common understanding resulting in agreed decisions of those involved during conscious meaningful communication, they are often manifested through steering media commodities like money and power (Habermas, 1987) that can compromise agreement. For instance, a power-centred role position held by a leader or manager may constrain behaviour by reprimanding or punishing individuals for certain types of behaviour, or facilitate and constrain behaviour by providing budgets to enable certain types of behaviour and not others. The three dimensions of culture, structure, and behaviour can be directly linked to Gardner's three types of intelligence (Table 4.3).

Table 4.3 *Organizational competence intelligence, catalysed from Gardner's classifications*

Gardner's Classification	Relation to Competence
Object related	Connected to the facilitation and constraints that are exerted by the structures (and their functional manifestations) of organizations and the objects that they adopt and operate through. Such objects have a physical manifestation even though they may be virtual in their nature, and thus derive from a cognitive or social construction that has behavioural consequences. They may, for instance, be myths, technologies, or other organizations in an operational environment.
Object free	Occurs through reflections of the structures and objects that are associated with an organization. Behaviour is facilitated and constrained by these reflections. If behaviour conforms to the facilitation and constraints, it is 'legitimate' for the culture in which it develops.
Personal intelligence	Defines a worldview that generates knowledge and manufactures symbols that can be used in social interactions. Another implication of this is that intelligence can be seen as the ability for an organization to be consciously aware of its culture, structure, and behaviour, its individual structures and processes, and the relationships between them.

Now, the need to understand the nature of intelligence, as depicted in the work of Chopra (1991), is linked with the idea of consciousness. This is clear from discussions on the cognitive nature of intelligence, which draw on the exploration of consciousness and self-knowledge in relation to computational process, and how information can be used in relation to behaviour (Sloman, 1985; McCarthy, 1995; Sloman & Chrisley, 2003). The tendency today appears to be to embrace cybernetic approaches to such studies (Ovum, 1994; Tecuci, 1998; Buchanan, 2005; Shoham et al., 2006; Triantis & Pintelas, 2006), connecting not only with self-processes, but also with goal-oriented thinking (Bonnet, 1984; Beaudoin, 1994; Jennings & Wooldridge, 1998). In such approaches rationality takes on an important role (Bonnet, 1985), defined within the context of such attributes as inference, morphogenic transposability (the ability to transfer intelligence to distinct contexts), reference identification, and self-awareness are brought into consideration.

Piaget (1963), in his attempt to explore the development of children, saw intelligence as the ability of an agency to adapt to its immediate environment. The agency is able to develop its intellect through mental schemas that are changed with a learning process, and this occurs through the attributes of assimilation and accommodation – both of which are forms of adaptation. Assimilation occurs as new information and experiences are fitted into existing schemas, while accommodation occurs as schemas are changed when new information cannot be assimilated. Piaget also developed the notions of operative and figurative intelligence.

Piaget (1950) saw that reality is a dynamic system of continuous change defined in reference to dynamic change through states and transformation (Demetriou, Doise & Van Lieshout, 1998). The states refer to the condition in which a thing or person can be found between the transformations which refer to any kind of change. The states are seen by Piaget as passive figurative representations that create what we may see as a figurative base of information and experiences, occurring through a set of figurative sedimentations developing from an agency's knowledge.

Piaget coined the term *operative intelligence* to refer to the dynamic process that frames how the world is understood by a sentient being. In particular it has relevance for the *informed cognitive manipulation and transformation of objects by a reflecting subject*, and exemplifies logical processes and freedom from domination by immediate experience (Jenks, 2005). The logical rules that are used are *constraining* in nature, and this very constraint allows one to understand how rational behaviour can progressively emerge from more primitive 'pre-rational' mechanisms (Paillard, 2000). Operative intelligence is directly connected with the representation and manipulation of the transformational aspects of reality, and it involves all actions that are undertaken so as to anticipate, follow, or recover transformations to the experienced world. It also refers to highly integrated and generalized sets of actions that are adaptive in nature (Schoenfeld, 1986). It can thus be thought of as the effective capacity of an agency to create a cycle of activity that manifests figurative objects (which exist in its figurative schematic base) as experiential objects. An illustration of operative intelligence occurs when an agency (like an organization) manifests elements of its schemas behaviourally. An example of an element of the schemas for one context may be political ideology, while for another, personality. In other terms, operative intelligence can also be seen as an indicative capacity for an agency to *reflect* the (figurative) decision models it maintains in its experienced world (thereby satisfying its intended potential for directed behaviour). Operative intelligence may fail when an organization is unable to 'adequately' manifest figurative objects experientially. We cannot be prescriptive about the nature of 'adequacy', which could relate to some degree of *acceptable* capacity for an organization to evidence its schemas through its normative modes of practice.

Piaget (1950) also proposed the term *figurative intelligence*. This provides a copy of states of reality or precise information about them, and involves any means of representation used to keep in mind the states that intervene between transformations, that is, it involves perception, drawing, mental imagery, language and imitation. Hence, figurative intelligence is a reflection of patterns of knowledge, and will exist through visual imagery and information. For us this can be seen as being housed in schemas of ideas and models, which entail structured relationships, information, and the sedimentation of epistemic properties. It is the capacity of an agency to adequately reflect its cognitive base of knowledge in its schemas and to maintain pragmatic interpretations that constitutes its *figurative intelligence* (Piaget, 1950; Piaget & Inhelder, 1969; Montangero & Maurice-Naville, 1997).

Piaget (1950) also attempted to measure intelligence in children using cognitive testing approaches to assess their concrete and formal operative strategies. In the context of children, the distinction between figurative and operative intelligence is simply shown in a map of cognitive development by Demetriou, Doise & Van Lieshout (1998: 186). The Piaget tests were designed to look for particular types of understanding and/or reasoning (Bybee & Sund, 1982). Outside the child learning context the concepts of figurative and operative intelligence have rarely been used. Within the context of organization theory, an equivalent to Piaget's examination of intelligence is the use of ethnographic methods. Interestingly, operative and figurative intelligence may be connected with an empirical approach (based on a fluid mechanics metaphor from physics) that distinguished between fluid and crystalline intelligence (Hooper, Fitzgerald & Papalia, 1971; Schonfeld, 1986). Here, operative intelligence involves the fluid ability of logical thinking and the formulation and elaboration of relations, while figurative intelligence involves the crystallized ability of everyday learning that reflect recordable experience. Measures for both fluid and crystalline intelligences have been proposed by Cattell & Butcher (1968), Cattell (1971) and Cattell, Barton & Dielman (1972) that may contribute to a more comprehensive approach in measuring organizational intelligence.

Let us return to the notion that there are both dynamic and passive attributes of intelligence. This effectively relates to the distinction between what can and cannot be immediately altered (Schutz, 1967: 208). Gustein (2007) notes that dynamic intelligence can be defined in terms of continuous processing and regularizing, flexible problem-solving, dynamic analysis, episodic memory, experience sharing, self-evaluation and self-regulation, simultaneity, flexible and contextual content use. They provide opportunities for growth, discovery, integration, and collaboration, and are regulatory in nature, involving continual evaluation as well as processes of adaptation. Static intelligence involves discrete processing, performing, absolute problem solving, static analysis, rote-procedural memory, instrumental communication, behavioural compliance, sequentiality, and content accumulation. This provides opportunities for requisite problem situation interventions with the dynamic provision of cues.

However, it is possible to revisit the difference between dynamic and static given here. To do this we can, for instance, refer to Nowak et al. (2000), who discuss the distinction between extrinsic and intrinsic dynamics that relate to agency self-organization. In distinguishing between the extrinsic and intrinsic, they differentiate between the dynamics of self-organization that experience external information, and those that do not. In the first instance, we can refer to extrinsic dynamics processes, while in the latter, where information is internally generated, we can refer to intrinsic dynamic processes that derive from passive figurative and cultural/epistemic states. So, we can distinguish between extrinsic dynamic processes that are receptive of, and responsive to, external interactions between an agency and its environment, and intrinsic ones that are purely internal, and may be connected with the notion of immanent change (as adopted, for instance, by Sorokin, 1937). Part of this intrinsic process involves the sedimentation of cultural and epistemic base elements into schemas, doing so through a network of implicit principles that are subject to change. For our purposes it is therefore useful to think of figurative intelligences as intrinsically dynamic as well as extrinsically static.

4.3 Organizational Intelligences

Choo (2002) explores the intelligent organization through its ability to manage information. He uses a definition of intelligence by Haeckel and Nolan (1993: 126) as the ability to deal with complexity by capturing, sharing, and extracting meaning from marketplace signals. The complexity is determined by the number of information sources it needs, how many business elements it must coordinate, and the number and type of relationships that connect these elements. A consequence is that an 'intelligence quotient' can be determined using three critical attributes:

- *Connecting* – the ability to access knowledge and information. This is facilitated through the linking of information sources, media, locations, and users such that accurate information can be captured and made available to the right users at the right time and place.
- *Sharing* – the ability to integrate and share information. This is facilitated by an ability to share and interpret data, in addition to understanding the core processes of the organization.
- *Structuring* – the ability to extract meaning from data. This is facilitated by matching and relating information from multiple sources so that some form of pattern or trend emerges. It can be achieved by recognizing how data are organized, related, and used, or through classification categories; indexes, tables of contents, and data models are some examples of filtering and structuring data.

Choo (citing Gregory, 1981) also notes that there are two distinct meanings to the concept of intelligence: possessing of knowledge and the creation of knowledge. Knowledge possession can solve problems and give understanding. Knowledge

Table 4.4 *Nature of cybernetic intelligence in organizations (based on Schwaninger, 2001)*

Characteristic	Intrinsic/ Extrinsic Attributes	Nature of Characteristic
Adaptability	Both	The impetus for change comes from extrinsic stimuli that the organization responds to, and so adaptable organizations must be responsive to change.
Extrinsic effectiveness	Extrinsic	The organization can effectively influence and shape its environment, and this implies the ability of market organizations to perform well in competitive environments
Virtuous	Intrinsic	The organization is virtuous in that it can reconfigure itself in relation to its environment.
Sustainable	Both	The organization can make positive net contributions to viability and development of the larger suprasystem (whole) in which it is embedded. It is thus able to sustain itself.

creation occurs with the resolution of issues, which implies performance in pursuit of goals. Thus, intelligence may be conceived as having two qualities: a quality of adaptive behaviour, this representing effective ways of meeting the demands of changing environments (Anastasi, 1986), and a quality of implementing own goals. Intelligent behaviour is therefore both goal- and action-directed and also adaptive (Sternberg, 1982; Sternberg and Detterman, 1986).

In common with Choo, Schwaninger (2001) sees intelligent organizations as those able to perceive their environments and respond appropriately to their imperatives. They also need to be proactive and socially interactive in ways that are consistent with interests and purposes. Schwaninger goes beyond Chopra's (1991) cybernetic vision, and suggests that the intelligent organization is adaptable, effective, virtuous, and sustainable (Table 4.4). Some of these attributes can be expressed in terms of intrinsic processes – that is, those that occur internally to the organization. Others are extrinsic since they are outwardly directed. Expressing the Schwaninger attributes in terms of intrinsic and extrinsic elements enables a linkage to be made to the ideas of Bourdieu about non-conscious processes. For instance, his idea of inculcation occurs through an extrinsic interaction between an agency and its environment. The environment can be seen in terms of physical or psychological structures that can facilitate and constrain extrinsic behaviour, and it is these that inculcate the agency.

While there are many possible approaches to defining organizational intelligence, a strategic pragmatic approach has been developed by Dealtry (2004) and considered by Yolles (2004). One of Dealtry's interests lies in knowledge intensification (in which identifiable knowledge is acquired and applied) within the context of corporate universities and the notion of Intellectual Equity (the effectiveness with which an organization utilizes the potential of its human capital). Often, it is implied, the potential and capabilities of an organization operate within the confines of organizational paradigms and routines of mechanistic strategy and planning thinking. To break out of this a model is proposed connecting purpose, properties, and practices. This is used to explain how an agency might become intelligent by re-defining itself and its people-development activities in much clearer terms that can be communicated for the mutual benefit of all the internal and external stakeholders. The model derives from the idea that each situation promotes a unique conceptual perspective of the firm's intellectual promise and what it has to do to develop its people and thereby fully materialize top management's vision. The model has three related conceptualizations that connect to this idea of the intelligent organization. They are intellectual:

> P1: purpose that is connected with organizational vision
> P2: properties that enable visions to be known and specified
> P3: practices that have phenomenal manifestations in development programmes that are timely and relevant

For Dealtry, these three Ps (P1–P3) engage all the potential and capabilities of an organization as a fully functioning business brain, and in so doing break out of the confines of organizational paradigms and mechanistic strategy and planning thinking routines. Each situation promotes a unique conceptual perspective of the firm's intellectual promise and what it has to do to develop its people and thereby fully materialize top management's vision.

The PPP model is sequential and cyclic. It is sequential in that each of the P1–P3 phases is activated sequentially, and after all have been activated the cycle restarts. Hence phase P2 will only be activated after phase P1, and this is a pre-requisite for the activation of phase P3. The P1, P2, and P3 occur sequentially as the system evolves. Hence this is a simple rational sequential model that is comforting for managers, but there is never any guarantee that strategic intelligence will be so well behaved. Suppose that P1, P2, and P3 do not operate together as a sequential and cyclic of development. Rather, they have a fundamental cybernetic interconnection and they may 'fire' out of sequence, or they may fire simultaneously, resulting in impact delays. Poor sequencing or impact delays may be due to the occurrence of pathologies, or due to external factors that the organization has not anticipated.

Albrecht (2003) is interested in what he calls general intelligence, adopting a model that lists seven key dimensions of an organization. These are taken to be independent variables on which organizational intelligence depends:

(1) strategic vision,
(2) shared fate,
(3) appetite for change,
(4) heart (giving more than contracted),
(5) alignment and congruence (relating to team-working),
(6) knowledge deployment, and
(7) performance pressure (which everyone owns with operational imperatives for shared success).

Independently from this, Gonyea & Kuh (2009) use three core dimensions of organizational intelligence:

(1) technical and analytical intelligence;
(2) intelligence of understanding procedural problems;
(3) context intelligence.

These have also been related to the notions of Erçetin et al. (2000) by Potas, Erçetin & Koçak (2010), from which the following set of independent variables arises:

(1) promptness in action and reaction;
(2) adaptation to changing situations;
(3) flexibility and convenience of operations;
(4) ability to detect prudence and being prudent;
(5) ability to use imagination;
(6) effective communication with stakeholders.

To some extent, these approaches can be connected with Schwaninger's notion of intelligence described above, for which the intelligent organization has:

(1) adaptability;
(2) effectiveness in shaping its environment;
(3) virtuosity (the ability to create a self-reconfiguration in relation to its environment);
(4) sustainability (the ability to make positive net contributions to viability and development of the larger suprasystem in which the agency is embedded).

Kihlstrom & Cantor (2000) provide a useful review of the notion of social intelligence and its relation with other theoretical constructs. Thorndike (1920) sees social intelligence as the ability of an agency to perceive its own and others' internal states, motives, and behaviours, and to act towards them in an appropriate way.

Cantor and Kihlstrom (1987) define social intelligence in terms of an agency's fund of knowledge about the social world, geared to solving the problems of social life and managing the life tasks, concerns, or personal projects which an agency either selects or is assigned. Weinstein (1969) sees it as the ability to manipulate the responses of others. Kihlstrom & Cantor (2000) further argue that *social intelligence* cannot be evaluated abstractly, but rather with respect to *context* and in relation to the *purposes* it serves from the agency's perspective.

This sets up criteria for the assessment of social intelligence through the use of empirical psychometric tests. For instance, Kosmitzki and John (1993) identified eighteen features of social intelligence, including six *core* attributes:

(1) understanding people's thoughts, feelings, and intentions well;
(2) being good at dealing with people;
(3) having extensive knowledge of rules and norms in human relations;
(4) being good at taking the perspective of other people;
(5) adapting well in social situations; being warm and caring; and
(6) being open to new experiences, ideas, and values.

Social perceptiveness is the capacity to be aware of the needs, goals, and feelings of others and the greater social environment, and this includes 'multiple others' in the organization. High levels of social perceptiveness are useful for:

(1) accurately evaluating a social situation and
(2) determining the needs of the social context,
(3) being aware of their social environment and of the intentions and sensitivities of others.

Gilbert & Kottke (2009) adopt a model of social ability which has to include the core sub-dimensions of the concept of social intelligence

(1) social perceptiveness and
(2) social affordance seeking.

The concept of cultural intelligence (Earley & Ang, 2003) posits that understanding the impact of an individual's cultural background on their behaviour is essential for effective business. Earley and Ang suggest that it is possible to measure an individual's ability to engage successfully in any environment or social setting and identify four basic aspects of cultural intelligence (see http://culturalq.com/fouraspects.html). Measures of cultural intelligence are provided by 'The Cultural Intelligence Center' based in East Lansing, Michigan (http://culturalq.com/measure.html). These include the identification of intelligence as Cultural Quotients (CQ), and a number of dimensions of these have been proposed that include drive, knowledge, strategy, and action, these being defined below.

The Intelligent Agency

CQ-Drive is the interest of an agency in experiencing other cultures and the extent to which one thinks to be capable of interacting effectively with people who have different cultural backgrounds. It includes:

- Intrinsic Interest – deriving enjoyment from culturally diverse experiences
- Extrinsic Interest – gaining benefits from culturally diverse experiences
- Self-efficacy – having the confidence to be effective in culturally diverse situations.

CQ-Knowledge is an agency's knowledge about how cultures are similar and how cultures are different. It includes:

- Business – knowledge about economic and legal systems
- Interpersonal – knowledge about values, social interaction norms, and religious beliefs
- Socio-linguistics – knowledge about rules of languages and rules for expressing non-verbal behaviours.

CQ-Strategy is how an agency makes sense of culturally diverse experiences. It occurs when people make judgements about their own thought processes and those of others. It includes:

- Awareness – knowing about one's existing cultural knowledge
- Planning – strategizing before a culturally diverse encounter
- Checking – checking assumptions and adjusting mental maps when actual experiences differ from expectations.

CQ-Action is an agency's capability to adapt verbal and nonverbal behaviour to make it appropriate to diverse cultures. It involves having a flexible repertoire of behavioural responses that suit a variety of situations. It includes:

- Non-Verbal – modifying non-verbal behaviours (e.g. gestures, facial expressions)
- Verbal – modifying verbal behaviours (e.g. accent, tone).

Given that wide diversity of approaches towards organizational intelligence, we aim at an approach that is capable to integrate the concept of organizational intelligence with different classes of organization theory and organizational culture theory. The first step is modelling the collective agency.

4.4 Agency Process Intelligences and Efficacy

Intelligence in a cultural agency is a function of its nature, giving it an ability to appreciate and harness its own knowledge as information about its environment, to construct new knowledge converted from information about its experiences, and to pursue its figurative schemas (like goals, ideology, and ethics) effectively and efficiently, enhanced by emotions. Intelligence enables the consideration of the interests and influences of an external environment, an agency's own goals, and the goals of others, and facilitation of the development of ideas about the possible reactions of others in relation to the action taken by the agency. Agency intelligence is reflected in the operation of its *self-system*, which, according to Bandura (1999: 2), lies at the very heart of its causal processes. It includes regulating attentional processes, schematic processing of experiences, memory representation and reconstruction, cognitively-based motivation, emotion activation, psychobiologic functioning, and the efficacy with which cognitive and behavioural competencies are executed in the transactions of everyday life.

Intelligence may be seen as the driver for and a constraint of the achievements that an agency may be able to materialize: no intelligence offers no achievement; low/high levels of intelligence equate to ineffective/effective achievement. Various forms of intelligence posited in the literature include general, cultural, social and emotional, and process. Process intelligence means Piaget's figurative and operative intelligence, both of which are core elements to agency, occurring as networks of processes that manifest *semantic-good* (e.g. types of knowledge or information) transversely – between systems in generically distinct domains. Placing this within the relatively simple context of *goal* achievement, this can be related to the capacity for performance. In cultural agency theory efficacy indicates the capacity of an agency's process intelligences to perform due tasks. In the strategic agency, figurative intelligence tasks are the capacity to manifest context-related cultural knowledge strategically for the development of schemas. Operative intelligence tasks refer to a capacity to manifest schemas for operative development. This is broader than Bandura's (1977) *self-efficacy* related to performance maintenance (Lindsley, Brass & Thomas, 1995). Self-efficacy is the belief an agency has in its own performance capacity and degrees of satisfaction.

Until now, no clear links have been established between the theories and empirical findings about organizational intelligences, organizational culture theory, and organizational theory. Here we address some of this, which is important because without well-defined links between the disparate classes of theory, generic theory is not accessible.

In general, when referring to agency intelligence, we shall mean process intelligence. This does not disregard other perspectives about the nature of intelligence. Process intelligence occurs as a network of processes that couple ontologically distinct systems. These networks manifest semantic-good (types of knowledge or information) through semantic channels, thereby allowing local meaning to arise from the manifested content in the receiving system. Where our interest lies in the intelligent strategic agency, the sematic-good refers to types of information that are able to update schemas, and its scope moves from cognitive schemas through activating to operative schemas. Where it lies in the cultural agency, the semantic-good refers to types of information, and we talk of cultural values, personality schemas, and operative potentials for behaviour. In either case, process intelligences take on relative meaning. *Operative intelligence* is a network of first order processes called autopoiesis (or self-production) that creates an *operative couple* between the figurative and operative systems, where the operative system is phenomenal in nature and resides in the phenomenal domain, and the figurative system is noumenal in nature and resides in the noumenal domain. The operative couple consists of a network of personality processes, which operatively manifests significant figurative information. It also creates improvement imperatives to adjust the figurative system. Connected with the network of processes that constitute operative intelligence is the capability of operatively manifesting feelings (or reactions to feelings). This capability can be called *'operative emotional intelligence'*. Here it is worth mentioning that in the modelling context emotional intelligence can be considered to be related to both figurative and operative intelligence. However, the specific detailed relationships are beyond the scope of this book.

The network of processes is itself defined by its figurative schemas, the decision imperatives in the figurative system and the improvement adjustment imperatives that arise from the operative system. *Figurative intelligence* is a network of second order processes called autogenesis or self-generation that *projects conceptual information into the operative couple*. Connected with this network is the capability of manifesting emotions into the operative couple, a capacity that can be called *'figurative emotional intelligence'*. However, this couple also creates improvement imperatives to adjust the cognitive meta-system, from which figurative intelligence emanates in the first place. This is taken to be existential in nature, and resides in the existential domain. This meta-system is composed of attitudes, emotions, and conceptual information that are harnessed to identify the network of meta-processes that define it, permitting significant conceptual information to be manifested in the operative couple. Intelligences are structured through personality perspectives and preferences. *Personality perspectives* arise in the personality meta-system from attitudes, emotions, and conceptual information, and are influenced by the adjustment imperatives carried through figurative intelligence from the operative couple. The perspectives are manifested across the personality through perspectivistic information carried by its intelligences, to be integrated into schemas in the figurative system, and structured into the operative system.

Personalities may experience intelligence limitation, which occurs when process information conduits become uncoupled, resulting in no information manifestations between generic systems. Under such a condition the personality may: (1) have its capacity reduced to conceptualize, schematize, or apply perspectivistic information; (2) have the orientation of its traits perturbed; and (3) can be drawn towards un-preferred or unintended conduct that may even 'corrupt' its proprietary strategic, ideological, or ethical orientations. When any of these conditions occur it is because *pathologies* have developed.

Piaget's operative intelligence, which we have been using as a representation of autopoiesis, is constituted as a network of (first order) processes of the personality that is able to manifest information between its trait systems. Coupling Piaget's and Bandura's terminology, **operative intelligence** has the efficacious capacity of a normative agency to create a cycle of activity that manifests figurative projections as operative objects. In other words, operative intelligence occurs in a personality as the capacity of a network of processes to efficaciously migrate appropriate information content between two analytically distinct traits, in relation to the beliefs that the agency has in this regard. This now leads us to the realization that it is efficacy that factors pathology, a notion to which we shall return later.

The notion of figurative intelligence (as adapted from Piaget, 1950) is a representation of autogenesis, and is constituted as a network of second order or meta-processes (like cognitive principles) that efficaciously enable and contextualize operative intelligence. It connects *identity* with *self-processes*, a notion indirectly supported by Markus and Nurius (1986), who proposed a theory of 'possible selves' which explains how the agency develops a connection between present self, motivation, behaviour, and possible or future self. In addition, it connects with Identity Process Theory (Breakwell, 1986; Sullivan, 2000; Twigger-Ross et al., 2003) where the conceptualization of identity is seen to involve four distinct principles of identity (self-esteem, self-efficacy, distinctiveness, and continuity) that together enable the maintenance of a positive self-view.

Now within the cultural agency there exists a strategic organizing component that, under the condition that the organization is seen to have a collective mind, represents its normative personality. It operates through strategic schemas which constitute the personality's resources, enable a capacity to adequately reflect the cognitive base of the agency's paradigm and maintain pragmatic interpretations, and constitute its figurative intelligence (Piaget, 1950; Piaget and Inhelder 1969; Montangero and Maurice-Naville, 1997) as indicated in Figure 3.2. **Figurative intelligence** can now be defined as providing precise information about states of reality, and involves all means of representation used to keep in mind the states that intervene between transformations, that is, it involves perception, drawing, mental imagery, language, and imitation. Hence, from patterns of knowledge figurative imagery and patterns of information will be manifested through figurative intelligence. In terms of the organization's paradigm the schema is composed of models, which entail structured relationships and epistemic and informational properties.

As we show in Figure 3.2, the coupling connections between personality and the social system are controlled by *social intelligence*. It is the network of operative processes that enables a personality to manifest its decisions from its operative orientation trait to be manifested socially as observable phenomena. Indeed, as far as other personalities in the social environment are concerned, the only observable phenomena are created through the operative orientation trait, and in the case of Boje's trait conceptualization (Figure 3.2), this is the technical-interest/power. While the other Boje traits (Figurative orientation of self-relational Ethics and cognitive orientation of knowledge disposition) may influence the personality, they cannot be directly observed. The coupling between the cultural environment and social intelligence (the latter occurring as a migratory dialogue between the personality and the social) is controlled by cultural intelligence.

Cultural intelligence, according to Earley and Ang (2003: 3), is defined as the ability of an agency to successfully adapt to a change in cultural settings attributable to cultural context. In cybernetic terms, it can be taken as the manifestation of the cognitive base as patterns of cultural knowledge (Thamas and Inkson, 2009). This definition requires a plurality of cultural beliefs, attitudes and values, which are in interaction and create a plural schema that implicitly has some level of cultural conflict within it. However, where there is no such conflict, then cultural intelligence simply reduces to 'the manifestation of the schemas as patterns of cultural knowledge'. Properly speaking this is actually what we might call 'cultural figurative intelligence' –the capacity to represent the cultural belief system (of values, attitudes, and beliefs) as a coalescence of normative ideological and ethical standards of the culture that ultimately defines what constitutes legitimate modes and means of social behaviour.

A plural agency is normally interested in a desired level of performance that is context specific. Performance is ultimately determined by the *efficacy* of the migrations of information between trait systems for given personality types. So any normative personality interested in changing preferences will also consistently want (at some preconscious level of awareness) to modify the efficacy by which cognitive information is migrated from one cognitive state to another (e.g. self-relational ethics to technical-interest/power or vice versa).

The efficacy of personality processes is important. Bandura (1986) defines the *collective efficacy* of the agency as the shared belief that a collective can, as a whole, attain goals and accomplish its desired tasks. The efficacy of agencies relates to 'the soundness of their thoughts and actions, and the meaning of their pursuits, and they make corrective adjustments if necessary'

(Bandura 2006: 165). Efficacy involves a belief or perception that efficacious collective actions are possible in relation to a social need. Problems with the cultural cohesion of an agency may affect its performance through lack of confidence in individual agencies and/or perceptual differences in collective efficacy (Bandura, 1995). It can be related to the cohesiveness or coherence of a collective agency, and thus can be indicated by a measure of degree or a measure of entropy of the agency. The efficacy of an agency will influence its ability to communicate, to set goals, and to persevere during adversity. Efficacy is conditioned by emotive imperatives (deriving from emotions in the cognitive domain and feelings in the figurative domain) that can be controlled (Adeyemo, 2007) by emotional intelligence (Salovey & Mayer, 1990). Efficacy therefore influences an agency's *capabilities* to produce designated levels of performance that exercise influence over events that affect life. Bandura (2006) also refers to empirical research that shows that perceived collective efficacy accounts for distinctions in the quality of group functioning in diverse social systems. He also refers to **perceived collective efficacy**, by which he means the common beliefs that reside in the minds of group members about their collective capability. The membership believes that they are acting on their common beliefs that contribute to the transactional dynamics, which promote group attainments.

Strategic agency operative intelligence may be seen as the migration of information between analytically distinct traits of personality. *Migratory effectiveness* relates to how well information is migrated from the figurative to the operative, and this is likely to be connected with knowledge and understanding. As an illustration of this, for example, how well does a normative personality manifest its self-relational information about ethics (the ethics trait) in the technical-interest/power trait information, and how well is its technical-interest power trait information manifested as a set of social events? In contrast, *efficiency* relates to the *capacity* of the channels through which the migrations occur in relation to the *resources* that are required to manifest the information as social action. These resources may be at some level of awareness inherently or intentionally limited. Hence in any personality the migratory capacities of each process channel may be more or less efficient, and when inefficiencies occur they will result empirically in different scores of the trait variables. From these variable scores we can derive information about preferred or predominant personality type.

Empirically, efficacy can be strong, modest, or weak. Scores on a scale indicate the degree of perceived efficacy/inefficacy that an agency might have. Perceived efficacy has an impact on the choices people make. Normally, with high efficacy status impediments to achievement will be seen as surmountable through improvement of self-regulatory skills and perseverant effort. Low efficacy status can negatively influence an agency's ability to communicate internally, to develop appreciations, and to set goals and cite tasks. It happens because of the way efficacy conditions the manifestation process and hence drives both local development and the adjustment imperatives for improvement. Efficacy can affect an agency's feeling, thinking, motivation, behaviour, and performance – including how it perseveres under adversity. Practically, it is the *perceived efficacy* that moderates the agency towards operative performance progression and hence achievement, and the adjustment imperatives that indicate the capability of this progression. The notion of efficacy assumes that every organization maintains some level of emotive impulse control, which might either dampen or enhance the emotive impulses. Blocked or perturbed intelligence processes (Pi,j in Figure 3.2) contribute to the formation of pathologies. They indicate the limited capacity of the agency to generate requisite responses to its perceived needs for achievement under environmental circumstances. Thus, the bars (Pi,j) of the intelligences shown in Figure 3.2 are indicative of emerging pathologies. Given combinations of these across the personality may well generate distinct personality dysfunctions.

The notion of efficacy applies to the network of processes that constitute the intelligences of the normative personality that determines either preferences or pathologies/dysfunction. In our model, while the traits are concerned with control and the epistemic attributes of a personality (within the meta-system and figurative and operative systems), efficacy is a conditional connector of the ontologically distinct traits systems. *Espoused values* are manifested as preferences from which requisite efficacy arises in the agency. An agency intuits and appreciates what is requisite from an understanding of its environment in relation to the imperatives from its values and attitudes and other emotive imperatives. Efficacy refers to the means by which figurative and operative intelligences develop, for instance through the coherence of a collective. Greater efficacy will result in an improved capacity for intelligence. The evaluation of efficacy could be done qualitatively through ethnographic qualitative or quantitative empirical techniques. Measures for perceived efficacy are provided by Adeyemo (2007), Alden (1986), and Lee (2005).

Since personality orientations are connected to both intelligences and efficacy it is now possible to collect our discussions as a set of proposition appropriate to the normative personality. We have already indicated that personality orientation arises through personality preferences. In the agency cultural/knowledge meta-system, espoused values indicate these preferences. These are manifested: (a) in the cognitive system of the personality as significant dispositional and state attitudes and information structured into cognitive schemas, (b) in the figurative system as figurative schemas, and (c) in the operative systems as operative schemas with structural/behavioural imperatives. These manifested preferences determine the set of trait orientations of the normative personality, which in the context of organizations we call organizational orientation. Preferences are thus responsible for the nature of a personality, being influenced by both its intelligences and efficacy, and indeed pathologies and dysfunctions. Pathologies Pi,j (Figure 3.2) that affect both intelligences and efficacy can fall into patterns that create agency dysfunctions.

4.5 Knowledge Strategy Agency Case

An approach that possibly is able to subsume many of the organizational approaches to intelligence comes from Inden, because it adopts a generic cybernetic model that is reminiscent of the living system. However, in particular it takes a knowledge approach to collective intelligence. Inden (2012) notes that the German word Anschlussfahigkeit, which in direct translation means 'connection ability', can be interpreted as 'contributing to the continuation of an autopoietic processes'. Linking autopoiesis with self-referentiality, he suggests that these operate through a knowledge-system. Anschlussfahigkeit, he thus notes, delivers reason that is able to question previous knowledge. From this perspective, he suggests, intelligence is equal to the effectiveness and efficiency of a self-referential knowledge-network to adapt to perceived change. As such, intelligence is the product of a network rather than of a single node of knowledge. According to Inkpen & Tsang (2005) knowledge-networks imply networks of processes by which knowledge is transferred. As such, knowledge-networks imply a network of processes, and this in turn links to Piaget's concept of intelligence. Further, self-referentiality enriches knowledge-networks and increases their efficiency – this implying increased efficacy in the network of processes that service them. Inden offers an example a colony of termites that is intelligent because of its network efficacy in pursuing its purposes. He suggests that the collective intelligence of termites is due to their ability to collaborate through social intelligence supported by common motivations and collective infrastructure. The self-reference of organizations is a prerequisite for the development of shared agendas, culture, mainstream thinking, rules of conduct and best practices, implemented business processes, and technologies. Other various attributes arise from these different dimensions of the organization, including trust and values. All go towards the creation of immanent information which contributes to the development of patterns of behaviour that are manifested in the environment.

Knowledge-networks occur in a collective agency as a distribution of patterns of knowledge, and facilitate knowledge creation through interactive processes (Migdadi, 2005: 28). This is connected with knowledge management, which for Wiig (1993) gives intellectual assets that can result in improved intelligence and performance. This view is supported by Gonçaloa, Burstein & Lezana (2002: 90), who explain that intelligence is the principal factor that links both knowledge and strategy within organizations. They continue by introducing a new term of *practical intelligence*, defined as a purposive adaptation in a real-world context. Hence practical intelligence is nothing other than a function of viable agency. Thus, setting up a knowledge management case, if approached in the right way, is also a case study of intelligence.

For Gonçaloa, Burstein, & Lezana (2002: 90), knowledge strategy is related to organizational intelligence, which contributes to a knowledge management practice. In demonstrating this they explore an organization located in Porto Alegre, capital of Rio Grande do Sul in Brazil. The corporation is involved in the design and production of assembly, test, and handling systems for companies manufacturing products such as automobile parts, as well as household appliances and electrical components. In undertaking their study, they distinguish between two types of organizational knowledge:

- formal structures, composed of rules, patterns, performance systems, or managerial models used for instance in strategic planning
- cognitive structures, found in learning processes, decision-making processes, leadership features, personnel flexibility, and informal communication systems.

From the perspective of agency theory, formal structures exist as cultural knowledge, with distinction made between core patterns of knowledge as a collection of knowledge nodes that each have specific experiential or thematic reference; rule-based schemas of knowledge that may be activated under specific conditions, and selected operative knowledge that has applicability to given immediate contexts. Cognitive structures are represented by the strategic dimension of the organization. The interest by Gonçaloa et al. was to explore the cognitive structures that support collective actions intrinsic to creating and transferring knowledge. In perusing this they wished to determine how a firm can provide conditions that will facilitate the expression of its intelligence in both cognitive and formal structures.

In developing their approach they distinguish between four cognitive systems that interact as part of the organizational cognitive perspective for promoting knowledge strategy. These are the organic system – the personnel-management problem that leaders must deal with; the analytic system – as the basis of the current structured knowledge and the practical process of accessing it; the intuitive system – that relates to intuition and experience during the strategic application; and the co-ordination system – facilitating harmonious interaction between people in an interconnected knowledge network. Applying these to the corporate case in question, they also identify observed principle categories and evidence for their existence. These categories and the related evidence have been assembled in Table 4.5, showing how they would migrate

Table 4.5 *Migrating conceptualizations of knowledge strategy to the cultural agency*

Cultural Agency	Gonçaloa et al.		Habitus	Gardner
Environment				Context
Agency operative system			Practices, perceptions	Behavioural awareness
Social intelligence			Inculcation – extrinsic conditioned from the environment.	Physical *object related* constraints. Process and relationship awareness
Cultural system				Context. Knowledge and creation of symbols used in social interactions.
Cultural intelligence			Transposable – (normative) practices can be acquired to other fields of attention or application.	Process and relationship awareness
Strategic Agency				
Cognitive system	Intuitive system	Unstructured and tacit knowledge, based on specific characteristics of each person. Information from the structured cultural memory to acquiring new insights.		*Object free* reflections of structures and objects. Personal intelligence worldview.
Cognitive system attitudes	Organic system	Based on how people are valued and managed. Provides perspectives on organizational future/development. Able to facilitate employee work satisfaction. Able to create trust. Facilitates understanding of the business' goals. Establishes project	Attitudes that are mental dispositions	Mythical *object related* constraints.

Figurative intelligence and its feedback	autonomy including decision making, with employee participation project structure. *Stimulation* to access and to inform structured knowledge. *Connecting* individual experience to a structured collective memory. Processes that structure the whole set of information of each project beyond the existing project memory to acquired knowledge. Sharing network of information about the evolution of each project. Organizational memory represented through a network of processes that maps individual experience to a structured collective memory.	Reflection of social circumstances. Generative – a plurality of attitudes are generated through feedback. Transposable – attitudes can be applied from one psychological field	Process and relationship awareness
Figurative system Analytic system	Structured and explicit knowledge-based information schemas from each project. Flexibility between project and building activities permanently combining different 'thoughtful minds'.		Virtual *object-related* constraints
Operative Intelligence and its feedback	Facilitates strong informal interchange of information to enable new historical insights. Used to access information from the structured memory for acquiring new insights. Processes that structure total information from each project (beyond the existing project memory) to acquired knowledge.	Generative – a plurality of practices are generated. Transposable – practices and perceptions from one psychological field to another	Technical *object-related* constraints. Process and relationship awareness

Table 4.5 (cont.)

Cultural Agency	Gonçaloa et al.	Habitus	Gardner
Operative system	Co-ordination system	Based on awareness of the whole range of organizational activities and organizational leadership features. Encouraging organizational conversation for sharing information. Issue-resulting in real-time with informal calls to relevant others. Embracing a business systemic view to initiate formally operative intelligence processes. Able to specify required knowledge for each part of the intelligence process.	Generative – a plurality of perceptions are generated.	Functional attributes of *object-related* constraints. Decision-making awareness.

to the strategic agency systems and intelligences, as discussed for the strategic agency. In addition we migrate the ideas of Habitus and Gardner that are intended to constitute intelligence, thereby relating them to Piaget's intelligences.

As a result it becomes clear from Table 4.5 that cultural agency theory links with a variety of views of the nature of intelligence. For instance it satisfies the needs of knowledge management as well as knowledge strategy. Gonçaloa et al., through their case study, have shown how knowledge strategy operates as a mechanism for intelligence, and this would in particular seem to be a case illustration of Habitus. It also becomes clear that there is a vast difference between Piaget's intelligences, Bourdieu's Habitus, and Gardner's ideas on intelligence. Having set Piaget's intelligences within the cultural agency therefore demonstrates that process intelligence is much more functionally specific and powerful than other ideas on intelligence. In contrast, Habitus is really a theory of personality development, while in Gardner's multiple intelligences, awareness is a cognitive function that occurs when activating figurative schemas are evaluated with feedback during their implementation. Thus for instance, there is often a difference between how an agency believes it is behaving, and how others in its social environment see its behaviour to be. Within a cultural agency multiple intelligences may also be seen to include a relationship to self-processes, including self-awareness and personality, that are normal for a living system. Gardner (1991) explains that intelligence is a context-related biological and psychological potential capable of being realized to a greater or lesser extent as a consequence of the experiential, cultural, and motivational factors. These factors cover all dimensions of the cultural agency, and this is perhaps still the easiest definition appropriate for intelligence that has been proposed.

5   Agency Traits and Types

5.1   Introduction

In Human Resource Management, personality indicators have become important because of the belief that they provide a way of connecting the demands of given social and task environments with individual potential behaviour, including performance. Their traditional primary utility is as screening vehicles for potential employees prior to more costly formal interview procedures. Connecting mind with decision-making and overt behaviour is conceptually axiomatic, and is traditionally the domain of cognitive theorists (Baron, 1982), who are seen as concerned directly with overt behaviour. However, connecting cognitive orientations with particular forms of behaviour for either individual or collective agencies is feasible using personality evaluations, given appropriate theory and a proper understanding of the pragmatic utility that can be created. Most generally, this field of study can be referred to psychosocial dynamics (Garcia, 2006), with those who work in this area often having a special interest in exploring the pathologies that drive socially problematic behaviour (Yolles, 2009a).

One of the earliest significant approaches to personality evaluation came from Jung in the early 1920s, when he developed a model of temperament. Temperament is basically connected to emotions and preferences (Gross, 2008), in contrast to cognitions which may be taken as being connected with epistemic meanings and processes of rationality. Cognition arises from epistemic beliefs and is a property of the mind which imparts the faculty of knowing, perceiving, or conceiving. It represents knowledge with degrees of certainty that are seen as 'truths' about our 'reality'. So cognitions are mental processes, and they may have attitudinal attributes that are the result of belief imperatives, with propositional content that is vectored towards some object of attention. Whether one is interested in temperament or in cognitions, both can be associated with personality differences. Jung linked this dynamic to YinYang processes of the mind, a term which he later replaced by the Greek word *enantiodromia*, and which we shall refer to by the use of the simpler word enantiomer. To explain these terms, Jung's *enantiodromia* are personality states that occur in dichotomously opposite and interactive pairs. Myers-Briggs Type Indicator (MBTI) is a development from this, but the term *enantiodromia* was dropped, and MBTI deals instead with psychological *functions* that together with paired values of social attitude combine in certain ways to generate personality patterns called *types* (Pittenger, 1993). In this chapter, and within the context of agency theory, we take a trait as being a personality control variable that can take one of a dyadic pair of values or degrees of balance between them (Gittinger, 1992; Fink, 2014) that determine the local 'state possibilities' of a personality. We refer to these values as enantiomers. When trait values are determined, personality traits will result in a 'personality condition'. Each dyadic pair of values for a given trait is in dynamic interaction.

Ryckman (2004) notes that Jung's theory models personality as a dynamic and organized set of characteristics possessed by a person that uniquely influences his or her cognitions, motivations, and behaviours in various situations. While motivations are emotionally based constructs, behaviour is constituted as the actions or reactions of cognitive individuals in relation to what they perceive within their environment. The behaviour may be conscious-unconscious, overt-covert, or voluntary-involuntary. Trait theorists (like Myers et al., 1998; Heinström, 2003) are interested in traits that adopt type values that together orientate personality, and create penchants towards decision making, and connect mental function with overt behaviour. Here, seemingly random variation in individual behaviours is seen as orderly and consistent due to distinctions in the ways they apply their cognitive functions. In developing his explicatory framework for personality, Jung (1923; 1957–79) articulates a number of propositions that can be summarized as:

(i) past experience and expectations about the future influence of behaviour and personality;
(ii) individuals are capable of constant and creative development; and
(iii) personality is an open system, which is receptive to inputs and exchanges.

He considers behaviour to be a sub-system of personality, which can change as a result of inputs from, and interactions with, the external environment of the individual. Thus, the influence of others can have a significant impact on an individual's behaviour, implicitly thereby recognizing the role of changing context.

In creating his thesis, Jung also established a basis for the development of a temperament theory of personality. It became the entry point for a number of other theoretical and empirical examinations of personality, most of which centre on personality differences between individuals. They include the MBTI (Myers Briggs, 2000), and its close relative Socionics (Müller et al., 1998), both relating to personal preferences. The latter of these two links

Jung's work with those of Freud and Kepinski. More empirical approaches include the Five Factor Model (Cattell, 1945), often referred to as FFM or the Big 5. There is a main distinction in the approaches adopted by MBTI and FFM: the former is a type approach that indicates personality states, and the latter is a trait approach that indicates a personality framework of indicative variables. The two approaches are not mutually exclusive, since the states that trait variables adopt can be represented as types (Eysenck, 1957). While all of these are temperament theories, in contrast both Harvey (1966) and Maruyama (2001) independently developed epistemic approaches based on cultural values that represent cognitive conditions. Maruyama was able to relate his approach, which he called mindscape types, to that of Harvey.

Support for the possibility of creating theory that links personality indicators with behaviour has not always been as strong as it is now. Social psychologists (e.g. Mischel, 1968) argue that behaviour is not stable but varies with context, a proposition which has been to some extent evidenced (Krupat, 2006). Theorists in the 1960s and 1970s suggested that predicting behaviour by personality tests was impossible (see, for instance, Borman et al., 2003). An explanation for this by some behavioural theorists was that personality is a perceived construct that people impose on others in order to maintain an illusion of consistency in the world. However, by the 1980s it was realized that while predicting single instances of behaviour may be unreliable, patterns of behaviour could be identified from an aggregate of a large number of observations. More generally, patterns are generically defined as an abstraction from a concrete form that keeps recurring in specific, non-arbitrary contexts. It is this very nature that enables a predictive capacity, even when it comes to their interaction with personal and situational variables. Another realization has also developed: that where it is possible to associate personalities with stable preferences, a consistent connection to behaviour can be discerned (de Oliveira, 2008; Hyldegård, 2009).

A theory of personality functioning reflects the personal narratives that individuals construct over the course of their lives (Tomkins, 1979; McAdams, 1996 & 2001). It contains not only a theory of persons but (at least implicitly) a theory of personality assessment through the identification and provision of a set of personality indicators – that is, a set of beliefs about the internal psychological structures and overt behavioural tendencies that must be measured in an assessment of personality and the procedures that are required to measure them. Personality theory and personality assessment are intertwined and manifested as the likelihood for behaviour through the use of personality indicators.

There is a divide between modern socio-cognitive approaches to personality assessment, and trait and types approaches, even though they can in principle be related (Eysenck, 1957; Van Egeren, 2009). Human agency is complex, and modelling its effective functionality requires theoretical pluralism (Bandura, 2008). However, the very plurality of personality schemas that coexist (Carver, 2005) creates an uncertain fragmented paradigmatic horizon that is unintegrated, with unrelated theories that are competitive and together demonstrate an undeveloped theoretical understanding of the nature of personality (e.g. Sharpley, 2006). For instance, Bandura's (1999: 229) agency theory is a socio-cognitive dynamic self-schema of personality that sees the individual as an autonomous system that interacts dynamically with its social environments. In contrast the trait schemas of personality like FFM (Buss, 1996) tend to be devoid of contextual connection, and have a static rather than dynamic nature (Bandura, 1986).

Earlier we set personality theory into a collective setting. Establishing organizations within a (social) psychological framework is not new. For instance, both Weick (1995) and Kets de Vries (1991) are interested in the psychology of the collective, and Bridges (1992) talks about the organizational character as a representative of a social personality. Maruyama (1988 & 2001) has applied his Mindscape concepts of personality to the collective. Bandura (1999) has applied his socio-cognitive concepts of the individual personality to the collective. Yolles (2006) also discusses the relationship between the individual and social collective, and notes that a social agency can develop a collective psyche that operates through normative processes.

Van Egeren (2009) is interested in a metaphor that links *agency* and *trait* schemas. Agency theory comes from the socio-cognitive notions of Bandura (1999), concerned with cognitive attributes like self-organization and self-reflection, with some significant interest also placed in the notion of efficacy. This is the cognitive *capability* of an agency to use its talents and abilities in its activities; it can enhance self-motivation through goal systems, and can be affected by positive or negative emotive orientation in such attributes as self-monitoring, cognitive representation, and recognition of capabilities in past successes and failures (Bandura, 1991). Efficacy is therefore conditioned by emotional intelligence (Adeyemo, 2007), itself defined as the ability of an agency to monitor its own and others' feelings and emotions, to discriminate among them and to use this information to guide one's thinking and actions (Salovey & Mayer, 1990).

Most work on traits is concerned with temperament (Mehrabian, 1991; Strelau, 2002; Carver, 2005; Van Ergeren, 2009). Thus, for instance, Mehrabian (1991) considers temperament as an *emotion trait*, this providing a potential for permanently linking trait and temperament theory with socio-cognitive theory. Van Egeren (2009) sees temperament as trait theory based on and reflective of emotional-motivational systems that are able to increase adaptation to classes of stimuli associated with positive and negative reinforcement (Depue

& Morrone-Strupinsky, 2005, p. 314). Thomas & Chess (1977, cited in Strelau, 2002) see temperament as a general term referring to the *how* of behaviour and *way* in which an individual behaves. More broadly, Davis (2000) notes that durable personality traits are usually tightly bound to qualities of emotions, but they may also be defined in terms of preconscious mental dispositions that affect the reflective processes and influence the different categories of cognitive and animated behaviour. They are focused at the reflective layer of personality and permeate it, providing the control patterns that create stability. They are also related to performance (Fleishman et al., 1999).

It has been said that the only cognitive trait approaches that centre on cultural values appear to come from Harvey (1966) and from Maruyama (1993). Whether adopting temperament or cognitive traits, the theoretical principles of trait immanence still have applicability. In discussing traits, Van Egeren (2009) develops a metaphor for agency, where personality traits are seen to be related to self-regulatory controls that underlie behaviour, rather than manifesting behaviour patterns themselves. Thus, for instance, he relates the central characteristics of traits to the central characteristics of self-regulatory processes underlying goal-directed behaviour. He also notes that personality traits appear to be connected to human action by self-regulatory functions that are inseparable from action itself. The traits are seen to have self-regulatory propensities or styles affecting how individuals characteristically pursue their goals. A set of traits should be seen to work together interdependently to exert control over human behaviour, and for him a principal task of personality theory is to describe this process of control. Our approach moves beyond metaphor to develop the basis of a formal psychosocial framework for the collective agency with a normative personality that, if durable, can maintain stable temperament preferences. In this case its behaviour may be anticipated.

Earlier we noted that personality is the result of orientations in the internal landscape of agency mind. It would therefore be useful to identify a typology for that orientation. This does not mean once a personality type has been allocated that changes are not possible. Change in personality type within agency theory is not like that of Jungian theory: personalities are deemed to be able to change type. Type is a general term that may include temperament which implies emotion/affect, but our interest here relates more to cognitive types. In what follows we shall first discuss traits, enantiomers, and agency types. This will explain how an agency is oriented in what it does, and provides explanation for why agencies take different orientations that affect how they see and respond to the world around them. However, agency types coalesce, and the way in which they coalescence creates a result that is sometimes referred to as individualism or collectivism. Therefore, it will be useful to discuss these two concepts in relation to agency traits.

5.2   Traits, Enantiomers, and Agency Types

The term *trait* as used here refers to the preferential variables of an agency that are formative in defining its functional nature. The traits may take one of two bi-polar enantiomer values that interact pairwise, thereby enabling balanced traits to arise, and orientate the agency in the way that it processes information and develops. These ultimately create a penchant towards particular forms of attitude, cognitive positioning, decision and policy making, and behaviour. For Van Egeren (2009) and Davis (2000), such traits operate as fundamental control and characterizing function. Traits arise from core properties of the agency that commonly exist within it, and its capability to create performance is a function of its capacity to process information efficaciously. The traits establish stable regulatory processes that enable the emergence of stable patterns of behaviour. Different traits therefore have different control functions and hence necessarily reflect different definitive characteristics (Yolles, 2009; Yolles & Fink, 2009; Yolles, Fink & Dauber, 2011).

MBTI as Agency

Following Yolles (2009a) and Yolles & Fink (2009b), it is possible to set MBTI within an agency substructure. The MBTI schema purports that seemingly random variation in behaviour is actually quite orderly and consistent, being due to basic differences in the way individuals prefer to use their perception and judgement, ultimately influencing behaviour. Perception involves ways of becoming aware cognitively and phenomenally. Judgement involves ways of concluding about what is perceived. If individuals differ systematically in what they perceive and in how they reach conclusions, then the rationale underpinning MBTI purports that they will correspondingly differ in their interests, reactions, values, motivations, and skills. The aim of the MBTI is to identify through its measuring instruments the basic preferences of people in regard to perception and judgement. The notion is that the effects of each preference, singly and in combination, can be established by research and put into practical use, especially in relation to decision-making behaviour.

The four preference dimensions of MBTI accumulate into a set of sixteen permutations dichotomies that result in the sixteen personality types. These form the basis of the Myers' model and therefore MBTI. To code these types, MBTI adopts a set of ordered letters: first letter E (extrovert) or I (introvert); second letter S (sensing) or N (intuition); third letter T (thinking) or F (feeling); fourth letter J (judging) or P (perceiving). There is a tendency is to understand each of the sixteen types as the sum of its essential parts, such as ESTJ=E+S+T+J. However, it is the interaction of the four preferences that is important and the unique mental patterns these interactions determine. Thus INTJ is taken to be the most independent minded of the sixteen types, while ISTP is seen as in particular having an intuitive investigatory aptitude. Thus, for instance, the sixteen types are listed as: ISTJ, ISFJ, INFJ, INTJ, ISTP, ISFP, INFP, INTP, ESTP, ESFP, ENFP, ENTP, ESTJ, ESFJ, ENFJ, and ENTJ. However, they can also be blocked into four stable patterns (Boje, 2004; Berens, 2007) and referred to as: Opinion (ENTJ, ENTP) and Government (ESTJ, ISTJ); Revolutionary (ENTJ, ENTP) and Reform (ESTJ, ISTJ); Prince (ENTJ, ENTP) and Bureaucratic (ESTJ, ISTJ); and Super (ESFJ, ISFL) and Heroic (ENFL, ENFP). So a personality will maintain a pattern of enantiomers that correspond to one of these patterns, in part because of the underlying socio-cognitive processes. These preference dimensions, which we refer to as personality traits, are described in Table 5.1 The shaded component of this table represents enantiomer values set within the context of social collectives that may be associated with Boje's (2004) perspective connected with the work of Maruyama (1988).

The Myers-Briggs schema is concerned with decision-making behaviour. However, there is a relationship between decision making and temperament orientation to the social that creates behaviour. This is determined by the connection between personality and the environment and is conditioned by its introvert/extrovert nature.

Using an agency substructure populated by MBTI schema superstructure, Yolles (2009a) modelled personality temperament that distinguishes individual differences in personality, attempting to migrate MBTI schemas into agency theory, and here we shall briefly follow his argument. Duncan (2005), who works in political psychology in relation to self-schemas, considers that a variable of individual differences has a political connection that comes from the propensity to attach personal meaning to social and historical events. Referred to as personal political salience, this is conceptualized as a self-schema and is seen to be related to efficient processing of political data. PPS in this context effectively provides a cognitive mechanism whereby people connect personal experiences to their wider social, historical, and political contexts. Such contexts are not only defined in connection with the formal governance in society, but also more informal governance in connection with the interrelation between individual agents, which is in part a function of the judging/perceiving enantiomers. Even though Duncan explores the *'individual differences self-schema'* in relation to politics, she does not appear to define what she means by this. Discerning what this might mean can be assisted through Dunbar & Abra (2008), for whom politics is seen in terms of the power associated with social interpersonal interactions. So it is possible to generalize Duncan's notion by drawing on Dunbar and Abra, and saying that where an 'individual difference personality self-schema' is projected into a social environment through social and interpersonal interaction, the result will

Table 5.1 *Trait variables and their enantiomers for personal political temperament in MBTI trait space, and its equivalent social trait space (shaded)*

Traits	Enantiomer	Nature	Enantiomer	Nature
Deconstraint (structure relating) for decision making towards increased viability	Judging	Normative values required. Drive towards closure. Need planned processes and regulation. Highly structured, adhering to plans.	Perceiving	Are flexible in a spontaneous way, seeking to experience and understand a plurality of phenomena. Allows for value changes. Open to environment.
	Monistic/ exclusive	Single normative narrative may be mediated from a plurality; demands exclusivity.	Pluralistic/ participatory	Pluralistic narratives servicing a multiplicity of requirements, demands participation.
Mindedness (decision modelling) using mental models, ideology and ethics	Thinking	Involves logical and rationality. Impartial based on normatively based ethical and ideologically based belief formulated by pre-defined rules.	Feeling	Involves evaluating information, and is associated with emotional responses. Connects with purely subjective perspective of situations, and orientated towards subjective processes based on personal ethical and ideological grounds.
	Objectifying	A normative externalized view of what is real. Subjective individual experiences are objectified. The normalization process may be associated with processes of monism and monocular vision (Maruyama, 2008).	Subjectifying	The post-modern process of individuals 'locally' interpreting reality through internalization. It can be associated with Piaget's notion of projection (Piaget, 1977: 20) and the coordination of perspectives, and provides for polyocular vision (Maruyama, 2008).

Table 5.1 (cont.)

Traits	Enantiomer	Nature	Enantiomer	Nature
Disposition (information gathering) through 'political' values and cultural norms.	Sensing	Preference for sensing relates to the tangible and manifest. Concerned with data that is literal and concrete. Noticing that an object exists without its pre-evaluation.	Intuition	Connected to the unconscious. Comes from complex integration of large amounts of information. Consequence is to see the bigger picture, focusing on the structured relationships and connection between facts and finding patterns. Tends to accommodate the abstract and conceptual from information that is gathered. Connected to possibilities, patterns and inherent meaning in an object.
	Transactional/ Confining	The construction of knowledge through three types of interaction: with subjects/objects in an environment; between those in the environment and outside world. Connected with the negotiated, collaborative, experiential, and jointly assessed. *Confining* personalities limit the distribution of power and retain it for themselves.	Transformational/ Liberating	Concerned with personal discovery, interconnectedness, social awareness, and change, and is connected with social justice. *Liberating* personalities listen to their own consciences rather than the dictates of convention.

be dynamics of personal politics. Here then, a self-schema is used to interpret information for general contexts and functions to organize, summarize, and explain an individual's behaviour in relation to the wider social, historical, and (power-related) interpersonal contexts. As a result, Yolles & Fink (2009b) are able to distinguish between enantiomers for an agency personality temperament model: identifying a cognitive trait as disposition, a figurative trait as mindedness, and an operative trait as deconstraining. The trait enantiomer values are described in more detail below:

(1) **Disposition**. The MBTI enantiomers of {*judging, perceiving*} can be migrated into this dimension. The domain is metasystemic in nature, and arises with a term that comes from Wollheim (1999). He discusses the distinction between unconscious mental state (relating to impulses, instincts, perceptions, imaginings, drives, and motivations) and disposition (relating to knowledge, emotion, and a filter to processes of knowledge migration). The enantiomers are taken as {*confining, liberating*}. *Confining* personalities limit the distribution of power and retain it for themselves. These also relate to transactional/transformational personalities as indicated in mindscape theory (Boje, 2004). Transactional personalities like to create clear structures that determine what is required of and delivered (as rewards) to others, and they prefer formal systems of constraint and discipline. Liberating personalities are those who, after Jung (Grossman, 1999, p. 93), listen to their own consciences rather than the dictates of convention, while transformational personalities are concerned with meaning, values, ethics, and like to form structures that satisfy purposes. Personality Temperament traits as defined here are set up within a trait space and are illustrated in Figure 5.1. It is feasible that the four blocks of MBTI personality states can be mapped into this space, as indicated by Boje (2004).

(2) **Mindedness**. The MBTI enantiomers of {*feeling, thinking*} can be migrated into this dimension. The dimension operates as a figurative ideate system, and has the enantiomer attributes of {*subjectifying, objectifying*}, in part as a reflection of the Foucauldian notion of the enantiomers *subjectification-objectification*. It defines a frame of reference that permits others to be seen as *subjects* (as others are subjectified) or *objects* (as others are objectified). Subjectifying is pluralistic since there are as many subjective perspectives as there are those who are capable of conscious awareness. Objectivism, however, is monistic in nature in that politically it is constituted within a single normative view of what is acceptable.

(3) **Deconstraining**. The MBTI enantiomers of {*sensing, intuition*} can be migrated into this dimension. This dimension operates within a power-related

148   The Agency

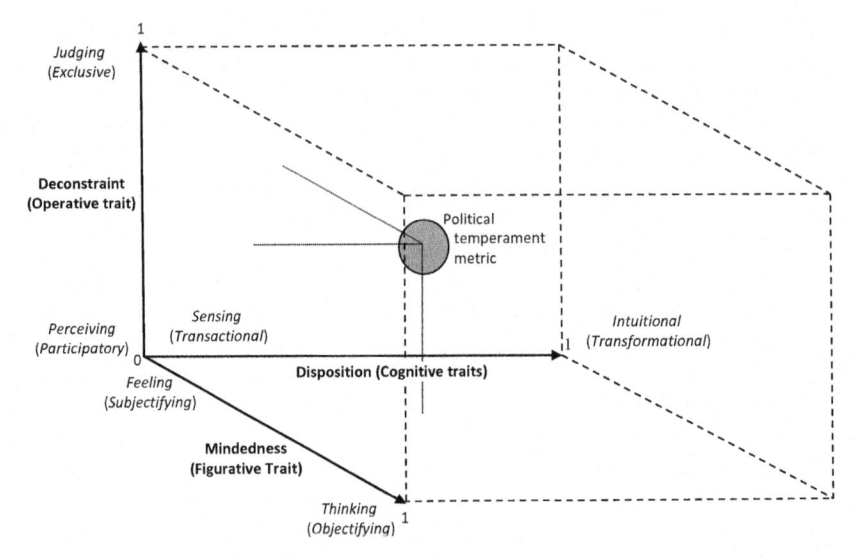

Figure 5.1 Illustration of personality temperament trait for a 'personal political' space showing trait enantiomers, with social collective terms shown in brackets

structural system. The definition of the enantiomers has been influenced by Eysenk (1957), and defined as {*pluralistic, monistic*}; when related to individuals within a political context they may also be seen as {*participatory, exclusive*}. Participatory means an agent establishing processes that allow others to participate in decision- and action-taking processes. Exclusive means establishing processes that the agent exclusively self-directs (the agent as the centre of political power), providing little opportunity for participatory access.

Boje's Foucauldian Personality Trait Types

A different approach to the creation of traits and their enantiomer values comes from Boje (2004). His exploration of personality traits relates to his interest in creating a generative trait basis for the mindscape theory types, and he chooses traits that arise from Foucault (1972) as shown below, each with a pair of enantiomers:

(1) **Knowledge trait**: Boje refers to an agency's will to historically constituted and informationally scripted patterns of knowledge, so that an agency is part of a *knowledge script system* and responds to and generates informational consequences. Boje also distinguishes between the bi-polar meta-types

within the context of a will to knowledge, and these correspond to *Transaction scripts* and *Transformation scripts*, respectively. Transactional scripting involves simple repetition and sameness that reflects on status quo, while transformation scripting is about embracing uniqueness and change in a system through emergence and deviation, and reflects on the possibilities that emerge through *autonomy*. The interaction between transaction–transformation involves Maruyama's notion of the dialectic of *deviation-counteracting* and *deviation-amplifying* in the scripts. This knowledge scripting is part of secondary socialization (e.g. by providing them with socially acceptable values). Through this, agents internalize the scripts, as well as the character type expected for agents in their environment. This script internalization is constituted as a means of formation, and enables an agent to be influenced by knowledge-based information that relates to its social environment.

(2) **Ethics trait**: Boje considers regulation within the context of Foucauldian ethics, which (unlike the normal definition of ethics) is connected with the relationships we have with ourselves and the mutual ways in which agents are both *controlled by others* and *control by self*. Control by a generalized other within a socio-cultural context is hence poly-ocular and perhaps more *social harmony*-oriented, while *achievement* is more connected with mono-ocularity self-interest and control by self. As such the bi-polar enantiomers that permit this trait to create an orientation are mono-ocularity (one view) and poly-ocularity (many views).

(3) **Power trait**: Boje notes that agents are not free to say just anything when or where they wish, and certain types of knowledge are forbidden in some social environments. This appears to be connected with a realization of the nature of the constraints and a technical ability to engage with the environment and to establish predictions and controls. This presupposes the existence of *a hierarchical structure* that both anticipates and constrains/facilitates behaviour. The enantiomer options that Boje assigns to this trait as an orientation to *power* may be related to hierarchy and *service*, and may be related to egalitarianism.

Agency Theory Traits Types

In contrast to both MBTI and Boje, in agency theory we adopt alternative traits with their own set of possible trait values. Personality interacts with its environment, and because of this we need also to consider influences that impinge from the environment on the agency. We distinguish two environmental traits: agency *cultural* and *social* orientation. Agency cultural orientation controls what is culturally legitimate in the agency, while social orientation controls how the agency reacts to the perceived needs of what it identifies as its environment, including others.

A set of five traits (cultural, cognitive, figurative and operative, and social) are identified, combinations of the enantiomers of three normative personality traits create *personality types*; and combinations of the five traits create *agency types*. These traits derive their bi-polar values from a cultural study by Sagiv and Schwartz (2007). This examines cultural values and illustrates how societal culture influences organizational values both directly and indirectly, and ultimately with respect to organizational tasks. An adaptation of their study drawing on Yolles & Fink (2011) provides the following explanation of the traits as summarized in Table 5.2.

These traits can be explained at greater length as follows:

Cultural orientation: This trait maintains three forms of knowledge: identification, elaborating, and executor knowledge (Yolles, 2006) that can each be manifested into the personality system as information. The enantiomers of this trait have been explored at some length in Yolles et al. (2008) and arise from the work of Sorokin (1939–1941), summarized in Sorokin (1962). As already explained, the two type orientations are Sensate and Ideational. Sensate epistemic attributes include appreciating the nature of the needs and ends that are to be satisfied in respect of a given object of attention; the degree of strength in pursuit of those needs; and the methods of satisfaction. The means of satisfaction occurs not through adaptation or modification of human beings, but through the exploitation of the external world. It is thus practically orientated, with emphasis on human external needs. With reality as perceived from senses, its operative nature is highlighted in that it views reality through what can be measured and observed rather than reasoned. Ideational cultural orientation epistemic attributes include: appreciating the conceptual and internal nature of an object of attention, and creating fulfilment or realization through self-imposed minimization or elimination of most physical needs. With reality as perceived conceptually, its operative nature is highlighted in that it views reality through what can be envisaged and reasoned. When we are considering the macro-economic context of a country and the policies that governments generate and implement to achieve efficacious performance, we will likely be referring to the political culture that drives its governance, which may adopt predominantly Sensate or Ideational perspectives. In cases of cultural instability, the ascendency of one type over the other may vary according to the means by which a particular regime is able to come to power and maintain it.

Cognitive orientation: This arises from cognitive and social psychology (Van Liere & Dunlap, 1981; Menary, 2009), is existentially connected with cognitive self-reference (Hannah et al., 2008 & 2010), and maintains a relationship with cognitive intention (Freeman, 2008). It might involve the effective realizing of potential, recognizing social and political structures and the

Table 5.2 *Cultural agency traits, strategic economic agency traits and social agency traits, and their possible polar orientations*

Orientations	Personality Type Enantiomers			
	Enantiomer	Nature	Enantiomer	Nature
Cultural	Senate	Appreciating nature of needs and ends to be satisfied. Means of satisfaction occurs through exploitation of the external world. Practically orientated, with emphasis on human external needs.	Ideational	Appreciating the conceptual and internal nature of an entity. Creating fulfilment or realization through self-imposed minimization or elimination of most physical needs.
Cognitive	Autonomy	Bounded entities should find meaning in their own uniqueness, encouraged to express their internal attributes like preferences, traits, feelings, and motives.	Embeddedness	Emphasizes maintenance of status quo and restraining actions or inclinations that might disrupt in-group solidarity or the traditional order.
Figurative	Mastery	Monistic in nature and encourages active self-assertion to attain group or personal goals and to master, direct, and change the natural and social environment, like values: ambition, success, daring, competence. May involve spontaneous decisions following from the spontaneous desires of the decision makers	Harmony	Pluralistic in nature. Tries to understand and appreciate rather than to direct or exploit. Connected with appreciations driving goal formulation as a process deriving from data collection and involving careful weighing of arguments

Table 5.2 (cont.)

		Personality Type Enantiomers			
Orientations	Enantiomer	Nature		Enantiomer	Nature
Operative	Hierarchy	Relies on hierarchical systems of ascribed roles for productive behaviour. Actors are socialized to take the hierarchical distribution of roles for granted and to comply with the obligations and their role's rules. Tends to adopt a chain of authority with well-defined roles. Actors expected to comply with role-obligations putting interests of the organization first. Unequal distribution of power, roles, and resources legitimate (values: social power, authority, humility, wealth).		Egalitarianism	Actors tend to recognize one another as moral equals sharing basic interests. Actors are socialized to co-operate and to feel concern for welfare of others. Expectation of action for benefit of others as a matter of choice (values: equality, social justice, responsibility, honesty). Organizations are built on co-operative negotiation among employees and management.
Social	Patterning	Persistent curiosity about the object world and how it works, is constructed, and is named, varied, or explored. It is connected to problems of symmetry, pattern, balance, and the dynamics of physical relationships between entities, and is likely to indicate relational connection.		Dramatist	Interested in sequences of interpersonal events, having dramatic or narrative structures that are likely to involve distinction and differentiation (e.g. distinguishing situations), and undertaking effective communications.

associated constraints imposed on the agency. The variable may be seen to take enantiomers that give the agency an *autonomy orientation* when an agency will follow less the guidance of its host culture, but might react more autonomously to the lessons drawn from (or opportunities offered by) environmental impulses; the other enantiomer of the variable might be *embeddedness orientation* (Sagiv and Schwartz, 2007). Autonomy refers to bounded entities that should find meaning in their own uniqueness and who are encouraged to express their internal attributes (preferences, traits, feelings, and motives). Embeddedness emphasizes the maintenance of the status quo and restraining actions or inclinations that might disrupt in-group solidarity or the traditional order. The trait is affected by attitudes, and emotive imperatives that may orientate the agency towards cognitive coherence or dissonance. It also has impact on perspectives that are associated with strategies, ideology, and ethics/morality. It, in addition, creates imperatives for the control of the patterns of behaviour through intention. The development of inefficacy can lead to lack of coherence and a demonstration of collective cognitive dissonance, and this can act as a driver for cognitive state/dispositional dysfunctions (Endler & Summerfield, 1995: 255). This can also be connected with patterns of information that arise from conceptual and cultural knowledge.

Figurative orientation: This has both cognitive and evaluative aspects, is influenced by attitudes and reflection, and connects with cognitive purpose and processes of cognitive self-regulation. As a trait variable it takes enantiomers that define a *harmony orientation* and a *mastery orientation* (Sagiv and Schwartz, 2007). Mastery is monistic in nature and encourages active self-assertion to attain group or personal goals and to master, direct, and change the natural and social environment (values: ambition, success, daring, competence). Harmony is pluralistic in nature and tries to understand and appreciate rather than to direct or exploit. We could further relate this to appreciations driving goal formulation as a process that derives from data collection and involving the careful weighing of arguments as opposed to spontaneous decisions following from the spontaneous desires of the decision makers. This trait maintains an interconnected set of more or less tacit standards which order and value experience, determines the way an agency sees and values different situations, and how instrumental judgements are made and action is taken. The trait facilitates how an agency as a decision maker observes and interprets reality, and establishes decision imperatives about it. As such the trait regulates the appreciations and resulting goals of the organization with respect to its intended operations, the potential for social interaction, and the ethical positioning that may occur as a response to opportunities provided or indicated by the social environment. Efficacy in this trait in relation to the operative orientation trait can lead to self-principled agencies with aesthetical, intuitive, or ethical/ideological positioning. It can provide preferred ideological images that may facilitate action. It orientates the agency towards a view of stages of historical development, with respect to interaction with the external environment. In-efficacy can lead to corrupt and sociopathic organizations (Yolles, 2009a), or more broadly agency misconduct (Greve et al., 2010).

Operative orientation: This provides the ability of an agency to be able to durably maintain a separate operative existence while coping with unpredictable futures. As a trait variable it is able to take one of two enantiomers. These are *hierarchy* and *egalitarianism*. Hierarchy relies on hierarchical systems of ascribed roles to ensure productive behaviour (Sagiv and Schwartz, 2007: 179). Through hierarchy, people are socialized to take the hierarchical distribution of roles for granted and to comply with the obligations and rules attached to their roles. In hierarchical cultures, organizations are more likely to construct a chain of authority in which all are assigned well-defined roles. Members are expected to comply with role-obligations and to put the interests of the organization before their own. Hierarchy defines the unequal distribution of power, roles, and resources as legitimate (values: social power, authority, humility, wealth). In contrast, egalitarianism seeks to induce people to recognize one another as moral equals who share basic interests as human beings. People are socialized to internalize a commitment to co-operate and to feel concern for everyone's welfare. They are expected to act for others' benefit as a matter of choice (values: equality, social justice, responsibility, honesty). Egalitarian organizations are built on co-operative negotiation among employees and management (Sagiv & Schwartz, 2007: 180). Hierarchy is also consistent with the formulation of strong control measures to accrue funds that might develop through the supposition that austerity measures are needed that must be directed to easily objectively controlled parts of a system through processes of mass taxation, while egalitarianism would rather challenge this by pointing to the unequal distribution of tax collection according to resources and capacity to pay. Challenges from the social system may require flexibility in the application of these rules. This trait can represent a durable and distinct personality orientation that is able to cope with unpredictable futures. It structures appreciative information-enabling adaptation, and enables the personality to facilitate responses to its social environment and predefine its behavioural penchant towards its operations. Agency efficacy in relation to the social orientation trait may contribute to the realizing of its full social orientation potential, to engage with the environmental predictions that it controls, and adjust its own operative processes. In contrast, in-efficacy may result in an agency inadequacy that can impact on its operative intelligence or the recognition of agency adjustment imperatives. This may occur through self-regulation and either the subordination to hierarchy or liberation away from power and bureaucratic regulations, allowing normative rule obedience to be defined at a sub-agency level. The distinction between hierarchy and egalitarianism is reflected in considerations of information power. This is constituted as the disciplining of information, and its control through, among other things, socialization and division of labour (Boje, 2004).

Social orientation: This directs action, interaction, and reaction that (re) constitutes the cultural environment in terms of (desired, welcome, undesired, not welcome) activities, and it determines the orientation that a society has towards its environment. In a stable Sensate culture the trait may orientate the agency towards a Dramatist (individual relationships, sequential, communication, contracts, individualist, ideocentric) social orientation, while in a stable Ideational culture it assumes a Patterning (configurations, relational pattern, balance, collectivist, allocentric) type orientation, and in a stable Idealist culture it assumes a balanced Dramatist Patterning type orientation. This connection arises since dramatizing is object-dependent, while patterning is object-independent (Park, 2005: 16). Adopting these enantiomers requires that social orientation must be seen as innate symbolic behaviour, thus creating a potential for actual behaviour. It is hence a response to the personality figurative schemas that at least in part represent an object (or situation) of interest – rather than the object (or situation) itself. The object has been internalized as figurative schemas, and social orientation then responds to this as though a cognitive projection that acts as a substitute for the object. This implies that social orientation has its roots in the normative personality and it responds more to its proprietary schemas than those from others in the social environment. The theory that this depends on arises from studies of children at symbolic play (Shotwell et al., 1980; Park, 2005: 4) under the influence of culture (Lillard, 2002). The trait is ultimately responsible for the way in which policy, deriving from the operative system, can be implemented. It may also reflect forms of democratic or autocratic administration. It is also reflective of introversion – with its focus on the inner world of ideas and experiences, reflecting on thoughts, memories, and feelings (and reflective of Ideational culture), and extraversion – with its focus on the external world and participatory activities and actions within it (and reflective of Sensate culture). It is unclear what the specific correlating relationship is between introverted/extraverted personalities and Ideational/Sensate cultural orientation, though a connection does seem to be possible.

These traits and their enantiomer characteristics are summarized in Table 5.3, also listing keywords that arise with respect to the enantiomers. The traits are instrumental in control aspects of the agency; the cultural orientation trait acts to constrain personality through normative self-reference and identity. The figurative orientation trait is concerned with normative self-regulation, and the operative orientation trait is concerned with normative self-organization – while the two together constitute a first-order operative couple, one of these drives the other cybernetically. There is also a second

Table 5.3 *Summary of the traits and their bi-polar enantiomers for an agency*

Trait	Trait Enantiomer	Nature
Cultural	**Sensate (S^e)** Sensory. Pragmatic. Instrumental.	Reality is sensory and material, pragmatism is normal, there is an interest in becoming rather than being, and happiness is paramount. People are externally oriented and tend to be instrumental and empiricism is important.
	Ideational (I^d) Supersensory. Moral. Creation.	Reality is supersensory, morality is unconditional, tradition is of importance, there is a tendency towards creation and examination of self.
Cognitive	**Autonomy (A^u)** Autonomy. Uniqueness (heterogenistic). Independent. Self-development.	People seen as autonomous, bounded entities who should find meaning in their own uniqueness and who are encouraged to express their internal attributes (preferences, traits, feelings, and motives). Intellectual autonomy encourages individuals to pursue their own ideas and intellectual directions independently (important values: curiosity, broadmindedness, creativity). Affective autonomy encourages individuals to pursue affectively positive experience for themselves (values: pleasure, exciting life, varied life). Likely to treat others as independent actors with their own interests, preferences, abilities, and allegiances. Others need autonomy to self-develop own ideas.
	Embeddedness (E^m) Social relationships. Traditional (homogenistic). Status quo. Order. Solidarity.	People are viewed as entities embedded in the collective. Meaning in life comes through social relationships, identifying with the group, participating in its shared way of life, and striving towards its shared goals. Such values as social order, respect for tradition, security, and wisdom are especially important. Embedded cultures emphasize maintaining the status quo and restraining actions or inclinations that might disrupt in-group solidarity or the traditional order. Embrace responsibility and duty and commit to shared goals. Connected with Transactional scripting that constitutes simple repetition and sameness.

Figurative	**Mastery (M^a)** Self-assertion. Mastery Monistic.	Encourages active self-assertion to attain group or personal goals and to master, direct, and change the natural and social environment (values are: ambition, success, daring, competence). It is basically monistic in nature.
	Harmony (H^a) Understanding. Unity Pluralism.	Trying to understand and appreciate rather than to direct or exploit. This orientation emphasizes the goals 'unity with nature', 'protecting the environment', and 'world at peace'. It is basically pluralistic in nature.
Operative	**Hierarchy (H^i)** Hierarchic. Inequality (heterogenistic). Authority. Humility. Power.	People are socialized to take the hierarchical distribution of roles for granted and to comply with the obligations and rules attached to their roles. In hierarchical cultures, organizations are more likely to construct a chain of authority in which all are assigned well-defined roles. There is an expectation that individuals operate for the benefit of the social organization. Sees the unequal distribution of power, roles, and resources as legitimate (values are: social power, authority, humility, wealth). This has an implicit connection with power and power processes.
	Egalitarianism (E^g) Moral equality. Cooperation. Equality (homogenistic). Social justice. Responsibility. Honesty. Service.	Seeks to induce people to recognize one another as moral equals who share basic interests as human beings. People are socialized to internalize a commitment to co-operate and to feel concern for everyone's welfare. They are expected to act for others' benefit as a matter of choice (values: equality, social justice, responsibility, honesty). Organizations are built on co-operative negotiation among employees and management. This has an implicit connection with service to the collective.

Table 5.3 (cont.)

Trait	Trait Enantiomer	Nature
Social	**Dramatism (D^r)** Relationalist. Sequential. Communication. Contracts. Individualist. Ideocentric.	Individual relationships to others are important, constituted as sequences of interpersonal events. Communication is important, as are individuals and their proprietary belief systems, and individual social contracts. Goal formation should be for individual benefit. **Ideocentric collectives are important, operating through** social contracts between the rational wills of individual members.
	Patternism (P^a) Configurations. Relational. Pattern. Balance. Collectivist. Allocentric.	Configurations are important in social and other forms of relationships. There is persistent curiosity. The social is influenced by relationships with individuals. Some importance is attached to symmetry, pattern, balance, and the dynamics of relationships. Goal seeking should be for collective benefit, and collective goal formation takes precedence over personal goal formation. Allocentric collectives are important, where the members operate subjectively.

order figurative couple that links the operative couple with its cultural environment and involves identity and self-reference.

While cultural orientation of a governing body refers to its political culture, it is in itself influenced by the ambient host culture in which the agency is embedded. Social orientation is an extension of the agency personality that orientates it within the social environment that hosts it. Both cultural and social traits are therefore part of the agency personality environment, and both are able to represent changing contexts that influence personality.

Maruyama's Mindscapes as Agency Trait Types

While there are various ways to characterize personality, most are typologies that distinguish between different classes of individuals (Furnham, 1996). The exception to this is the mindscape theory of Maruyama. This represents personalities through one of at least four basic cognitive types or *epistemological meta-types* (Maruyama, 2001 & 1988).

Tung (1995) notes that for Maruyama (1993), mindscapes constitute epistemological structures that refer to the way in which people process and interpret information, and this is therefore a form of cognitive processing (e.g. Galavan, 2005). Maruyama identified four epistemological meta-types, *H* (hierarchical bureaucracy), *I* (independent prince), *S* (social revolutionary), and *G* (generative reformer) to differentiate agencies on the basis of logical processes and the way in which they analyse and synthesize information. These four epistemological types are claimed to account for nearly two-thirds of all peoples in the world (Maruyama, 1993). While the four epistemological types are universal, one mode tends to dominate in a given country. Consequently, Maruyama theorized that cultural differences arise from the way in which the epistemological meta-types evolve and become dominant in one country. These mindscapes provide a link between seemingly separate activities such as decision process, criteria of beauty, and choice of science theories. They do not line up on a single scale, nor do they fit in a two-by-two table. Mindscape theory is relational, rather than having a classificational typology, since its purpose and use 'lie in interrelating seemingly separate aspects of human activities such as organizational structure, policy formulation, decision process, architectural design, criteria of beauty, choice of theories, cosmology, etc.' (Maruyama, 1988:2).

Following Yolles & Fink (2012), mindscapes can be formulated through Sagiv–Schwartz traits as shown in Table 5.3. The strategic economic agency is shown in its three-dimensional space in Figure 5.2, though the additional two traits are symbolically indicated as arguments of each mindscape mode. Now, two mindscape modes that take leading institutional roles are *I* and *H*. These are very closely connected, Individualism and Collectivism, adopting the recognition that they are cognitive conditions that can be described through mindscapes.

Mindscape modes are responsible for the potential cognitive patterns that can and do arise, both in and across different cultures. This is clearly the case with the rise of, for instance, *I* or *H* modes and their respective connection with Individualism and Collectivism. Having said this, it should be noted that some of the attributes of these modes may change, as Oyserman, Coon, & Kemmelmeier (2002) note, the specific meanings of Individualism and Collectivism tend to change across cultures. Yolles & Fink (2014) have developed a more sophisticated form of mindscape theory that has eight types of mindsets, partly related to the four of Maruyama. However, there is not sufficient space here to explore these and the way in which they have been created and developed. As a final note here, individualism and collectivism (which are often confused as being politically right wing and left wing) should be seen as the result of trait value adherence. Such trait values in reality represent pathological orientations (as opposed to traits that balance extreme values), since each extreme necessarily ignores vital aspects that are part of the opposite view. As in our trait theory, Nozick (1977) notes that individualism and collectivism are positions that are unconnected with rational choice.

The mind-set values shown in Table 5.3 can give greater transparency to mindscape types (Yolles & Fink, 2014a, 2014b, 2014c). The Sagiv-Schwartz trait values can be compared with the Maruyama mindscape type values using an epistemic mapping technique. Combinations of trait values are created and epistemically compared to the given mindscape values. The result is given in Table 5.4. In Figure 5.2 the four mindscape types are located in corners of the two-dimensional trait space where question marks indicate that Maruyama had not found types with the respective value combinations and that further research is needed to characterize the missing value combinations.

5.3   Individualism and Collectivism

Tamis-LeMonda et al. (2007) recognize that Individualism and Collectivism are macroscopic overarching value systems, and agencies may adopt either value system according to the context in which they find themselves. Consistent with this, Yoon (2010) notes that culture affects individuals' political attitude and behaviour through cultural values and through perspectives of environments that facilitate thought and action, and are formed into agency orientations towards individualism or collectivism. Now individualism and collectivism are indicative of *I* and *H* mindscapes. It is not so simple as to say that a particular agency has embraced individualism or collectivism, since context is also important. Three distinct contexts are identified by Dockens (2012), who argues that agencies often shift the mindscape that they adopt

Table 5.4 *Nature of the Maruyama mindscapes*

Sagiv–Schwartz Mindscape	Nature
Hierarchical bureaucrat $H(E^m H^a H^i D^r T^d)$	Social relationships. Traditional. Status quo. Order. Solidarity. Understanding. Unity. Pluralism. Hierarchical. Inequality. Authority. Humility. Power. Relationalist. Sequential. Communication. Contractivist. Individualist. Ideocentric. Supersensory. Moral. Creation.
	Prone to Ideational collectivism.
Independent prince $I(A^u M^a E^g D^r S^e)$	Autonomy, Uniqueness, Independent, Self-development, Self-assertion, Mastery, Monistic,
	Moral equality. Cooperation. Equality (homogenistic). Social justice. Responsibility, Honesty. Service, Relationalist, Sequential.
	Prone to Sensate individualism.
Social reformer $S(A^u H^a E^g P^a S^e)$	Autonomy. Uniqueness. Independent. Self-development. Order. Understanding. Unity. Pluralism. Moral equality. Cooperation. Equality. Social justice. Responsibility. Honesty. Service. Configurations. Relational. Pattern. Balance. Collectivist. Allocentric. Sensory. Pragmatic. Instrumental.
	Prone to Sensate individualism.
Generative revolutionary $G(A^u H^a E^g P^a I^d)$	Autonomy. Uniqueness. Independent. Self-development. Understanding. Unity. Pluralism. Moral equality. Cooperation. Equality. Social justice. Responsibility. Honesty. Service. Configurations. Relational. Pattern. Balance. Collectivist. Allocentric. Supersensory. Creation.
	Prone to Ideational collectivism.

according to differentiable *public*, *private*, and *personal* contexts, these respectively related to Habermas' (1987) distinction between the *social, external, and internal* worlds that define our social reality.

Individualism and collectivism are very broad constructs. While integration of all values of a society into one bipolar dimension is seemingly 'parsimonious', the terms individualism and collectivism mean different things to different people. As a guiding position we may refer to Sagiv & Schwartz (2007), who present three constructs which are clearly related to 'Individualism': *Intellectual Autonomy* {broad-mindedness, freedom, creativity, security}, *Affective Autonomy* {exciting life, varied life, pleasure, enjoying life, self-indulgent}, *Mastery* {capable, successful, ambitious, independent, influential, social recognition, choosing own goals, daring}, and two others that are clearly related to 'Collectivism': *Harmony* {accept my portion in life, world at peace, protect environment, unity with nature, world of beauty}, and *Embeddedness* {polite, obedient, forgiving, respect tradition, self-discipline, moderate, social order, family security, protect my public image, national security, honour elders, reciprocation of favours}. There is also the construct of *Hierarchy*

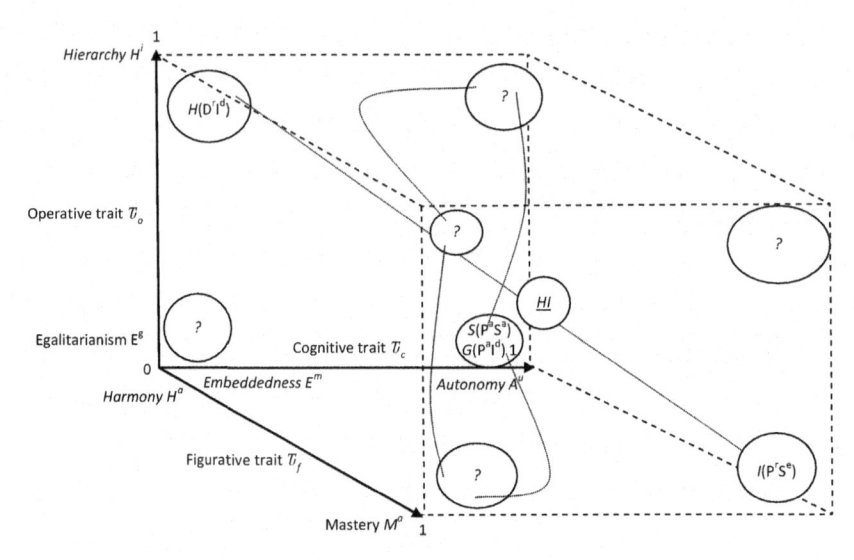

Figure 5.2 Distribution of strategic economic agency (normative personality) meta-types in a three-dimensional trait space, each displaying its cultural and social trait natures

{authority, wealth, social power}, which is opposed to *Egalitarianism* {loyal, equality, responsible, honest, social justice, helpful}, and it is unclear whether hierarchy or egalitarianism should be seen as orthogonal to, or linked with, individualism/collectivism. This is because hierarchy appears to have some correlation with both mastery and embeddedness. As such there are apparently some forms of hierarchy which are practiced by individualists, in particular in mastery-oriented society; and there are other forms of hierarchy which are practised by collectives, in particular in embeddedness-oriented societies. Similarly, egalitarianism may on the one hand refer to the ideal that all humans are equal beings and, thus, are intellectually free to say what they want, but on the other hand it could also mean that equality implies that everyone should get a reasonable share in available resources, irrespective of the individual contribution to achieving those resources.

Different authors give different weight to specific aspects of the 'value universe' and more often than not illustrate their perceptions of individualism and collectivism with 'two-word' constructs, like for instance *methodological individualism* versus *methodological institutionalism* (Davis, Marciano & Runde, 2004), or more common to politics, *transactional individualism* versus *relational collectivism* (Herrmann-Pillath, 2009; Tangen, 2009; Glasman et al., 2011; Yolles, 2009). However, we also find the use of the same term to describe different constructs, like conservative individualism as opposed to socialist (or collective) individualism or transactional individualism as opposed to relational collectivism. Both pairs depend on the ideological position of those who adopt the terms. Here, different weight may be given to the intellectual, spiritual, economic, or social aspects of 'individualism', or on the spiritual, intellectual, economic, or social aspects of 'equality', or on the right to enjoy individual achievements without boundaries or responsibilities to take care of other human beings and of natural resources.

There is necessarily a connection between economics and the social since it is the social that hosts economics, and without the host there would be no economics. The *methodological individualism* adopted in economics has an impact at the social level through the behaviour of individual persons (Frey & Benz, 2004). In methodological individualism not all human beings are considered to be isolated entities, their behaviour being perceived to be the result of interactions with their surroundings – other people and institutions.

This perspective might recognize that social groups are *complex* systems with dynamic interactive processes that result in the development of *systemic emergence* (Archer, 1982; Cohen & Stewart, 1994; Yolles, 2006) – where such emergence results in an autonomous social system having propriety properties. However, methodological individualism tends to assign little value or significance to this.

So, perspectives of methodological individualism differ fundamentally from theories in which collectives are emergent and act as autonomous units. This latter view embraces the more collectivistic *methodological institutionalism* which is concerned with the constructed sets of institutional rules that 'regulate' and 'stabilise' human behaviour, a view that is more consistent with notions of culture theory (e.g. Hofstede, 2001), where it is seen that it is through the development of cultural values and norms that collectives develop more or less uniform styles of perception and collective behaviours.

The recognition by Costanza et al. (1993) that the economic system is a subset of the cultural system is here of interest. The cultural system has a dynamic that is a result of the interaction between its coupled types, and hence these ultimately determine the orientation that an agency may have. It would be of interest, therefore, to be able to identify how this cultural orientation can impact on the cultural system, something that we shall return to in due course. However, if orientations exist within a cultural system, perhaps they also exist elsewhere, for instance in the economic system.

Some indication of this is provided by Davis, Marciano, & Runde, (2004:1), when they say: 'For some, economics is identified with individualism. But close examination of the underlying claims making such explanations raise a number of difficult philosophical issues...' They continue by noting that 'adherence to the principles of economic individualism and laissez-faire (cast in the natural law tradition) is a doctrinal and dogmatic commitment...' (Ibid., 2004: 10).

That such orientation exists in socio-cultural organizations is illustrated by Best & Widmaier (2006). They note that in recent decades there have been recurrent financial crises; an increasing gap between the rich and poor; and an intensified global debate concerning the appropriate responses to globalization. Yet, in the midst of this debate they suggest that 'tensions persist between economists' claims to apolitical value-neutrality and their often-passionate commitments to classically liberal ideals. From an ostensibly technocratic vantage, the legitimacy of institutions such as the International Monetary Fund and the World Bank has come to rest on their claim to the neutrality of expertise. Their various programs, whether emphasizing the importance of surveillance, conditionality, structural adjustment or technical assistance, have been presented as "tool kits" for states in need of guidance — value-neutral means to whatever ends a state determines. However, this claim to have divorced economics from any ethical biases coexists with a recurring resort to a classically liberal rhetoric that stresses the need to enhance the scope for individual choice and autonomy.... [consistent with the single political position of Individualism that results in] tensions between...liberal ethical principles and the continued claims of ethical neutrality?' (Best & Widmaier, 2006: 609).

Individualism is apparent elsewhere, as explained by Best & Widmaier (2006), when they note that it embraces the idea that the social world has no independent meaning outside the action of individuals, and micro-classical approaches consider the individual to be *responsible* for his or her own economic welfare. However, it is not only Individualism that is of interest, as noted by Yoon (2010) in reference to its conceptual opposite Collectivism. Individualism and Collectivism occur at two levels of analysis. Yoon, drawing on Schwartz (2004) and following Hofstede (2001: 215–216), distinguishes between these two levels: the *individual level* (with its history of little empirical inquiry), and the *cultural level* (with its history of significant empirical inquiry). The individual level supports multidimensional constructs (e.g. multiple key attributes and orthogonal classifications). At the cultural level there are unidimensional bi-polar constructs relating to cultural values, allowing analysis of how collectivistic or individualistic a nation is (e.g. ecological factor analysis based on the aggregate survey data). However, within such a unidimensional construct, multidimensional constructs can be discovered at a lower systemic level thereby allowing individual and cultural level analysis to be matched.

Most academics who write about *Individualism and Collectivism* appear to centre their studies on the individual level of analysis. At this level, Yoon (2010) notes that Triandis (Triandis et al., 1985; Triandis et al., 1988; Triandis, 1994) distinguishes between two attributes of personality that drive the view of individuals: allocentric personality attributes of collectivism where people operate subjectively, and idiocentric attributes of individualism where people operate through social contracts that develop through the rational wills of its individual members. Triandis also established the psychological study of Individualism and Collectivism, explaining how these cultural orientations affect the psychology of the individual (Hock 2002). Triandis (1995) largely speculated the implications of these cultural syndromes for politics in Individualism and Collectivism. Such an approach also enables a connection to be made between micropolitics and macropolitics; and recognises that culture (specified as Individualism and Collectivism) 'affects an individual's political attitude and behaviour as internalized values at the individual level and as "human-made" environments under which people think and act' (Almond & Verba, 1963: 32).

If particular penchants are apparent in supposedly neutral bodies like the International Monetary Fund and the World Bank, then we surely need to understand more fully what the terms Individualism and Collectivism actually mean. For Bandura (2006), Individualism is part of a duality with Collectivism that arises from the same value set. Tamis-LeMonda et al. (2007) also note that the duality is theoretically and empirically limiting. The two perspectives are culturally embedded and affect how people respond to the world (Shulruf, Hattie & Dixon, 2011), even though how they are manifested also depends on the contextual situation (Triandis, 1988). Oyserman, Coon, & Kemmelmeier (2002) explain Individualism as the doctrine that all social phenomena (their structure and potential to change) are in principle explicable only in terms of individuals – for instance their properties, goals, and beliefs. In contrast, Collectivism in principle and ideally relates to people coming together in a collective to act unitarily through normative processes in order to satisfy some commonly agreed and understood purpose or interest. Bodies that adopt Individualism and Collectivism have realities that are differently framed, and hence maintain ontologically distinct boundaries that constitute frames of reality, and these represent barriers for coherent meaningful mutual communications. While Collectivists are interested in society as such, Individualists deny that society may have any coherence beyond that of the individual, and in this sense Individualism and Collectivism are ontologically distinct.

For Individualism, reality frames the development goal of *autonomy/ independence* while Collectivism frames *relatedness/interdependence* (Tamis-LeMonda et al., 2007; Schartz, Luychx & Vignie, 2011). Individualism and Collectivism both embrace distinct cultural identities (from which organizational structures are a reflection) that are manifested within individuals as self-identity that impacts on basic motives for action (Earley & Gibson, 1998). Viskovatoff (1999) also notes that Individualism–Collectivism represents a dualism, and recognizes attempts to overcome it that:

(a) Adopt a post-structuralist approach (where, due to complexity in human systems, the reduction of things to simple structures is inadequate, and meanings are relative and subject to change);
(b) Recognize that reality should be seen as chaotic (and hence subject to chaos), disorganized, and fragmented (hence affecting the framing of development goals);
(c) View the social world in terms of the *decentred* subject (thus impacting on self-identity).

Collectivism and Individualism each have their own value ranges, but the boundaries between their differentiations can become merged. Thus, the notions of Toennies (1957), Triandis (1995, 2003) and White & Nakurama (2004) connect through *transactional* and *relational* forms of Collectivism (Yolles, 2009), where *Transactional Collectivism* is constituted as a boundary for Individualism. Thus, in a complex society in which the collective exists and operates politically through civil society, the form of individualism that is prevalent in Western societies is (a) *Transactional Individualism,* and the form of collectivism is (b) *Relational Collectivism.* Yolles (2009) has further claimed that the two orientations of Transactionalism and Relationalism constitute polar political forces that are in interaction with each other, and from which balances may emerge even temporally. He also creates definition for the bi-polar positions: in Transactionalism the collective is not seen to be separable from the individual, relationships to other individuals are important and must be honoured, individuals and their proprietary belief systems are important, individual social contracts are important, and goal formation should be for individual benefit and **ideocentricity**; in Relationalism the collective is a superior organic whole, the relationship to the whole is important and must be honoured, the whole is influenced by relationships with individuals and influence in relationships with particular collectives, goal seeking should be for collective benefit, collective goal formation takes precedence over personal goal formation, and allocentric collectives are important, where the members operate subjectively.

Considering that *Transactionalism* and *Relationalism* constitute an orientation towards others in a social environment, it is possible to reconsider them within the light of Shotwell et al. (1980), who were interested in the development of symbolization in children as they engaged in play. The significance of studying children is that they operate without the constructed fabric of a defensive social consciousness, and hence their basic cognitive information processes can be more easily inferred. Symbolic play is the ability to represent actual or imagined experiences through the combined use of objects, motions, and language that can develop into the building of structures, and as such, symbolization therefore has an impact on operative functionality. Two distinct polar styles of symbolization were defined: (a) *dramatists* and *(b) patterners*. Dramatists are interested in sequences of interpersonal events, having dramatic or narrative structures that are likely to involve distinction (e.g. the distinction of scenes or chapters), and undertaking effective communications. Patterners show strong interest and skill in configuration, deriving from persistent curiosity about the object world and how it works, how it is constructed and is named, varied, or explored. It is connected to problems of symmetry, pattern, balance, and the dynamics of relationships between entities. These bi-polar orientations can drive transactional and relational orientations, broadening their very basis. So linking these types with Transactionalism and Relationalism, we can now define Dramatism and Paternism as follows:

(1) *Transactional Dramatism* refers to individual relationships to others, constituted as sequences of controlled interpersonal events. Communication is important, as are individuals and their proprietary belief systems, and individual social contracts. Goal formation should be for individual benefit. Ideocentric collectives are important, operating through social contracts between the rational wills of its individual members.
(2) *Relational Patternism* refers to the importance of configurations of social and other relationships. The social is influenced by relationships with individuals. Some importance is attached to symmetry, pattern, balance, and the dynamics of relationships. Goal seeking should be for collective benefit, and collective goal formation takes precedence over personal goal formation. Allocentric collectives are important, where the members operate subjectively.

Returning again to Individualism, it can be considered in the same way as we have considered Collectivism. In doing this it might be useful to refer to Ron Allen[1], who relates forms of Individualism and Collectivism to the political right and left respectively. Thus he refers to political: (1) *Conservative Individualism*, which he argues is based upon (a) an unquestioned acceptance of the capitalist status quo which is concerned with competitive and possessive individualism, (b) the individual and their properties and needs, and (c) individual accomplishment/achievement. In contrast, (2) *Socialist Individualism* is defined as being concerned with the role of the individual to facilitate the collective, with respect, for instance, with the distribution of goods. Socialist Individualism may therefore more correctly be seen as a boundary form of Collectivism in which the role of the individual is represented.

Extending Allen's considerations, might it be the case that a universal connection can be made between Individualism and the political right, and

---

[1] Posted in 2003 at www.usenet.com/newsgroups/talk.politics.libertarian/msg08333.html, accessed July 2007.

Collectivism and the political left? If so then a logical problem arises. If, as indicated by Sorokin, Sensate culture is associated with Individualism and Ideational culture with Collectivism, then stable Sensate cultures will necessarily tend to embrace the political right while stable Ideational cultures will tend to embrace the political left. Now stable Idealistic culture (which is a precursor for stable Sensate culture: Sorokin, 1941, Vol. 4: 265), would need to be connected with a political balance point between Individualism and Collectivism. Such a balance does exist, and has been called *Collective Individualism* (Limerick & Cunnington, 1993), and this would need to embrace centre-ground politics. If such restriction on the political left, right, and centre are deemed unlikely, and it is taken that what constitutes the right and left are always universally well defined, then the only apparent way out of the dilemma is to suggest that the epistemological boundaries (and thus the very meaning) of what constitute Individualism and Collectivism are different under Sensate and Ideational cultures. This conforms to the realization that Sensate and Ideational normative epistemologies are different, and hence any frames of reference that are created during such stable periods will be different. This view can be supported by recognizing that the current epoch Individualism delivers *Transactional Dramatizing*, and Collectivism delivers *Relational Patterning*. As an extension of this argument, we also need to refer to unstable cultural periods, when political regimes are likely to oscillate between the right and the left.

The distinction between the *Dramatizing Political Right* and the *Patterning Political Left* leads to a consideration of their main opposing characteristics: (1) the *Dramatizing Political Right* tends to disavow the collective and its processes in favour of the individual, so that a phrase like 'there is no such thing as society' (voiced by a UK Conservative prime minister: see Thatcher, 1987 & 1987a) may not be a surprise, and where society's sacrificial lambs are those who do not have personal resources or capacity to make their individual lives sustainable to some level of personal dignity; and (2) the *Patterning Political Left* tends to disavow the individual and its human rights for the sake of the collective and the sustainability of its directing executive (World Report, 2012: China, 2012). The commonality between both extreme positions is always the potential abuse of the individual and its human rights.

While cultural type orientations are important to the political orientation of Individualism and Collectivism, Ball (2001) explains that the Individualist/ Collectivist orientation of a society will on one hand influence its course of economic development; on the other hand, economic growth and changes in economic structure will alter the orientation of the society towards Individualism/ Collectivism.

We have argued that durable collective bodies like societies or corporations adopt orientations that are Individualistic or Collectivistic. As such they have realities that are differently framed.

The durable collective may adopt an Individualist or Collectivist (cultural level) orientation, but individuals also do this. The connection between the collective and the individual is not only that the individual makes up the collective, but that the collective develops socio-cultural norms that derive from the population of individuals (Bandura, 2006; Yolles, 2009a). It is thus that the individual level of Individualism/Collectivism informs the cultural level. Tamis-LeMonda et al. (2008) are interested in the socialization of children by their parents, and note the dominating influence in this of Individualistic and Collectivist perspectives. Each of these perspectives operates through a set of traits that inform the socialization process. Tamis-LeMonda et al. are also interested in examining if and how this duality might *coexist* is some form of continuity. Exploring the behaviour of parents during the socialization of their children within changing contexts, they find that the Individualism–Collectivism duality is a dynamic: (i) coexistence of the two cultural value systems as forms of association change over time; (ii) that may be better viewed as conflicting, additive, or functionally dependent; (iii) the dual parts of which are individually dynamic, changing across situations, developmental over time, and being so in response to social, political, and economic contexts. The idea that the Individualism–Collectivism duality coexists and maintains a dynamic changing relationship implies that the dominant cultural set in a given situation should be seen as a variable that is sensitive to fluctuating contexts, and is contained within a single continuum which maintains characteristics that embrace both value sets. In their study of child socialization processes, Tamis-LeMonda et al. also note that the dynamic nature of the Individualism–Collectivist relationship implies discontinuities in parenting practices. This is consistent with work elsewhere (de Oliveira, Croson & Eckel, 2008; Hyldegård, 2009; Myers Briggs, 2000) in which, while the traits may be subject to continuous variation, they coalesce into only a few stable personality states that can result in particular modes of behaviour.

Parents emphasize individualistic attitudes when children's education should foster children's achievement orientation, but they emphasize collectivist attitudes and the long term aspect of social responsibility when care for elderly parents is an issue.

While the context of the Tamis-LeMonda et al. analysis relates specifically to the short-term individual processes of child socialization, it has a much broader implication when it comes to the group, as illustrated by other research. Taking a leaf out of personality theory and following Eysenck (1957), the orientations of Individualism and Collectivism may be seen as type conditions that arise from a trait, reflective of Sorokin's model of culture. The trait is able to change its representation for the group because of the principle of immanent change (Sorokin, 1962; Yolles, 2006; Yolles, 2009; Yolles, 2009b; Yolles, Fink & Dauber, 2011). During this, the types that each of the two subgroups hold may be in conflict and create a chaotic cultural environment, but for durable groups one condition develops where either one of the types achieves a stable dominance, or some form of stable balance between the two types may arise. Within this cultural continuum the ascendency of one type over the other may change periodically through immanent change. The duration of the period depends upon the size of the population (creating social momentum) associated with the affiliation (Yolles, Frieden & Kemp, 2008). Hence for the case of individual parents as considered by Tamis-LeMonda et al., periodicity may be indiscernible and fully dependent on changing situations, while in the case of Sorokin's study of civilizations, it may occur over generations.

In the current corporate paradigm the dominant cultural value set is Individualism, a view supported, for instance, by the economist Milton Friedman in his article in *The New York Times Magazine* in 1970. Thus in corporate environments, dealing with structures that are populated by individuals, and dealing with them as single instances from which derive a problematic issue, seems to dominate the diagnosis of organizational problems. However, Collectivism seems to be important too, as illustrated by Rosenhead (1998), who notes that one of the characteristics of the well-managed organization is that it has cohesive management teams. The main distinction between Collectivist and Individualist orientations in seeking the resolution of problematic issues is that in the case of the former, organizational culture is important, while in the latter it is organizational structures and individual roles and the search for individual responsibility and blame. Within this frame of reference, the fact that perhaps 90 per cent of all joint alliances fail due to lack of consideration of cultural factors (Kelly & Parker, 1997) is likely an illustration of the dominant Individualist corporate orientation.

As in Sorokin's sociocultural dynamics, the two polar value types of Individualism–Collectivism can result in an intermediate balance, thus implying that the trait to which they belong is a continuum, as highlighted by Limerick & Cunnington (1993). This balance point was earlier called *Collective Individualism*. It refers to network organizations in which a corporation may be seen to have a reality frame of reference that supports the development goal of *collaboration*. Here, individuals work together with others towards a common vision and mission, and their emancipation, their freedom from groups, organizations, and social institutions. The organization is also seen as a host for learning the development of shared values and beliefs among its participants. One of the features of Collective Individualism is shared value, and a process of decentring already referred to in relation to Viskovatoff (1999). From the cultural identity of Collective Individualism is manifested the self-identity of individuals that is referred to as *liminality* – a decentring that constitutes a threshold-like quality of the personality as people lose their group identity. This constitutes an emancipated identity defined not by the external agencies of social and institutional Individualist or Collectivist membership, but by self. Here, self is defined in terms of a number of characteristics within a corporate context, which include: (i) identity, where self is continuity; (ii) psychological contracts which are issue related; (iii) cultural values which include integrity, maturity, and field independence (perhaps implying empowerment); and (iv) processes which include negotiation, career responsibility of self, the traversing of many systems, and collaborating with others on issues.

For Bandura (2006), Individualism and Collectivism allow views to be taken that encompass territorial culturalism (as well as the more personal parochial interests), and drawing in their balance of Collective Individualism. This continuum establishes an orientation that creates partiality and more generally limits any capacity to undertake a balanced analysis, including that of sustainability. In concert with this, each of the value sets drives specific development goals that exclude the rise of alternatives that might be more suitable, especially under conditions of chaos when ontological boundaries and the related development goals may need to change. Bandura (2006) therefore looks towards an alternative that does simply not lie on the Individualism–Collectivism continuum. In doing this he proposes that a broader view needs to be taken that is directed towards human development, adaptation, and change, and this can provide guiding principles and the creation of innovative practice in complex situations, and assist with creating sustainability.

An illustration of this lies in the Western economic crisis that emerged in 2007/8. This is perceived differently by Individualists and Collectivists. In a Sensate culture, and in particular in countries where the rule of law has value and is not a political football, Individualism has a transactional *dramatist* nature that adopts a rule-based control approach intended to resolve the crisis through a policy of social austerity. In resolving the debt crisis, society is seen as an object of attention, and as such is simply regarded as a financial source that needs to be drained in order to balance debt. The Greek situation in this crisis has been representative of how bad things can get for individual and social development (Humphries, 2012), resulting in severe individual hardship and the endangerment of economic sustainability to a level of dignity in a large proportion of the economically disadvantaged society. Under the same conditions of rule of law, the Collectivist alternative is relational *patterning*, operating through a policy of relational growth stimulation, where the state facilitates the encouragement of enterprise, ignoring the indebtedness, and assuming that the economic system will self-adjust. The balance point between Individualism and Collectivism is Collective Individualism, a midway compromise in which austerity and stimulation are parallel policy options. However, neither of these policy options responds to the concerns of Bandura (2006), who seeks analysis and diagnosis devoid of territorial culturalism and parochial interests. Such a 'proper' analysis seems rarely to enter into any political framework. Noting the apparently corrupt nature of Western banks referred to in the introduction of this book, such an analysis and diagnosis might lead in an unexpected direction, for instance by redefining of the social nature and role of banks. It is likely such a development is consistent with the need for an economic paradigm shift, as described by Dolphin & Nash (2011).

5.4   Some Thoughts

There is an argument that distinguishing Individualism and Collectivism as the only alternatives to political and economic decision-making policy may be inadequate, even if balanced positions are found. Shalom Schwartz (1992, 1994) was interested in moving away from such a dichotomous perspective in favour of a broader cultural perspective, and developed his 'Schwartz Value Inventory' based on a survey of 60,000 respondents. Its intention was to identify common values that act as guiding life principles, and which lie beyond the relatively simple notions of Individualism and Collectivism. In doing so he identified ten 'value types' that gather multiple values into a single category.

These Schwartz value types create orientations that determine the nature of an agency and enable them to be related to mindscapes. It is interesting, therefore, that this study, when formulated within the context of Maruyama's mindscapes, takes us back to variations of Individualism and Collectivism. Within a political context these personality types may incorrectly be represented as right and left wing political classifications. While agency orientations can tend towards either extreme Individualism or Collectivism, they may also take a balance between them. However, where these perspectives (or variations between the extreme values) take a particular political orientation, proper understanding of the complex problematic situations may be lost due to assumptions buried in the political position.

We can elaborate on this further in respect of extreme value personality positioning. When agencies adopt a political orientation towards extreme Individualism or Collectivism, they normally do not realize that they are living a pathology that causes psychosis which, in some cases, could promote sociopathic personalities. Psychosis, as explained, for instance, by Laurent (2007: 116), is a condition of certainty and delusion where everything can be explained according to an order of reason, and which gives rise to the adage *the madman has lost everything but reason*. But can one identify psychosis simply? Perhaps a suspicion of psychosis arises from the form of speech, where third person pronouns are used to refer to self (Van Staden & Fulford, 2004; Weiland & Legg, 1964). Perhaps also this can be illustrated with Margaret Thatcher, the UK prime minister in the 1980s, who is thought of as an extreme individualist (Sutcliffe-Braithwaite, 2013; Brand, 2013). She publically used the third person singular to refer to herself when she said 'The lady's not for turning' (Thatcher, 1980). If this is true, even where a single example does not generate a general condition, it would be consistent with the view that extreme political positioning also embraces psychosis.

6 Agency Consciousness

6.1 Introduction

A living system agency is represented through a meta-theory of *substructure*, constructed through a *generic system hierarchy*. The substructure has various dynamic properties that include autonomy and a potential for viability through adaptability. It can maintain a *superstructure* that conceptually enriches it, and an example is personality. This is detailed through a cognitive-affective landscape that creates orientations, houses consciousness and awareness, and constitutes strategic agency. One of its functions is to deliver a potential for behaviour that is influenced by that landscape. So, consciousness, personality, and behaviour are all closely tied together.

Plural agency behaviour is *structure determined* because its structure inherently determines patterns of possible behaviour, including a range of possible responses or reactions to both external (environmental) and internal (immanent) influences. Primary interest here lies in internal influences that are the result of processes that derive from interactions between the sub-agencies that compose the cultural agency. Immanent dynamics are a function of processes of internalization, where an agency observes its environment and, in an attempt to understand it, internalizes conceptualizations that become represented in consciousness. This internalization is perspective dependent and may occur through perception or apperception (interpretative observation). The representations occur through cognitive images/schemas. Sometimes, how one sees the world is transformed through consciousness elaboration, thereby generating improved understanding of issues being faced in an environment. This can give improved decision-making abilities concerning potential action. When this occurs, we say that *undecidability* has been reduced since new ways of explaining problematic issues emerge that facilitate improved decision making.

6.2 Undecidability and Generic System Hierarchies

Cultural agencies exist in context-related complex changing situations to which they have an adaptive potential. Consider that such situations have a set of unclear issues that require resolution. Appropriate interventions for issue resolutions are undecidable because outcomes are non-deterministic. Since knowledge about issues, their conditions, and the formulation of responsive constructs may be uncertain or unknown, the provision of higher order explanations, if they can be found, can provide resolution by reducing uncertainty.

An illustration is the concept of *cultural intelligence* (Earley & Ang, 2003), which explains resolutions for problematic cross-cultural issues that arise due to a multiplicity of values/beliefs within culturally pluralistic agencies. This term is used to explain the ability of an agency to successfully adapt to a change in cross-cultural settings. It recognizes the existence of ethnocentricity, where those in a given culture are resistant to any movement from their substantive existent values and beliefs (Triandis, 1990). It also provides guidance for overcoming cross-cultural issues (Triandis, 2006). For Seed & Tomasello (2010), cultural intelligence is responsible for perspective shifting during collective interaction and communication through processes of internalization, thereby facilitating internal symbolic cognitive representations. For Priddy (1999), these representations are constituted as dynamic schemas. This impacts creatively on how given situations may be construed where they relate to different purposes. It may further be noted that cultural intelligence implies a strong orientation towards adaptation, that is, in relation to the feedback processes of our agency model. There is no comparably strong emphasis on action orientation, that is, the feed-forward processes of our model. However, our related concept of cultural figurative intelligence does not have the same orientation.

Reduction in uncertainty is an interest of living system agencies since this improves their viability in given contexts. They do this through anticipation (Rosen, 1985) by creating strategic models that determine potentials for behaviour. Such models require environmental conditions to be determined through the use of strategic techniques like environmental scanning. However, adapting a concept from Dubois (2000), strategic modelling anticipation is subsidiary to substructural anticipation. This is because substructural formative processes (which can establish an agency's status as a living system) directly influence agency patterns of behaviour and viability.

Undecidability is thus a basic attribute of agencies. It has been discussed by Boxer and Cohen (2000: 21) in terms of adaptability, where an agency is capable of 'successfully adapting to its environment by tracing out *trajectories* through a space of agency theories via successive elaborations of its articulations.' For them, *undecidability* refers to multiple possible elaborations of agency articulations, each of which induces mutually inconsistent closures within which to anticipate. The nature of closure, according to van de Vijver (1999), is that it provides stability, giving protection from colonizing stimuli, leaving openness to new potentially meaningful stimuli, and providing a context from which to interpret surroundings.

The idea of undecidability has developed through a number of perspectives. It was discussed by Gödel (1931) in his development of *formal theory*, where it refers to statements in a formal system (with its operative rules) which cannot be refuted or proved from within the system. In *cybernetics* (Beer, 1975; Boxer & Cohen, 2000), it refers to a higher order system (e.g. a metasystem with its meta-language and meta-rules) that is able to resolve undecidabilities and influences adaptation (since the metasystem is not strictly speaking part of the system but rather its observing supersystem). In *organization theory* (Seidl, 2003: 21) undecidability occurs in relation to behaviour, and deference is made to meta-rules in complex decision-making processes where decision options have similar value. In *learning theory* (Wertsch, 1979), higher or deeper levels of conscious symbolic thought arise through processes of internalization that may *enrich* (Williams & Imam, 2006) situational explanation by cognitively elaborating on and transcending what has been observed, just as it may *reduce* this through limiting options, for example, by identifying some options as non-legitimate and by that bounding the available repertoire of behaviours.

The systemic meta-level therefore has an important place in responding to undecidability. Every system may have a meta-level system, and each meta-level may be seen as a (higher order generic) system in its own right. This leads to the concept of the generic system hierarchy: where higher order meta-level systems each have their unique way of bounding undecidability and assisting adaptation through complex decision-making, resulting from contextual internalizations. These internalizations can result in deeper levels of consciousness, partly *enriched* by higher order situational explanation, that have the capacity to condense complexity into understandable concepts.

Looking more generally at generic system hierarchies, they may be seen to be connected to the more traditional idea of the *system hierarchy* (see for instance, Bahm, 1981). In system hierarchies, systems are seen in terms of their particular behavioural functionalities (their properties or specific things they do), have both imposed and emergent causation, and can indicate transactional relationships. System functionality is conditioned by the properties and relationships between the parts that compose a system, as well as the functional relations it has to other systems in its environment. This explains the mutual conditioning between a system and its environment.

In contrast, generic system hierarchies express both imposed and emergent causation in terms of *generic* functionality (i.e. the *classes* or *types* of things they do), for instance by differentiating between cognitive processes and physical behaviour. It is structured through an axiomatic substructure that distinguishes between ontological hierarchical distinctions each with a class of functionality, interconnected through transitive networks of processes. In contrast, superstructure modelling enables commensurable theoretical appendages to be added. These facilitate the explanation of complex detail that may include system hierarchies. Such hierarchies entail principles of living systems through their network of processes.

6.3 Substructure Modelling

Following Yolles & Fink (2015a, 2015b, 2015c), one can distinguish between at least five substructural agency models that can increasingly represent higher levels of complexity with higher generic orders of type system, and where undecidability is increasingly bounded. In the following we shall deal with the instrumental agency, the cognitive-affective agency, the defining socio-cultural agency, and an illustration of superstructure modelling.

The Instrumental Agency

As discussed in Chapter 2, the instrumental agency is really a misnomer in that it is a pre-living-system, and it is only legitimate to introduce it formally into agency theory since it provides an entry point to generic systems hierarchies. This is in contrast to the living system, which, while being able to respond to situations instrumentally, also has the capacity to learn, thereby creating novelty. As an elementary substructural model, the instrumental agency has a generic class of metasystem functionality which is limited to the holding of cognitive schemas and decision making. This is connected with an operative system from which behaviour stems. These are connected by autopoietic operative intelligence (Figure 6.1), as explained by Yolles (2009). This allows for the production of cognitive/psychic structures and behaviour, from cognitive networks, and networks of structured information and misinformation. It also establishes a substructural autopoietic dialogue that is a reflection of an

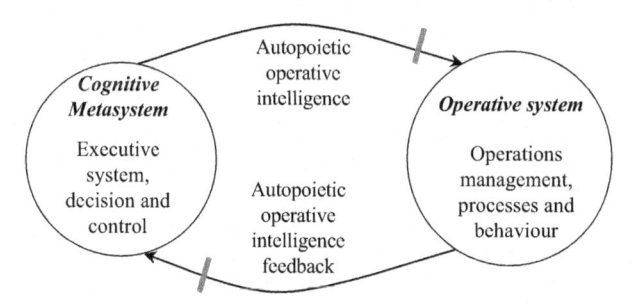

Figure 6.1 Agency with a single cognitive metasystem, which controls its operative system, showing potential generic pathologies as bars across operative intelligence (including feedback)

agency capacity to reflect decision models schemas phenomenally. Regeneration of the relational networks through agency behaviour is influenced by: (a) motivational pressures satisfying cognitive need (like rituals, power, honour, and money), (b) social/environmental pressures.

Specified as an instrumental couple, Figure 6.1 does not permit higher order attributes like learning by knowledge acquisition, but it is rather a strategic regulating couple. This leads to a problem with existing theory in cybernetics. Glanville (2004) explains that there are two classes of what we call generic hierarchy in cybernetics, first and second order. The former is the cybernetics of observed systems, and the latter is the cybernetics of observing systems. This distinction is shown in Figure 6.1:

(1) The observed system is the operative system, which taken alone (where the bars constitute potentially isolating pathologies) constitutes first order cybernetics that is only concerned with the way operative system function, perhaps in interaction with others.
(2) The cognitive system is an observing system of the operative system, with the link between them being represented by Piagetian regulatory operative intelligence. As such, it should in principle constitute second order cybernetics.

Following von Glasersfeld (1984), second order cybernetic systems are deemed to be knowledge-based learning systems implicitly reflective of Piagetian theory, this necessarily in principle involving figurative intelligence. This leads to the recognition of a contradiction in the instrumental agency: the cognitive system is an observing system and so must be able to learn figuratively, but it only regulates. This dilemma can be understood (Yolles & Fink, 2015b) by recognizing that Figure 6.1 has as its origin Schwarz's paradigm of viable systems, while second-order cybernetics arises from Beer's (1972, 1975, 1979) paradigm of management cybernetics. The anomaly can be resolved by proposing that there is a distinction between a formal instrumental couple as indicated in Figure 6.1, and an informal generalized couple in which the cognitive metasystem allows inherent extensions with implied learning processes. Formally, such learning arises from higher generic orders like the cultural agency, but if we can regard the cognitive system to inherently embrace higher generic orders that facilitate figurative learning, we informally extend the instrumental agency.

Showing autopoiesis as a network of processes in Figure 6.1 is a feature of Schwarz's theory of viable systems, but it cannot be so represented in Beer's management cybernetics. It is a network of processes that transitively connect two generic classes of system. It may be seen as a network of processes that manifest strategic content of the metasystem (like goals, ideology, ethics, and self-schemas) operatively. This network is otherwise referred to as operative intelligence, and functions with some degree of efficacy. With limitations in efficacy come deficiencies in the quality of operative intelligence. This may occur because of communication or process inadequacies, when transitive pathologies arise as indicated by the bars on the intelligences Figure 6.1.

The introduction of the generic higher order metasystem reduces undecidability by explaining the instrumental control behaviour of the operative system. The nature of instrumentality is that the strategic elements of the metasystem, like goals and self-schemas, are manifested operatively by the autopoietic operative intelligence, and feedback from the operative system creates imperatives for either further development or retrenchment. Generic pathologies indicated as bars across the networks of processes limit the instrumental capacity of the agency, making it less effective in responding to change.

Understanding the regulatory interaction between the system and metasystem can enrich action explanations and bound undecidability. Agency thus has a structured operative system that generates interactive behaviour with others, with transitive feedback as a generic set of learning loops (with generic pathologies).

The Cultural/Cognitive-Affective Agency

The cultural/cognitive-affective agency is classed as a living system (Figure 6.2) since it has both instrumentality and learning. The cultural/cognitive system of this agency enables the creation of novelty and provides a stability anchor for the agency. Culture is a collective attribute of the living system involving cultural knowledge and cognitive and behavioural norms. It has a collective personality, and cognition-affect becomes the driver through which cognitive-affective attitudes are established and maintained, influencing the strategic nature of the agency. While cognition relates to thinking and rationality, affect relates to emotion (Figures 6.3 and 6.4).

Cognitive-affective agencies are classed as living systems since they possess both instrumentality and learning. Their instrumentality occurs as figurative schemas are manifested as operative schema potentials, while learning occurs with novel attitudes and conceptual information as inputs to cognitive schemas (Figure 2.10) from mental disposition migrated from the cultural system.

Cognitive and affective dimensions are intimately related since cognition and emotion control each other when agency consciousness can become modified. Both necessarily operate with autogenetic figurative and autopoietic operative intelligence (Yolles, Fink & Dauber, 2011). The introduction of figurative intelligence demonstrates that a double-loop of generic learning (with generic pathologies potential) occurs, as well as feedback that delivers imperatives to the cognitive system. Where this system creates information-based attitudes

180   The Agency

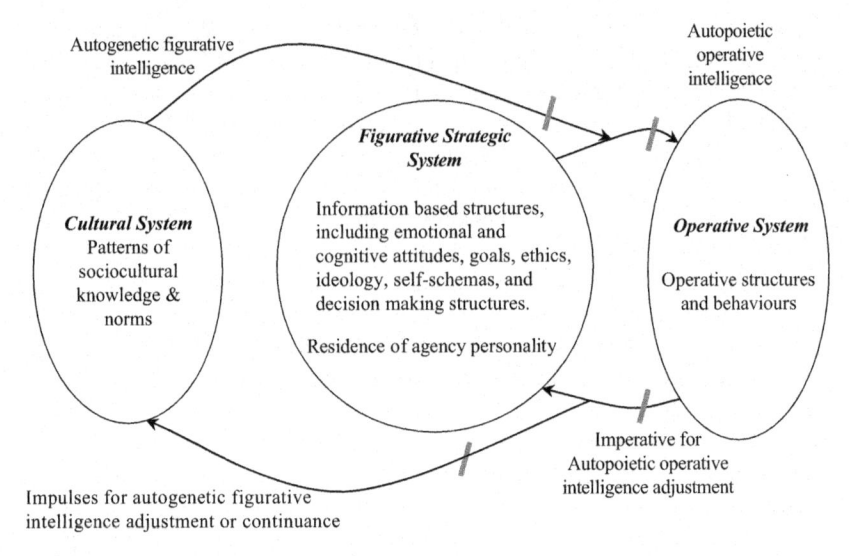

Figure 6.2 Core concept for the Cultural Agency

(emotional attitude in the affective agency and cognitive attitude in the cognitive agency), patterns of (emotional or cognitive) information are accumulated that enable the agency to respond to a known context determined by an understanding of the environment. More broadly, figurative intelligence establishes patterns of social elaboration that can be used to project identity. In the cognitive personality, the knowledge is constituted as patterned coherence in information gathering. The nature of figurative intelligence may be extended to include the metacoupling that occurs between cognitive being and the autopoietic dialogue. It is responsible for the influence that is created by the network of cognitive principles that define 'I' and result in the agent's own rules of production. Figurative intelligence involves the metacoupling between the autopoietic dialogue (operative intelligence) and the cognitive outcome of the dialogue. Personality creation, regeneration, evolution, or cognitive transformation can continuously develop, affecting figurative and operative intelligence.

The Defining (Socio-Cultural) Agency

The model of Figure 6.3 may be elaborated through the introduction of higher generic orders of metasystem. The explanation for such elaboration of the core model comes from Wertsch (1979), as he explains the Vygotsky School of learning. Two propositions are: (a) agencies are always directed towards an object or motive; (b) internalization of the external environment has an important function – activity motivated by a goal is mediated by physical and

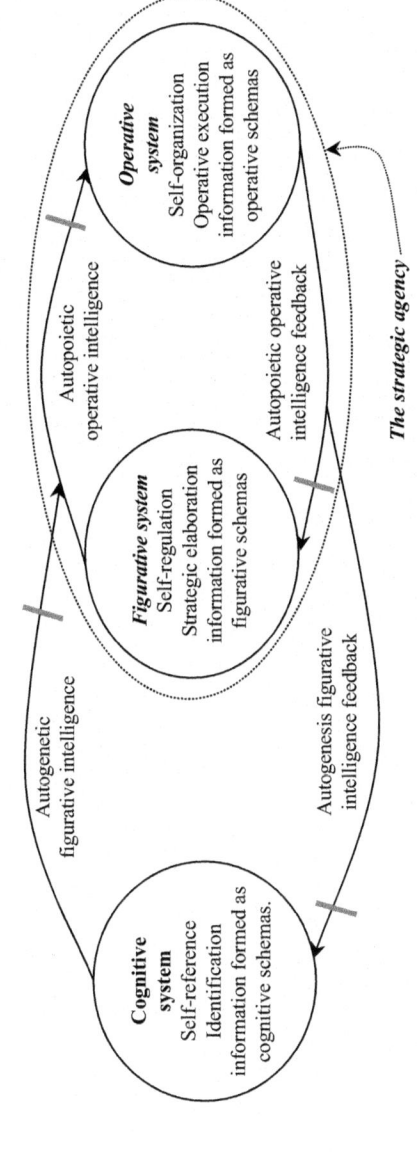

Figure 6.3 The Cognitive Agency with a knowledge creating cognitive system and instrumental figurative system, illustrating generic pathologies

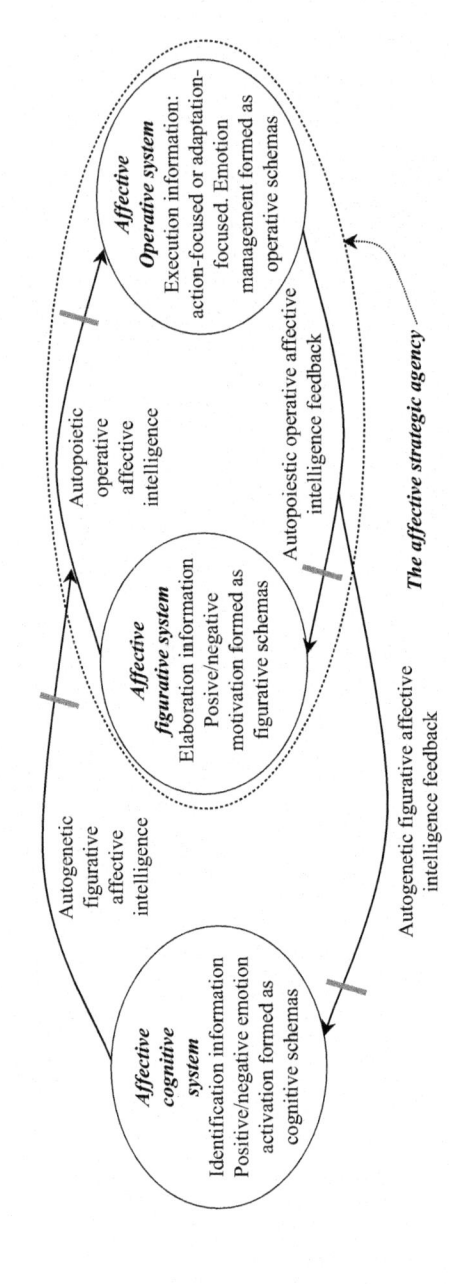

Figure 6.4 The Affective Agency indicating the role of emotions in the agency, and their connection with the cognitive agency

psychological tools (including language) that allow and lead to the creation of types of activities that otherwise would not exist. These instrumental activities have at their basis the values, behaviours, and opinions that they encounter. Deci & Ryan (2009) note that agencies maintain a natural tendency to take these in. For Verenikina and Gould (1998), internalization is the transition in which external processes with external material objects are transformed into processes that take place mentally at the level of consciousness. During this transition these processes become generalized, verbalized, and abbreviated; importantly, they also become the means for further development and transcend what is possible with external activity. For Wertsch (1979), it is through external motivational social activities that a plane of consciousness emerges. This links with Lucas' (2002) exploration of plural levels of cognitive consciousness. It offers an explanation for the ontological emergence of higher generic orders of the agency and of the recognition that consciousness may be seen as a social phenomenon (Shanon, 1993; Praetorius, 2000). This explanation highlights why it is possible to legitimately propose any number of higher generic orders of metasystem that lie beyond the core agency model. Such higher orders provide greater facility for the further bounding of undecidability, and as we shall explain in due course, may also provide social facility for social science paradigm shifts.

In the elaborated agency model shown in Figure 6.5 there is a self-identification system involving a higher level of consciousness. It is connected to the lower generic order through a network of higher order processes that we have called autogenetetic defining intelligence. Autogenetesis comes from the word *genetic* meaning 'relating to or determined by the origin, development, or causal antecedents of something'. So it refers to a self-defining network and triple generic learning loop of simplex processes. This defining system is often associated with knowledge creation. This agency generic system hierarchy constitutes a fourth order agency model with generic triple-loop learning (and generic pathologies as indicated by the grey bars in Figure 6.5).

Following Yolles & Fink (2015c), autogenetic defining intelligence can also be referred to as cultural intelligence where the context of the model is socio-culture, and this relationship is shown in Figure 6.6. Where feedback occurs, we have a first-order system. Here, however, there is an implied *instrumental agency* with a second-order generic hierarchy (operative intelligence plus feedback), and a cognitive agency with third-order generic hierarchy (operative and figurative intelligence plus feedback). Consistent with the explanation of Verenikina and Gould (1998), higher orders can be argued to arise as deeper levels of social consciousness for the individual agency. This is also the case with cultural agency with its indicative cultural intelligence. The latter is a social learning model that occurs through the network of feed-forward and

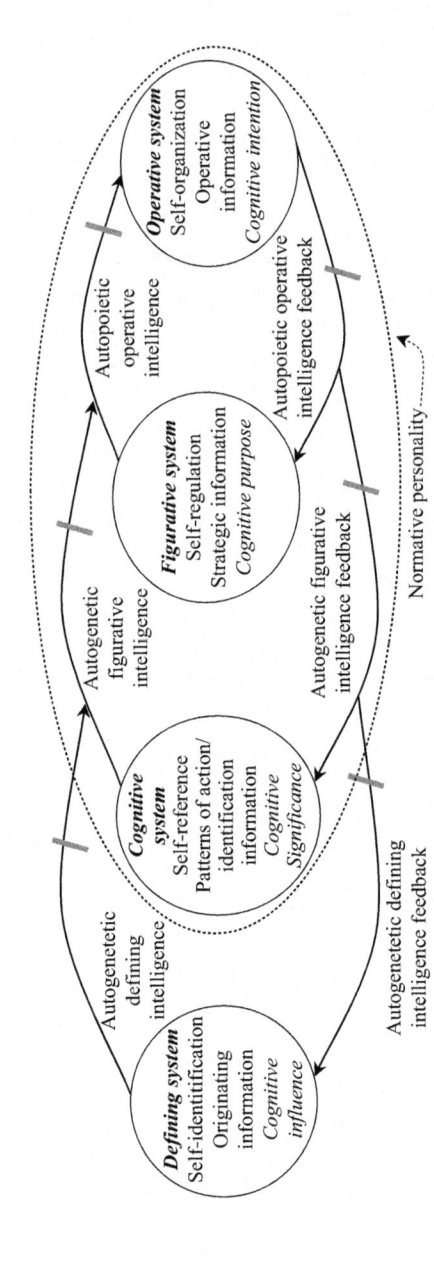

Figure 6.5 The Defining Plural Agency, with new generic autogenetesis (self-defining), showing generic triple-loop learning (with generic pathologies) and feedback

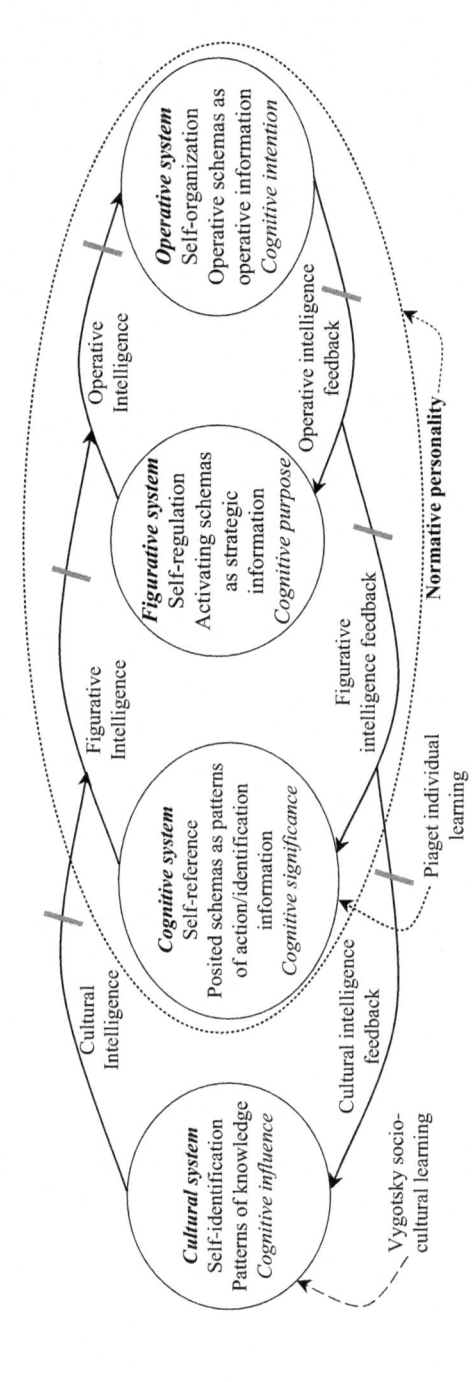

Figure 6.6 Learning theory terminology permits seeing the Defining Agency as a Cultural or Socio-Cultural Agency

feedback processes. Figure 6.6 allows one to distinguish between two types of knowledge: idiosyncratic knowledge that is created by and belongs to the individual in the sense of Piaget (1950) that is socially provisional since it is awaiting social confirmation, and social knowledge in the sense of the Vygotsky School (Wertsch, 1979) that allows us to establish paradigms that influence how we collectively perceive, operate, and behave.

At this stage it is worth noting that the generic system hierarchy is able to maintain agency stability. Let us explore this briefly in relation to Figure 6.6 in a way that is a reflection of Yolles & Fink (2014). Each system in Figure 6.6 is subject to conditions of stability. Thus, the cultural system creates a stabilizing anchor for the personality. Similarly, the cognitive system creates a personality anchor. Instability in the cultural system will leave the personality without any stabilizing influence, which it will have to create itself, resulting in attributes that may not be context relevant. Similarly, cognitive system instability will leave the instrumental dimension of the personality without any influencing stability, and it will have to try to generate stability by itself. When the agency is not culturally anchored it is incapable to creating knowledge-based novelty, thus limiting the degree of personality cognitive schema novelty, that is, by limiting the capacity to alter dispositional attitudes and information. Where the personality is not anchored by its cognitive system it is not able to create cognitive schema novelty.

These systems are all connected together through intelligences, which become epistemically useful when issues of complexity require resolution. This occurs incidentally by creating increasingly stronger bounds on undecidability. These intelligences exist by virtue of the higher order generic states and may be defined as follows:

- Operative intelligence consists of a *network of first-order processes* that manifests significant figurative information operatively, but also creates improvement imperatives to adjust figurative schemas. On its own this creates instrumental forms of adaptation.
- Figurative intelligence projects conceptual information to the instrumental agency through a *network of second-order processes*, allowing novel forms of adaptation to occur.
- Cultural Intelligence projects socio-cultural information to the cognitive (and by implication its related affective) agency through a *network of third-order processes*, directing it and offering the option to adapt to change in socially acceptable ways while at the same time having an ability to function efficiently under cultural diversity.
- Feedback for each of the intelligences provides living system control capacity at different generic orders, which may include imperatives for change or continuance.

Table 6.1 *Literature support for paradigm shifts of different agency intelligences*

Generic Network	Paradigm Shift	Literature
Autopoiesis	Yes	Li, Clark & Winchester (2010)
Autogenesis	Perhaps	Schwalbe & Schwalbe (1991), Paecht-Horowitz (1973), Csányi & Kampis (1985), Drazin & Sandelands (1992)
Autogenetesis	Not yet indicated	New concept, no publications so far
Learning Theory Network		
Operative intelligence	Yes	
Figurative intelligence	Yes	DeVries (1991)
Cultural intelligence	Yes	Seed & Tomasello (2010), Chen, Liu & Portnoy (2012), Blum (2009)

Where they provide entry points to tightening the bounds on undecidability and hence more effectively responding to unanswered questions, their application can be seen to cause a paradigm shift – that is, new ways of seeing and explaining complexity. This is illustrated in Table 6.1. To explain this table, the generic learning loops of autopoiesis, autogenesis and autogenetesis constitute a basis for a family of paradigm shifts since each offers new ways-of-seeing. There is support in the literature that this happens. In particular, autopoiesis has caused a paradigm shift (e.g. Li, Clark & Winchester, 2010). There is no clear view that autogenesis constitutes a paradigm shift (Schwalbe & Schwalbe, 1991), probably because of the lack of agreement concerning its nature (Paecht-Horowitz, M., 1973; Csányi & Kampis, 1985; Drazin & Sandelands, 1992). However, the functional equivalents to autopoeisis/autogenesis, defined as Piaget's operative/figurative intelligences, *have* constituted a paradigm shift (DeVries, 1991).

The concept of *autogenetesis* is a new and unsupported term that requires a little closer examination. Through recursive modelling and the use of Piaget's (1950) intelligences, autogenetesis takes the contextually sensitive name *cultural figurative intelligence*. So has this triple level generic learning loop the potential to generate a family of paradigms creating greater simplicity in complexity?

At this point it is useful to reflect again on Vygotsky's third level network of processes. There appears to be no clear generic learning loop that facilitates the indicated social learning process. If we assign this social constructivist process to the cultural environment, then we can similarly identify cultural figurative intelligence as the network of processes that facilitates this level of learning. While there is no place to pursue this here, it would be interesting to further explore this.

A reduced form of cultural figurative intelligence is called *cultural intelligence* (Earley and Ang, 2003: 3; Thamas & Inkson, 2009), referred to earlier. For Ang, Van Dyne, & Tan (2011) this offers an agency the ability to adapt to different cultural frames and the ability to function efficiently under cultural diversity. If *cultural intelligence* is a basis of a new family of paradigms, then so is cultural figurative intelligence. With 'cultural figurative intelligence' we go beyond cultural intelligence at large, and introduce a strategic concept that complements adaptation. Thus, cultural figurative intelligence may be concerned with design of creative strategies to influence values and beliefs in a cross-cultural environment. So, for instance, strategic attempts to induce cultural change may help to reduce murder rates in some national contexts, or reduce the incidence of rape in places like India.

Cultural intelligence was introduced by Earley & Ang (2003) and conceived during a period of unprecedented globalization and interconnectedness (Held, et al., 1999). According to Ionescu (1975) this represents an increasingly complex *centrifugal society*. However, the attendant increase in intercultural interactions enhances the probability of cultural misunderstandings, tensions, and conflicts (Ang, Van Dyne & Tan, 2011). The concept of cultural intelligence can now provide compressed explanations for resolving such situations, thus creating a simpler view of complexity and *contributing to* the rise of new paradigms (Seed & Tomasello, 2010; Chen, Liu & Portnoy, 2012). For Blum (2009), the multiple cultural perspectives highlighted by cultural intelligence *do* constitute a paradigm shift. However, support for this construct as the basis of new paradigms may take time to materialize social support, and may currently rather be a 'virtual paradigm' (Yolles, 1999) on the way to become a paradigm.

There is another form of intelligence that we have not referred to, and which has some importance: behavioural. This may be defined as an agency's capability to function effectively in phenomenal situations characterized by diversity. It does this with a behavioural efficacy: *a task-specific potency that refers to general effectiveness across multiple tasks in a complex behavioural environment.* Behavioural intelligence in particular occurs as a 'structural coupling' (Maturana & Varela, 1987) that represents interaction between two (or more) living system agencies in a plural environment, and which have had a past and future historical relationship. One of the manifestations of behavioural intelligence is social intelligence, which is used to orient interaction with others in a social environment.

6.4   Illustration of Superstructure Modelling

We have explained that given a generic substructure it is possible to elaborate a model with theoretical superstructure accoutrements. These provide conceptual detail which may be migrated from other paradigms as long as this migration process resolves any potential theoretical incommensurability.

An illustration of theoretical accoutrement can be provided by populating a third-order generic system hierarchy substructure with a superstructure of paradigm concepts was given in Figure 2.10. A paradigm is basically a cognitive map carried by a durable autonomous 'living' purposeful and adaptive human activity group that has a culture and normative operative processes; and a representation of the organization which creates an imperative towards collective behaviour. A change in the organization is always represented by a change in its dominant paradigm, so that each reflects the other.

Another illustration of the provision of theoretical detail is provided in Figure 6.7, which is an elaboration of Figures 1.3, 3.2, and 4.1. This is a third-order generic agency model. However, the context is different and builds on Figure 6.2 through the elaboration of cognitive theory. We wish to elaborate on this model using a principle of recursion that strictly relates to a proposition of viability adapted for agency from Beer (1959) and recognizes (Yolles & Fink, 2015a) that an agency has viable system properties: *that every viable agency contains and is contained in a viable agency with context-dependent meaning*. It implies that the core agency model of Figure 6.3 (the cognitive agency) can be recursively set into the figurative system of Figure 6.2, this now being referred to as the cultural agency normative personality. While the cognitive agency may be a living system in its own right, it is unable to be maintained meaningfully within a social context without cultural agency support, since without this it becomes isolated from the social environment and hence exists there only as a theoretical construct. The figurative system now becomes a *cognitive contextual environment* and harbour for the (cognitive agency) normative personality (Yolles, Fink & Dauber, 2011). Its control processes are maintained through traits which ultimately influence agency patterns of behaviour. If we wished to include the *affective agency* as well (see Figure 6.4), then we could talk about the normative personality influences on cultural agency instances of behaviour. The values that these traits take represent its capacity for transeunt behaviour. This is because the traits are manifestations of the cognitive structure of the agency, and as such within given environmental contexts determine the range of possible responses that an agency is capable of.

An additional attribute of Figure 6.7 is the connection between the agency operative system and its social environment. This constitutes an extrinsic aspect of the agency through explicit modelling of interaction with the Social Environment. This therefore illustrates the structure determination of behaviour in the substructure. This relates to cultural structure, cognitive structure involving the transeunt function of the cognitive-affective agency (where mental acts create causative effects outside the collective personality), and

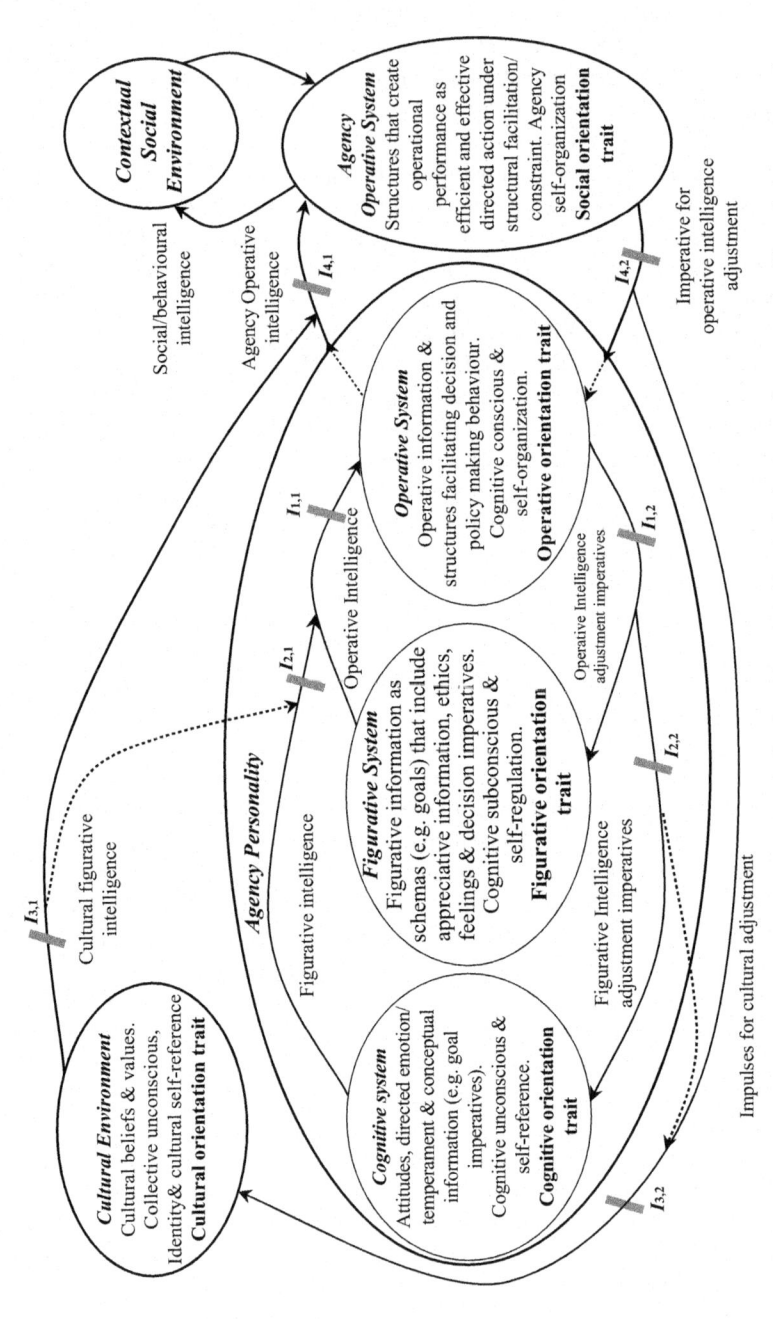

Figure 6.7 Cultural Agency involving a Collective 'Personality' using superstructure modelling in the Cultural Agency substructure, I's indicating intelligences with possible generic pathologies (Source: Yolles & Fink (2015c: 317))

Note: intelligences $I_{i,j}$, order $i=1,4$ have feedforward/feedback $j=1,2$ & if pathologies occur they create intelligence *limitation* and impeded *efficacy* organizational structure relating, for instance, to the nature and purpose of divisions or departments. All of these influence the agency in its social operative behaviour, through the lifeworld processes that populate the intelligences ($I_{i,j}$) and also may be subject to pathologies shown as bars. This modelling approach is possible because the base living system model is recursive (Yolles & Fink, 2015a). As recursions develop, so contexts and hence meanings associated with higher order generic systems change. We note that the Ii,j (for all I and j) are quite equivalent to the Pi,j shown in Figure 6.7, though the former relate to intelligences and the latter to that pathologies that they are subject to.

6.5   Internalization as Knowledge Migration

The development of agency superstructure often occurs through a movement of knowledge from other paradigms. This occurs through a process of *knowledge migration* which, when engaged, allows meanings to be manifested from a remote to a local agency paradigm. This is also a process of internalization that corresponds to the creation of a knowledge-based perspective of the observed. The meanings are predicated on normative beliefs rather than facts, since people are 'belief-seeking rather than fact-seeking' (Jastrow, 1927: 284), a notion connected with apperception. The implication is that only those elements of meaning that have a common belief basis across two paradigms can be migrated. Thus meanings cannot be fully manifested from one paradigm to another since paradigms are essentially distinguished by their embedded beliefs, though seemingly similar paradigms may have different modes of practice. So, by the term *migration* we, strictly speaking, refer to the process by which existent knowledge, when manifested across to agency, becomes a *catalyst* for the local creation of knowledge extensions. Thus, the term knowledge migration implies that there is an epistemological distance between a knowledge source (a distant paradigm) and knowledge sink (here, the local agency paradigm). The catalytic process is engaged through an oscillatory process initially engaging an analysis to establish the basis of new theory, and is then followed by a synthesis to create paradigmatic extensions that satisfy various essential propositions identified as appropriate in the sink. Migration, like internalization, is therefore a complex process that embraces analysis and synthesis. So, migrated knowledge is not just an epistemic reconstruction from a distant source, but rather a re-creation into the local paradigmatic context that allows for meaning extensions.

There are a couple of issues about migrating knowledge that need to be explored. One comes from Burrell & Morgan (1979) and has been referred to as paradigm incommensurability – a concern relating to the legitimacy

Table 6.2 *Characteristics of Paradigms*

Characteristics	Meaning
Propositions	Paradigms are formally expressed through propositions. A proposition is a statement of assertion that includes an illustration of its truth, unless that truth is self-evident (axiomatic). The propositions of a paradigm therefore enable it to be described as a "system of truths". Propositions are created through the use of concepts and conceptual schemes.
Concepts	Concepts are (Tiryakian, 1963:9) the name for the members of a class or the name of the class itself. Conceptual schemes are groups of concepts used in conjunction for a particular purpose. Concepts are precise, may have empirical referents, and are fruitful for the formation of theories to a situation under consideration. They are intended to represent aspects of reality.
Extension	The extension of a paradigm is defined by the set of concepts that it adopts.
Coextension	Two paradigms are coextensive when they occupy the same spaces of extension and have empirical referents that can be measured on a common platform. This does not necessarily mean that they must have a form of interrelationship, though this is possible.
Qualitative similarity	If the measurements of the empirical referents of concepts are qualitatively similar then they can be measured on the same scale of values and are commensurable. However, if they are qualitatively different, then two paradigms are qualitatively dissimilar and therefore incommensurable.

of comparing knowledge across different paradigms, and one that is also applicable to knowledge migration. Following Yolles (1999), to understand incommensurability one needs to first understand the nature of commensurability. Things that are commensurable can be described as being coextensive and qualitatively similar. To see this we define a set of relevant characteristics of paradigms in Table 6.2.

In the migration of constructs (e.g. as theory conceptualizations) from a remote to a local paradigm, coextension is not an issue since after the migration the source paradigm is no longer of interest. But if there a need for coextension, the paradigms are incommensurable if their concepts cannot be measured on the same scale of values – that is if they are qualitatively dissimilar. Qualitative similarity is not an issue since when knowledge is recreated, new approaches to measurement will normally be required. If each paradigm has its own set of knowledge, a consequence of paradigm incommensurability is that the different sets of knowledge that occur across two paradigms may in some way and to some degree be contradictory. One of the tasks of the migratory process is to safeguard against contradiction, or to reconfigure it so that it is seen differently. An illustration of the latter is easy to find, even within the same paradigm. Eisenhardt (2000: 703) writes: 'Paradox is the simultaneous existence of two inconsistent states ... This duality of coexisting tensions creates an edge of chaos, not a bland halfway point between one extreme and the other.' In the same Special Topic Forum of the Academy of Management Review, Lewis (2000:769) concedes that 'managing paradoxical tensions denotes not compromise between flexibility and control, but awareness of their simultaneity'.

Now a paradigm is a generator of knowledge that derives from the propositions that compose it, and the problem of incommensurability arises if migrated knowledge creates the possibility of contradictions in meanings – which will, if exposed, develop into epistemic conflicts. However, where we deal with a complex plurality of paradigmatic knowledge, we may never be able to determine if they maintain contradictions because of that very complexity. As argued by Yolles (1999), this is supported by Gödel's *incompleteness theorem* that suggests that in any formal system (like a paradigm defined through propositional knowledge) there exist (local) truths that may be indicated but cannot be captured.

The creative synthesizing aspect of knowledge migration broaches on the connection between objectivity and subjectivity, as does, therefore, internalization. This is because if one considers that a meaning structure that constitutes knowledge in one paradigm is an object of attention, then the nature of that object is determined from a knowledge-created perspective by the subject making the evaluation. The subject and object are thus irrevocably bound together. It is through the dialectic interaction between the object and subject that the propositional nature of the object is discovered that frees knowledge of its subjective illusions. This dialectic interaction enables the subject to organize its actions into a coherent system. This union between the objective and subjective in relation to the migratory process can be further amplified. Whewell (1860) (cited in Snyder, 2001:1) proposed that all knowledge has both a subjective and an objective dimension, making them commensurable conceptualizations. He argues that this is because one can re-conceptualize subjectivism such that it is seen to arise not from experience (and the cognitive schemas that it induces) alone, but rather as an interaction between the phenomena experienced and the consciousness that experiences it. The mind, therefore, is not merely a passive recipient of sense data, but an active participant in its attempts to gain knowledge of what is perceived in the world. As a result, different ways of seeing arise, as people develop individually invented meanings (Crotty, 1998), consistent with *synthesis* in the development of new knowledge. In other words, the process of internalization is synthesized through the interactions between experience and the migration/internalization of those experiences into a plane of consciousness resulting in schemas that represent those experiences. Thus, there is inherently a distinction between the objective and its subjective reconstruction, but these are frequently commensurable.

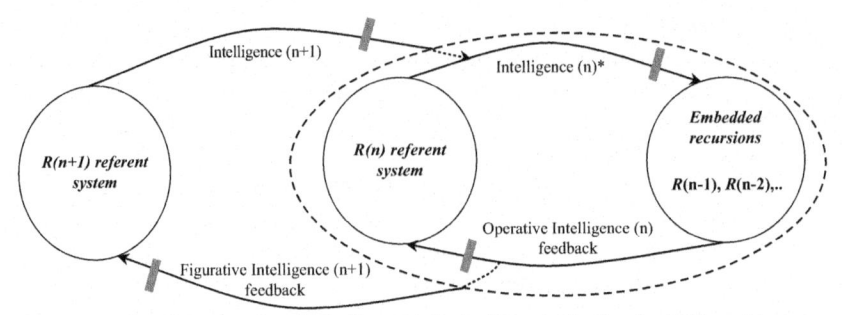

*Where if Intelligence (n) = Operative Intelligence (n), then Intelligence (n+1) = Figurative Intelligence (n)

Figure 6.8 Recursive simplex generator for an nth order simplex model through the generation of (n+1) higher order generic constructs in an implied autopoietic hierarchy

6.6 Generic System Hierarchy Generator

We offer here a generator of higher order generic system hierarchies (due to Yolles & Fink, 2015c), shown in Figure 6.8. To understand the model we begin by considering the meaning of n=1. This gives the instrumental agency – a second-order generic system hierarchy, the order determined by the number of networks of intelligence listed (operative intelligence) plus the feedback as a generic attribute. With n=2, we have the cognitive agency – a third-order generic system hierarchy (indicated by *R(n+1)*), and the *core agency* model that defines the basis of a living system according to Schwarz (1994). Higher orders must be expressed through recursions. Recursion is a modelling process by which a response to a statement raises that statement again, relating to all things that are applied to themselves (Glanville, 2002: 25). It is also the application of a whole concept or set of actions that occur at one systemic level of consideration to a lower logical systemic level of systemic consideration (Yolles, 1999). If *action* as a functional operator is applied to some *object/subject* at one focus in a generic system hierarchy, then applying the same action to an object/subject at a lower focus constitutes recursion. However, epistemic content that is part of those actions changes with local context during the transformation from one focus to the other. Viability is important to agency recursion. This is due to the axiom that 'every viable living system contains and is contained in a viable living system'.

Recursions can be represented through the referent system *R(n-1)*, *R(n-2)*,….. Higher orders than n=2 are possible, but are normally expressed recursively as indicated in Figure 6.7. There is a relationship between higher orders of agency for increasing n and reduction in undecidability with explanation potential for events in *R(1)* – the agency operative system for the real

Agency Consciousness 195

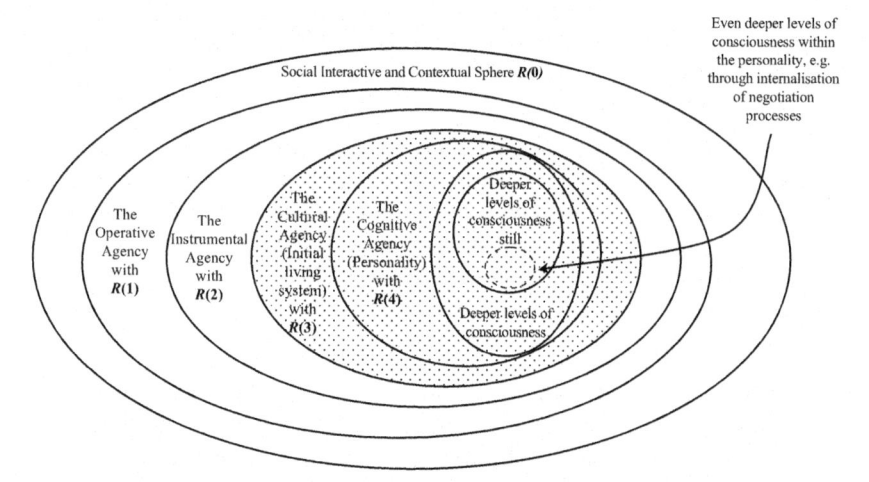

Figure 6.9 Illustration of levels of consciousness from an action context to the living system and onwards, where the dotted area indicates living system occupation

world. In the case of i>n+1, higher orders of generic system hierarchies create *informal* functional influences $R(1)$ – agency structure, and hence behaviour in the social environment $R(0)$. These higher orders are thus relevant to anticipation only as *qualitative inference* (Yolles & Fink, 2015c).

Relating this to Figures 6.5/6.6, there is an implied missing system – the cultural agency operative system $R(1)$. The dotted lines shown represent a recursive component within the agency indicative of normative personality.

Each higher order that develops in a generic systemic hierarchy results from processes of internalization that can result in deeper levels of consciousness emergence. While generic systems have higher orders, consciousness is said to have deeper levels, and so there is a correspondence between degree of higher order system and depth of consciousness. That is, a system of hierarchically embedded ontological differentials express sequentially increasing depths of consciousness as shown in Figure 6.9. This Figure begins with the action context, moving sequentially inwards to greater degrees of generic system hierarchy and levels of consciousness. The operative system is indicated next, followed by the instrumental agency. The first living system in this hierarchy is that of the cultural system. A recursion within the figurative system is the cognitive agency, also called the personality or the strategic agency. Deeper levels of consciousness follow. During consciousness emergence an agency with an $R(n)$ level of consciousness may experience a shift to a deeper level $R(n+1)$ that reflects the appearance of a higher order of generic system in the hierarchy.

6.7 The Case of Negotiation and Agency Internalization

The Construct

Consider a cross-cultural collective Eurozone agency involved in a negotiation through Eurogroup creditors. The creditors are autonomous socio-political sub-agencies with diverse cultural backgrounds and political orientations. They have come together for a strategic negotiation with Greece to help it resolve its financial crisis after the 2007/8 recession. Lax & Sebenius (2006) have proposed a generic model that inherently underpins all negotiation process, and has the following components:

- *Value creating and claiming,* relating to the orientation an agency takes within a negotiation. Two such orientations are individualist win-lose that create value, and a collectivist win-win that claim value. Win-lose games are usually those in which the game is bounded by predetermined constraints, such as zero-sum games. However, win-win games have no predefined constraints that bound what might develop. It is feasible in a win-win game for all participants to profit in one way or the other, and often win-win games are the result of conflict resolution strategies that embrace the needs of all disputants, suggestive of negotiation tendencies.
- *Set-up*, which defines a full set of actual and potential participants, each of which perform their own processes and in so doing mutually interact to deliver some mutually 'desired' outcome.
- *Deal design,* which refers to the interests of the parties involved in the negotiation.
- *Audit* is intended to overcome potential barriers to achieve a successful negotiation.
- *Tactics* – operative manipulation intended to facilitate a desirable decision.

Since the Lax & Sebenius schema is generic for the negotiation process, the following schema can be migrated to a general agency model:

(1) The Eurozone seeks stability and establishes a strategic negotiation between the sub-agency participants of Eurogroup creditors and Greece, each being *value creating and claiming* – broadly having collectivist or individualist (Triandis, 1995) orientation. Each implies a spectrum of values and goals that facilitate anticipatory futures.
(2) *Set-up* is responsible for a 'plural culture' involving all the partner sub-agencies and their values and norms. Cultural intelligence manifests this to the sub-agency personality, delivering attitudes and other relevant context sensitive information to the cognitive system.

(3) From the cognitive system, figurative intelligence manifests a complex of 'common' goals and more or less opaque negotiator schemas that represent *deal design* for the parties involved in the negotiation. Where commonality fails, negotiations are doomed.
(4) From the figurative system, operative intelligence manifests selected elements of this complex together with *audit* (Yolles & Fink, 2011) to the operative system, drawing on available schemas associated with the involved negotiators.
(5) The manifestations deliver options for operative decision-making for the Eurozone agency. It is in the operative system that negotiation *tactics* develop for each sub-agency through operative decision-making, resulting in negotiator communicative interactions.

Consider now a given negotiator who wishes to determine strategy to satisfy a wished-for outcome. The negotiator's strategy will be based on two intimately connected cognitive schemas (Chapter 3): (1) reproductive, which evokes already known events; (2) anticipatory, that imaginatively elaborates on this, and offers a potential on which future actions are predicated. Both are dependent on perspective and apperceptions. Where there is some degree of certainty in the outcome of the negotiation a deterministic outcome will be feasible. However, where there is significant uncertainty, other options occur. These include consciousness transformation. If this occurs it will deliver new emergent conceptualizations, resulting in perspective and apperception shifts. Hence an alternative negotiation strategy can result.

The Lax & Sebenius schema can now be used to model the internalization process to underpinning both reproductive and anticipative schemas in the negotiating strategy, from the perspective of a given sub-agency wishing to satisfy the desired negotiating outcome:

(1) Through *value creating and claiming,* constructed sub-agencies are perceived to have a personality orientation that is broadly individualist or collectivist, thereby providing some insights about their negotiation stance, and facilitating some degree of anticipation about the future.
(2) Initially a constructed plural culture is *set-up* with apperceived sub-agency participants and their values. Pathologies here can be disastrous for any negotiation since if negotiator orientations are misperceived misunderstanding of intent or purpose occurs, with consequences.
(3) Figurative intelligence now manifests through *deal design* the self-goals and perceived apperceptive goals of other negotiators. Another attribute is self-schema and postulated or apperceptive negotiator schemas that determine the set of possible strategic options and processes in the negotiation. These goals and schemas constitute a theory-based complex that can

provide negotiation options, and constitutes a new level of consciousness which lasts for the duration of the negotiation.
(4) Operative intelligence now manifests selected elements of this complex to the operative system, delivering relevant context sensitive options, conditioned by *audit*.
(5) In the operative system decisions are made about options, and *tactics* are determined that may be modified under intelligence feedback.

A Theoretical Background to Eurozone Financial Policy

Donskis (2015) explains that there is a loss of sensitivity through *liquid modernity*[1], where one can withdraw from our ability to empathize with other individuals' pain and suffering, reducing human beings to things or non-persons that awaken only when we or 'one of us' (Young, 2003) are hit by the same kind of calamity or aggression. This withdrawal-and-return mechanism only shows how vulnerable and unpredictable life is. Objectivizing people is a facilitation of political individualism and its associated policy of austerity, which operates through budgeting and revenue, as explained by Wildavky's cultural theory of budgeting (Van Nispen, 2007). The model arises from the Cultural Theory of Risk (GGCT, 2015), developed by Douglas (1986), and formalized by Thompson, Ellis, & Wildavsky (1999):

(1) Collectivism: they can manage revenues but not expenditures, due to many echelons (levels of command) between the top and the bottom where the spending occurs.
(2) Egalitarianism: such regimes can control expenditures but cannot manage revenues due to a lack of internal authority to make large demands on the members.
(3) Fatalistism: such regimes can manage neither expenditures nor revenues and, therefore, suffer from apathy and no action.
(4) Individualism: such regimes can manage both revenues and expenditures (at low levels); the state is kept poor by making resources available only for collective goods; this leads to revenue and expenditure reductions.

These are set-up in a 2 × 2 matrix, and measure belief systems along grid and group (thus sometimes called Grid-Group Cultural Theory). *Grid* indicates group interaction, while *group* indicates expectation for belief and behaviour constraint in relation to risk perception (Marris, Langford & O'Riordan, 1998). Boholm (1996) notes it is an ambiguous opaque theory. While the theory has

---

[1] Bauman (2000) used the term to characterize highly developed global societies as an extension of modernity.

had a facelift (Mamadouh, 1999), it still has issues. For Yolles & Fink (2014a, 2014b, 2014c) egalitarianism is a fundamental attribute of collectivism and cannot be separated out, while fatalism is an emotion of helplessness emerging from hierarchy and power leaving no optional courses for fatalistic individuals. Van Nispen (2007) explains that following Wildavsky and assuming that European member states have a 'policy mix' of measures of both revenues and expenditures to meet the budget deficit reference value set at 3 per cent of GDP, there are basically three choices to reduce a budget deficit and to balance the budget:

(i) The introduction of new taxes and/or an increase of existing rates to enable a high level of spending;
(ii) A reduction of expenditures, for instance by the postponement of investments and/or spending cuts;
(iii) The promotion of economic growth as the budget deficit will disappear when the economy expands.

Extreme individualism and extreme collectivism (and their budgetary options of austerity/growth) are pathological conditions, delivering policies that do not recognize all the needs of a society – unlike an individualism–collectivism (austerity–growth) balance. Such a balance would permit the creation of policies that are not dogma centred, and recognize the need for deeper processes of analysis that fully respond to issue resolution. So, individualism in the Eurozone, even with some suggestion of selectively applied collectivism, is not to the benefit of all of Europe as a whole, especially with respect to the economic issue countries of Portugal, Ireland, Italy, Greece, and Spain (PIIGS).

After the onset of the Western economic crisis in 2007/8 that bailed out the miscreant banking system, the Eurozone adopted a policy of austerity to manage the vast bank support debt incurred in virtually all of Europe. This hit the PIIGS harder than others, damaging their infrastructures and saving the rich from capital losses, while hurting incomes of the poor and middle classes. In 2015 a new anti-austerity government was voted in to power in Greece, perhaps to be followed in other PIIGS countries. Rather than maintaining the socially crippling debt, the government decided it wished to renegotiate with its Eurogroup creditors away from austerity relief packages.

Case Situation of Greece and Eurozone Negotiations

Greece joined what became the European Union (EU) in 1981. With EU funding it improved its industrial enterprises and heavy infrastructure, after which it experienced economic growth, especially in tourism (GDCT, 2015). In 2001 it joined the Eurozone, and experienced further growth (almost tripling its GDP by 2007/8: World Bank, 2015). This created optimism, and with the European Commission, the European Central Bank (ECB), private banking institutions, and the Greek business community, loans were taken out to pay Greek and foreign infrastructure companies for various projects, like the 2004 Olympic Games. Then came the crises caused by the wayward banking system. By 2010 Greek GDP had dropped about 20 per cent, leaving creditor repayment issues. During this period its credit rating was downgraded by the three major commercial credit rating companies, making credit more expensive and aggravating the Greek situation. EU bank bailouts were deemed to be required that were to be recouped through measures of austerity. Between 2008 and 2013 the Eurozone creditors (EU, ECB), and International Monitory Fund (IMF)) has overseen three (2010, 2012, 2015) austerity packages to Greece (GDCT, 2015). Between 2010 and 2013 government employee salaries were frozen/cut, layoffs made, bonuses and worker overtime cut, pensions frozen, and VAT, working hours, and taxes (on fuels/luxury-goods) increased. The social impact of this resulted in public demonstrations and rioting, corporate closures, and even one public suicide (GDCT, 2015). Elections in early 2015 saw the rise of the anti-austerity Syriza government led by Alexis Tsipras, and a new round of negotiations began. One issue for Greece's inability to meet forecasts is that expectations for income through taxation were not met, due principally to corporate tax evasion (Guillot, 2015).

Eurozone officials believed that the EU held all the trump cards in its negotiations with Tsipras, including allowing the collapse of Greek banks (Waterfield, 2015). However, Tsipras seemed determined to find a way to overcome political individualism with new proposals for debt repayment, especially since not all creditors were individualists: 'I think that European history is full of disagreements, negotiations and at the end, compromises. So, after the comprehensive Greek proposals, I am confident that we will reach a compromise that will help Eurozone and Greece to overcome the crisis' (Tsipras' statement upon arriving at the EU Summit, 25 June 2015, (www.primeminister.gov.gr/english/category/person/primeminister).

This attitude was encouraged since in 2012 the EU had made small moves towards collectivism: 'After two years of austerity, growth is suddenly back in fashion in Europe, following calls by the incoming French president, François Hollande, for measures to boost the economy. But the EU's planned "growth pact" is likely to be too small to help the crisis-hit countries of southern Europe... Disappointing economic data in southern Europe and the recent Greek election...has apparently led to a rethink. European leaders have come to the realization that austerity alone just makes the situation worse. Now, the time to invest has arrived' (Volkery, 2012). This shift in orientation is supported elsewhere: Olivier Blanchard, chief economist of the IMF, had been privately urging the Eurogroup creditors for several months that sizeable debt relief was the only credible option (Robertson, 2015). If Tsipras had been trying to turn this orientation to his benefit, he had not realized the degree of Eurogroup reluctance to service severe cases of debt with growth policies, especially in Germany. Nor did he realize the degree to which the Eurozone wanted to retain Greece as a member: 'During a pivotal meeting with Merkel, French President François Hollande and European Council President Donald Tusk, Tsipras at one point received a thinly veiled threat that if he walked away and left the euro, Greece risked going it alone geopolitically, too' (Faiola & Mui, 2015).

In terms of the Lax & Sebenius model, Tsipras' strategy of forcing an orientation change during negotiations with the Eurogroup creditors implies moving from a win-lose to a win-win negotiation. In win-lose, Europe would win by feeling that they were keeping the Eurozone stable, and Greece would lose through continued austerity measures. The negotiation is bounded by the creditors, who determine austerity constraints. A likely outcome would be Greece continuing to decline economically and socially without immediate hope for growth potential, unless of course the creditors in some way balanced/eased their requirements. Tsipras' intention to abort further austerity policies on Greece (FT, 2015) would therefore have required a bargaining chip to distract them from Eurozone individualism. On 27 June Tsipras announces a referendum to be held on 5 July. As part of this announcement he says 'Greece, the birthplace of democracy, should send a resounding democratic message to the European and global community. And I personally commit that I will respect the outcome of your democratic choice, whatever it may be... Greece is, and will remain, an integral part of Europe, and Europe an integral part of Greece. But a Europe without democracy will be a Europe without an identity and without a compass' (www.keeptalkinggreece.com/2015/06/27/tsipras-speech-on-referendum-full-text-in-eng-video-with-eng-subtitles/).

The snap election was seemingly intended to create a 'democracy' bargaining chip against the austerity measures, and the Greeks voted 'no' decisively to the proposed Eurozone austerity measures (GDCT, 2015). However, this had no effect on the final agreement of austerity, which included additional pension cuts, taxes, and a fire sale of state assets through privatization.

This history allows one to second guess the process of internalization that occurred for Tsipras, following the Lax & Sebenius generic negotiation model.

(1) Through *value creating and claiming,* the schema representing the Eurogroup creditors in Tsipras' consciousness were negotiators with mixed individualist and collectivist orientations. The need was to find a way to shift the creditors further towards collectivism to facilitate measures for growth instead of debilitating austerity.
(2) Initially, a constructed plural culture is *set-up* with apperceptive negotiators with posited values and beliefs. Pathologies occurred here for

Tsipras, who misjudged the tendency among the creditors and their aversion to take risks over Greece, especially where the stability of the EU project was concerned. He also believed that the destabilizing threat of Greece leaving the Eurozone, and perhaps even EU membership, was greater than he believed.

(3) Figurative intelligence now manifests through *deal design* the self-goals and apperceptive goals of the negotiators. Another attribute is self-schema and postulated negotiator apperceptive schemas that determine the set of possible strategic options and processes in the negotiation. As a result of the conceptual inaccuracies, Tsipras determined a set of goals and schemas that constituted the negotiation tactic. Options included a referendum to convince the creditors that the Greek population was behind him.

(4) Operative intelligence now manifests selected elements of this complex to the operative system, delivering relevant context-sensitive options, conditioned by *audit*. This included decision options for a referendum.

(5) In the operative system decisions are made about options, and *tactics* are determined that may be modified under intelligence feedback. The decision to have a referendum was pathological since it created expectations in the population that were distressed, established a delay for economic revival that was highly problematic for Greece, and aggravated the creditors.

Tsipras clearly had no intention of leaving the Eurozone, weakening his Eurogroup negotiating position. As such its fears of Greece leaving the Eurozone, thereby destabilizing the European project, were not significant in the negotiation. However, did his negotiation tactics arise through an emergent deeper level of consciousness? If yes, one would expect to see a *new order of novelty* appearing in the negotiation process, and a consequential apparent shift in perspective and apperception. Tsipras' decision to call a referendum and offer a 'democratic dimension' as part of the negotiation tactics may have been the result of the emergence of such a new level. It would have also embraced a shifted perspective and apperception concerning the theme of the negotiation. Since his later political stance constituted an 'about turn' on his original position, it seems possible that he did pass through a process of consciousness transformation. The actual explanation would have to be validated through inference from secondary data inquiry, or directly through primary interview.

Part II

Agency Change

7 Joint Alliances

7.1 Introduction

So far we have considered the development of the cultural agency, its social nature, its strategic nature, its consciousness, and what it is that makes it intelligent. Perhaps rather as in a Monty Python comedy sketch ... now for something completely different. Instead of exploring the immanent attributes of the agency, we shall instead explore the way in which two or more autonomous agencies in an external environment might connect for their mutual benefit.

Two or more organizations entering into a voluntary co-operation can be called joint alliances, joint ventures, and partnerships (Kelly and Parker, 1997; Fitzgerald, 2000). While the term alliance may be seen as a generic form of cooperation (Glaister and Buckley, 1997: 200), a joint alliance may take on forms that include joint ventures, mergers and acquisitions. They occur when legally distinct organizations come together purposefully through two or more sponsoring partners (Geringer, 1991; Muralidharan & Hamilton, 1999).

When organizations enter into a joint alliance, they always face a potential for change. However, the nature of that potential depends on the type and purpose for the joint alliance that is intended or develops. Alliances always address Human Resource Development (HRD), since the capacity of the organization to respond to the change implied directly involves the human resources that compose the organization(s) involved. The nature of the alliance will depend upon how it has been formed, for instance through stimulation by host government insistence, the desire for rapid market entry, increased economies of scale, risk-spreading, gaining, and knowledge transfer. They have become important, (Schuler, 2001), even though they entail risk (Shen, Wu & Ng, 2001).

In this chapter we shall review theoretical and empirical studies of alliances. One brief study will examine Mauritius as part of an interest in developing an analytical framework for understanding alliance foundation, formation, development, implementation, and restructuring, with particular reference to human resources issues. Another study will examine a particular case in Central and Eastern Europe. A framework will develop that will be applied to a specific case study of an alliance. This involves the Czech Academic Link Project (CZALP) between Liverpool John Moores University, UK, and the Technical University of Ostrava in the Czech Republic. This will illustrate the usefulness of the framework and theory, and identify principles relating to the development of alliances to guide further research in this area.

Most approaches to joint alliance studies have been based on transaction-cost and resource-based theories or on technology transfer, knowledge diffusion, and organizational learning perspectives (Glaister and Buckley, 1997). The resource-based view focuses on motivations for alliance formation, especially needs to exploit excess or idle under-performing resources and acquire or access new resources for growth. Alliances are thus seen as bundles or portfolios of resources contributed by partners, not as coalitions of business activities, enabling selective access to required resources and phased approaches to resource acquisition and transfer (e.g. termination with acquisition by one partner: Zhai, Shi, and Gregory, 1999). Since knowledge is increasingly seen as a key resource, this perspective is aligned with those perspectives emphasizing the 'transfer' and 'diffusion' of knowledge in alliances, especially technological knowledge. Such knowledge processes, and particularly knowledge innovation, are advantaged in cross-national alliances (Zhang et al., 2010), even if this entails more risk of failure. Some risks for failure are visible and correctable, for instance when there are poor or inadequate partner relations (Büchel, 2003).

'Technology transfer', first applied to the reconstruction of Europe and Japan after World War II, was later applied to the transfer of technology between 'developed' and 'developing' countries in the late 1950s (Klauss, 2000). Discussion of technology transfer in international alliances is dominated by a 'hardware orientation', involving the application and transfer of 'hard' technologies in relatively unproblematic ways. Even when applied to so-called soft technologies, such as the transfer of American-style Master in Business Administration (MBA) and management training programmes into Central and Eastern Europe, 'transfer of management and educational technology' metaphors and analyses predominate (e.g. Hull, 2000). Such studies fail to question the mission (e.g. to assist economic transformation) or the process (e.g. one way transfer of modern management and educational technology from the 'Western' to the 'Eastern' partner in the alliance).

'Knowledge diffusion' emerged in the 1950s as a way of understanding how alliance formation was driven by knowledge assets, especially technologies and management systems. Unidirectional flows of knowledge are assumed from the corporation's home base (e.g. research and development function) to its subsidiaries and alliances, with a rigid separation, as in technology transfer, between knowledge generation and application. Recent 'knowledge leveraging' perspectives focus more on the links between generation and application, forms of productive knowledge other than technology, and the need to acquire and access knowledge from outside the firm's boundaries (Grant et al., 2000). Knowledge is seen as created in many sites and functions and accessed in many locations, and its creation and exploitation are seen as linked or complementary processes. New knowledge needs to be aligned with existing knowledge, dependent on the recipient's 'absorptive capacity', linking this perspective with organizational learning perspectives (e.g. Hamel, 1991).

In the knowledge diffusion view, knowledge generation is equated with knowledge creation, and knowledge application with knowledge transfer or diffusion. Grant et al. (2000: 113) see alliances as inferior to firms in terms of 'knowledge integration': 'it is the very absence of investment in common language, social norms, organizational routines and institutionalised modes of decision making that limit their capacity to conduct the low-cost knowledge-integration activities that characterise firms ....in supporting "higher organising" principles, alliances are inevitably inferior to firms'. Grant et al. (2000: 115–116) also argue that 'the movement of knowledge between different geographical locations is central' to the process of adding value in knowledge development. Here we conceive of this 'movement' of knowledge not as 'transfer' but as 'migration', where meanings are manifested in a receptor of knowledge that is relative to its current knowledge base. This implies issues of misunderstanding or misperception that may easily occur during the communication of complex patterns of knowledge. We also analyse 'higher organising principles' in alliances through the concepts of suprasystems, metasystems, and suprametasystems, based on systems theory (e.g. Yolles, 1999 & 2006). Our approach seeks to build on resource-based, organizational learning and knowledge, leveraging perspectives by regarding knowledge as a critical resource, where *knowledge migration* occurs across distinct cultural domains – as meanings are manifested relatively from one domain to another through communications. Local knowledge development also occurs. These replace the idea that knowledge transfer or diffusion occurs as key processes in alliances.

7.2   International Alliances in Central and Eastern Europe

In the international arena joint ventures usually have duration, a contractual basis, and a strategic nature. Many issues and factors identified as important variables in research on alliances in general may be also of importance to alliances in particular, and useful in developing a framework to guide further research. So, a developing a theory of alliances can be useful to the enhancement of specific instances of alliance formation.

A major issue for empirical research has been partner selection, as performance outcomes are influenced by the nature of the partner selected, influencing the mixture of skills and resources available to the alliance, and so its ability to achieve its strategic objectives (Geringer, 1991). Joint alliance partners are likely to have different and/or asymmetrical objectives. Alliances may be more likely to succeed when partners possess complementary missions, resource capabilities, managerial capabilities, and other attributes that create a 'fit' in which the bargaining power of the partners is evenly matched (Harrigan, 1985). This draws attention to issues of power in alliances. Further attention for the reader may be directed towards distinguishing between task-related and partner-related criteria (Geringer, 1991; Glaister & Buckley, 1997).

A central focus of research has been in the strategic interests of partners. This has been especially the case for the strategic interests of the partner seeking aid, that is, the local partner. The interests of local partners have also often been overlooked. This is surprising since the strategic objectives of local partners also impact on the choice of both partner and structure, with a potential for conflict if objectives differ (Li & Shenkar, 1997). Partners in an intended alliance become the metaphorical 'parents' of an alliance 'child' when it has been born after conception. Some partners may engage in alliances where knowledge and competencies match each other (compatibility); others may look to alliances where they add to or build on those of the partner (complementarity). Gray & Yan (1997) found that the institutional environment, the relative bargaining power of the parents, the nature and extent of their prior relationships, and the level of initial success of the alliance to satisfy objectives were all important factors in affecting alliance performance.

A particularly important issue is that of *trust* in alliances. One can distinguish between personal, procedural, and institutional trust (Butler & Gill, 1997). The maintenance of parent trust is dependent on both alliance performance and developed over time. Trust can also be enhanced by high and increasing levels of autonomy granted to the alliance, its physical separation, its distinct geographical and organizational identity, parent forbearance during problems, and their consistent support. As ambiguity and interdependence increase, there is a likelihood for a greater need for personal trust, with the formal contract most useful to alliance partners at foundation, for developing mutual understanding (Gill & Butler, 1996).

A particular geographical region of the world that has been susceptible to joint alliances is Central and Eastern Europe. This is because since 1989 there has been a political and social transformation with the demise of the Soviet Union, and the consequential interest in management and management development in the context of a discourse of market fundamentalism and 'transition' (Henderson and Whitley, 1995). Examples of international alliances in the Countries of Central and Eastern Europe (CCEE) having management interests include the Krakow Consortium Initiative, formed between Teesside University, various North East England companies, and Polish universities and companies to develop Polish academics as trainers in Polish industry (Jankowicz & Pettit, 1993).

Official policy and rhetoric in relation to CCEE development, supported by the International Monetary Fund and the European Bank for Reconstruction and Development, favoured free-market 'restructuring'. However, while enterprise managers may have subscribed to the need for technological, financial, and structural restructuring, they did not tend to see the need for managerial restructuring (e.g. Kelemen and Lightfoot, 1999). In Poland, the business press offered positive if parochial images of successful 'modern' enterprises contrasted with old, failed enterprises (always Polish). They also offered a strongly gendered, idealized, and Americanized image of management (Kostera, 1995 & 2000). 'Moral crusades' were promoted by Western political and financial institutions, trainers, and consultants. They adopted non-reflexive 'knowledge transfer' views of management development 'missionaries'. These missionaries made simplistic and unproblematic assumptions about management learning, often neglecting or disparaging the heritages of the countries in which they worked (e.g. Kostera, 1995 & 2000; Jankowicz, 1994; Henderson & Whitley, 1995). Host partner trainees or students were required to 'comply' in class with Western models, while rejecting such ideas privately as being inappropriate (e.g. Kostera, 1995 & 2000; Kelemen, 1999). Against this background, it seems clear that a more useful way forward is for *alliances to be seen as networks (implying cooperative processes) that increase performance* (Mitsuhashi & Greve, 2009).

Alliances can be jarred by managerial style and cultural differences (Iborra & Saorin, 2001; Fedor & Werther, 1996). Differences in teaching, training, and learning styles were a particular issue for alliances. For example, Jankowicz & Pettit (1993) have discussed how both Western trainers and Polish academics 'colluded' in accepting directive, 'expert' services from Western trainers as being functionally suitable for both parties. Jankowicz (1994) comments in a similar fashion on Holden and Cooper's (1994) account of training Russian construction managers, whose tendency to learned helplessness, a preference for authoritative exposition, and a lack of a common managerial vocabulary. This has led Western trainers to develop a *directive* hierarchical 'modelling' approach to training where the foreign partner *instructs* the local partner. This is as opposed to a more organic interactive approach in which interchanges are common and knowledge migration occurs in both directions. Such a directive approach does not best facilitate meaning transfer, self-directed learning, or long-term application and transfer of learning for autonomous organizations in the host country. Voros & Schermerhorn (1993) point to the need to build on the strengths of the system (e.g. with respect to mathematics or critical debate) in order to avoid the dual traps of 'dependence' and 'local convenience' in alliances, both of which may inhibit sustainable development of learning. There is another issue that is usefully referred to, which is that experience in the development of joint alliances in at least one of the partners reduces risk (Heimeriks, 2010).

In post-communist CCEE there have been various studies of management education and managerial learning that result from Western alliances (including acquisitions and joint ventures) with Western companies in Hungary (Lee et al., 1996; Simon & Davies, 1996; Villinger, 1996). They identify various barriers to learning, including language problems, different cultures and attitudes to business, and foreign expatriate managers making little attempt to learn Hungarian or familiarize themselves with the culture or country. This importance of language and culture to international alliances is emphasized by Cseh and Short (2001). They produced a case study of a British–Hungarian collaboration between 1994 and 1997 – to design and deliver training in change and crisis management and team building – in a large Hungarian public sector organization using interpreters and translators. Understanding the meaning attributed by participants to their environment is necessary, but more difficult when communication is mediated by a translator. This is because it is through language that meaning is created and social reality created, managed, and shared. Jankowicz (1999) uses metaphors of 'export sales' and 'new product development' to discuss knowledge transfer across cultural and linguistic boundaries. In the first case, the assumption is made that both parties share the same conceptual background and assumptions, whereas in the second case, the two parties are seen as co-equal collaborators. Every language encodes phenomena differently, so the meanings encoded by one party may be subtly different from that encoded by the other. Jankowicz (1999: 319) argues that knowledge development occurs through 'mutual knowledge creation', rather than knowledge transfer, this (like our term knowledge migration) referring to the negotiation of new understanding.

7.3   Knowledge Management and Knowledge Transfer in a Cross-Cultural Context

Exploring culture and cross-cultural management from a *knowledge management* perspective results in a rejection of the dominant approach to culture in international management, with its roots in anthropology and social psychology (Holden, 2002). This is because it over-emphasizes cultural differences, culture shock, culture clashes and collisions, and problems in cross–cultural communication and negotiation. An alternative is to view cross–cultural management in terms of knowledge management, associated with a knowledge domain. Culture is seen as an organizational knowledge resource, and knowledge transfer is crucially seen as occurring through a process of migration to an acquiring parent in an alliance. This allows the exploration of capacities of migration in cross-cultural know-how, and the conceptualization of the cross–cultural worker as a form of knowledge worker. Cross-cultural management is thus seen as a form of interactive osmosis, and international knowledge transfer then becomes a form of cross-cultural migration.

Newell (1999), in a discussion of the use of Western-style management education in China (for instance, in relation to the MBA), points out that much of the knowledge base in China has been imported in a linear fashion from the West through the translation of Western textbooks and the use of Western teachers and trainers. She presents an alternative model of knowledge involving social construction, knowledge-sharing, participation in social networks, and interaction between Chinese and Western ideas and people. Social technologies like tools of Human Resource Management (HRM) are less codified and even more interdependent with the social context than physical technologies. She refers to the 'mental models' developed by people to make sense of their experiences and the difficulty of articulating and transferring tacit knowledge, essential to effective management. Knowledge has to be continually 'reinterpreted', 're- created', or 're- constituted' rather than 'transferred', to 'create a unique bundle of management knowledge, deeply embedded in the unique social, political, cultural and economic context of China' (Newell, 1999: 290). Western management may also have much to learn from China in terms of its emphasis on networks and stakeholders: knowledge flows are not simply one-way, from the Western source to the Eastern destination. There have been concerns over whether 'knowledge' of Western HRM and management practices can be unproblematically 'transferred' in the way suggested by many proponents of 'technology transfer'. However, a further question arises as to whether it is appropriate to attempt to 'transfer' Western HRM practices. These are primarily derived from attempts by American private sector companies in the 1980s and 1990s to respond to increasing global competition (especially from Japan) to other contexts. Such contexts include the public services of developing countries facing different problems and in different contexts in the twenty-first century. We will consider this issue with particular reference to the case of HRM in the Mauritian Civil Service.

Mauritius, a small island ex-colony of the UK in the Indian Ocean off Southern Africa, presents a particularly interesting case study of knowledge migration in a cross-cultural context, especially in terms of the 'transfer' of Western knowledge of HRM policies and practices. It is a country with a growing industrial export sector, especially in textiles and clothing, as well as growing financial services and tourism sectors. This exposes it, along with the presence of Western multinationals and joint ventures, to global influences on its management and HRM practices. In addition, though it is conventionally placed with the developing countries of Southern Africa, where it is an active player in various regional political and economic groupings, its status as an upper-middle income, recently industrialized country links it more closely with the newly industrialized countries of South and East Asia (McCourt & Ramgutty-Wong, 2003). This position is reinforced by its geographical situation and in particular by its population mix. As an ex-colony of the Netherlands, France, and latterly Britain, it retains a small but economically still important Francophone community from the sugar plantocracy alongside large numbers of people drawn from Africa (Creoles) and Asia, especially India and China. These communities have recently begun to exploit their geographical, religious, family, and ancestral ties to Asia to develop trading and other economic relationships, including the importation of Chinese and other workers into the textile, tourism, and financial services sectors.

In terms of management and HRM practice, the Mauritian Civil Service is officially committed to a merit-based, bureaucratic system, though there is the belief that ethnic-based nepotism, client-based patronage, and political favouritism are pervasive. Though a number of reports have advocated 'reform' in the management of the Civil Service, and a number of task-forces have been set up to evaluate such issues as performance-related pay, it appears from a review of documentation and a series of interviews and focus groups held with Civil Servants at all levels that the service remains largely unreformed and that HRM as practised is largely non- strategic, with many features persisting from the colonial era (McCourt & Ramgutty-Wong, 2003).

The Western Strategic HRM model is often seen in terms of human resource policies and practices being strategically integrated horizontally and vertically with corporate strategy, with a substantial degree of devolution of responsibility for HRM to line managers. However, in the Mauritian Civil Service salaries are primarily determined by the Pay Research Bureau, staffing matters by the Public Service Commission, and training by the Mauritian Institute for Public Administration and Management. Line ministries, let alone line managers, have little role to play in managing staff. In addition, in two other areas often cited as essential to strategic HRM, staffing, and performance management, there is little evidence of reform. There appeared to be a lack of transparency in recruitment and selection, an absence of clear criteria, and a lack of scrutiny of selection decisions. There is still general use of annual 'confidential reports' for promotion and the use of seniority as the basis for promotion decisions (indeed, the Public Service Commission demands a written explanation if an official is recommended for promotion 'over the head' of a more experienced colleague). Performance-related pay systems are also absent, and there is a general feeling that ethnic and political patronage remain pervasive (alluded to in the phrase 'Mauritian specificities').

It would appear then that despite the exposure of Mauritius to global influences and despite the efforts of the University of Mauritius in running Master's programmes in HRM that there has been little 'transfer' of knowledge about HRM policies and practices into the Mauritian Civil Service.

However, this case also raises the general question of the limits to knowledge migration of HRM practice in a cross-cultural context. It is difficult to see how strategic HRM could be adopted without the political will to bring about structural reforms and constitutional amendments to the role of the Public Service Commission. It may be that 'Mauritian specificities' and especially the ethnically based and clientilistic nature of current Mauritian politics means that any devolution of responsibility in HRM to line managers will result in their discretionary powers being abused to favour their own ethnic group. The role of the Public Services Commission, whilst problematic, may therefore be positive in containing or reducing nepotism and patronage that may otherwise flourish, and in addition line managers may not currently have the skills or training to operate a devolved system successfully. Thus 'transfer' of knowledge and technology in HRM from the West to Mauritius may not only not be feasible, it may also be undesirable in the Mauritian context; 'Mauritian specificities' may require HRM responses that take the specific needs of the Mauritian context into account, rather than the wholesale importation of models of managing people designed in other socio-cultural contexts to address other problems.

7.4 Viable Knowledge Creation and Learning in International Alliances

The knowledge translation process is here considered to be a process of knowledge migration from knowledge source (the knowledge base, often in the 'West') to knowledge destination or sink, often in the 'South' or 'East' (Figure 7.1). Knowledge can be seen as potentially able to migrate in both directions, not only from source to destination but also destination to source. A 'knowledge intermediary', or KI, may assist in this process as a knowledge broker working in partnership in an international alliance (Iles and Yolles, 2003) to migrate knowledge across cultural boundaries.

Learning is critical to alliances: at its very foundation, and as the parents learn more about each other, from each other, and from the alliance itself (Schuler, 2001). This learning can also be useful for other units and alliances. Competitive alliances appear to be the most challenging, leading to greater priority for alliance learning; as Pucik (1988: 81) says, 'shifts in relative power in a competitive partnership are related to the need at which the partners can learn from each other'. Some partners may emphasize learning, others may not; 'the behaviours and styles of managers in organizations have a significant

214   Agency Change

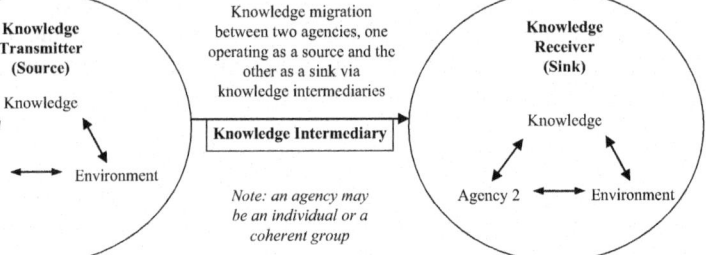

Figure 7.1 Knowledge migration between two agencies, one operating as a source and the other as a sink via knowledge intermediaries (adapted from Steenhuis & de Boer 1999: 86)

impact on the ability and willingness of a firm to learn' (Schuler 2001: 317). A lack of openness, a need for control, low cultural awareness, and ethnocentricity may reduce the ability of organizations and managers to learn, while flexibility and a willingness to take risks may promote it. HRM policies and practices may support or inhibit knowledge flow, sharing, and development. Asymmetry in learning capability may lead to alliance instability and dissolution, despite short-term gains for one partner. Inkpen & Currall (1997) discuss issues of relative bargaining power and learning asymmetry, and suggest that if partners learn at equal rates or engage in forbearance, need for control diminishes and trust increases. Learning about an alliance partner provides the basis for increased trust, as trust is the vehicle for knowledge migration. Learning from a partner provides the basis for increased bargaining power and reduced dependence. Opportunistic behaviour may lead to instability and greater efforts at control by the other partner.

Alliances can therefore provide significant opportunities for organizational learning, especially the transfer of culturally embedded knowledge, if personal, procedural, and institutional trust are developed and substantial non-contractual inputs invested (Fitzgerald, 2000). Benefits are likely to be appropriated asymmetrically, according to the organizational learning capacity or absorptive capacity of the partners (Pucik, 1988).

A number of alliance issues of relevance in respect of human resources can be identified (Schuler, 2001). These occur at a two levels:

- The organizational level, involving parent to parent relationships, parent-alliance relationships, alliance-context relationships, and parent characteristics.
- The individual/group level, involving staff learning and sharing knowledge, staff competencies, staff attitudes and behaviours, staff motivation and commitment, and recruitment to the alliance.

Joint Alliances

A number of stages can be identified in the formation of an alliance: formation, development, implementation, and learning. At its formation stage a number of important issues arise, including:

- the reasons for the alliance,
- how its benefits will be utilized (e.g. how knowledge is managed),
- the selection of managers,
- the selection of partners,
- the building of trust,
- negotiating the alliance.

During its development a few crucial issues include:

- locating the alliance,
- establishing the right structure,
- getting the right senior managers.

During implementation there are a number of essential attributes to embrace, which include:

- establishing alliance vision, mission, values, strategy, and structure,
- developing human resource policies and practices and staffing and managing employees are critical, especially in supporting and rewarding learning and knowledge sharing.

The learning stage is of paramount importance for restructuring, and involves:

- learning from the partners,
- migrating the new knowledge to the parents,
- migrating the new knowledge to other locations.

As part of this stage three key issues also need to be addressed: control, trust, and conflict. Learning and trust are positively related, while trust and the use of informal and formal controls are negatively related, so establishing mechanisms to enhance trust may benefit the relationship between alliance partners (Schuler, 2001).

A framework summarizing empirical research theorizing into alliance and venture performance and identifying a future research agenda is presented in Figure 7.2 (Iles & Yolles, 2002), where it is specifically applied to the CZALP case to be discussed later. The initial foundation or formation of the alliance is seen as influenced by the respective partners' motives, objectives, resource contributions, relative bargaining power, prior relationship, expected returns, organizational and national cultures, management styles, training/learning styles, and environmental and organization-specific HRM issues. The development and implementation phases of the alliance are seen as influenced by ongoing partner inputs, such as levels of partner interaction,

216 Agency Change

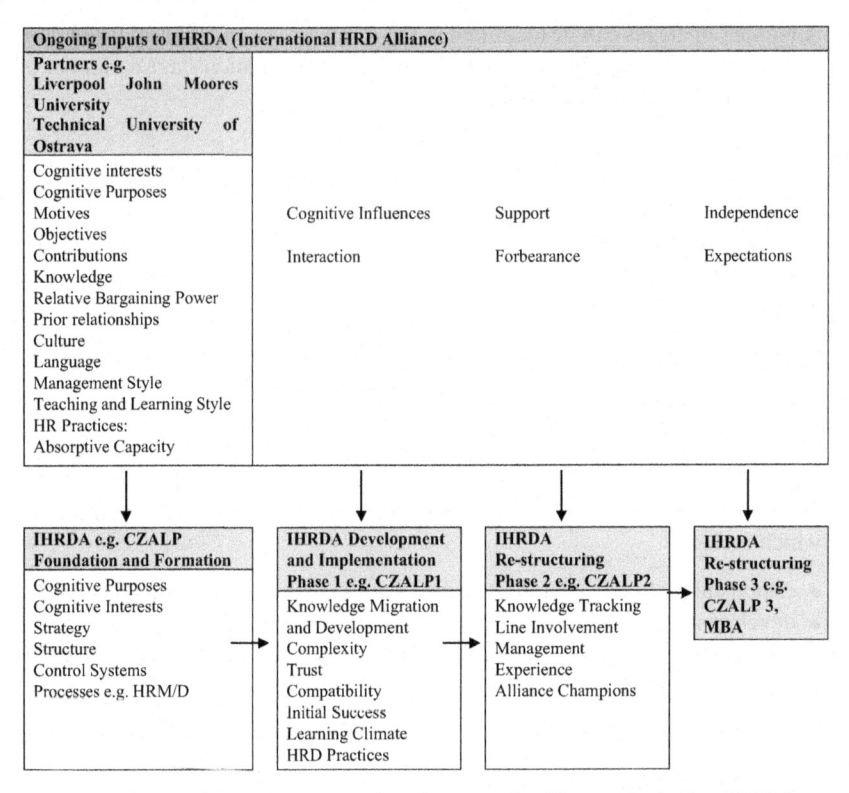

Ongoing Inputs to IHRDA (International HRD Alliance)			
Partners e.g. Liverpool John Moores University Technical University of Ostrava			
Cognitive interests Cognitive Purposes Motives Objectives Contributions Knowledge Relative Bargaining Power Prior relationships Culture Language Management Style Teaching and Learning Style HR Practices: Absorptive Capacity	Cognitive Influences Interaction	Support Forbearance	Independence Expectations

IHRDA e.g. CZALP Foundation and Formation	IHRDA Development and Implementation Phase 1 e.g. CZALP1	IHRDA Re-structuring Phase 2 e.g. CZALP2	IHRDA Re-structuring Phase 3 e.g. CZALP 3, MBA
Cognitive Purposes Cognitive Interests Strategy Structure Control Systems Processes e.g. HRM/D	Knowledge Migration and Development Complexity Trust Compatibility Initial Success Learning Climate HRD Practices	Knowledge Tracking Line Involvement Management Experience Alliance Champions	

Figure 7.2 Development and performance in alliances, including CZALP

the development of mutual trust, partner capability (e.g. resource complementarity), degree of inter-partner learning, level of knowledge development and migration, as well as the cognitive purposes and interests of the alliance itself. Of particular relevance to knowledge migration are the cognitive influences brought to bear by the agencies. Evaluation of alliance performance may then lead to restructuring, such as the phases 2 and 3 identified in Figure 7.2. As Cyr (1995) notes, goals and expectations between the parents and between the parents and the alliance change over time, necessitating a process of building relationships, establishing channels of communication, and engaging in continuous learning. A decision to re-structure is seen in Figure 7.2 as dependent on knowledge tracking, line management involvement, management experience, and the presence of alliance champions in the management team (Muralidharan and Hamilton 1999). Inter-partner trust may contribute to successful restructuring, as various changes may affect partners' incentives to continue with the alliance.

The criteria for defining alliance success or failure will depend on the parents' expectations and motives and the viewpoints of the various stakeholders involved, issues taken up in the case study which will discuss the various phases of CZALP (1, 2, and 3, represented as CZALP1-CZALP3) in more detail to illustrate the applicability of the framework presented in Figure 7.2.

Figure 7.2 presents a simplified model of an alliance formed between two partners. In reality, of course, there may be multiple partners and numerous restructurings. In addition, a comprehensive model needs to consider the relationship of the alliance to funding bodies (e.g. the British Council, the European Union). Figure 7.2 highlights the importance of organizational learning, knowledge migration, and cognitive interests, purposes, and influences. According to Yolles (2006), cognitive interests connect with cultural knowledge and paradigms, cognitive purposes are strategic schemas, and cognitive interests relate to behaviour. This figure points to a number of issues and factors important to a future research agenda, especially the analysis of knowledge migration and learning in alliances. These will next be explored through viable systems theory.

7.5   Modelling Alliances

Alliances, including joint ventures, are children of complexity, particularly susceptible to examination by methodologies from management systems, as they represent structured approaches to inquiry that are capable of reducing complexity (Yolles, 1998 & 1999). According to Yolles (1999) there are two types of worldview: *weltanschauung* and paradigm. We recall that paradigms exist when they maintain cognitive constructs that give a complete view of reality or way of seeing through the development of theory, a social organization that supports a school of thought, and concrete use of tools and texts for the process of scientific puzzle solving. The theory formalizes the paradigm. *Weltanschauungen* are socially unsupported informal constructs of the mind that may become *paradigms* when formalized (Yolles 1999), that is, when theory is built up around them; this occurs as it passes through a semi-formalized shared *weltanschauung* stage called a *virtual* paradigm that may become a paradigm with social support.

Worldviews operate through culture (beliefs, values, attitudes, and language), established within 'rational' organized structures called propositions and norms. They have a relationship with each other, and with the behavioural world. This relationship is shown in Figure 7.3 (Yolles, 1999), where we have collected together the two types of worldview into the existential domain, referred to here as the metasystem, and differentiated from the phenomenal domain within which it is defined by the 'real' or perceived behavioural world.

218   Agency Change

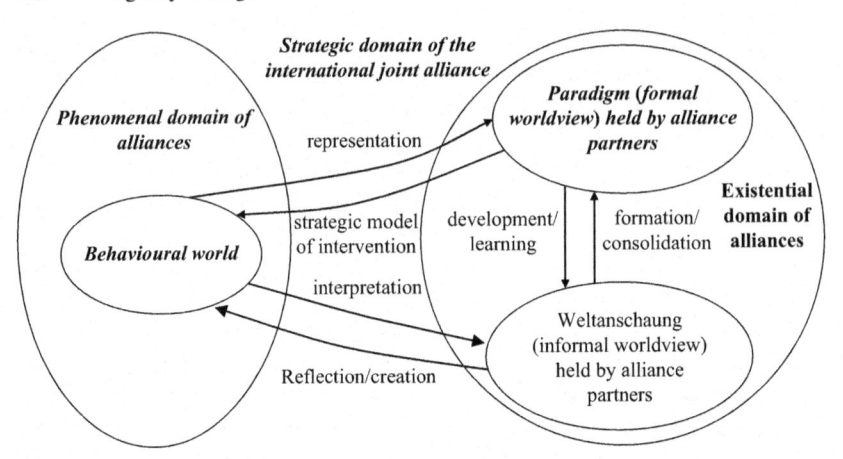

Figure 7.3 Relationship between types of worldview and behaviour

The phenomenal domain is made up of structures and actions that define the behavioural world and are created within a frame of reference defined by the existential domain. Connection occurs between the two domains through an implied strategic noumenal domain, responsible for strategic agency attributes. Each of the three domains has cognitive properties associated with it. The behavioural domain has cognitive interests, the strategic domain cognitive purposes, and the cognitive domain cognitive influences. We shall return to this shortly.

Our interest lies with purposeful adaptable organizations in interaction in an alliance; they can be modelled as agencies in a suprasystem of agencies themselves in an environment. Each agency has an operative system that exists within a phenomenal domain, and a metasystem defined in terms of the existential domain, from which develop decision-making processes (Figure 7.3). This metasystem may be referred to as the 'cognitive consciousness' and 'observer' of the system (Yolles, 1999).

Agencies manifest behaviour when viewed from the perspective of the alliance operative suprasystem shown in Figure 7.4, but internally they display social, cultural, and political processes. They also possess an economy that facilitates operative behaviour.

Traditionally, the interactive behaviour of agencies in an operative suprasystem (e.g. partners in an alliance) is explained in terms of agency attributes, needs, and the individual characteristics of policy-makers. The external environment, and particularly the structure of power and influence in a suprasystem, may have profound effects on the general orientations of one agency towards another. Thus, the major characteristics of any operative suprasystem can be used as one set of variables to help explain the typical actions of an agency.

Joint Alliances 219

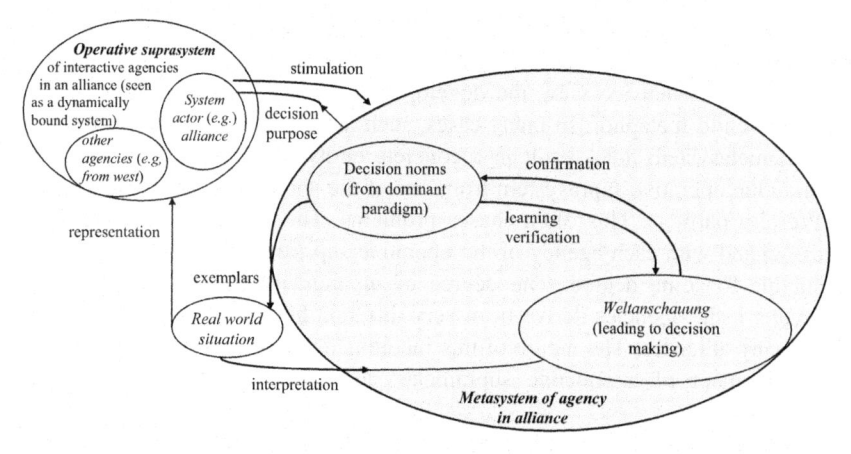

Figure 7.4 An operative suprasystem of agencies in an alliance and a decision making imperatives metasystem of one partner

While an operative suprasystem such as an alliance may simply be a collection of agencies in interaction, it can also have associated with it a purposefulness and be seen as an agency in its own right. In such cases, it is essential that a new virtual suprametasystem is implied that takes the same standing as a virtual paradigm. As Yolles (2006: 125–126) explains:

An actor may be a unitary individual or plural collective. The unitary focus enables the model to refer to a person's worldview in eventual relation to their behaviour. The plural focus is represented by a multiplicity of people forming a coherent social community through their interactions, mediated by cultural structure[1] that enable corporate organization (for instance) to possess and maintain worldviews. This enables claims about reality to be normatively understood, purposefulness to be developed through shared understanding, and actions to be formulated, agreed on and performed. If these worldviews are at least semi-formalised[2] and socially shared with a significantly large social community, then they may be seen as virtual paradigms that may become paradigms in the sense of Kuhn (1970). Paradigms are the result of a sufficiently large plurality of individuals (a group). They are culturally generated, responsible for the formation and maintenance of the organization's patterns of knowledge, and form the basis of an actor's behavioural procedures and thus its bureaucratisation. It is through this that the orthodoxy that defines acceptable behaviour in an organization is defined. The worldview/paradigm is not only a cultural manifestation; it arises with the knowledge that coalescences around the cultural belief system.

---

[1] Piaget (1972) refers to cultural structures as normative symbolic structures.
[2] This occurs when their cultural basis of attitudes, values, and beliefs, and the set of propositions that they hold are at least partly expressed.

So, while a suprametasystem is simply a virtual construction, it does have the potential to emerge as a cultural entity itself, a process that we shall explain in due course when we view the development of an alliance in terms of the parent–child metaphor. In many cases, such as may occur with alliances, the suprametasystem does result in a concrete entity, and attempts are made to drive the operative suprasystem from one of the agency metasystems (e.g. the Western partner). This often causes problems. The assembly of worldviews associated with each agency of the operative suprasystem will be incommensurable to some degree. The degree of incommensurability will likely be greater if the agencies derive from very different host cultures, as is common in many alliances. The nature of this incommensurability is important for the development of a concrete suprametasystem that results in a successful alliance.

When two or more worldviews come together during attempts for meaning to be shared between groups of view-holders, some cognitive strands become coincident, providing for commonalities of understanding (Yolles, 1999). With worldview incommensurability a cognitive pattern emerges entailing a 'cognitive turbulence', becoming a source for the manifestation of conflict, arising from the interference that occurs because of incommensurable differences in cognitive organization and knowledge.

Alliances often begin life as intended purposeful operative suprasystems, and fail for a number of reasons, often centring on cultural differences (Kelly & Parker, 1997). Alliance parents may have cognitive purposes that are different, or will likely be expressed differently because of problems of language that are culture dependent. The cognitive interests may also be divergent or misinterpreted. Finally, and perhaps most importantly, they may fail because cognitive turbulence is not dealt with, and as such no concrete suprametasystem is able to form. Cognitive turbulence will impact on the strategic noumenal and operative phenomenal domains. The phenomenal domain is the place where worldview differences are contested (Yolles, 2001). The contesting process defines a cognitive purpose that will be directly responsible for the manifestation of conflict. In so doing, intention is realized through the creation and strategic pursuit of goals and aims that may change over time, and this enables agencies through control and communications processes to redirect their futures. The strategic process derives from a relational logic that in turn derives from agency rationality. This will likely be different for each of the agency partners in a suprasystem involved in contesting differences. Each agency may pursue its own missions, goals, and aims, resulting in an organization of thought and action that ultimately determines the behavioural possibilities of the agencies. Finally, ideology defines the manner of thinking. This intellectual framework enables policy makers to interpret reality politically, involving ethical and moral orientations, and providing an image of the future that enables action through 'correct' strategic policy. It also gives a 'correct' view of the stages of historical development in respect of interaction with the external environment (e.g. Western views of free market 'restructuring' and 'transition' in Central and Eastern Europe, Henderson & Whitley, 1995, where 'market fundamentalism' is commonly found).

Failure in international joint alliances may have a broader catch-all explanation. Issues may arise that endanger their survival, and these are likely to be unanticipated by the alliance parents, which therefore do not have adequate governance and policies to respond adaptably to the instabilities that arise. Related consideration has been raised by Reuer et al. (2011), who explain that in more recent years a view has arisen concerning senior executive responsibilities in both corporate enterprises and public organizations. Interest in this has moved towards the structure, functions, and performance implications of corporate boards, and these have been directed towards issues involving international joint alliances. Making parents responsible for child failures is perhaps not too different from metaphorically blaming child pathologies on the capacity of its parents to suitably nurture it. As Shute et al. (2011) explain, while parents can leverage appropriate design of policies and practices for the benefit of the child, this cannot tell the whole story. The proposition assumes that it is possible for the parents to get together and make appropriate policy and practice agreements, something that may be more difficult where they are socially, cognitively, and culturally divorced – as is usually the case in international joint alliances. Since joint alliance behaviour is to some extent constrained by its parents, issues due to this separation can easily arise.

Gray and Yan's (1997) analysis of four Sino-American joint ventures explored the impact of 'founding' environmental and inter-organizational factors on the development of alliance ownership and control structures. The institutional environment, the relative bargaining power of the alliance parents, the nature and extent of their prior relationships, and the level of the initial success were all found to be important. In terms of the effect of culture on the formation of alliances, cultural differences influence negotiation outcomes through the behaviour adopted by negotiators during the negotiation process (Iborra and Saorin, 2001). A particular issue raised here is that of trust in joint alliances, which Kelly and Parker (1997) indicate is essential. Butler and Gill (1997: 6) have also applied the concept of trust to research on alliances. A joint alliance can be seen in terms of an autonomous purposeful adaptive activity system that arises through the sustained actions of two or more parents. This idea links in with a classification of types of joint venture based on Kelly and Parker (1997), which, following Yolles & Iles (2006), can be one of three types:

1. Horizontal alliances occur between competitors in an industry through functional need that contributes to the direction or the alliance. Collaboration across specific functions can produce benefits, like: (a) research and development that can reduce both costs and risks by sharing expertise, (b) cross-licensing agreements that can enable risks across international markets to be reduced.
2. A vertical alliance between organizations that share the control of operations contributes to the kinematics of the alliance. In so doing it utilizes the specialist skills associated with the partner organizations that act as joint alliance parents. Such a distribution can aid operational efficiency, as it can aid effectiveness; examples of such partnerships occur between organizations in the supply–delivery chain that may be composed of suppliers, marketers, or distributors.
3. Diagonal alliances across organizations in different sectors of operational activity can occur by their pooling knowledge, expertise, resources, or technology; this establishes an optional set of possibilities/potential for the alliance. Diagonal alliances represent a form of operational convergence between the partner organizations when, for instance, the technologies of IT and telecommunications come together through such a partnership.

The class of alliance being sought determines its strategic nature, and this is defined by operative interests and reflected in strategic purposes. The cultural attributes of each agency that partners an alliance constitute an influence on both its strategic and operative attributes. The partner agencies are considered to be autonomous, and the way in which they connect in an alliance is illustrated symbolically in Figure 7.5. Here it is shown that agencies can be constituted across three ontological components: the phenomenal domain within which communication and action occur interactively, the noumenal domain that maintains strategic schemas, ideology, ethics and goals, as well as systems of thought, and a metasystem (the existential system) that operates through culture and worldview (and supports strategic ways of seeing). When two such agents come together in a joint alliance the outcome can fail. When parents maintain different cultural, ethical, and ideological positions they maintain a separateness that only permits the development of a joint history of experiences through phenomenal structural coupling. This is because the parents can be structurally coupled at the systemic level (Maturana and Varela, 1979), permitting a (past and future) history of experiences. Systemic structural coupling only enables parent organizations to understand each other through communication and the observation of behaviour, both of which are prone to error in complex situations. Where communication is made between a message sender and a receiver, if the messages are complex a distinction may develop between the meanings assigned to a message by the sender and

Joint Alliances 223

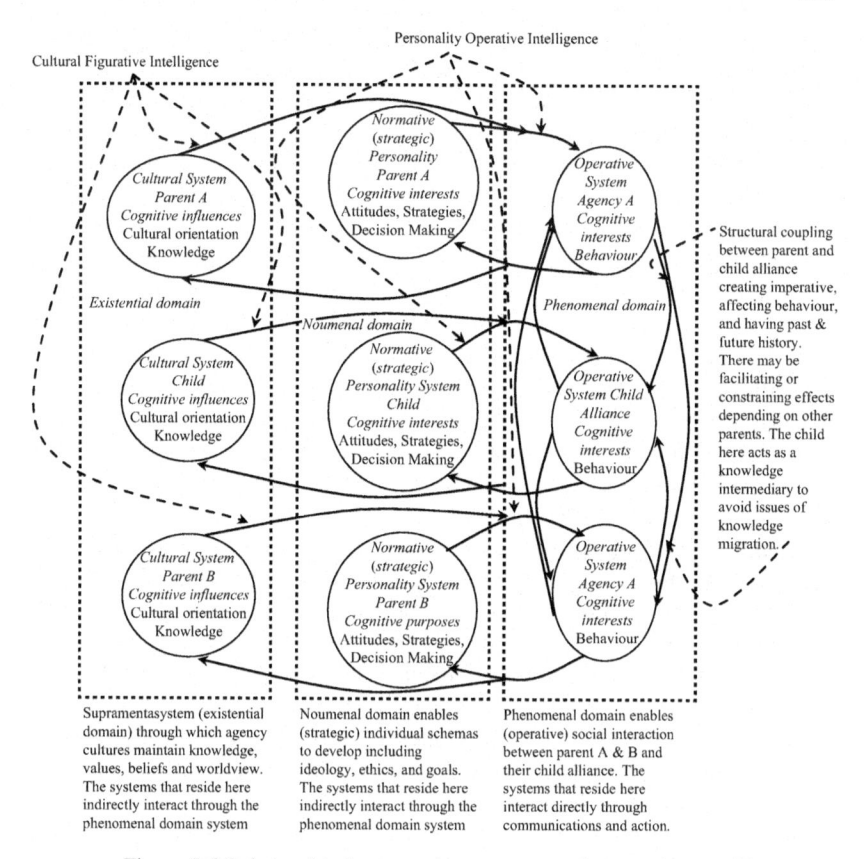

Figure 7.5 Relationship between the parent agencies entering an alliance and the resulting child agency

meanings apprehended by a receiver, and this will result in a mismatch in understanding. Where complex patterns of behaviour are observed, misunderstanding may develop because of a horizon of meanings for one partner that another does not have access to. This may be additionally complexified by other factors, like the projection by one parent of fears related to the actions of another.

Figure 7.5 also shows two agencies in interaction, creating a joint alliance child which now takes the role of a knowledge intermediary for both parent agencies. This child provides the means by which any suprametasystem incommensurability may be addressed since it acts as a translating mediator for the parents. This is because the supramentasystem is a virtual construction that simply implies a cultural boundary that encloses the cultural potentials of each parent in an intended alliance. It becomes concrete, however, through the emergence of the child agency culture which emerges from its cognitive/strategic development. Austin (2005) (citing Piaget, 1966) explains that cognitive development unfolds in a way that is independent of culture, and the alliance child develops cognitively through the emergence of effective strategic schemas. As the schemas form and are found to be effective through implementation and action, they become reflected in the development of cultural norms that also enables it to operate within the context of both parents. This develops through an evolutionary process and is dependent on the emergent processes of cultural figurative intelligence. This is broader than Earley & Ang's (2003) definition of cultural intelligence, and it subsumes it. In particular, Ang, Van Dyne & Tan's (2011) adjusted definition of cultural intelligence as an agency's capability to function effectively in situations characterized by cultural diversity provides an accurate description of evolutionary cultural development of an alliance child, where it is referring to the diversity of the child's two parents.

Cognitive interest, purposes, and influences are located respectively in the operative systems, strategic normative personality, and the cultural system for both parents and the alliance child. We also show systemic structural coupling as occurring between the operative systems of each parent, but it also occurs *only indirectly* existentially and noumenally through the process intelligences that manifest behaviour. This is because noumenal attributes are only seen through such things as cognitive attitudes towards objects of attention that are manifested through language, while existential attributes are only seen through cultural manifestations like artefacts.

The parent organizations have come together to create a joint alliance child, and through its durability it has been allowed to develop both noumenal and existential dimensions. Here too, coupling at the noumenal and existential level of existence is possible, but as already explained this only occurs indirectly through the phenomenal domain. If the parents have spawned a viable child organization, it is allowed to develop autonomously under guidance through the creation of a past and future history of interaction resulting from structural coupling. Its culture is likely to reflect aspects of the cultures of the parents, and when mature it will be capable of mediating between the parents. The child does need some degree of independence to operate successfully, given that it maintains a set of operational constraints and a modus operandi that have been formulated initially by parental agreement. However, this independence should encompass the capacity to evolve.

The child agency is formed by the parents, but is in a difficult position since it needs to balance its operations in a way that satisfies the demands of both parents, but still responding to the operational demands that are applied to it. To do this they need to be both implicitly self-observing viewers with self-observed worldviews (see Yolles & Fink, 2015a–c). The child agency may find it problematic to explain needs that can be understood by the parent, who in an international context has cultural and hence epistemic problems appreciating the demands of the alliance environment, or even if there is some level of understanding, being able to respond to the needs in a coherent way. Direct communication between the parents is often culturally bound and hence problematic. Indirect communication between the parents and the child may well be less problematic since they constitute an intermediary that should be able to map meanings between the parents. An illustration of such a development comes from an examination of the international joint alliance in the telecommunications industry. The break-up of the US telecommunications group AT&T (American Telegraph and Telephone) and the privatization of BT (British Telecom) stimulated an alliance process (Musso, 1998) that proved itself culturally unstable, with disjointed relationships across the set of beliefs and values. The joint alliance that formed was called *Concert* and resulted in failure after two years of operation at a cost of USD800 million annually before it shut down in 2001. The published rationale for the closure was a downturn in the global telecommunications market, but the dysfunction appears clear (Jatras, 2001). Clearly, the issue here was the inability of the parent agencies to form a suitable alliance child.

7.6   Application of the Model to a Case Study of the Czech Academic Link Project (CZALP)

This case study is of an alliance between Liverpool John Moores University (LJMU) in the UK, and the Technical University of Ostrava in the Czech Republic. It began in 1992 in order to develop resource-based learning, and it later came to involve other Czech partners. It is referred to as CZALP and will first be analysed in terms of the framework presented in Figure 7.2.

The Technical University of Ostrava, Faculty of Economics, offers both undergraduate and postgraduate courses in the region of Moravia. Within the last few years in association with LJMU it has been able to develop its management and business activities significantly as an outward looking institution interested in expanding its campus-based courses to a wider market throughout the region using distance learning.

The Faculty has connections with all of the medium-sized and large organizations in the region, and is a provider of education for their employees. For example, it services the needs of Vitkovice s.p., a steel company with about 20,000 employees, and the smaller organization Investicni Banka, both of which are organizations within the immediate catchment area of the University. Since distance teaching is new to the University, care needed to be taken in how it could manage course delivery for students at a distance.

The project brought together the expertise of both the Liverpool Business School and the Learning Methods Unit, Liverpool John Moores University. The Business School had a track record in a variety of international developments, including two Know How Fund projects, one with the Russian Federation and another with the Czech Republic.

Later we will refer to the viable systems perspective on knowledge migration discussed above as it relates to the whole CZALP project to identify directions for future research.

The CZALP Project: Phase 1

This phase lasted from 1992 until 1995. It was funded by the UK Know-How Fund, and the long-term goals of the project were directed towards helping the Czech economy in its development, with the realization that since the socio-political shifts business-related higher education had a unique and important role to play.

The parents shown in Figure 7.5 in this international joint alliance were Liverpool Business School in the UK and the Faculty of Economics in the technical University of Ostrava, Czech Republic. The Liverpool team was aware of the need to demonstrate cultural sensitivity in all of its joint activities, and the Czech leadership showed itself to be very aware of its new social roles and responsibilities, and keen on providing guidance on how to provide maximum assistance to the project. This leadership was in addition able to take its staff with it in this enthusiasm, as shown, for instance, by the good representation at presentations made by the Liverpool partners. This also applied to the managers of their commercial contacts, who have not only attended these presentations, but also visited Liverpool.

During the initial three-year CZALP phase 1 project 1992–1995, work focused on the development of management education in three areas, namely Banking, Information Technology, and Management. This was successful in that new courses were prepared and supported by extensive packs of learning materials suitable for full-time students. In parallel with these developments, LJMU and the Faculty shared ideas and experiences on wider aspects of their activities. In particular, the Faculty was interested in LJMU's long experience of face-to face part-time education. In the Czech Republic regional universities such as Ostrava have had little involvement in this form of education. The constraints of the traditions of curriculum design and delivery and costs mean that continuing education has not been very developed.

Through their contacts with Western countries, there was a growing Faculty recognition that reaching the 'stock' of current managers should be part of their efforts to underpin economic development. The Faculty now has a part-time degree delivered at weekends, consistent with government policy to encourage this form of access.

Another stimulus for development arose from the split of what was Czechoslovakia. Czech Telecom had been developing an in-company programme with a university now in Slovakia. These developments, together with local business contacts, led to a recognition of a demand for both short up-date courses and an undergraduate degree to be available throughout the region, to include some face to face tuition supported by learning materials. Consequently, the Faculty began setting up an Open Learning Unit, planned to have a full-time member of staff with up to ten associates based in member departments.

In terms of Figure 7.2, the Czech partners' motives in CZALP included demonstrating how it could play a role in Czech economic development in the 1990s, especially in Moravia. It particularly wished to develop expertise in open and distance learning and in management education, banking, and information technology (IT) in collaboration with its partner, as well as developing part-time courses in business and management education. It offered senior management commitment and financial and staff support to the project, as well as contacts with local enterprise managers.

LJMU could offer expertise in part-time education and in open and distance learning, and was interested in applying its expertise in new market opportunities in Central and Eastern Europe. Both partners recognized the impact of their national and professional cultures on their management and training and learning styles, and were committed to understanding and respecting their partners' respective styles. Frequent interaction, visits, and attendance at workshops led to a degree of trust and feelings of compatibility, examples of successful learning and knowledge migration, and successful delivery of project outcomes (e.g. development of a part-time degree, setting up of an Open Learning Unit, and development of new courses and open learning packs for full-time students in the areas of Banking and IT).

Both partners were also committed to knowledge tracking, monitoring, and scanning developments in pedagogy, IT, and the evolving Czech economic and social situation. CZALP1 enjoyed alliance champions in the form of the Dean and leadership of the Faculty of the Technical University of Ostrava on the one hand and the two authors of this chapter on the other. As a result, a need for restructuring the project was recognized, leading to the development of the second phase of the project, CZALP2 (Figure 7.2). Phase 3 of the Project, the development of a franchised MBA, is not the subject of the present chapter.

The CZALP Project: Phase 2

Phase 2 of the CZALP project lasted from 1997 until 2002. This was a restructuring phase that had three main objectives. One was to build on work carried out in the three areas of banking, information technology, and management by developing open learning modes. The second was to advise and support the nascent Open Learning Unit through sharing experience gained at LJMU. The third was to participate in, and facilitate, the establishment of a network of institutions in Moravia capable of delivering open learning, according to market demands. The broader objectives of CZALP2 included the creation of staff-centred development groups for resource-based learning in areas relating to managing in a market economy. This became a Business School in Ostrava and was the alliance child that now took its own responsibility for the development and maintenance of courses, developing its own cognitive purposes and interests. It was through this unit that all communication relevant to the development with the University was now funnelled since this group was familiar with the cultures and strategic orientations of both alliance parents.

As part of this process, evaluation of the development needs and schedule of activities as perceived by the Faculty of Economics in Ostrava was necessary. The local environment demanded part-time education using open learning. Some of these needs had been filled within the previous CZALP project, yet there was little provision in most areas. Exploration of ways to satisfy the developing needs of the Faculty in respect of the above was seen as necessary in CZALP2.

A major reorganization of enterprises in Moravia had taken place, helped by the Faculty alliance unit and less directly by LJMU. The Faculty enjoyed excellent relations with its local and distant enterprises, and provided courses in various areas to satisfy their needs. It aimed to continue to develop these links and enhance its role in developing Management Education in respect of its catchment area. Jointly, LJMU and the Faculty intended to take advantage of the best practices available for both effective and efficient course delivery and curricula development.

Almost every sector of Czech industry has been facing up to the challenge of competition and liberalization of regulations, with an emphasis on improvements in productivity, value for resources invested, and new ways of monitoring performance. All sectors have been involved in a major change of culture. The aim of CZALP2 was to continue to work closely with the partners to identify the training needs for improved enterprise performance within a competitive environment. In addition, this was also intended to relate to the wider European objectives of the Technical University of Ostrava. CZALP3 was an elaboration of CZALP2 through the development of autonomous programmes by the successful alliance and began in 2002 with the launch of the (child) alliance's own MBA programme, though since the Czech alliance parent did not have MBA degree awarding powers, the Western parent was involved in the validation process and was the degree awarding agency.

Table 7.1 Example alliance situations and their cognitive attributes as viable systems

Situation	Cognitive Interest (may be divergent or mis-interpreted)	Cognitive Purpose (may differ or be differently expressed)	Knowledge Migration through Cognitive Influence
Cooperation in research and development e.g. on open learning	Share cost of innovation	Lead time to development	Share basic knowledge of innovation
New markets in Central Europe e.g. Moravia	Joint working with host country organization to develop market	Developing joint control and logico-relational processes with host country organization	Share product and market knowledge
Accessing segmented specialist local market e.g. Czech Telecom	Help in facilitating access to local markets		Share product, market knowledge
Guide technical knowledge to keep up with development in e.g. technology (OL, IT)		Develop new goals e.g. Open Learning	Share technical knowledge e.g. IT
Expand market share in stagnant or crowded markets e.g. part-time, in-company degrees	Help by facilitating market access to new markets	Develop market share	Share marketing knowledge for given sectors
CZALP1 1997–2002 Representatives of alliance parents identified, and interact/	Management education (IT, Banking, Management) Part-time education Open Learning Unit	Develop new markets. Support restructuring of Czech economy especially in Moravia	Share knowledge of local market Share experience in part-time education Open learning
CZALP2 1997–1999 Alliance child formed.	Open learning Open learning support network	Develop new approaches Support Czech Telecom	Share knowledge of Open learning
CZALP3 1999–2002 Alliance child launches its own programme.	Launch franchised MBA. Develop Ostrava as self-standing professional University.	Develop Company Links. Demonstrate Ostrava as mainstream Business School within European standards.	Share knowledge of MBA modes. Knowledge migration to facilitate autonomous development.

7.7 Outcome

International joint alliances that arise can be volatile, with many dissolving prematurely, and may have limited cognitive influence, purpose, or interest, and an intended limited life span and domain of action; examples are the single projects described earlier. Alternatively, they may be instances of an enduring general agreement intended for the long term, as in CZALP. If this occurs, it is usually the case that a paradigm will have developed that will have associated with it recognizable patterns of behaviour.

The strategic motivation for alliances varies with the organizations involved and their cognitive purposes and interests (Kelly and Parker, 1997). In Table 7.1 we selected five of these as applying to alliances, and supposed that each of the types of alliances had a capability of becoming viable systems in their own right. As a result, we have proposed their associated cognitive properties. We note that in Table 7.1 the last column is referred to as knowledge migration, which is cognitive influence dependent. In Table 7.1, we have also applied these three domains specifically to the three CZALP phases in the latter half of the table.

We propose that alliances may occur between agencies that are cognitive and adaptive, having cognitive influence, purpose, and interest which are strategic in nature. Within alliance theory it is also common to talk of project mission and goals. The notion can, however, also be applied to other partnerships, such as between Small to Medium sized Enterprises (SMEs) and academia (Iles and Yolles, 2002), and international joint ventures (Iles and Yolles, 2002b) as when a cognitive domain is established, from which emerges a new concrete suprametasystem that forms a child of the alliance parents, and which directs the child alliance system.

It is essential that a cognitive interest or purpose exists to facilitate an alliance. However, it cannot work without the formation of a local frame of reference from which derives the child cultural metasystem. This will be formed through the cognitive influences of all the worldviews involved, and will be a formation of the whole rather than any one part of the agencies of the alliance suprasystem. It is through the locally defined cultural metasystem that the agencies can deal with paradigm incommensurability, and thus the formation of cognitive turbulence and manifest conflict. With it, local purposefulness and direction can develop, but without it, behaviour will be prone to chaos.

Alliances between organizations are therefore considered to be purposeful adaptive activity systems, analysable in terms of three domains: cognitive, transformational, and behavioural, each with the cognitive properties of influence, purpose, and interest. This may provide the potential for further developing the theory associated with alliances, enabling us to formulate a more general viable systems theory of alliances, including International alliances such as CZALP, and identify issues and directions for further research.

8 Agency Dynamics

8.1 Introduction

Agencies naturally pass through processes of change, and pressures to do so might come from within the organization and/or from its environment. A relatively simple way of evaluating the change process through which the imperatives for change can be explored is through its dominant paradigm, where it has one. The idea of the paradigm became well known through the work of Kuhn (1970) in his exploration of the development and dynamics of scientific paradigms. However, plural agencies also have paradigms that constitute a map of their natures. Where there is a dominant paradigm, then there is no ambiguity in this nature, but where there are competing paradigms, so we enter the realm of dynamic complexity and perhaps even organizational chaos. In the latter case the agency will likely experience cultural cleavage that will interfere with the capability to perform. The demise of a dominant paradigm is not the demise of the agency, which can shift to a new paradigm in order to maintain viability.

Paradigms are conceptual patterns of thought, ideology, and pragmatism that begin life through an agency's appreciations of their apprehended epistemic truths. Any coherent autonomous durable human activity group has the ability to form a culture, and develops both cognitive interests and purposes that will form a paradigm which lives through, and represents the nature of, that agency. Within it, ideological appreciations are formulated which guide the group operationally. These appreciations are meant as a somewhat reflective view of a situation, with both cognitive and evaluative aspects. They might also be called attitudes with reflection that under the special conditions may be transformed into goals. Formulated systemically, they become appreciative systems (Vickers, 1965) that appear as generalized versions of appreciations that allow the membership of a plural agency to give accounts of a variety of situations.

Paradigms exist through their set of belief-based propositions, and it is this that creates their conceptual form. Following Duverger (1972), when the beliefs are logically rationalized and systemized so that they coalesce figuratively (in the sense of Piaget, 1950) to establish a phenomenal potential to explain experience, they may be referred to as ideology. The ideological system of thought is manifested as narrative when the potential for experience is used to shape knowledge into story (Yolles, 2007). According to this view, paradigmatic narrative is ideological dogmatism when it not only facilitates story, but also logically constrains it. However, story has both epistemic and contextual elements, and so paradigmatic narrative also has the capacity to formulate and deliver a multiplicity of distinct knowledge-based stories that it shapes.

A plurality of paradigms in a given constellation interact, and as their stories ring out they contribute to a concerto of meanings; where there is little semantic harmony paradigm conflicts and wars often develop (Kuhn, 1970; Casti, 1989; Hatch & Cunliffe, 2006; Chari et al., 2009), though this is always impossible where the paradigms are incommensurable. In such conditions the paradigmatic songs generate a cacophony or sound that may be referred to as *antenarrative*, a pre-coherence narrative reflective of cultural dissonance and indicative of cultural cleavage. Every constellation has the potential for chorus, but this has evolutionary imperatives that must necessarily eliminate incommensurability.

As an illustration of paradigmatic cacophony in science, in *organizational theory* there have been calls for a return to an intellectual orthodoxy (Clegg et al., 2006: 44), while failure in existing paradigms and the rise of meta-paradigms suggest the development of a more chaotic antenarrative phase. This is represented by uncertainty in the development of its dominant epistemology. Another example occurs in *personality theory*, which in any case is developing a presence in organizational theory, at least since Kets de Vries (1991) and implying some level of potential convergence. Since human agency is complex, modelling its effective functionality requires theoretical pluralism (Bandura, 2008). The plurality of personality schemas that coexist (Carver, 2005) create an uncertain fragmented constellation of paradigms that are uncoordinated, competitive, and together demonstrate an undeveloped theoretical understanding of the nature of personality (e.g. Sharpley, 2006). For instance, Bandura's (1999: 229) sociocognitive theory is a dynamic self-schema of personality that sees the individual as an autonomous system that interacts dynamically with its social environments. In contrast, there are trait schemas of personality like the Five Factor Model (FFM) that tend to be devoid of contextual connection and have a static rather than dynamic nature (Bandura, 1986). To deal with fragmentation, some seek a 'magic bullet' unique schema that can explain everything, and for Boje (2004) this would likely constitute a monistic horizon that is monophonic in that it offers a single general narrative and at least one story. Others seek synergistic theoretical and methodological pluralism (a 'horses for courses' perspective), which Boje (2004) would likely refer to as a plural horizon that is polyphonic since it offers many narratives each telling its own story. These narratives often have no point of interconnection, and while their stories (that are intended to explain 'reality') may be on a similar theme, their content reflects no relationship. Reflecting on such monism/pluralism and commenting on the distinctive natures of the Five Factor Method and sociocognitive theory, Cervone et al. (2001: 36) note that 'If five-factor and social-cognitive theories of personality were closely related and could easily be integrated, then there would be no need for a unique social-cognitive theory of personality assessment in the first place. Social-cognitive principles simply could be subsumed under the theoretical umbrella of five-factor theory, as McCrae and Costa (1996) have explicitly proposed. A distinct theory of personality assessment is required only if the personality theories differ fundamentally, and they do.' It would appear that here the word distinctive refers to a coherent and embracing theory, though not necessarily all-embracing.

8.2   Kuhn, Piaget: From Paradigm Crisis to Transformation

The novel ideas of Kuhn (1970) on paradigmatic change have led to not only gentle criticism connected, for instance, with the way paradigmatic incommensurability is dealt with (e.g. Budd & Hill, 2007), but also to the elaboration of notions about paradigm change through the cognitive properties and functioning of the human groups who socially carry them (e.g. Fischer, 1992).

According to Kuhn the paradigm involves four dimensions of common thought: common symbolic generalizations; shared commitment to belief in particular models or views; shared values; shared commitments of exemplars (concrete problem interventions), and is constituted as 'the set of views that the members of a...community share' (Kuhn, 1970: 176).

The paradigmatic development process first explored in depth by Kuhn (1970), argues that science passes from a *normal* mode through one of *crisis* and then to one of *revolution*. Normal science is realist in nature (Rauterberg, 2000), and has its history in the ideas of Descartes, who believed that foundational concepts are known intuitively through reason, and that truths can be deduced with absolute certainty from our innate ideas. In essence, the development of normal science embraces processes of continuous change in theory when the implications of its logical base pass through a morphogenesis. It operates in a thematic application domain that supports a dominant epistemology that allows for only a unitary perspective for the construction of knowledge. It also assumes certainty, and the possibility of making predications. The term *normal science* refers to the routine work of scientists within a paradigm, slowly accumulating knowledge in accord with established theoretical assumptions. For Kuhn it involves puzzle-solving, through which it becomes enlarged as its frontiers of knowledge and techniques are pushed forward.

Revolutionary science refers to a transformative mode for paradigms, and is connected with the idea of scientific revolutions (a metaphor that Kuhn appears to have adopted from political science). It tends to be limited to specific (thematic) subdivisions of a field of science that has passed through the prerequisite sense of crisis. The transformative mode arises when paradigms, with a normative epistemology, have poor operative intelligence, with inadequacy in their ability to support their figurative base through the normal inquiry process. The revolutionary period results in confusion within a framework of presuppositions about what constitutes a problem, a solution, and a method, and where the rationality of issues are replaced by emotionality, and are settled not by logic, syllogism, and appeals to reason, but by irrational factors like group affiliation and majority or 'mob rule' (Casti, 1989: 40).

The failure of a dominant epistemology impacts on its family of paradigms, leading to their operative intelligence impoverishment. Thus for instance, in the case of theories for personality assessment, the Big Five, the FFM, and Myers Briggs Type Inventory all adopt a common epistemology that has its critics (e.g. Maruyama, 1980; Bandura, 1986). In a similar vein Calás and Smircich (1999: 658) refer to *postmodernism* 'that it has become partially exhausted ... [and] ... has opened space for other theoretical approaches to appear'.

Beyond Kuhn, Ravetz (1999) and Funtowicz and Ravetz (1993) introduced the notion of *post-normal* science, indicating a condition where situational facts are uncertain, values in dispute, stakes high, and decisions urgent. This definition arises because of the realization that post-normal science: 'lies at the contested interfaces of science and policy' (Ravetz, 1999: 3). The idea that decisions are urgent comes from the specific context that Ravetz adopts in the field of ecology and the political urgency for decisions that might address the possibility of environmental disaster. However, more generally it arises at the dissipative edge of cultural crisis, involving competing values, uncertainty, and relativism. In such situations defenders of challenged paradigms usually refer to 'paradox', that is, a false dichotomy that can be supported by the dominant paradigm, and thus should serve to silence the critics who apparently are incapable of logical thinking.

Hessels and van Lente (2008) in their discussion of post-normal science recognize that it refers to the limitations of rational decision-making and engages with value plurality and public participation in attempts to facilitate outcomes to complex public policy decisions. In a broader sense than that posited by Ravetz, post-normal science engages with uncertainty for complex situations in which there exist plural relativist political processes.

Since paradigms are dynamic, it should be possible to track their viability – those able to maintain a high level of operative intelligence and survive the four possible modes of existence: from normal to post-normal through to critical and further on to transformational science. Understanding and tracking such changes is feasible using the viable systems modelling approach of Schwarz (1997). It is this model that explains in detail the characteristics that would be expected in each mode.

8.3 Understanding Paradigms

Scientific theories normally arise from metaphors (Brown, 2003) that begin with literal everyday experiences, and are then mapped into a domain of application to enlarge and enhance an inquirer's understanding of it. Conceptual extensions are identified and abstracted, enabling an analytic framework to develop. Within this, core theory results, with the formation of a logical base of propositions, principles, models, and narrative, the veracity of which are grounded in evidence. These are formulated as schemata which, when they become pragmatic and gather support, develop as domain application paradigms. During this process the metaphors may become lost at some horizon of meanings, and only the theory remains. A constraint on the development of theory may be that the initial metaphor may not be sufficiently rich to adequately represent the application domain, resulting in bounded paradigms that limit descriptive and explanatory capability.

Hessels and van Lente (2008) note that normal science is also referred to as academic science or mode 1 science, and is epitomized by the dominance of the 'Mertonian CUDOS norms' (Merton, 1942) that include *communalism* (the common ownership of scientific discoveries within which scientists give up intellectual property rights in exchange for recognition and esteem); *universalism* (according to which claims to truth are evaluated in terms of universal or value-free criteria); *disinterestedness* (according to which scientists are rewarded for acting in ways that appear to be selfless); and *organized scepticism* (where all ideas must be tested and are subject to structured community scrutiny).

While mode 1 science can be described as the place for the equilibrium development of paradigms, it is also the relatively simple narrative mode created through epistemic imperatives that drive stories as songs that rise and fall to the academic niche *music of the spheres*. The songs maintain their own dynamic, where incremental changes enable the equilibrium to move linearly. Even so, they maintain inbuilt limitations driven by the ideological dogma that creates the paradigm in the first place.

The use of *normal science* has not proved itself adequate for the social sciences (Manuel-Navarrete, 2001), and this includes Organization Theory. Here the plurality is unable to account for the whole of a thematic *Reality* (Hatch & Cunliffe, 2006). As an illustration, this also appears to be the situation in the thematic domain of personality research, where each schema operates as a distinct and unconnected narrative resulting in disjointed storytelling.

The concept of *post-normal science* goes beyond the traditional assumptions that science is both certain and value-free. In addition to the application of routine techniques, judgement also becomes necessary, as well as involvement of extended peer communities. Kuhn had already emphasized the important role of human factors, such as intuition, imagination, and receptivity to new ideas, in the exercise of scholarly activities. Karl E. Weick's article on 'Theory Construction as Disciplines Imagination' in the 1989 American Management Review special issue proves a perfect match with Kuhn's ideas.

In contrast to normal science, *post-normal science* (also called *post-academic science*) is concerned with complexity and has interests that relate to uncertainty, assigned values, and a plurality of legitimately argued perspectives. These attributes are antenarrative in nature, from which narratives may arise, and where a plural collective co-construction of multiple voices develop, each with a narrative fragment and none with an overarching conception of the story that is becoming. 'Feminist Organizational Theorizing', 'Postcolonial Analysis' and 'Actor-Network Theory' are excellent examples provided by Calás and Smircich (1999). Mode 2 science may also be linked intimately with Boje's (2001) notion of antenarrative, where a constellation of paradigms exist in an incoherent disjoint discordant space.

Mode 3 science is that of *crisis*, a condition in which paradigmatic narrative reflects the crisis that the paradigm is passing through and is thus incapable to hosting coherent stories. It is a boundary condition for transformation and a prerequisite for revolution (Kuhn, 1970). It attenuates the role of paradigms since their carriers become estranged from them. As the crisis deepens, carriers commit themselves to some concrete proposal for reconstruction to a new framework. Where different frameworks exist, communication fails and loses its semantic content as polarization develops, when members of the different camps become constrained by the boundaries of their paradigm (Hatch & Cunliffe, 2006). Crisis is closely related to the 'incredulity toward meta or master narratives – and to a continuing question of *how to write* legitimate knowledge' (Calás and Smirchich, 1999: 664).

For Fischer (1992) crisis corresponds to an unstable cognitive strategy that oscillates between the constraint of normal science and a search for a better frame of thought – one that might allow a novel integration of fragmentary representational structure that exists across a plurality of paradigms on a higher level of abstraction, differentiation, and integration. It is here that the social forces of unity, consensus, and commitment become more fluid, and new social ties, circles, and networks form, while new virtual paradigms may rise or fall.

The *transformative* mode 4 defines paradigms' pre-narrative condition, where new virtual paradigms may arise or old paradigms may be reborn, though they might not necessarily be in conflict with any of their predecessors. After Kuhn, two forms of conceptual extension are possible: (a) lateral, so as to be able to identify phenomena not previously known; or (b) transitive, where a higher level of theory (referred to as meta-theory) than those known before arises that may be linked to a whole group of lower level theories without substantially changing any. As such, for Fischer (1992) a crystallization of the support occurs when the emergence of a new cognitive consensus becomes concretized.

The rise of paradigms as a part of normal or post-normal science is a function of the realistic or relativistic perspectives that an academic community takes. To recognize their distinctions, we can call on two epistemologically distinct examples referred to earlier that might be usefully returned to: *grand theories* and *mixed methods theories*. As part of realism, grand theories tend to exist in normal science and are theoretically unitary in their development. In contrast, the mixed methods approach is relativist and adopts a plural theoretical approach that operates in post-normal modes of science (cf. Lewis and Grimes, 1999). We have already indicated that through their transitive development some grand theories entertain mixed methods.

Perhaps *mixed methods approaches* can be seen as the result of groups trying to reduce uncertainty in a post-normal science environment. Such approaches have gathered significant support in a variety of thematic areas (e.g. Alvesson, 2000; Mingers, 2001; Lindlof, 2002). The approach is represented by Modell (2007) as a boundary cross-over between realism and relativism, and is referred to as critical realism. Here, two forms of input are accepted: primary qualities of realist data (that are objective and independent of any observer) which accurately represent external objects, properties, and events; and secondary qualities of relativist data that have subjective attributes.

Grand theories seek to describe or explain very broad features of their area of interest (Donelan, 2004), and ascribe to problem situations a few broad unifying conceptual categories (Llewellyn, 2003). Oakley (2004) refers to grand theories as being doctrine rather than problem driven. While they may be developed laterally through elaboration of their conceptualizations, for Jokisch (2001) they are susceptible to four problems: simplifying generalizations, which may have totalitarian aspects, and which provide the possible difficulty of assigning specific concrete situations; the 'emptiness' of its central concepts; a lack of empirical connection; and the lack of allowing for internal changes.

Such problems are likely to be diminished when paradigms become transitively extended and their dogmas become meta-theoretic (Mowen, 1999). Meta-theory may be seen as having three dimensions: it acts to connect different mid-range theories (Bacharach, 1989); it improves parsimony by accounting for a broader array of phenomena with fewer constructs than was previously possible (Morgan & Hunt, 1994; Tybout, 1995); and it generates new knowledge (Kaplan, 1964) by producing new empirically testable hypotheses. Realist meta-theory is unitary and concerned with principles from which particular theory can develop, as in the case of Bandura's (1986) Social Cognitive Theory. Relativist meta-theory is pluralistic, connecting different relatable theories (e.g. Jackson & Keys, 1984; Jackson, 1991; Adams & Hyon, 2005). Relativist meta-theory building needs principles that can distinguish between paradigmatic differences, similarities, and interrelationships to be comprehended (Gioia & Pitre, 1990). Approaches are required that allow their distinctions to be explored (Parker & McHugh, 1991; Scherer, 1998).

Lewis and Grimes (1999), exploring their meta-triangulation approach, adopt a relativistic meta-theory strategy that they claim can explore divergent theoretical views, challenging taken-for-granted assumptions, and portraying organizations in new light. However, such approaches have both limitations and dangers (Lewis & Grimes, 1999: 686–687), for which two problems may arise: bracketing and lensing. We have already in passing referred to bracketing. Paradigm bracketing arises when different paradigms are classified according to what they do, which may reproduce the very dualisms that the approach tries to overcome (Deetz, 1996). The lensing perspective rises from the realization that each paradigm has its own lens from which meaning arises, and across which there are both complementarities and disparities (Poole & van de Ven, 1989; Gioia & Pitre, 1990; Ybema, 1996).

Earlier we referred to the development of meta-theory. This constitutes an alternative transitory evolution that occurs when paradigms are formulated through the use of higher level frameworks or *meta-frameworks* that reflect 'a theory of meaning' (cf. Weick, 1989) through the formulation of meta-theory, and these can respond to both doctrinal and problem-based issues (Oakley, 2004). For Oakley, such a framework demands a theory of attention, which involves the development of a cognitive semiotic that demands both self and context awareness, and reflection on theory development process. The doctrine of this framework requires cognitive and cultural processes that are subjugated by attention. There may be many alternative meta-theories on which to build a theory of meaning, where one may develop a more successful theory of attention on which to ground a theory of meaning, while simultaneously being attached to a defined context which is in some way problem-driven (Cheng, 2007). The creation of a meta-theory framework thus enables paradigmatic connections that operate on a semantic level, rather than one which is connected with more local paradigmatic propositions. Examples of such frameworks are Management Cybernetics (Beer, 1981), and Complexity Theory (Hemaspaandra & Ogihara, 2002).

8.4 Paradigms under Change

While realist paradigms may arise spontaneously, they may also pass through processes of developmental change. The idea that paradigms may survive different modes of existence, from normal to post-normal and through crisis to transformation, raises the question whether paradigms can, and if so how they may be able to, survive shifts in their phases of existence. To begin to respond to this, one really needs to appreciate the distinction between the processes of change that a paradigm goes through when it is part of normal and post-normal science. For Kluver et al. (2003), their distinction can be highlighted by the realization that in normal science there is the tendency for paradigms to change incrementally, beginning with rather simple models and developing complexity. In contrast, post-normal science is often transformative, embracing the early capture of as much of the complexity that a conceptual framework is capable of.

We have already referred to the paradigm as a group affair that has a logical base of theory and embedded normative modes of practice. It is defined in the Kuhnian sense as a 'disciplinary matrix' composed of shared beliefs, values, models, and exemplars that guide a 'community' of theorists and practitioners (Kuhn, 1977). The exemplars contribute to its modes of practice, while its community nature suggests that it operates through a culture that drives it as a coherent group. This group culture operates through a belief system (of beliefs, values, and attitudes) and language; and it has both group norms and a cognitive space of conceptualization associated with it (Yolles, 1999). So the paradigm operating as a viable human activity system is much more than a theory and is susceptible to change.

This idea of the paradigm can be further extended using process intelligences. We may be reminded that figurative intelligence provides a copy of states of reality or precise information about them, and involves any means of representation used to keep in mind the states that intervene between transformations, that is, it involves perception, drawing, mental imagery, language, and imitation. In terms of the paradigm there is a figurative base that is composed of models, which entail structured relationships and epistemological and information properties. The capacity of the figurative base to adequately reflect the cognitive base of the paradigm and maintain pragmatic interpretations constitutes its figurative intelligence (Piaget, 1950; Piaget & Inhelder, 1969; Montangero & Maurice-Naville, 1997). In contrast, operative intelligence is dynamic and intimately connected to understanding. It is responsible for the representation and manipulation of the transformational aspects of reality. It involves all actions that are undertaken so as to anticipate, follow, or recover the transformations of the objects or persons of interest. Within the context of the paradigm, operative intelligence provides an indication of the ability of its holders to map its figurative base pragmatically. So, figurative intelligence involves experiential reflections from operative intelligence. Since states cannot exist independently from the transformations that interconnect them, figurative intelligence derives its meaning from operative intelligence. Strategies 'for sensemaking' in detection of 'patterns in processes or their driving mechanisms', as well as with respect to 'prediction' or 'detection of meaning of processes for people involved' (Langley, 1999: 695) are related to figurative and operative intelligence.

As a reflection of agencies, paradigms that survive the trials and tribulations that its holders experience over time and thus are durable are said to be *viable*. Viable paradigms are able to survive both normal and post-normal situations. To understand how this may occur, paradigms should be seen as autonomous systems which define, create, and manage their own futures. Through their holders, they are also able to self-organize and hence alter their own logical base. They produce the laws that rule them (Schwarz, 1997), and they do this because they are logically closed, a condition that occurs, according to Parsons (1937), when: all its propositions are interdependent in that each has implications for the others, and each of these implications finds its statement in another proposition of the same system.

While paradigms may be logically closed, they are also open systems in that they take in data from their environment that comes from measurement, knowledge, and narratives from experiences and other paradigms. Their outputs are knowledge and narrative. If the paradigm is to be able to provide a narrative through its advocates who adequately explain all of the inputs that relate to their interests and purposes, then its propositions must be able to conceptually respond to the inputs. Where it cannot do this, the paradigm fails.

In normal science paradigms operate as equilibrium systems that are deterministic and hence certain in their patterns of knowledge. Over time paradigms change deterministically and reversibly (Prigogine & Stengers, 1984). Processes of change involving randomness or irreversibility are exceptional. However, when uncertainty occurs within the paradigm in relation to its paradigmatic inputs, the paradigm shifts to a far from equilibrium state. Here, the paradigm's logical structure defined by its propositions and principles becomes dissipative and subject to fluctuation, and it is unable to provide a stable narrative that adequately explains its environment. Demand for phenomenon-driven research is emerging (Cheng, 2007). New types of structures may originate spontaneously as the paradigm moves from organizational chaos to greater order. A viable paradigm that is able to survive this experience can become classed as part of post-normal science.

In agency theory there is a noumenal domain. Here there resides the logical base, models, and information that operate as the theoretical patterns that the paradigm holds; and in the phenomenal domain reside the normative modes of practice that emerge from the theory and become manifest as observable phenomena. The connection between logical structures and practice/modes of behaviour in the paradigm is autopoietic and defines its operative intelligence. It is through operative intelligence that viable systems can pass through processes of emergence and evolution towards complexity and more developed autonomy; by that they maintain themselves, change, and survive.

Schwarz (1997) identifies a set of principles that identify three inseparable primal categories present in all systems: (1) there is a connection between objects, relations, and wholes; (2) every dynamic system consists of a dual principle governing change, a drift towards disorder, and a capacity to increase order (and complexity) through self-organization; (3) as the complexity of the system increases and *operational closure* develops that can lead successively to self-organization, self-production (autopoiesis), self-reference, and autonomy in durable viable systems. Self-organization is the source of morphogenesis within which structures change, autopoiesis is the source of the overall coherence of the living organisms, and self-reference is at the root of consciousness.

Paradigms only exist through the holders who define and maintain them. As such, durable paradigms may be seen as viable human activity systems that are both complex and adaptive, and able to maintain a separate existence within the confines of their existential or other constraints. Their existential nature consists of the belief system and patterns of knowledge that arise through the coherent group of people who maintain them. They have an at least potential independence in their 'self-processes' for regulation, organization, production, and cognition. Schwarz notes that viable systems can pass through processes of emergence and evolution towards complexity and autonomy, though autonomy does not mean that there is no interactive influence from its environment. This occurs through the development of patterns of self-organization that accommodate phenomenal change in the paradigmatic practices and behaviours that paradigm holders pursue. This occurs through morphogenesis and new forms of complexity; patterns for long-term evolution towards autonomy; and patterns that lead to systems functioning viably through their capacity to create variety and indeed respond to environmental situations with the matching *requisite variety* (Ashby, 1956), which is required to maintain balance and enable a paradigm (through its carriers) to respond adequately to its environment.

The dynamic process that viable paradigms can pass through as they change is illustrated in Figure 8.1 and Table 8.1 (adapted from Schwarz, 1997). They explain the cycle of change for viable paradigms that are able to survive by transforming their natures, initially by developing through normal science, experiencing uncertainty, and moving into post-normal science and hence to metamorphosis. During this process, non-viable paradigms decease, while a

242   Agency Change

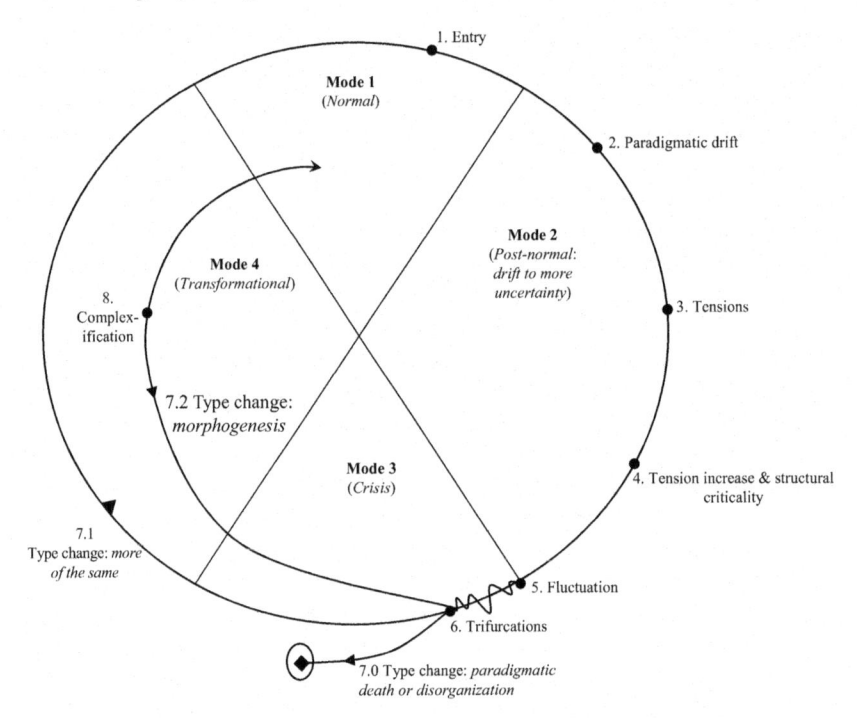

Figure 8.1 Cycle of paradigmatic change, and the relationship between four modes of science

viable paradigm will become complexified as it develops more attributes and explanatory power in its theory.

8.5 Transformation of Paradigms

In our cycle of change we have said that paradigms pass through a transformational mode. The question may be asked, how does the shift from one mode to another develop?

The rise of paradigms is intimately connected with the rise of paradigmatic cultures, which are influenced by the micro-actions of individuals, and which become symbolized and hence normatively anchored into the paradigm (Staw, 1991). As a result, it develops a cognitive base. This base is both culture and knowledge-centred, and is hence sensitive both to knowledge and cultural challenges, the two necessarily being related.

The normal mode of a paradigm exists through its adoption of a normative epistemology, which lies at the basis of its formalized patterns of knowledge. This may be challenged with the development of doubt about its veracity

Table 8.1 *Explanation of the options for paradigmatic change*

Mode of Being	Step	Movement towards Evolution
Mode 1: Normal	1. Stable equilibrium	The paradigm exists with a stable belief system and logical base, though during normal development the base may change its form (morphogenesis). Where there are too many distinct narratives with competing stories, equilibrium is lost.
Mode 2: Post-normal	2. Paradigmatic drift 3. Tension development 4. Tension increase and structural criticality	Antenarrative develops as dissipative processes are introduced and a constellation of paradigms result in a cacophony of voiced stories. In a complex application domain, drift enables unexpressed potentials to be actualized. The drift takes the paradigm away from its stable position and gives rise to tensions between its ability to explain and predict, and questions about its methods in relation to observations.
Mode 3: Crisis	5. Fluctuations	The tensions, following the tropic drift that moved the paradigm away from its stable narrative position, are leading it to structural criticality. If the paradigm loses robustness, fluctuations are amplified. Fluctuations occur internally, or in the environment as noise. Through amplification of fluctuations due to tensions following uncertainty drift, a discontinuity occurs in the causal sequence of events/behaviour. This likely will be accompanied by debates about utility of the epistemological basis for the paradigm.
	6. Trifurcations	When trifurcations occur the paradigm is able to take one of three possible paths in its pragmatic behaviours.
	7.0 Paradigmatic death (post-narrative)	In type 7.0, decay represents a process of disorganization, regression, or extinction of the paradigm, ultimately leading to the possible loss of group member carriers. This can be seen as the start of a catastrophe trifurcation.
	7.1 Type 1 change 8.	In type 7.1 the process of change begins with 'more of the same' small changes that maintain its current state but do not resolve issues. Complexification of the logical base and modes of practice can occur during a process of iteration.
Mode 4: Transformation	7.2 Type 2 change	In type 2 change, metamorphosis occurs through emergence that begins in the logical base of paradigm, and is amplified within its critical structure leading to a new logical base of propositions that induce new forms of practice.

244   Agency Change

Table 8.1 *(cont.)*

Mode of Being	Step	Movement towards Evolution
		This is referred to as morphogenic change, occurring through amplification and differentiation. It is a relational process that develops in the paradigm through positive and negative feedback, and integration, when the new cognitive base is manifested figuratively and pragmatically.

(e.g. Meehl, 1997). Such challenges can result in structural changes that lead to pragmatic adjustment when modes and mechanisms of practice alter. When a paradigm exists in normal mode and is challenged in this way, the result can be a shift into a post-normal mode. We can adapt an argument from Rummel (1979) to explain how this can happen in one of two ways.

First, change can occur more rapidly than the ability of a culture has to adjust. This creates a *cultural lag* that leads to instability and conflict. It occurs when the realization of values fails, and values disparities develop. Now cultural lag is constituted as the difference between what is and what some segments of a culture consider *ought to be*. Interestingly, this engages with ideology and ethics, since both involve a coalescence of values. In the case of ideology the values are orientations towards action, but this is constrained by ethics, which identifies what ought to happen and involves processes of judgement. New modes and means of practice create the means to satisfy certain values, even while existing norms, attitudes, or institutions inhibit or block such satisfaction.

Second, the effect of new modes and means of practice can also be considered through the idea that within periods of normal science, paradigms fall into an equilibrium of values that relates to the complex of desires and attitudes. Values in a culture may be seen here to ultimately balance out, and a general equilibrium emerges between wants and costs, investments and rewards, capabilities and power. Among possible states of a system, it is the balance of power that Rummel (1979) sees as such equilibriums.

This explanation can be elaborated on through the notion of *culture shock* (Dahl, 2000). Culture shock is normally taken to mean the anxiety and related feelings that arise when people are faced by a sudden change in their sociocultural environment, and it grows out of an inability to assimilate new elements within it. Thinking beyond the initial shock Adler (1987: 29) considered that culture shock is the opportunity of a 'profound learning experience that leads to a high degree of self-awareness and personal growth' as adaptation to new situations arise.

So, when a paradigm resides in normal mode its gradual development occurs through equilibrium processes that many consider to represent its 'advancement'. The rise of challenge to the use of a particular normative epistemology results in cultural uncertainty, when predominant values become challenged. This leads to the onset of culture shock and cultural instability, and the eventual development of new modes and means of practice. During this process conflicts and relativisms are likely to arise, and the paradigm shifts into post-normal mode. This process may not be inevitable, particularly when the holders of a paradigm are imbued with *cultural intelligence*: defined as the ability for an individual to successfully adapt to a change in cultural settings attributable to cultural context (Earley & Ang, 2003: 3).

There is another quite distinct issue of interest to do with paradigmatic change. It occurs when one realizes that paradigms do not develop in isolation, but rather are responsive to their ambient host culture. Through the human activity groups that carry their paradigm, an individual culture is created that determines its orientation and possibilities. This culture, however, is influenced by the ambient cultural environment in which the paradigms sit. This happens in the case of corporate cultures which exist within a cultural framework (e.g. Sørnes et al., 2004, Sagiv & Schwartz, 2007).

This notion of ambient culture having an influence on paradigmatic culture can also be extended using the notions of socio-cultural dynamics proposed by Sorokin (1939–42). In his theory cultures shift through their own internal dynamics (referred to as immanent change) between two states of being, Sensate and Ideational. *Ideational cultures* are ideas-led, while *sensate cultures* are led by the senses. Cultural values can be explored in this light. They are manifested as a coherent set of ideological values that drive modes or practice, and a set of ethical values that drive judgements. According to Zetterberg (1997), in an ideational culture ethics is concerned with unconditional moral principles. In a sensate culture ethics is concerned with the pursuit of happiness. The former thus preaches value fidelity, the latter preaches pragmatism. In a sensate culture human activity is extroverted; in an ideational culture it is introverted.

Following Rummel (1979), as a culture shifts from one stable state to another it becomes unstable since opposing interests arise. In terms of Sorokin's theory, this leads to a loss of ideological and ethical stability, affecting the paradigms and their development.

So ideational culture drives a normal science, epitomized for instance by Bacon who (in the late sixteenth Century at the boundary shift towards sensate culture and in the Industrial Revolution) popularized inductive methodology for scientific inquiry. It is through his notion of inductive reasoning that scientists are led from fact to axiom. Before beginning this induction, the inquirer is required to free his or her mind from certain false notions or tendencies which distort the truth. Later, with the development of stable sensate culture, normal science shifted towards an empirically orientated science.

Where the ambient host culture of a paradigm is *sensate*, it results in the encouragement of paradigms that conform to the ambient normative (and dominant) epistemology that maintains realist perspectives. Where the ambient host culture is *ideational*, paradigms that conform to the ambient normative (and dominant) epistemology are driven towards relativist epistemologies. Where the ambient host culture is unstable (as a discontinuous change between cultural states occurs) then the dominant epistemology starts to lose its dominance (as is likely happening now for organization theory). It is in such periods that paradigms shift into post-normal science, crisis, and transformation, wholesale. This does not of course mean that paradigms do not pass through the cycle when the ambient normative culture is stable. It just means that the nature of post-normal, crisis, and transformation modes are likely to be different.

8.6 Agency Life-Cycle

By now we should be aware that agency is not a static body, but changes through both external and internal processes. Internal change that is due to internal processes is referred to as 'immanence'. Immanent change is important to normal organizational developments, and can have significant impacts on any capacity to function effectively, especially in a changing environment. For sufficiently large organizations, their *immanent dynamics* begin with small changes that influence its culture, and hence its dominant paradigm.

An illustration of the impact of immanent dynamics comes from the idea that an agency passes through processes of change as it grows (Greiner, 1998/1972). This idea goes back at least to 1912 with Ludwig von Mises's work on the theory of money. In his article on 'Evolution and Revolution as Organizations Grow' Larry Greiner (1998) reasserted major findings of his 1972 article, namely that organizations as they grow also pass through a series of developmental phases. Each phase begins with a period of evolution, with steady growth and stability, and ends with a revolutionary period of substantial organizational turmoil and change. As firms age and grow over a long period, they may pass through several stages of evolution, each of which will end in revolution, since a major solution in one period becomes a major problem in a later period. Greiner originally (1972) distinguished five pairs of evolution-revolution, and in his 1998 paper with *extra-organizational solutions* he added one more *solution attempt* as source of growth, but did not explicitly attach

Table 8.2 *Sources of firm growth and evolving crises (Greiner, 1998)*

Phase	Sources of Growth	Emergent Crises
1	Creativity and innovation	Incoherence of action and need for leadership.
2	Leadership: direction and hierarchy	Rigid hierarchical decisions and need for delegation.
3	Decentralization (delegation)	Parochial attitudes and need for coordination.
4	Formalization of coordination	Precedence of procedures and need for collaboration.
5	Collaboration and social control	Exhausting teamwork procedures and social pressures, no internal solution found.
6	Seeking extra-organizational solutions	Crises of cultural conformity (only mentioned as typical for service firms)

crisis of cultural conformity to it as the counterpoise, which he mentioned later in that paper in the context of the professional service firm (Table 8.2).

Greiner's early views stimulated conceptualizations of life-cycle models (Rink & Swan, 1979; Miller and Friesen, 1984; Hanks, 1990; Adizes, 1999; Lester et al., 2003). Yan (2006) notes that (1) there is no consensus on the methodologies to be used to identify whether the corporate body has achieved a given life-cycle stage, and (2) the various life-cycle models are quite distinct having from between three to eleven different stages, but mostly three to five stages (Quinn and Cameron, 1983; Yan, 2006). All life-cycle models are variations of a cyclic pattern of birth, growth, maturity, and demise, but there are a variety of particular stage models to represent this. For instance Miller & Friesen (1984) identify an empirically supported five-stage life-cycle, while Adizes (1999) produces an eleven-stage cycle, Greiner (1998) expanded the general five-stage model to *six sources of growth* stages, but for the professional service his team identified only four stages. With respect to crises emerging from *seeking extra-organizational solutions* one may also refer to the reported high failure rates of foreign direct investments and international mergers and acquisitions (e.g. Child et al., 2001).

There are some criticisms of life-cycle models (Stubbart & Smalley, 1999; Phelps, Adams & Bessant, 2007). A larger more comprehensive study by Levie & Lichtenstein (2008) performed an in-depth analysis of 104 scholarly studies of life-cycle papers published over a 45-year period. They argue that organizations grow like organisms and pass through dynamic processes of complexity, which involve non-equilibrium conditions. This facilitates their entry into different life-cycle configurations, but not necessarily set to any order. Levie & Lichtenstein (2008) note that Miller & Friesen (1984) undertook some empirical test of a configuration life-cycle model that arose as a composite from a number of other models and tested it on longitudinal data from thirty-six firms. It was uncovered that much organizational growth and change was discontinuous in nature, with varying periods of organizational 'momentum', in which there were quantum leaps in organizational form. Also detected was a tendency for firms to adopt a limited number of organizational forms, which differed from one another in multifaceted ways. These different forms were not necessarily connected to each other in any deterministic sequence. Levie & Lichtenstein also note that Raffa, Zollo, & Caponi (1996) found that growth paths of thirty-two young Italian software firms were quite complex, with the firms moving between seven different identifiable configurations, but not in any set order.

Considering the variety of presumed stages and the lack of a clear sequence of stages one important issue remains: the issue of *immanence*. Immanence refers to the implicit dynamics that emerges from the interaction and microbehaviours of humans within an organization. As Greiner (1998) put it: any *solution* is at the core of the consequent *crisis*. Thus, cycles go through the stages *solution – crisis – solution – crisis – and so on*.

The immanent dynamics that is referred to may be seen as an outcropping from the cultural research of Sorokin (1962). He shows that cultures naturally pass through a never ending sequence of changes which have an impact on social life. The 'immanent' sources of change are contrasting cultural orientations that necessarily exist simultaneously in any social system. However, emphasis on the one or the other contrasting cultural orientation necessarily changes as issues within the social system change. This stands to reassert the existence of manifest corporate life-cycles. Within the organization different cultural orientations exist, which interact in problem resolutions, but if taken to the extreme they become problem causes. This view, which can be found in the reflections of Greiner (1998), is consistent with that of Cameron & Quinn (2006), who emphasize that if taken to the extreme any of the four basic leadership styles which they have identified is counterproductive. Only constructive interaction between alternate styles is productive.

Swings between stable and unstable periods in organizations are accompanied by swings in emotional climate in the organization. For example, when owners/managers take recourse to authoritarian styles, they aim at generating an emotional climate of fear. Thus Boje (2002), in his analysis of the ENRON case, refers to a 'rank and yank performance review method, in which the lowest 15 per cent performers were let go.' Thus, ENRON top management created a climate of fear, 'accentuating its more "Yes-Sir subservience, risk-proneness, and its overt macho sexism"' (Boje, 2002). As to cultural effects of a climate of fear Deming (1982, 1993, 2000) and Joiner (1994) (cited by Curiouscat, 2015) noted that: *where there is fear you do not get honest figures*, and *data* ('the results') can be improved by (1) *distorting the system*, (2) *distorting the data,* (3) *improving the system* (which tends to be more difficult, though likely what is desired). Beyond that some staff might take subversive or even hostile sabotage action against owners and managers, which might be driven by the desire to act against the *dominance emotions* displayed by their masters (Mars, 2001; Fink, Holden & Lehmann, 2007).

By contrast, a climate of security is perceived to be positively related to a communication culture (Ashkanazy & Nicholson, 2003). Creating a positive emotional climate often is strongly recommended (Ashkanazy & Ashton-James, 2007). A positive emotional climate is a precondition for collaboration and social control, which help to mobilize innovative potentials, that is, openness to new values and ideas, openness to trust and mutual dependence, that is, working together for the greater good; and integrative potentials, that is, communication, direction, and leadership. (Appelbaum, Roberts & Shapiro, 2009).

Taking a broader perspective we might posit that any insolvency of a firm and the consequent closure of a firm is necessarily preceded by uncoordinated *within-firm* communication at all levels about the emergence of crisis signals, conflicting interpretations of causes of an emerging crisis, and conflicting views about possible solutions. Thus, for a more general model of organizational crises and change we might need to extend Greiner's model with roots of crises that are not tied to prevailing strategies and managers who cling too long to outdated strategies. To demonstrate this within a comparative context, we collect relevant information from Germany and Austria concerning causes of insolvency (Table 8.3).

Since we can relate the causes of insolvency to constituting elements of an organizational culture (attitudes and values, figurative intelligence, operative intelligence), taking a cultural perspective allows one to consider corporate life-cycle stages as a reflection of cultural state and development.

We can elaborate on the cultural view by extending the agency model to introduce an additional generic order in the hierarchy. Let us consider a corporate cultural agency embedded in an ambient national socio-political culture as shown in Figure 8.2. Let us suppose that this ambient culture has been internalized by the agency, therefore creating for it a higher order of consciousness in its generic systemic hierarchy. Where internalization has occurred pathologically, then the nature of the ambient culture is somehow misunderstood, thereby influencing capacity for corporate performance. Consider now that the ambient culture may be under gradual change through incremental adjustments such that it maintains its overall stability. This stability occurs because the ambient value system and semantic norms are stable (in the former case individual values in the system maintain their relationships, while in the latter case norms maintain their meaning). As previously indicated, culture has the capacity to create a stable anchor for the corporate

Table 8.3 *Causes of insolvency – information collected in Austria and Germany (Sources: KSV1870 2013; Rotter, 2014; Sicking, 2011)*

1. **External sources of crisis (insolvency) beyond control by firm owner or manager:**
   - Poor payment morale of clients (poor counterparty risk management),
   - Market change, decline in demand, new foreign or domestic competitors,
   - Credit constraints,
   - Strong wage increase,
   - Changes in taxation system or tax increase,
   - State bureaucracy, labour law, and social policy implementation,
   - Accident or severe health problem of owner/manager.
2. **Internal sources of crisis (insolvency)**
   2.1 *Attitudes and values*
   - Authoritarian rigid leadership style of owner/manager,
   - Lack of transparency and deficient communication,
   - Lack of essential personality characteristics such as: reliable, honest, fair, creative, loyal, and open,
   - Fraud.

   2.2 *Strategy (lack of figurative intelligence)*
   - Lack of vision and foresight, wrong images of the future,
   - Incapability to make appropriate market assessment,
   - Unfounded investment decisions and excessive investment,
   - Lack of rational decision making,
   - Too long clinging to outdated strategies.

   2.3 *Implementation (lack of operative intelligence)*
   - Lack of financial resources,
   - Lack of market observation, ignorance of market feedback,
   - Lack of operative knowledge about accounting system and business practices,
   - Lack of controlling or inefficient corporate controlling.

agency, which assists in maintaining agency viability. Part of the anchor values and norms will be a projection for certain expectations in corporate development to corporate culture. Such expectations will reflect a variety of ambient agency regulations through its norms.

Our interest lies in two situations here. One is that the ambient culture is stable and the other is that it is unstable. In both cases values and norms still exist, though in the latter case the value system and semantic norms are likely to become unstable (when individual values in the system lose their relationships and norms lose meaning). A stable ambient culture provides a feasible platform for a normal sequence of phases in an evolutionary corporate life-cyclic pattern of birth, growth, maturity, and demise. With ambient cultural instability, anchors are no longer provided for corporate culture. Thus, any phases it passes through will be dependent on local corporate context-sensitive issues that are likely to involve uncertainty. As such, any phase shifts that a corporation settles to may be more a function of circumstance rather than a corporate life-cycle evolution. These two cultural conditions provide an

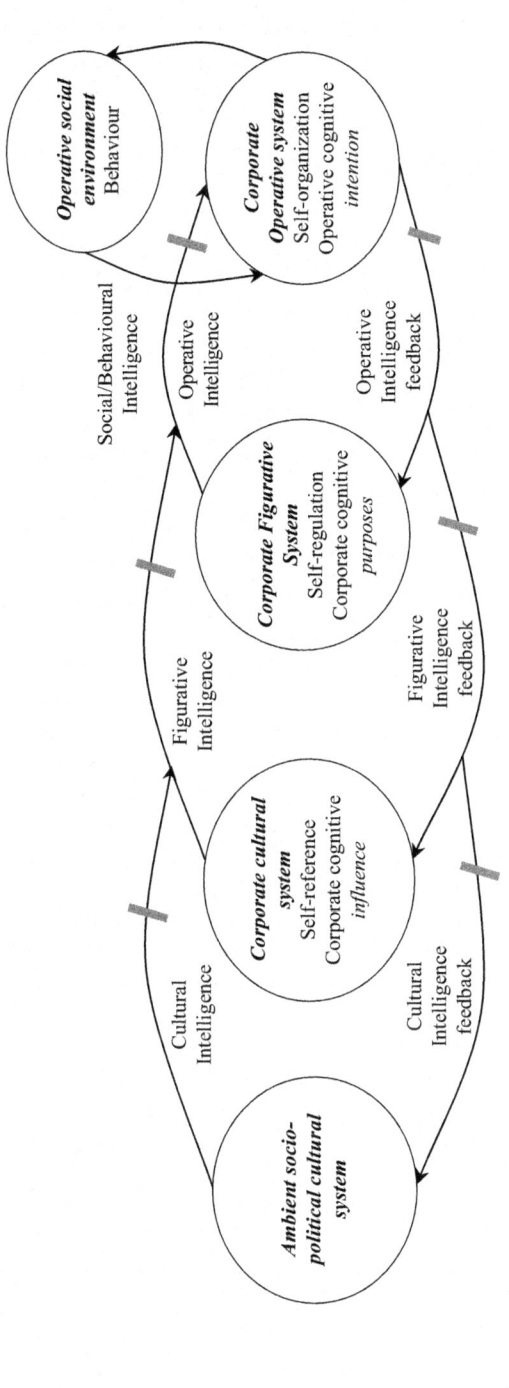

Figure 8.2 Corporate body embedded in an ambient national culture

explanation as to why a predictive sequence of life-cycles are sometimes seen, and other times not. It would be interesting, therefore, to consider ambient cultures as an additional variable in the light of studies like that of Levie & Lichtenstein (2008) referred to above, and see how ambient cultural stability might impact on their results.

Kuhn (1975) was also interested in cultural change through paradigmatic shifts and the change in normative practice that accompanies them. We elaborate on his idea in the next section since they are relevant to explaining the change process. Here, then, we posit a model that is capable of describing solution–crisis–solution–cycles, irrespective of the initial contextual shape of a stable solution and of the type of a crisis which may emerge, and explains corporate change in a stable ambient culture as it moves from one phase to another.

8.7 Baoshang Bank Case Study

Background to Baoshang Bank

Baoshang Bank is a joint-stock commercial bank that was established in 1998 and originated in Inner Mongolia, but it has successfully developed a trans-regional development with presence in more than 14 regional areas, and it has business activity in a number of important cities, including Beijing, Ningbo, Chengdu, and Shenzhen. Among the 147 city commercial banks, 39 of them have realized trans-regional development, with first-tier cities such as Beijing, Shanghai, and Shenzhen being first choice of trans-regional development. Among non-listed banks, Bank of Dalian, Bank of Shanghai, Bank of Hangzhou, Harbin Bank, Baoshang Bank, and Shengjing Bank rank top in terms of branches number outside the province.

The bank has more than a dozen autonomous regional offices located across China, each with their own distinct culture. With around 6000 employees, it is a relatively small bank by Chinese standards, compared to say the Bank of Communications, which is one of the top five Chinese banks with around 90,000 employees.

It is a rapidly growing bank that was bootstrapped towards improved performance through its tripartite agreement in 2005 with the National Development Bank (NDB) and the German International Project Consultant (IPC) company. The NDB is a state-owned enterprise that is overseen primarily by the Ministry of Treasury and Finance, with shareholding held in-trust by Independent Public Business Corporation (IPBC) and is based in Papua New Guinea. The IPC has been involved as a corporate body since the 1980s, having been offering consultancy advice to organizations in transnational economies. This tripartite partnership delivered a micro-loan project that led to is accelerating micro-loan business. After 6 years, in September 2011, Baoshang Bank had accumulated nearly 120 billion yuan from its small and micro-enterprise loans by serving the needs of nearly 80,000 small and micro-enterprises, as well as individual businesses and farmers or herdsmen. The non-performing business loans ratio is only 0.46 per cent.

The bank's special interest in Small to Medium Enterprises (SMEs) and in particular micro-funding has therefore been demonstrated to be a successful strategy. Micro-enterprises are enterprises with fewer than ten employees and a turnover or balance sheet total of less than €2 million (Europa, 2007). However, the bank's leadership in micro-enterprise loan funding became challenged in 2011. The reason is that smaller businesses in China contribute to 80 per cent of its employment (Deng, 2011), and a policy approach was suggested (Luo, 2009) for the improvement of the small business horizon. Government policy was then developed, as a consequence, to support this horizon. This resulted in a number of large state-owned banks leaning towards this market. As a response, Baoshang Bank needed to differentiate itself from other banks. Having said this, the large banks have not embraced micro-financing since they appear to believe that this accrues a high cost. They would also be unlikely candidates for such a development because of the difficult culture change that they would need to pass through in order to implement it.

Thus, unlike the large longer established banks, Baoshang Bank was prepared to embrace a culture change. Its partner IPC recommended that the bank altered its credit culture. Rather than the original centralized approach that required all loan issues to be approved by head office, a more distributed approach was adopted that enabled greater speed and flexibility. This involves decision making by a loan officer and two members of the credit censoring committee, a process that takes the much shorter time of three days. This is an important change since a significant portion of the bank's business is dependent on micro-financing. As a measure of this commitment, almost 30 per cent of its staffing is dedicated to micro- and small enterprise finance.

With this cultural shift, a new principle was engaged where more importance was attached to analysis as opposed to mortgages; and to credit as opposed to guarantees. More, micro-enterprise applicants could apply using their ID cards for business licenses. Loans varied between 3000 and 10 million yuan, and qualifying applicants would receive their loans within between 3 and 7 working days. This business model is particularly directed towards potential applicants in remote areas, as in vast Inner Mongolia. It operates in this region through its subsidiary, the Baoshang Benefit Farmer Finance Company, which is responsible for the setting of the interest rate loans and their variation for agriculture-related small enterprises and rural farming. These rates vary from between 11.8 per cent and 18 per cent, and since September 2011, the

Company had issued 12,122 loans, with a total loan size of 577,690,000 yuan and a total loan balance of 200,216,400 yuan.

The bank has extended its micro-financing policy by delivering its micro loan business to Ningbo and Shenzhen, which sit on the southeast coast of China, and Chengdu located on the southwest coast of China, as well as Beijing. These developments pose problems to the bank, which, since it is trans-regional, needs to evaluate it cultural coherence across all of its regional branches.

In order for Baoshang Bank to transfer its micro-financing business to the new regions, it required a training programme that would transfer knowledge and values to designated micro-financing teams. Any such training programme of course requires the support of its executives, selected from branches earmarked for knowledge transfer. However, special care needs to be taken in a Confucian society like China to take account of levels of power and authority. As such, beyond this executive level, a number of senior loan officers were involved who would ultimately be responsible for the new teams, and junior loan officer who would engage with the new teams. This titular group oversaw the selection of forty core training supervisors from head office and selected branches becoming responsible for the training of local trainers for micro business finance. These trainers then trained staff for the transfer of knowledge to establish micro-financing teams.

To accompany the training programme, the bank wished to install performance appraisal to evaluate its programme. As such it appraises loan officers, not according to the total amount of the loans issued, but rather according to the number of loans. This has had an impact on the commission that a loan officer accrues. This is calculated monthly, so that loan officers can obtain 3000 yuan commission on a monthly loan rate of fifteen loans per month. This new appraisal approach appeared to be popular with loan officers. On average the officers maintain as many as seventy-eight customers. A single loan officer is able to maintain up to 200 customers. As a result, the per capita annual profit created by loan officers has become greater than one million yuan.

The per capita cost of small and micro-financing is more than 100,000 yuan with the per capita profit able to reach 700,000 to 800,000 yuan. Annual yield rate of this business can reach 7 per cent to 9 per cent, a significantly larger figure than 3 per cent on more normal corporate loans. In addition, micro loans require lower investment funding, loan periods are short, and there is fast capital turnover but high risk-based pricing. With more loan officers, a critical cost barrier is passed and costs drop.

The issue that Baoshang Bank now faces in its labour-intensive microloan business is to integrate the ever-growing credit team. This is a typical problem that is faced by distributed organizations, and embraces the same problem as the cultural partitioning and distinct paradigms across the regions of China, and the potential for conflicts that can arise in part from distinct perspectives and miscommunications.

The Issue

While Baoshang Bank has been keen to develop a culture change in being able to respond to its business strategy, the creation of a coherent bank that operates through a single culture is still problematic. There are ways of evaluating the values of a culture, and a committed investigation that would be most useful comes through the Schwartz cultural value instrument (1994). However, the investigation undertaken in this case was not the result of a brief to test cultural differences. Rather, our brief was much more directed towards promoting a branch awareness of the imperative for change. Instead, then, of delivering a cultural measuring instrument to members of the bank across the regions, a series of awareness-raising lectures was delivered that explained the change process within the context of the corporate life-cycle. The conclusion to this was the delivery of a life-cycle questionnaire that was to inquire how the different branches saw the development stage of the bank. An inference of coherence would then result by a comparative analysis of where each branch saw itself in the cycle of change.

To do this it was explained that in the more traditional corporate life-cycle adapted from Daft (2008), each phase is subject to change as indicated by Figure 8.3. For this life-cycle to have any chance of being representative of the way in which the bank changes, **a core assumption is that its ambient national culture is in a *normal* stage of stability**. The life-cycle is composed of a number of phases including 'morphing', implying the organization's capacity to change is not an adequate representation of the change process. The shift from the entrepreneurial to the collectivity phases in Figure 8.3 is the result of agency immanent dynamic processes. The upper part of the figure shows how the immanent dynamics shown in Figure 8.1 acts to create new phases. Due to the trifurcation of the dynamic process, it also indicates that a new phase may or may not arise, depending on a variety of internal conditions. Thus three outcomes were possible: the organizational system dies; or it continues as it was before; or it transforms into a new phase, for instance in the first phases from entrepreneurial to collectivity. Similarly with the other phases, where: (collectivity→fomalization), (formalization→elaboration), (elaboration→morphing). Beyond this, the organization again passes through a whole system change rather than a phase change.

As a result of this, a number of questions were to be put to members of each of the branches visited in order to stimulate their thinking process in identifying where they are in the cycle of change, which they would indicate in a table. These questions are:

256   Agency Change

1 Supposing that Baoshang Bank is in an early cycle of growth, using the Table 8.4 and Table 8.5, suggest where the Bank may be in the cycle.
2 What periods of tensions and crises has it passed through to get there?
3 Please highlight if you believe that the phases of change have occurred in Baoshang Bank.
4 Explain these changes, and indicate approximately when they likely occurred.
5 List your reasoning.

Prior to the request for the questionnaire to be responded to, a Chinese facilitator (Zhu Wen) was used to explain in simple terms the request being made and she would also assist staff to complete the forms, respond to

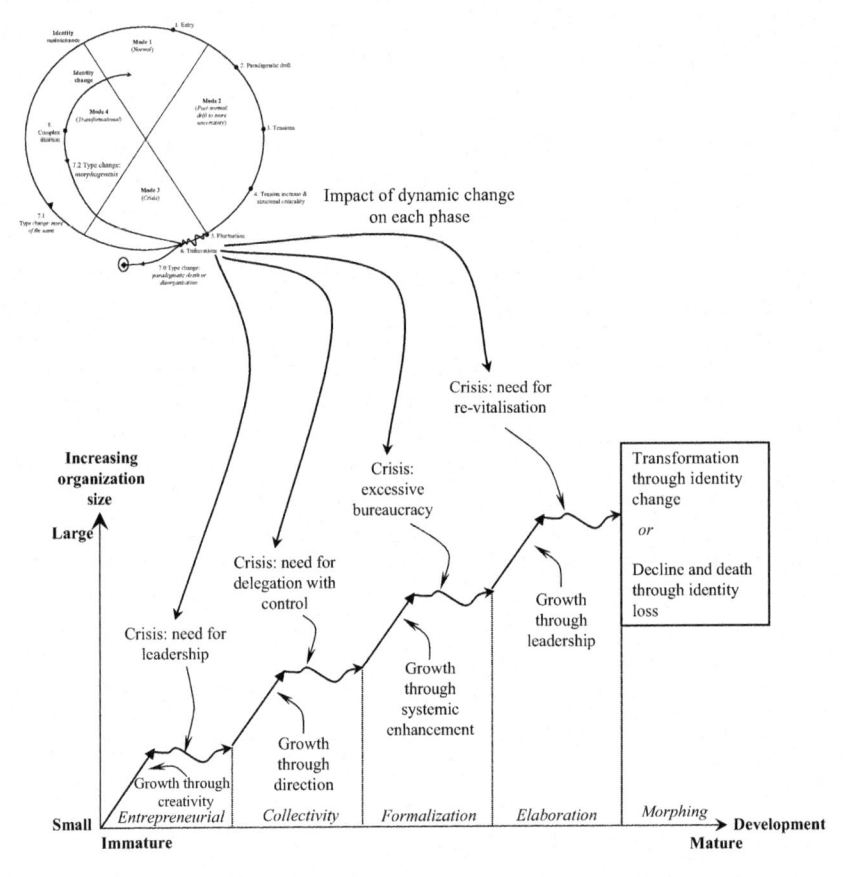

Figure 8.3 Adaptation of the corporate life-cycle (assumption: ambient culture is in *normal* phase of stability)

Table 8.4 *The phases of the corporate cycle*

Phases of Life-Cycle	Considerations	
Entrepreneurial	Personal control systems	
	Innovation by owner/manager	
	Goal: Survival	
	Management style: Entrepreneurial	
	Crisis: Lack of/Need for leadership	
Collectivity	Personal rewards aimed at individuals who	
	Innovation from employees and managers	
	Goal: Growth	
	Management style: Charismatic, directive	
	Crisis: Lack of/need for delegation	
	Pressures for Growth	Organization goals
		Economies of scale
		Executive advancement
		Economic health
Formalization	Impersonal rewards through formalized systems	
	Innovation from separate innovative groups	
	Goal: Internal stability/market expansion	
	Management style: Delegation with control	
	Crisis: Too much red tape	
Elaboration	Extensive rewards tailored to product and department success	
	Innovation by institutionalized R & D	
	Goal: Image/reputation-building	
	Management style: Team approach	
	Crisis: Lack of/need for revitalization	
Morphing (Decline or transformation)	Resizing, restructuring, merging, re-definition?	
	Decline	
	Organizational Atrophy	Inability to respond to changing environment
	Organizational Vulnerability	Inefficient, bureaucratic, fat, and happy
		Loss of resources
		Loss of market share
	Environmental decline	Loss of legitimacy/ethics
		Stagnating economy
		Flat/shrinking market
		Increased competition

questions, and in due course translate and summarize the outputs. Typically, a meeting would have more than 100 participants in the audience. A request was made to separate into groups and appoint a leader. The group would then discuss each question and then make a decision about how to respond.

258   Agency Change

Table 8.5 *Illustration of the connection between the first two phases of the corporate life-cycle and its dynamic development process*

Phase of Cycle	Step	Date	Explanation
Entrepreneurial	Entry		
	Paradigm shift		
	Tension		
	Criticality		
	Fluctuation		
	Trifurcation		
	Paradigm demise		
	Type change		
Collectivity	Etc....		

Analysis and Conclusion

Each of the regional branches of Baoshang Bank is an autonomous unit. This can cause problems for internal processes like meaningful communications, correct apprehension of goals, and coherent collective actions. The development of the important micro-financing activity has been handled sensitively, taking into account the nature of Confucian society and the positions of authority. However, it has resulted in an over-complex approach to the implementation of a training scheme. As a result, due to the number of administrative layers that exist between the trainers and the executive, feedback misinformation is quite likely, and serious issues may be overlooked.

The different regional branches do not contribute well to the development of a coherent culture for the bank as whole. In some cases they see themselves principally as autonomous units that just so happen to be part of a larger organization. Examination of the perspectives that arise from the group responses in each branch meeting has shown through inference where these views lie. The word 'infer' is used since the exercise was not intended to seek out such issues and problems. A more detained exercise would be more likely to do this.

It has already been said that the outcome of this study was the delivery of a life-cycle questionnaire that was to inquire how the different branches saw the development stage of the bank. An issue here is that different perceptions by each group may be the result of a misunderstanding of what is required in responding to the perception inventory. As such, the approach adopted is to take a dominant view, and where there are two such views, rational argument is created to gain an improved inference of the situation. The only issue that might arise with deducing cultural differences from this is that different branches were opened up or acquired at different times, and their development phase in the Baoshang Bank may differ to that of the bank as a whole.

However, such differences do show one thing: that there is little inter-branch communication through which the Baoshang Bank story can be told. It may be that appropriate iconic tails should be generated that are memory catching and which reinforce the story of the bank development.

The inferential analysis for each branch's response to how it saw itself placed in the cycle of change would be compared, and would overall indicate the coherence of the bank as a whole. In addition, one of the whole system change approaches (see for instance Burns, 2007; or Leonard, 1996) should be used to create greater cultural coherence.

The Beijing head office only opened in 2011, after the new push towards greater efforts towards micro-financing. The questionnaire was passed to members of the department of strategy who are responsible for Baoshang Bank policy. They recognize a lot of challenges that result from the addition of new systems, new members, and new leaders. Throughout, their intention is to promote a one-brand culture, and one operative mode that includes new technology. These challenges have resulted in a number of tensions between departments of the bank, which are increasing rather than reducing. However, they believe that this is a consequence of the phase of change that they are currently in. For them, the dominant phase is **formalization**, as the department has struggled (under crisis) with developing a needed strategy for delegation and control of the organization. This is not surprising since there are many new branches that have arisen since 2007. Additional internal systems are being added to the organization in an attempt to bring more integration. This may require a human resource programme to 'develop' the culture of each autonomous branch. There may be issues to consider, and conflicts to address. For instance there is a view in the Chifeng branch that cultural diversity is a benefit to the organization. However, there is a distinction between allowing a distinct culture to maintain its independent trajectory, and the encouragement of autonomous thought, this latter being a function of empowerment rather than cultural diversity.

The Chengdu branch was the third to have been opened outside Inner Mongolia. They have no accord with head office since they do not recognize that the bank as a whole is in the **formalization** phase, and rather see it in a **collectivity** phase. Perhaps this is because they are not looking towards the bank as a whole, but rather towards their own branch. Clearly there appear to be communication problems between this branch and head office. There are issues related to the provision of clear direction, telephone banking, staff commitment, and organizational cohesion. It has been said that the dominant perception is that the bank is in a phase of **collectivity**. This is the case since branch direction would appear to be consistent with the development of an autonomous organization. In other words the branch would seem to see itself to be independent of the Beijing branch.

The Chifeng branch was acquired in 2007 having taken over a local bank, and their perception is that they retain their original culture. It was the first branch outside of Inner Mongolia. This is potentially problematic since there is likely to be significant misunderstanding with head office and any interchanges with other branches. As such, the benefits of coherence are lost to both the branch and the bank. The branch is not forthcoming, however, in explaining the problems of non-synergistic development with the organization as a whole. Staff moving into the branch from outside will likely experience cultural change problems, and this will impact on their capacity to operate properly and on their performance. This will also have an impact on the development of the micro-funding initiative as staff find themselves in conflict with more senior management. So, this branch is likely to have significant operative problems that are difficult to resolve. For those moving from other branches to the Chifeng branch, there will be a cultural cleft, and different reference points for information and goals will result. A deeper analysis of the branch is on the cards to determine where the cultural clefts occur, and how they impact on performance. The branch has a majority (50 per cent) that sees that its phase of development is 50 per cent **formalization**, consistent with the perspective of head office.

The Hohhot branch was newly established in 2005, and since then has developed its own product base, apparently with only some reference to the bank as a whole. Due to the fact that it was a new branch, it has an employee population that is relatively young and well qualified. It does not perceive there have been historical issues of clear direction, and this may be because head office maintained particular interest in the development of the new branch. The perception of where the bank is in the dynamic of change is confused among the different respondent groups. This might be a reflection of the way in which the respondents self-selected themselves into respondent groups. Likely, they did this according to departments, and perhaps this indicates departmental cultural differences. A significant proportion of the respondent groups (30 per cent) have a perception consistent with that of the head office, seeing the bank as having a **formalization** phase. However, the highest percentage response (45 per cent) is that the bank is in a **collectivity** phase, a view consistent with the Chengdu branch.

The Erdos branch was established in 2011. Erdos is a very rich city full of natural resources and with a small population. The profitability of this branch is high in comparison to other branches of the bank, and it is therefore a valuable asset. As a new autonomous branch, they are likely in the **entrepreneurial** phase; however, the strategic component of the organization that is in contact with the head office may identify **formalization**. There is a clear split in perception in the branch as to whether the organization is in a **formalization** or an **entrepreneurial** phase of development (41.7 per cent in both cases). This may, as in the case of the Hohhot branch, be the result of cultural cleavage in the branch, and hence problems of adherence to common goals, and misunderstanding during processes of communication.

The Ningbo branch in Inner Mongolia opened in 2011. It is a city well known for small factories and manufacturing, and hence offers a useful opportunity for the development of small-enterprise financing. There is an overwhelming perception that the bank is in an **entrepreneurial** phase (52 per cent). There is a less significant faction that sees it in the **collectivity** phase (37.5 per cent). Again, this difference may be due to lack of cultural integration at the branch level.

Overall, therefore, there are significant challenges in the bank that relate to culture diversity among the branches. The differences in the phase of development are indicated in the listing below:

Branch	Perceived Phase
Beijing	Formalization
Chengdu	Collectivity
Chifeng	Formalization
Hohhot	Collectivity
Erdos	Formalization or Entrepreneurial (equal split)
Ningbo	Entrepreneurial

These differences are indicative that the bank has some significant development to integrate its culture. This problem may well therefore impact on the new micro-financing initiative that the bank is progressing, and it should be attended to.

8.8   Conclusion

In this chapter we started with the observation that organization theory as a discipline can be identified through three theoretical and practical components: organizational structure and environment, management and purposive behaviour, and organizational change and dynamics. However, there are few attempts to connect each of these aspects together to enable organization theory to develop in a holistic rather than a piecemeal way. With respect to the expectation that a new organization theory might emerge, we refer to the rise of the complexity view and the need for explicit examination of control and communication within organizational situations. The current economic crisis might have unforeseeable effects on the persistent societal dissatisfaction with respect to environmental and social concerns and unethical management behaviour, which ultimately makes clear that the current paradigms of various organization theories do not satisfy societal demands.

Predominant paradigms in organization theory (as in other fields) may go through a cycle from *normal* mode to *post normal* mode, fall into *crisis* and finally to one of *revolution*. As a paradigm enters its post-normal mode, the normal prevailing confirmatory mode approaches to theory must be considered to have lost their capability to make useful predications, something that is not always recognized by researchers. This leads to crisis that may result in a scientific revolution that would be needed to transform or replace extant theories. New sets and systems of classifications, emphasis on relations between events and occurrences rather than on substances, and new motivation-oriented theories might emerge that emphasize motivational aspects and address the concerns of individuals with newly emphasized shared needs and desires. A meta-view of phenomena and the ability to identify redundancies and variety in a system create views of patterns of change and capabilities to adapt to new challenges by self-organization.

Paradigms may die, when normal science continuously tends to fail with its applications to radically changing societal domains, or at least needs substantial transformation. The emerging theories are then considered to be post-normal and value laden. In this sense, post-normal science is concerned with complexity and has interests in aspects which relate to uncertainty, assigned values, and a plurality of legitimately argued perspectives.

In conclusion, we note that paradigms only exist through the human activity systems that create, carry, define, and maintain them. Durable paradigms may be seen as viable human activity systems that are complex and adaptive, and able to maintain a separate existence within the confines of their existential and other constraints. In essence, in this chapter we do not deal with such constraints.

We might distinguish aspects of economic and existential viability. Economic viability would mean that an organization has to achieve a surplus or at least balance between revenues and expenses. Existential viability refers to the fact that some organizations, if they fail, may cause enormous damage to mankind, for example, exploding nuclear power stations. Economic viability is subject to classical business administration, and safety has both a technological and psychological aspect, for example, in terms of safety culture. But this, in our mind, would constitute stories for a different set of academic arguments.

Life-cycles have also been considered. These may be valid in normal situations, but under ambient cultural uncertainty they are likely to be unrepresentative of the way in which agencies change.

Part III

Agency as Society

9 The Sociological and Political Agencies

9.1 Introduction

In this chapter we distinguish between the sociological and political views of agency, though the two constitute different perspectives of the same thing that enhance each other. Both approaches are basically systemically based. We shall introduce the social action theories of Parsons, Luhmann, and Habermas, which are shown to be synergistic with agency. This will also include Habermas' perspective on the distinction between Parsons' approach and that of living systems theory. The discussion of Luhmann's work will also direct us to a brief introduction of semiotics. Practical illustration of the use of Luhmann and Habermas' approaches will be made, this requiring them to be reduced to their essences. A brief examination of how the living system cultural agency theory relates to these approaches will be made. It may be noted that for both Luhmann and Habermas, communication takes a central position, while in agency theory it is just one additional feature of social existence. The political agency is also considered here, and for consistency we briefly consider systemic, sociological, and institutional perspectives, and connect them with agency. To finalize the chapter we present a case study regarding the Military of Guatemala, modelling this through the use of sociological political theory, and relating this to agency.

9.2 The Sociological Approach

We previously discussed knowledge migration, and recognized that it is constituted as an interplay between the subjective and the objective, resulting in the creation of a local paradigm. Even effective processes of knowledge migration into a local paradigm can sometimes be problematic in that they can establish a dichotomous unintegrated theory due to unexplored distinctions. This was the conclusion of Ken Menzies (cited in Habermas, 1987), when he commented on Parsons' theory of action, which establishes a model that connects a cultural system with a personality system, with a social system and a behavioural system. Menzies notes that Parsons' theory has a theoretical cleavage:

> Running throughout his work are two different programs – a social action one in the idealist tradition and a social system one in the positivist tradition. The action program focuses on the meaning of an action to an actor, while his social systems program focuses on the consequences of an activity or a system of activity. Parsons does not have an action system, as he claims, but only a behavioural system and a separate action theory. One can see a peculiar tension between systems theory and action theory in the history of Parsons' influence as well. Most of his older disciples and readers who approach him from the side of his writings on socialization theory assert (or tacitly assume) a methodological primacy for basic action-theoretical concepts. Most of his younger disciples and readers who approach him from the side of his macrosociological works assert that systems-theoretical concepts are fundamental to his theory construction. To illustrate these different assessments: for the one group the key to understanding his work as a whole is *Toward a General Theory of Action* and the relations between culture, society, and person (with institutionalization and internalization as the most important mechanisms of interconnection); for the other it is *Economy and Society* (with the schema of intersystemic interchange relations). When Parsons reprinted his two encyclopaedia articles entitled 'Social Interaction' and 'Social System' one after the other, he justified the order by noting that 'the subject of social interaction is in a fundamental sense logically prior to that of social system' (Habermas, 1987: 201).

The interplay between the objective and subjective assumptions can be commensurable as proposed by Whewell (1860) (cited in Snyder, 2001: 1). For instance Schutz and Luckmann (1974) were concerned with semantic communication processes in the lifeworld, and the objectivation of knowledge (§7.2.2). For them the lifeworld is 'the province or reality in which man continually participates in ways which are at once inevitable and patterned. The everyday lifeworld is the region of reality in which man can engage himself and which he can change while he operates in it by means of his animate organism' (Schutz and Luckmann, 1974: 3). From a knowledge perspective they see that in the lifeworld each individual has their own pattern of knowledge, but when they try to form cohesive local social groups they need to develop shared knowledge that enables common meanings to emerge. In this conceptualization, the objectivating process is relative to the social group. For us lifeworld is a context-related thematic culturally transmitted stock of interpretative patterns that have interconnection with knowledge and meaning, and which is enabled through communications.

Parsons' General Theory of Action provides a well-developed entry into a systemic view of the nature of society, and therefore provides a useful springboard to explore a number of significant issues that highlight the distinctions between Parsons' model and more modern approaches.

9.3 Parsons

Parsons created what appears at first sight to be a general (equilibrium) theory of social action. It is a structural-functional approach that creates a framework for building theory, where society is seen as a complex system whose parts work together to promote solidarity and stability. The functionalities include a cultural system, social and personality system, and in due course a behavioural system was added. These are constituted as structures that facilitate relatively stable patterns of social behaviour. Each social structure has a functional attribute that plays its part in the society as a whole.

Parsons' theory comes out of the sociological tradition, and it conceptualizes that (Parsons, 1951: 6): 'the social system is only one of three aspects of the structuring of a completely concrete system of social action. The other two are the personality systems of the individual actors and the cultural system which is built into their action. Each of the three must be considered to be an independent focus of the organization of the elements of the action system in the sense that no one of them is theoretically reducible to terms of one or a combination of the other two. Each is indispensable to the other two in the sense that without personalities and culture there would be no social system and so on around the roster of logical possibilities. But this interdependence and interpenetration is a very different matter from reducibility, which would mean that the important properties and processes of one class of system could be theoretically *derived* from our theoretical knowledge of one or both of the other two.' This can be elaborated on (Parsons and Platt, 1973: 57) as: the cultural system includes norms, values, and knowledge, and facilitates the definition of a contextual situation; the personality system includes cognitive competence and performance capacity; the social system includes obligation to rationality and affect. In addition, action is conditioned by learning capacity and intelligence, these (Parsons and Bales 1956) now being assigned to a newly identified behavioural system.

A useful explanation of Parsons General Theory of Action arises from an adaptation of that provided by Eckstein (1988: 802), represented as Figure 9.1, and explained as follows. Parsons sees societies as complexes of interaction. An agency exists in an objective situational context that cognitively decodes the context and enriches it with temperament giving it meaning. This occurs through a process of socialization that arises through early learning and which delivers modes of understanding and value that arises through the socio-culture. Also delivered are cognitive and affective meanings that become internalized, making the culture personal. It is through institutionalization that an expectation for behaviour arises through social roles. Where there is deviation from expected behaviour, sanctions arise, enabling smooth and regular patterns of interaction possible. Cognitions and affective responses to them enable goals to be defined

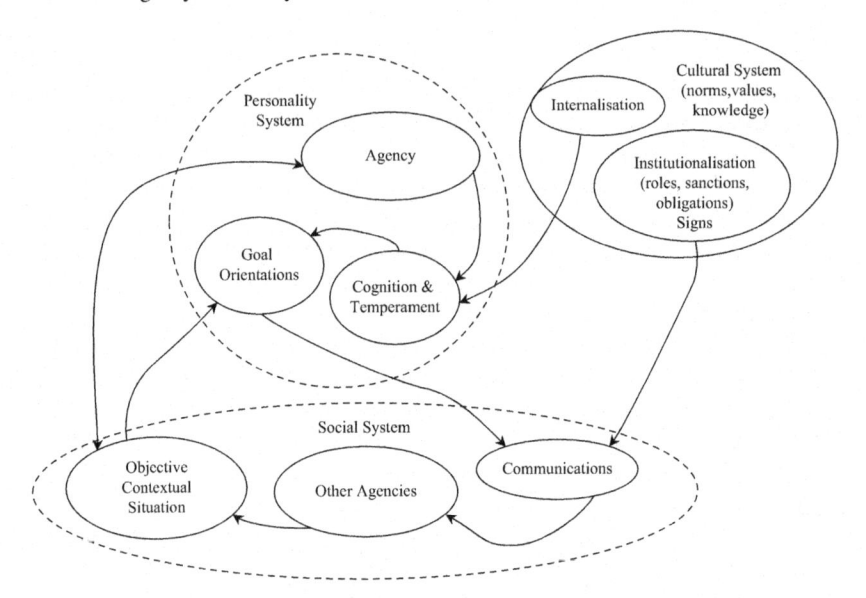

Figure 9.1 An interpretation of Parsons General Theory of Action Model (adapted from Eckstein, 1988)

and pursued. Cognitions, feelings, and goals are communicated to other agencies through symbolic expressions of the culture (signs) that enable an agency's actions to be intelligible to the other. Such actions also depend on objective facilities that are part of any agency's situation and which independently affect the choice of goals. Other agencies respond, changing the situation in some respect, and so the process continues. The General Theory of Action emphasizes neither subjective nor objective factors, but rather their interaction. Thus people cannot choose goals and the means to manifest them operatively without society, and social norms provide meaning. For this to occur, they require both intention and awareness of society's norms, which they are unable to escape. However, he does not explain how social norms and values change, thereby influencing the way in which people operate.

Habermas notes two issues of interest in Parsons' General Theory of Action. The first is that it does not engage a theory of pathology (Habermas, 1987: 203). The other issue relates to a theory cleavage as referred to earlier. He notes (Habermas, 1987: 201) that in a process of theory construction it should be possible to combine the basic concepts of action systems and theory. His resolution initially distinguishes between two types of integration: social and system. It rests on the notion that societies should be conceived in terms of *social integration* (of action contexts) operating through systemically stabilized complexes of action. Habermas believes that social integration is established through a normatively secured consensus (that is, through cultural values and norms). In contrast, *system integration* occurs through a non-normative regulation of self-maintenance processes, that elsewhere, in social cybernetics, authors like Beer (1979) were more pertinently referring to in terms of viability.

Habermas (1987: 151) notes that *social integration* attaches consensus to action orientations, independent of whether the consensus is normatively guaranteed or communicatively achieved. In contrast, *system integration* reaches through social integration non-normatively, steering decisions that are not subjectively coordinated – that is, Habermas notes, without accessing the lifeworld. This twin needs for integration arises, he sees, because if the integration of society occurs exclusively through system integration, then society is seen only in terms of a self-regulating system. This results, he notes, in an analytic study of society through the external perspective of an observer. This approach also poses the problem of interpreting the concept of a system in such a way that it can be applied to interconnections of action.

It would seem that Habermas' view that system integration is non-normative arises because he sees no capacity for the direct entry to the system of the cognitive processes belonging to the appropriate 'those' who compose it. This explicitly maintains an analytical divide between social and system integration that is not only unnecessary, but has already been shown to be problematic. This is because normative processes establish a basis for the broad orchestration of sub-agencies to harmonize with the plural agency to which they belong (e.g. lifeworld-like), thereby allowing for the development of social integration. However, once the basis for social integration is in place, such orchestration now allows for the intelligent recognition in the plural agency of its systemic needs, including its ability to adapt. This brings us back to Parsons and his structurally limiting the function of intelligence to the behavioural system. There is much richer theory than this, which would likely render the problem sociological issues of the Parsonian theory cleavage less than significant.

This cleavage was noted by Habermas and provides with him an opportunity to insert into the horizon of Parsons' theory the notion of lifeworld. It is in the lifeworld where purposeful communications are undertaken – a global place in the plural agency where embedded singular agencies maintain their proprietary local worldviews and communicate with intention over a theme. In so doing they create messages that are knowledge laden. According to Yolles (2006) the lifeworld only comes into being through the worldviews that populate it, which are independent (local) topological cognitive-affective spaces that interact through communication processes involving the exchange of messages. Each locality has both a cognitive and an affective content that enables it to maintain a capacity to develop enhanced meanings, and through its interaction to create mutual local understanding that offer a potential for the formation of common agreements. Lifeworld can be seen to have localities that can be divided into two generic messaging classes: message sources and message sinks. Both engage in aspects of message *transfer* that occurs from one locality to another within their global plural agency. The phenomenal syntactic structures that constitute communication are not perceived to change as they are displaced from one locality to another. However, the thematic knowledge embedded in the messages is not linearly transferred, but rather non-linearly *migrated* between the lifeworld localities. It is from this that the idea of *knowledge migration* arises that is in particular important for the social communication of complex issues. All movements of knowledge occur through message transfer, and the function of the communicated message is to act as a catalyst for the local creation of knowledge triggered by the message content. It is this local creation process that is referred to as knowledge migration and allows for migrated meanings embedded within that message to be misunderstood from the perspective of the message source. Every lifeworld locality is a bounded worldview that is uniquely shaped through life experiences. The concept of lifeworld therefore allows for the mechanism by which Parsonian communication processes develop and connect with social integration. Indeed, Habermas (1987: 225) purports that without the implicit operation of lifeworld that connects communication with action, the interconnection between culture, society, and personality fall apart. This requirement is unlikely since there will be alternative, perhaps lifeworld-like, structures. Commenting on such issues brings to mind the note by Alexander (1984) that Habermas (among other German sociologists) creatively misread the work of Parsons for strategic point-accruing purposes in his public discussions of theory with Luhmann and others.

Broadening the issue of the cleavage in Parsonian theory, Habermas considers that action systems should be considered to be a special case of living systems. For him, living systems are understood as open systems, maintaining themselves while contained within an unstable and hyper-complex environment through interchange processes across their boundaries. States of the system are viewed as fulfilling functions of maintenance. The distinction, Habermas notes, between action and living systems is that the structural patterns of action systems are not accessible to purely external observation. Rather they must be accessed hermeneutically – from the internal perspective of participants. The need then, we are told, is to subsume systems-theoretical concepts from the external perspective of an observer by embracing lifeworld processes and grasping the symbolic structures of those who use it. He continues by suggesting that the viewing of societies in terms of boundary maintaining structures, as supposed in living systems, limits the capacity to embrace processes of cultural reproduction, social integration, and socialization.

This brings us to an essential question that goes to the heart of Habermas' view. Is it adequate for living systems to be seen to be devoid of lifeworld-like processes, and simply in terms of boundary maintaining structures? Even if the living system is seen purely through Maturana & Varela's (1980) conception of autopoiesis, then Habermas' understanding of the living system appears to be severely limiting, neglecting the internal processes that, by their very nature, may be argued to draw on some lifeworld-like mechanisms.

This brings us to a further question. If living systems are not just concerned with boundary maintenance, then could we instead refer to action systems as social living systems? First, living systems should not just be seen as autonomic processes, but rather as being cognitively mediated. In other words, they will have some lifeworld-like structures available to them. The involvement of autopoiesis is central to the living system, connecting a strategic system that creates an action potential for an agency, and an operative system that enables it to manifest those actions. Both systems have states of being that are representations of condition, but not only limited to the fulfilment of functions of maintenance as supposed by Habermas. Autopoiesis may also be viewed as a network of processes underpinned by the very lifeworld-like functions that Habermas is so concerned with. Having said this, the Maturana & Varela's idea of a living system is itself limited in that it does not draw in access to some existential patterns that deliver identity, and that might stabilize and inform a social living system. Therefore, it does not establish the living system as having the potential to represent an action system. Maturana and Varela, who developed their idea in relation to biological organisms, were never convinced that their idea of autopoiesis through which the living system is constituted could be applied to the social system. However, Beer (1980: 1) notes in the introduction to Maturana & Varela's book *Autopoiesis: The Organization of the Living,* that:

> The fact is that if a social institution is autopoietic (and many seem to answer to the proper criteria) then, on the authors' own showing, it is necessarily alive. That certainly sounds odd, but it cannot be helped. It seems to me that the authors are holding at arms-length their own tremendously important discovery. It does not matter about this mere word 'alive'; what does matter is that the social institution has identity in the biological sense; it is not just the random assemblage of interested parties that it is thought to be.
>
> When it comes to social evolution then, when it comes to political change: we are not dealing with institutions and societies that will be different tomorrow because of the legislation we passed today. The legislation – even the revolution – with which we confront them does not alter them at all; it proposes a new challenge to their autopoietic adaptation. The behaviour they exhibit may have to be very different if they are to survive: the point is that they have not lost their identities.

Schwarz' (1997) elaboration of the living system, beyond that of Maturana & Varela, has the capacity to clearly represent social systems as living since the ability to represent identity is explicit. For the social system this identity can be represented through culture that can establish a basis for society, or through patterns of cognition that can establish a basis for personality. It thus allows one to recognize that Habermas' limited view of the living system is denuded of the attributes of culture and personality that embrace inherent lifeworld and indeed strategic intelligence processes as explored by Piaget (1950), and provides for the possible redefinition, even under chaos, of identity and boundary that can enter into the exploration of viability, a condition that suggests that an agency is durable, and able to survive over time.

9.4   Luhmann

Habermas' interest in lifeworld processes necessitates communications, an interest that was grasped by Luhmann (1982). The antecedents of Luhmann's theory of social systems arise through social action, within which observed regularities emerge and evolve through collaborative and collective behaviour. Collective action is dependent upon meaningful communication, and it is this aspect of collaborative action and discourse that Luhmann's work centres on. For Luhmann, it is from systems of communication that systems of action arise. Communication is the basic unit for the self-reproduction of social systems, and action as the basic unit for their self-description and self-observation. Action is socially constructed rather than being unilaterally produced. The shift from action to communication is the elementary unit of social systems, and therefore is the basic unit of analysis for sociological theory. Unlike other theories of action he proposed the operation of communication as an element of social systems which always needs the participation of at least two processors (participants) for an individual communicative act to come about.

Following Kneer & Nassehi (1993, cited in Kirsch, 1998), Luhmann considered his constructs to constitute a functional-structural systems theory, unlike Parsons' functional-structural theory. Here, a social system is a coherence of social actions that are in mutual reference to one another, this enabling them to be distinguished from an environment. Unlike Parsons' *causal functionalism* that identifies connections between system operations and system maintenance, Luhmann rather adopts *equivalence functionalism,* where specific operations may be associated with functions, and where functionally equivalent substitutions are feasible. Maintenance is dealt with since cause and effect is replaced by seeing the social in terms of problem situations and their interventions. Unlike Parsons' General Theory of Action, Luhmann's theory embraces the concept of self-reference that is a property of living systems, which are able to observe and reflect on themselves, and make decisions as a consequence.

Table 9.1 *Types of autonomous system in Luhmann's theory*

System Type	Nature
Living	Living systems reproduce themselves from their own bio-physical operations (metabolism).
Psychic	Psychic systems reproduce themselves from their own mental operations (thinking, mind, feelings).
Social	Social systems reproduce themselves from their own communicative operations.

In the foreword to Luhmann's (1995) book on social systems, Eva Knodt remarks that he lays out a theoretical groundwork that provides a frame of reference for a description of modern society as a complex system of communication. This is differentiated horizontally into a network of interconnected social subsystems. Each of the subsystems reproduces itself recursively on the basis of its own system-specific behaviour, and how this occurs is expressed in terms of the cybernetic theory of autopoiesis. Regarding this behaviour, Luhmann's concept is strictly operational and avoids any form of ontology. Each of the systems is autonomous, and named as living, psychic, and social, and each is differentiated in Table 9.1.

While the three systems are each autonomous, they are interconnected. The connection between psychic and social systems creates what Luhmann (1995) calls meaning. Psychic systems and social systems are structurally coupled: that is, they co-evolve together through their mutual interaction. The rationale for this co-evolution is that social systems cannot exist without persons, while persons require social systems to maintain existence. The co-evolution operates as an ordering process for both systems, and enables achievement. It is evolutionary achievement between the psychic and social systems that specifically defines Luhmann's idea of meaning. It is an approach that stands against behaviourism in which human beings are seen as mechanical responsive devices that react to stimuli.

In this theory, social systems and individuals exist as environments for each other. The environment for the social system has complementary and competing physical, biological, psychological, and social influences, and it generates novelties. Additionally, the social system adapts to these novelties through a self-selection process (Bausch, 2001).

Selection is fundamental to all social systems, and operates as the basis of communication that is the basis for their very definition. Following the notions of Shannon and Weaver (1964), communication involves *information* that is a selection of possibilities from a known or unknown repertoire of possibilities (Luhmann, 1995: 140). For them, communication principally involves the mechanical transmission of data (rather than context-sensitive meaningful information) from a source to a sink. Its interpretation as information occurs later, at the sink. While the Shannon and Weaver approach sees sources and sinks as postivistic, in Luhmann's theory their connection is constructivist. Basically, each system has to create its own information. Information-creating processes can be triggered by external irritations. But there is no direct transfer from one system to another, from one head to the other. Thus, while information is important to communication, it cannot be *transferred* between a source and a sink as in the theory of Shannon and Weaver. Rather, an explicit message containing coded information acts as a catalyst that enables the sink to create new information. Thus, we could envisage information to be *acquired* by a sink from a message sent by a source through a process of what we shall call *information migration*. This occurs because for Luhmann a source and a sink have an ordered structural coupling, and information (embedded in a message) is an irritation to the sink that has the task of ordering it. Brier (2001) explains that since structural coupling can coordinate behaviour, messages carrying information can coordinate behavioural coordination itself. It should be noted that when we refer to behaviour, we are also referring to a behavioural response from a structural coupling.

When behaviour occurs in the social system it is expressed in terms of communication, which can occur either intentionally or unintentionally between a source and a sink. This behaviour occurs as *utterance*, defined as a selection from a repertoire of intentional acts. The sink is referred to as 'ego'. Utterance occurs through a source (in Luhmann's terms an 'alter'). Luhmann introduced the terms 'alter' and 'ego', it seems, to enable him to discuss the 'alter ego'[1] of a social system. In the core of the alter/ego conception of communication lies the idea that the operation of communication requires two autonomous participants, alter and ego. This makes communication a genuine social operation/process. Luhmann conceptualizes communication from alter's side, from the completion of the operation, not so much from ego's side. Ego's intention is less important.

An outcome of utterance and information is: 'understanding', defined as the observation of the distinction between utterance and information. Communication is not only one or the other of these elements; it is a synthesis of all three, as summarized in Table 9.2.

Brier (2001a,b) notes that for Luhmann *understanding* is distinct from *meaning*. Understanding is a property of an autonomous whole system (or holon) that develops only when the experiences of meaning or of

---

[1] The alter ego is defined in the online Webster dictionary as a second self, a trusted friend, or the opposite side of a personality.

Table 9.2 *Communication is a synthesis of three elements*

Communication Element	Responsible	Nature of Element
Utterance	Source as an 'alter'	A selection from a repertoire of intentional acts
Information	Sink as an 'ego'	A selection from a repertoire of possibilities
Understanding	An autonomous 'self', e.g. a source or sink	Observation of the distinction between utterance and information. Understanding (or more properly in Luhmann's concepts, interpretation) is a form of meaning that occurs through reflection.

meaningful action are projected into another autonomous system (Luhmann, 1995: 73). This holon can be a communication source or sink, and it is enabled through the process of reflection. Understanding takes on its particular character through experiences, clearly indicating Luhmann's adherence to a subjectivist epistemology. Since communication is a synthesis of utterance, information, and understanding, it is integrally tied to meaning.

Meaning has an important place in Luhmann's theory. Here both psychic and social systems use meaning as a medium. The nature of meaning is phenomenal and connects to the work of Husserl (1950), enabling, as Luhmann indicates, concepts like intention, reference, expectation, experience, and action to be taken in. Each of these indicates elements or structures that can be assigned to either psychic or social systems, as expressed in Table 9.3, and each provide attributes for meaning.

Meaning plays a part through access to experience, and guides selectivity in communication. This meaning can only occur through a structural coupling with the psychic system. As such, it is not necessary to consider roles played by individuals in social systems. To be maintained, social systems need to continue the production of further communication. If a social system were to cease communicating, it would cease to be seen as an autonomous system that satisfies its own purposes.

Within the context of agency theory, with its links to mainstream cognitive psychology, meaning is connected with worldview that is established through culture. Luhmann's cybernetics of the social system does not diverge from this, since meaning can be connected to culture through semantics. Having said this, it does appear that his theory diverges, and perhaps significantly, from what we would normally accept as a definition of culture. For him culture is defined in terms of a limitation of meanings that make it possible to distinguish what constitute the appropriate/correct from inappropriate/incorrect contributions to a communication.

Table 9.3 *Concepts associated with meaning in social systems*

Phenomenon	Nature
Intention	This holds open the world as a whole, guaranteeing actuality through access
Reference	This establishes a relationship with phenomenal reality, and connects to what is possible (the conditional reality)
Expectation	Expectations are behavioural in nature, and thus connected to operations. The social system has a structure that is composed of generalized behavioural expectations. A network of expectations organize experiences, excludes possibilities, and bridges discontinuities in action.
Experience	This is expressed as selection that is attributed to the environment that provides a point of reference.
Action	This occurs where selection is attributed to the system itself, as opposed to the environment.

There are other problems in Luhmann's theory. One is concerned with meaning itself. All three of his autopoietic systems are needed (if on very different levels) to create meaning in a message, and one needs the sign concept to understand their interaction. Brier (2002) refers to the lack of a sign and signification concept as a problem of Luhmann functionalism, where the role of body and mind in the production and meaning of social communication has not been adequately grasped by the theory.

Another view comes from Viskovatoff (1999), who sees that Luhmann has understood better than other theorists the centrality of the concept of meaning to social theory, and has extensively worked out its implications. However, his embedded theory of meaning cannot coherently make the social domain autonomous as he desires because he does not take into account the distinction between syntax and semantics. Viskovatoff develops on this distinction by highlighting the idea that social systems consist of rules, not just communications. By raising the rule concept to take the same prominence in social theory as those of actor and system, autonomy can be maintained while avoiding the counterintuitive aspects of Luhmann's theory.

This concept of social rules, when they are recognized by an individual, is embraced through a process of internalization. Verenikina and Gould (1998) explain that this is a process by which external processes associated with external material objects are transformed into processes that take place mentally at the level of consciousness. It is a transition in which these processes become generalized, verbalized, abbreviated. Importantly, they also become the means for further development that transcends what is possible with external activity. For Wertsch (1979), it is through external social activities that a plane of consciousness is *constructed* (i.e. ontologically emerges. This process explains how many levels of cognitive consciousness can develop, as posited by Lucas (2002). For Vygotsky (1978), all higher mental functions are internalized social relationships. This allows for a variety of analytic and related processes to occur that begin with abstraction. In Piaget's theory of learning, a process of abstracting actions allows an individual to replace perceptual judgements for those based on reasoned internalized actions (Elkind, 1976).

In pursuing this line of thought, Viskovatoff first recalls the three ways by which information can be represented in Luhmann's theory:

- in the mind of a source,
- in the mind of a sink,
- as an 'utterance' in some kind of symbolic form.

Utterance is a physical token that allows a corresponding meaning to be conveyed between a source and a sink. For utterances to be understood they must involve signs that conform to a code that is understood by both the source and the sink. An utterance only has meaning when a sink can interpret and thus gain meaning from it through that code. Thus semantics occurs as a mental attribute of communication in social systems. Communications as utterances are signified syntactic forms that do not take meaning in themselves. However, there is also a role for semantics here. For Viskovatoff, when studying human behaviour it is legitimate and indeed unavoidable to use a level of analysis that deals with the semantics that comprises people's (subjective) beliefs and desires. While Viskovatoff does not see that Luhmann adopts such a semantic level, he argues that it is feasible to introduce it because it is consistent with his definition of meaning. Accepting a physical behavioural level of analysis that is the basis of Luhmann's work does not require the rejection of a semantic level.

In Luhmann's theory behaviour is only composed of acts of communication. This is composed of selections of utterance, information, and understanding. Language is one (of several other) medium of communication. Language has a syntactic nature that makes it amenable to a description by means of a relatively small number of rules. These rules are reflected in the structures of a social system that are expressed in terms of expectation. These expectation structures of social systems are differentiated into functional subsystems through the formation of local collections of rules. The rules, Viskovatoff argues, can take a similar autonomous ontological status to communication in Luhmann's theory. In particular, he argues that rules have physical (or behavioural), syntactic, and semantic levels of analysis. They can take an existence apart from the intentions of the actors who follow them, and are capable of evolution on their own apart from their interpretation by actors.

We have said that expectations can structure communication. The expectation structures are maintained over time, and can both facilitate and constrain

Table 9.4 *Equivalence between Shannon and Weaver's and Lynn's models of communication*

Shannon and Weaver Model: representing message delivery, meaning and use		Lynn Model: representing message meaning conditioned by social context	
Phase	Concern of Phase	Phase	Concern of Phase
Pragmatics	Effectiveness of message transmission relating to its use or consequence	Influence	Behavioural or psychological consequences of communication
Syntax	Technical, implying control and predication of the success of message transmission	Encounter	Decoding of symbols that define a transmitted message in a communication
Semantic	Transmission of meaning	Exchange	Flow of meaning through exchange of a set of symbols

communicative behaviour through the collections of rules. This idea leads to Viskovatoff's stress that in Luhmann's theory it is *structural expectation* that enables social systems to endure. This notion of expectation is consistent with Dubois' concept of strong anticipation, where rules are a formalized potential for behaviour that are a consequence of structure. Within this context we shall therefore consider the terms expectation and anticipation to be interchangeable.

Anticipation structures are also important to an understanding of the way information is acquired by autonomous sinks. Let us elaborate on this a little. Communication is the process of message transmission between a source and a sink. However, the meaning of the message is subjective and will differ for the source and sink. Consider that a message is composed of signs that are syntactically structured. Now in the theory of autonomous systems message transmission occurs between an autonomous sink and source when they are structurally coupled. Thus, the information embedded in a message transferred between a source and a sink is an anticipated disturbance to the sink.

Explanations about information can vary when a syntactic and semantic perspective is adopted. This is supported by Flueckiger (1995), who tells us that information carried by signs can be examined in different ways, depending upon whether a syntactic, semantic, or pragmatics perspective is adopted. These different perspectives can only be reconciled within the framework of a broadly defined semiotics.

Semiotics is a general theory of signs and symbolism, usually divided into the branches of pragmatics, semantics, and syntactics, terms originally adopted by Shannon and Weaver (1964), and for which Lynn (1973) provides an alternative model (Table 9.4). Lynn's proposition shows how semiotics provides an understanding of how dynamic communications occur as a means by which social systems develop and survive. In particular, it is concerned with how messages become meaningful in the context of other components. It is concerned with social context that can condition at least interpersonal, intergroup, intragroup, and mass communication. These areas connect to social and cognitive psychology, organizational development, change and knowledge management, as well as areas such as sociology, journalism, and political science.

When we talk of semantic communication, we mean the communication of thematised meanings that are migrated between connected sources and sinks in the lifeworld. Part of this process is a semiotic one, in which there is an attempt to examine the texts that compose the messages being communicated, and which can attempt to deal with the cultural and temporal subjectivities embedded in communication processes and the migration of meaning. Semantics refers to meaning, and in the nineteenth century Peirce (Hartshorne et al., 1972) used the term semiosis to refer to the *process* of 'meaning making'. Brier (2001) tells us specifically that semiosis is connected to meaningful cognition and communication as exchange of signs in autonomous[2] organizations.

Sonesson (2000) recognizes the distinction between the Shannon and Weaver, and the Lynn approaches to communication, by distinguishing between the *Tartu* and the *Prague* schools of thought. According to him, the Tartu school sits firmly on the foundation of the classical information theory, and takes interest in the obstacles to communication. It is concerned with *how* communication entities (sources and sinks) are differently distributed in space; culturally, how a text becomes deformed when the code applied to it at the sink is different from that at the source; and whether a text in the culture of a source has become a non-text in the culture of the receiver.

In contrast, the Prague school supposes that communication is an action that takes place successfully. It does not tell us anything about the degree of the activity required, or its nature. It does suppose, however, that even where messages are spatially displaced, the sender *and* the receiver also have to take an active part. In addition, the Prague school models focus on the relationships between different temporal phases of the same culture: what is accomplished by a source as well as by the sink are acts across time, which may be close but will not coincide. This apparently underscores that the actions of a source and a sink are autonomous. Sonesson indicates that it is an adaptation of the conception of perception propounded by Husserl: lean phenomenology[3] (and the lifeworld) with an added social dimension (Sonesson, 2008).

---

[2] Brier actually refers to autopoeitic systems, but we have already indicated that autonomy is a function of autopeisis.

[3] Husserl's phenomenology claims that our access to reality is conditioned by how we understand it. Our common language plays a significant role in that understanding, as our statements about

A distinction between the Prague temporal and Tartu spatial models can be easily illustrated. While the Prague model says that two subjects involved in a process of communication may initiate their acts in time using different sets of norms, the Tartu model says that they may initiate their acts in space using different cultural systems. This is another way of saying that the meaning for a message sink is not exactly the same as the meaning for the message source, and that a process of knowledge migration has occurred because local culturally based coding or decoding processes have occurred.

The Prague and Tartu models together give a more satisfactory account of the complexities of communication than the Shannon & Weaver model because, for Sonesson, they add, for instance, active subjects and cultural norms. A basic problem with the classical foundation for information theory is that it is concerned with the transformation of a communication through message transmission coding, not as in cultural semiosis with the emergence of meaning that links directly to conceptualizations of the lifeworld.

9.5 Habermas

Following the tradition of Mead, Habermas (1987) in his theory of Communicative Action rejected the Parsonian model of structural-functionalism, and adopted the model of society as a self-regulating system. Here, every event or state is ascribed a meaning that arises from its functional significance in relation to a communication-theoretic model. It is through this that actors orient their actions through their own interpretations. Implicit to his theory lies the distinction between social behaviour and communication, where communication is seen to be a social need. The theoretical basis has a number of axioms that underpin social communications. These include:

- Meaningful communication, which occurs in the socially shared lifeworld, is essential to the process of understanding – this being a pre-requirement for purposeful social action.
- The lifeworld offers commonly accepted background knowledge within which action can be coordinated.
- Communication between social actors is directed towards the formation of agreement.
- Disagreement occurs when communication is distorted or unresolved.
- Communication needs speech-acts that occur through language composed of signs and symbols that conform to a code of understanding.

---

what we 'observe' are interpretations that derive from theory. We can extend this to saying that a language-dependent view of reality in understanding and explanation is an application of a general principle to be found in all uses of languages.

Table 9.5 *Types of rationality in Habermas' theory of communicative action*

Rationality Type	Nature of Rationality Type
Cognitive-instrumental	This conducts action that aims at the successful realization of privately defined goals. These action types are either *instrumental* (when they are directed at efficient interventions in a state of affairs in the world through labour, for instance), or *strategic* (when they guide attempts to successfully influence the decisions of other actors such as in relations of domination).
Communicative	This underlies action that is aimed at mutual understanding, conceived as a process of reaching agreement between speaking subjects to harmonize their interpretations of the world.

- It is through the mediation of language and with rational argumentation that social actors can coordinate their actions in terms of an orientation to mutual understanding.

According to Deflem (1996), Habermas' theory rests on a distinction between two concepts of rationality that shape knowledge to guide action (Table 9.5).

It is clear that lifeworld is important to Habermas. Lifeworld can be expressed in terms of patterns of meaning in a social environment. These patterns represent a transcendental site where speakers and hearers meet for intersubjective affairs, like dealing with validity claims, settling disagreements, and achieving agreements. Habermas sees lifeworld as a reservoir of taken-for-granteds, or as unspoken convictions that participants in communication draw upon in cooperative processes of interpretation. Single elements of the lifeworld are mobilized as consensual knowledge when they are relevant to a situation. He defines lifeworld to be a culturally transmitted linguistically organized stock of interpretative patterns. One presumes that since they are interpretative we are dealing with subjective patterns of meaning.

The notions of lifeworld that derive from Schutz and Luckmann (1974) are of particular interest here. For us, when a social group of worldview holders enter together into a given lifeworld they define a suprasystem of communicative actors. The communication occurs with the others over a particular theme, and according to some dynamic logical structure that satisfies a need, goal, or purpose. Within this suprasystem they become involved in semantic communication that:

(a) involves the transmission of thematised meanings,
(b) permits the development of common understandings to occur.

Those in the suprasystem can disengage from the lifeworld, and thus exclude themselves from the possibility of acquiring flows of communicated meaning, when they are replaced by steering media like power or money (Habermas, 1987). This redirects behaviour by eliminating rational argument. As part of this it reduces the making of statements that involve information or challenges to other statements involving information that is part of the meaningful communication processes.

The actors in the lifeworld are supposed to have corporeal existence. This means that they are not taken as figments of each other's imagination, and while they may be seen in relative ways, they exist either physically or virtually. Further, the actors are supposed to be endowed with essentially similar consciousnesses, otherwise common meanings will not be able to develop. They have meaning-strata that transform 'natural' things into cultural *object of attention*. This may be an object like an artefact, an action, a gesture, or a communication, any of which can have attention attracted.

Objects of attention are seen through a kernel of determinable and common meanings. This kernel has a cognitive *horizon* of unidentified meanings in a message[4], and will be uncertain and indeterminate. This can cause particular problems for culturally diverse actors in a given lifeworld. When we talk of cultural diversity, we may be referring to different ambient cultures that differentiate distinct social organizations. Thus, two enterprises in a given society may be very different, but there may well be a degree of magnitude of difference between two different organizations that stand across two different societies because they are likely to have very distinct normative patterns. Even if the kernel of meanings is common (and this is often not the case in very diverse situations), there will be distinct culturally assumed horizons that will lead to very different understandings. Normally, the horizon is experienced as being determinable and capable of explication if the need is seen to arise. However, this is often not possible in situations that involve remote and virtual communications (e.g. letters and emails) where the need for explication may not be realized. Where communication involves interrelations and reciprocal actions, feedback control on the translation of meaning can enable improved understanding between the actors in a lifeworld. They are more easily able to create a stratified social and cultural world that is historically pre-given as a more or less common frame of reference that defines the 'natural world' view of things.

The lifeworld is a social phenomenon, and not therefore only a function of self. It becomes part of the experiences of all social actors at any moment. 'The lifeworld is not my private world nor your private world, nor yours and mine added together, but rather the world of our common experience... The component of the self-evidences which is the underpinning of the lifeworld to

---

[4] This is sometimes referred to as subtext.

which we are accustomed is, for instance, endangered in solitary confinement, even often demolished.' (Schutz and Luckmann, 1974: 68).

When talking of experiences, it should be realized that it is through their *sedimentation* that knowledge is acquired. The process of sedimentation is conditioned by cognitive organization that lies at the basis of our worldviews, and is moderated by the lifeworld. It occurs where the conditions that define the limits of a situation also determine the possibilities for the acquisition of knowledge. Lifeworld experiences may also be expressed in terms of boundaries. 'In our description of the experience of the lifeworld we stumbled on the boundary conditions for this experience which are imposed on everyone. They form the limits within which subjective experiences of the lifeworld are arranged in certain structures. Subjectively, they can be experienced as transcendences of the everyday world. World time limits subjective duration: one ages in it and it forms the absolute boundary of life-spans' (Schutz and Luckmann, 1974: 92). The structures referred to represent finite provinces of reality, are defined in terms of meanings, and are important to the acquisition of knowledge. They are consistent with the relevant structures of Habermas, defined as interconnections of meaning that hold between a given communicated utterance, the immediate context, and the cognitive horizon of meanings.

In the lifeworld the communicative aspects of situation management occur where it is interpreted and some agreement is arrived at. Here participants pursue their plans cooperatively on the basis of a shared definition of the situation that we shall suppose is commonly understood. Habermas refers to consensus as normally a condition for pursuing goals. It occurs when a hearer:

(a) accepts the truth of an assertion,
(b) accepts the normative validity of a command.

Commonality (of lifeworld) rests on consensual knowledge, on the cultural stock of knowledge that members share. Having seen that Habermas' view of communicative action is consensus based, we can highlight a problem with it as a social condition. According to Yolles (2001) it is better to talk of agreement rather than consensus. This is because consensus is often a function that involves attitude or position engineering. A simplified Habermasian argument can explain this. An action system involving lifeworld should be coextensive with the social elements of values, norms, goals, and behaviour. However, if these elements become divorced from one another and thus individually differentiated from the lifeworld, then they lose their significance to the social process. As a result, actors behave towards the formally organized action system in a way that is steered by, for example, a process of exchanges and power. In other words, steering media-like power (e.g. threats), exchanges (e.g. bribes), emotion (e.g. fear or love), or ego (e.g. not wanting to be diminished by admitting a lack of understanding) may perturb the lifeworld and disrupt meaningful communications, rendering it inadequate. As a result, the transmission of meaning is irrelevant. Even if we do have co-extensivity in the social elements so that consensus is possible, it may never occur because of the problem of knowledge migration, which implies that we may never really know if a social group has unanimity of thought over a given thing.

There is another problem that interferes with the lifeworld. Formal regulation (e.g. sets of procedure) reduces the need to achieve consensus by means of communication, and so action that results from this in the lifeworld has its validity forfeited. Formal regulation constitutes an argument, from Ionescu (1975), that with increasing social complexity and through centripetal politics (occurring with the distribution of power to autonomous bodies with their own agendas) both communicative action and lifeworld can be suspended. This, one supposes, has an impact on the reproduction of knowledge and thus the renewing of potential liberated by that knowledge, and hence requisite variety and viability.

Habermas' (1987) theory of communicative action hinges on lifeworld. For him, action results from the interaction of four social elements[5]: values, norms, goals, and behaviour. For us, values and norms are associated with the cognitive domain, goals with the noumenal/organizing domain, and behaviour within the phenomenal domain. These elements come together through actors in the lifeworld, illustrating that each of the domains can be represented within it. Actors disappear as acting subjects, and are absorbed into units to which the decisions and thus the effects of action are attributed. In so far as actions are viewed in terms of their internal analytical structure and conceived of as the outcome of a complex joint operation among the specific subsystems, actors are represented in terms of the four elements.

Reiterating that communication is central to the creation of action, participants pursue their plans cooperatively on the basis of shared definition of the situation. The cooperative processes of interpretation involve the 'three worlds' of lifeworld. According to Giddens (1984), Habermas' three worlds view entails the notion that an act of communication involves four claims: that a communication:

1 is intelligible
2 has a true propositional content

---

[5] Habermas talks not of elements, but of the four subsystems [each of which have attributes]: culture (that determines values), society (that creates norms), personality (that form goals), and organism (that creates behaviour). We can also refer to each subsystem as systems [that have functions associated with their attributes]. Cultural systems specialize in pattern maintenance, social systems around integration of acting units (human individuals/personalities engaged in roles), personality systems around goal attainment, and behavioural organism around adaptation. These derive from traditional Parsonian thinking in sociology. We do not adopt these terms here because the said subsystems are not explicitly defined in ways that we find satisfactory, and our purposes are different from this.

Table 9.6 *Habermas' three worlds model of communications*

Type of World Relevancy	Nature of World	Communication Claim
The external natural (object) world	Material objects have relations between them and between individual actors (and their strategies), in a cognitive knowledge-based frame of reference.	Content is propositionally true
The social world	Actions associated with actors in a social group derive from common values expressed as a set of norms. The norms take on special status that includes moral validity and facts.	Content is justified
The internal (subjective) world	The sphere of internal personal experiences and meanings associated with the individual psyche.	Content is sincere

3 is justified in being said
4 has a content that is sincere, without an intent to deceive.

Midgley (2000) explains that intelligibility is a precondition for effective communication. When made explicit, the other items (2)–(4) can all be questioned and justified through rational argument. The nature of rational argument is that it enables us to distinguish each of the three worlds, each of which are concerned with the external or objective, the social, and the internal or subjective (Table 9.6). The three dimensions thus form a frame of reference that enables a rational act of speech (Figure 9.2). The creation of the boundaries that distinguish between each of these worlds is a function of agreement that has occurred through semantic communication that is dependent upon rational argument. Interestingly though, according to Koegler (1996), the theory is devoid of the notion of semiotic power.

A non-rational argument occurs where the boundaries between each world are faulty, and it results in myth that entails confusion of distinctions between the three worlds. Thus, a true view of the external natural world implies a justified view of the social world. Midgley (2000) has highlighted an interesting example of this that we shall elaborate on. Consider the proposition that competition is essential for evolution. In this case it is necessarily right to act competitively in social relationships. However, from Habermas' three world's model this view is both mythical and irrational. This is because while competition may be essential to evolution, there is no requirement that people should be always be competitive. The moral justification (moral, operative, ...) for competitive activity needs to be assessed separately from the claim that competitive activity is a truth of the external natural world. Such an argument is sometimes called neo-Darwinian. Kauffman (1993) suggests that while this

```
                    External natural (object) world
                              ▲
                              │
                              │   A speech act
                              │      ○
                              │
                              └──────────► Social world
                             ╱
                            ╱
                           ▼
                    Internal (subjective)
                           world
```

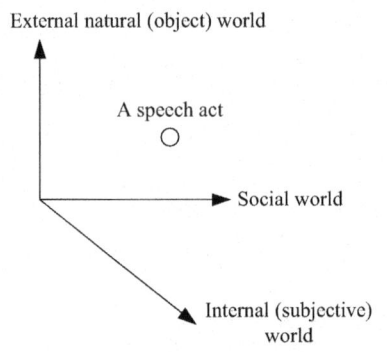

Figure 9.2 The frame of reference enabling a rational speech act

type of thought considers that natural selection is the prime factor of evolution, it would have better taken into account processes of self-organization. In particular, he tells us that it is inadequate because it 'fails to notice, fails to stress, fails to incorporate the possibility that simple and complex systems exhibit order spontaneously' (Kaufman, 1993: xiii).

9.6   Agency and Socio-Cultural Processes

In agency theory communication originates in the noumenal domain (which houses the figurative system) through self-schemas, but is manifested in the operative lifeworld. Communication has cognitive influences that connect to knowledge and meanings that develop during lifeworld processes. We have previously said that this is a phenomenon of thematic semantic communications. Influences occur from our interpretation of transmitted knowledge that derives from the cognitive organization (the beliefs, attitudes, values) of other worldviews. It ultimately determines how we interact, defines our rational understandings, and provides the means by which thematic meaningful communications can occur.

In the noumenal domain communications processes are purpose related and logically connected. In intelligent organizations these attributes are socially derived through the process of knowledge objectification. For instance, with respect to the rational attributes communications can influence individual beliefs and formulate socially defined and approached common organizational missions, goals, and aims. This requires logical and rational abilities on behalf of each participant in the communication. People are relationally linked to those who have logical connections to the organization and form part of its network. They can contribute to the organizing process of thought and action, thus defining sets of possible systemic and behaviour possibilities.

Behavioural communications are concerned with the physical or virtual structure of communications, and the nature of the set of communication acts. It drives interaction and enables people as individuals and social groups to gain and develop the possibilities of an understanding of each other's subjective views. It is therefore consistent with a practical interest in mutual understanding that can address disagreements, which can be a threat to the social form of life. Communication may not only be direct. It may be indirect, for instance through the perceived association of two texts. It may not be verbal either. For instance, when we meet and talk, part of the communication process is verbal, but a large part of it is visible, through body language and facial expression. This can provide feedback that gives an indication as to whether or not a semantic communication has been successfully understood or not. This can be a problem in virtual communications through the Internet, where there is no implicit feedback mechanism, and where many more misunderstandings are therefore possible.

According to Deflem (1996), Habermas' concept of the lifeworld is that it provides a set of cultural values, ensures that social actors abide by the normative standards of their society, and that social actors are enabled to act as competent personalities in harmony with their social environment (referred to as identity formation). Three structural components of the lifeworld therefore correspond to the functions: culture, society, and personality.

Culture can be reproduced through the transmission of schemes of interpretation that are consensually shared by the members of a lifeworld. In social interaction, social integration refers to the legitimate ordering of interpersonal relations. This occurs through the coordination of actions via shared norms that are intersubjective. In personality, socialization processes seek to ensure that personalities with interactive capabilities are formed. Thus, culture, society, and personality are all structural components of the rationalized lifeworld. As such, the process of societal rationalization entails a differentiation of the lifeworld into different structural domains and specialized social institutions. The lifeworld, then, has a twofold meaning: on the one hand, the horizon-forming contexts of culture, society, and personality within which communicative action takes place, and, on the other hand, the resources of possibilities from which participants in communicative action can transmit and renew cultural knowledge, establish solidarity, and build social identity.

Other attributes of Habermas' (1987) conceptualizations are also relevant to agency theory. One of these is that both see society as a self-regulating system. Unlike Habermas, who ascribed meaning that arises from functional significances to a communication-theoretic model, here meaning is ascribed by context, and the nature of any operative processes like actions are relative to that context, as are interpretations. Social behaviour is socially constructed, and while communication is seen to be an essential component, this does not need to be an explicit component of systemic processes.

288   Agency as Society

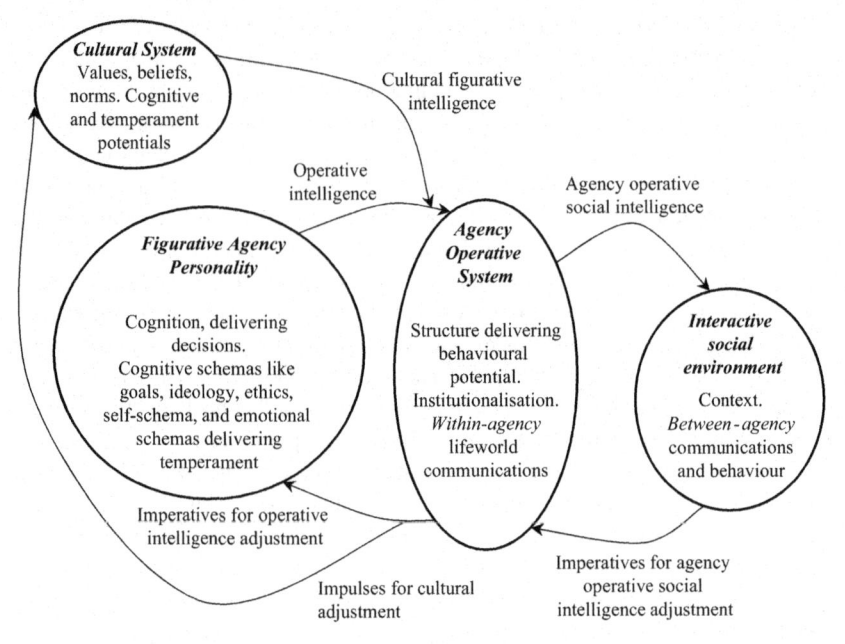

Figure 9.3 A representation of the cultural agency interacting in a social environment

Agency theory differs from that of Parsons in that it is not structural-functional. Its interest in communication distinguishes between *within-agency* lifeworld communication that satisfies the needs of Habermas, and *between-agency* lifeworld communications that occurs in the agency's environment as it interacts with other agencies (though the frame of reference of the model determines what is *within* and what is *between*), as indicated in Figure 9.3. There is a distinction between the two. Within a coherent agency (one that has a dominant common culture), communication is a lifeworld process that maintains semantic processes that are more or less understood by those who are part of that lifeworld, and therefore deliver meaning, making agreement a durable and hence viable construct. In the agency's interactive social environment, there are likely to be more differentiable cultures having semantic distinctions, and for complex situations agreement may be misunderstood and transitive.

Whereas Parsons considered the personality to be associated with the individual, the very existence of a cultural anchor for a social system suggests that there may be more than this at work. Culture houses values as well as the norms that enable members of a society to regularize their institutional modes of thought and behaviour. Culture assembles patterns of meanings embodied in symbols through which people communicate, perpetuate, and develop their knowledge about and attitudes towards cognitions and emotions, and hence provides a potential for cognitive processes and emotion/temperament.

The cognitive and temperament norms that emerge from a dominant culture influence the social, creating a potential for the development of what we refer to as the normative personality. The nature of this normative personality is strategic, delivering to the agency as a whole a variety of schemas that it has created, which include goals, ideology, ethics, and self-schemas that determine its modes of decision making and action behaviour, as well as emotional schemas that arise from emotional attitude, structure feelings, and apply emotions to contextual situations.

The agency operates through its intelligences that constitute a network of information-carrying processes that interconnect the different parts of the agency, and which facilitate the potential for coherence promised by culture. These process intelligences are central to the agency operating as a living system.

9.7   The Political Agency

Arguments concerning political structures and processes are closely connected with sociocultural ones, something usually seen through modern approaches to politics. What is sometimes referred to as traditional approaches to politics have tended to emphasize the study of the state and government, adopting grand narratives in the normative and idealistic study of the organization and the activities of the state and principles and the ideas that underlie political organizations and activities. They also tend to include philosophical, historical, institutional, and legal perspectives. Modern approaches tend to be concerned with theory (including methodology where appropriate) and practice, often finding observations and evidence important, and they embrace interdisciplinarity. These approaches tend to be placed into formal classifications, these sometimes being arbitrary because much political research cannot be uniquely pigeonholed due to its various disciplinary strands. Illustrations of classifications of modern politics include behaviouralist, sociological, psychological, decision making, economic, quantitative, systems, social class, structural-functional, and communication.

The earliest modern approach to politics came with behaviouralism, followed by its more problem-oriented sibling, post-behaviouralism. Related approaches, like simulation (mathematical, statistical, stochastic, or human interaction), can be subsumed within these, but they can also often be associated with systemic approaches. Another area of interest is that of political culture, for instance through the work of Chilton (1991) on political development. While, like the systemic work of Habermas and Parsons that Chilton follows, this could also be labelled a sociological or systems approaches. Behaviouralism examines political behaviour. Its focus is on the individual as voter, leader, revolutionary, party member, etc., and the influences of the group or the political system on the individual's political behaviour. In some cases, mathematical modelling (i.e. game theory) has been applied here to political systems, but it has tended to be highly restrictive in its propositions. It often adopts statistical methods to provide evidence, and one of its achievements here is the use of analytical statistics to anticipate election results from small regional samples of the electorate and official election results. However, while such models indicate relationships they are unable to offer deeper explanation. In general, behaviouralism looks for regularities that assume certain uniformities in political behaviour which can be expressed in generalizations or theories in order to predict political outcomes. It embraces processes of verification that emphasize testing and evidence, providing systematic approaches, and hence making it into a 'pure' science. Quantitative techniques are believed to be satisfactory in delivering such evidence. Facts tend to be distinguished from values and objectivity is paramount, these features therefore embrace a positivist perspective. It is also seen to be connected with other social sciences like history, sociology, and economics. It has given way in many quarters to post-behaviouralism. One of the tenets for its arrival included the belief that behaviouralism failed to offer solutions to many social and political problems. This approach may more particularly be seen as being associated with post-positivism, still embracing objectivity, but subject to the relative perspective of observers.

The sociological approach to politics is connected with new institutionalism or neo-institutionalism, a theory that focuses on developing a sociological view of institutions and explains why and how they emerge in a certain way and within a given context. The sociological approach comes to terms with claims by sociologists like Weber, Merton, Parsons, Habermas, and Foucault, examining power and the state from the social perspective. The psychological approach is interested in the quest for power and its use to influence others. The decision-making approach is interested in the characteristics of decision makers as well as the type of influence individuals have on the decision making. The economic approach relates political study to the economic necessity of life. The social class approach embraces theories of the political system, like Marxism, which itself embraces both social and economic dimensions. Here, economics creates a substructure, while politics, social, and cultural attributes become superstructural complements to this. Rather in the sense of the later work of Sorokin (1937–1942), whose theory of sociocultural change centres on the interplay between sensate and ideational attributes of culture, Marxism is founded on an interplay between (sensate) materialism and (ideational) idealism. The Marxian approach identifies political issues about social equity that are due to the state oppressing a class of society. It offers a resolution to this that comes from the argument that revolution to overthrow the oppressors and establish a classless and stateless society can resolve these issues. However, this approach does not examine the impact of sociocultural instabilities that also develop. Post-Marxian analysis has been pursued by people like Horkheimer and Habermas. This new tradition is responsible for the development of Critical Theory, which was intended to explain 'mistaken' Marxian evaluations without breaking with its fundamental intentions. Beyond Marxism, the class approach also has other dimensions, like the relationship between pluralism, elitism, and class analysis. This is closely related to the structural-functional approach, where society is treated as a single inter-related system, and each part of the system has a well-defined role. The communication approach is interested in the relationship between part of the political system through the use of communication, highlighting Luhmann and Habermas. The systems approach attempts to explain the relationship of political life with other aspects of social life, for instance through Parsons' or Easton's approaches. The idea of a system in sociology was originally borrowed from biology by Talcott Parsons, who first popularized the concept of the social system. According to Easton, it is not possible to analyse political events in isolation from other aspects of the society. In other words, influences from society shape the political process.

Important to the development of political thought, Easton's (1965) system model has inputs that may demand or support change for the status quo, while outputs are political decisions that might result in new policies (see Figure 9.4). The political system has demands and supports through political behaviour for action and non-action (i.e. the status quo) that are formulated as inputs. The demands and supporting groups stimulate competition in the political system, and decisions or outputs result that are directed towards some aspect of the social or physical environment. A policy decision (or output) is made in relation to a specific policy which interacts with its environment. Any change is an outcome. Outcomes may generate new demands or supports through feedback.

What has been called the *New Institutionalism* is due to its interdisciplinary discussions of the *institution* Huntington (1968a: 12) is interested in institutionalization which explains how organizations acquire value and stability. *Institutions* constitute stable, valued, recurring patterns of behaviour that arise from culturally based *customs*, and highlight the structural-behavioural aspects of an agency. *Institutionalization* is the process of institutional development that encompasses political culture and embeds it in a structure and modes of behaviour. It is from this that stable, valued, recurring patterns of behaviour arise. The development of stable patterns of behaviour are also tied to a need for cultural stability.

292   Agency as Society

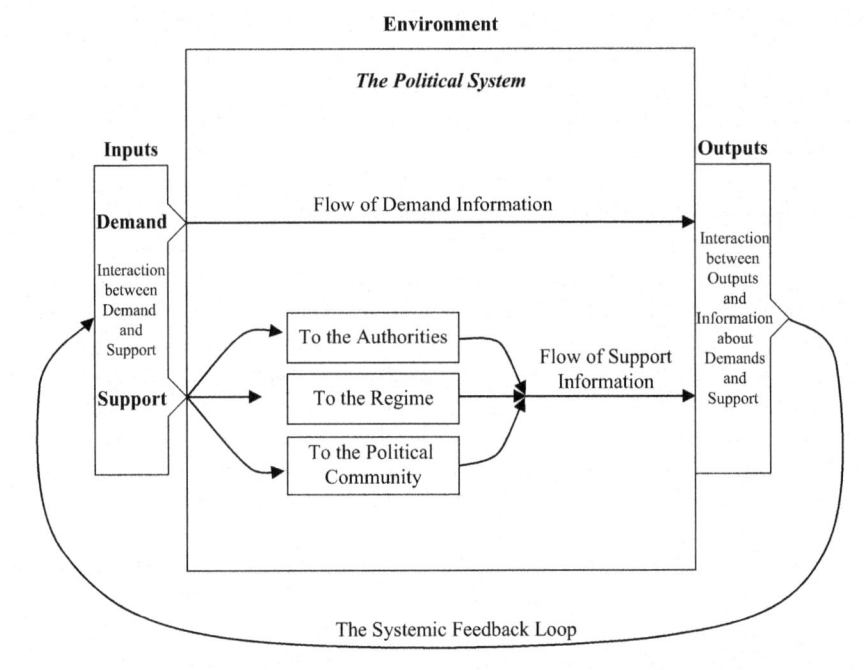

Figure 9.4 Basic systems model for political policy making (adapted from Easton, 1965)

Huntington also discusses the strength of a political organization and its procedures, and argues that this strength varies in its *scope of support* and its *level of institutionalization*. For him, *scope* refers to the extent to which the political organizations and procedures encompass activity in a society, that is, the proportions of social *mass* involved in a political organization. Huntington is also interested in issues of adaptability, which in a political agency would be a central attribute. Huntington (1965: 394) additionally notes that 'the level of institutionalisation of any political system can be defined by the adaptability, complexity, autonomy, and coherence of its organizations and procedures. So also, the level of institutionalisation of any particular organization or procedure can be measured by its adaptability, complexity, autonomy, and coherence. If these criteria can be identified and measured, political systems can be compared in terms of their levels of institutionalisation. Furthermore, it will be possible to measure increases and decreases in the institutionalisation of particular organizations and procedures within a political system.'

Huntington notes that *adaptability* is directly related to *degree of institutionalization*, and the *degree of institutionalization* is also a function of *time*.

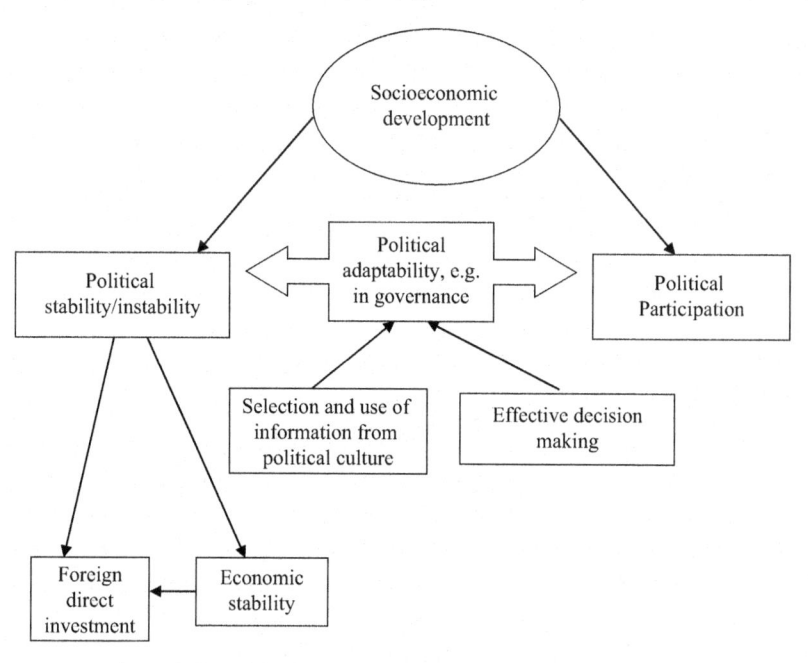

Figure 9.5 Model of socioeconomic development deriving from political arguments of Huntington (1968) (based on Rautakivi, 2014)

These two positions are likely flawed in that they do not take into consideration the possibility of cultural instability, when de-institutionalization may be a longer term consequence, for instance through decline in capability (as illustrated, for instance, by Asimov, 1951), or adaptation during declining institutionalization. Other elements of the political process are also discussed by Huntington besides political stability, and these include political participation, economic stability, and foreign direct investment. These have been represented in Figure 9.5, adapted from Rautakivi (2014).

Another interest of Huntington (1965) is political development, and he notes that there are a number of perspectives that account for it (e.g. rationalization, competitiveness, and nation-building, mobilization, and participation). He further notes that development is not normally discussed as a reversible process. Rather, if political development is expressed in terms of the mobilization of people into politics, political de-development can also take place, where people are demobilized out of politics. He further notes some manifestations of political development: urbanization is likely to give way to ruralization; literacy improvement is not normally followed by sharp declines; capital once invested into industry stays invested; increases in per capita gross national product are often permanent, except for minor dips or destruction caused by war or natural catastrophe. In the last example, reference to conflict situations as the cause of decline is totally a function of in/stability. By the same token, the forms of development highlighted by Huntington may be subject to de-development over the longer term when cultural stability is endangered. By political culture is meant the particular pattern of orientations to political action (Almond, 1956: 396). Culture arises through values, beliefs, knowledge, and norms. These become oriented and manifested as ideologies, attitudes, and practices that are held by a political membership. This may include political myths and beliefs that shape their political behaviour, and which result in moral and ethical judgements, and self-schema and goals that they believe creates for them a good society. This can then be related to political development, where political culture may be subject to change. For Huntington (1965: 393) 'a theory of political development needs to be mated to a theory of political decay...theories of instability, corruption, authoritarianism, domestic violence, institutional decline, and political disintegration may tell us a lot more about the "developing" areas than their more hopefully defined opposites...[Appropriately] political development [should be seen] as the institutionalization of political organizations and procedures. This concept liberates development from modernization. It can be applied to the analysis of political systems of any sort, not just modern ones. It can be defined in reasonably precise ways which are at least theoretically capable of measurement. As a concept, it does not suggest that movement is likely to be in only one direction: institutions, we know, decay and dissolve as well as grow and mature. Most significantly, it focuses attention on the reciprocal interaction between the on-going social processes of modernization, on the one hand, and the strength, stability, or weakness of political structures, traditional, transitional, or modern, on the other.'

The Easton model of Figure 9.4 can be migrated directly to agency theory, allowing discussion of networks of political operative processes of Figure 9.6 (that in Figure 9.3 are represented as political operative intelligence and its feedback imperatives) and feedback to try to maintain operative stability. This view of the Easton model can be placed in the context of Huntington's political development, resulting in Figure 9.6. Operative stability can, in cultural agency, be referred to as instrumental stability since it is concerned with the efficacious manifestation of strategic aims like political goals. Outputs are carried through operative intelligence – a network of processes that specify through attendant information (and sometimes hype) how demand is satisfied by support. Inputs occur along the operative intelligence feedback and create imperatives that respond to the monitoring of how well

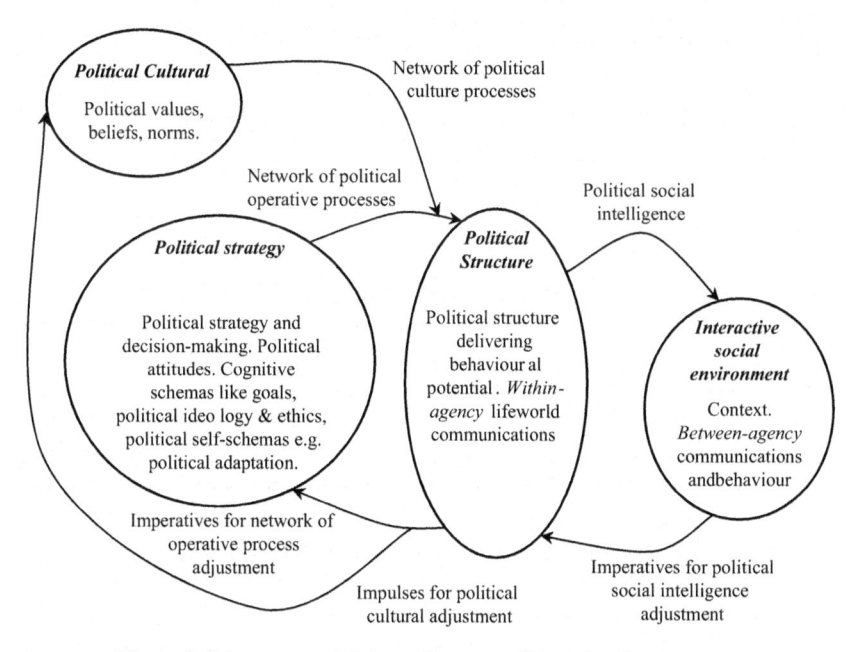

Figure 9.6 Agency model that relates to political development

demands have been supported. When talking of efficacy, Easton (1967: 25) means political efficacy, referring to 'a norm, as a psychological disposition or feeling, and as a form of behaviour', this leading (for Easton) to contradiction and confusion. According to Yolles & Fink (2011) in cultural agency theory, there is no contradiction since all three of these are related to the intelligences, and how well these work is measured as efficacy.

Huntington's approach to political development can also be migrated to cultural agency and linked commensurably to that of Easton. Thus for instance, Huntington's concept of political development might be discussed in terms of supporting demands through effective strategic decision making, and the cultural instabilities that might eventually result when these demands are not perceived to be satisfied in a way that is appropriate to at least some segments of the membership of the political environment. Such arguments can be deepened. Not all political regimes may be subject to political cultural instabilities, especially those that disregard the political environment and maintain autocratic/despotic decision processes. The attribute of participation may be determined by political social intelligence as a function of how arguments are put into the membership of the political process through the between-lifeworld processes. Political agency in/stability is ultimately determined by political culture in/stability.

9.8 Luhmann, Habermas, Agency, and Practice

While the conceptualizations of both Luhmann and Habermas are expressed highly theoretically, there are some clear applications of them. Here we shall indicate one practical application for each.

Luhmann and the Military of Guatemala

Kirsch (1998) explores the political and military strategy of Guatemala's armed forces during the 1960s–1990s civil war from the perspective of Luhmann's autopoietic theory, an approach that attempts to show the promise that his work could have in providing an improved understanding of Third World politics.

In 1956 around 200 mercenaries in the 'liberation' movement of colonel Carlos Castillo Armas, trained by the CIA, invaded Guatemala from Honduras, and in due course replaced the incumbent elected president. During the next 42 years Guatemala suffered from pervasive militarization and civil war with the Unidad Revolucionaria National de Guatemala (URNG).

Kirsch applied Luhmann's communication theory to this case, citing Yin (1989) as a means to validate the approach, which adopts a single case (the military of Guatemala's functional structure), which is seen holistically (the military as an autopoietic social system) and longitudinally (relevant time period: from 1954 until 1997).

Attributes of Luhmann's work that are highlighted for application to the case include Kneer & Nassehi's (1993) realization that understanding (like action) is a component of communication and not a phenomenon of consciousness. Psyche and behaviour do not interact directly, only indirectly through communication. The only way therefore of assessing the connection between psychic and behavioural phenomena is through communication, and methodologically, one way of assessing communications is through an observational approach, a notion supported by Luhmann.

Kirsch summarizes Luhmann's theory in relation to its application to the case as follows:

- A system is a quantity of interacting elements that delineates itself from its environment.
- No system can operate beyond its boundaries. Autopoietic systems are operatively closed, self-referential, and self-reproductive.
- The function of a social system is to mediate between the overwhelming complexity of the world and the feeble complexity processing capacity of the individual through reduction of indeterminable complexity into determinable complexity. Trust is an important means of reduction of complexity.

- Autopoietic social systems are systems of communication. Although both types of systems are structurally coupled, there is no interface between communication and consciousness.
- Actions are products of social descriptions. Systems of communication usually perceive themselves as systems of action.
- What is communicated as an understanding is a property of communication rather than of consciousness. The only indicators of how previous conversations have been understood are connecting conversations.
- What distinguishes psychic and social systems from other systems is that they operate meaningfully. Meaning is the constant reiteration of selections from within a horizon of potentialities referred to by actuality. It is operatively closed and self-referential. Semantics is meaning that is generalized on a higher level in a society system.
- An autopoietic social system observes the world through designation by distinction. Its observation is confined to a fundamental distinction expressed in a binary code.
- Binary code of the military can be assumed to be national security/lack thereof. An autopoietic social system's fundamental distinction is its blind spot: it can't see that it can't see what it can't see. A second-order observation – an observation of an observation – can see the blind spot of the observation it observes.
- The theory of autopoietic social systems is a second-order observation of society (i.e. it provides better understanding of what is happening).
- Through system differentiation, social systems divide themselves into sub-systems, repeating the difference between system and environment within the system. The operations of a society's sub-systems is controlled through programmes.

The position taken by the parties to the conflict, social and psychic and in an environment, are theorized as being expressed through a binary code that is used to construct communications. Hence both the social and psychic systems make sense of the world exclusively through system-specific and accessible binary code. Within the context of this conflict it results, Kirsch posits, in the following relationships: the purpose of national security is to preserve existing structures, therefore demanding counterinsurgency, and insurgency is seen to be a threat to existing structures, implying a lack of national security. This limiting frame of reference resulted in Guatemala's military taking on a counterinsurgency–insurgency perspective. Consequently, tactics and strategies of counterinsurgency became its programme. Since an operative system cannot observe itself, it requires a higher order system to do so and guide it (Glanville, 2004). As such, the military is therefore unable to determine whether its counterinsurgency–insurgency frame of reference provides an adequate mode or behaviour. This is a problematic view that generates paradox if one considers the argument of agency theory: that self-reference requires the involvement of higher orders of observation (Yolles & Fink, 2015a, 2015b, 2015c).

The obvious outcomes of this study are that:

- The military of Guatemala opposed the peace negotiations with the URNG because it depended on the civil war as its *raison d'être*.
- It was capable of a dirty war with scorched earth strategies of unprecedented proportions because of its internal structure and ideological orientation, both of which were shaped in an evolutionary process controlled by the State Department and the CIA in cooperation with domestic economic and political elites.

The Luhmann approach to the study of this conflict conceives of the military as an autopoietic communication system with its impact on the psychic and social systems. However, two alternative studies of this conflict have also developed. One is by Martínez de León (1994), whose approach was to conceive of it as a group of individual actors seeking to maintain their social and political status. The other was by Jonas (1996), which was to conceive of the conflict as a corporate actor seeking to maintain the power positions of international elites. All approaches provide overlapping results in the political analysis, even though all of the three inquirers studying this case take distinct definitions of the 'social' and the 'political'.

While it is validating for the Luhmann approach that different analytical approaches to the study of this conflict produced similar results, there is perhaps an elementary reason for this. From agency theory it can be said that in an ongoing conflict situation in which two groups have already been polarized and 'locked-in' to entrenched oppositional positions, the conflict becomes an equilibrium one that maintains itself 'normally'. A sophisticated living systems approach is not really essential to explore such situations. It is only when new instabilities arise that the conflict may change, where more sophisticated approaches to analysis and diagnosis may contribute to its resolution. In sum, it is difficult for such conflicts to become resolved without disrupting the stability that has developed in the relationship between the parties.

Reflection

It has been said that 'all approaches provide overlapping results in the political analysis'. It is possible to create a diagram that shows where each of those approaches might fit in the agency model of Figure 9.3. As a guideline for delivering the proposed diagram, we first identify the three approaches specified:

- A Luhmann approach conceives of the military as an autopoietic communication system with its impact on the psychic and social systems.
- A Martínez de León approach conceives there to be a group of individual actors seeking to maintain their social and political status.
- A Jonas approach conceives the military conflict in terms of a corporate actor seeking to maintain the power positions of international elites.

These three perspectives may be integrated through agency theory. In the case of Luhmann, communication as an autopoietic system arises because an agency has a figurative and cognitive (psychic) system that links with its operative system through autopoiesis to deliver optional statements that can be selected and delivered to other agencies. The agency can be a corporate actor that develops through figurative and operative norms. However, these norms arise through a cultural development that emerges through a stable collection of individuals.

Habermas, Alienation, and Domination

Cecez-Kecmanovic & Janson (1999) are interested in eliminating causes of unwarranted alienation and domination in organizations within an Information Systems context, thereby enhancing an opportunity to realize human potential.

To do this, Cecez-Kecmanovic & Janson note that Habermas (1984) defines communicative action as the interaction of social actors pursuing goals. They do this by achieving shared understanding and coordinating their plans of action. Referring to shared understanding suggests inter-subjective interpretation of aspects of social reality. This occurs when the actors agree on a common understanding of what exists (the objective world of facts, events, and states of affairs), what is right and legitimate (the social world of norms), and what they prefer or desire, relating to the internal worlds of personal experiences and emotions. Communicative action assumes the validity claims of truth of facts, rightness of norms, and sincerity of expressions. Understanding is achieved by social actors through cooperative interpersonal interpretation of the situation under examination. Since consensus is a core feature of Habermas' approach, seeking this through rational argumentation is a requirement. However, this does not assume that social actors have shared goals. Rather actors are seen to pursue their own goals that may have potentially divergent interests. However, the coordination of plans of action through processes of interpretation is still feasible in Habermas' theory. This is distinct from the more common view in the Information Systems community that communicative action just points the actors involved to achieving mutual understanding and consensus. For Habermas (1984: 94), achieving understanding in language becomes a mechanism for coordinating action.

Cecez-Kecmanovic & Janson continue by noting that an essential requirement for successful communicative action is that *ideal speech situation* conditions exist. These refer to communicative practice that is free from any kind of distortion, coercion, and ideology. This is because these attributes only include force of argument, rather than any other constraining impulses. Thus, everyone capable of speech and action is entitled to participate. More, everyone is equally entitled to query any assertion, to introduce new topics, and to express attitudes, needs, and desires. In other words, there needs to be both transparency and openness. The Interactive System for Information Dissemination (ISID) was developed on this basis, designed to meet the company's desire for open, clear, and efficient communication, and providing efficient and effective access to information. This includes information about all decisions, actions, and events, as well as interoffice correspondence, outbound and inbound communication, and minutes of meetings. Supporting documents are retrievable by keywords, authors, and recipients.

A breakdown in the system can be overcome through a Habermasian approach. This is illustrated as follows. A manager subverted the communicative action process, making it into a strategic action type or process. He achieved this during the absence of a key member of staff who was on holiday. When this was detected and analysed from the documentation stored in the information system, a public discussion ensured. While it left the outcome untouched, it did establish a constraint that inhibited this outcome in the future. This situation demonstrates a situation where corporate members with potentially different goals are able to realize goals by engaging in communication action.

A summary, arising from Cecez-Kecmanovic & Janson, is that the company first created conditions which approximate the ideal speech situation, that is: in-house company training to engender communicative competence in individuals, the capacity for self-reflection, sanctioned responsibility to actively participate in discussions, free inquisition of claims, and the ability to reason rationally using appropriate argumentation. The validity claims of truth, rightness of action, and sincerity of actors may be questioned, as are the underlying values, policies, and assumptions. Argumentation can, therefore, establish the basis for shared understanding of a problem situation, as well as in achieving consensus in relation to potential actions. However, such consensus is not always achievable. A single individual makes decisions, but those affected are still involved and capable of influencing the decision and its implementation. This ensures coordination of individual action plans. This more or less constitutes, according to Cecez-Kecmanovic & Janson, Habermas' ideal speech situation.

Reflection

Referring to Figure 9.3, it can be shown visually how and where communications occur in the agency, and how failed communication might be represented as a pathology. This can be left to the reader as an exercise, noting that one way of doing this is to consider the following. The speech act is a phenomenal process of communication that occurs between two or more agencies in the social world. However, the social world is seated in the external natural world. The relationship has been discussed previously in this chapter in terms of internalization. This is a process by which external processes associated with external material objects are transformed into processes that take place mentally at the level of consciousness. These processes become generalized, verbalized, abbreviated, and become the means for further development that transcends what is possible with external activity. It is through external social activities that a plane of consciousness spontaneously emerges. Higher mental functions are internalized social relationships, allowing for a variety of analytic and related processes to occur that begin with abstraction, and when applied to social actions allows an individual to replace perceptual judgments for those based on reasoned internalized actions. This explanation has implication on the modelling, through agency, of the speech act:

- Individuals experience the external world, aspects of which they internalize.
- Individuals use their internalized conceptualizations to create figurative schemas that may become associated with self.
- Figurative schemas become manifested as decision potentials from which processes of social communication arise.
- Transitive pathologies may occur instrumentally (between the figurative and operative system), or during the process of communication in the social world.
- Lateral pathologies may occur when internalized cognitive structures or related figurative schemas are developed with faults that may arise, for instance, through misperceptions or misunderstandings.

Cultural Agency Theory in Relation to Habermas and Luhmann

Following Habermas, Parsons' General Theory of Action is a special case of agency theory involving a cultural, psychic/cognitive/personality and social system. However, agency theory is significantly broader than the General Theory of Action, and is not an equilibrium model like that of Parsons. Nor is it subject to the theoretical cleavage that Menzies has noted in Parsons' theory.

The use of cultural agency theory enables what has until now been seen to be complex explanations of living systems to be expressed simply in terms of a substructure, and in particular in terms of basic learning systems. Superstructure can be migrated into agency theory where there is no incommensurability with existing propositions. This is the case for both Luhmann's theory and that of Habermas. Luhmann's ideas can be directly migrated into agency theory since they are both living systems constructs. However, agency theory does not require the restrictions that Luhmann has introduced. This is because psychic and social events are not necessarily only the result of communications, but they together form an interactive set that can influence one another mutually. Habermas' theory was used as a basis in the initial establishment of agency theory in Yolles (2006), so that its propositions are consistent. However, there are limits to Habermas' construction that are not prevalent in agency theory. It is not specifically a theory concerned with communication, though this is seen to be a feature that is necessarily a part of the agency. Honneth (1995, cited in The Loch Journal, 2011), uncovers another attribute, relating to the inability to ensure that within the historic-cultural context, true understanding can occur between individuals when they fully appreciate or comprehend the deeper aspects of each other's 'life ideals and modes of orientation'. Another issue that Habermas does not engage in is the influence and management of emotion, which is an important attribute. Habermas' perspective on this only embraces emotions in terms of socio-psychological costs (www.stefan-szczelkun.org.uk/phd402.htm) that touch on emotion. This is taken further by Crossley (2002: 18), who tells us that Habermas' position 'can be criticised...for failing to give sufficient attention to the affective [emotional] dimension of communicative action [and that] communication is...more than an exchange of symbols and ideas: that is it is a process of mutual affecting in which interlocutors make emotional as well as cognitive appeals. Furthermore, he fails to consider that communications can and do take place within the context of different types of emotional relationship.' Crossley further considers that these limits to Habermasian theory are due to inclusion, but are not inconsistent with his broader ideas. In contrast, agency theory has a well-developed affective dimension (Fink & Yolles, 2015a).

Agency theory expresses autopoiesis in terms of a simple instrumental learning and provides a capability to explain, for instance, how a network of operative processes can be used to represent goals and ideologies operationally. Where these processes work well, then the agency may be said to be operatively efficacious. Similarly, expressing autogenesis in terms of cognitive learning where contextually sensitive information is selected from patterns of cultural knowledge can be applied to goals, for instance, and provide guidance of how those goals may be implemented in that context. Operative intelligence feedback may instrumentally adjust the goals or the way in which operative intelligence responds to them, which figurative intelligence feedback can create imperatives for changes in cultural knowledge, or to adjust the way in which figurative intelligence deals with the selections of contextual information. Other illustrations of agency theory will be provided in due course, in particular showing the application of its embedded personality theory to employee job screening.

10 The Economic Agency

10.1 Introduction

The 2008 Western recession resulted from the failure of financial institutions, including banks, due to their uncontrolled self-indulgent financial practices leading to a severe economic crisis. Policy options to resolve the recession that have resulted from the crisis included financial sector restructuring or bail-outs on the assumption that the banks are generally moral and trustworthy organizations. A bail-out policy required debt servicing which has led in the European Union to measures of austerity, damaging social fabrics and hurting the more vulnerable. An alternative policy in the United States has been to borrow more to stimulate economic growth, the result of which should be a servicing of the debt. The economic crisis was not predicted by any economic models. Prediction of the crisis by economic models failed. After the Lucas Critique, which says that economic and political processes are both important to economic theory, political processes have tended to be reflected in economic models. The policy options of austerity and investment can be associated respectively with the culturally based political modes of Individualism and Collectivism. The making of economic policy arising from either of these political modes is seen by some to be an inadequate basis for developing a sustainable economic society, implying the need for an improved socio-economic modelling basis that reflects culture. A new culturally based economic meta-model is developed, where cultural orientation is a driver for a strategic economic agency and the formation of economic policy. The meta-model enables the modelling of the relationship between cultural, economic, and political processes using cybernetic agency theory, and specific propositions can be introduced to generate specific models. The meta-model that arises can assist in the understanding of complex socio-economic processes. The meta-model adopts trait-based agency theory, the strategic economic agency that is constituted as an agency's normative personality from which political orientations and the anticipation of classes of decision-making behaviour can develop. The chapter shows that Individualism and Collectivism can be seen as a subset of the broader mindscape theory, reformulated here for the meta-model.

The US/European economic crisis that was manifested in 2007/8 was not predicted by any mainstream economic models. Following the *Lucas Critique* (Lucas, 1976), economic theory began to embrace issues of policy, and this has led to explorations that connect macroeconomics and policy making (Coats, 1969; Dolphin & Nash, 2011: 13). While this leads to the realization that there is a need to explore both human and political dimensions, by extension economic policy also needs to embrace cultural theory (Costanza, Wainger, Folke & Miler, 1993).

To take this forward, we shall present cultural agency theory formulating a relationship between culture, sociocultural dynamics, and socio-political orientations that contribute to the formation of economic policy. As part of this, personality is then explored in terms of Maruyama's mindscape theory (Chapter 5).

The situation of interest relates to 2008 and 2009 when the world economy experienced its worst ever financial crisis caused by a US relaxation of the constraints on financial institutions and their responsibility in making loans, resulting effectively in unsecured lending and in due course a collapse in the sub-prime market, resulting in uncountable failures and financial disasters. It has resulted in the deepest recession since the 1930s. According to the IMF in 2011, global GDP contracted by 0.5 per cent in 2009 – the first annual fall in GDP in the post-war period (Dolphin & Nash, 2011). More, real GDP in the advanced countries fell by 3.4 per cent, and the banks were bailed out by their host nations, thus creating a mountain of debt that has been responsible for an economic disaster in Europe and the United States, and has destabilized the Euro.

To deal with the crisis there has been argument that the policies which have been pursued are politically distinct, there being two approaches: austerity and stimulation. These policy positions can be related, not so much to right and left politics, but rather to one of two ideological positions: Individualism and Collectivism. This drives us to look more critically at these two cognitive positions. For some, economics is identified with individualism, a theme that Davis, Marciano & Runde (2004: 21) have interest in when they say that 'close examination of the underlying claims [of Individualism] making such explanations raise a number of difficult philosophical issues. One of the most challenging concerns the requirements for reducing statements about social phenomena to statements about individuals...Another fundamental issue involves what constitutes the "best" explanation in science or in economics. These more philosophical questions return us to economic methodology's epistemological concerns, but no less important are the ontological ones the topic of individualism raises. When we privilege individualist explanations in economics, do we believe that only individuals exist? That society itself does not exist?' Nozick (1977: 359; cited in Davis, Marciano & Runde, 2004: 121) notes critically that methodological individualism is quite distinct from the more Collectivistic methodological institutionalism, so why are economists not equally methodological institutionalists? Neither individual nor institutional factors have legitimate explanatory primacy, and the idea that all explanations have ultimately to be in terms of individuals (or institutions) is thus unfounded. This leads us to consider that the nature of Individualism and Collectivism, and the consequential political, and hence policy, dynamics that result.

An agency model will be presented which reflects on Bandura's (2006) realization that Individualism, Collectivism, or indeed a Collective Individualism balance between the two, cannot hope to respond to the sort of challenge that the economy is passing through. More, it is explained that, given the right model, it should be possible to anticipate policy tendencies and hence macroeconomic processes. Finally, an indicative case study will be provided that shows how agency personality can be used to anticipate policy outcomes and their consequences. We say indicative since to do a full in-depth study would require much more space than is available to us in this book.

10.2 Economics and Policy

Economic crises are often the result of government policy failure, giving rise to the perception that there is a need for policy change and reform, and as a result there is also a need for (Bolt et al., 2003):

(i) sufficient sector diagnosis to understand the contextual concerns of policy changes;
(ii) improved ex-ante assessment of likely impacts of policy reforms and related analysis of the costs of adjustment;
(iii) sufficient attention to institutional capacity building, before, during, and after the implementation phase of policy reform.

Reforms represent changes to the underlying framework that govern the behaviour of different stakeholders. How these may respond to policy changes must be taken into account in policy analysis.

Reforms centre on the removal and replacement of alternative constraints and facilitations or encouragements. Understanding of the nature and dynamics of policy changes and institutional reforms is therefore an essential need in policy formulation. This tends to conform to an evolutionary process that Bolt et al. (2003) explain in simple terms as:

(1) macroeconomic stabilization and the parametric policy changes (like price liberalization);
(2) structural policy and the underlying market and institutional changes;
(3) a formative stage, although it is exemplified by an emphasis on the political economy of policy reforms.

The appreciation of the nature of reforms so characterized facilitates reinforcement for the need for more systematic policy and deep institutional analyses.

The European Project offers an illustration of the need for institutional reforms. The creation of effective economic policy to manage the recently developed debt crisis has been threatening the Project's integrity (Veron, 2011), and Europe seems to have had some difficulty in responding to the issues that need to be addressed. One reason for this has been given by William Rhodes, who predicted the great financial crisis in the last decade. To deal with debt crises like this one policy makers need to (Rhodes, 2012):

(1) manage it;
(2) be time sensitive since delays deepen crises;
(3) provide political leadership;
(4) undertake fast decisions, clear communication, prompt action, and persistence;
(5) recognize in a plural economic system that each country is a unique case;
(6) realize that there is no single recipe for all borrowers;
(7) allow the private sector and public and private sectors to work together, calling on trust between all stakeholders, with consensus;
(8) avoid panic, which often arises from outside perception, from the rescued stakeholders and public opinion;
(9) provide measures for contagion, noting that every sovereign debt crisis is followed by banking crises;
(10) recognize that reforms take time to develop.

A number of these principles, Rhodes claims, have been lost within the European Crisis.

An alternative more macroscopic perspective of this situation comes from Dolphin & Nash (2011) who, drawing on Hall (1993) and Hill (2010) among others, argue that the current debt crisis has arisen due to an adherence to an old and now inappropriate economic paradigm that needs to be replaced. In particular they note (Dolphin & Nash, 2011: 13):

> ...the economics profession continues to resist change because it has invested so much intellectual capital in the wrong models and is reluctant to admit its mistake. James Galbraith describes 'a kind of Politburo for correct economic thinking' that has been 'on the wrong side of every important policy issue' (2009: 95). This 'Politburo' resists new ideas. Consequently, new economic thinking, or anything that challenges the consensus, is marginalised. Those outside the current mainstream, he argues, cannot get a place at a top US university, cannot get published in top academic journals and are reduced to publishing their ideas in newsletters and blogs.

They also note that in the 'real world' democratic political systems, economic paradigm change is likely to be associated with a shift of power, possibly within the ruling party, but more likely through a change in the party in charge, that is, resulting in a policy regime shift. Most of the time the 'old guard' will be too closely associated with the old paradigm to credibly put forward the new one, although 'conversion' is not impossible (Coats, 1969). Broadly, they note the distinction between the 'utopian economics' that centres on notions of rational expectation, and 'reality economics' that does not.

However, the likelihood that a new paradigm will emerge can only be the result of what Dolphin & Nash refer to as an extended period of little-to-no economic growth, something that is likely to occur, at least in Europe. In support of this they note a letter written by Richard Koo, Chief Economist at Nomura (www.economist.com/node/21 5262 89) to *The Economist*, when he says:

The economics profession has never considered a recession that could be caused by the private sector minimising debt in order to repair balance sheets after a debt-financed bubble in asset prices. As a result, the profession has no clue as to what is the right thing to do.

However, Dolphin & Nash also note the possibility of a way forward that draws on an evolutionary approach to economic history proposed by Lent (2009). Here, 'advanced economies are seen to be entering a "synergy" phase during which productive (rather than financial) capital will have the central role in determining growth. But, he [Lent] argues, the level of investment needed to ensure that strong growth occurs will only be forthcoming if companies are reasonably confident about future levels of demand. This will require that "demand is consciously encouraged through public policies and business strategies" (ibid. 61). The outcomes of these policies should include a reversal of the trends that have seen real median wages stagnate in recent years and a steady decline in the share of wages in national income over the last three decades' (Dolphin & Nash, 2011: 16).

Lent's (2009) notion arises from the work of Carlota Perez (2002, 2004a, 2009a), who has studied the tensions and patterns that prefigured major crashes and recessions in the past. In particular, Perez is interested in the historical economic processes that drive the volatility of capitalism, and their shift through historical phases of boom, bust, stagnation, and radical reinvention. These historical periods can be split into four phases, and between phase 2 and 3 there is the often troubled turning point created by a financial crash. These phases are:

1 *irruption*, when a new cluster of technologies and an associated business paradigm emerges and begins to spread;
2 *frenzy*, when finance capital invests ever more heavily in the new technology and linked businesses and greatly expands its political influence;
3 *synergy*, when the new technology and paradigm spreads more fully across all spheres of society leading to economic benefits;

4 *maturity*, when the technology and paradigm reaches the point at which it stops producing major productivity gains and achieves market saturation.

So far we have learned that economic issues can arise when crises appear and when policy makers do not respond in a timely and appropriate way to the crises, or when there is a change in policy thinking resulting from a shift in political power or political regime change. However, what profoundly determines how we address economic issues is the dominant economic paradigm that informs the current wisdom of policy making thought that is likely currently in transition. The cyclic theory proposed by Perez may be new for economics, but it has its theoretical basis elsewhere, in the study of sociocultural dynamics by Pitrim Sorokin (1938–42). Here, consistent with Costanza, Wainger, Folke & Miler (1993), changes in culture have the capacity to change everything else in their social system, including economics. Culture, Sorokin argues, passes through a cycle of change for which we recall (Chapter 5) that two modes of thought are responsible, Sensate and Ideational. The tensions that arise between these two cultural orientations result in an outcome from which all of a society's strategic and behavioural processes derive. This tension between two cultural orientations is manifested, for instance, in the political orientations that arise in the European Parliament, and which are ultimately responsible for its very cohesion. This is explained by Yolles (2009), who argues that the European Project is able to make decisions because its membership falls into two basic political divisions, Individualists and Collectivists. In what follows, we shall introduce Sorokin's theory, and then discuss Individualism and Collectivism.

10.3   Macroeconomic Modelling

Macroeconomics can be broadly distinguished into two areas of interest: (1) the causes and consequences of short-run fluctuations in national income (the business cycle); (2) the attempt to understand the determinants of long-run economic growth (increases in national income). In order to be able to make future forecasts for these areas, macroeconomic models are used by both governments and large corporations to assist in the development and evaluation of economic policy and business strategy.

Early macroeconomic models like the IS-LM (Investment-Saving/Liquidity preference-Money supply) model, the Mundell–Fleming model of Keynesian macroeconomics, and the Solow model of growth theory tend to be static rather than dynamic models describing the economy over many time periods (Blanchard, 2000). The simplicity of such models, however, while satisfying useful illustrative macroeconomic purposes, does little to assist any capacity to make useful anticipatory forecasts of macroeconomic change.

Neoclassical approaches to macroeconomic modelling (Veblen, 1898) tend to dominate microeconomics, and seek to determine prices, outputs, and income distributions in markets through supply and demand. These often centre on propositions of utility maximization by individuals with bounded resources, and of profits by firms with budget constraints which assume rational choice theory with available information and factors of production. Such approaches suffer from certain questionable assumptions, which include accurate anticipations; determinable states of knowledge; and decisions made through bounded rationality. Now boundedness in rationality supposes that a decision maker does not know all alternatives and all outcomes; makes a limited search to discover a few satisfactory alternatives; makes decisions which satisfy his or her aspirations; and is an objective (rather than subjective) entity. In bounded rationality decision makers may wish to act rationally but their ability to do so is constrained because they have a limited ability to absorb and handle information. Inquirers are further supposed to have limited cognitive ability to perceive alternatives and their consequences, so that there is a limit on the search for alternatives, and hence the first alternative to satisfy the problem constraints is generally accepted. As such a search for optima in given problem situations to various problems may occur (e.g. through profit maximization, utility maximization, or cost minimization) – where the performance of an economy is judged in terms of how close it is to some theoretical optimum.

Empirical approaches have also been evident, resulting in a model called the Phillips curve (Phillips, 1958), in which unemployment and inflation were seen to have an inverse relationship. Friedman (1968), among others, argued that this relationship was due to unexpected past inflationary episodes, and that such a simple relationship should not be seen to be generally valid. In addition, he argued, there was a need to build in human perceptions and resulting behaviours. Less than a decade later Lucas (1976) argued, in what has come to be called the *Lucas Critique*, that empirical results in macroeconomics are seen to be unreliable due to their being derived from observed relationships between various macroeconomic quantities that varied over time, but that they were in fact dependent on the macroeconomic policy regime that was currently in place. So, now not only was human perception to become part of macroeconomic theory, but also policy regime. Lucas further argued that it would not be possible to predict the effects of new policies unless models were created independent of policy changes, based on deep parameters that constitute such economic fundamentals as preferences, technology, and budget constraints.

As a result of the Lucas Critique, two types of model arose: dynamic stochastic general equilibrium (Phelps, 1970) and computable general equilibrium (Kehoe & Kehoe, 1994). The dynamic modelling approach makes the assumption that all agents of given classes (for instance, the class *corporations* or the class *households*) are identical, so that outcomes arise from an averaging process. They also centre on assumptions about preferences, technology, and budget constraints, and are often interested in business cycles and the cyclical effects of monetary and fiscal policy. In contrast, computable general equilibrium approaches centre on long-run relationships, typically exploring the long-run impact of permanent policies like the tax system or the openness of the economy to international trade. Both approaches attempt to represent the relationships between the various macroeconomic variables each from their own set of propositions and with the intention of anticipating behavioural outcomes. In doing this, both classes of model make assumptions that the economic system being modelled is both in equilibrium and closed.

Where modelling processes centre on conditions of general equilibrium, the analysis of economic growth tends to be grafted on to the theory, and this can pose a problem where growth does not conform to general equilibrium (Nelson, 2004). Where an economic system is postulated to be closed, then it cannot be directly influenced by other economic systems, a proposition which in the current global crises is blatantly wrong. As implied by Friedman and the Lucas Critique, closure is a proposition that sits uneasily with the recognition that economics only exists through the open human activity systems that carry them. In equilibrium systems there is normally an assumption of rational determinism, so that everything that needs to be known about the situation is, or at least can be, known. Equilibrium and closedness are often connected. Leijonhufvud notes that *closure* in modern macroeconomics 'stems from the commitment to optimising behaviour as the "microfoundations" of the enterprise. Models of "optimal choice" render agents as automatons lacking "free will" and thus deprived of choice in any genuine sense.... Whatever happens, they are always in equilibrium' (Leijonhufvud, 2011: 3).

Trosby (2001) notes that despite its intellectual imperialism, neoclassical economics is quite restrictive in its assumptions, is highly constrained in its mechanics; and is limited in its capacity to provide explanations. He further argues that economics comprises a plurality of paradigms that each offer uncoordinated alternative ways of analysing the functioning of the economy or the actions of the individual.

Consistent with Postpositivism (and unlike Constructivism), the positivist rational determinism of neoclassical economic modelling has given way to a principle of rational expectation that allows for randomness. Hence the core proposition is as follows. Expectations occur such that: *if* (a) an analysis and model can be in some way validated, *and* (b) an intervention strategy can be deduced that allows problem situations to be resolved in some way, *and* (c) the analysis arises from a view that comes out of the perspective demanded by the model, *then* (d) during implementation of the intervention strategy the specifications are honoured such that that monitoring occurs to ensure that (b) and (c) are valid. Under such conditions the result will satisfy the perceived needs of the situation. Leijonhufvud (2011) relates the idea of rational expectation to George Soros' (2008) use of the term 'reflexivity', where for instance, at the start of an analysis of financial markets one recognizes that present beliefs about the future induce actions that create the future (Soros, 2008). As such an investor who can assess current market sentiment and consequently infer how it will produce a future (different from that which is generally expected) can make a profit. A bad reading of the market or poor inferences will result in a loss. Agents do not only have to form expectations about a future objective reality, but they must also form an opinion of their own about the expectations of other market participants, and implicit to this there are other higher degrees of expectation that can result. In rational expectation the postulated randomness is assumed to be well behaved, conforming to a normal (Gaussian) distribution, and hence allowing the future to be known with some well-known degree of confidence. Hence, the certainty about a situation is transferred from having full knowing of the nature of a situation to having full knowledge about the bounds of its variations. For Leijonhufvud (2011), rational expectations is a special degenerate case of reflexivity, where the future actually realized is always a random draw from the universally believed and true Gaussian distribution of possible futures. This assumption makes the economy a closed system, where agents are supposed to possess at least probabilistic knowledge of the *objective* reality about which they must learn.

In contrast to rational expectation, one needs to accept that the future cannot be known with certainty, even as a Gaussian probability distribution (Leijonhufvud, 2011). This then implies that the economy must be seen as an open system. Agents in such a system have to *adapt* to events the probability of which they had not estimated correctly, or which may be totally surprising. Once behaviour is seen as resulting from adaptive processes, then the need arises to consider non-linear behaviour that entertains complex system dynamics. Approaches that draw on these ideas may be referred to as post-neoclassical.

An entry point to post-neoclassical modelling comes from *mercantile* agency theory (Spence, 1975) – an information system-based approach that supposes outcome uncertainty, where it is assumed that an agency operates through self-interest and bounded rationality, risk attitudes of the principal and agent, and where agency hierarchies roughly correspond to behaviour-based contracts, while markets correspond to outcome-based contracts. In a conceptual development of this, human activity systems can be modelled mathematically as complex adaptive systems (Prigogine & Stengers, 1984). Computational approaches have developed from this, such as Agent-based computational economics (Spence, 1975; Tesfatsion, 2003, Tesfatsion & Judd, 2006), which operates through computer simulations and decomposes aggregate macroeconomic relationships into microeconomic decisions for predefined individual economic agents. The classes of agent interactions that occur with the market and each other are also specifiable. There is a tendency to ignore agent preferences, and rather to concentrate on outcome strategies. The agent is constituted as an objective computer-based bundle of data and behavioural methods that is intended to represent an entity residing within the world[1]. Such agents may be classed as individuals (like consumers and producers); social groups (like families, firms, communities, and government agencies); institutions (such as markets and regulatory systems); biological entities (like crops, livestock, and forests); and physical entities (such as infrastructure, weather, and geographical regions). They may also be composed of other agents.

Nelson (1982, 2004, 2005) discusses a relatable approach called the evolutionary theory of economic change, which has its roots in biology (Kauffman & Johnson, 1991). Costanza, Wainger, Folke & Miler (1993) note that just as biological systems maintain their information in biological genes so these systems evolve with changes in the genes that define them. Taking this as an analogy to explain evolutionary change in social systems, Costanza, Wainger, Folke & Miler explain that in social systems the genetic structures can be replaced by cultural ones, and economic systems are seen as a subset of cultural systems.

The evolutionary theory of economic change (e.g. Dopfer, 2005) concerns the principles of economic growth in relation to both scientific and social technologies (the latter referring to business practice, organizational forms, and institutions). Consistent with earlier approaches, this also embraces the idea of bounded rationality, but here the actors also have the capability to do something new, to innovate, if they think they see an opportunity, or when what they have been doing becomes clearly inadequate in a changed context. This approach is hence capable of embracing non-equilibrium processes. Unlike neoclassical theory, in evolutionary theory there is no theoretical optimum that acts as a comparative base line, since the possibilities for economic action are perceived to be in flux, and this disallows detailed prediction. Rather, economic performance is seen in terms of the rate and nature of progress, recognizing that it arises through a learning process that belongs to the human activity system that maintains the economic system. This approach to the modelling of economics has frequently drawn on the work of evolutionary game theory (Weibull, 1995; Hofbauer & Sigmund, 2003; Nowak, 2006).

The idea of prediction may be problematic within the context of non-equilibrium systems. In its place, however, one may again refer to *anticipation*.

---

[1] www2.econ.iastate.edu/tesfatsi/ace.htm

Within the context used here this refers to an anticipating system, which Schwarz (2001) takes to mean the systems which (thanks to their structure and organization) have the ability to make predictive models, to influence or to generate the future, and to anticipate the future functioning of real-life systems. We recall that this notion arises with Robert Rosen (1985), who proposes that *anticipatory systems* are those which contain predictive models of themselves and/or of their environments and which allows them to change state at an instant in accord with the model's predictions pertaining to a latter instant, consistent with the notion of adaptation. Such anticipation, Rosen tells us, is typical for 'living systems'. Dubois (2000) developed on Rosen's notion to distinguish between weak anticipation (where the anticipation is based on a model of the system and thus is capable of model-based prediction) and strong anticipation (part of anticipatory systems where the anticipation is self-produced by the system itself and not by a model). Moreover he has shown that any model is implicitly anticipatory. For instance, economic planning is constituted through weak anticipation when it is based on a strategic economic model. In complex situations long-term economic planning and thus long-term deterministic anticipation normally fails. As a result, weak anticipation must be seen as an incremental (step by step) process that is necessarily associated with adaptation. In an adaptive system strong anticipation is both evolutionary and is accompanied by systemic cognitive change. As such, new structures can arise, enabling new forms of behaviour to occur that can relate to changes in the environment. Anticipation is thus a dynamic process in constant renewal.

For Geels (2011), evolutionary economic theory includes the following substantive propositions:

- a focus on populations of agents like firms in industries that compete for scarce resources (money) in market environments, and which exert selection pressure;
- the use of behavioural theory as a tool for providing foundational concepts, alternative to neoclassical theory, on which to build a theory of industry and technological change – here, routines and bounded rational search have limited foresights, and use routines and rules of thumb for decision-making productive knowledge, and unresolved conflict provides an alternative to profit maximization and optimal agency contracts;
- the use of mercantile agency comes from the behavioural theory of the firm, and this has been complemented with the resource-based view of the firm in which capabilities and knowledge also arise;
- competition is technology-based through product and process, and companies can acquire competitive advantage by offering improved products or doing things better, faster, more efficiently, more reliably than others;

- capabilities and knowledge tend to gradually accumulate over time through 'behavioural learning' or 'trial-and-error learning' with search processes providing variations to which markets provide performance feedback.

According to Goldspink & Kay (2004), the capacity for theory to explain the relationship between the constitutive elements of social systems (people) and the emergent phenomena that result from their interaction (i.e. organizations, societies, economies) is limited unless there exists a substantive theory of sociality that is sometimes regularly referred to as the 'micro-to-macro problem'. This idea has been responded to through evolutionary economics and the development of a meso-economic level of analysis. For Dopfer, Foster & Potts (2004), meso-economics is able to embrace microeconomics, and provide a link to macroeconomics. This arises by seeing the knowledge of an agency not as conceptual structures that are able to inform strategic processes (as occurs in learning theory), but rather more reminiscent of Knowledge-Based Computing Systems in which strategic models (that presumably arise from these conceptual structures), are constituted as an information base of rules from which strategic outputs can result given appropriate inputs. A generic rule has a population of actualizations which arise from this base, and which is referred to as a 'meso unit'. Generic rules are carried by agency hosts, and when focussing on a single generic rule for an agency, a 'micro' perspective on the rule in its local environment arises. Here, particular interest tends to lie in the connective structure between:

(1) the carriers of the rule;
(2) the efficiency and efficacy of the rule in relation to particular processes;
(3) with the socio-psychological processes that shape the origination, adoption and adaptation, and retention of a rule in a carrier.

At the meso level, abstracts are generated such that the population of rule actualizations can be observed, where issues of population size and state of development of the meso unit and the composition of the carrier population are of interest.

Geels (2011) has proposed a development of evolutionary economics that is sensitive to:

(a) agency strategy and interpretation;
(b) environment and civil society;
(c) social problems and normative issues.

It does this by coupling in disciplines and fields such as neo-institutional sociology, organization theory, economic sociology, and strategic management, and synthesizes these into a new co-evolutionary theory. Here, actors are perceived as being embedded in external task and institutional environments. In an industry regime the core elements of technology, beliefs, mission, and strategic orientation guide actions towards the external environments. The external environments are linked to core elements and types of action through a number of 'enactment-adaptation cycles': an evolutionary cycle that embraces behavioural learning; a sense-making cycle that embraces cognitive learning; a political cycle; a cultural cycle; and a normative cycle. These cycles are recursive and link external pressures with endogenous strategic responses, allowing for destabilization processes in transitions, industry responses to social problems, and longitudinal industry trajectories.

Taking a different route within complexity, Frieden and Hawkins (2009) have developed a dynamic information theory that is able to model complex adaptive systems using *Extreme Physical Information* (EPI). Here the interaction between information and economic agents in a price discovery process can result in the uncovering of the dynamic laws of an economic system. On its own this is just illustrative of the potential that EPI has of representing the dynamics of economic systems. However, its broader potential to represent a wide variety of situations can be made apparent through its intimate link with Knowledge Cybernetics (Yolles, 2006), which centres on a graphical 'living system' cybernetic theory. Such theory has the capacity to model growth, and hence has an implicit ability to connect with evolutionary economic theory. It also has the capability to anticipate future outcomes. Illustrations of the use of this theory are provided by Yolles, Frieden & Kemp (2008) for the context of cultural dynamics, and by Yolles, Fink & Frieden (2012) in the exploration of behavioural processes for human activity systems. Our interest in this chapter is to return to this general approach in due course.

10.4 Economic Agency

We recall that Costanza, Wainger, Folke & Miler (1993) note that changes in culture have the capacity to change everything else in their social system, and economic systems are seen as a component of cultural systems. So, while Geels (2011) draws on evolutionary economics to embrace a variety of other complementary theoretical streams that embrace complexity, we draw on a cybernetic approach that:

- centres on Schwarz's (1997) 'living system' theory of adaptive organization;
- incorporates Habermas' (1971, 1987) theory of knowledge and communication;
- addresses Bandura's (2006) agency theory of human development;
- incorporates Piaget's (1950) theory of cognitive development;
- delivers a theory of normative personality that within an economic context can be seen as a strategic economic agency, and which has embedded within it strong anticipation (Dubois, 2000) as one of its features;

- adopts as a propositional aspect of its formalization Frieden's (1998) mathematical information theory EPI, itself deriving from Fisher Information theory.

Established as a recursive modelling system, it also has the capacity to introduce disparate modelling features from complementary theoretical streams. This work has its basis in a variety of studies, including Yolles (2006), Yolles, Frieden & Kemp (2008), Yolles & Fink (2009), Yolles (2009a), Yolles (2009b), Yolles, Fink & Dauber (2011) and Yolles, Fink & Frieden (2012).

The theory constitutes a formal psychosocial framework for the 'collective mind' of an agency that is its *normative personality* that formulates in decisions and results in agency behaviour. Within the context of this chapter, behaviour is constituted as the implementation of macroeconomic policy.

We note again that the term normative personality is not new, being usually used within the context of the ambient normative social *influences* that exist during the formation of personalities, and that *mould* them (Mroczek & Little, 2006). Our interest lies in recognizing that the norms in a collective may together coalesce into a unitary cognitive structure such that a collective mind can be inferred, from which an *emergent* normative personality arises. To explain this further, consider that stable collectives develop a common dominant culture within which shared beliefs develop in relation to the capacity of the collective power to produce desired outcomes. Cultural anchors are created that are represented within the paradigm that the agency carries, which enables the development of formal and informal norms for patterns of behaviour, modes of conduct and expression, forms of thought, attitudes, and values that are more or less adhered to by its membership. When the norms refer to formal behaviours, then where the members of the collective contravene them, they are deemed to be engaging in illegitimate behaviour which, if discovered, may result in formal retribution – the severity of which is determined from the collective's ideological and ethical positioning. This develops with the rise of collective cognitive processes that start with information inputs and through decision processes result in orientation to action. It does this with a sense of the collective mind and self. It is a short step to recognize that the collective mind is associated with normative personality. Where a normative personality is deemed to exist, it does not necessarily mean that individual members of the collective will conform to all aspects of the normative processes: they may only do so 'more or less'.

Strong anticipation arises in the normative personality through a set of core traits which function as personality control variables (Van Egeren, 2009), where the values/states that they adopt refer to personality types (Eysenck, 1957), and where the type values of a personality derive from the state of its traits. Thus, the cultural orientation traits discussed by Sorokin can take values of Sensate and Ideation that determine cultural type. However, within the personality, Sensate cultural type is manifested as forms of Individualism, while Ideational cultural type is manifested as forms of Collectivism (Sorokin, 1962). The trait theory that emerges is based on and reflective of emotional-motivational systems that are able to increase adaptation to classes of stimuli associated with positive and negative reinforcement (Depue & Morrone-Strupinsky, 2005: 314, cited in Van Egeren, 2009). For Davis (2000) durable personality traits are usually tightly bound to qualities of emotions, but they may also be defined in terms of preconscious mental dispositions that affect the reflective processes and influence the different categories of cognitive and animated behaviour. They also provide the regulatory patterns that create agency stability. For Fleishman, Constanza & Marshall-Mies (1999) they are also related to performance, and within the context of this chapter we can also refer to economic performance. In corporate theory the traits have generic characteristics that are domain dependent, and may be seen as normative personality variables that regulate the importance attributed to different classes of information. They are indicative of personality styles that arise from a combination of personality *types,* and which suggest a collective agency's expected behavioural orientation in relation to that class of information. The types have a special role in personality theory. They are deemed to be responsible for the patterns of behaviour that a personality generates. Patterns of behaviour are generically defined as an abstraction from a concrete form that keeps recurring in specific, non-arbitrary contexts. It is this very nature that enables an agency's behaviour to be strongly anticipated, even when it comes to their interaction with personal and situational variables. Where it is possible to associate personalities with stable type preferences, a consistent connection to behaviour can be discerned (de Oliveira, 2008; Hyldegård, 2009), and this includes the likelihood of determining economic behaviour, even under conditions of uncertainty.

In Figure 6.7 (see Chapter 6 on agency consciousness) we show a generic model representing a durable collective agency that has a culture, a normative personality, an operative capacity, operates intelligently, can adapt to changing situations, creates and implements policy, and hence becomes responsible for macro-economic processes. It enables specific relationships to be introduced within and across domains, as necessary and according to the logical processes that may be proposed within a socio-political situation. This economic 'living system' is designed to satisfy the context of economic performance, which following the *Lucas Critique* is sensitive to political regime and particular policy orientations.

Figure 6.7 is also a result of thematic combinatorial conceptualizations from which the collective agency maintains its normative personality (Yolles, 2006;

Yolles, Fink & Dauber, 2011b) and which is fundamentally relational, allowing for the modelling of more or less complexity. It does this through what some refer to as a *systemic hierarchy*: where systems are structured as a hierarchically nested set of recursively embedded systems, one within another creating more complexity in the modelling process (Williams and Imam, 2006). Thus, complex 'bottom-up' interpersonal interrelationships can be modelled that 'cause' (through a complex multiplicity of reasons that often are taken as a principle of *emergence*) higher order systemic forms in which complexity becomes reduced to an invisible horizon of meanings. At the same time, top-down influences can be made to constrain, under normal (as opposed to post-normal uncertain and perhaps chaotic) circumstances, the nature of the interactions that are legitimized at the bottom level. Thus, the modelling approach can represent networks of processes at the individual and small group level, as well as their impact on the higher level social influence networks of processes and vice versa (Yolles, 2006).

An agency is not isolated, but interacts with an environment, or with other agencies in an environment, as illustrated in Figure 6.7. Here, the agency is shown to have behavioural intelligence, as represented through its *overt actions* (Ang, Van Dyne, Koh, Ng, Templer, Tay & Chandrasekar, 2007: 6). This is constituted as a structural coupling (Maturana and Varela, 1987) that is responsible for past, present, and future interactive history.

The agency also has internal intelligences, also indicated in Figure 6.7, which are constituted as forms of autogenesis and autopoiesis (Schwarz, 1997). These internal intelligences include a form of cultural intelligence (Yolles et al., 2011), and personality intelligences – concepts originally drawn from Piaget (1950). The autogenetic function operates as figurative intelligence, enabling it to *self-create* its collective cognition, and the autopoietic function operates as an operative intelligence that enables it to operatively *self-produce* its collective cognition. In cybernetic terms, intelligence may thus be seen as a network of relational processes of transformation of a definable set of components of a given domain of the living system: (i) through their interactions and transformations continuously regenerate, realize, and adapt the relations that produce them; and (ii) constitute its socio-cognitive nature as a concrete unity.

Such a concrete unity represents an open socially viable economic system, because: (a) the development path of the system is open in the sense that it maintains permanent system dynamics driven by the internal *autopoietic* (or self-producing) and *autogenetic* (or self-creating) processes and the sub-units within the system; and (b) it is open in the sense that the system by itself is to be seen as a sub-system of a larger system.

Figure 6.7 embraces the idea that a concrete 'living' economic system is embedded into a cultural environment and interacts with a social environment, a notion extended by reflecting on the recognition that there are consequential influences and interactions with these environments. Central to the understanding of the model in Figure 6.7 are two principal features: (1) the living system can be seen as an agency equipped with a necessary and sufficient set of intelligences that has the capacity to create and pursue the system's own goals, and (2) it may self-organize and respond to a changing environment through adaptation (Bandura, 2006). Under complexity, the dynamics of change for this living system are generically well defined (Yolles, Fink, Iles & Sawagvudcharee, 2013).

The intelligences may be seen as the driver for and the constraints of the achievements that a 'living' economic system may be able to materialize: without intelligences there are no achievements; with low levels of intelligence poor results develop; and with high levels of intelligence good results can be achieved. Several forms of intelligence are widely referred to in the literature, including: intelligence at large (general intelligence), cultural, social, and emotional intelligence. In the context of strategic thinking and operational activity, we further distinguish between figurative (self-creational) and operative (self-producing) intelligence. Bandura's (2006) notion of efficacy is also useful, and can be differentiated as desired and actual efficacy as it relates to performance, the efficacy gap impacting on work satisfaction and emotions.

The figurative system in Figure 6.7 operates as a Strategic Economic Agency. As such it also has 'strategic' figurative and operative intelligences represented by $I_{2,1}$ and $I_{2,2}$, and $I_{3,1}$ and $I_{3,2}$. The nature of these intelligences is due to their sensitivity to contexts that arise from the meanings of the systemic domains, and since different components of the model have different meanings, so they are distinct from other figurative and operative intelligences in other parts of the model.

This allows us to consider intelligence as a systemic function. Such a notion has been identified by Hämäläinen & Saarinen (2007) as intelligent action in real time and within complex, interconnected, and changing structures, in contexts and environments, where human agents tune to, react to, and influence one another in those subtle and sometimes-not-so-subtle ways that are unique to us as human beings. We may develop on this by proposing an enhanced definition for intelligence within the context of an economic system as: the general ability of an agency (a living economic system) to appreciate and harness its own knowledge as information about its environment (feedback processes), to construct new knowledge and to generate new or better capabilities through the *manifestation* (resulting in forms of internalization) of information about its experiences (feedback from the external environment – counterparts in the task environment, feedback from agents within the society/economy – stakeholders, institutions – and overall evaluation) into other parts of the system, and from that manifested information, to pursue its goals effectively and efficiently.

Into this definition, we can integrate all extensions and differentiations of intelligences, as far as cultural intelligence, socio-economic (behavioural) intelligence and agency operative intelligence are concerned, and as long as a) there is an action or application oriented network of processes (feed-forward process) and a corresponding feedback network of processes, and b) each type of intelligence weights the relevance, importance, efficiency, and effectiveness of these processes and can attach different importance to forward linkages and feedback linkages in the processes of self-reproduction and self-organization.

While agency operative intelligence is constituted as a network of self-producing processes that occur between the normative personality of the agency and its operative system (through its bureaucracy – this being responsible for the implementation of policy that arises from the normative personality), behavioural intelligence then maps this implementation into the social environment. Economic intelligence may be operative in that it is autopoietic – as part of the agency that is responsible for economic policy and determining the principles that are to be pursued. In contrast, behavioural economic intelligence is connected with how this policy is applied, and it is constituted as a structural coupling that maintains a past and future relationship between the agency operative system and its social environment.

Figure 6.7 also indicates that there are five traits in any agency that we regard as *formative*, one of which defines its cultural orientation, three of which define its normative personality (the cognitive, figurative, operative orientations), and the last of which defines its social orientation.

As indicated by Yolles et al. (2011) and Fink et al. (2012), in the context of organizational culture research, these are bi-polar value dimensions which typify an agency and establish strong anticipation. Within the context of a national economy, this agency is therefore able to make use of the concept of bi-polar traits, and indicate preferences in the respective domains for the forward linkages (i.e. action-oriented processes) or feedback linkages (i.e. information collection, adaptation, and learning processes). As a result, understanding the five type values that an agency has adopted can enable strong anticipation to be manifested, thereby creating macro-economic expectations. While these five traits are representative of the agency as a whole, particular aspects can be examined individually. The recursive nature of the modelling process that delivers Figure 6.7 enables a drilling down to permit a more detailed examination of microscopic socio-economic phenomena, to which macroeconomic policy should be responsive. Sensitivity to more microeconomic features can be lost with pathologies (indicated by the bars of $I_{i,j}$, where $i=1,4$ and $j=1,2$) that arise in the agency system. These pathologies inhibit the normal functioning of the intelligences, and degrade the performance capability of an agency.

10.5   Traits, Policy, and Macroeconomics

The capacity to anticipate variations of economic policy created by a governing body is driven by the ability to evaluate the stable type values that emerge for each of the five traits of the personality. Each system of the agency needs to be carefully assessed, likely enantiomers identified, and an evaluation made of the relationships between the traits that occurs. There is also a relationship between that governing body and civil society as a force for adjustment, and external stakeholders who are constituted as voters. Consistent with Geels formulation, agents have not only an internal environment composed of their culture, personality, and operative system, but they are also interactive with external task environments, and the agency is sensitive to all of its strategic attributes. However, unlike Geels' theory, the external environments are not necessarily restricted to types of action through 'enactment-adaptation cycles' that may be susceptible to pathologies that are able to interrupt the cycles or inefficacies that may ameliorate them. Behavioural learning is fundamental to the nature of agency through its cybernetic processes, and cognitive learning and adaptation as part of personality development are also core to the conceptualization. Other forms of cycle may develop, but what is central is that all agency processes are tied in some way to cultural and personality dynamics.

Now we have modelled how values, defined in terms of bi-polar traits, guide and legitimate policies. Policies at large and economic policies have the same roots within a society, are driven by internal interest groups, and are subject to cultural influences. To understand the interplay between the forces it is of importance to refer to the mutual auxiliary function of the alternative poles of the bipolar traits. This was identified by Jung in the 1930s within the development of his theory of Psychological types (though not as part of trait theory), was strongly re-emphasized by Blutner & Hochnadel (2010), and at family level was empirically identified by Tamis-Le Monda et al. (2007).

With emphasis on the auxiliary function of the bi-polar traits we can define process intelligence as the ability of an agent to appreciate and harness its own knowledge as information about its environment, to construct new knowledge converted from information about its experiences, and based on the information to pursue its goals effectively and efficiently, these terms subsumed within the concept of efficacy.

Such intelligences enable the consideration of the interests and influences of the external environment (stakeholders, institutions, counterparts in the task environment), an agency's own goals, and the goals of others, and facilitation of the development of ideas about the possible reactions of others in relation to the action taken by the agency. In an economic policy context intelligences become manifest in the behaviours and actions of politicians, civil servants, and other economic agents and in the outcomes of these behaviours. These intelligences are facilitated through degrees of efficacy or inefficacy, determinants for the manifestation of information between the distinct systems of an agency. Adapting the notion of efficacy from Bandura (2006), it relates to the soundness of an agency's collective cognitive processes (e.g. as discussed by Heylighen, Heath & Van Overwalle, 2012) and actions, the meaning of its pursuits, and its ability to take corrective adjustments where necessary. Efficacy is conditioned by emotive imperatives that derive from emotions and feelings (Adeyemo, 2007) that can be controlled by emotional intelligence (Salovey & Mayer, 1990). Efficacy therefore influences an agency's *capabilities* to produce designated levels of performance that exercise influence over events that affect economic life. By assigning such capability to the intelligences, inefficacy can be taken as the performance capability of the intelligences to connect the ontologically distinct systems of the agency in a coherent way. While efficacy is the performance capability of the intelligences to connect the ontologically distinct systems of the agency in a coherent way, inefficacy limits that performance capability.

For illustration of our thoughts on economic intelligence and efficacy we drafted a stylized table of national accounts. With these illustrations we also deliver some insights for the empirical remark of Siegel et al. (2012: 24) why '...FDI tends to flow to countries higher on cultural harmony'. This is shown in Table 10.1, where all data are expressed in unspecified currency units. One currency unit corresponds to a claim on one product unit. In the baseline 'balanced scenario', the basic assumptions are that functional distribution of income between labour and capital is 70:30 per cent, assuming that this corresponds to marginal and average labour and capital productivity, and that this distribution of income corresponds to the levels of consumption and investment. Workers pay 50 per cent of their income for taxes and social insurance to the government. Capital owners pay 20 per cent tax on incomes, and spend 24 units for investment to maintain production of 100 units. Governments invest 25 per cent of private investment into infrastructure, maintenance investment, etc. Government receipts of taxes and social insurance contributions from wages are necessary to maintain adequate education, health care, safety, public security, etc., and ascertain political and social coherence.

Next, in the second part of Table 10.1, for the 'Mastery case' we assume that due to organizational and technological progress, labour and capital productivity increased by 10 per cent. However, trade unions are weak and capital owners can take it all. The mastery guided case illustrates generation of capital surplus through wage 'discipline', increasing relative poverty. After productivity increase, capital owners can invest the same amount as before (24) to maintain the higher output level of 110 units. Since they pay

Table 10.1 *Illustration of economic intelligence to figurative trait value options*[2]

Figurative Trait "Balanced" case of "Harmony" and "Mastery":
[all data in unspecified currency units, one currency unit corresponds to a claim on one product unit]

	Workers	Capital Owners	Government	Total of Rows	Available Goods
Income from goods production	70	30		100	100
Taxes and social insurance	−35	−6	41	0	
Expenditure for consumption	−35	0	−35	−70	Total Demand
Investment	0	−24	−6	−30	−100
Balances [external balance]	0	0	0	[0]	[0]

Figurative Trait "Mastery"' case after 10 units labour productivity and production increase, but stagnant wages:
[all data in unspecified currency units, one currency unit corresponds to a claim on one product unit]

	Workers	Capital Owners	Government	Total of Rows	Available Goods	Excess Supply
Income from goods production	70	40		110	110	
Taxes and social insurance	−35	−8	43	0		
Expenditure for consumption	−35	0	−37	−72	Total Demand	
Investment	0	−24	−6	−30	−102	[+8]
Balances	0	8	0	8	[+8]	
[external surplus = excess capital gains = capital export]						

more taxes (8 units), a capital surplus of 8 units remains, which cannot be reasonably invested into the domestic economy, because demand for consumer goods increases less than output. Demand for consumer goods increases only by 2 units, because the government spends the increase of

---

[2] General Assumptions: Workers pay 50 per cent of their income for taxes and social insurance to the government. Capital owners pay 20 per cent tax on incomes, and spend 24 units for investment to maintain production of 100 units. After productivity increase capital owners can invest the same amount as before and maintain higher output level. Governments invest 25 per cent of private investment, e.g. infrastructure maintenance investments.

Table 10.1 (cont.)

Figurative Trait "Harmony" case after 10 units wage increase, but stagnant production:
[all data in unspecified currency units, one currency unit corresponds to a claim on one product unit]

	Workers	Capital Owners	Government	Total of Rows	Available Goods	Excess Demand
Income from goods production	80	30		110	100	
Taxes and social insurance	−40	−6	46	0		
Expenditure for consumption	−40	0	−40	−80	Total Demand	
Investment	0	−24	−6	−30	−110	[−10]
Balances [external deficit]	0	0	0	0	[−10]	

[external deficit = capital import]

A "Harmony" case after 8 units wage increase (after tax) through budget deficit, but stagnant production:
[all data in unspecified currency units, one currency unit corresponds to a claim on one product unit]

	Workers	Capital Owners	Government	Total of Rows	Available Goods	Excess Demand
Income from goods production	70	30		100	100	
Taxes and social insurance	−35	−6	41	0		
Expenditure for Consumption	−35	0	−43	−78	Total Demand	
Investment	0	−24	−6	−30	−108	[−8]
Balances [external deficit]	0	0	−8	−8	[−8]	

[external deficit = capital import]

tax income from capital owners for consumptive purposes. Thus, excess capital of 8 units can be used to provide export credits or to be invested abroad, which is needed, because excess output of 8 units must be exported.

In the third part of Table 10.1, we illustrate a specific form of a harmony (and more egalitarian) case. Trade unions are very strong and 'welfare' increase of the masses of population takes place through wage and employment increase (wage indiscipline), which are not supported by productivity increase. Production stagnates at the previous level of 100 units. Excess demand of 10 units can be met only through imports. What will be feasible if in another country the 'mastery case' prevails? In the 'mastery' country capital owners are looking for export opportunities, which they can finance through excess capital gained through wage discipline in their home country. In the 'harmony' country they cannot afford imports, but they need imports to balance supply and demand, so they take the offered export finance opportunity and incur foreign debts.

In the fourth part of Table 10.1, the second harmony case is constructed to show how the twin deficit emerges. From wages paid by government 50 per cent directly flow back to the government through taxes and social insurance payments. Thus, only after tax wage payments increase the state budget deficit. In this case, we assume that government increases employment by 16. It suffers only from an 8 unit deficit. Consumption increases by 8 units through increase in net wages.

Of course, one also could construct many variants and also a merger of the two harmony cases: employment increase through budget deficit and wage increases beyond productivity gains.

Considering the 'mastery case' and the two 'harmony cases' it seems to be clear that neither unconditional mastery strategies nor any of the stylized harmony cases would be feasible for a longer period. Both strategies imply that other societies pursue the alternative pole strategy. Without deficit countries, capital surplus countries would not know where to export their capital surplus – and vice versa. But, one day capital owners of mastery countries may want their money back, and, even in mastery countries poverty cannot be increased endlessly. Inevitably there will come the riot point (cf. Roe and Siegel, 2011).

Thus, economic (process) intelligence is a function of long-term efficacy of economic policy action. Intelligence weighs possible direct outcomes of behaviours induced by both types of 'single pole' policies and also the negative side-effects. Consequently, it mostly will aim at a more balanced approach, since single pole driven behaviour may not be sustainable in the long run. Here, in a 'mastery' driven society, concerns about emerging poverty and social coherence put constraints on mastery driven behaviours of profit and income maximization of a small group of extremely rich individuals. In a 'harmony' driven society concerns about lack of achievements (e.g. lack of productivity gains and innovation) constrain 'harmony' driven behaviour towards more equal distribution of income, which may be pursued irrespective of different contributions of different classes of individuals to goods and services production and to future productivity gains.

Beyond intelligence, we can see the agency orientation globally represented through its personality mindscapes (discussed earlier in this book), and to see its use we offer an illustrative narrative about decision-making behaviour in respect of economic policy. This narrative needs to link combinations of enantiomers across traits, but how this can be done has not been fully

10.6 Case Situation: The 2007/2008 European Recession and Mindscapes

Interest here now rests in offering an illustration of how mindscapes can be used within a social psychological context. To do this we will create a short political-economic story, that is, *'The Situation'* that can be explored in a way that indicates how a mindscape macro analysis might develop.

First we describe *'The Situation'*: Let us consider the following story as an illustration of how mindscape theory can be used. In exploring this story, it will not be important whether we adopt Maruyama Mindsets or Sagiv-Schwartz mindsets, since they are epistemologically equivalent. However, for clarity we shall adopt the Sagiv-Schwartz symbolism.

Financial deregulation allowed financial institutions to make investments without responsibility, and in due course this led to a sub-prime meltdown (Ferguson, 2010) and the 2008 global economic crisis. The banks were found to be under-funded, and so were bailed out by their host nations, thus creating a mountain of debt that has been responsible for an economic disaster in Europe and the United States, and has destabilized the Euro. This debt crisis arose because of the way in which the banks had conducted (or misconducted) their business.

The approach to the resolution of the economic crisis that the EU intended to adopt in 2009 is clearly defined in a report published in 2009 by the European Union (EU, 2009):

The European economy is in the midst of the deepest recession since the 1930s, with real GDP projected to shrink by some 4% in 2009, the sharpest contraction in the history of the European Union. Although signs of improvement have appeared recently, recovery remains uncertain and fragile. The EU's response to the downturn has been swift and decisive. Aside from intervention to stabilise, restore and reform the banking sector, the European Economic Recovery Plan (EERP) was launched in December 2008. The objective of the EERP is to restore confidence and bolster demand through a coordinated injection of purchasing power into the economy complemented by strategic investments and measures to shore up business and labour markets. The overall fiscal stimulus, including the effects of automatic stabilisers, amounts to 5% of GDP in the EU.

So the perceived need was to restore confidence. At this stage there was no question as to whether there might be a need to change the very nature of the banking system. If the strategy taken was found not to work, or if the banks were found to be sociopathic or corrupt (Yolles, 2009), then perhaps an alternative strategy might have been sought.

Interestingly, there has been some indication that the banks might be analytically (as opposed to clinically) sociopathic (Yolles, 2009a) – where pathologies develop that result in organizational dysfunctions that create antisocial outcomes such as consistent acts of pollution and amoral behaviour that verges on, or is a central part of, corrupt practices. This may be illustrated through the realization that they have maintained amoral high executive pay-outs (Finance and Investment, 2012) in the face of vast public pay-outs to support them, and there is evidence that they may also be corrupt. This is seen by Barclays bank being fined £290m in June 2012 by the Financial Services Authority in the UK, and the Commodity Futures Trading Commission and Department of Justice in the United States. For four years between 2005 and 2009 Barclays had lied about the interest rate it had to pay to borrow, to make the bank look more secure during the financial crisis and, sometimes – working with traders at other banks – to make a profit[3]. This was one of the pegs that encouraged the UK Member of Parliament Steve Collins[4] to say that banking is 'a sewer of dishonesty'. As a consequence, Barclays Bank lost its Chairman, CEO, and COO, forced out of office for corrupt practice in relation to Libor[5]. Investigations into various other possible bank frauds of this type have also been undertaken across the world (Vaughan & Finch, 2012). At the same time, JPMorgan Chase, the largest US bank, is being investigated for energy-market manipulation (Klimasinska & Kopecki, 2012), while the US-based HSBC bank is being accused of drug money laundering[6].

This leads to a new question. Is the policy of austerity the correct course of action (Roe, 2012), or are there alternatives? According to Joseph Stiglitz (2012), the Nobel Prize winner for economics, the German diagnostic pre-occupation with a policy of austerity to overcome the crisis has been wrong. He notes that Spain and Ireland had a surplus before the crisis, and it was the crisis that caused the deficit, not vice versa. An incorrect diagnosis leads to an incorrect prescription which will not redirect the economic misfortune creatively. Europe, he says, rather requires a comprehensive set of reforms for growth, which would necessitate more spending, a European-wide banking system and euro bonds. The notion of more spending is, of course, an alternative to austerity to maintain the status quo, in which the government spends money in order to stimulate growth. So, we have two opposing positions: austerity and stimulation. There is, of course, a clear alternative as practised currently by the US government: a combined policy of stimulation and

---

[3] www.bbc.co.uk/news/business-18622264
[4] twitter.com/TradeDesk_Steve/statuses/218311507447001088
[5] Libor is the London Interbank Offered Rate, the average interest rate estimated by leading banks in London that they would be charged if borrowing from other banks. It is determined by a daily poll carried out on behalf of the British Bankers' Association asking banks to estimate how much it would cost to borrow from each other for different periods and in different currencies.
[6] www.aljazeera.com/news/americas/2012/07/2012716213139157207.html

austerity (Orszag, 2012). Which of these positions might be the way to move forward then, if any?

The '*Situation*' requires '*An Analysis*': The European Community (EU) established its European Project in the 1950s, and while it is composed of diverse nations each of which send political representatives, it still maintains political cohesion (Yolles, 2009a) that stems from its dichotomous Individualist-Collectivist political culture. This is consistent with a mindscape examination where the EU leaders are representing the European Economic Community through its agency. Recall from chapter 5 that Maruyama identified four Mindsets: *H* (hierarchical bureaucracy), *I* (independent prince), *S* (social revolutionary), and *G* (generative reformer). Now both the *I* and *H* mindscapes are representative of the agency as a whole. It is currently a sensate organization and since 'like begets like' its leadership is constituted by leaders who must necessarily have mindscapes that are cognitively similar. In sensate organizations senior/leadership *I* (related to Individualist) roles succeed in the EU political administration, seen to be similar to Individualism and obverse to the *H* mode (and Collectivism). Now, in a political context it is relatively easy to see mode *I* and *H* mindscapes in terms of Individualism and Collectivism, especially where, as Bandura (2005, 2006, 2007), recognizes, there are *parochial interests* because politicians wish to ensure their political survival. So then how do parochial interests develop in an agency? They arise within the personality's operative system, when they impact on the agency's operative intelligence. When we refer to mode *I* and *H* mindscapes from here on, we shall take them to be represented respectively by Individualism and Collectivism, recognizing that they are prone to *parochial interests*.

While the EU may be a stable collective that began with the will to political stability, even though it is composed of diverse cultures, the bi-polar nature of its politics is stable (Yolles, 2009a). This does not mean that its culture is necessarily Sensate or Ideational, since during a period of post-sensate period and cultural decline, its mindscape orientation will likely oscillate, leading to the ascendency of either a mode *I* or *H* mindscape depending on circumstances, or a trait balance that applies to *I* and *H* mindscapes making them equivalent to Collective Individualism (Limerick & Cunnington, 1993; Viskovatoff, 1999).

The debt crisis is perceived differently by *I* and *H* mode mind-sets. In a Sensate culture and in particular in countries where the rule of law has value and is not a political football, the mode *I* mind-sets has a transactional *dramatist* nature that adopts a rule-based control approach intended to resolve the crisis through a policy of social austerity. In the current debt crisis, society is seen as an object of attention, and as such is simply regarded as a financial source that needs to be drained in order to balance debt. As we have seen within the Greek saga (Humphries, 2012), this can result in severe individual hardship and the endangerment of economic sustainability to a level of dignity in a large proportion of the economically disadvantaged society. Under the same conditions of rule of law, the mode H mind-set alternative is relational *patterning*, operating through a policy of relational growth stimulation, where the state facilitates the encouragement of enterprise, ignoring the indebtedness, and assuming that the economic system will self-adjust. The balance point between Individualism and Collectivism is Collective Individualism, a midway compromise in which austerity and stimulation are parallel policy options. However, neither of these policy options responds to the concerns of such a 'proper' analysis seems at present unavailable. Noting the apparently corrupt nature of Western banks referred to earlier, such an analysis and diagnosis might lead in an unexpected direction, for instance by redefining of the social nature and role of banks. It is likely such a development is consistent with the need for an economic paradigm shift, as described by Dolphin & Nash (2011).

Mode I and H mindscapes are quite distinct in the way in which policy provisions are designed and implemented. The reason lies in the S^e and I^d enantiomer distinctions between them. S^e agencies like to maintain clear control since they like to see results appearing, and this is why in a financial crisis such as the current one they tend to favour measures of austerity to alleviate debt that impose strict controls on a mass 'controllable' portion of the population, rather than the stimulation of growth, which rather constitutes relational and uncertain processes. This drives us to look more critically at these two cognitive positions. For some economic policy is identified with individualism, a theme that Davis, Marciano & Runde (2004: 21) have interest in when they note that 'close examination of the underlying claims [of I mindscapes] making such explanations raise a number of difficult philosophical issues. One of the most challenging concerns the requirements for reducing statements about social phenomena to statements about individuals...Another fundamental issue involves what constitutes the "best" explanation in science or in economics. These more philosophical questions return us to economic methodology's epistemological concerns, but no less important are the ontological ones the topic of individualism raises. When we privilege individualist explanations in economics, do we believe that only individuals exist? That society itself does not exist?' Nozick (1977: 359; cited in Davis, Marciano & Runde, 2004: 121) notes critically that methodological individualism (or the driving of I mindscape economic policy) is quite distinct from the more Collectivistic methodological institutionalism (that drives policies that come from the H mindscape), so why are economists not equally methodological institutionalists? Neither individual nor institutional factors have legitimate explanatory primacy, and the idea that all explanations have ultimately to be in terms of individuals (or institutions) is thus unfounded. This leads us to consider the nature of Individualism and Collectivism, and the consequential political and hence policy dynamics that result.

The policy highlighted by the EU (2009) report was promoted by a mode H mindscape since it embraced the stimulation of growth. However, the post-2009 policy that emerged, and which was driven by the German Chancellor Angela Merkel, was quite alternative to this, leading to cries that austerity measures cannot work (Arestis & Pelagidis, 2010). According to Arbabzadeh (2012), Germany's relative financial and economic power and its creditor position is allowing it to drive EU policies. This leads to a validation of Bandura's view of parochialism, as explained by Pastor (2012). He argues that in the making of economic policy, 'confidence' has more political power than actual epistemological wisdom, so that the post-crisis economic recovery is being driven by a narrative crafted through the power of parochial economic interests.

The resolution to the debt crisis was still not in sight (Arbabzadeh, 2012; Schmidt, 2011). It is unlikely to be solved by an I mode mindscape, through commitment to policies of austerity (Arestis & Pelagidis, 2010). However, there are also problems with the H mindscape to resolve the current crisis. Following Dockens[7], the H mode cannot deal with the diversity and change that is demanded by complex information-driven societies. A prediction by Dockens is that changing demography, social networks, and climates will combine to produce a twenty-first century that precludes the survival of H mode thinking. Even the fantastic ability of the H mode mindscape to rationalize defeat as victory has its limits. It is therefore also unlikely that a trait balance in the mindscape will succeed by drawing on both stimulation and austerity in succession, as has been attempted by the US President Obama. Dockens' prediction of the failure of the H mindscape would appear to point significantly to the resurgence of a Sensate culture in this period of cultural oscillation. Much later, however, we shall see the ascendency of a stable form of Ideational culture, when the H and perhaps G mode mindscape will dominate.

Returning to the current situation, while a G mode mindscape could resolve the issues through processes of transformation and emergence, the likelihood of such a mindscape being harnessed in this way to resolve the crisis is unlikely, unless as Dolphin & Nash (2011) imply, the crisis continues to a point where the validity of the dominant economic paradigm is destroyed. However, if the onset of a collapse like that of the Soviet Union is not on the cards, resolution may occur as the EU is forced to take advice from external consultants or involve the civil society. If it does occur, however, we may well see a sudden and unexpected shift into Ideationalism that might materialize over the next few generations.

---

[7] William Dockens III personal communication in relation to this case study during August 2012.

10.7 Observations

The economic crisis of 2007/8 has provoked impetus to examine the capability of economic theory in creating useful predication and its connection with political and cultural processes, and the control connections that occur between them in the formulation and deployment of macro-economic policy. In so doing it has shown that current approaches are left wanting. For instance, while there has been a tendency for economic theory to embrace paradigms that encompass complexity, there are still problems in their ability to represent a reality that is constituted by human activity systems from which culture and mindscapes determine macroeconomic policy. Further, while some approaches are interested in connecting economics with policy making and politics, no other approaches additionally connect with culture. Some argument has been made that it has arisen because of a shift from Collectivist to Individualist strategic policy. However, supposing the role of Individualism/ Collectivism in any social dynamic does appear to be a questionable proposition.

The chapter has embraced agency theory to build a meta-model that can assist in obtaining an improved understanding of the complexities of cultural socio-economic systems. It adopts a trait-based agency approach in which the agency has a normative personality within which its socio-political orientations arise, enabling the anticipation of classes of decision-making behaviour and hence economic policy, even under crisis. It is through the trait nature of the agency that a set of scenarios can be postulated for possible futures in complex situations. For this to work, however, there is a need to appreciate the meaning and function of trait orientations. In a simple illustration of the way in which trait orientations work, we offered a small case that explores the financial condition of different orientations.

The theory for the meta-model has developed through a cybernetic 'living system' approach that allows us to examine different aspects of an agency. It is designed to represent collectives which have an observable (through their manifestations) culture and normative personality from which in principle one is able to anticipate patterns of behaviour, and illustrates the intimate connection between culture and the economic policy processes that, following the Lucas Critique, should be seen as a significant influence on economic processes.

The model has then been coupled with Maruyama's mindscape theory, and we have developed an alternative to this which we have referred to as Sagiv-Schwartz mindscapes theory since it derives from their extensive empirical research. The mindscape modes should be seen as emerging from the interactive nature of the five traits that construct the agency. There are at least four mindscape modes, and two of them, I and H, are relatable to Individualism and Collectivism. However, if we accept that Individualism and Collectivism are just two modes of mindscape theory, then this sets the scene for a broader view about likely anticipation of macroeconomic policy than has been so far apparent.

Taking a cultural view, the West is currently experiencing post-Sensate instability, resulting in an interactive conflict between Sensate and Ideational orientations, either of which is able to achieve short-lived ascendency that does little to add to social coherence. However, within this there is still a dominating orientation towards hierarchy. Dominant orientations can be examined in terms of mindscapes allowing us to explore context sensitive patterns of behaviour. To illustrate this, we have provided a very sketchy approach in telling the story of the European debt crisis through mindscape modes applied to a leadership role, showing how an analysis can create broad explanations. The next step would be to undertake a deep analysis that would move beyond a cursory examination, and seek remedies; however, this would need to be left to a future study.

As a final comment, this chapter results in an emergent argument that has three strands. The first strand is the argument that the recession is due to fundamental change in policy. This comes about because even though there is so much research that tries to tease out how Individualism and Collectivism contribute to socio-cultural dynamics, there is no research outcome that is able to do this. Rather, the research points to dramatic shifts in policy orientations that occur where societies and organizations have not developed norms that constrain their greedy and egocentric behaviour. The second strand argues that current macroeconomic modelling is not up to the task of anticipating economic processes. Perhaps the most promising has been in evolutionary economics, but one of the few pieces of work that suggested the oncoming 2007/8 recession has been Perez's historical work, and this has only been generally indicative, being unable to identify the policy specifics that might be expected from a macroeconomic theory. The chapter has further argued that a good macroeconomic theory should include culture as an element, and a meta-model has been proposed to satisfy this need. The third strand argues that the strategic orientations of Individualism and Collectivism, while potentially important, are only two options of a broader base of mindscape modes that can arise under different socio-cultural and trait conditions. Any preoccupation with these two strategic orientations alone will necessarily lead researchers further into an analytical *cul de sac*, especially where such analysis is solely empirical. It also suggests that researchers should rather consider culturally derived mind sets (like mindscape theory) to identify strategic and operative issues that drive macroeconomic processes.

11 The Financial Agency, Society and Corruption

11.1 Introduction

This chapter is reflective of the financial agency, including the banking and shadow banking industry that have been so important for China's socio-economic revolution. The country has moved from being a state-owned to a private enterprise market economy, and as a result a growing class of entrepreneurs that has made China a global hi-tech manufacturing leader. During this process it has experienced social instability, this resulting in 'financial and banking crises, corruption, massive unemployment, a rising crime rate, uncontrolled urbanization and overpopulation' (Lewis & Litai, 2003: 927). Of these attributes, corruption has a major impact on socio-economic environments. Beyond the discussion of the financial environment then, this chapter will also consider corruption and its social consequences.

So to begin, let us consider the context for examining the financial system. In the introduction to this book we discussed the Western economic crisis as it emanated from a banking system with issues. It is fitting, therefore, that for the close of this book, we return to this topic. Here, however, we shall examine the Chinese situation, exploring the possibility of a Chinese crisis emanating similarly from a banking system with issues. Recognizing (after Robert Lucas Jr. Nobel prize winner for economics in 1995) that studies on economics also require studies on politics since the two are so interlinked, it is appropriate to begin with a political perspective on China. However, the economy is also supported by a financial system which is dominated by banking processes, and this therefore plays an even more significant role. To understand the economy, one must therefore also understand the financial system. This includes financial institutions like banks, financial markets, and clearing and settlement systems, and it is through the financial system that most commercial activity occurs. In this chapter our interest lies in banking. Banks contribute to the financial system through an intended role that allows them to work conjointly with others to promote and maintain safe and efficient financial operations through financial market infrastructures, as well as to provide a variety of other services to different elements of financially concerned society.

The remarkable success in China's economic reforms has not been paralleled by political reforms, at least as far as democratic representation is concerned. This may perhaps have no consequences on the continued economic development of China, all things being equal, but were it faced with unexpectedly hard times, perhaps occurring with a severe recession like that of the West in 2007/8 and a population demanding new and immediate resolution, there may be a perceived need for wholesale reversal of the reforms. Montinola, Qian & Weingast (1996) argue that even though there has been no development towards democratic processes, other factors play well for it. China is a nation that operates through political decentralization, having enhanced the powers of local government. At the same time it has altered central-local government relations in several critical ways that are difficult, though not impossible, to reverse. Another significant change has occurred in the ideology that underpins its reforms, with a move away from the dogmatic Marxism-Leninism to a more pragmatic, market-oriented approach that is embraces neoliberal principles, with its attendant socio-economic issues related to bounded wealth distribution (Harvey, 2005; Kumar, 2008). As a result, a new political federalism has arisen which offers political protection for China's reforms, and this includes placing limits on central government. In today's China there is a division of authority between the central and local governments. Local governments have primary control over all economic matters that are legitimately connected with their jurisdictions, and this has been set up in such a way as to make such self-determination politically durable. Montinola et al. (1996) refer to this form of political governance as market-preserving federalism, which forms what they also refer to as a Chinese 'common market'. There are five principles to this:

> P1: China has a hierarchy of governments with a delineated scope of authority. This leads to subnational autonomy for each political unit within its own sphere of authority.
> P2: Subnational governments have primary authority over the economy within their jurisdictions.
> P3: Central government has the authority to police the common market and to make sure that there is mobility for goods and factors across sub-government jurisdictions.
> P4: There is revenue sharing among governments, but it is limited, and borrowing by governments is constrained so that all governments should face hard budget constraints.
> P5: The allocation of authority and responsibility has an institutionalized durability that disallows it to be changed by the central government either unilaterally or under pressure from subnational governments.

Montinola et al. note that P1–P5 constitute an ideal institutional arrangement for market-preserving federalism, designed to limit the degree to which a political system can encroach on markets. They also note that other federalisms do not have such a market-preserving structure. They cite, for instance, Argentina, Brazil, and India as not having conditions P2 and P5, implying that political discretion and authority are not distributed – a requirement for market-preserving qualities.

The idea of administrative decentralization in China, referred to earlier in this chapter, has a history. The first decentralisation of the modern period occurred in 1958, andis known as the Great Leap Forward. It was discontinued in 1961, and is considered to be responsible for the great famine in China, with the loss of millions of lives. It highlights the consequences that can occur from misguided political policy. It was envisaged to be a distributed developmental strategy which recognised that China had more human resources than investment capital for high end industrial technology. It was aimed at rapidly transforming China from an agrarian economy by embracing collectivization and lower end technological industrialisation. It introduced mandatory agricultural collectivisation, and those who did not participate were considered counter revolutionaries and subject to persecution. Coercion, terror and systematic violence were its cornerstones, from which millions of people died (Gabriel, 1998; Dikotter, 2010). The failure of the Great Leap forward diminished Chairman Mao Zedong's political authority, and he sought a remedy for this in a second decentralisation.

The second wave of adminstrative decentralization occurred in 1966, and was known as the Great Proletarian Cultural Revolution. This provided a degree of provincial autonomy to the administrative and market reforms (Breslin, 2000). It was intended as a means by which Mao Zedong attempted to reassert his authority over the Chinese government, though it ended with his death in 1976. It paralyzed China politically, and had a major impact on its economy and society, with millions of people being persecuted in the violent struggles which claimed the lives of somewhere between 1.5 million (McFarquhar and Schoenhatls, 2006) and 40 million (Scaruffi, 2009) Chinese. The death toll was due to both the radicals who supported the revolution, and the army who attempted to restore order towards the end of the cultural revolution,

In 1978, two years after the death of Mao Zedong, a new initiative arrived. The Open Door policy was a new concept of administrative decentralization that, according to Montinola et al., was combined with financial incentives, reliance on market mechanisms, increased control for lower governments over their economies, and a new openness to international markets. These features, we are told, generate far-reaching consequences for political institutions and economic performance. Thus the distinction between the Great Leap Forward, the Cultural Revolution, and the consequence of the Open Door decentralization lies in an embracing of marketization.

It is not only the power of governance that has been distributed. In the Chinese banking system a central bank (the People's Bank of China) which issues currency, acts as the financial hub of each five-year State Economic Plan (its 12th plan or mission being from 2011–2015: Caploe, 2011), and supervises the big four major state banks, each with their particular specialization. The central bank and each of the big four have established a branch in every province, municipality, and county. Within the federal system regional governments at provincial, municipality, and county levels also hold influence over credit decisions through the regional branches. Localities also have power in credit-plan formulation, being able, for instance, to impose loans on specialized banks, and to decide whether an enterprise should pay back a loan.

The importance of the banking industry is that it provides fiscal lubricant for economic development. However, not all is sunshine and brightness in the Chinese economy under its current regulatory position. The big four state-owned banks service the requirements of the state apparatus. Commercial banks also exist, which are intended to satisfy evolving and increasing business activity. Development problems were faced by the big four after China joined the World Trade Organization (WTO) (Liu et al., 2005; Allen et al., 2006; Iles & Yolles, 2006; Podpiera, 2006; Qu & Leung, 2006), but in recent years the banks have become more efficient, more or less following Western practices (Rowe, Shi & Wang, 2011), resulting in China's status as a 'tiger economy' (Fu & Heffernan, 2009), which, like that of Malaysia, Singapore, and Indonesia, underwent rapid economic growth that is usually accompanied by an increase in the standard of living.

In this part of the chapter we explore the Chinese banking system and the problematic issues it faces. Part of this relates to the shadow banking system in China. However, China is not alone in this. The Western recession of 2007/8 is also credited with suffering from the effects of shadow banking (Gorton, 2010; Nersisyan & Wray, 2010; Sanches, 2014), though until recently this would seem to have been something of a public whisper. As part of an exploration of the issues we shall explain how the coupling of regulated and unregulated banking has resulted in corrupt practices that the Chinese government is trying to tame. Beyond this we shall model the banking system through agency, explaining its weaknesses and why corrupt practices have developed.

11.2 The Chinese Context

China is currently passing through at least two imperatives for change (Figure 11.1). One is the imperative from globalization that it is experiencing through its membership of the WTO, and the other is informatization, as

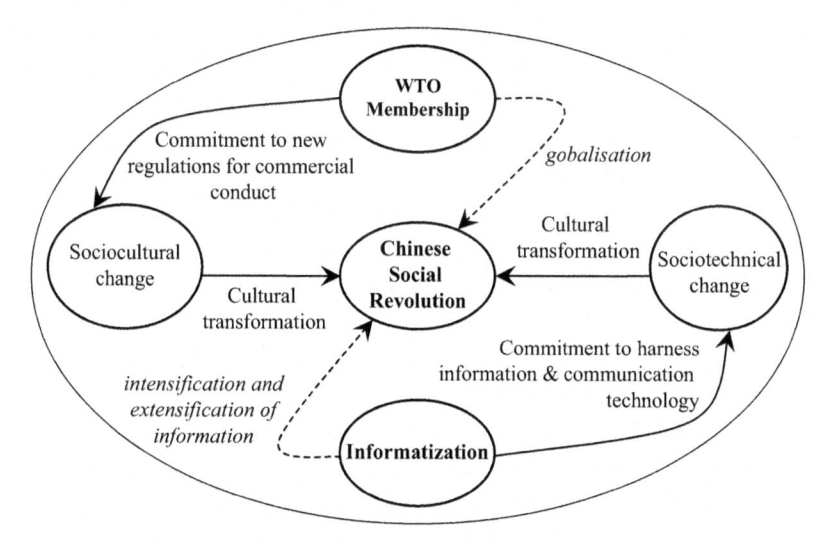

Figure 11.1 Impact of change on China

information technology takes hold and pushes forward new ways of working and connecting with potential customers for Chinese organizations (Xie, 2001; Iles and Yolles, 2005).

While the latter has generated a very large number of studies on the impact of new technology within the last decade, particularly with the rise of the Internet, the interest in this chapter lies more with the globalizing imperative that constitutes a drive for change, and therefore viability, within a new competitive and regulatory environment. Broadly speaking, it is possible to identify a number of interrelating attributes of interacting organizations that enable it to function in a changing environment; these are outlined in Figure 11.2. This is a relationship diagram that indicates the connection between culture, paradigmatic/worldview perspective and knowledge, figurative aspects like ideas, and polity-based order, and behavioural/material aspects.

In the autumn of 1898, US President McKinley stated his desire for the creation of an 'open door' that would allow all trading nations access to the Chinese market. It was not until December 1978, however, that China established its own 'open door' policy through the Chinese leader Deng Xiaoping that set in train the transformation of its economy. Prior to this, China's main trading partners had been the USSR and its satellite countries. This new policy coincided with the recognition that China needed Western technology and investment, opening its door to foreign businesses setting up in China. Four special economic zones were authorized in southern China, with tax incentives

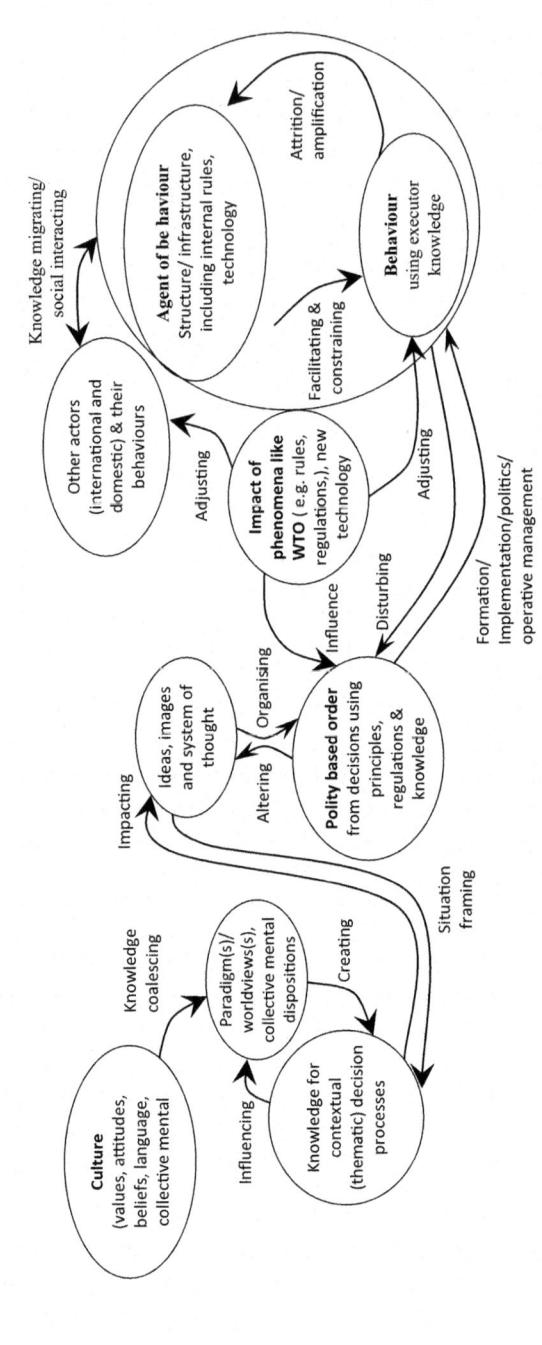

Figure 11.2 Interrelating attributes of organizations and impact of World Trade Organization (WTO)

to attract foreign capital and businesses, often from overseas Chinese in Hong Kong and Taiwan.

11.3 The Chinese Banking Industry

As China's economic growth continued, its financial system also experienced dramatic growth. Before 1978, the Chinese economy was centrally planned and production was exclusively conducted by state-owned enterprises(SOEs). The financial system consisted of a single bank, the People's Bank of China (PBC), which served both as a Central Bank and as a commercial bank. Most long-term investment financing was not channelled to enterprises through the banking system, but financed with budgetary grants. The PBC only provided working capital to enterprises (Guariglia and Poncet, 2007).

In 1978, the single bank was split, the PBC operating as a Central Bank; three state-owned banks were created: the Bank of China, the People's Construction Bank of China, and the Agriculture Bank of China, respectively dealing with foreign currency transactions, investment in manufacturing, and banking in rural areas. A fourth state-owned bank was created in 1984, the Industrial and Commercial Bank of China, which took over all commercial transactions from the PBC. In 1980, China once again joined the World Bank and returned to the International Monetary Fund. In 1984, it established business relations with the Bank for International Settlements. In 1986 it officially became a member of the Asian Development Bank.

After 1984, a number of non-state owned banks also entered the financial system, including commercial banks, urban and rural credit cooperatives, trust and investment companies, financial companies, and other institutions. However, in 1994 state-owned banks still dominated the financial sector: their total assets covered around 78 per cent of the total assets of the entire financial sector. Major banking reforms were initiated in 1994 when the central government decided to separate policy banks from commercial banks, and established three policy-lending banks and four specialized commercial banks. The banking reforms thereafter included, among others: transforming the urban credit cooperatives into commercial banks (1996–1998); granting limited licenses to some foreign banks; reducing government intervention in credit allocation; loosening interest rate controls; and recommending standard accounting norms (Guariglia and Poncet, 2007).

The system was liberalized at the end of the 1990s, when the Constitution acknowledged the private sector to be an integral part of the economy. Since the 1980s China has steadily broadened its finance sector. A group of foreign-capital and Sino-foreign joint venture financial organizations were established in the special economic zones and coastal open cities, as well as in major inland cities, and the right to do RMB business was given to some foreign-investment banks. The Chinese government enlarged the regions where foreign-invested banks are able to establish business operation organizations from twenty-three cities and Hainan province to all major cities. By the end of 1999, a total of 177 commercial financial banks had set up branches abroad to develop international credit business. Among them, the Bank of China has the most, and the largest, branches.

Despite the large size of the banking sector in China, until recently, most bank credit has been directed to inefficient state enterprises, with efficient private enterprises lacking access to external funding. Until 1998, the four state-owned commercial banks were instructed to lend to SOEs. The Chinese state enterprises submitted investment plans and funding requests that had to be approved at the provincial and central authority level. Based on this, lending quotas were issued to enterprises. Since private enterprises were excluded from submitting investment plans, they were, naturally, also excluded from lending quotas. In addition, there was also a legal bias against private domestic firms, which made it riskier for banks to lend them money (Huang, 2003).

A major impulse for changes in the banking sector came about with China's entry into the WTO in 2001 (relevant to Figures 11.1 and 11.2), bringing fewer restrictions on ownership and increasing operational freedom. After WTO access, foreign banks have explored opportunities in Chinese financial markets, resulting in intensified competition and such changes as deregulation, technological change, and globalization (Xie, 2001). The banking system was also characterized by significant non-performing loans (Podpiera, 2006). As a consequence of the reforms, by the end of 2002, the state-owned banks' market share had declined to 68 per cent, and non-performing loans had also significantly declined (Allen et al., 2006; Podpiera, 2006; Guariglia and Poncet, 2007).

However, in practice, banks still considered private enterprises to be risky, due to their short credit history or lower chance of being bailed out by the government. Lending by state banks is still determined by policy reasons, rather than by commercial motives. Allen et al. (2005) characterize China as a counter example to the finance-growth literature: in spite of a malfunctioning financial system it has been one of the fastest growing economies. The Chinese case suggests therefore that there might be circumstances under which financial distortions do not represent an impediment to growth. Foreign Direct Investment (FDI) may be used to alleviate the costs associated with an inefficient banking sector. China's financial resources are therefore often directed to the least efficient firms (SOEs), while denied to more efficient firms (private enterprises) in terms of access to external funding, property rights protection, taxation, and market opportunities (Guariglia and Poncet, 2007).

Therefore, after joining the WTO, China's financial firms, especially state-owned Commercial Banks, found themselves in a competitive international market, with the financial system experiencing some turmoil because it is unsure of what to expect from the change, or how to deal with it. Even where it may know how to respond, it often lacks the structured approaches by which it can enable change to be developed. The Chinese banking sector is still dominated by four large state banks that allocate most of their financial resources to the inefficient and loss-making state-owned enterprise sector (Boyreau-Debray, 2003). As such, the transition to a modern and profit-oriented banking sector was far from being achieved. However, the development of more recent commercial banks has tried to address this, and it is possible to see some sort of evolutionary movement in the banking sector not only in its sphere of activities, but also in its governance.

11.4 Finance and the Evolution in Chinese Banking

Yueh (2010) notes that membership of the WTO introduced elements of international economic law. This further developed the legal reforms and contributed to greater decentralization because of the accession terms that China signed up to. The resulting global integration demanded additional laws and regulations to govern fast-changing markets. As a result, Yueh sees this process has resulted in an evolutionary framework for economic and legal reform in China that is common to a development pattern for young economies and starts with an underdeveloped legal system. In the case of China, institutionally and contractually defined rights were adequate to support early gradual developmental growth. As part of this Yueh recognizes that informal institutional reforms have resulted in economic incentives that in due course became formal legal reforms. This process is highlighted with increasing marketization, in which informally defined rights are also replaced. However, since the informal contractual and institutional rights do not extend from the Chinese legal system, they can be enforced informally through: (a) social relationships, (b) business relationships, and (c) contractually defined measures such as binding arbitration. Yueh provides an illustration of this. Villagers recognize the implicit ownership of farm land independent of public ownership, while foreign investors recognize that their rights in relation to contracts and disputes are often settled without litigation. This said, Chinese–foreign joint alliances, even those entered into with trusted parties, may be subject to externally enforced international arbitration procedures.

Yueh also notes that informal institutional processes are often problematic for foreign investors in China, especially in relation to property rights. In the 1980s the first laws governing corporate forms came into being to facilitate Chinese–foreign joint alliances, and, in some rare cases, wholly foreign-owned enterprises. The alliance and foreign enterprise laws contractually defined the rights and obligations of these enterprises, thereby giving some level of security. Increasing market development embraced increasing complexity with a perceived need for new protection through law for the rights of both foreign and domestic firms. Thus, for instance, new laws covering mergers and acquisitions came into force in 2003, and new bankruptcy laws came about in 2006. Additional laws came in the area of governing as well, to improve the governance of the increasingly complex Chinese economy. As such, formal legal reforms began to replace the informal institutions that had underpinned China's economy.

This development has, according to Lin & Zhang (2009), also been reflected in the banking industry. In the last three decades, Chinese government-owned banks have passed through a privatization programme that has also followed an incremental approach to change. This raises questions about the role of domestic private ownership and foreign private ownership in relation to banking performance relative to state ownership. In their study of banking from 1997 to 2004, Lin & Zhang found that the Big Four state-owned banks have had poorer long-term performance on average than the city-level commercial banks, domestic joint-equity banks, and the newly established Chinese–foreign joint-equity and exclusive foreign capital banks. Banks in viable joint alliances that have also become public corporations outperform others Lin & Zhang suggest that, in order to help the reform process, the government has sold the equity of better banks first to attract foreign and private investors. In other countries, like Argentina, improved banking performance has arisen through placing non-performing loans into residual entities. In China, partially privatized banks cannot do this, while the Big Four state-owned banks can place non-performing loans into assets management companies, resulting in an injection of funds from the government. Overall, Lin & Zhang have found that state ownership of banks is negatively related to bank performance, with the Big Four banks having the worst performance. This recognition encourages the formation of joint alliances with foreign banks. For instance, in 2005 the Construction Bank of China sold some of its equity to foreign investors, as did the Bank of China in 2006.

Lin & Zhang conclude from their empirically based study that there are politically oriented state-controlled corporation investment issues, but these are mitigated by regulatory reform in relation to foreign joint alliances in the management of Chinese banks. Underinvestment in private corporations is alleviated with increased bank lending. As such, Chinese banking reform has increased the efficiency of resource allocation, easing corporate investment issues and reducing financial constraints. In accord with this, Tsai et al. (2014) note that recent regulatory efforts have overall been positive for the corporate governance of Chinese corporations, as well as on the efficiency of asset allocation. Continuing deregulation and liberalization should, they say, enhance the liquidity and maturity of markets. This should attract more international capital and stimulate economic growth. This, they note, underlines the need to increase our understanding of regulatory reform through a governance structure.

11.5   The Impact of Shadow Banking

Welborn (2002), in his review of Tsai's (2002) book on 'back-alley' banking, notes that private enterprise growth at around 20 per cent per annum has been the driving force behind China's new economy since 1978. The non-state sector in China is responsible for around two-thirds of Gross Domestic Product. Traditionally, China has been antagonistic to the private sector. Private-sector growth in China has taken place in an environment that is openly hostile to entrepreneurs and private businesses, and official state banks have extended credit principally to state and collective enterprises, rather than private ones. According to Tsai, this development has occurred through the stubborn persistence of the private sector, by accessing development funding from informal sources. Much of this informal financing has its basis at local levels, where there has been significant variation in funding sources. The reluctance of state banks to support private business occurs because the banks are pressured to respond to the needs of SOEs to encourage unemployment stability. Also, policies of central and local governments tend to encourage certain industries through 'policy loans'. There have also been structural constraints of the provision of formal credit. Historically, state banks have not been very effective in responding to administrative and technical loan requirements, principally due to lack of understanding. As a result, the formal loan process has been highly restricted for private businesses. Therefore, a variety of non-governmental funding mechanisms have been developed.

This informal financing system is frequently referred to as shadow banking. Das (2014) supports the earlier argument of Tsai (2002) by recognizing the very significant shadow banking sector in China. Here, by shadow banking is meant those institutions and economic structures used to perform banking functions that are beyond existing regulatory processes. It may also be defined (adapted from Li, 2013) as the system of credit intermediation that involves entities and activities fully or partially outside the regular banking system. It is thus serviced by nonbank financial organizations which provide services similar to traditional commercial banks but without regulation or supervision.

Das (2004) notes that in recent years China has evolved its own substantial shadow banking system. This system has several layers, which include the informal sector and the larger sector. The informal sector facilitates direct lending between individuals and underground lending, often by illegal loan sharks (also called curbside capitalists or back-alley bankers), providing high interest loans to small businesses. In the larger sector, there are a range of non-banking institutions, which are subject to various degrees of regulation. The sector involves direct loans of surplus funds by companies to other borrowers or trade credit, often being delivered for extended periods. The non-bank financial institutions include finance companies, leasing companies and financial guarantors. In addition, there are more than 3,000 private equity funds, which are supported by foreign investors. Micro-credit facilities also occur for personal finance, involving micro-credit providers, consumer credit institutions, pawn shops, trust companies, Wealth Management Products (WMP), and finally supportive capital markets that permit insurance companies and institutional investors to purchase debt and equity securities. The credit market is dominated by the four major state-controlled banks who tend to lend principally to SOEs that are associated with the government and officially sanctioned projects. Outside this sphere of activity there is a gap filled by the shadow banking sector businesses, which have more limited access to bank credit. The relationship between the larger shadow banking sector and the banks is illustrated in Figure 11.3 (adapted from Li, 2013). It explains the connection between deposits, purchases, investments, and loans that occur between the banks and the shadow banks in China. Here, banks have investors and create trust assets, which include loans, stocks, bonds, exchange traded funds (EFTs) which are similar to indexed mutual funds and trade like stocks and may refer to commodities or a pool of assets, and private equity (PE). EFTs are used as entrusted loans, trust loans, or indirect credit extensions to the property sector, which includes SOEs, Small to Medium sized Enterprises (SMEs), Local Government Financing Vehicles (LGFVs), real-estate property developers, and households. There are a variety of investors, which may be individual, qualified wealth individuals, and institutional investors like SOEs and LGFVs.

Shadow banking is enlarging at the expense of traditional banking. Das (2014) notes that the share of new lending in Chinese banks has fallen in recent years to about 50 per cent, from a higher 90 per cent around a decade ago. As a result, the economy is becoming more dependent on unregulated shadow banks, especially true for local governments, property companies, and SMEs.

The financial system is complex in China, as one can infer from Figure 11.3. This is because formal banking mechanisms are mixed in with informal shadow banking, where the former is fairly well regulated and the latter is not. There are also important issues that relate to the interconnection between central government and local governments. As Das (2014) explains, China's provinces, regions, and centrally controlled municipalities are more or less autonomous, beyond security and foreign policy issues that are the province of government.

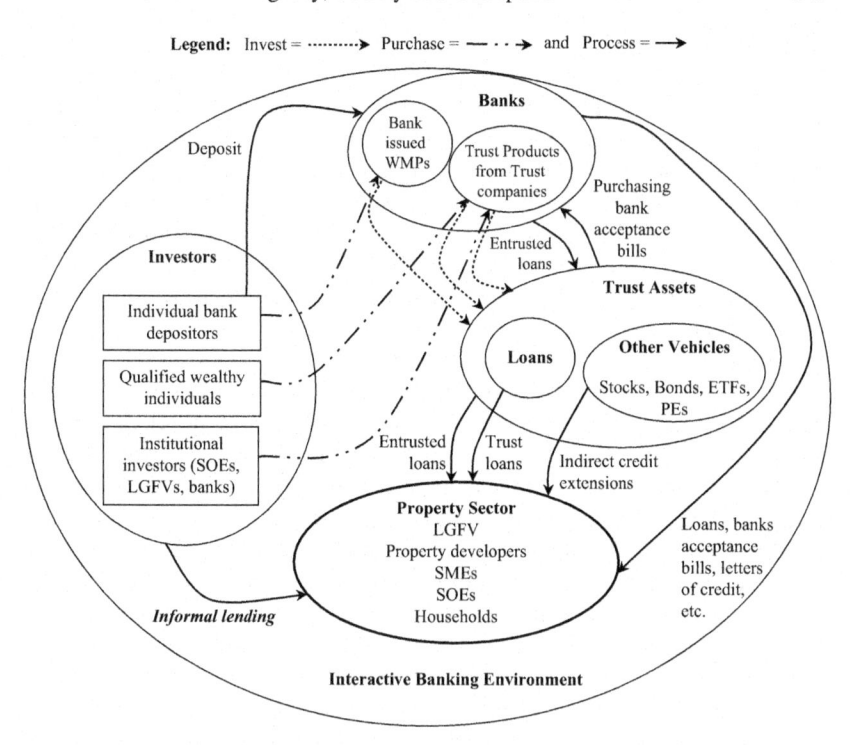

Figure 11.3 Typical relationship between Chinese banks and larger sector shadow banks (adapted from Li, 2013)

After the Western financial crisis in 2007/2008 with its global influences, the Chinese government relaxed controls on local government spending, allowing them to enter into processes of growth for which they required capital. However, under Chinese law (principle P4 indicated earlier), local governments are not permitted to borrow, and therefore needed to find creative solutions that might be informally agreed by the government. Their innovative solution was to create LGFVs, also known as Urban Development and Investment Companies (UDICs). While local governments were unable to borrow, LGFVs could. They make loans from banks, primarily, as well as by issuing bonds or other equity instruments that might refer to insurance companies, institutional investors, and individuals. More recently, Das (2014) explains, with pressure on banks to curtail loans, the LGFVs have borrowed from the shadow banking system, often making public projects trophy images and more expensive, and resulting in high levels of unsustainable debt that can result in possible insolvency. Few LGFVs have sufficient cash flow to service debts.

They rely on land sales and high property prices to satisfy debt requirements. LGFVs also may fall into vicious cycles of creating new debts to service maturing ones. More problematic, it is not always the case that local governments have a financial capability to guarantee LGFV solvency. It thus becomes clear that China's local governments are facing pathological financial issues that arise from the combination of excessive borrowing, capital misallocation, and debt servicing based on increasing property prices. The property sector may be seen as a sink for investments, loan, and other financial goods. The implication is that the system is likely to operate as required, all things equal (with respect to the banks, investors, and trusts), as long as there is stability in the property market.

Das (2014) continues by noting that local governments that want to grow revenue increase their loans and create increasingly large development projects. This amplifies the supply of new properties and land inventory that the LGFVs hold. As a result, land and property sales slow and prices come under pressure, thereby limiting their ability to liquidize assets to respond to maturing debts. As a result, lenders have their credibility strained, which limits cash flows. As a result, LGFVs have reduced funds, resulting in incomplete projects or delayed completion deliveries. Ultimately, local governments and their LGFVs will require government assistance or become insolvent. This is likely to happen due to political allegiances. Local governments, through their debt acquisitions, have helped maintain China's growth. This assisted China's government to save face, and to maintain social stability. Core or 'special' relationships (in Chinese called *guanxi*) among other things in the Chinese Communist Party (CCP), make it difficult for Beijing to refuse in the longer term.

The connection between banks and shadow banks shown in Figure 11.3 can be elaborated on to explain how this is creating issues that (like the onset of the Western economic crisis as explained in the introduction to this book) could result in a Chinese economic crisis. What seems to be happening in China perhaps gives a hint of the Enron crisis (Axtman & Sherer, 2002). In cahoots with their regulators and before its eventual demise, Enron was a leading US company that used a network of holding companies to create a hollowed out façade with off-the-balance-sheet partnerships (many in the Cayman Islands, and other sites where surveillance is lax) that made it appear, fraudulently, to be financially solid (Boje, 2002). Returning to the Chinese situation, Das (2014) explains that the banks frequently use shadow banking to take loan assets off their balance sheets. This presents stronger financial statements for regulators and investors, though it is unclear how regulators do not see this unless the shadowy fiscal inputs are hidden, when the activities may be regarded as fraudulent. That fraud does occur is reflected in a report by Tam (2008), who notes that the Banking Regulatory Commission in China found there to be fraud and other irregularities in China's financial institutions for the year 2005 that accumulated to about US$95 billion – a 31 per cent increase over the previous year. The government disciplined 6826 people, including 325 senior executives. Punishment was also administered to 1205 institutions for fraud and other illegal activities. Those involved included top level leaders and local managers in China's state-owned commercial banks. Tam concludes that the current rules and regulations covering corporate governance have been inadequate to engineer effectiveness. Having said this, Rowe, Shi & Wang (2011) note that corporate requirements in governance are continuing to develop, and as the Chinese banking system continues towards privatization, bank objectives have evolved to both maximize shareholders returns and protect the interests of the depositors and other creditors. Western governing structures have also often been adopted by the banks to establish appropriate standards and practices.

In order to sidestep regulations, banks use Trust Companies and WMPs to facilitate high-interest loans to companies like property developers. The banks also collaborate with Trust Companies and Security Brokers, Das (2014) tells us, thereby creating investment products for depositors who are looking for higher returns. Banks tend to rely more and more on such products to maintain their market share and their earnings. They do this through returns made from the distribution of shadow banking products. The mechanism functions as follows. Banks sell shadow loans to a trust that is now presented as a WMP and sold to bank clients. This can be used by the client to borrow from a bank. The banks, trusts, and WMPs occasionally combine their fiscal goods (deposits and assets or securities) from different schemes, and in order to meet repayments then generate new fiscal products. This vicious circle can result in economic problems. Thus, for instance, if a riskier trust or WMP fails, new fiscal products may not be available, and a sponsoring bank would therefore need to offer support. This occurred, Das (2014) tells us, during the onset of the Western 2007/2008 crisis. Any consequences of loss could result in wider problems within the financial system that would have consequences for business growth and solvency.

Investors are not protected here since WMPs offer only *expected* returns, and they are usually asked to guarantee any financial shortfall if the assets funded by the pool default. Partly, this ensures that transactions are hidden from the balance sheet, limiting transactional transparency. Sometimes the investors believe that they are fiscally protected from loss because of the risk that trusts may lose their operating license if their financial products make losses. Such losses have in the recent past been concealed by applying their own capital, and getting state-owned entities to take over problematic loans, or using proceeds from new trusts to repay maturing investments. Investors may also make the assumption that banks will guarantee repayment and returns on shadow banking investment, a perception supported by the transfer of bank assets to trust companies and WMPs, and by the distribution of shadow bank products by banks. Das (2014) notes that a high political risk exists that could end in government forcing banks to support fiscal structures to avoid any threat to social stability.

Das (2014) has also noted that the government in Beijing has recognized the problem, and taken steps to address this. Moves have been made to reduce the growth in debt and the expansion of shadow banking. Quantitative measures are now applied to credit creation and, having learned from the Western recession, banks are required to increase their reserves, thus limiting lending. Centring on shadow banking, in 2014 the government proposed a policy the intention of which is to limit the success of shadow banking. Their proposals can be summarized as follows:

- Banks would be exposed to increased scrutiny of existing rules.
- Banks would be unable to hide transactions by migrating some loans and assets away from the balance sheet.
- Bank wealth management would be more limited.
- Cooperation between banks, trusts, and security brokers would be restricted.
- The pooling of deposits by trusts from more than one product or investing in non-tradable assets would be constrained.
- Clients would not be able to borrow from private equity (PEs) firms.
- Between three to five new private banks will be created, thereby increasing capacity in the banking system beyond the dominant state-owned lenders.

Other government actions include intervention in money markets by draining liquidity and increasing interest rates. This restricts excessive credit growth and limits bank risk management practices. A result in June 2013 was a jump in interest rates. What showed up was an increase in financial volatility, and weaknesses in the structure of the financial system, especially recognizing that the shadow banking system was not stable.

The state banks control the major proportion of customer deposits. In contrast, other banks usually have more limited deposits, being more reliant on wholesale funding, for example from the interbank market. In this market, liquidity tends to depend on the larger banks, even with the participation of the smaller banks. When liquidity becomes reduced, higher rates can rapidly become amplified, resulting in instability. Placing greater constraints on the interbank market puts pressure on the smaller banks and initiates redemption of WMPs. This in turn limits access to funding in interbank markets. The result can be a cycle of increasing interest rates. The smaller banks maintain lower levels of government bonds than do the larger banks. This limits their ability to raise funds guaranteed by securities, and endangers their viability, forcing them to liquid asset distress selling, resulting in falling prices, and they might then become subject to insolvency proceedings. Das notes that the onset of the recent Western recession showed fund scarcity and payment issues which, when combined with payment or solvency issues in small banks and the shadow banking system, can rapidly result in larger economic problems.

Some issues may be raised here that have required resolution:

- Dealing with the growth in debt is problematic since it is a source for economic growth.
- Increase in the size and complexity of the shadow banking sector reflects structural issues.
- A need is for major and widely based economic, financial, and structural reform, which is politically unpalatable.
- Attempts to slow credit growth, to regulate the shadow banks, and to reduce levels of speculation are not currently fully determined.
- Where the central banks fail to resolve issues, government authorities intervene to promote liquidity to disband worries about a slowdown in growth and associated financial problems.

There appears to be some difficulty for government in properly responding to the needs of regulations that are able to resolve debt created through the shadow banking industry, and hence end the vicious growth–debt cycle.

11.6 Understanding Agency Issues and Corruption

Corruption, Alon & Kellerman (1999) note, affects an economy by setting private preferences into the public domain. This is because, they say, it cheats members of one group (e.g. taxpayers, shareholders, or Sunday supplement readers), and applies whatever is accrued to a privileged group. Ren (2016) notes that the Chinese financial sector is peppered by wasteful spending, bribe-taking for loan making, and pocketing off-book gains. Such practices are relevant to the whole of the financial sector, including banking (e.g. state owned commercial banks), securities, insurance, financial conglomerates, the stock exchange, and foreign exchange administration. Recognising this, it is therefore of interest for the financial context to explore corruption and its capacity to be modelled.

In order to examine the Chinese banking system through agency, we shall formulate a general model and populate it with appropriate superstructure. To do this we shall need to revisit the strategic agency, coupling its ideas with the cultural agency. However, here we model the politico-economic agency (for China as an illustrative nation) that operates in a global economic context (Figure 11.4). The operative system in the agency is populated by a number of sub-agencies (banks, shadow banks, investors, and government authorities) that interact, and this interaction is subject to a strategic system directed and

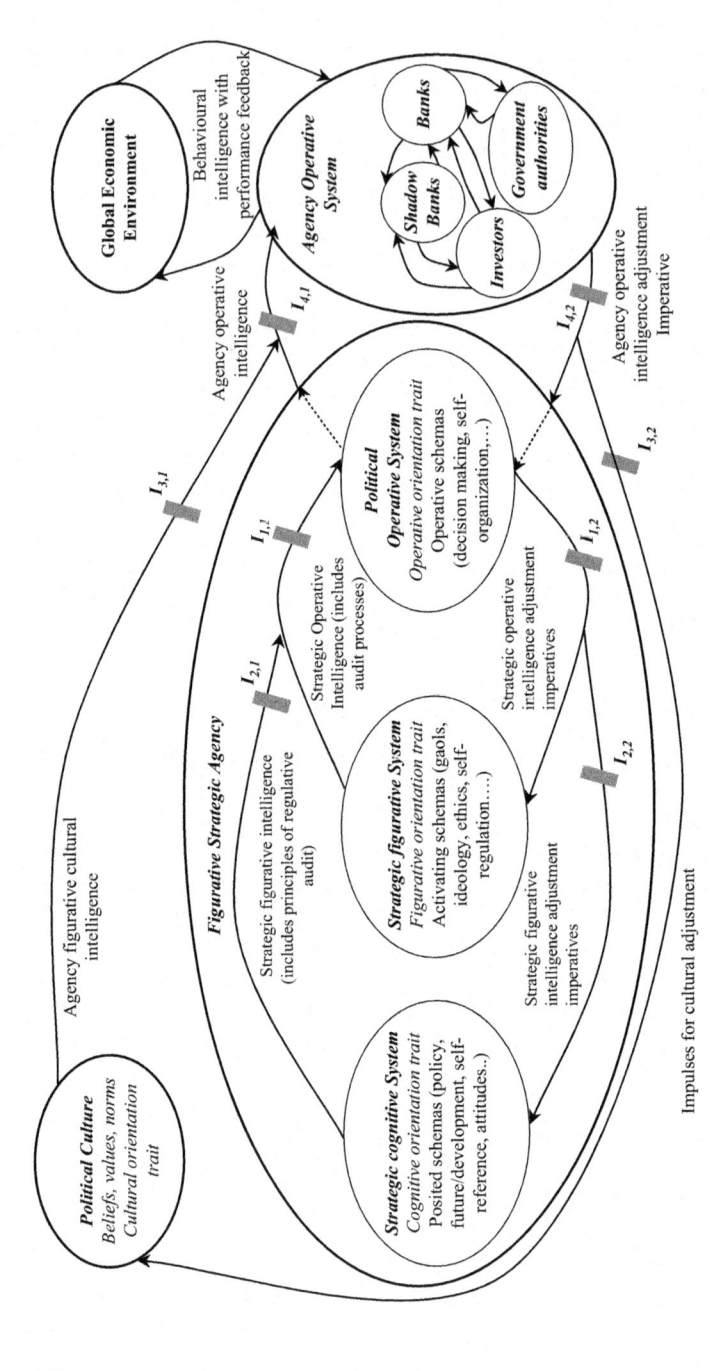

Figure 11.4 The national (Chinese) politico-economic agency

Note: $I_{i,j}$ (with possible pathology type $i=1,3$ and order $j=1,2$) may have *transitive* pathologies that can arise through both *intelligence limitation* and *efficacy distinction*, or where *semantic blocks* develop stabilized by a political culture, which we shall return to shortly. First, however, we shall consider the figurative strategic agency as considered earlier.

As a development of earlier arguments, we note that the figurative strategic agency in Figure 11.4 is a venue for the potential formation of schema, as they are deemed to be needed. They are created as a consequence of the interaction between environmental context and political culture. The potential for a schema is realized when agency figurative cultural intelligence is activated by agency operative intelligence, and appropriate political and economic patterns of knowledge are selected and manifested in the strategic cognitive system to form specific cognitive schemas. Selections are influenced by the cultural orientation trait, and this contributes towards the creation of political attitude. The way in which information arriving in the cognitive system of the figurative strategic agency is used to form cognitive schemas is influenced by the agency cognitive orientation trait.

Figurative schemas have been manifested from cognitive schemas through strategic figurative intelligence to create a strategic 'blueprint' definition involving all facets of a cognitive schema, and collective interactions of the whole set of strategic schemas intended for operative processing. How figurative schemas are constructed is also influenced by the figurative orientation trait, which biases construction, determining what is more important to agency. The operative schemas are manifested through operative intelligence, and constitute a schedule of decision option specifications from which decisions can result. Not all cognitive schemas will be manifested as figurative schemas, but rather create a potential for being figurative schemas.

In Figure 11.4 we also introduce the idea of behavioural intelligence that connects the agency to its global economic environment. Behavioural intelligence is constituted as the *overt actions* of an agency (Ang, Van Dyne, Koh, Ng, Templer, Tay & Chandrasekar, 2007: 6), and it contributes to the capacity of the agency to function as it requires, with aims that include finding common ground for economic success using opportunistic, exploitive or cooperative relations. Whichever moves towards 'common ground' are taken will be determined by the agency's social orientation trait, itself influenced by the cultural orientation trait.

The traits across the agency are also a function of the intelligences, since the system orientations are ultimately determined by the cultural orientation trait as satisfying varieties of either individualistic or collectivistic orientations. As such the traits are also subject to transitive pathologies that may either influence agency efficacy, or in more serious cases of dysfunction, perturb agency nature.

We may recall that political culture is the set of attitudes and practices held by its political membership that include political myths and beliefs that shape their political behaviour, and which results in moral and ethical judgements, and self-schema and goals that they believe create for them a good society. In fact in a society like that of China, political culture extends beyond 'membership' since not all members of a society are party members, and hence do not have authority to participate in permitted political processes. However, the ambient political culture still delivers values and norms to them. Political culture not only creates socio-political norms that influence a number of attributes (including decision-making structure and behaviour) of the agency. We have already noted that it also acts as a field directive that orients the whole agency towards degrees of either individualism or collectivism. The political system in China has been, and still is, in principle collectivist. With economic reform, however, wealth has become an important facet of Chinese society, and this is consistent with embracing individualism. Political and economic power are close bed fellows, since political decisions have economic consequences, and economic decisions have political consequences. This is inherent in the Lucas Critique, which says that economic and political processes are together important (Lucas, 1976; Yolles & Fink, 2013), and beyond this realization that all of the social sciences are intimately connected (e.g. Yoon, 2010). The connection between economics and politics can, for instance, be illustrated when discussing types of despotism. In political despotisms, decisions are made by an executive through the use of political power. In economic despotisms, decisions are made by an executive through economic power. As a result, political and economic power can mutually challenge each other, and may conflict. Where they do conflict, values and norms may be lost, resulting in cultural instability. This change referred to earlier from collectivism to individualism will therefore be reflected in political culture, creating cultural instability.

Something similar happened in the West. A shift in political culture occurred in the United States (and following this, Europe). More than two decades later in 2007/8 the West experienced a major recession. Political culture had changed from one that supported some degree of collectivism, to an extreme form of individualism where regulatory authorities were emasculated. Any form of extremism is implicitly pathological to an agency, being unhelpful in achieving its wants and needs in developing a society. This is because extreme individualism ignores positive attributes of collectivism, and extreme collectivism ignores positive attributes of individualism. There is some evidence that such extremism can be viewed as a (normative) personality abnormality. Normal and abnormal personality can be treated within a single structural framework (Markon, Krueger & Watson, 2005), and abnormal personality can be modelled as extremes of normal personality variation (O'Connor & Dyce, 2001). An illustration occurs with a shift in political orientation, when the normative personality loses its stability, this perhaps resulting in mild psychosis. This may have occurred with a political shift from a soft form of individualism that 'respected' collectivism to a more extreme form. Using the same model as explored earlier, during this shift culture became unstable and norms lost their relevance to be replaced after some gestation period by new norms once a set of values had become accepted. Gestation always takes time as the culture moves from cultural instability to stability. In political processes, this instability can last years or even decades, resulting in a loss of overall direction for the agency since a new system of values has not been fully recognized and potential norms are still under semantic development. In this case, the strategic system is no longer controlled by the political culture, and the politico-economic agency becomes a strategic *instrumental agency* that loses any meaning that could arise from political culture. A strategic instrumental agency is only capable of adjusting its schemas in response to imperatives from the strategic operative system and the agency operative system, rather than being able to create new knowledge and understandings about the nature of problematic issues and their corrective interventions.

Another important attribute of agency concerns pathologies, of which there are two forms that we shall discuss: transitive and lateral.

Transitive and Lateral Pathologies

While it is all very well to try to create a formal theory of the nature and cause of plural agency pathologies, organizational ill-health is a condition that is ultimately recognized from operationally sick behaviour.

In the theory so far we have paid little attention to pathologies that can be described as *transitive*. That is, the connection between the different domains or modes of *Being* (phenomenal, noumenal, and existential) in some way limits the migration process that is essential for the modes to operate coherently as a whole, a unity. This unity has an overall meaning that is defined by context, as is the nature of the domains/modes. Changing the context necessarily changes the meaning of the modes, and this also reflects on the idea that each mode, because of its special nature, has its own context. Relating these contexts can be useful in contributing to a better understanding of the whole complexity.

Formally, *laterally* based pathologies relate to *within domain* interactions, where interest in improving the collective is restricted to understanding from a knowledge perspective the nature of what is happening within domains or modes of Being. However, in *transitive*-based pathologies we are concerned with *between domain* interactions and interest in improving the collectives concerns how their distinct domains or models of *Being* are coupled together.

Lateral pathologies represent conditions that are internal to the ontologically differentiable systems in a plural agency, and this is the more usual way of exploring pathologies. When exploring collectives from a lateral perspective it is useful to recognize that two orientations for their pathologies may develop. They may be inwardly directed, creating general conditions affecting the internal operations of the collective adversely, and they may be outwardly oriented, affecting the social environment in which they exist.

This distinction in orientation can be formalized, allowing us to define the two orientations of lateral pathology: autopathic, with internally directed pathologies, and sociopathic, with external socially directed pathologies. While autopathology may have an unintended impact that is external to the plural agency, it primarily affects the internal working environment of a collective. It can therefore have a significant influence on the ability of the collective to operate intelligently. It can also affect the capacity of individuals and groups to operate effectively and efficiently. So, for instance, in the plural agency Claver et al. (1999) explore problems of development that arise because of the restrictive hierarchical nature of organizations and their authoritarian governance and relationships that operate through power-based leadership roles.

In contrast, sociopathic collectives contribute to the creation of pathologies within their external environment, sometimes through strategic motivations. In general, they maintain egocentric as opposed to sociocentric behaviour, and have exogenously oriented attitudes that are likely to include callousness and a conscience-defect. That a plural agency is sociopathic does not mean that it is not also autopathic, so that being a member of one category does not exclude it from being a member of the other.

In passing it may be noted that laterally represented pathologies can ultimately be expressed in terms of a transitive model. While transitive pathologies are normally expressed graphically, lateral pathologies can also be graphically represented, thereby helping a corporate therapist to explain the processes at work. It is possible to illustrate this by exploring the pathology of the plural agency in terms of its capacity for *associative projection*, an important property for any cognitive entity, as we shall explain now.

Following Yolles (2006) (who cites Piaget (1977: 20) in a discussion of human cognitive processes), plural agencies have an associative projective capacity when they are active in forming an image of reality, and as already indicated it involves the two kinds of properties: (a) an interrelation or coordination of viewing points; and (b) the possibility for deductive reasoning. In (b) there are logical processes at work that enable the consequences of relationships to be determined. A pre-requirement for this in (a) involves the ability to develop an *object conception*. For Piaget (1977: 87) object conception derives from the coordination of the schemes that underlie the activities with objects. This is in contrast to the notion of *objectivity*, which more generally is seen as a derivative of the coordination of perspectives. The capacity of an agency to change the relationship between object and subject through the coordination of perspectives results in an ability to shift roles (or to use the theatre metaphor, change characters). The ability to assume the role of another is seen as a special case of a more fundamental capacity to decentre or departicularize the focus of an agency's conceptual activities to consider and coordinate two more points of view.

One of the apparent facets of the coordination of viewing points is the necessity to subjectify the object, thereby connecting an agency's own comprehension and deductive reasoning from actions or operations that have been subjectively assumed. This leads us to want to consider further the subject–object relationship. It has in particular been explored by Foucault (see Rabinow, 1984) and the process of subjectification. For Foucault, subjectification is the creation of an association between an emotional perceiver and a phenomenal object that is beyond the boundary of subjective perception. The process of subjectification is one of shifting the boundaries of what constitutes the subjective. The two are irrevocably bound together, and it is from this association that social action originates. The object and subject are in dialectic interaction, and this enables properties of the former to be discovered, freeing knowledge of its subjective illusions. This dialectic interaction enables the subject to organize its actions into a coherent system that constitutes its intelligence and thought.

By now we should be aware that the real natures of the subject and object are distinct, and this very distinction is fundamental to associative projection. It is explained by Piaget (1977: 62) in the following way. The subject appears to be formulated through tacit knowledge, while objects are only seen as pictures that have been theorized such that they can be interpreted. As a consequence of this explanation we can formulate Figure 11.5, which is related to Figure 2.12 with pathology types F (for figurative intelligence) and O (for operative intelligence).

A type pathology is primary in nature, when the agent is incapable in some way of normally relating the noumenal (or 'collective mental') image of an object to its phenomenal actions within a context indicated by the tacit subject. Now, the collective coexists within the phenomenal environment with which it interacts. However, the object is external to its own behavioural system. As a result, any of the type F or O pathologies or their combination constitutes a condition of collective sociopathology. Sometimes pathologies that arise may be disguised through the personality orientation of the agent towards the object.

There is an obverse of this proposition. Let us take it that associative projection is a normal attribute of those individuals who populate a plural agency. Within the collective it occurs through the normative processes. So when associative projection is bounded because of an inhibited ability to adequately create subjective association, then the collective at least has the behavioural potential to be sociopathic. It comes from the inability of the

356   Agency as Society

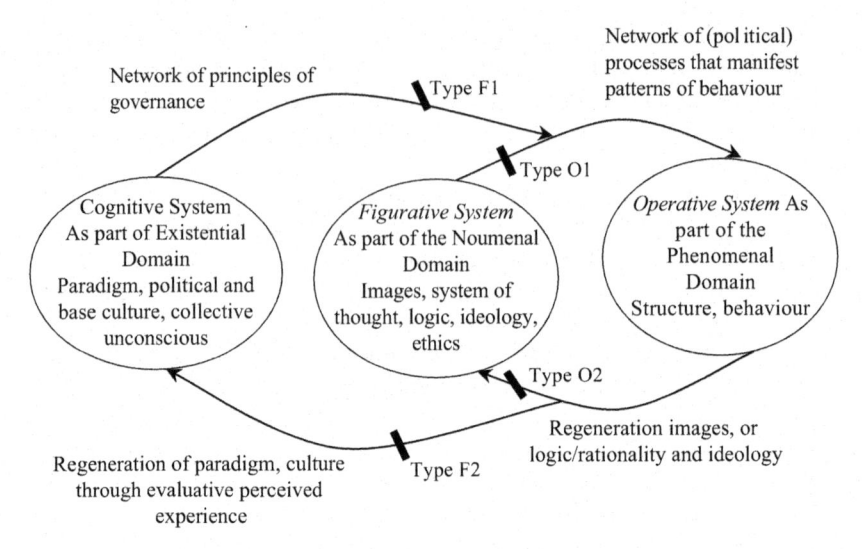

```
                                        Network of (political)
    Network of principles of            processes that manifest
    governance              Type F1     patterns of behaviour

                                 Type O1
   ┌─────────────┐    ┌─────────────────┐    ┌─────────────────┐
   │ Cognitive System │ │ Figurative System │ │ Operative System As │
   │ As part of Existential │ │ As part of the Noumenal │ │ part of the │
   │ Domain │ │ Domain │ │ Phenomenal │
   │ Paradigm, political and │ │ Images, system of │ │ Domain │
   │ base culture, collective │ │ thought, logic, ideology, │ │ Structure, behaviour │
   │ unconscious │ │ ethics │ │ │
   └─────────────┘    └─────────────────┘    └─────────────────┘
                                         Type O2
                                           Regeneration images, or
    Regeneration of paradigm, culture       logic/rationality and ideology
    through evaluative perceived   Type F2
    experience
```

Figure 11.5 Type F and O pathologies

collective agent to recognize objects, thereby limiting the inclusiveness of the perspectives that need to be coordinated.

In Figure 11.6 we illustrate the nature of associative projection according to Piaget. This is shown as a transitive process in which distinct levels of reality are connected. However, the coordination of perspectives arises from a more detailed lateral process that occurs in the virtual domain and is shown in Figure 11.6. It may be noted that the image of the objects as depicted in this figure is constructed from ideological viewing points that arise from the collective agent's ideology, and its ethical position reflects this and guides behavioural responses.

In particular, in Figure 11.7 we show the potential for the images of the objects to be strategically coordinated as they become structurally coupled to each other, with the image of one object influencing the images of the others.

This interconnection can and often does fail totally, at least with respect to its efficacious capacity for performance. Consider an illustration of this. Each department in a complex organization maintains an image of the other departments as objects in their local environments. Because of the all-consuming egocentric pursuit of its own behaviour, each department sees the local objects as opaque images. Their purpose and function may be known, but what they actually do and the policies that they generate and pursue are not of much concern or interest. As a result, the object-images are isolated from each other by being relegated to a virtual horizon that lies beyond immediate awareness and disallows the possibility of structural coupling. Remedies to such a situation are sometimes expressed through the search for 'joined up

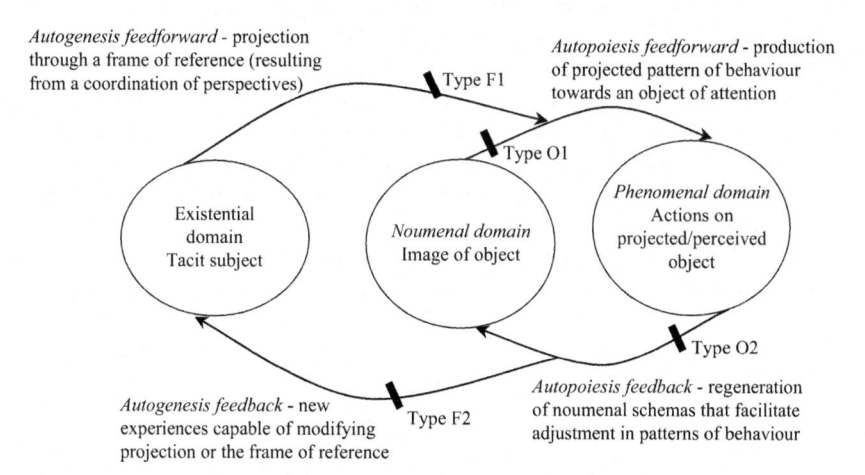

Figure 11.6 Interpretation of Piaget's notion of the relationship between subject and object

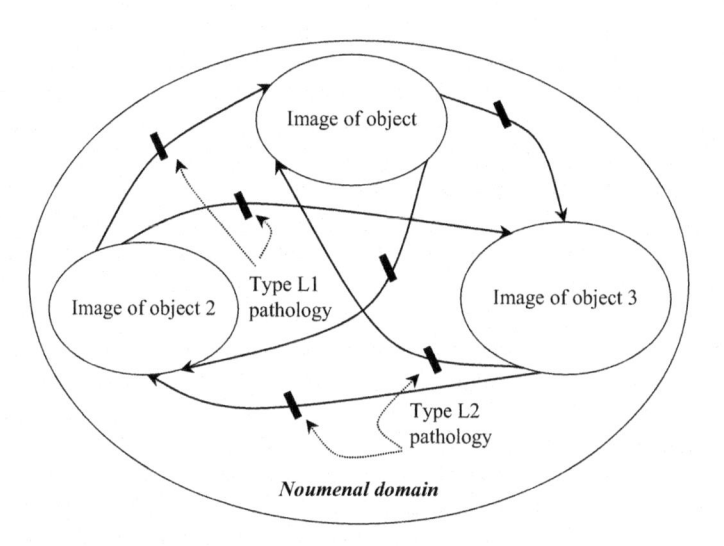

Figure 11.7 Interactive relationship between distinct images of objects, each interaction susceptible to (type L1 or L2) lateral pathologies that interfere with the deductive reasoning processes that affect perspective coordination

governance'[1], a term intended to convey the impression of organizational cohesion through policy and action research processes.

Where structural couplings are possible in Figure 11.6, they may become susceptible to type L (lateral) pathologies, so that the coordination of perspective fails. The seriousness of the inability to undertake associative projection of an agent is a function of the number and type (L1 or L2) of pathological breaks that exist.

When type L pathologies occur, sociopathic responses may arise because of the inability of the agency to coordinate perspectives. However, this situation can be made more complex when transitive pathologies are also engaged. This can occur by developing the transitive nature of each of the objects in Figure 11.6.

Autopathologies

Autopathologies may arise in the cultural agency together with structural and process problems. Thus, for example, Claver et al. (1999) explore problems that reflect on the development of social pathologies that arise because of the restrictive hierarchical nature of organizations, their authoritarian governance, and relationships that operate through power-based leadership roles. Such environments inhibit viable processes by creating emotional and rational bases for pathologies.

There are three dimensions that should be considered in this regard: culture, structure, and behaviour. Behaviour is facilitated and constrained, but not caused by structure, but they are otherwise independent. Both are, however, conditioned by culture. When talking of culture we mean a general existential condition that maintains a belief system and supports patterns of knowledge and understanding. Culture may be argued to be composed of more than one aspect. An example is political culture with its embedded political knowledge that can be manifested as ideology and ethics. Another manifestation is empowerment that 'formally' if not practically liberates the individual or group potential to perform certain types of operational behaviour. Thus, in some corporate environments, employees are empowered to make certain types of decision that directly result in behaviour, without having recourse to request permission from more senior roles. However, when push comes to shove the degree of such empowerment is often highly limited by the collective's bureaucracy, and is therefore more apparent than substantive.

Another problem often comes with structures. Many plural agencies maintain restrictive hierarchical structures. They are the result of a political culture that is responsible for political awareness. For Rosenbaum (1972: 13), political culture is 'learned behaviour', implying processes of socialization involving

---

[1] For example see http://news.bbc.co.uk/1/hi/special_report/1998/11/98/e-cyclopedia/211553.stm

the creation of values, attitudes, and beliefs that influence a political positioning and the formation of political ideology and ethics. According to Hunter (2002) political culture is the normative context within which politics occur. This context includes the ideals, beliefs, values, symbols, stories, and public rituals that bind people together and direct them in common action. Political culture is ultimately responsible for political processes that establish power distributions, which act to constrain and facilitate certain types of politically acceptable behaviour. This occurs through political structure with relatable action that is a reflection of that culture's ideals, and, in turn, reinforces that culture's normative boundaries.

Political culture also provides the boundaries of political legitimacy and the horizons of political possibility, and defines modes of operations that reside in the political structures that are defined and that constrain social processes. These structures normally maintain political executives (in a pluralistic political environment there may be more than one executive, which can result in competition and conflict) supported by a political bureaucracy. This mediates between members of the plural agency subjected to the political processes, and the executive(s). However, the bureaucracies also maintain political cultures with resulting power structures and modes of operation that may be, but are unlikely to be, a complete reflection of the plural agency's political culture in which they reside. Let us explain this.

The nature of bureaucracy is that that it controls meaning and develops systems of administration (Mazlish, 1990). This is different from the usual notion that a bureaucracy will simply reflect a given ideology. In other words, there is an interaction between a bureaucracy and an ideology that affects the development of both the bureaucracy and the ideology. One explanation for the interaction between them is that bureaucracies operate through the subjectivity of leaders, and both the leaders and the led define themselves and their relationship through their association within their shared culture (Fromm, 1961). During this process, a selection is made from their shared culture that is codified by ideology. It is made real and alive through the leader's image, but is also subject to the manifesting developmental potential of those being led. It is the bureaucracy that helps decide on ethical issues, that is, what is right and wrong thinking in a social community. While ethical issues provide for moral judgements, ultimately such judgements can be used to identify who is faithful to a political bureaucracy and who is not. Used in a political process, it determines who of the ideologically unfaithful is a heretic. Thus for Mazlish (1990), the manipulation of ideologies becomes one of the most important means for the control of people, through the control of their thoughts.

The bureaucracy is subject to lateral pathologies. In Figure 11.7 the object images may be seen as departments that need to interact but are unable to do so because of type L pathologies. We have already referred to this in terms of 'joined

360   Agency as Society

up governance'. A transitive formulation of Figure 11.7 will allow other more fundamental pathologies (type F or type O) to be explored. It is feasible to name pathology types. For instance, cybernetic pathologies can easily emerge and develop unintentionally when departments do not invest sufficient time or effort into communications processes, or ensure that control processes in complex situations are sufficiently clear, untangled, well defined, or coherent. This has a significant cost for operational effectiveness and collective viability.

Corruption as an Illustration of Autopathology

A version of Figure 11.7 provides an explanation for the development of corrupt practices. It begins by considering the relationship between ideology and ethics. In considering the former, values are manifested from culture to create firstly, noumenal cognitive attitudes, and second, noumenal orientations towards action that constitute ideology. Action is in turn constrained by ethics, which creates processes of judgement that can result in what ought to happen. Though ideology may be seen as schema, its capacity to facilitate action arises when it conforms to both legitimacy that satisfies meaningful norms including standards of conduct (we shall return to this shortly) and opportunity that is manifested from the operative environment. Here, Figure 11.8 (explained in Table 11.1) lists three laterally connected attributes of any political system.

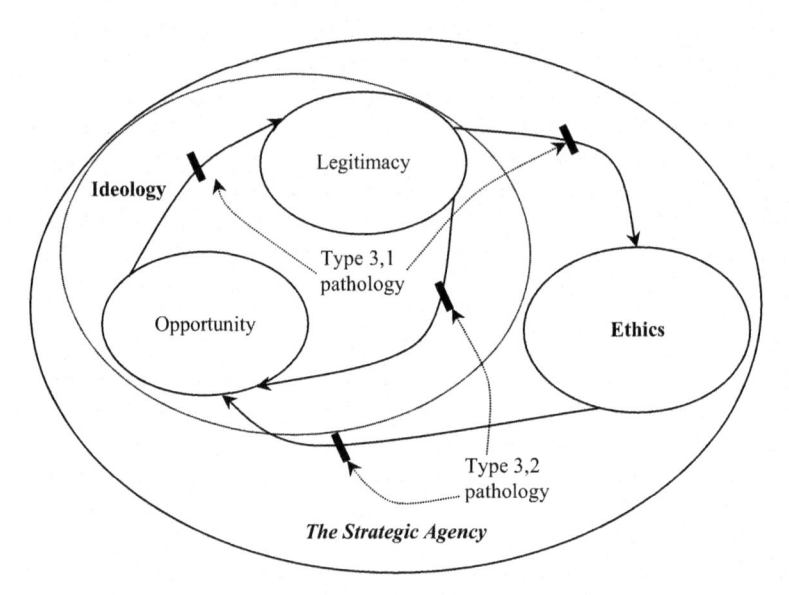

Figure 11.8 The Strategic Agency expressed in terms of the interaction between Ideology (Legitimacy, Opportunity) and Ethics

Table 11.1 *Nature of the terms and coupling relationships in Figure 11.5*

Term	Nature
Ideology	A collection of rationalized and systemized beliefs that coalesce into an image that establishes a potential for social action
Opportunity	The capacity to engineer favourable circumstances, for instance in respect of economic or political structures or conditions
Legitimacy	The capacity to engineer a body of regulations and rules by a governing executive operating under a constitutional right
Opportunity–legitimacy coupling	Legitimate regulations and the creation of opportunity (e.g. economic or political) mutually influence each other and develop through a shared history. Breaking the connection means that illegitimate opportunities can develop, resulting in illegitimate or corrupt practices.
Ethics	A value system that can be used to explore moral value judgements and create what a plural agency may call justice.
Ethics–ideology coupling	Ideology is connected to ethics through the identification of what is right and wrong, and involves the notion of judgement and justice based on ideological values.

These are *legitimacy*, *opportunity*, and *ethics*. A deepening of the relations in Figure 11.8 can occur, for instance as shown in Figure 11.9, where we note that economic, political, and financial conditions are all intimately connected and combine to create opportunities in the combined spheres of activity, and in Figure 11.10 we note the nature of legitimacy as being composed of regulations, normative standards, and accountability.

During a period of political cultural instability values are confused and norms need to be re-generated. The result is often that the connection between ideology and ethics can also therefore become disrupted. When this occurs, corrupt practices may develop. The Western crisis of 2007/8 is an illustration of this, as is the connection between banking and shadow banking in China. We can detail this argument further to more fully explain the rise of corruption. Figure 11.9 shows three laterally connected attributes of any political system. Ideology is connected with ethics, but ideology can also be distinguished into legitimacy and opportunity.

Legitimacy is concerned with the creation and implementation of a body of rules and regulations that facilitate and constrain the behaviours of those who populate the structure of a plural agency. These rules and regulations are legitimate when they are created in accordance with recognized or accepted standards or principles that conform to the dominant paradigm of the collective. The behaviours are facilitated from another factor too: opportunity and in particular economic opportunity. Legitimacy is also connected with accountability (Ackerman, 2005). There is also a close connection between ideology

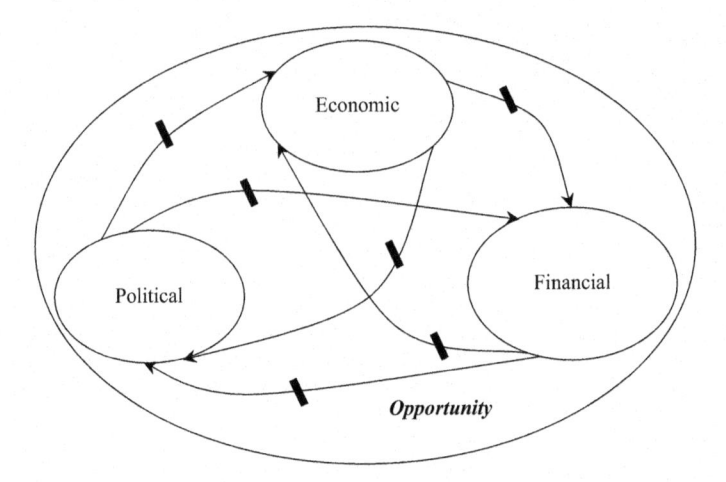

Figure 11.9 The nature of opportunity in a politico-economic agency

and ethics: ideology establishing a context for ethical developments. The ideological schema for legitimacy and opportunity is therefore intimately connected with an ethics schema. This relationship appears to be implicitly supported, for instance, by the 'White Paper' On New Foreign Aid Policy published in 2006 by the UK's Department of International Development, which outlines a foreign aid policy that focuses on promoting good governance and anti-corruption as a means to reducing poverty. The problem in legitimacy is that in an instrumental politico-economic agency where there is no stable political culture, it is not possible to create new knowledge, and hence the ability to be creative with legitimacy is limited where there are problematic issues to contend with. In the case of China, there would appear to be legitimacy issues with shadow banking. Corrupt practices are therefore more likely when the interactive relationship becomes pathological with type L pathologies when the coordination of perspective fails and when sociopathic responses may arise because of the inability of the agency to coordinate perspectives (Yolles, 2009b). There are indirectly supporting arguments for this. Thus for instance, in Figure 11.9 we posited the nature of opportunity, and in Figure 11.10 we do something similar for legitimacy. In this latter case, where normative standards have been lost due to cultural instability, then it is whether a pathology has occurred that disconnects it from regulations and accountability. In the case of the well-known Enron crisis, legitimacy failed because the regulators were part of the corruption process, and the connection between regulations and accountability were discounted.

The fraud that we have considered is only part of the problem. The Chinese central government is on a bent against severe corruption in

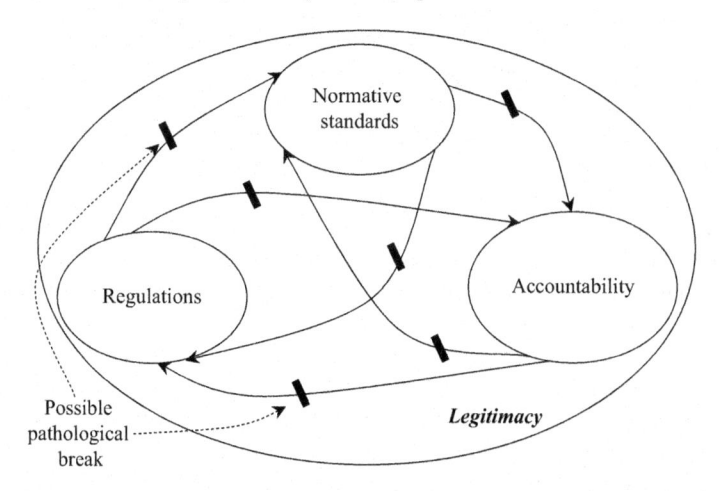

Figure 11.10 Deeper notion of legitimacy with possible pathological breaks

general (Tao, 2015). Political structures that are either devoid of cultural orientation or are invested with pathological faults facilitate the development of corruption, and this provides an illustration of pathological conditions. Often corruption is seen in terms of a moral imperative, but there is more to it than just this. For instance, Goorha (2000) tells us that anti-corruption not only has a moral imperative, but also an economic one. Corruption has been generally vilified because it is indicative of governance that is failing to perform its chief function of limiting transaction costs, and indeed there is a direct relationship between corruption and transaction costs (Murphy et al., 1993). This relationship tells us that low transaction costs encourage economic growth through institutions being able to exploit opportunities by engaging in economic exchange and transformation of resources (Goorha, 2000).

According to the World Bank, corruption is constituted as behaviour (on the part of officials in both the public and private sectors) in which people improperly (and in the context of the State, unlawfully) enrich themselves and/or those close to them, or induce others to do so, by misusing the political role in which they are placed. This definition really should be followed by an extensive examination since it raises questions about what constitutes legitimacy, and what is the nature of improper or unlawful behaviour.

For Anderson and Gray (2006) there are at least two dimensions of corruption (and both relate in some way to processes of *legitimacy*, a term we can easily define). Generalizing from this, we posit two forms of corruption as:

- *constructional* – which refers to bribery to influence the *formulation* or *content* of rules and regulations that are institutionally legitimized within the collective
- *administrative* – which refers to bribery by individuals or collectives to influence the *implementation* of legitimate rules and regulations.

While conceptually different, both types of corruption can have major impacts on the business environment. Constructional corruption weakens the legitimate administrative rules (e.g. State laws) that are deemed to support the plural agency and facilitate its interests and purposes. Corruption undermines the collective's capacity to pursue due processes of governance, and to implement its legitimate rules and regulations. Both forms of corruption can pre-orientate preferences and reduce the likelihood of identifying or accessing opportunities that may enable the collective to operate more viably.

Corruption is higher where political opportunities are not realized: for example, where policies and institutions are weak (Anderson and Gray, 2005). Weak institutions do not have the capacity to enforce facilitating or constraining processes in relation to policy provisions, or where the policies themselves do not cater for the legitimate needs that a collective has. Collectives in transition, like the countries of Asia or Countries of Central and Eastern Europe, are also likely to be subjected to higher levels of corruption, though this proposition implies that the definition of corruption in each collective is the same. In periods of fast growth, formulation of corruption may be exacerbated, particularly if such growth is lubricated by the provision of wealth inducing resource.

The viability of a plural agency is ultimately determined by the way it is able to respond to the challenges that arise from its environment. We are aware that this is called requisite variety, referring to the different problem states that a complex situation may develop that the complex collective must respond to through action. The capacity of the collective to identify and respond to such action imperatives can be diminished by its pathologies, especially when they reduce the possibility of generating appropriate options that can contribute to requisite variety. The most effective way of ensuring that there is a significant potential for the creation of options is for the collective to prime as much of its populous for this task. This goes hand in hand with the need to ensure that members of the populations also have access to the core facilitating resources of the collective. Examples of such resources are education, health, and opportunity. Thus in a corporate environment, providing health plans or access to new knowledge for only the senior management does little to motivate lower ranks to participate in the search for a requisite variety of options. In a national context the same elements occur, with appropriate policy implications.

The accessibility of resources in many plural agencies are dependent upon two vital attributes: economics and communication, and there is evidence to show that economic and communication deficits are causes for the rise of corrupt practices. There are two measures for this (McAdam, 2004), one from Transparency International and the other from Passau University with their Corruption Perception Index (CPI). For instance, according to Transparency International (2006) there is a strong correlation between corruption and poverty. When corruption occurs within the mechanisms that evaluate the legitimacy rules and regulations within the collective then this too has its own potentially significant impact on the viability of the collective. For instance, a corrupt judiciary 'erodes the ability of the international community to tackle transnational crime and terrorism; it diminishes trade, economic growth and human development; and, most importantly, it denies citizens impartial settlement of disputes with neighbours or the authorities. When the latter occurs, corrupt judiciaries fracture and divide communities by keeping alive the sense of injury created by unjust treatment and mediation' (Transparency International, 2007).

Corruption is a core inhibiting the ability of a plural agency to maintain its viability. It is thus a pathological condition of a collective that will ultimately impact on the way that it operates within its social environment.

Various studies of corruption and their causes, particularly within the context of the nation state, have been undertaken. For instance, You (2005, 2005a), in a comparative study on corruption between Korea and the Philippines, finds that *inequality of income* and *wealth* is the overriding variable that best explains the relative level of corruption among these countries and across time. In addition, You finds that there are other rules that appear to apply which we can generalize as follows:

- High inequality can lead to greater incentives for corruption.
- Lower inequality can lead to more equal opportunity for education.
- In a meritocratic bureaucracy education can result in lower levels of corruption.
- Monitoring and accountability can reduce corruption.
- Economic growth is not a cause of corruption.
- Economic growth can be a consequence of corruption.

In another study, this time on police corruption in India, Verma (1999) shows that longer term corruption becomes cultural, and from his study we can attempt to generalize on his findings as follows. In organizations with elitism, politicization, unaccountability of behaviour, and outdated management practices a culture of corruption can emerge over the longer term. This can only be addressed through transformational change, such as organizational structure (including roles and functions), management practices, supervision procedures, decentralization of power, and creation of a local accountability system.

More, exploring corruption and ethics within globalized society, Zekos (2004) identifies a number of propositions that can be generalized as follows:

- ethics can lead to value maximization in the long run while corruption can lead to value minimization in the long run regardless of short-term value maximization.
- ethical norms are influenced by culture, technology, and religion, affecting in parallel the conception of the wrong doing of corruption.
- ethical standards are essential across different parts of social life.
- corporate environments need personnel policy and codes of conduct that mirror ethical principles rather than just rules, and which aim to induce employees to feel that they ought to 'comply with' rather than 'obey' company-imposed rules.
- the introduction of codes of conduct enforceable internationally and not voluntarily, defining the fundamental principles of business contacts will establish a harmonized view regarding corruption tactics and ethical principles and prohibiting the establishment of corruption methods and not baptizing them as ethically necessary for business.

In another study on corruption in the Russian Federation, Dininio and Orttung (2004) argues that corruption: *increases* with the growth of the regional economy, decrease in per capita income, and population decreases; can be *reduced* by (a) encouraging economic development away from the political centre, and (b) fostering political accountability.

Ng (2006) in yet another study, this time of corrupt international financial markets, finds that corruption can be associated with a firm's higher borrowing cost, lower stock valuation, and worse corporate governance.

Overall therefore, it seems that corruption whether inside government or in corporate or civil interaction with government has some common principles. We can try to extract these, in particular by examining a study undertaken by Anderson and Grey (2006) for the World Bank on corruption to countries in transition, in particular, with respect to the Countries of Central and Eastern Europe and in Asia. It uses data from the European Bank for Reconstruction and Development – the World Bank Business Environment and Enterprise Performance Survey (BEEPS). Their study provides an in-depth look at how corruption in business-government interactions is changing in the transition countries and what factors might be influencing those trends. In Table 11.2 we summarize and generalize on their findings.

11.7 Society, Development and Corruption

There is a clear connection between the political, economic, and financial systems in society. The Chinese economy is in dynamic movement, requiring

Table 11.2 *Variables to fight corruption, illustrations/explanations deriving from Anderson and Grey (2006)*

Variable	Need	Illustration	Explanation
Economic access	Positive economic pressure (e.g. against conditions of poverty)	Taxation as a negative economic pressure	Countries with less burdensome tax regimes tend to have lower levels of corruption in tax administration
Openness (in communication; egalitarian/flat access to governance)	Meaningful communications; low levels of complexity in rules/regulations; participatory opportunities to acquire power	Closed political systems with constraints on elitist access to steering media (e.g. power & money).	Opening up closed political systems can lead to an expansion of some forms of corruption in the short-term, but over time more political and economic competition helps foster the transparency and accountability that is essential for controlling corruption
Accountability	Control & operational audit	Law and the judiciary	Judicial independence without accountability can open the door to widespread corruption
Transparency	Mode of operations with control operational/asset audit	Government procurement contracts	Improving procurement systems with independent corporations by having transparency, competition, and standardization, together with financial audit and control; though asset monitoring does not always work
Operational efficiency & effectiveness	Operational means, e.g. competition, standardization, sound policy	Customs	Streamlined customs procedures and improved efficiency at border crossings reduced clearance times at the borders while also helping to lower corruption
Political support	Strong advocates	Purposeful leadership	Strong purposeful leadership is essential in shaping and pushing reform against corruption, especially in transitional countries.

appreciation of both political and financial system attributes. The intention in this chapter has been to centre initially on the financial system, and in particular banking. We have discussed the connection between formal and informal (shadow) banking, and shown that economic development could be threatened by the issues that this relationship throws up.

We have explained that political reform has occurred in China, though the reform has not taken a democratic path that many China watchers in the West would recognize. Rather, it has taken a path of decentralization that is difficult to dismantle, and which fundamentally supports China's 'economic miracle'. However, analysing it through agency theory, we find that it could be subject to both transitive and lateral pathologies that may inhibit it from reaching its performance potential. Lateral pathologies arise, for instance, when a break occurs between economic, political, and financial processes, so that, for instance, political policy is unconnected with financial or economic functionality, perturbing the potential for the creation of opportunity. It may also occur when ideology becomes corrupted through pathologies that disconnect legitimacy from opportunity or disconnect ethics from ideology. However, by adopting agency theory, we have been able to show that such pathologies may not just be internal issues of efficacy, but may rather arise from something more fundamental. It has been argued here that there is a clash between Chinese political collectivism and economic individualism, resulting in political cultural instability, where values become confused and certain cultural norms become abandoned. This does not differ much from the clash that occurred in the West in the build-up to its economic crisis in 2007/8. This, we have argued, disconnects culture from having an influential anchoring role in development, and results in instrumental development that allow strategic attributes to be adjusted, but does not allow strategy to be influenced by the creation of new knowledge. In modelling the banking system, we have explained that the instrumental financial agency is subject to instrumental change, so that no new strategic mechanisms are possible – only adjustments of existing ones, norms become lost as valued become confused, and strategic schemas may lose their interactive coherence, resulting in corrupt practices.

Like bad governance corruption inhibits economic growth (Wei, 2001; Forgues-Puccio & Blackburn, 2009). It can also diminish benefit from the inward FDI that results from globalization (Wei, 2001). Thus, China attracts a large amount of foreign investment, but its FDI is relatively low given its size and growth rate.

Wei explains that international capital flows (like FDI, international bank loans, portfolio investment, and official debt to other governments or intergovernmental institutions) may be volatile, and subject to reversals that can be responsible for currency crises, and even establish a basis for recession. While different types of capital inflow imply a different risk level for a recipient country, its level of corruption has an important impact on the composition of capital inflows, pointing them away from the more stable FDI towards less stable bank borrowing.

China, like other countries in East and Southeast Asia, experienced an economic crisis in 1997. This is attributed to high levels of corruption, poor corporate governance and doubtful business practices (Arvis & Berenbeim, 2003). The outcome, resulting from a combination of corrupt political leaders and unscrupulous business consortia, contributed to the financial market collapse and resulted in poverty for millions.

The Asian crisis was connected with structural problems in the banking and corporate sectors (Knowles et al, 1999). It included high levels of financial leverage, weak supervisory and regulatory frameworks, and excessive risk-taking by both lenders and borrowers, and these permitted corrupt practices to seep into organizational processes. An outcome was high rates of nonperforming loans leading to highly vulnerable and unexpected capital outflows. This in turn resulted in a sudden loss of confidence that saw widespread panic, massive capital withdrawal, and a fast unravelling financial system in a number of Asian economies. Alon & Kellerman (1999) explain that in China's collective, familistic and guanxi (personal connections) setting, the individualism of neoliberalism that it has embraced had permitted abuses, collusion, lack of transparency, poor banking practices, and corruption, resulting in significant economic weaknesses and crisis. However, this new individualism is also resulting in new political perspectives that encourage individual and political rights (Hansen and Svarverud, 2010). This brings us back to the cultural instability referred to earlier, and enables us to note that such a dichotomy will likely take some decades to resolve. The cultural dichotomy is manifested phenomenally, where the power of collectivistic governance is being challenged by the power of individualistic money, and where power and money are two steering media of society.

Asian collectivism embraces authoritarianism and hierarchy which combined to create what Knowles et al. (1999) called moral hazard. Such collectivism also embraces the desire for group harmony, and this too increases moral hazard. Corrupt practices like expensive gift baskets, million dollar payoffs, corporate bribes, payoff to low-level functionaries, nepotism, cronyism, or lack of transparency all arise from collectivism. These are also seen in individualist societies, since no society is purely individualist or collectivist, even though the types of collectivism may be different. While collectivism may contribute to moral hazard, it does not mean that all collectivistic cultures are corrupt (Li, Triandis, & Yu, 2006).

The form of collectivism in China tends to avoid legislative regulation for civic control in favour of people-centred regulation (Sargeson, 2002). This is in contrast to the West where legislative regulatory civic control is more commonly in evidence (Rose, 1991; Majone, 1994; Sneeringer & Key, 2011; Baldwin, Cave & Lodge, 2012). These distinct orientations have led to a different orientation for Chinese economic growth than in the West. Government in China tends to cooperate closely with the private sector, this reducing the perceived need for regulatory frameworks, taxation and public consumption (Sargeson, 2002). However, while arbitrary and perhaps piecemeal collectivist approaches provide a potential for flexibility, they also provide greater opportunity for biased or corrupt practices.

China's treatment for corruption is anticorruption policy, designed to strengthen transparency and the rule of law in both the public and private sectors. This began in 1978 (Cole, Elliott & Zhang (2009) and has been continuing ever since. It currently has a Transparency International perceived corruption ranking of 83, which may be related to North Korea and Somalia, these being the most corrupt globally with a rank of 167. Making comparison with Singapore, which began its measures against corruption in 1952 with the establishment of the Corrupt Practices Investigation Bureau, it is now within the top ten 'cleanest' countries in the world (rank 8, that compares with Denmark rank 1, and the USA rank 16) countries in Southeast Asia.

Bibliography

Abrena, M., Epstein, G., & Power, D. (2003), Trends in the Rentier Income Share in OECD Countries, 1960–2000, Working Papers wp58a, Political Economy Research Institute, University of Massachusetts at Amherst.

Ackbar, M., Abbot, J., & Bakan, J., (2005), *The Corporation*: A film by Mark Ackbar, Jennifer Abbot, and Joes Bakan, www.thecorporation.com/index.php?page_id=2, accessed January 2006.

Ackerman, J.M., (2005), Social Accountability in the Public Sector: A Conceptual Discussion, Social Development paper 82, World Bank.

Ackoff, R.L., (1971), Towards a System of Systems Concepts, *Management Sciences*, 7 (11) July: 27.

Adams, K., & Hyon, J., (2005), Towards a System of Systems Methodologies, Once Again, 26th ASEM National Conference Proceedings, October, see www.asem.org/conferences/2005conferenceproceedings/92.pdf, accessed January 2009.

Adeyemo, D.A., (2007), Moderating Influence of Emotional Intelligence on the Link between Academic Self-Efficacy and Achievement of University Students, *Psychology Developing Societies*, 19(2): 199–213.

Adizes, I., (1999), *Corporate Lifecycles*, Prentice Hall, New Jersey. Also see www.adizes.com/corporate_lifecycle.html, accessed April 2010.

Adler, P.S., (1987), *Culture-Shock and the Cross-Cultural Learning Experience*, Newbury, Cambridge.

Albrecht, K., (2003), *The Power of Minds at Work: Organizational Intelligence in Action*, Amacon, New York.

Albrow, M., (1997), *Do Organizations Have Feelings?* Routledge, London.

Alden, L., (1986), Self-Efficacy and Causal Attributions for Social Feedback, *Journal of Research in Personality*, 20: 460–73.

Alexander, J.A., (1984), The Parsons Revival in German Sociology, *Sociological Theory*, 2: 394–412, www.jstor.org/stable/223356, accessed June 2014.

Allaire, Y., & Firsirotu, M.E., (1984), Theories of Organizational Culture, *Organization Studies*, 5(3): 193–226.

Allen, C.T., Machleit, K., & Schultz Kleine, S., (1992), A Comparison of Attitudes and Emotions as Predictors of Behaviour at Diverse Levels of Behavioural Experience, *Journal of Consumer Research*, 18 (March): 493–504.

Allen, F., Qian, J., & Qian, M., (2005), Law, Finance, and Economic Growth in China, *Journal of Financial Economics*, 77: 57–116.

(2006), China's Financial System: Past, Present, and Future. In Brandt L., & Rawski T., (Eds), *China's Economic Transition: Origins, Mechanism, and Consequences*, Cambridge University Press, Cambridge.
Allik, J., & Realo, A., (2004), Individualism-Collectivism and Social Capital, *Journal of Cross-Cultural Psychology*, 35 (1, January): 29–49.
Allport, F.H., (1924), *Social Psychology*, Houghton Mifflin Co., Boston.
Almond, G.A., (1956), Comparative Political Systems, *The Journal of Politics*, 18(3): 391–409.
Almond, G.A., & Verba, S., (1963), *The Civic Culture: Political Attitudes and Democracy in Five Nations*, Princeton University Press, Princeton, NJ.
   (1980). The Intellectual History of the Civic Culture Concept. In Almond, G.A., & Verba, S., (Eds), *The Civic Culture Revisited: An Analytic Study*, Little, Brown, Boston.
Alon, I., & Kellerman, E.A., (1999), Internal Antecedents to the 1997 Asian Economic Crisis, *Multinational Business Review*, 7: 1–12.
Alvesson, M., & Deetz, S., (2000), *Doing Critical Management Research*, SAGE, London.
Alvesson, M., & Willmott, H., (1996), *Making Sense of Management*, Sage, London.
Amagoh, Francis (2008), Perspectives on Organizational Change: Systems and Complexity Theories, *The Innovation Journal: The Public Sector Innovation Journal*, 13(3): 1–13.
Amburgey, T.L., & Dacin, T., (1994), As the Left Foot Follows the Right? The Dynamics of Strategic and Structural Change, *Academy of Management Journal*, 37(6): 1427–52.
Anderson, J.R., (1993), *Rules of the Mind*, Erlbaum, Hillsdale, NJ, also see http://act-r.psy.cmu.edu/, accessed June 2003.
Anderson, J.H., & Grey, C.W., 2006, Anticorruption in Transition 3: Who Is Succeeding and Why? The World Bank. Available at http://siteresources.worldbank.org/INTECA/Resources/ACT.pdf, accessed January 2014.
Anderson, P., (1999), Complexity Theory and Organizational Science, *Organization Science*, 10(3): 216–32.
Andrews, H., Roberts, L., & Selwyn., (2007), Hospitality and Eroticism, *International Journal of Culture, Tourism and Hospitality Research*, 1(3): 247–62.
Ang, S., Van Dyne, L., & Koh, C., (2006), Personality Correlates of the Four-Factor Model of Cultural Intelligence, *Group & Organization Management*, 31(1): 100–23.
Ang, S., Van Dyne, L., Koh, C.K.S., Ng, K.Y., Templer, K.J., Tay, C., & Chandrasekar, N.A., (2007), Cultural Intelligence: Its Measurement and Effects on Cultural Judgment and Decision Making, Cultural Adaptation, and Task Performance, *Management and Organization Review*, 3: 335–71.
Antony, M.V., (1999), Outline of a General Methodology for Consciousness Research, *Anthropology and Phylosophy*, 3(2): 43–56.
Appelbaum, S.H., Roberts, J., & Shapiro, B.T., (2009), Cultural Strategies in M&As: Investigating Ten Case Studies, *Journal of Executive Education*, 8(1): Article 3. Available at: http://digitalcommons.kennesaw.edu/jee/vol8/iss1/3, accessed May 2013.

Archer, M.S., (1982), Morphogenesis versus Structuration: On Combining Structure and Action, *The British Journal of Sociology*, 33(4, December): 455–83, The London School of Economics and Political Science, www.jstor.org/stable/589357, accessed February. 2013.

Argote, L., & Todorova, G., (2007), Organizational Learning: Review and Future Directions, In Hodgkinson, G. P., & Ford, J K., (Eds), *International Review of Industrial and Organizational Psychology* (pp. 193–234). Wiley, New York.

Argyris, C., (1976), Single Loop and Double Loop Models in Research on Decision Making, *Administrative Science Quarterly*, September, 21: 363–375.

(1977), Double Loop Learning in Organizations, *Harvard Business Review*, September–October.: 115–124.

Argyris, C., & Schön, D., (1978), *Organizational Learning: A Theory of Action Perspective*, Addison-Wesley, Reading, MA.

Arvis, J.F., & Berenbeim, R., (2003), *Fighting Corruption in East Asia: Solutions from the Private Sector*, World Bank, Washington, DC.

Ashby, W.R., (1956) (reprinted 1961), *An Introduction to Cybernetics*, Methuen, London.

(1961) (reprinted 1964), *An Introduction to Cybernetics*, Wiley, New York.

(1968), Principles of Self Organising Systems. In Buckley, W., (Ed.), *Modern Systems Approach for the Behavioural Scientist* (pp. 108–18), Adline Pub. Co., Chicago, USA.

Ashkanasy, N.M., & Ashton-James, C.E., (2007), Positive Emotion in Organizations: A Multi-Level Framework. In Nelson, D., & Cooper, C.L., (Eds), *Positive Organizational Behaviour* (pp. 58–73), SAGE Publications, Thousand Oaks, CA.

Ashkanasy, N.M., & Nicholson, G.J., (2003), Climate of Fear in Organizational Settings: Construct Definition, Measurement, and a Test of Theory, *Australian Journal of Psychology*, 55: 24–29.

Asimov, I., (1951), *Foundation*, Doubleday, New York.

Atkinson, R.C., & Shiffrin, R.M., (1968), Human Memory: A Proposed System and Its Control Processes. In Spence, K.W., & Spence, J.T., (Eds), *The Psychology of Learning and Motivation: Vol. 2, Advances in Research and Theory* (pp. 90–196), Academic Press, New York.

Austin. T.L., (2005), A Comparison of the Cognitive Development of Outcome Based versus non Outcome Based Education: An Exploration of South African Learners, Doctoral Thesis, Rand Afrikaans University, South Africa. Also see http://etd.uj.ac.za/theses/available/etd-05232006–145736/restricted/Thesis.pdf, accessed April 2007.

Aveleira, A., (2004), (October), Consciousness and Reality: A stable-Dynamic Model Based on Jungian Psychology, Metareligion, www.meta-religion.com/Psychiatry/Analytical_psychology/consciousness_and_reality.htm, accessed December 2005.

Averill, J.R., (1980), A Constructivist View of Emotions. In Plutchik, R. and Kellerman, H., (Eds), *Emotion: Theory, Research and Experience*; Vol. 1 (pp.305–339), Academic Press, New York.

Axtman, K., & Scherer, R., (2002), Enron Lapses and Corporate Ethics, *The Christian Science Monitor*. www.csmonitor.com/2002/0204/p01s01-ussc.html, accessed May 2015.

Baars, B.J., (1997), In the Theatre of Consciousness: Global Workspace Theory: A Rigorous Scientific Theory of Consciousness, *Journal of Consciousness Studies*, 4 (4): 292–309.

Bacharach, S.B., (1989), Organizational Theories: Some Criteria for Evaluation, *Academy of Management Review*, 14(4): 496–515.

Baecker, D., (2001), Why Systems? *Theory, Culture and Society*, 18: 59–74.

Baer, J., Kaufman, C., (2008a), Toward an Agentic Theory of the Self. In *Self-Processes, Learning, and Enabling Human Potential* (pp.15–49), Information Age Publishing: Charlotte, NC, USA.

Bahm, A.J., (1981), Five Types of Systems Philosophy, *International Journal of General Systems*, 6(4): 233–237.

Bakhtin, M.M., (1984), *Problem of Dostoevsky's Poetics*, University of Minnesota Press, Minneapolis.

Baldwin, R., Cave, M., & Lodge, M., (2012), *Understanding Regulation: Theory, Strategy, and Practice*, Oxford University Press on Demand.

Bales, R.F., (1965), The Equilibrium Problem in Small Groups. In Hare, A.P., Borgatta, E.F., & Bales, R.F., (Eds), *Small Groups: Studies in Social Interaction*, Knopf, New York.

Ball, R., (2001), Individualism, Collectivism, and Economic Development, *The ANNALS of the American Academy of Political and Social Science*, 573(1): 57–84.

Bandura, A., (1977), Self-Efficacy: Toward a Unifying Theory of Behavioural Change, *Psychological Review*, 84: 191–215.

(1986), *Social Foundations of Thought and Action: A Social Cognitive Theory*, Prentice-Hall, Englewood Cliffs, NJ.

(1988), Organizational Application of Social Cognitive Theory, *Australian Journal of Management*, 13(2): 275–302.

(1991a), Social Cognitive Theory of Moral Thought and Action. In Kurtines, W.M., & Gewirtz, J.L., (Eds), *Handbook of Moral Behaviour and Development* (Vol. 1, pp. 45–103), Erlbaum, Hillsdale.

(1994), Self-Efficacy. In Ramachaudran, V.S., (Ed.), *Encyclopedia of Human Behaviour* (Vol. 4, pp. 71–81), Academic Press, New York. (Reprinted in H. Friedman, (Ed.), *Encyclopedia of Mental Health*. 1998). See www.des.emory.edu/mfp/BanEncy.html, accessed January. 2010.

(Ed.), (1995), *Self-Efficacy in Changing Societies*, New York: Cambridge University Press.

(1997), *Self-Efficacy; The Exercise of Control*, Freeman, New York.

(1999) A Social Cognitive Theory of Personality. In Pervin, L., & John, O., (Eds), *Handbook of Personality* (2nd edn., pp. 154–196), Guilford Publications, New York. (Reprinted in D. Cervone and Y. Shoda (Eds), The Coherence of Personality, Guilford Press, New York.)

Bandura, A., & Locke, E., (2003), Negative Self-Efficacy and Goal Effects Revisited, *Journal of Applied Psychology*, 88: 87–99.

Barber, B., (1963), Is America Business Becoming Professionalised. In Tiryakian, E.A., (Ed.), *Sociological Theory, Values, and Sociocultural Change* (pp. 121–145), Free Press, New York.

Barley, S.R., (2007), Corporations, Democracy, and the Public Good, *Journal of Management Inquiry*, 16(3): 201–215.

Barney, J.B., (1991), Firm Resources and Sustained Competitive Advantage, *Journal of Management*, 17. Jg., H. 1, S: 99–120.
Baron, J., (1982), Intelligence and Personality. In Sternberg, R., (Ed.), *Handbook of Intelligence*, Cambridge University Press, Cambridge.
Barry, Brian. (1978), *Sociologists, Economists, and Democracy*, University of Chicago Press, Chicago.
Batini, N., Callegari, G., & Melina, G., (2012), Successful Austerity in the United States, Europe and Japan, International Monetary Fund Working Paper WP/12/190, www.imf.org/external/pubs/ft/wp/2012/wp12190.pdf, accessed November. 25, 2012.
Batra, Rajeev, & Stayman, Douglas M., (1990), The Role of Mood in Advertising Effectiveness, *Journal of Consumer Research*, 17 (September): 203–214.
Bauman, Z., (2000), *Liquid Modernity*, Polity Press, Cambridge. http://english.360elib.com/datu/J/EM353297.pdf.
Bausch, K.C., (2001), *The Emerging Consensus in Social Systems Theory*, Kluwer Academic Publishers. Dordrecht.
Beaudoin, L., (1994), Goal Processing in Autonomous Agents. PhD. Dissertation, School of Computer Science, The University of Birmingham. www.sfu.ca/%7Elpb/tr/Luc–95.html#38.
Beer, S., (1959), *Cybernetics and Management*, English University Press, London.
(1966), *Decision and Control: The Meaning of Operational Research and Management Cybernetics*, John Wiley, Chichester.
(1972), *The Brain of the Firm*, Wiley, Chichester.
(1975), *Platform for Change*, Wiley, Chichester.
(1979), *The Heart of Enterprise*, John Wiley & Sons, Chichester, UK.
(1980), Preface to *Autopoiesis: The Organization of the Living, by* Maturana, H., Varela, F.J., Boston Studies in the Philosophy of Science, Vol. 42.
(1981), *Brain of the Firm: The Managerial Cybernetics of Organization* (2nd edn.), John Wiley and Sons, Chichester, UK.
(1985), *Diagnosing the System for Organizations*, John Wiley & Sons, Chichester, UK.
(1989), The Viable System Model: Its Provenance, Development, Methodology and Pathology, *Journal of Operational Research Society*, 35: 7–26.8.
(1994), *Beyond Dispute: The Invention of Team Syntegrity*, John Wiley & Sons, Chichester, UK.
(2002), What is Cybernetics? *Kybernetes*, 31(2): 209–19.
Berreby, D., (1998), Complexity Theory: Fact-Free Science or Business Tool? *Strategy & Business, Booz, Allen & Hamilton*, First Quarter 1998.
Bertalanffy, L. von, (1968), *General Systems Theory*, Penguin, Middlesex, UK.
Before it's news, (2012), Bank Cabal Exposed, July 6th, http://beforeitsnews.com/economy/2012/07/2353556-2353556.html, accessed December 2012.
Berens, L.V., (2007), Essential Qualities of the Personality Patterns, see www.interstrength.com/faculty/lindaberens.html, accessed June 2008.
Berger, P., & Luckmann, T., (1966), *The Social Construction of Reality*, Penguin, Middlesex, UK.
Bertalanffy, L.V., (1951), General Systems Theory: A New Approach to the Unity of Science, *Human Biology*, 23(December.): 302–361.

Best, J., & Widmaier, W., (2006), Micro- or Macro-Moralities? Economic Discourses and Policy Possibilities, *Review of International Political Economy*, 13(4) October 2006: 609–31.

Birch, D., Haggerty, A., & Parsons, W., (1995), *Corporate Evolution*, Cognetics, Inc., Cambridge, MA.

Blanchard, O., (2000), *Macroeconomics* (2nd edn.), Prentice Hall, New Jersey, USA.

Blum, E., (2009), Cultural Intelligence: Cultural Complexity Is Today's Business Reality, http://iloapp.culturalintelligence.org/blog/www?Home, accessed May 2014.

Blutner, R., & Hochnadel, E., (2010), Two Qubits for C.G. Jung's Theory of Personality, *Cognitive Systems Research*, 11: 243–259., www.blutner.de/Jung.pdf, accessed March 2012.

BMJ, (1970), Epidemic Malaise, British Medical Journal, London, Saturday 3 January No. 5687, pp. 1–2.

Bogilovic, S., Ceren, M., & Škerlavaj, M., (2014), 'Building the Babylon Tower: Knowledge Hiding', IACCM Conference, Cultural Intelligence and Creativity, Warwick University, Warwick, 26–28 June.

Boholm, Å., (1996). Risk Perception and Social Anthropology: Critique of Cultural Theory. *Ethnos*, 61(2), 159–178.

Boisot, M., & Child, J., (1988), From Fiefs to Clans and Network Capitalism: Explaining China's Emerging Economic Order, *Administrative Science Quarterly*, 41: 600–628.

Boje, D.M., (2000), Transformational Leadership, http://business.nmsu.edu/~dboje/teaching/338/leader_model_boje.htm.

(2001), *Narrative Methods for Organizational and Communication Research*, Sage, London, also see http://cbae.nmsu.edu/, dboje/papers/narrative_methods_intro.htm, accessed June 2008.

(2002), *Enron Metatheatre: A Critical Dramaturgy Analysis of Enron's Quasi-Objects*. Paper presented at Networks, Quasi-Objects, and Identity: Reintegrating Humans, Technology, and Nature session of Denver Academy of Management Meetings. Tuesday August 13, 2002. http://business.nmsu.edu/~dboje/ Revision Date: 9 August 2002. http://business.nmsu.edu/~dboje/papers/enron_theatre_LJM.htm, accessed 23 February 2009.

(2004), Welcome to Mindscapes, http://peaceaware.com/mindscape/, accessed December 2007.

(2011), *Storytelling and the Future of Organizations*, Routledge, New York.

Boje, D.M., Oswick, C., & Ford, J.D., (2004), Language and Organization: The Doing of Discourse, *Academy of Management Review*, 29(4): 571–577.

Boje, D.M., & Rosile, G.A., (2003), Theatrics of SEAM, *Journal of Organizational Change Management*, 16(1): 21–32.

Bolender, J., (2010), *The Self-Organising Social Mind*, MIT press, Cambridge, MA.

Bolt, R., Fujimura, M., Houser, C., De Guzman, F., Nixson, F., & Weiss, J., (2003), *Economic Analysis of Policy-Based Operations: Key Dimensions*, Asian Development Bank.

Bond, M.H., (1988), Finding Universal Dimensions of Individual Variation in Multicultural Studies of Values: The Rokeach and Chinese Value Surveys, *Journal of Personality and Social Psychology*, 55(6): 1009–1015.

Bonnet, A., (1985), *Artificial Intelligence; Promise and Performance*, Prentice Hall, New Jersey, USA.

Borger, R., & Seaborne, A.E.M., (1966), *The Psychology of Learning*, Penguin Books, Harmondsworth, Middlesex, U.K.

Borman, W.C., Hedge, J.W., Ferstl, K.L., Kaufman, J.D., Farmer, W.L., & Bearden, R.M., (2003), Current Directions and Issues in Personnel Selection and Classification, *Research in Personnel and Human Resources Management*, 22, 287–355.

Bormann, G., (1985), Symbolic Convergence Theory: A Communication Formulation, *Journal of Communication*, 35(4, Autumn): 128–138.

Boulding, K.E., (1956), General Systems Theory – The Skeleton of a Science, *Management Science*, 2(April): 197–208.

Bourdieu, P., (1971), Systems of Education and Systems of Thought. In Young, M.F.D., (Ed.), *Knowledge and Control: New Directions for the Sociology of Education* (pp. 189–207), Collier-Macmillan, London.

(1984), *Language and Symbolic Power*. Polity Press, Cambridge, UK.

Bowlby, J., (1980), *Attachment and Loss: Sadness and Depression*, Basic Books, New York.

Boxer, P.J., & Cohen, B., (2000), Doing Time: The Emergence of Irreversibility, *Annals of the New York Academy of Sciences*, 901(1): 13–25.

Boyreau-Debray, G., (2003), 'Financial Intermediation and Growth: Chinese Style.' World Bank Policy Research Working Paper No. 3024.

Brand, R., (2013), Russell Brand: Margaret Thatcher Was an Icon of Individualism, Radio Times, www.radiotimes.com/news/2013-04-10/russell-brand-margaret-thatcher-was-an-icon-of-individualism.

Brandenburger, A., & Nalebuff, B., (1996), *Co-Opetition*, Currency/Doubleday, New York.

Breakwell, G.M., (1986), *Coping with Threatened Identities*. Methuen, London.

Breslin, S., (2000), Decentralisation, Globalisation and China's Partial Re-Engagement with the Global Economy, *New Political Economy*, 5(2): 205–226.

Bridges, W., (1992), *The Character of Organizations: Using Jungian Type in Organizational Development*, Consulting Psychologists Press, Palo Alto, CA.

Bridoux, F., (2004), A Resource-Based Approach to Performance and Competition: An Overview of the Connections between Resources and Competition. *Luvain, Belgium Institut et de Gestion, Universite Catholique de Louvain*.

Brier, S., (2001), Cybersemiotics: A Reconceptualisation of the Foundation for Information Science, *Systems Research*, 18(5): 421–427.

(2002), Intrasemiotics and Cybersemiotics, *Sign System Studies*, 30(1): 113–127.

Briggs Myers, I., (2000), *An Introduction to Types: A Guide to Understanding Your Results on the Myers-Briggs Types Indicator*, CPP, Palo Alto, CA. Revised from the 1998 edition.

Brodbeck, F.C., Frese, M., & Javidan, M., (2002), Leadership made in Germany: Low on compassion, high on performance, *Academy of Management Executive*, 16(1): 16–29.

Brown, J., (2000), Critical Reasoning, Understanding and Self-knowledge, *Philosophy and Phenomenal Research*, LXI(3): 659–676.

Brown, J.A.C., (1961), *Freud and the Post-Freudians*, Penguin Books, Harmondsworth, Middlesex.

Brown, S.R., (2001), Structural Phenomenology: A Top-Down Analytic Methodology, URL http://cogprints.ecs.org/1762/ last access 2016-09-03, 12:00.

Brown, T.L., (2003), *Making Truth: Metaphor in Science*, University of Illinois Press.

Brugha, C., (1998), The Structure of Qualitative Decision Making, *European Journal of Operational Research*, 104(1): 46–62.

Bucchi, M., (2002), *Science in Society: An Introduction to Social Studies of Science*, Routledge, London.

Buchanan, B.G., (2005), A (Very) Brief History of Artificial Intelligence, AI Magazine: 53–60. www.aaai.org/AITopics/assets/PDF/AIMag26-04-016.pdf.

Büchel, B., (2003), Managing Partner Relations in Joint Ventures, MIT Slone Management Review, July 15, http://sloanreview.mit.edu/article/managing-partner-relations-in-joint-ventures, accessed January 2015.

Buckner, R.B., (1983), *Surveying Measurements and Their Analysis*, Landmark Enterprises, Cordova, CA.

Budd, J.M., & Hill, H., (2007), The Cognitive and Social Lives of Paradigms in Information Science. In *Proceedings of the Annual Conference of the Canadian Association for Information Science*, Ed. Clement Arsenault and Kimiz Dalkir, 11, McGill University, Montreal, Quebec, www.cais-acsi.ca/proceedings/2007/budd_2007.pdf, accessed January 2009.

Burge, T., (1988), Individualism and Self-Knowledge, *Journal of Philosophy*, 85: 64963.

Burnes, B., Cooper, C., & West, P., (2003), Organizational Learning: The New Management Paradigm? *Management Decision*, 41(5): 452–464.

Burns, D., (2007), *Systematic Action Research: A Strategy for Whole System Change*, The Policy Press, Bristol, UK..

Burrell, G., & Morgan, G., (1979), *Sociological Paradigms and Organizational Analysis*, Heinemann, London.

Buss, D.M., (1996), Social Adaptation and Five Major Factors of Personality. In Wiggins, J.S., (Ed.), *The Five-Factor Model of Personality: Theoretical Perspectives* (pp. 180–207), Guilford, New York.

Butterfield, F., (1982), *China: Alive in the Bitter Sea*, Times Books, New York.

Bybee, R.W., & Sund, R.B., (1982), *Piaget for Educators* (2nd edn.), Charles E. Merrill Publishing Co., New York.

Calás, M.B. & Smircich, L., (1999), Past Postmodernism? Reflections and Tentative Directions, *Academy of Management Review*, 24(4): 649–671.

Cameron, K.S., Quinn, R.E., De Graff, J., & Thakor, A.V., (2006), *Competing Values Leadership: Creating Value in Organizations*, Edward Elgar Publishing, Cheltenham, UK.

Cantor, N., & Kihlstrom, J.F., (1987), *Personality and Social Intelligence*, Prentice-Hall, Englewood Cliffs, N.J.

Caploe, D., (2011), China 5-Year Plan: All Prosperity to the People !!!, Economy Watch, www.economywatch.com/economy-business-and-finance-news/china-5-year-plan-all-prosperity-to-the-people.06-04.html, accessed August 2015.

Caporael, L.R., (1997), Vehicles of Knowledge: Artifacts and Social Groups, *Evolution and Cognition*, 3(1): 39–43.

Carter, V., Dohrer, T., Duque, G., Fulton, T., & Shipley, C., (1997), *Critical Theory and Qualitative Research*, www.ed.psu.edu/ci/cs597/definition.html, accessed 2000.

Carver, C.S., (2005), Impulse and Constraint: Perspectives from Personality Psychology, Convergence with Theory in other Areas, and Potential for Integration, *Personal Social Psychology Review*, 9(4): 312–333.

Casti, J.L. (1989), *Paradigms Lost*, Abacus, London.

Cattell, R.B., (1945), The Description of Personality: Principles and Findings in a Factor Analysis. *American Journal of Psychology*, 58, 59–90.

(1971), *Abilities: Their Structure Growth and Action*, Houghton Mifflin, Boston.

Cattell, R. B., & Butcher, J., (1968), *The Prediction of Achievement and Creativity*, BobbsMerrill, Indianapolis, IN.

Cattell, R. B., Barton, K., & Dielman, T. E., (1972), Prediction of School Achievement from Motivation, Personality and Ability Measures, *Psychological Reports*, 30: 35–43.

Caves, R.E., (1980), Industrial Organization, Corporate Strategy, and Structure, *Journal of Economic Literature*, 18: 64–92.

Cecez-Kecmanovic, D., & Janson, M., (1999), Re-Thinking Habermas's Theory of Communicative Action in Information Systems. *Paper Posted to University of Missouri-St. Louis. Retrieved March, 30*, 2007.

Cervone, D., Mor, N., Orom, H., Shadel, W.G., & Scott, W.D., (2004), Self-Efficacy Beliefs and the Architecture of Personality. In Baumeister, R.F., & Vohs, K.D., (Eds), *Handbook of Self-Regulation: Research, Theory, and Applications* (pp. 188–210), Guilford Press, New York.

Cervone, D., Shadel, W.G., & Jencius, S., (2001), Social-Cognitive Theory of Personality Assessment, *Personality and Social Psychology Review*, 5(1): 33–51.

Chandler, A.D., (1962), *Strategy and Structure*, MIT Press, Cambridge, MA.

Chandler, D., (1997), *Semiotics for Beginners*, Gerd-Andreas Tiede, www.aber.ac.uk/media/Documents/S4B/the_book.html, accessed 2001. *Also published as Chandler*, 2001.

(2001), *Semiotics: The Basics*, Routledge Kegan Paul, London. Also see www.aber.ac.uk/media/Documents/S4B/semiotic.html, accessed June 2005.

Chapman, P., Evans, J., Crundall, D., & Underwood, G., (2000), Anger and Aggression in Driving and Non-Driving Contexts. In *Proceedings of the International Conference on Traffic and Transport Psychology*, Berne, Switzerland, 4–7 September.

Chari, V.V., Kehoe, P.J., & McGrattan, E.R., (2009), New Keynesian Models: Not Yet Useful for Policy Analysis, *American Economic Journal: Macroeconomics*, 1(1): 242–266.

Checkland, P.B., (1981), *Systems Thinking*, Systems Practice, Wiley, Chichester.

Checkland, P.B., & Scholes, J., (1990), *Soft Systems Methodology in Action*, John Wiley & Sons, Chichester.

Chen, X.P., Liu, D., & Portnoy, R., (2012), A Multilevel Investigation of Motivational Cultural Intelligence, Organizational Diversity Climate, and Cultural Sales: Evidence from US Real Estate Firms, *Journal of Applied Psychology*, 97(1): 93–106.

Chen, Z.X., & Francesco A.M., (2000), Employee Demography, Organizational Commitment and Turnover Intentions in China: Do Cultural Differences Matter? *Human Relations*, 53(6): 869–887.

Cheng, J., (2007), Critical Issues in International Management Research: An Agenda for Future Advancement, *European Journal of International Management*, 1(1/2): 23–38.

Child, J., (1972), Organizational Structure, Environment, and Performance: The Role of Strategic Choice, *Sociology*, 6: 1–22.

Child, J., Faulkner, D., & Pitkethly, R., (2001), *The Management of International Acquisitions*, Oxford University Press, Oxford.

Chilton, S., (1991), *Grounding Political Development*, Lynne Rienner Publishers, London.
Ching, L., & Yu, D. J., (2010), Turning the Tide: Informal Institutional Change in Water Reuse, *Water Policy*, 12(S1): 121–134.
Chomsky, N., (1975), *Reflections on Language*, Pantheon Books, New York.
Choo, C.W., (2002), *Information Management for the Intelligent Organization: The Art of Scanning the Environment*, Information Today, Inc., Medford Township, NJ.
Chopra, D., (1990), *Quantum Healing, Exploring the Frontiers of Mind/Body Medicine*. Bantam Books, New York.
  (1991), *Creating Health: How to Wake Up the Body's Intelligence*, Houghton Mifflin, Harcourt.
Christianson, S.A., (1992), Emotional Stress and Eyewitness Memory: A Critical Review, *Psychological Bulletin*, 112: 284–309.
Churchman, C.W., (1971), *The Design of Inquiring Systems*, Basic Books, New York.
  (1979), *The Systems Approach* (2nd edn). Dell, New York.
Churchman, C.W., Arnoff, E., & Ackoff, L.R., (1957), *Introduction to Operations Research*, Wiley, New York.
Clark, A., (2008), *Supersizing the Mind: Embodiment, Action, and Cognitive Extension*, Oxford University Press, New York.
Clark, A., & Chalmers, D., (1998), The Extended Mind, *Analysis*, 58(1): 7–19.
Clark, P., (2000), *Organizations in Action: Competition between Contexts*, Routledge, London.
Clark, P., & Staunton, N., (1989), *Innovation in Technology and Organization*, Routledge, London.
Claver, E., Llopis, J., Gascó, J.L., Molina, H., & Conca, F.J., (1999), Public Administration: From Bureaucratic Culture to Citizen-Oriented Culture, *International Journal of Public Sector Management*, 12(5): 455, 464.
Clegg, S., Barrett, M., Clark, T., Dwyer, L., Grey, J., Lemp, S., & Marceau, J., (1996), Management Knowledge for the Future: Innovation, Embrios, and New Paradigms. In Clegg, S., & Palmer, G., (Eds), *The Politics of Management Knowledge*, Sage, London.
Clegg, S., Hardy, C., Lawrence, T., & Nord, W., (2006), *The Sage Handbook of Organization Studies*, SAGE, London, UK, New York, USA, Thousand Oaks, California, USA, New Delhi, India.
Coats, A., (1969), Is There a "Structure of Scientific Revolutions" in Economics? *Kyklos*, 22(2): 289–296
Cobb, P., & Yackel, E., (1996), Constructivist, Emergent, and Sociocultural Perspectives in the Context of Developmental Research, *Educational Psychologist*, 31(3/4): 175–190.
Cocchiarella, N., (1991), Formal Ontology, Handbook of Metaphysics and Ontology. In Smith, B., & Burkhardt, H., (Eds), *Philosophia* (p. 640), Verlag, Munich.
Coghlan, (1993), In Defence of Process Consultation. In Mabey & Mayin-White (Eds), *Managing Change*, Paul Chapman Publishing Ltd, London.
Cohen, J., & Stewart, I., (1994), *The Collapse of Chaos: Discovering Simplicity in a Complex World*, Viking, London.
Cohen, M.S., Freeman, J.T., & Thompson, B.T., (1998), Critical Thinking Skills in Tactical Decision Making: A Model and a Training Method. In Canon-Bowers,

J., & Salas, E., (Eds), *Decision-Making under Stress: Implications for Training & Simulation*, American Psychological Association Publications, Washington, DC.

Cole, M.A., Elliott, R.J., & Zhang, J., (2009), Corruption, Governance and FDI Location in China: A Province-Level Analysis, *The Journal of Development Studies*, 45(9): 1494–1512.

Coleman, J.W., (1987), Toward an Integrated Theory of White-Collar Crime, *American Journal of Sociology*, 93: 406–439.

Collier, J., (2006), Conditions for Fully Autonomous Anticipation. In *Computing Anticipatory Systems, CASYS'05(AIP Conference Proceedings)* (Vol. 839, pp. 282–289). www.academia.edu/download/30868284/collier-Corrected-April-8-2006.pdf, accessed June 2014.

Commission of the European Communities, (2001), Promoting a European Framework for Corporate Social Responsibility, available at: http://europa.eu.int/eur-lex/en/comgpr/2001/ com2001_0366en01.pdf.

Connor, K., (1991), A Historical Comparison of Resource Based Theory of Five Schools of Thought within Industrial Organization Economics: Do We Have a New Theory of the Firm? *Journal of Management*, 17(1): 121–154.

Cooley, C.H., (1962), *Social Organization: A Study of the Larger Mind*, Charles Scribner's Sons, New York. Originally published in 1909.

Cornelisson, J.P., C. Oswick, L.T., Christensen, & Phillips, N., (2008), Metaphor in Organizational Research: Context, Modalities and Implications for Research Introduction, *Organizationa Studies*, 29(7): 7–22.

Costa, P.T., & McCrae, R.R., (1992), NEO PI-R. Professional Manual, FL: Psychological Assessment Resources, Inc., Odessa.

Costanza, R., Wainger, L., Folke, C., & Miler, K.G., (1993), Modeling Complex Ecological Economic Systems: Toward an Evolutionary, Dynamic Understanding of People and Nature, *BioScience*, 43(8): 545–555.

Coveney, J., (1998), The Government and Ethics of Health Promotion: The Importance of Michel Foucault, *Health Education Research Theory & Practice*, 13(3): 459–468, also see http://her.oxfordjournals.org/content/13/3/459.full.pdf, last access 2016-09-03, 12:18.

Crossley, N., (2002), Emotion and Communicative Action. In Bendelow, G., & Williams, J., (Eds), *Emotions in Social Life: Critical Themes and Contemporary Issues (chapter 2)* (pp. 17–36), Taylor & Francis, Abingdon, UK.

Crotty, J., & Epstein, G. (2008). *Proposals for Effectively Regulating the US Financial System to Avoid yet Another Meltdown* (No. 2008-15). Working Paper, University of Massachusetts, Department of Economics.

Crotty, M., (1998), *The Foundations of Social Research: Meaning and Perspective in the Research*, Sage, London.

Crouch, C., (2004), *Post-Democracy*, Polity Press, Cambridge.

Csányi, V., & Kampis, G., (1985), Autogenesis: The Evolution of Replicative Systems, *J. theor. Biol.*, 114: 303–323.

Cseh, M., & Short, D., (2001), The Facilitation of Learning in a Hungarian Organization: The Challenges of Training with Interpreters and Trainers. Proceedings of the 2nd Conference on HRD, Research and Practice across Europe, University of Twente, Eschede, Netherlands, 26–27 January 2001, 41–52.

Cullen, J. (1999), Socially Constructed Learning: A Commentary on the Concept of the Learning Organization, *The Learning Organization*, 6(1): 45–52.

Cummings, T.G., & Worley, C.G., (1993), *Organization Development and Change* (5th edn.), West Publishing Co, St Paul, Minneapolis, MN.

Cupchik, G., (2001), Constructivist Realism: An Ontology that Encompasses Positivist and Constructivist Approaches to the Social Sciences [33 paragraphs]. *Forum Qualitative Sozialforschung/Forum: Qualitative Social Research* [On-line Journal], 2(1). Available at: www.qualitative-research.net/fqs-texte/1-01/1-01cupchik-e.htm, accessed 2003.

Curiouscat, (2015), http://curiouscat.com/management/deming/management_by_target. Last accessed 18 May 2015 18:20.

Daft, R.L., (2008), *Organization Theory and Design*, 10th edition, South-Western Cengage Learning, Mason, OH, USA.

Dahl, S., (2000). *Communications and Culture Transformation: Cultural Diversity, Globalization and Cultural Convergence*, ECE, London. Also see Dahl, S (1998,2000): Communications and Culture Transformation: Cultural Diversity, Globalization and Cultural Convergence, London: ECE.4.

(2004), *Intercultural Research: The Current State of Knowledge*, Middlesex University Discussion Paper No. 26, Middlesex University Business School, London, UK. Also see http://papers.ssrn.com/sol3/papers.cfm?abstract_id= 658202, accessed November 2005.

Dalmau, T., & Dick, B., (1987), *Politics, Conflict and Culture: A Journey into Complexity*, Interchange, Chapel Hill, Qld. Also see www.uq.net.au/~zzbdick/ dlitt/DLitt_P23pcc.pdf.

Daly, M.C., & Valletta, R.G., (2008), Cross-National Trends in Earnings Inequality and Instability, *Economics Letters*, 99: 215–219.

Damasio, A., (2000), *The Feelings of What Happens*, Vintage, London.

Darvas, G., (1998), Laws of Symmetry Breaking, *Symmetry: Culture and Science*, 9: 2–4, 119–127. http://www.bu.edu/wcp/Papers/Scie/ScieDarv.htm, last access 2016-09-03.

Das, S., (2014), China's Shadow Banking System, April 16th, A Roubini Global Economics Project, accessed May 2015 at www.economonitor.com/blog/2014/04/ chinas-shadow-banking-system/.

Dauber, D., (2010), Study on Individual Value Preferences and Personality Traits, Unpublished work in process.

Dauber, D., Fink, G., & Yolles, M.I., (2010), A Generic Theory of Organizational Culture, Conference Paper Delivered to The Southern Management Association Annual Meeting, Auburn University, October.

(2012), A Configuration Model of Organizational Culture, SAGE Open 2012 2: Originally Published Online 22 March, http://sgo.sagepub.com/content/2/1/ 2158244012441482.

Davenport, B., Shuler, S., & Whiiten, P.A., (1997), Making Sense out of Creativity and Constraints. In Davenport Sypher, B.D., (Ed.), *Case Studies in Organizational Communication 2: Perspectives on Contemporary American Work Life* (pp. 11–31), Guilford Press, New York.

Davis, A.K., (1963), Lessons from Sorokin. In Tiryakian, E.A., *Sociological Theory, Values, and Socio-Cultural Change* (pp. 1–7), Free Press.

Davis, D.N.(2000), Agents, Emergence, Emotion and Representation, Emergent Behaviour of Complex Human-Machine Interaction (Session Chair), IEEE International Conference on Industrial Electronics, Control and Instrumentation (IECON2000), Nagoya, Japan, www2.dcs.hull.ac.uk/NEAT/dnd/papers/iecon.pdf.
  2000, Minds Have Personalities - Emotion is the Core, CiteSeer, accessed July 2010, http://citeseerx.ist.psu.edu/viewdoc/summary?doi=10.1.1.124.419.
Davis, J., Marciano. A., & Runde, J., (2004), *The Elgar Companion to Economics and Philosophy*, Edward Elgar Publishing Limited, UK.
De Bono, E., (1977), *The Happiness Purpose*, Penguin Books Ltd., Harmondsworth, ISBN: 0140220585.
De Oliveira, A.C.M, Croson, R.T.A., & Eckel, C., (2008), Are Preferences Stable Across Domains? An Experimental Investigation of Social Preferences in the Field, Center for Behavioural and Experimental Economic Science (CBEES) Working Paper #2008-3. www.aeaweb.org/annual_mtg_papers/2009/retrieve.php?.
De Rivera, J.H., (1977), *A Structural Theory of the Emotions*, International Universities Press, New York.
  (1992), Emotional Climate: Social Structure and Emotional Dynamics, *International Review of Studies on Emotion*, 2: 197–218.
De Rivera, J. H., & Grinkis, C., (1986), Emotions as Social Relationships, *Motivation and Emotion*, 10: 351–369.
Deal, T.E., & Kennedy, A.A, (1988), *Corporate Cultures - The Rites and Rituals of Corporate Life*, Penguin Books, London.
Dealtry, R., (2005), Achieving Integrated Performance Management with the Corporate University, *The Journal of Workplace Learning*, 16(1): 65–78.
Deci, E.L., & Ryan, R.M., (2009), Self-Determination Theory: A Consideration of Human Motivational Universals. In Corr, P.J., & Matthews, J., (Eds), *The Cambridge Handbook of Personality Psychology* (pp. 441–456).
Deetz, S., (1996), Describing Differences in Approaches to Organization Science: Rethinking Burrell and Morgan and Their Legacy, *Organization Science*, 7: 1991–2007.
Deflem, M., (1966), *Habermas, Modernity and Law*, Sage, London. Also see www.sla.purdue.edu/people/soc/mdeflem/zhablaw.htm, accessed December 2002.
Demetriou, A., Doise, W., & Van Lieshout, C.F.M., (1998), *Life-Span Developmental Psychology*, John Wiley & Sons, New York.
Deming, W.E., (1982), *Quality, Productivity, and Competitive Position*, Massachusetts Institute of Technology, Center for Advanced Engineering Study, Cambridge, MA.
  (1993), *The New Economics for Industry, Government, and Education*, MIT Press Boston, MA.
  (2000), *Out of the Crisis*. Cambridge, Mass.: MIT Press, Cambridge, MA. ISBN 0262541157.
Deng, S.H., (2011), Policy Fine-Tuning Helps China's Small Businesses through Tough Times, Business China Weekly, No. 19, 8th November, http://news.xinhuanet.com/english2010/indepth/2011-11/08/c_131235568.htm, accessed February 2014.
Denison, D.R., & Mishra, A.K., (1995), Towards a Theory of Organizational Culture and Effectiveness, *Organization Science*, 6(2): 204–223.

Depue, R., & Morrone-Strupinsky, J., (2005), A Neurobehavioural Model of Affiliative Bonding: Implications for Conceptualizing a Human Trait of Affiliation, *Behavioural and Brain Sciences*, 28: 313–395.

Dewey, J., (1937), *Democracy and Education: An Introduction to the Philosophy of Education*, Macmillan, New York.

(1938), *Experience and Education*, Macmillan, New York.

(1966), *Democracy and Education*, Free Press, New York.

Dikotter, F., (2010), *Mao's Great Famine: The History of China's Most Devastating Catastrophe, 1958-62*, Walker & Company, New York and London.

Dininio, P., & Orttung, R.W., (2004), (November), Explaining Patterns of Corruption in the Russian Region, Working Paper Number 727, William Davidson Institute, University of Michigan Business School, USA.

Dockens III, W.S., (2012), Private communication.

Dockens, W.S., (1999), Four Brand New Colors: Information Nullification in Psychology and the Humanities, www.ceptualinstitute.com/genre/dockens/newcolors.htm, accessed March 2012.

Dodd, C., (1995), *Dynamics of Intercultural Communication*, Brown & Benchmark Publishers, Dubuque, IA.

Dodge, H.R., & Robbins, J.E., (1992), An Empirical Investigation of the Organizational Life Cycle Model for Small Business Development and Survival, *Journal of Small Business Management*, 30(1): 27–37.

Dodgson, M., (1993), Organizational Learning: A Review of Some Literature, *Organization Studies*, 14(3): 375–394.

Dole, J. A., & Sinatra, G. M., (1998), Reconceptualizing Change in the Cognitive Construction of Knowledge, *Educational Psychologist*, 33 (2/3): 109–128.

Dolphin, T., & Nash, D., (2011), All Change: Will There Be a Revolution in Economic Thinking in the Next Few Years? Discussion Paper at the Institute for Public Policy Research, UK.

Domingo, P., (1998), Occam's Two Razors: The Sharp and the Blunt, *Proceedings of the Fourth International Conference on Knowledge Discovery and Data Mining* (pp. 37–43), AAI Press, New York, NY. Winner of the Best Paper Award for Fundamental Research, www.martinsewell.com/occam/Domi98.pdf.

Donelan, C., (2004), Teaching Film Theory in a Post-Film Era, *Academic Exchange Quarterly*, Spring, http://findarticles.com/p/articles/mi_hb3325/is_/ai_n29089786, accessed May 2006.

Donskis, L., (2015), From Person to Nonperson: Mapping Guilt, Adiaphora, and Austerity, *Deeds and Days*, (62): 109–125.

Doolittle, P.E., & Camp, W.G., (1999), Constructivism: The Career and Technical Education Perspective, *Journal of Vocational and Technical Education*, 16(2). Also, http://scholar.lib.vt.edu/ejournals/JVTE/v16n1/doolittle.html, accessed April 2000.

Dopfer, K., (2005), Evolutionary Economics: A Theoretical Framework, In Dopfer K., (Ed.), 2005, *The Evolutionary Foundation of Economics*, Cambridge University Press.

Dopfer, K., Foster, J., & Potts, J., (2004), Micro-Meso-Macro, *Journal of Evolutionary Economics* 14: 263–279.

Douglas, M., (1986), *How Institutions Think*, Syracuse University Press, Syracuse, NY.

Drazin, R., & Kazanjian, R.K., (1990), A Reanalysis of Miller and Friesen's Life Cycle Data, *Strategic Management Journal*, 11: 319–325.

Drazin, R., & Sandelands, L., (1992), Autogenesis: A Perspective on the Process of Organising, *Organization Science*, 3(2): 230–249.

Drucker, P. F., (1985), *Innovation and Entrepreneurship: Principles and Practice*, Heinemann, London.

Du, R., Ai, S., & Brugha, C.M., (2011), Integrating Taoist Yin-Yang Thinking with Western Nomology: A Moderating Model of Trust in Conflict Management, *Chinese Management Studies*, 5(1): 55–7.

Dubois, D., (2000), Review of Incursive Hyperincursive and Anticipatory Systems - Foundation of Anticipation in Electromagnetism, CASYS'99 - Third International Conference. Edited by Dubois, D.M. Published by The American Institute of Physics, AIP Conference Proceedings 517, pp. 3–30.

Dunbar, N., & Abra, G., (2008), Observations of Dyadic Power in Interpersonal Interaction, Paper presented at the annual meeting of the International Communication Association, TBA, Montreal, Quebec, Canada, May 22, www.allacademic.com/meta/p234228_index.html

Duncan, L.E., (2005), Personal Political Salience as a Self-Schema: Consequences for Political Information Processing, *Political Psychology*, 26(6): 965–976.

Duverger, M., (1972), *The Study of Politics*, Thomas Nelson and Son, London. Originally published in 1968 as *Sociologie Politique*, Presses Universitaires de France, Paris.

Earley, P.C, (2002). Redefining Interactions across Cultures and Organizations: Moving Forward with Cultural Intelligence, *Research in Organizational Behaviour*, 24: 271–299.

Earley, P.C., & Ang, S., (2003), *Cultural Intelligence: Individual Interactions across Cultures*, Stanford Business Books, Stanford, CA.

Earley, P.C., & Gibson, C.B., 1998, Taking Stock in Our Progress on Individualism-Collectivism: 100 Years of Solidarity and Community, *Journal of Management*, 24(3): 265–304.

Earley, P.C., & Mosakowski, E., (2004), Cultural Intelligence, *Harvard Business Review*, (10): 139–146.

Easton, D, (1951), The Decline of Modern Political Theory, *The Journal of Politics*, 13 (1, February): 36–58.

(1965), *A Systems Analysis of Political Life*, Wiley, New York.

Easton, D., Dennis, J., (1967), The Child's Acquisition of Regime Norms: Political Efficacy, *The American Political Science Review*, 61(1, March): 25–38.

Eckstein, H., (1988), A Culturalist Theory of Political Change, *The American Political Science Review*, 82(3, Sep): 789–804.

Eichacker, N., (2012), European Financial Deregulation, Liberalization, and the EMU: The Financial Underpinnings of the European Crisis, Economics Graduate Student Workshop, Dept. Economics, University of Massachusetts Amherst, 3–4 November 2012.

Eisenhardt, K.M., (2000), Paradox, Spirals, Ambivalence: The *New Language* of *Change* and *Plura*lism, *Academy of Management Review 2000*, 25(4), 703–705.

Elfenbein, H.A., (2007), Emotion in Organizations: A Review in Stages, *Annals of the Academy of Management*, 1: 315–386. See www.irle.berkeley.edu/workingpapers/144-07.pdf, accessed July 2011.

Elkind, D., (1976), *Child Development and Education: A Piagetian Perspective*, Oxford University Press, Oxford.

Ellis, L., & Smith, K. (2007), *The Global Upward Trend in the Profit Share*, BIS Working Papers 231, Bank for International Settlements.

Endler, N.S., & Summerfield, L.J., (1995), Intelligence, Personality, Psychopathology, and Adjustment. In Saklofske, D.H., & Zeidner, M., (Eds), *International Handbook of Personality and Intelligence* (pp. 249, 284), Plenum Press, NY.

Erçetin, S.S., (2000), Organizational Intelligence, *Educ. Admin. Theory Appl.*, 24: 509–526.

Espejo, R., (1993), Management of Complexity in Problem Solving. In Espejo, R., & Schwaninger, M., (Eds), *Organizational Fitness: Corporate Effectiveness through Management Cybernetics*, Campus/Verlag, Frankfurt/New York.

Espejo, R., & Harnden, R., (1989), *The Viable System Model: Interpretations and Applications of Stafford Beer's VSM*, Wiley, Chichester.

Espejo, R., Schuhmann, W., Schaniger, M., & Bielello, U., (1996), *Organizational Transformation and Learning*, Wiley, Chelmsford.

Espejo, R., & Schwaninger, M., (1993), *Organizational Fitness: Corporate Effectiveness through Management Cybernetics*, Campus Verlag, Frankfurt am Main.

EU, (2009), Economic Crisis in Europe: Causes, Consequences and Responses, *European Economy*, 7|2009, European Commission Directorate-General for Economic and Financial Affairs, Brussels.

Europa, (2007), Definition of Micro, Small and Medium-Sized Enterprises, http://europa.eu/legislation_summaries/enterprise/business_environment/n26026_en.htm, accessed February, 2014.

Evaristo, J.R., Scudder, R., Desouza, K.C., & Sato, O., (2004), A Dimensional Analysis of Geographically Distributed Project Teams: A Case Study, *Journal of Engineering and Technology Management*, 21(3): 175–189. See www.sciencedirect.com/science/article/pii/S0923474804000293, accessed February 2014.

Eysenck, H. J., (1957), *Sense and Nonsense in Psychology*, Penguin Books Ltd, Harmonsworth, Middlesex, UK.

(1991), Dimensions of Personality: 16, 5 or 3? – Criteria for a Taxonomic Paradigm, *Personality and Individual Differences*, 12: 773–790.

Factor, A., (2001), Eco-Economic Theory Building: Implications for Researching Small and Medium-Sized Enterprises, Report of the The Danish Environmental Management Survey (DEMS) project, working paper No. 7, April, http://research.asb.dk/fbspretrieve/531/0003089.pdf, accessed April 2010.

Faiola, A., & Mui, Y.Q., (2015), Greek Leaders Debt Deal Ignites Revolt at Home from Austerity Opponents, The Washington Post, July 13th, www.washingtonpost.com/world/greece-agrees-to-a-punishing-ultimatum-from-european-leaders/2015/07/13/4b6c2f2a-28f3-11e5-960f-22c4ba982ed4_story.html.

Fan, Y., (2002), A Classification of Chinese Culture, *Cross Cultural Management*, 7(2): 3–10.

Fedor, K.J., & Werther Jr., W.B., (1996), The Fourth Dimension: Creating Culturally Responsive International Alliances, *Organizational Dynamics*, (Autumn) 39–52.

Ferguson, C., (2010), Inside Job: How Bankers Caused the Financial Crisis, USA, Cert 12A, 108 mins, Documentary, narrator: Mat Damien, reviewed at: www.guardian.co.uk/film/2011/feb/17/inside-job-review, last access 2016-09-03, 11:44.

Fernández-Dols, J.M., Carrera, P., De Mendoza, A.H., & Oceja, L., (2007), Emotional Climate as Emotion Accessibility: How Countries Prime Emotions, *Journal of Social Issues*, 63(2): 339–352.

Feyerabend, P., (1975), *Against Method: Outline of an Anarchistic Theory of Knowledge*, New Left Books, London.

Fiegenbaum, A., & Thomas, H., (1995), Strategic Groups as Reference Groups: Theory, Modeling and Empirical Examination of Industry and Competitive Strategy, *Strategic Management Journal*, 16(7): 461–476.

Finance and Investment, (2012), (July 18), The End of Exorbitant CEO Exit Packages? Don't Hold Your Breath, Knowledge Wharton, http://knowledge.wharton.upenn .edu/article.cfm?articleid=3052, last access 2016-09-03, 11:45.

Fink, G., (2014), Type Building and Mappings in Organizational and Cultural Studies, *European Journal of Cross-Cultural Competence and Management*, 3(1): 95–96.

Fink, G., Dauber, D., & Yolles, M., (2012), Understanding Organizational Culture as a Trait Theory, *European Journal of International Management*, 6(2): 199–220.

Fink, G., Holden, N., & Lehmann, M., (2007), Survival by Subversion in Former Socialist Economies: Tacit Knowledge Exchange at the Workplace. In Oesterle, M.-J. (Hrsg.), *Internationales Management im Umbruch – Globalisierungsbedingte Einwirkungen auf Theorie und Praxis Internationaler Unternehmensführung*, Tagungsband der Kommission Internationales Management.

Fink, G., & Yolles, M.I., (2011), Understanding Normative Personality and Its Intelligences, International Association of Cross Cultural Competence and Management, Proceedings of IACCM Conference 2011, Ruse, Bulgaria, pp. 82–106, https://www.wu.ac.at/iaccm/conferences/2011-ruse-bulgaria/online-proceedings-2011/, last access 2016-09-03, 11:48.

(2012), Narratives, Paradigms and Change – the Issue of Relevance, *European Journal of Cross-Cultural Competence and Management*, 2(3/4): 191–208.

(2015), The Affective Agency: an Agency with Feelings and Emotions, Working paper of the Organizational Orientation, Coherence and Trajectory (OCT) Project, http://papers.ssrn.com/sol3/papers.cfm?abstract_id=2463283, last access 2016-09-03, 11:50.

(2015a), Collective Emotion Regulation in an Organization – A Plural Agency with Cognition and Affect, *Journal of Organizational Change*, 28(5): 832–871

Fischer, F., (1998), Policy Inquiry in Postpositivist Perspective, *Policy Studies Journal*, 26(1): 129–146.

Fischer, G., (2001, August). Communities of Interest: Learning through the Interaction of Multiple Knowledge Systems. In *Proceedings of the 24th IRIS Conference* (Vol. 2001). Department of Information Science, Bergen.

Fischer, K., (1992), *The Social and Cognitive Dynamics of Paradigmatic Change: A Scientometric Approach Science in Context*, Cambridge University Press.

Fitzgerald, S.P., (2000), Building Personal and Procedural Trust through Sino-American joint Ventures: The Transfer of Culturally Embedded Knowledge. Paper presented to the 7th International Conference on Advances in Management, Colorado Springs, USA July 2000.

Fivaz, R., (2000), Why Consciousness? A Causalogical Account? *Systems Research and Behavioural Science*, 17: 6.

Fleishman, E.A., Constanza, D.P., & Marshall-Mies J., (1999), *Abilities*, In: Peterson, N.G., Mumford, M.D., Borman, W.C., Jeanneret, R.P., & Fleishman, E.A., (Eds), *An Occupational Information System for the 21st Century: The Development of ONET*, American Psychological Association, Washington, DC.

Flood, R.L., & Romm, N., R.,A., (1996), *Critical Systems Thinking: Current Research and Practice*, Plenum, New York.

Floridi, L., (2003), *Ontology, Blackwell Guide to the Philosophy of Computing and Information*, (pp. 155–166) Blackwell, Oxford.

Flueckiger, F., (1995), *Contributions Towards a Unified Concept of Information*, Faculty of Science at the University of Berne, Swizerland. Also available at www.mypage.bluewin.ch/federico.flueckiger/Uci/Ctrb2uci/Preface/Preface.htm, accessed April 2003.

Fontaine, R., & Richardson,S., (2005), Cultural Values In Malaysia: Chinese, Malays and Indians Compared, *Cross Cultural Management*, 12(4): 63–77.

Forgues-Puccio, G.F., & Blackburn, K., (2009), Why Is Corruption Less Harmful in Some Countries than in Others? *Journal of Economic Behaviour & Organization*, 72: 797–810.

Foucault, M., (1972), *The Archaeology of Knowledge and the Discourse on Language*, Pantheon Books, NY Originally published in French, 1969.

(1974), Human Nature, in Elders F., (Ed.), *Reflexive Water: The Basic Concerns of Mankind*, Souvenir Press, London.

Frappaolo, C., (2008), Implicit Knowledge, *Knowledge Management Research and Practice*, 6: 23–25. www.knowledgeharvesting.com/documents/C%20Frappaolo%20-%20Implicit%20knowledge.pdf, last access 2016-09-03, 11:52.

Fraser-Mackenzie, P.A.F., & Dror, I.E., (2009), Selective Information Sampling: Cognitive Coherence in Evaluation of a Novel Item, *Judgment and Decision Making*, 4(4): 307–316.

Fredrickson, J.W., (1986), The Strategic Decision Process and Organizational Structure, *Academy of Management Review*, 11(2): 280–297.

Freeman, M.H., (2008), Reading Readers Reading a Poem: From Conceptual to Cognitive Integration, *Cognitive Semiotics*, 2(Spring): 102–128.

Freud, S., (1962), *Two Short Accounts of Psycho-Analysis*, Penguin Books, Harmondsworth, England, originally published in English in 1926 under the title *The Problem of Lay-Analyses*, Maerker-Branden, NY.

Frey, B.S., & Benz, M., (2004), From Imperialism to Inspiration: A Survey of Economics and Psychology. In Davis, J., Marciano. A., & Runde, J., (Eds), *The Elgar Companion to Economics and Philosophy*, Edward Elgar Publishing Limited, UK.

Frieden, B.R., & Hawkins, R.J., (2009), Asymmetric Information and Economics, *Physica A*, 389 (2010): 287–295.

Frieden, R., (1998), *Physics from Fisher Information: A Unification*, Cambridge University Press, Cambridge.

Friedman, M., (1968), The Role of Monetary Policy, *American Economic Review*, 58 (1): 1–17.

Fromm, E., (1961), *May Man Prevail? An Inquiry into the Facts and Fictions of Foreign Policy*. Doubleday, Garden City, NY FT, 2015, Greek Debt Crisis, Financial Times, 10 July, www.ft.com/indepth/greece-debt-crisis, accessed 10th July, 2015.

Fu, X., & Heffernan, S., (2009), The Effects of Reform on China's Bank Structure and Performance, *Journal of Banking & Finance*, 33: 39–52.

Fudjack, J., (1999), The Structure of Consciousness – Liminocentricity, Enantiodromia, and Personality, September issue of The Enneagram and the MBTI e-journal, see http://tap3x.net/EMBTI/j6structures.html, accessed June 2008.

Funder D., (1997), *The Personality Puzzle*, Norton, New York.

Funtowicz, S. O., & Ravetz, R., (1993), Science for the Post-Normal Age, *Futures*, 739–755. http://www.uu.nl/wetfilos/wetfil10/sprekers/Funtowicz_Ravetz_Futures_1993.pdf, last access 2016-09-03, 12:46.

Furlong, G., (2005), Knowledge Management and the Competitive Edge, Doctoral dissertation, University of Greenwich Business School, www.gre.ac.uk/schools/business/Dissertation/TOC.html, accessed February 2006.

Furnham, A., (1996), The Big Five versus the Big Four: The Relationship between the Myers-Briggs Type Indicator (MBTI) and NEO-PI Five Factor Model of Personality, *Personality and Individual Differences*, 21(2): 303–307.

Gabriel, S.J., (1998), Political Economy and the Great Leap Forward: Permanent Revolution and State Feudal Communes, China Essay Series, Essay Number 4, www.mtholyoke.edu/courses/sgabiel/economics/china-essays/4.html, accessed June 2015.

Gagan, J.M., (1998), *Journeying Where Shamanism and Psychology Meet*, Rio Chama Publications, PO Box 4276, Santa Fe, NM 87502.

Galavan, R., (2005), *Exploring the Belief Systems of Senior Managers: Antecedents of Managerial Direction*, Cranfield University School of Management, UK.

Galbraith, J., (2009), Who Are These Economists, Anyway? *The NEA Higher Education Journal*, Fall, 85–97. http://www.nea.org/assets/docs/HE/TA09EconomistGalbraith.pdf, last access 2016-09-03, 12:55.

Galbraith, J.R., & Nathanson, D.A., (1978). *Strategy Implementation: The Role of Structure and Process*, West, St. Paul.

Galbraith, P., (2004), Organizational Leadership and Chaos Theory: Let's Be Careful, *Journal of Educational Administration*, 42(1): 9–28.

Garcia, L., & Quek, F., (1997), Qualitative Research in Information Systems: Time to be Subjective. Presented at the IFIP WG8.2 Working Conference on 'Information Systems & Qualitative Research. 31 May-03 June 97, Philadelphia, USA. Proceeding available in book published by Chapman Hall.

Garcia, M.J., (2006), Social Movements: Between Resistance and Confrontation, between Private and Public, *POLLIS*, 2(1): 329–332.

Gardner, H., (1983), *Frames of Mind: The Theory of Multiple Intelligences*, Basic Books, New York.

(1991), Intelligence in Seven Steps. In Dickinson, D., (Ed.), *Creating the Future: Perspectives on Educational Change*, Accelerated Learning Systems Limited. http://education.jhu.edu/PD/newhorizons/future/creating_the_future/crfut_gardner.cfm, last access 2016-09-03, 13:02.

GDCT, (2015), Greek Debt Crisis Timeline, Wikipedia, https://en.wikipedia.org/wiki/Greek_government-debt_crisis_timeline, accessed July 2015.

Geels, F.W., (2011), Towards a neo(co)evolutionary theory of industry, civil society, polity and technology: Enriching evolutionary economics with insights from institutional theory, organization theory, economic sociology and strategic management, pre-published paper available from www.sussex.ac.uk/spru/documents/frank-geels-entire/doc, last access 2016-09-03, 13:05.

Gell-Mann, M., (1994), *The Quark and Jaguar*, Little, Brown and Company, London.

Gennaioli, N., Shleifer, A., & Vishny, R.W., (2013), A Model of Shadow Banking, *The Journal of Finance*, 68(4): 1331–1363.

Geringer, J.M., (1991), Strategic Determinants of Partner Selection Criteria in International Joint Ventures, *Journal of International Business*, 22(1): 41–62.

GGCT, (2015), Changing Minds, http://changingminds.org/explanations/culture/grid-group_culture.htm, accessed July 2015.

Giacalone R.A., & Thompson, K.R., (Eds) (2006), Ethics and Social Responsibility, *Special Issue of Academy of Management Learning & Education*, 5(3) 266–277.

Gibson, B., (2008), The Current Macroeconomic Crisis, Working Paper 2008-02, Dept. Economics, University of Massachusetts Amherst, www.umass.edu/economics/publications/2008-02.pdf, last access 2016-09-03, 13:07.

Gibson, H., (2000), In the Image of Leibniz's God: of Metanarratives and Congeries, Academic Forum 2000-01/Number 18, www.hsu.edu/interior2.aspx?id=6367, accessed April, 2012.

Giddens, A., (1984), *The Constitution of Society*, Polity Press, Cambridge, MA.

Giep, F., & Borgmann, M., (2001),*The Mental World of Brands*, ACR, Reading.

Giglioli, P.P., (1972), *Language and Social Context*, Penguin Books, Middlesex, UK.

Gilbert, J.A., & Kottke, J.L., (2009), Developing a Measure of Social Perceptiveness, Presented at the Annual Conference of the Association for Psychological Science, May 24, San Francisco, California.

Gill, J., & Butler, R., (1996), Cycles of Trust and Distrust in Joint-Ventures, *European Management Journal*, 14(1): 81–89.

Gindis, D., (2009), From Fictions and Aggregates to Real Entities in the Theory of the Firm, *Journal of Institutional Economics*, 5(1): 25–46.

Gioia, D.A., & Pitre, E., (1990), Multiparadigm Perspectives on Theory Building, *Academy of Management Review*, 15: 584–602.

Girod, S., & Bryane, M., (2003), Branding in European Retailing: A Corporate Social Responsibility Perspective, *European Retail Digest*, 38(2): 1–6.

Gittinger, J., (Ed.), (1992), *PAS Atlas*, MARS Assessment Technology Inc., Sterling, Virginia.

Gladstone, J., & Reynolds, T., (1999), The Role of EAP Group Work in Promoting Self-Reliant Employees, *Employee Assistance Quarterly*, 14(4 June): 53–63

Glaister, K.W., & Buckley, P., (1997), Task Related and Partner-Related Selection Criteria in UK International Joint Ventures, *British Journal of Management*, 8(3): 199–222.

Glanville, R., (2002), Second Order Cybernetics. *Encyclopaedia of Life Support Systems*. www.facstaff.bucknell.edu/jvt002/brainmind/Readings/SecondOrderCybernetics.pdf, last access 2016-09-03, 17:25.

(2004), The Purpose of Second-Order Cybernetics, *Kybernetes*, 33(9/10): 1379–1386.

Glasman, M., Rutherford, J., Stears, M., & White, S., (2011), The Labour Tradition and the Politics of Paradox, *The Oxford London seminars*, 2010–11, www.scribd.com/doc/55941677/Labour-Tradition-and-the-Politics-of-Paradox, last access 2016-09-03, 17:29.

Glassman, R.B., (1973), Persistence and Loose Coupling in Living Systems, *Behavioural Science*, 18(2, March): 83–98.

Gleick, J., (1968), *Chaos*, Sphere Books Ltd., London.

Glezos, M., (2012), Life and Debt: A Greek Tragedy, Reporter John Humphries, Panorama, 25th July, www.youtube.com/watch?v=Nu_cYB60xFY.

Gödel, K., (1931), *Kurt Godel: Collected Works*, Oxford University Press, Oxford.

Godkin, L., & Allcorn, S., (2009), Institutional Narcissism: Arrogant Organization Disorder and Interruptions in Organizational Learning, *The Learning Organization*, 16(1): 40, 57.

Goldberg, L.R., (1993), The Structure of Phenotypic Personality Traits, *American Psychologist*, 48, 26–34.

Goldkuhl, G., (2000), The Validity of Validity Claims: An Inquiry into Communication Rationality, Proceedings of the Fifth International Conference on Language-Action Persspectives on Communications Modelling (LAP 2000), Aachen, Germany. (Also see www-i5.informatik.rwth-aachen.de/conf/lap2000/paper171-191.pdf), last access 2016-09-03, 17:32.

Goldspink, C., & Kay, R., (2004), Bridging the Micro-Macro Divide: A New Basis for Social Science, *Human Relations*, 57(5): 597–618.

Gonçaloa, C., Burstein, F., & Lezana, A., (2002), Towards an Organizational Perspective to Promote Knowledge Strategy. *Proceedings* of the Australasian Conferences on Information Systems (ACIS), pp. 90–110, http://aisel.aisnet.org/acis2002/, last access 2016-09-03, 17:36.

Gonsowski, J.C., (1999), (27 April), The Myers-Briggs Type Indicator: Mapping to Circumplex and Five-Factor Models, The Enneagram and the MBTI Electronic Journal, Issue 8, tap3x.net/EMBTI/j8gonsowski.html, accessed May 2004.

Gonyea R.M., & Kuh G.D., (2009), NSSE organizational intelligence, and the institutional researcher. New Direction for Institutional Research No. 141.

Good, T.L., & Brophy, J.E., (1990), *Educational Psychology: A Realistic Approach* (4th edn.), Longman, White Plains, NY.

Goorha, P., (2000), Corruption: Theory and Evidence through Economies in Transition, *International Journal of Social Economics*, 27(12): 1180–1204.

Gordon, S.L., (1989), Institutional and Compulsive Orientations in Selectively Appropriating Emotions to Self. In Frans, David & McCarthy, E. Doyle (Eds), *Sociology of Emotions: Original Essays and Research Papers* (pp. 115–135), JAI Press, Greenwich, CT.

Gorton, G.B., (2010), *Slapped by the Invisible Hand: The Panic of 2007*, Oxford University Press, New York.

Goshal, S., (2005), Bad Management Theories Are Destroying Good Management Practices, *Academy of Management Learning & Education*, 4(1): 75–91.

Gottfredson, M.R., & Hirschi, T., (1990), *General Theory of Crime*, Stanford University Press, Stanford, CA.

Gouveia, V.V., & Ros, M., (2002), The Hofstede and Schwartz Models for Classifying Individualism at the Cultural Level: Their Relation to Macro-Social and

Macro-Economic Variables, www.cchla.ufpb.br/pospsi/autores/valdiney/the_hofstede_and_ schwartz_models.htm. Accessed June 2015.

Govan, G.V., (2005), *Breaking the Corporate Paradigm in the Military: Using a Military Innovative Approach to Enhance Enterprise Behaviour within the Services, Report of the Air Command and Staff College*, Maxwell Air Force Base, Alabama.

Grant, R.M., Almeida, P., & Song, J., (2000), Knowledge and the Multi-National Enterprise. In Millar, C.J.M., Grant, R.M., & Choi, C.J., (Eds), *International Business: Emerging Issues and Emerging Markets* (pp. 102–114), MacMillan Press Ltd, Basingstoke.

Gray, B., & Yan, A., (1997), Formation and Evolution of International Joint Ventures: Examples from U.S.-Chinese Partnerships. In Beamish, P.W., & Killing, J.P., (Eds), *Cooperative strategies: Asian Pacific perspectives* (pp. 57–88), The New Lexington Press, San Francisco.

Gray, J.B., Matear, M.S., & Matheson, K.P., (2000), Improving the Performance of Hospitality Firms, *International Journal of Contemporary Hospitality Management*, 12(3): 149–155.

Greiner, L., (1998), Evolution and Revolution as Organizations Grow, Harvard Business Review, May–June, https://hbr.org/1998/05/evolution-and-revolution-as-organizations-grow/ar/1, accessed May 2015.

Green, D., & Griffith, M., (2002), Globalization and Its Discontents, *International Affairs (Royal Institute of International Affairs 1944)*, 49–68.

Greenwood, R., Suddaby, R., & Hinings, C.R., (2002), Theorizing Change: The Role of Professional Associations in the Transformation of Institutionalized Fields, *Academy of Management Journal*, 45(1): 58–80.

Gregory, R., (1981), *Mind in Science*, Cambridge University Press.

Greiner, L.E., (1972), Evolution and Revolution as Organizations Grow, *Harvard Business Review*, 50 (July–August 1972): 37–46.

(1998), Evolution and Revolution as Organizations Grow, *Harvard Business Review*, May–June 1998

Issue. https://hbr.org/1998/05/evolution-and-revolution-as-organizations-grow/ar/1 (last accessed 25 May 2015, 09:40 a.m.).

Greve, H.R., Palmer, D., & Pozner, J., (2010), Organizations Gone Wild: The Causes, Processes, and Consequences of Organizational Misconduct, *The Academy of Management Annals*, 4(1): 53–107.

Gross, J.J., (2008), Emotion Regulation. In Lewis, M., Haviland-Jones, J.M., & Feldman Barrett, L., (Eds), *Handbook on Emotion* (pp. 479–512), The Guilford Press, New York & London.

Grossman, S., (1999), C.G. Jung and National Socialism. In Bishop, P., (Ed.), *Jung in Context: A Reader*, Routledge, London and New York.

Guariglia, A., & Poncet, S., (2007), Could Financial Distortions Be No Impediment to Economic Growth after All? Evidence from China Paper presented to CEA conference Nottingham April 2007.

Guastello, S.J., (1997), Science Evolves: An Introduction to Nonlinear Dynamics, Psychology, and Life Sciences, *Nonlinear Dynamics, Psychology, and Life Sciences*, 1(1): 1–6.

Guba, E.G., & Lincoln, Y.S., (1994), Competing Paradigms in Qualitative Research, In Denzin, N.K, & Lincoln, Y.S., (Eds), Handbook of Qualitative Research (pp. 105–117), Sage, Thousand Oaks.

Guillot, A., (2015), Greece Struggles to Address Its Tax Evasion Problem, *The Guardian*, 24th February, www.theguardian.com/world/2015/feb/24/greece-collecting-revenue-tax-evasion, accessed July 2015.

Guilford, J.P., (1977), *Way Beyond the IQ: Guide to Improving Intelligence and Creativity*, Creative Education Foundation, Buffalo, NY.

(1982), Cognitive Psychology's Ambiguities: Some Suggested Remedies, *Psychological Review*, 89: 48–59.

Guo, K.J., (2006), *Strategy for Organizational Change in State-Owned Commercial Banks in China: A Developing Organizational Development View*. Doctoral Thesis, Faculty of Business and Law, Liverpool John Moores University.

Guo, K., Yolles, M.I., & Iles, P., (2011), *Understanding Organizational Fitness: The Case of China*, Information Age Publishing, Charlotte, NC.

Gupta, A.K., & Govindarajan, V., (2000), Knowledge Flows within Multinational Companies, *Strategic Management Journal*, 21(4): 473–496.

Gustein, S., (2007), RDI Programme. In Smith, B., & Smith Myles, B., (Eds), *Autism Spectrum Disorders: A Handbook for Parents and Professionals* (pp. 289–298), Greenwood Publishing Group. Santa Barbara, California, USA

Haapasaari, P., Kulmala, S., & Kuikka, S., (2012), Growing into Interdisciplinarity: How to Converge Biology, Economics and Social Sciences in Fisheries Research, *Ecology and Society*, 17: 1, 6.

Habermas, J., (1970), Knowledge and Interest. In Emmet, D., & MacIntyre, A., (Eds), *Sociological Theory and Philosophical Analysis* (pp. 36–54), MacMillan, London.

(1971), *Knowledge and Human Interests*, Beacon Press, Boston.

(1979), *Communication and the Evolution of Society*, Heinemann, London.

(1984), *The Theory of Communicative Action*. Vol. 1, Polity Press, Cambridge, UK.

(1987), *The Theory of Communicative Action*. Vol. 2, Polity Press, Cambridge, UK.

Habito, R., (1999), *Healing Breath*, Orbis Books, Maryknoll, NY.

Haeckel, S.H., & Nolan, R.L., (1993), *Managing by Wire, Harvard Business Review*, 71(5, September–October): 122–132.

Haimes, G.A., (2006), *Organizational Culture and Identity: A Case Study from the Australian Football League*, A thesis submitted in total fulfilment of the requirements for the degree of Doctor of Philosophy, Victoria University, School of Human Movement, Recreation and Performance Faculty of Arts, Education and Human Development.

Hall, E.T., (1984), *The Dance of Life: The Other Dimension of Time*, Anchor, Garden City, NY.

Hall, P., (1993), Policy Paradigms, Social Learning, and the State: The Case of Economic Policymaking in Britain, *Comparative Politics*, 25(3): 275–296. Comparative Politics, Vol. 25, No. 3 (Apr., 1993), 275–296.

Hall, W., (1995), *Managing Cultures: Making Strategic Relationships Work*, John Wiley & Sons, New York.

Hämäläinen, R.P., & Saarinen, E., (Eds) (2007), *Systems Intelligence in Leadership and Everyday Life*, Systems Analysis Laboratory, Helsinki University of Technology, Espoo.

Hamel, G., (1991), Competition for Competence and Inter-Partner Learning within International Strategic Alliances, *Strategic Management Journal*, 12: 83–103.

Hamel, G., & Prahalad, C.K., (1989), Strategic Intent, *Harvard Business Review*, 67(3): 63.

Hameroff S.R., (1994), Quantum Coherence in Microtubules: A Neural Basis for Emergent Consciousness, *Journal of Consciousness Studies*, 1: 91–118.

Han, Zhao-Hong, & Kim, Ji Hyun, (2008), Corrective Recasts: What Teachers Might Want to Know, *Language Learning Journal*, 36(1): 35–44.

Hanks, S., (1990), An Empirical Examination of the Organizational Life Cycle in High Technology Firms. Doctoral dissertation, University of Utah.

Hannah, S.T., Balthazard, P., Waldman, D., & Jennings, P.L., (2010), The Neurological Basis for Leader Complexity, in Preparation for Journal of Applied Psychology (see early version at www.brainmappingforsuccess.com/resources/pdf/Basis-for-Complexity.pdf); and 2008, A Neuroscientific Analysis of Complexity Leadership, in proceedings of Academy of Management Conference, Anaheim, CA, August).

Hannah, S.T., Balthazard, P., Waldman, D., et al., (2008), A Neuroscientific Analysis of Complexity Leadership, Proceedings of Academy of Management Conference, August, Anaheim, CA.

Hansen, F., & Christensen, L.B., (2005), A New Paradigm in Communication, *Journal of Business Research*, 58(10): 1426–1436, www.cerog.org/lalondeCB/CB/2003_lalonde_seminar/201–228_pap_68-rev_hansen_christensen.pdf, accessed June 2011.

Hansen, M.H., & Svarverud, R., (2010), *iChina: The Rise of the Individual in Modern Chinese Society*, NIAS – Nordic Institute of Asian Studies, Copenhagen.

Harrigan, K.R., (1985), *Strategies for Joint Ventures*, Lexington Books, Lexington MA.

Harris, I.C., & Ruefli, T.W., (2000), The Strategy/Structure Debate: An Examination of the Performance Implications, *Journal of Management Studies*, 37(4): 587–604.

Harrison, Lawrence E., (2000), Introduction – Why Culture Matters. In Harrison, L.E., & Huntington, S.P. (Eds), *Culture Matters: How Values Shape Human Progress*, Basic Books, New York.

Harrison, M.I., (1994), *Diagnosing Organizations*. Applied Social Science Methods Series Vol. 8, Sage Publications, London.

Hartshorne, C., Weiss, P., & Burks, A.W., (1972), *Charles Sanders Peirce (1931–58): Collected Writings* (8 Vols.), Harvard University Press, Cambridge, MA.

Harvey, D., (2005), *A Brief History of Neoliberalism*, Oxford University Press, Oxford.

Harvey, O.J., (1966), *Experience, Structure and Adaptability*, Springer, New York.

Harvey, R.J., (1999), Item Response Theory, *The Counseling Psychologist*, 27(3): 353–383.

Haslam, N., & Baron, J., (1994), Intelligence, Personality and Prudence. In Sternberg, R.J., & Ruzgis, P., (Eds), *Personality and Intelligence* (pp. 32–58), Cambridge University Press, Cambridge.

Hatch, M.J., (1993), The Dynamics of Organizational Culture, *Academy of Management Review*, 18(4): 657–693.

(1997), *Organization Theory: Modern, Symbolic and Postmodern Perspectives*, Oxford University Press, Oxford.

Hatch, M.J., & Cunliffe, A.L., (2006), *Organization Theory*, Oxford University Press, Oxford, UK.

Hatfield, E., Cacioppo, J., & Rapson, R.L., (1994), *Emotional Contagion*, Cambridge University Press, New York.

Hatfield, E., & Rapson, R.L., (2004), Emotional Contagion: Religious and Ethnic Hatreds and Global Terrorism. In Tiedens, Larissa Z., & Leach, Colin Wayne (Eds), *The Social Life of Emotions* (pp. 129–143), Cambridge University Press, Cambridge, UK.

He, H.W., & Balmer, J.M.T., (2007), Identity Studies: Multiple Perspectives and Implications for Corporate-Level Marketing, *European Journal of Marketing*, 41 (7 and 8): 765–787.

Heath, R., (2001), *The Hidden Power of Advertising*, Admap Publications. London, UK

Heidegger, M., (1927), *Sein und Zeit*, and also published as Heidegger, M., Stanbaugh, J., *Sight and Time*, 1996, State University of New York Press.

(1962), *Being and Time*, trans. Macquarrie, J., & Robinson, E., Harper & Row, New York.

(1978), Die Lehre vom Urteil im Psychologismus (1913). In *Frühe Schriften*, Vittorio Klostermann, Frankfurt am Main (GA 1).

Heinström, J., (2003), Five Personality Dimensions and Their Influence on Information Behaviour, *Information Research*, 9(1) paper 165, see http://InformationR.net/ir/9-1/paper165.html, accessed May 2006.

Held, D., (1980), *Introduction to Critical Theory*, Hutchinson, London.

Held, D., McGrew, A., Goldblatt, D., & Perraton, J., (1999), *Global Transformations: Politics, Economics and Culture*, Polity Press, Cambridge, Also see www.polity.co.uk/global/globocp.htm, accessed May 2003.

Hemaspaandra, L.A., & Ogihara, M. (2002), *The Complexity Theory Companion*, Springer-Verlag, http://books.google.co.th/books?id=JCwIaB8Z-wAC, accessed January 2009.

Hentschel, U., & Sumbadze, N., (2002), Individual Differences in Mindscapes and Attitudes, *Social Behaviour and Personality*, 30(3): 213–222.

Herrmann-Pillath, C., (2009), Social Capital, Chinese Style: Individualism, Relational Collectivism and the Cultural Embeddedness of the Institutions-Performance Link, Working Paper Series no 132, Frankfurt School of finance and Management, http://d-nb.info/997649216/34.

Hessels, L. K., & van Lente, H., (2008), Re-Thinking New Knowledge Production: A Literature Review and a Research Agenda, *Research Policy*, 37: 740–760.

Heugens, P.P.M.A.R., & Lander, M.W., (2009), Structure! Agency! (and other Quarrels): A Meta-Analysis of Institutional Theories of Organization, *Academy of Management Journal*, 52(1): 61–85.

Heylighen, F., Heath, M., & Van Overwalle, F., (2012), *The Emergence of Distributed Cognition: A Conceptual Framework*, Proceedings of Collective Intentionality IV, Siena (Italy), to be published as a special issue of Cognitive Systems Research.

Higgins, T.E., (2000), Does Personality Provide Unique Explanations for Behaviour? *Personality as Cross-Person, Variability in General Principles European Journal of Personality*, 14: 391–406.

Hill, C.W.L., & Jones, G.R., (2001), *Strategic Management*, Houghton Mifflin, Boston, MA.

Hill, M., (2010), The Economic Crisis and Paradigm Change, available at www.socialpolicy.org.uk/lincoln/Hill.pdf. Accessed May 2015.

Hirschheim, R.A., (1992), Information Systems Epistemology: An Historical Perspective. In Galliers, R., (Ed.), *Information Systems Research* (pp. 28, 60), Blackwell, Oxford.

Hirschman, E.C., & Stern, B.B., (1999), The Roles of Emotion in Consumer Research, *Advances in Consumer Research*, 26: 4–11, www.cob.unt.edu/slides/Paswan/emotion.pdf, accessed May 2011.

Hirshleifer, D., & Teoh S.H., (2003), Herd Behaviour and Cascading in Capital Markets: A Review and Synthesis, *European Financial Management*, 9(1): 25–66.

Ho, M.W., and Fox, S.W., (1988), *Evolutionary Processes and Metaphors*, Wiley, London.

Hochstetler, A., & Copes, H., (2001), Organizational Culture and Organizational Crime. In Shover, Neal, & Wright, John Paul, (Eds), *Crimes of Privilege*, Oxford University Press, New York.

Hock, R.R., (2002), *Forty Studies that Changed Psychology: Explorations into the History of Psychological Research*, Prentice Hall, Upper Saddle River, NJ.

Hofbauer, J., & Sigmund, K., (2003), Evolutionary Game Dynamics, *Bulletin of the American Mathematical Society*, 40(4): 479–519. See http://homepage.univie.ac.at/josef.hofbaucr/03bams.pdf, last access 2016-09-03, 17:59.

Hofstede, G., (1980), *Culture's Consequences – International Differences in Work-Related Values*, Sage Publications, Newbury Park.

(1981), Culture and Organizations, *International Studies of Man and Organization*, 10(4): 15–41.

(1984), *Culture's Consequences: International Differences in Work-Related Values*, Sage.

(1987), The Cultural Relativity of Organizational Practices and Theories. In Dymsza, & Vamberly (Eds), *International Business Knowledge*, Routledge, London, New York, NY.

(1991), *Cultures and Organizations, Software of the Mind, Intercultural Cooperation and Its Importance for Survival*, McGraw Hill, New York.

(1994), Management Scientists Are Human, *Management Science*, 40(1): 4–13.

(2001), *Culture's Consequences: Comparing Values, Behaviours, Institutions and Organizations across Nations*, Sage, Thousand Oaks, CA.

(2002), Dimensions Do Not Exist: A Reply to Brendan Sweeney, *Human Relations*, 55(11): 1355–1361.

(2005), Dimensionalizing Cultures: The Hofstede Model in Context, www.ac.wwu.edu/~culture/introduction.htm, accessed January 2007.

Hofstede, G., Hofstede, G.J., & Minkov, M., (2010), *Cultures and Organizations: Software of the Mind* (3rd edn.), McGraw-Hill, New York, NY.

Hofstede, G.J., Pedersen, P., & Hofstede, G., (2002), *Exploring Culture, Exercise, Stories and Synthetic Cultures*, Intercultural Press, Yarmouth, Maine.

Hofstede, G., Neuijen, B., Ohayv, D.D., & Sanders, G., (1990), Measuring Organizational Cultures: A Qualitative and Quantitative Study across Twenty Cases, *Administrative Science Quarterly*, 35: 286–316.

Holbrook, M.B., & Hirschman, E.C., (1982), The Experiential Aspects of Consumption: Consumer Fantasies, Feelings, and Fun, *Journal of Consumer Research*, 9 (September): 132–140.

Holden, N.J., (2002), *Cross-Cultural Management: A Knowledge Management Perspective*, Financial Times/Prentice Hall, Harlow.

Holden, N.J., & von Kortzfleisch, H., (2004), Why Cross-Cultural Knowledge Transfer Is a Form of Translation in More Ways than You Think, *Knowledge and Process Management*, 11(2): 127–138.

Holden, P.J., & Cooper, C., (1994), Russian Managers as Learners: Implications for Theories of Management Learning, *Management Learning*, 25(4): 503–522.

Homburg, C., & Pflesser, C., (2000), A Multiple-Layer Model of Market-Oriented Organizational Culture: Measurement Issues and Performance Outcomes, *Journal of Marketing Research*, 37(4): 449–462.

Honneth, A., (1995), The Other of Justice: Habermas and the Ethical Challenge of Postmodernism. In White, S.K., (Ed.), *The Cambridge Companion to Habermas* (p. 3011), Cambridge University Press, Cambridge.

Hooijberg, R., & Choi, J., (2001), The Impact of Organizational Characteristics on Leadership Effectiveness Models: An Examination of Leadership in a Private and a Public Sector Organization, *Administration & Society*, 33(4): 403–431.

Hooper, F.H., Fitzgerald, J., & Papalia, D., (1971), Piagetian Theory and the Aging Process: Extensions and Speculations, *Aging and Human Development*, 2: 3–20.

House R., Javidan, M., Hanges, P., & Dorfman, P., (2002), Understanding Cultures and Implicit Leadership Theories Across the Globe: An Introduction to Project GLOBE *Journal of World Business*, 37:1,3.

Howard, N., (1999), *Confrontation Analysis: How to Win Operations other than War*, CCRP Publications, Washington. http://www.dodccrp.org/files/Howard_Confrontation.pdf, last access 2016-09-03, 18:05.

Huang, Y., (2003), *Selling China: Foreign Direct Investment During the Reform Era*, Cambridge University Press, New York.

Huchingson, J.E., (2001), *Pandemonium Tremendum: Chaos and Mystery in the Life of God*, The Pilgrim Press, Cleveland.

Hull, G.S., (2000), US MBA and Management Training Programs in Central and Eastern Europe, *Journal of Technology Transfer*, 25: 319–327.

Humphries, J., (2012), (25th June), Panorama, BBC1, www.youtube.com/watch?v=Nu_cYB60xFY, accessed July 2012.

Hunter, J.D., (2002), *Politics and Political Culture: The Critical Difference*, an essay available on www.nd.edu/~isla/ISLA/webpages/thearts/sikkink/, accessed June 2005.

Huntington, S.P., (1965), Political Development and Political Decay, *World Politics*, 17 (3, April): 386–430.

(1968). *No Easy Choice: Political Participation in Developing Countries*, Harvard University Press, Cambridge, MA.

(1968a), *Political Order in Changing Societies*, Yale University Press, New Haven, CT.

Huse, E., & Cummings, T., (1985), *Organization Development and Change*, West, St. Paul.

Husserl, E., (1950), *Ideen zu einer rseinen Phanomenolgie und phanomenologischen Philosophie*, Vol. 1, in *Husserliana*, Vol. 3. Also see Husserl, 1950-, XIX. 1911: *Philosophie als strenge Wissenschaft*, Logos, Vol. 1. English translation by Lauer, Q., 1965, *Husserl*, Harper and Row, New York.

Hutchings, K., & Weir, D., (2004), Networking in China and Arab Nations: Lessons for International Managers Presented at British Academy of Management Conference 2004.

Hutchins, E., (2010), Enculturating the Extended Mind, *Philosophical Studies*, 152(3): 437–446.

Huy, Q.N., (2001), Time, Temporal Capability and Planned Change, *Academy of Management Review*, 26(4): 601–623.

Hyldegård, J., (2009), Personality Traits and Group-Based Information Behaviour: An Exploratory Study, *Information Research*, 14(2) paper 402, http://www.informationr.net/ir/14-2/paper402.html, last access 2016-09-03, 18:10.

Iborra, M., & Saorin, C., (2001), Cultural Effects on Negotiation Process: The Interorganizational Situation. *Proceedings of the 16th Workshop on Strategic Human Resource Management*, EIASM brussels, 15–16 April, 2001, 1–21.

Iles, (2006), Culture and Transformational Change with China's Accession to the WTO: The Challenge for Action Research, *Journal of Technology Management in China*, 1(2): 147–158.

Iles, P., Feng, Y., & Hao, B., (2011), Re-Conceptualizing Distributed Leadership: Knowledge Management, Information Integration and the Leader-Task-Context Framework, BAM Conference Aston September 2011.

Iles, P., & Yolles, M., (2005), WTO Entry, Culture and Employment Relations in China: Action Research Approaches to HRD and Knowledge migration in Transforming SOEs, The 16th Annual Conference of the Chinese Economic Association (UK).

Inden, U., (2012), Effectiveness and Efficiency of Autopoietic Systems Improving Organizational Adaptiveness by Enriching and Augmenting Autopoietic Cycles, XIV International Conference: Problems of Management and Simulation in Complex Systems (PUMSS-2012), Samara (Russia) 19–22 June 2012, Russian Academy of Sciences.

Inglehart, Ronald, (1990), *Culture Shift in Advanced Industrial Society*, Princeton University Press, Princeton, NJ.

(1997), *Modernization and Postmodernization: Cultural, Economic, and Political Change in 43 Societies*, Princeton University Press, Princeton, NJ.

Inglehart, R., & Baker, W.E., (2000), Modernization, Cultural Change, and the Persistence of Traditional Values, *American Sociological Review*, 61(1): 19–51.

Inglehart, R., & Oyserman, D., (2004), Individualism, Autonomy, Self-Expression and Human Development. In Vinken, H., Soeters, J., & Ester, P., (Eds), *Comparing Cultures, Dimensions of Culture in a Comparative Perspective* (pp. 74–96), Brill, Leiden, The Netherlands.

Inkpen, A.C., & Tsang, E.W.K., (2005), Social Capital, Networks, and Knowledge Transfer, *Academy of management review*, 30(1): 146–165.

Ionescu, G., (1975), *Centripetal Politics*, Hart-Davis, MacGibbon, London.

Ionesco, M., (1989), Regional Cooperation for Research Collections, *Collection Building*, 9(2): 7–11.

Isen, A.M., (1987), Positive Affect, Cognitive Processes, and Social Behaviour, In Berkowitz, L., (Ed.), *Advances in Experimental Social Psychology* (Vol. 20, pp. 203–253), Academic Press, New York.

Izard, C.E., (1977), *Human Emotions*, Plenum, New York.

Jackson, M., (1991), *Systems Methodology for the Management Sciences*, Plenum Press, New York.
Jackson, M., & Keys, P. (1984). Towards a System of Systems Methodologies. *Journal of the Operational Research Society*, 35(6): 473–486.
  (1992), *Systems Methodologies for the Management Sciences*, Plenum, New York
  (2000), *Systems Approaches to Management*, Plenum Pub Corp; ISBN: 030646506X.
Jackson, T., (2001), Cultural Values and Management Ethics: A 10 Nation Study, Human Relations, 54(10): 1267–1302.
Jacobs, K., (2013), *The Ethics of Corporate Social Responsibility, Ethical Inquiry*, November, Brandeis University, www.brandeis.edu/ethics/ethicalinquiry/2013/November.html. December 2015.
James, K., Jarrett, M., & Lucas, D., (1996), Psychological Dynamics and Organizational Learning: From the Dysfunctional Organization to the Healthy Organization, *Canfield School of Management Working Papers Series*, ISBN 1 85905 086 7.
Janis, I.L., (1972), *Victims of Groupthink*, Houghton Mifflin, Boston.
Jankowicz, A.D., (1994), Holden and Cooper's 'Russian Managers as Learners': A Rejoinder, *Management Learning*, 25(4): 523–526.
  (1999) Towards a Meaningful HRD Function in the Post-Communist Economies of Central and Eastern Europe, *Proceedings of the Academy of Human Resource Development*, 318–326.
  (2000), From 'Learning Organization' to 'Adaptive Organization', *Management Learning*, 31(4): 471–490.
Jankowicz, A.D., & Pettit, S., (1993), Worlds in Collusion: An Analysis of an Eastern European Management Development initiative, *Management Education and Development*, 24(1): 93–104.
Jantsch, E., (1980), *The Self-Organising Universe: Scientific and Human Implications of the Emerging Paradigm of Evolution*, Pergamon Press, New York.
Jastrow, J., (1927), The Animus for Psychical Research. In Murchison, Carl (Ed.), *The Case for and Against Psychical Belief*, Clark University Press, Worcester, MA.
Jeffcutt, P., (2004), *The Foundations of Management Knowledge*, Routledge, London.
Jenkins, R., (2004), *Social Identity*, Routledge, NY, originally published in 1996.
Jenks, C., (2005), *Childhood*. London: Routledge.
Jennings, N.R., & Wooldridge, M., (1998), Applications of Intelligent Agents. In Jennings, N.R., & Wooldridge, M.J., (Eds), *Agent Technology Foundations, Applications, and Markets*, Springer-Verlag, New York, NY. Also see http://agents.umbc.edu/introduction/jennings98.pdf. December 2015.
Jessop, B., (1990), *State Theory*, Polity Press, Cambridge, UK.
Johannessen, J.A., Olaisen, J., & Olaisen, B., (2000), *Mismanagement of Tacit Knowledge: Knowledge Management, The Danger of Information Technology, and What to Do About it*. http://program.forskningsradet.no/skikt/johannessen.php3, accessed April 2002.
Johnson, G., & Scholes, K., (1999), *Exploring Corporate Strategy*, Prentice Hall, Harlow, England.
Joiner, B.L., (1994), *Fourth Generation Management: The New Business Consciousness*, McGraw-Hill.

Jokisch, R., (2001), Problems with Theory-Construction of Grand Theories; Niklas Luhmann's Theory of Social Systems, as An Example, Contained in SysteMexico, Special Edition: *The Autopoietic Turn: Luhmann's Reconceptualisation of the Social*, Tecnológico de Monterrey – Tec – Campus Ciudad de México: 16–23. Also see www2.tu-berlin.de/~society/Jokisch_SocialSystems_DistinctionsTheory.htm, accessed January 2009.

Jolton, J.A., & Geisert, T.L., 2009, Corporate Identity Crisis, *Kenexa*, available from www.kenexa.com/getattachment/80585796-3458-472c-b923-87b3d097c10a/Corporate-Identity-Crisis.aspx, accessed *Nob* 2011, accessed February 2012.

Jonas, S., (1996), Dangerous Liaisons: The US in Guatemala, *Foreign Policy*, Summer (103): 144–161.

Jones, P., Comfort, D., Hillier, D., & Eastwood, I., (2005), Corporate Social Responsibility: A Case Study of the UK's Leading Food Retailers, *British Food Journal*, 107(6): 423–435.

Joseph, H.W.R., (1946), (reprint of second edition 1916), *An Introduction to Logic*, Clarendon Press, Oxford.

Joslyn, C., (1992), Foundational Concepts of Metasystem Transition Theory. In Heylighen, F., Joslyn, C., & Turchin, V., (Eds), *Principia Cybernetica Web* (Principia Cybernetica, Brussels), URL: http://pespmc1.vub.ac.be/FOUNDCONC.html, accessed May 2003.

Jung, C. (1923). *Psychological Types*, New York: Harcourt Brace.

Jung, C.G., (1916), Psychoanalysis and Neurosis. In Read, H., Fordham, M., & Adler, G., (Eds), *The Collected Works of C.G. Jung*, Pantheon Books, New York.

(1923), *Psychological Types*, Harcourt Brace, New York.

(1936), *The Archetypes and the Collective Unconscious*, Collected Works, Vol. 9.i. (also see www.geocities.com/Athens/Acropolis/3976/Jung2.html). December 2015.

(1971), *Psychological Types* (H. G. Baynes, Trans., revision by R. F. C. Hull), The Collected Works of C. G. Jung (Vol. 6). Princeton University Press, Princeton, NJ. (Original work published 1921).

Kahn, B.E., & Isen, A.M., (1993), The Influence of Positive Affect on Variety Seeking among Safe, Enjoyable Products, *Journal of Consumer Research*, 20(September)(2): 257–270.

Kahn, W.A., (1998), Relational Systems at Work. In Staw, B.M., & Cummings, L.L., (Eds), *Research in Organizational Behaviour*, Vol. 20 (pp. 39–76), JAI Press, Greenwich, CT.

Kaplan, A., (1964), Chapter VII: Models. In Chandler, *The Conduct of Inquiry: Methodology for Behavioural Science* (pp. 258–291), San Francisco, CA, USA.

Kauffman, S.A., (1993), *The Origins of Order: Self-Organization and Selection in Evolution*, Oxford University Press, Oxford.

Kauffman, S.A., & Johnson, S., (1991), Coevolution to the Edge of Chaos: Coupled Fitness Landscapes, Poised States, and Coevolutionary Avalanches, *Journal of Theoretical Biology*, 149: 467–505.

(1993), *The Origins of Order: Self-Organization and Selection in Evolution*. Oxford University Press, Oxford.

Keen, P.G.W., & Scott Morton, M.S., (1978), *Decision Support Systems: An Organizational Perspective*, Addison-Wesley, Reading.

Kehoe, P.J., & Kehoe, T.J., (1994), A Primer on Static Applied General Equilibrium Models, *Federal Reserve Bank of Minneapolis Quarterly Review*, 18(1), 2–16.

Kelemen, M., & Lightfoot, G., (1999), Discourses of Entrepreneurship, Pricing and Control: The Case of Romania. Presented to the British Academy of Management, September 1999 (change in text).

Kelly, A., & Parker, N., (1997), *Management Directions: Joint Alliances*, Institute of Management Foundation, Corby, Northants NN17 1TT, UK.

Kemp, G., (1997), Cultural Implicit Conflict: A Re-Examination of Sorokin's Socio-Cultural Dynamics, *Journal of Conflict Processes*, 3(1): 15, 24.

Kepner, C.H., & Tregoe, B.B., (1965), *The Rational Decision Maker*, McGraw-Hill, New York.

Kets de Vries, M.F.R., (1991), *Organizations on the Couch: Clinical Perspectives on Organizational Behaviour and Change*, Jossey-Bass Inc (a Wiley publication), NY, USA.

Kihlstrom, J.F., & Cantor, N., (2000), Social Intelligence. In Sternberg, R.J., (Ed.), *Handbook of Intelligence* (2nd edn., pp. 359–379), Cambridge University Press, Cambridge, UK. Also see http://socrates.berkeley.edu/~kihlstrm/social_intelligence.htm, accessed November 2011.

Kincheloe, J.L., & Horn, R.A., (2008), *The Praeger Handbook of Education and Psychology: Volume 1*, Greenwood Publishing Group, Westport, CT, USA.

Kinley, D., Nolan, J., & Zerial, N., (2007), The Politics of Corporate Social Responsibility: Reflections on the United Nations Human Rights Norms for Corporations, *Company and Securities Law Journal*, 25(1): 30–42.

Kirsch, J.H.C., (1998), The Military of Guatemala and Niklas Luhmann's Theory of Autopoietic Social Systems. Master thesis in Political Science, Virginia Polytechnic Institute and State University, USA.

Klauss, R., (2000), Technology Transfer in Education – Application to Developing Countries, *Journal of Technology Transfer*, 25: 277–287.

Klimasinska, K., & Kopecki, D., (2012), (July 4), Bloomburg, Dimon Faces Image 'Nightmare' with Energy Probe at JPM, www.bloomberg.com/news/2012-07-03/jpmorgan-probed-over-potential-power-market-manipulation-1-.html.

Kluckhohn, C., (1962), Universal Categories of Culture. In Tax, S., (Ed.), *Anthropology Today: Selections* (pp. 304–20), University of Chicago Press, Chicago.

Kluckhohn, F., & Strodbeck, F., (1961), *Variations in Value Orientations, Evanston*, Ill., Row Peterson, Evanston, IL.

Kluver, J., Stoica, C., & Schimdt, J., (2003), Formal Models, Social Theory and Computer Simulations: Some Methodical Reflections, *Journal of Artificial Societies and Social Simulation*, 6(2). http://jasss.soc.surrey.ac.uk/6/2/8.html, accessed January 2009.

Kneer, Georg, & Nassehi, Armin, (1993), *Niklas Luhmanns Theorie sozialer Systeme: Eine Einführung (Niklas Luhmann's theory of social systems: an introduction)*, Fink, München.

Knowles, J.C., Pernia, E.M., & Racelis, M., (1999), Social Consequences of the Financial Crisis in Asia, Asian Development Bank, Economic Staff paper no. 60. https://openaccess.adb.org/bitstream/handle/11540/2484/esp060.pdf?sequence=1, accessed April 2016.

Koch, C., (2009), A "Complex" Theory of Consciousness, *Scientific American*, 1st July, www.scientificamerican.com/article/a-theory-of-consciousness/, accessed September 2015. Originally published at www.klab.caltech.edu/koch/CR/CR-Complexity-09.pdf.

Koegler, H.H., (1996), Critical Speech Act Theory or Semiotic Power? Habermas and the Wittgenstein tradition. *University of Illinois RK Urbana Champaign file name: 12-1-96.txt*.

Koestler, A., (1967), *The Ghost in the Machine*, Picador, London.

Kolb, D.A., (1974), *Organizational Psychology: An Experiential Approach*, Prentice-Hall, Englewood Cliffs, New Jersey.

Kolodner, J.L., (1993), *Case-Based Reasoning*, Morgan-Kaufmann Publishers, Inc, San Mateo, CA.

Koontz, H., & O'Donnall, C., (1968), *Principles of Management*, (4th edn.). McGraw-Hill, New York.

Koot, W., (2004), Hybridisation and Dis-Identification: Fatal Modernisation Strategies in Organizations In Jeffcutt, P., (Ed.), *The Foundations of Management Knowledge* (pp.188–207), Routledge, London.

Kosmitzki, C., & John, O.P., (1993), The Implicit Use of Explicit Conceptions of Social Intelligence, *Personality & Individual Differences*, 15: 11–23.

Kostera, M., (1995), The Modern Crusade: Missionaries of Management Come to Eastern Europe, *Management Learning*, 26(3): 331–352.

(2000), Reclaiming the Voice: A Reflection on Some Silenced Ones, *Human Resource Development International*, 3(1): 9–13.

Kostova, T., Roth, K., & Dacin, M.T., (2008), Understanding Radical Organizational Change: Bringing Together the Old and the New Institutionalism, *Academy of Management Review*, 33(4): 1022–1105.

(2009), Theorizing on MNCs: A Promise for Institutional Theory, *Academy of Management Review*, 34(1): 171–173.

Kotter, J.P., & Schlesinger, L.A., (1979), Choosing Strategies for Change, *Harvard Business Review*, 106–114.

Kroeber, A.L., & Kluckhohn, C., (1952), Culture: A Critical Review of Concepts and Definitions. *Papers. Peabody Museum of Archaeology & Ethnology, Harvard University*.

Krupat, E., (2006), Context Matters, But Let's Not Go Too Far, *Journal of General Internal Medicine*, 21(10): 1129–1130.

KSV 1870, (2013), *Insolvenzursachen 2013: Der Chef ist schuld!* www.ksv.at/insolvenzursachen-2013-der-chef-ist-schuld. KSV = Kreditschutzverband von 1870. Last accessed 21 June 2015, 16:10.

Kuhn, S.T., (1970), *The Structure of Scientific Revolutions*, University of Chicago Press, Chicago.

(1977), *The Essential Tension*, University of Chicago Press, Chicago.

Kumar, A., (2008), Housing for Low Income Families, *Space*, 13(2): 14–48.

Kuppens, P., Ceulemans, E., Timmerman, M.E., Diener, E., & Kim-Prieto, C., (2006), Universal Intracultural and Intercultural Dimensions of the Recalled Frequency of Emotional Experience, *Journal of Cross-Cultural Psychology*, 37(5): 491–515.

Ladrière, J., (2002), *Technical Universe in an Ontological Perspective, Society for Philosophy & Technology*, 4(1) http://scholar.lib.vt.edu/ejournals/SPT/v4n1/LADRIERE.html, accessed 2003.

Landemore, H., (2012), Democratic Reason: Politics, Collective Intelligence, and the Rule of the Many. In Landemore, H., & Elster, J., (Eds), *Collective Wisdom: Principle and Mechanisms*, Cambridge University Press, Cambridge.

Langley, A., (1999), Strategies for Theorizing from Process Data, *Academy of Management Review*, 24(4): 691–710.

Lasn, K., & Liacas, T., (2000), Birth of the Corporate "I", *Adbusters*, No. 31, Aug/Sept, www.nancho.net/corperson/adbcorpI.html, accessed May 2002.

Laurent, Eric, (2007), Three Enigmas: Meaning, Signification, Jouissance,in Vontz, V. (ed), The Lacan: An Introduction, Albany State University of New York of New York Press, pp. 116–127.

Lax, D.A., & Sebenius, J.K., (2006), *3D Negotiation: Powerful Tools to Change the Game in Your Most Important Deals*, Harvard Business School Press, Boston, MA.

Le Doux, J., (1998), *The Emotional Brain*, Simon & Schuster, Phoenix.

Lee, F.L.F., (2005), Collective Efficacy, Support for Democratization, and Political Participation in Hong Kong, International Journal of Public Opinion Research, Vol. 18 No. 3, http://ijpor.oxfordjournals.org/content/18/3/297.full, accessed January 2011.

Leijonhufvud, A., (2011), Nature of an economy, Policy Insight, Centre for Economic Policy Research, February 2011, No. 53.

Leman, P.J., (1998), Social Relations, Social Influence and the Development of Knowledge, British Psychological Society, Developmental Section Conference, Lancaster University, Lancaster, UK, September.

Lent A., (2009), A New Economic Paradigm, *Renewal*, 17(4), www.renewal.org.uk/articles/a-new-economic-paradigm/.

Leonard, A., (1996), Team Syntegrity: A New Methodology for Group Work, *European Management Journal*, 14(4): 407–413.

(1999), Consideration of Knowledge Management, *Journal of Knowledge Management Practice*, August, available at: www.tlainc.com/articl12.htm, accessed December 2007.

(1999a), A Viable System Model: Consideration of Knowledge Management, *Journal of Knowledge Management Practice*, August, www.tlainc.com/articl12.htm, accessed February 2006.

(2000), The Viable System Model and Knowledge Management, *Kybernetes*, 29(5/6): 710–715.

Lester, D.L., Parnell, J.A., & Carraher, S., (2003), Organizational Life Cycle: A Five-Stage Empirical Scale, *International Journal of Organizational Analysis*, 11(4): 339–354.

Leung, K., Bhagat, R.S., Buchan, N.R., Erez, M., & Gibson, C.B., (2005), Culture and International Business: Recent Advances and Their Implications for Future Research, *Journal of International Business Studies*, 36: 357–378.

Levin, C., & Coburn, T., (2011), Wall Street and The Financial Crisis: Anatomy of a Financial Collapse (Majority And Minority Staff Report), United States Senate Permanent Subcommittee on Investigations Committee on Homeland Security and Governmental Affairs, accessed November 2012 from www.ft.com/cms/fc7d55c8-661a-11e0-9d40-00144feab49a.pdf.

Levie, J., & Lichtenstein, B.B., (2008), From "Stages" of Business Growth to a Dynamic States Model of Entrepreneurial Growth and Change, Working paper,

University of Strathclyde Hunter Centre, available at: www.strath.ac.uk/media/departments/huntercentre/research/workingpapers/media_146530_en.pf, accessed November 2011.

Lewicki, P., Hill, T., & Czyzewska, M.,(1992), Nonconscious Acquisition of Information, *American Psychologist*, 47(6): 796–801.

Lewin, A.Y., (1999), Application of complexity theory to organizational science, *Organization Science*, 10(3): 215.

Lewis, J.W., & Litai, X., (2003), Social Change and Political Reform in China: Meeting the Challenge of Success, *The China Quarterly*, 176: 926–942.

Lewis, M.W., (2000), Exploring Paradox: Toward a More Comprehensive Guide, *Academy of Management Review 2000*, 25(11): 760–776.

Lewis, M.W., & Grimes, A.J., (1999), Metatriangulation: Building Theory from Multiple Paradigms, *The Academy of Management Review*, 24(4): 672–690.

Leydesdorff, L., & Dubois, D.M., (2004), Ancitication in Social Systems: The Incursion and Communication of Meaning, *International Journal of Anticipatory Systems*, 15: 203–216.

Li, C., (2013), Shadow Banking in China: Expanding Scale, Evolving Structure, Third Conference on Chinese Capital Markets, December 6th, New York University.

Li, J., Lam, K., & Fu, P.P., (2000), Family-Oriented Collectivism and Its Effects on Firm Performance: A Comparison between Overseas Chinese and Foreign Firms in China, *International Journal of Organizational Analysis*, 8(4): 364–379.

Li, J., & Shenkar, O., (1997), The Perspectives of Local Partners: Strategic Objectives and Structure Preferences of International Cooperative Ventures in China. In Beamish, P.W., & Killing, J.P., (Eds), *Cooperative Strategies: Asian Pacific Perspectives* (pp. 22–56), The New Lexington Press, San Francisco.

Li, P., (1998), Towards a Geocentric Framework of Organizational Form: A Holistic, Dynamic and Paradoxical Approach, *Organization Studies*, 19(5): 829–861.

Li, Q., Clark, B., & Winchester, I., (2010), Instructional Design and Technology Grounded in Enactivism: A Paradigm Shift? *British Journal of Educational Technology*, 41(3): 403–419.

Li, S., Triandis, H.C., & Yu, Y., (2006), Cultural Orientation and Corruption, *Ethics & Behaviour*, 16(3): 199–215.

Liang, S.Y., & WU, W.C., (2001), The Roots of Illness Part 1 – Jing, Qi, and Shen, Syl Wushi Newsletter, Vol.1, No. 4, www.shouyuliang.com/newsletter/v1n4/v1n4a1.shtml, accessed June 2005.

Lillard, A., (2002), Pretend Play and Cognitive Development. In Goswami, U., (Ed.), *Blackwell Handbook of Childhood Cognitive Development* (pp. 188–205).

Limerick, D., & Cunnington, B., (1993), *Managing the New Organization*, Business & Professional Publishing, Chatswood.

Lin, X.C., & Zhang, Y., (2009), Bank Ownership Reform and Bank Performance in China, *Journal of Banking & Finance*, 33(2009): 20–29.

Lindlof, T.R., & Taylor, B.C., (2002), *Qualitative Communication Research Methods*, Sage, London.

Lindsley, D.H., Brass, D.J., & Thomas, J.B., (1995), Efficacy-Performance Spirals: A Multilevel Perspective, *Academy of Management Review*, 213(3): 645–678.

Lipsey, R.G., (1963) (reprinted 1987), *An Introduction to Positive Economics*, Weidenfield and Nicolson, London.

Liu, M.T., Liu, C.H., Jing J., & Huang L.J., (2005), Internet Banking: Strategic Responses to the Accession of WTO by Chinese Banks, *Industrial Management and Data Systems*, 105(4): 429–442.

Liu, R., (2002), Competitiveness Analysis of Shareholding Commercial Banks, *Journal of Financial Research*, 8: 82–91.

Liu, S., (2003), Cultures within Culture: Unity and Diversity of Two Generations of Employees in State-Owned Enterprises, *Human Relations*, 564): 387–341.

Llewellyn, S., (2003), What Counts as Theory in Qualitative Management and Accounting Research? Introducing Five Levels of Theorizing, *Accounting, Auditing and Accountability Journal*, 16: 662–708.

Loomis, C.P., (1963), Social Change and Social Systems. In Tiryakian, E.A., *Sociological Theory, Values, and Sociocultural Change* (pp. 187–215), Free Press, New York.

Lowe, E.J., (2006), *A Survey of Metaphysics*, Oxford University Press, Oxford.

Lowe, S., & Oswick, C., (1996), Culture: The Invisible Filters. Ch. 6, 90–116. In Gatley, S., Lessem, R., & Altman, Y., (Eds), *Corporate Management: A Transcultural Odyssey* (Ch. 6, 90–116), McGraw-Hill, London.

Lucas C., (2002), A Logic of Complex Values. In Smarandache, F. (Ed.), Proceedings of the First International Conference on Neutrosophy, Neutrosophic Logic, Neutrosophic Set, Neutrosophic Probability and Statistics, pp. 121–138. Xiquan, Phoenix. (www.calresco.org/lucas/logic.htm), also see www.calresco.org/lucas/eiem.htm.

Lucas, R.E., Jr. (1976), Econometric Policy Evaluation: A Critique, *Carnegie-Rochester Conference Series on Public Policy*, 1: 19–46.

Luhmann, N., (1986), The Autopoiesis of Social Systems. In Hofstede, G., & Sami Kassem, M., (Eds), *Sociocybernetic Paradoxes*, Sage, London.

(1995), *Social Systems*, Stanford University Press, California. Translated from the German edition on 1984.

Lundberg, C., (1985), On the Feasibility of Cultural Interventions in Organizations. In Frost, P.J. et al.(Eds), *Organizational Culture*, Sage Publications, Beverley Hills.

Luo, S. (2009). How American Government Promotes Small Business: Lessons for China. *Dissertations, Theses and Capstone Projects*, 43. Also see http://digitalcommons.kennesaw.edu/cgi/viewcontent.cgi?article=1037&context=etd, accessed February, 2014.

Lyden, J.A., & Klengales, W.E., (2000), Supervising Organizational Health, *Supervision*, 61(12): 3–6.

Lye, J., (1996), Some Principles of Phenomenal Hermeneutics www.brocku.ca/english/courses/4F70/ph.html, accessed 2002.

MacFarquhar, R., & Schoenhals, M., (2006), *Debating the Cultural Revolution in Vhina*, Belknap Press of Harvard University Press, Cambridge, MA.

MacIsaac, D., (1996), The Critical Theory of Jurgan Habermas, www.physics.nau.edu/~danmac, accessed 2000.

Mahoney, J.T., & Pandian, J.R., (1992), The Resource-Based View within the Conversation of Strategic Management, *Strategic Management Journal*, 13: 363–380.

Majone, G., (1994), The Rise of the Regulatory State in Europe, *West European Politics*, 17(3): 77–101.
Malik, F., (2002), Introduction to Management Cybernetics, Cwarel Isaf Institute, www.kybernetik.ch/en/fs_intromankyb.html, accessed October 2015.
Mamadouh, V., (1999), Grid-Group Cultural Theory: An Introduction, *GeoJournal*, 47 (3): 395–409.
Mandelbrot, B., (1982), *The Fractile Geometry of Nature*, Freeman, New York.
Mánuel-Navarrete, D., (2001), *Approaches and Implications of Using Complexity Theory for dealing with Social Systems*, paper given at the Conservation and Sustainable Development – Comparative Perspectives workshop, held at the Yale Center for Comparative Research, Yale University, New Haven, USA, 30–31 August.
Markon, K.E., Krueger, R.F., & Watson, D., (2005), Delineating the Structure of Normal and Abnormal Personality: An Integrative Hierarchical Approach, *Journal of Personality and Social Psychology*, 88(1): 139–157.
Markus, H., & Nurius, P., (1986), Possible Selves, *American Psychologist*, 41(9): 954–969.
Marris, C., Langford, I. H., & O'Riordan, T., (1998), A Quantitative Test of the Cultural Theory of Risk Perceptions: Comparison with the Psychometric Paradigm, *Risk analysis*, 18(5): 635–647.
Mars, G., (2001), Introduction to Workplace Sabotage. In Mars, G., (Ed.), *Workplace Sabotage* (pp. 11–26), Aldershot, UK., Burlington, US.: Ashgate, Aldershot, UK., Burlington, US.
Marsden, S., (2012), Rupert Murdoch flies to UK to tackle News International crisis, 16th February, *The Independent*, UK, www.independent.co.uk/news/media/press/rupert-murdoch-flies-to-uk-to-tackle-news-international-crisis-6983510.html. June 2015.
Marshall, S.P., (1995), *Schemes in Problem Solving*, Cambridge University Press, Cambridge, UK.
Martin, J., (1992), *Cultures in Organizations: Three Perspectives*, Oxford University Press, New York.
Martínez de León, L.E., (1994), *La Democracia de las Armas, Gobiernos Civiles y Poder Militar*, Nueva Imagen Guatemala, Guatemala.
Maruyama, M., (1963), The Second Cybernetics: Deviation-Amplifying Mutual Causal Processes, *American Scientist*, 5(2): 164–179.
 (1965), Metaorganization of Information: Information in a Classificational Universe, Relational Universe, and Relevantial Universe, *Cybernetica*, 8(4): 224–236.
 (1972), Non-Classificational Information and Non-Informational Communication, *Dialectica*, 26(1): 51.
 (1974), Hierarchists, Individualists, and Mutualists: Three Paradigms among Planners, *Futures*, 6: 103–113.
 (1977), Heterogenics: An Epistemological Restructuring of Biological and Social Sciences, *Acta Biotheoretica*, 26: 120–136.
 (1980), Mindscapes and Science Theories, *Current Anthropology*, 21: 589–599.
 (1988), Dynamics among Business Practice, Aesthetics, Science, Politics and Religion, *Cultural Dynamics*, 1: 309–335. http://cdy.sagepub.com/cgi/content/abstract/1/3/309. June 2015.

(1993), Mindscapes, Individuals and Cultures in Management, *Journal of Management Inquiry*, 2(2): 140–154. June 2015.

(2001), Individual Types: Subcultural or Transcultural, *The General Psychologist*, 36 (3): 64–67.

(2002), Individual Heterogeneity, Human Resources and Management Policy, *Metamorphosis*, 1(2): 155–183.

(2008), Poly-Ocular Vision: Individual Cognitive Types and their Implication in Human Resources Management, *Indian Journal of Management Technology*, 1(2): 79–94.

Massey, C., Lewis, K., Warriner, V., Harris, C., Tweed, D., Cheyene, J., & Cameron, A., (2006), Exploring Firm Development in the Context of New Zealand SMEs, *Small Enterprise Research: The Journal of SEAANZ*, 14(1): 1–13.

Maturana, H.R., (1975), The Organization of the Living: A Theory of the Living Organization, *International Journal of Man-Machine Studies*, 7: 313–332.

(1988), Reality: The Search for Objectivity or the Quest for a Compelling Argument, *Irish Journal of Psychology*, 9: 25–82.

Maturana, H.R. Maturana, H., (1996), Metadesign, *Instituto de erapia ognitiva*, Publicaciones, www.inteco.cl/articulos/006/doc_ing4.htm, accessed 2000.

Maturana, H., & Varela, F.J., (1979), *Autopoiesis and Cognition*, Boston Studies in the Philosophy of Science, Boston.

(1980) (1st edition 1973), Autopoiesis and Cognition: The Realization of the Living. In Cohen, Robert S., & Wartofsky, Marx W., (Eds), *Boston Studies in the Philosophy of Science* (p. 42), D. Reidel Publishing Co., Dordecht.

Mazhar, F., (2011), Emotional Competence, Boddunan, June 11, www.boddunan.com/miscellaneous/51-general-reference/17879-emotional-competence.html, accessed July 2011.

Mazlish,B., (1987), *The Tree of Knowledge*, Shambhala, London.

(1990), *The Leader, the Led, and the Psyche: Essays in Psychohistory*, University Press of New England, Hanover, NH.

McAdam, P., (2004), Corruption: A Non-Parametric Analysis, *Journal of Economic Studies*, 31(6): 509–523.

McAdams, D.P., (1996), Personality, Modernity, and the Storied Self: A Contemporary Framework for Studying Persons, *Psychological Inquiry*, 7: 295–321.

(2001), The Psychology of Life Stories, *Review of General Psychology*, 5(2): 100–122.

McAuley, J., Duberley, J., & Johnson, P., (2007), *Organization Theory: Challenges and Perspectives*, Prentice-Hall, Harlow, UK.

McCann, J.E., (1991), Patterns of Growth, Competitive Technology, and Financial Strategies in Young Ventures, *Journal of Business Venturing*, 6: 189–208.

McCarthy, J., (1995), Making robots conscious of their mental states. In AAAI Spring ymposium on Representing Mental States and Mechanisms. AAAI. www-formal.stanford.edu/jmc/consciousness.html. June 2015.

McCrae. R.R., & Allik, J., (2002), *The Five-Factor Model of Personality across Cultures*, Kluwer Academic Publishers, New York.

McCrae, R.R., & Costa, P.T., (1996), Toward a New Generation of Personality Theories: Theoretical Contexts for the Five-Factor Model. In Wiggins, J.S., (Ed.), *The Five-Factor Model Of Personality: Theoretical Perspectives* (pp. 51–87), Guilford, New York.

McGraw, K.L., & Harbison-Briggs, K., (1989), *Knowledge Acquisition: Principles and Guidelines*, Prentice-Hall International, London, UK.

McKenna, M.K., Shelton, C.D., & Darling, J.R., (2002), The Impact of Behavioural Style Assessment on Organizational Effectiveness: A Call for Action, *Leadership & Organization Development Journal*, 23(6): 314–322.

McMahon, R.G.P., (2001), Deriving an Empirical Development Taxonomy for Manufacturing SMEs using Data from Australia's Business Longitudinal Survey, *Small Business Economics*, 17(2001): 197–212.

McSweeney, B., (2001), The Essentials of Scholarship: A Reply to Geert Hofstede, *Human Relations*, 55(11): 1363–1372.

(2002), Hofstede's Model Of National Cultural Differences and Their Consequences: a Triumph of Faith – a Failure of Analysis, *Human Relations*, 55(1): 89–118.

McWilliams, A., Siegel, D.S., & Wright, P.M., (2006), Corporate Social Responsibility: Strategic Implications, *Journal of Management Studies*, 43(1): 1–18.

Mead, G.H., (1934), *Mind, Self and Society from the Standpoint of a Social Behaviourist*, Ed. Morris, C.W., University of Chicago Press, Chicago.

Mead, R., (1994), *International Management: Cross-Cultural Dimensions*, Blackwell, Oxford.

Meehl, P.E., (1997), The Problem is Epistemology, Not Statistics: Replace Significance Tests by Confidence Intervals and Quantify Accuracy of Risky Numeral Predictions. In Harlow, L.L., Mulaik, S.A., & Steiger, J.H., (Eds), *What If There Were No Significance Tests?Mahwah, NJ: Lawrence Erlbaum Associates* (pp. 393–425).

Mehrabian, A., & Russell, J.A., (1974), *An Approach to Environmental Psychology*, MIT Press, Cambridge, MA.

Menary, R., (2009), Intentionality Cognitive Integration and the Continuity Thesis, *Topoi*, 28: 31–43.

Merton, R.K., (1942), The Normative Structure of Science. In: Merton, R.K., (Ed.), *The Sociology of Science: Theoretical and Empirical Investigations*, University of Chicago Press, Chicago.

Meyer, A.D., Tsui, A.S., & Hinings, C.R., (1993), Configurational Approaches to Organizational Analysis, *Academy of Management Journal*, 36: 1175–1195.

Meyer, R., (2003), *Systems, Sustainability and Design*, 6th Asian Design International Conference, 14–18 October, Tsukuba International Congress Centre, University of Tsukuba, Japan, accessible at www.idemployee.id.tue.nl/g.w.m.rauterberg/conferences/CD_doNotO pen/ADC/final_paper/348.pdf. April 2015.

Midgley, G., (1991), Pluralism and the Legitimation of Systems Science, *Systems Practice*, 5(2): 147, 172.

(1995), Mixing Methods: Developing Systemic Intervention. Research Memorandum no. 9, Centre for Systems, University of Hull.

(2000), *Systemic Intervention: Philosophy, Methodology, and Practice*, Kluwer Academic/Plenum Publishers, NY.

(2004), Personal communication.

Midgley, G., Munlo, I., & Brown, M., (1998), The Theory and Practice of Boundary Critique: Developing Housing Services for Older People, *Journal of Operational Research Society*, 49(5): 467–478.

Migdadi, M.M., (2005), An integrative view and empirical examination of the relationships among knowledge management enablers, processes, and organizational performance in Australian enterprises, PhD thesis, School of Economics and Information Systems, University of Wollongong, Australia.

Miller, A., (2002), Realism, *The Stanford Encyclopedia of Philosophy*, Zalta, Edward N., (Ed.), http://plato.stanford.edu/archives/win2002/entries/realism/, accessed 2002.

Miller, D., & Friesen, P.H., (1984), A Longitudinal Study of the Corporate Life Cycle, *Management Science*, 30(10, October): 1161–1183.

Miller, G.A., Galanter, E., & Pribram, K.H., (1960), *Plans and the Structure of Behaviour*, Holt, Rinehart & Winston New York.

Miller, J.G., (1995), *Living Systems*, University of Colorado Press, US.

Miller, N.E., & Dollard, J., (1941), *Social Learning and Imitation*, Yale University Press, New Haven.

Minai, A.T., (1995), Emergence, a Domain Where the Distinction between Conception in Arts and Sciences is Meaningless, *Cybernetics & Human Knowing*, 3(3): 25–51.

Minder, R., (2012), Spain's Banking Crisis Moves into the Courtroom, New York Times, July 4, www.nytimes.com/2012/07/05/business/global/spains-banking-crisis-moves-into-the-courtroom.html?pagewanted=all, accessed May 2013.

Mingers, J., (1995), *Self-Producing Systems*, Plenum Press, New York and London.
(2001), Combining IS Research Methods: Towards a Pluralist Methodology, *Information Systems Research*, 12(3), September 2001.

Mingers, J., & Gill, A., (1997), *Multimethodology*, Wiley, Chichester.

Minkov, M., (2011), *Cultural Differences in a Globalizing World*, Emerald, Bingley, UK.
(2013), *Cross-cultural Analysis; The Science and Art of Comparing the World's Modern Societies and Their Cultures*, with contributions by Geert Hofstede, Sage, Thousand Oaks, CA.

Minkov, M., & Blagoev, V., (2014), Cultural Maps of the World, *European Journal of Cross-Cultural Competence and Management*, 3(1): 4–17.

Minkov, M., & Hofstede, G., (2011), The Evolution of Hofstede's Doctrine, *Cross Cultural Management: An International Journal*, 18(1): 10–20.

Mintzberg, H., (2007), *How Productivity Killed American Enterprise*, mimeo, www.henrymintzberg.com/pdf/productivity2008.pdf download (23 February 2009).

Mischel, W., (1968), *Personality and Assessment*, Wiley, New York.

Mitchell, G.D., (1968), *A Dictionary of Sociology*, Routledge & Kegan Paul.

Mitsuhashi, H., & Greve, H.R., (2009), A Matching Theory of Alliance Formation and Organizational Success: Complementarity and Compatibility, *Academy of Management Journal*, 52(5): 975–995.

Modell, S., (2007), *Mixing Qualitative and Quantitative Methods in Management Accounting Research: A Critical Realist Approach*, Social Science Research Network, http://papers.ssrn.com/sol3/papers.cfm?abstract_id=997194, accessed January 2009.

Montangero, J., & Maurice-Naville, D., (1997), *Piaget, or the Advance of Knowledge: An Overview and Glossary*, Lawrence Erlbaum Associates, Mahwah, NJ.

Montinola, G., Qian, Y., & Weingast, B.R., (1996), Federalism, Chinese Style: The Political Basis for Economic Success, *World Politics*, 48(1): 50–81.

Morgan, G., (1986), *Images of Organization*, Sage, California.
Morgan, S.D., & Hunt, R.M., (1994), The Commitment-Trust Theory of Relationship Marketing, *Journal of Marketing*, 58(3): 20–38.
Mowen, J.C., (1999), *The 3M Model of Motivation and Personality: Theory and Empirical Applications to Consumer Behaviour*, Springer.
Mroczek, D.K., & Little, T.D., (2006), *Handbook of Personality Development*, Lawrence Erlbaum Associates.
  (2006), Theory and Research in Personality Development at the Beginning of the 21st Century. In Mroczek, D.K., & Little, T.D., (Eds), *Handbook of personality development* (pp. 3–8), Lawrence Erlbaum Associates, Mahwah, NJ, USA.
Müller, H.J., Malsch, T.H., & Schulz-Schaeffer, I., (1998), Socionics: Introduction and Potential, *Journal of Artificial Societies and Social Simulation*, 1(3). Retrieved from: www.soc.surrey.ac.uk/JASSS/1/3/5.html, 2006.
Muralidharan, R., & Hamilton, R.D., (1999), Restructuring International Joint Ventures, *International Journal of Organizational Analysis*, 7(4): 307–332.
Murphy, K.M., Shleifer, A., & Wishny, R.W., (1993), Why Is Rent-Seeking So Costly to Growth? *American Economic Review*, 83, Papers and Proceedings: 409–414.
Murtagh, M.J., (2008), A Funny Thing Happened on the Way to the Journal: A Commentary on Foucault's Ethics and Stuart Murray's "Care of the Self", *Philosophy, Ethics and Humanities in Medicine*, www.peh-med.com/content/3/1/2, accessed April 2008.
Mwaura,G., Sutton, J., & Roberts, D., (1998), Corporate and National Culture – an Irreconcilable Dilemma for the Hospitality Manager? *International Journal of Contemporary Hospitality Management*, 10(6): 212–220.
Myers Briggs, I., (2000), *An Introduction to Types: A Guide to Understanding Your Results on the Myers-Briggs Types Indicator*, CPP, Palo Alto, CA. Revised from the 1998 edition.
Myers, I.B., & McCaulley, M.H., (1985), *MBTI Manual: A Guide to the Development and Use of the Myers-Briggs Type Indicator*, Consulting Psychologists Press, Palo Alto, CA.
Myers, I.B., McCaulley, M.H., Quenk, N.L., & Hammer, A.L., (1998), *A Guide to the Development and Use of the Myers-Briggs Type Indicator* (3rd edn.), Consulting Psychologist Press, Palo Alto, CA.
Myers, M.D., (1999), Qualitative Research in Information Systems, www.auckland.ac.nz /msis/isworld/index.html, accessed 2001.
Myers-Briggs Foundation, (2001), The Auxiliary Function, www.myersbriggs.org/my-mbti-personality-type/understanding-mbti-type-dynamics/the-auxiliary-function.asp.pen/ADC/final_paper/348.pdf. June 2015.
Nadler, D.A., (1993), Concepts for the Management of Organizational Change. In Mayon-White, B., (Ed.), *Planning and Managing Change*, Harper & Row, London.
Nadler, D.A., & Tushman, M., (1977), *Feedback and Organizations Development: Using Data Based on Methods*, Addison-Wesley, Reading, Massachusetts.
  (1979), A Congruence Model for Diagnosing Organizational Behaviour. In Kolb, D., Rubin, I., & McIntyre, J., (Eds), *Organizational Psychology: A Book of Readings* (3rd edn.), Prentice-Hall, Englewood Cliffs, NJ.

Napier, N., (2005), Knowledge Transfer in Vietnam: Starts, Stops, and Loops, *Journal of Managerial Psychology*, 20(7): 621–636.
Nash, J., (1996), *Essays on Game Theory*, Edward Elgar Publishing Ltd, Cheltenham, UK.
Nash, R., (2005), Cognitive Habitus and Collective Intelligence: Concepts for the Explanation of Inequality of Educational Opportunity, *Journal of Education Policy*, 20(1): 3–21.
Nelson, R.R., (2004), Economic Development from the Perspective of Evolutionary Economic Theory, SLPTMD Working Paper Series, No. 001, Department of International Development, University of Oxford., given as the Presidential Lecture, Schumpeter Society, December 7.
  (2005), Where Are We Now on an Evolutionary Theory of Economic Growth, and Where Should we be Going? Center on Capitalism and Society The Earth Institute at Columbia University, www.earth.columbia.edu/ccs, Working Paper No. 3, February.
Nelson, R.R., & Winter, S.G., (1982), *An Evolutionary Theory of Economic Change*, Harvard University Press, Cambridge, MA.
Nersisyan, Y., & Wray, L.R., (2010), The Global Financial Crisis and the Shift to Shadow Banking, Working Paper no. 587, Levy Economics Institute of Bard College, Annendale-Hudson, NY.
Newell, P., (2005), Citizenship, Accountability and Community: The Limits of the CSR Agenda, *International affairs*, 81(3): 541–557.
Newell, S., (1999), The Transfer of Management Knowledge to China: Building Learning Communities Rather Than Translating Western Textbooks? *Education and Training*, 41(6/7): 286–293.
Nicolis, G., & Prigogine, I., (1989), *Exploring Complexity: An Introduction*, W.H. Freeman and Co., New York.
Nobre, F.S., (2003), Perspectives on Organizational Systems: Towards a Unified Theory. *Doctoral Consortium on Cognitive Science at the ICCM 2003*. Bamberg-Germany, April.
Nonaka, I., & Takeuchi, H., (1995), *The Knowledge-Creating Company: How Japanese Companies Create the Dynamics of Innovation*, Oxford University Press, New York.
Novak, J.G., (1993), (March), How Do We Learn Our Lesson? *The Science Teacher*, 60: 50–55.
Nowak, A., Vallacher, R.R., Tesser, A., & Borkowski, W., (2000), Society of Self: The Emergence of Collective Properties in Self-Structure, *American Psychological Review*, 107(1): 39–61.
Nowak, M., (2006), *Evolutionary Dynamics*, Harvard University Press, Cambridge, MA.
Nozick, R., (1977), On Austrian Methodology, *Synthèse*, 36: 353–392.
Nunn, C.H.M.H., (1994), Collapse of a Quantum Field May Affect Brain Function, *Journal of Consciousness Studies*, 1: 128, or for summary see www.abrupt.org/LOGOS/consc.html, accessed 2004.
Oakley, T., (2004), Elements of Attention: A New Approach to Meaning, *Construction in the Human Sciences*, www.mind-consciousness-language.com/articles%20oakley1.htm, accessed January 2009.

Ochsner, K.N., (2000), Are Affective Events Richly Recollected or Simply Familiar? The Experience and Process of Recognizing Feelings Past, *Journal of Experimental Psychology. General*, 129: 242–261.

O'Conner, B.P., & Dyce, J.A., (2001), Rigid and Extreme: A Geometric Representation of Personality Disorders in Five Factor Model Space, *Journal of Personality and Social Psychology*, 81: 1119–1130.

Oesterle, M.-J., & Laudien, S., (2007), The Future of International Business Research and the Relevance Gap: A German Perspective, *European Journal of International Management*, 1(1/2): 39–55.

O'Farrell, P.N., & Hitchens, D.M.W.N., (1988), Alternative Theories of Small Firm Growth: A Critical Review, *Environment and Planning A*, 20(10): 1365–1383.

Olins, W., (1978), *The Corporate Personality: An Inquiry into the Nature of Corporate Identity*, Design Council, London, UK.

Orszag, P., (2012) (May 23), History Shows U.S. Can Stimulate Now, Cut Later, Bloomburg Buiness Week, www.bloomberg.com/news/2012-05-22/history-shows-u-s-can-stimulate-now-cut-later.html. May 2015.

Osborn, A., (1934), *Edmund Husserl and His Logical Investigations*, International Press, New York.

Ovum Report, (1994), *Intelligent Agents: The New Revolution in Software*.

Oyserman, D., Coon, H.M., & Kemmelmeier, M., (2002), Rethinking Individualism and Collectivism: Evaluation of Theoretical Assumptions and Meta-Analyses, *Psychological Bulletin*, 128(1): 3–72.

Ozcelik, H., Langton, N., & Aldrich, H., (2008), Doing Well and Doing Good: The Relationship between Leadership Practices that Facilitate a Positive Emotional Climate and Organizational Performance, *Journal of Managerial Psychology*, 23 (2): 186–203.

Pabst, A., (2012), The National, Arab Emirates, July 18th, www.thenational.ae/ thenationalconversation/comment/rot-of-corruption-in-banking-industry-poisons-investors#ixzz2F44Xj2LG, accessed December 2012.

Paecht-Horowitz, M., (1973), The Origin of Life, *Angewandte Chemie*, 12(5): 349–438.

Paillard, J. (2000), The Neurobiological Roots of Rational Thinking. In Cruse, H., Dean, J., & Ritter, H., (Eds), *Prerational Intelligence: Adaptive Behaviour and Intelligent Systems without Symbols and Logic*, Kluwer, Dordrecht.

Pajares, F., (1999a), Moral Disengagement in the Perpetration of Inhumanities, *Personality & Social Psychology Review*, 3(3): 193–209.

(2005), Guide for Constructing Self-Efficacy Scales. In Pajares, F., & Urdan, T., (Eds), *Self-Efficacy Beliefs of Adolescents* (pp. 1–43), Information Age Publishing, Greenwich, CT.

(2006), Toward a Psychology of Human Agency, *Association for Psychological Science*, 1(2): 164–80.

(2007), Impeding Ecological Sustainability through Selective Moral Disengagement, *International Journal of Innovation and Sustainable Development*, 2(1): 8–35.

(2008), The Reconstruction of 'free will' from the Agentic Perspective of Socialcognitive Theory. In Baer, J., C. Kaufman, J.C., & Baumeister, R.R., (Eds), *Are We Free? Psychology and Free Will* (pp. 86–127), Oxford University Press, Oxford.

Papadakis, S., (2007), Technological convergence: Opportunities and Challenges, www.itu.int/osg/spu/youngminds/2007/essays/PapadakisSteliosYM2007.pdf, accessed September 2015.

Paris, C., Hall Johnston, J., & Reeves, D., (1998), *A Theoretical Framework and Measurement Strategy for Training Team Tactical Decision Making*. Available at: www.dodccrp.org/proceedings/DOCS/wed00000/wed000e6.htm, accessed April 2002.

Park, Hye-Jung, (2005), The Relationship between Teacher-Perceived Children's Play Styles and Their Pretend Play Behaviours, PhD of the Graduate School. University of Texas at Austin.

Parker, M., & McHugh, G., (1991), Five Texts in Search of an Author: A Response to John Hassard's 'Multiple Paradigms and Organizational Analysis', *Organization Studies*, 12: 451–456.

Parliamentary Commission, (2012), Banking Standards, Parliamentary Commission on Banking Standards: A joint Committee of the House of Commons and the House of Lords (December), UK, www.parliament.uk/documents/joint-committees/ Banking_Standards/Written%20Evidence%2019%20December%202012.pdf, accessed January 2013. London, UK.

Parsons, T., (1937), *Structure of Social Action*, McGraw Hill.

(1950), *The Social System*, Free Press, Glencoe. London, UK.

Parsons, T., & Bales R.F., (1956), *Family, Socialization, and Interaction Process*, Routledge & Kegan, London.

Parsons, T., & Platt, G.M., (1973), *The American University*, Harvard University Press, Cambridge, MA.

Pascale, R.T., (1999), Surfing the Edge of Chaos, *Sloan Management Review*, 83–94.

Pateman, Carol, (1980), The Civic Culture: A Philosophic Critique. In Almond, G.A., & Verba, S., (Eds), *The Civic Culture Revisited: An Analytic Study*, Little, Brown, Boston.

Paul Pasquier, P., Rahwan, I., Dignum, F., & Sonenberg, L., (2006), Agumentation and Persuasion in the Cognitive Coherence Theory. In Dunne, P.E., & Bench-Capon, T.J.M., (Eds), *Frontiers in Artificial Intelligence and Applications*, Vol. 144, Proceedings of a Conference on Computational Models of Argument – COMMA.

Peirce, C.S., (1931–58), *Collected Papers Vol. I–VIII* (Eds), Hartshorne & Weiss, Harvard University Press, Cambridge, MA.

Perényi, Á., Selvarajah, C., & Muthaly, S., (2011), Investigating the Applicability of the Firm Life-Cycle Model to SMEs in the Hungarian ICT Sector, Conference on Emerging Forms of Entrepreneurship and Innovation, held at the Small Business Advancement National Center, Sweden, accessed from http://sbaer.uca.edu/ index.php/research-archive/icsb/2011-2/, accessed November 2011.

Perez, C., (2002), *Technological Revolutions and Financial Capital*, Edward Elgar, Cheltenham.

(2004), Technological Revolutions, Paradigm Shifts and Socio-Institutional Change. In Reinert, E., (Ed.), *Globalization, Economic Development and Inequality*, Edward Elgar, Cheltenham.

(2005), Respecialisation and the Deployment of the ICT Paradigm, paper for the IPTS FISTERA Project, available at www.carlotaperez.org.

(2009a), After Crisis: Creative Construction, available at www.opendemocracy.net.
(2009b), The Double Bubble at the Turn of the Century: Technological Roots and Structural Implications, *Cambridge Journal of Economics*, 33(4): 779–805.

Peters, T., (1987), *Thriving on Chaos: Handbook for a Management Revolution*, Macmillan, London.

Pettigrew, A., Massini, S., & Numagami, T., (2000), Innovative Forms of Organizing in Europe and Japan, *European Management Journal*, 18(3): 259–273.

Pfeffer, J., & Salancik, G.R., (1978), *The External Control of Organizations: A Resource Dependence Perspective*, Harper and Row, New York, NY.

Phelps, E.S., (Ed.), (1970), *Microeconomic Foundations of Employment and Inflation Theory*, Norton and Co., New York.

Phelps, R., Adams, R., & Bessant, J., (2007), Life Cycles of Growing Organizations: A Review with Implications for Knowledge and Learning, *International Journal of Management Reviews*, 9(1): 1–30.

Phillips, A.W., (1958), The Relationship between Unemployment and the Rate of Change of Money Wages in the United Kingdom 1861–1957, *Economica*, 25 (100): 283–299.

Phillips, N., & Tracey, P., (2009), Institutional Theory and the MNC, *Academy of Management Review*, 34: 169–173.

Phillips, N., Lawrence, T.B., & Hardy, C., (2004), Discourse and Institutions, *Academy of Management Review*, 29(4): 635–652.

Piaget, J., (1950), *The Psychology of Intelligence*, Harcourt and Brace, New York.
(1963), *The Psychology of Intelligence*, Routledge, New York. Republished in 2001.
(1972), *The Principles of Genetic Epistemology*, Routledge & Kegan Paul, London.
(1977), *The Development of Thought: Equilibration of Cognitive Structures*, Viking, New York.

Piaget, J., & Inhelder, B., (1969), *The Psychology of the Child*, Basic Books, New York.

Pickering, A., (1987), Forms of Life: Science, Contingency and Harry Collins, *The British Journal for the History of Science*, 20(2): 213–221.

Piquero, N.L., (2002), Low Self-Control, Organizational Theory, and Corporate Crime, *Law Society Review*, January 1.

Pittenger, D.J., (1993), Measuring the MBTI...and Coming Up Short, *Journal of Career Planning and Employment*, 54(1): 48–52.

Podpiera, R., (2006), Progress in China's Banking Sector Reform: Has Banking Behaviour Changed? IMF Working Paper No. 06/71.

Polanyi, M., (1962), *Personal Knowledge*, Routledge & Kegan Paul, London.
(1997), Tacit Knowledge. Chapter 7 in Prusak, Laurence, (Ed.), *Knowledge in Organizations*, Butterworth-Heinemann, Boston.

Poole, M.S., & Van de Ven, A.H., (1989), Using Paradox to Build Management and Organization Theories, *Academy of Management Review*, 14: 562–578.

Porter, M., (1980), *Competitive Strategy*, Free Press, New York.
(1985), *Competitive Advantage*, Free Press, New York.

Postmes, T., & Spears, R., (1998), Deindividuation and Anti-Normative Behaviour: A Meta Analysis. Summary of: Deindividuation and Anti-Normative Behaviour,

Psychological Bulletin, 123: 238–259. Also see www.cooperationcommons.com/node/350.

Potas, N., Erçetin, S.S., & Koçak, S., (2010), Multi Dimensional Organizational Intelligence Measurements for Determining the Institutional and Managerial Capacity of Girls' Technical Education Institution (Diyarbakir, Sanliurfa and Konya/Turkey), *African Journal of Business Management*, 4(8): 1644–1651.

Praetorius, N., (2000), *Principle of Cognition, Language and Action: Essays on the Foundations of a Science of Psychology*, Kluwer Academic Press, Dordrecht/Boston/New York.

Priddy, R., (1999), *The Human Whole*, http://home.no.net/rrpriddy/P/11percept.html, accessed, January 2003.

Priem, R.L., & Butler, J.E., (2001), Is the Resource-Based 'View' a Useful Perspective for Strategic Management Research? *Academy of Management Review*, 26(1): 22–40.

Prigogine, I., (1989), The Philosophy of Instability, *Futures*, August: 396–400.

Prigogine, I., & Stengers, I., (1984), *Order Out of Chaos: Man's New Dialogue with Nature*, Flamingo, London.

Pritchard, W., (1993), What's New in Organization Development, Contained in Mayon-White, B., (Ed.), *Planning and Managing Change*, Harper & Row, London.

Privatisation International, (1998), Thailand to raise US$13 bn through privatization, www.faqs.org, accessed April 2010.

Pye, L., (1992), *Chinese Commercial Negotiating Style*, Quorum Books, New York, NY.

Qu, W., & Leung, P., (2006), Cultural Impact on Chinese Corporate Disclosure: A Corporate Governance Perspective, *Managerial Auditing Journal*, 21(3): 241–264.

Quinn, R.E., & Cameron, K., (1983), Organizational Life Cycles and Shifting Criteria of Effectiveness: Some Preliminary Evidence, *Management Science*, 29 (1983): 33–51; and Larry E. Greiner, "Evolution and Revolution as Organizations Grow," Harvard Business Review 50 (July–August 1972): 37–46.

Rabinow, P., (1984), *The Foucault Reader: An Introduction to Foucault's Thought*, Pantheon Books, NY.

Raffa, M., Zollo, G., & Caponi, R., (1996), The Development Process of Small Firms, *Entrepreneurship & Regional Development*, 8: 359–371.

Rauterberg, G.W.M., (2000), How to Characterize a Research Line for User-System Interaction, *IPO Annual Progress Report*, 35: 66.

Rautakivi, T., (2014), The Role and Effects of Efficacy in Socio-Economic Development and Foreign Direct Investment: A Comparative Study of South Korea and Singapore, *Journal of Organizational Transformation and Social Change*, 11(3): 230–245.

Ravetz, J.R., (1999), What Is Post-Normal Science, *Futures*, 31(7): 647–653.

Redding, G., (1998), The Changing Business Scene in Pacific Asia. In McDonald, F., & Thorpe, R., (Eds), *Organizational Strategy and Technological Adaptation to Global Change* (pp. 22–36), Macmillan Business, Basingstoke.

Redding, P., (2002), Georg Wilhelm Friedrich Hegel, *The Stanford Encyclopaedia of Philosophy*, Zalta, Edward N., (Ed.), http://plato.stanford.edu/archives/sum2002/entries/hegel/ accessed 2003.

Ren, D., (2016), Corruption Found across China's Financial Industry, *South China Morning Post*, 4 June, www.scmp.com/news/china/policies-politics/article/190972/corruption-found-across-chinas-financial-industry.html, accessed June 2016.

Rensch, B., (1972), *Homo Sapiens; From Man to Demigod*, Methuen & Co, London.

Reuters, (2013), INSIGHT-How Colombian drug traffickers used HSBC to launder money, January 1, www.reuters.com/article/2013/01/01/hsbc-idUSL1E8NU0L820130101.

Reuer, J.J., Klijn, E. Frans, Van Den Bosch, A.J., & Volberda, H.W., (2011), Bringing Corporate Governance to International Joint Ventures, *Global Strategy Journal*, 1: 54–66 (2011).

Rhodes, W.R., (2012), *Banker to the World: Leadership Lessons from the Front Lines of Global Finance*, Kindle Books.

Rickards, T., & Moger, S., (2000), Creative Leadership Processes in Project Team Development: An Alternative to Tuckman's (1965) stage model, *British Journal of Management*, 4: 273–283.

Rink, D.R., & Swan, J.E., (1979), Product Life-Cycle Research: A Literature Review, *Journal of Business Research*, 219–247. Vol. 7 issue 3.

Robertson, J., (2015), The Greek Crisis Is Shaking the IMF to Its Core, *BBC World News*, 15 July, www.bbc.com/news/business-33537445. Vol. 7 issue 3.

Robbins, S.P., & Barnwell, N., (1998), *Organization Theory: Concepts and Cases* (3rd edn.), Prentice Hall, New Jersey.

Roe, M., (2012) (19 June), Greece and the Limits of Anti-Austerity, Project-syndicate, www.project-syndicate.org/commentary/greece-and-the-limits-of-anti-austerity.

Roe, M.J., & Siegel, J.I., (2011), Political Instability: Its Effects on Financial Development, Its Roots in the Severity of Economic Inequality (February 3, 2011). Journal of Comparative Economics, 39: 279–409, Available at SSRN: http://ssrn.com/abstract=963214. Accessed June 2015.

Rokeach, M., (1968), *Beliefs, Attitudes, and Values: A Theory of Organizational Change*, Josey-Bass Inc., San Francisco.

Rose, C.M., (1991), Rethinking Environmental Controls: Management Strategies for Common Resources, Faculty Scholarship Series. Paper 1820. http://digitalcommons.law.yale.edu/fss_papers/1820.

Rosen, R., (1985), *Anticipatory Systems*, Pergamon Press, Oxford.

Rosenbaum, W.A., (1972), *Political Culture*, Thomas Nelson and Sons Ltd, London, UK.

Rosenblueth, A., Wierner, N., & Bigelow, J., (1943), Behaviour, Purpose and Teology, *Philosophy of Science*, 10(S): 18–24.

Rosenhead, J., (1989), *Rational Analysis for a Problematic World: Problem Structuring Methods for Complexity, Uncertainty, and Conflict*, John Wiley and Sons, New York.

(1998), Complexity Theory and Management Practice. www.human-nature.com/science-as-culture/rosenhead.html, accessed June 2009.

(2001), Complexity theory and management practice, *Science as Culture*, http://human-nature.com/science-as-culture/rosenhead.html, accessed February 2006.

Rotter, W., (2006), IFORS' Operational Research Hall of Fame Stafford Beer, *International Transactions in Operational Research*, 13(6): 577–578.

(2014), *Managementfehler sind die häufigsten Ursachen für Insolvenz und Fluktuation.* www.personalmanagement.info/hr-know-how/top-trainerinformieren/detail/managementfehler-sind-die-haeufigsten-ursachen-fuer-insolvenz-und-fluktuation/; Online since 29.09.2014, Last accessed 21 June 2015 16:20.

Rowe, W., Shi, W., & Wang, C., (2011), Board Governance and Performance of Chinese Banks, *Banks and Bank Systems*, 6(1): 26–40.

Ruiz, M., (1997), *The Four Agreements*, Amber-Allen Publishing, San Rafael, California, USA.

Rummel, R., (1979), *Understanding Conflict and War*, Sage Publications, Beverly Hills, CA. Also see www.hawaii.edu/powerkills/CIP.CHAP8.HTM, accessed February 2009.

Russell, J.A., (1980), A Circumplex Model of Affect, *Journal of Personality and Social Psychology*, 39: 1161–1178.

Ryckman, R., (2004), *Theories of Personality*, Thomson/Wadsworth, Belmont, CA.

Sagiv, L., & Schwartz, S.H., (2007), Cultural Values in Organizations: Insights for Europe, *European Journal of International Management*, 1(3): 176–190.

Salovey, P., & Mayer, J.D., (1990), Emotional Intelligence, Report for the NTH Biomedical Research Support Grant S07 RR07015, NIH grant CA42101, NCHS Contract 200-88-7001, Haywood Publishing Co., Inc.

Samuel, Y., (2010), *Organizational Pathology: Life and Death of Organizations*, Transaction Publishers, New Brunswick, New Jersey.

Saninno A., & Ellis, V., (2013), *Learning and Collective Creativity: Activity-Theoretical and Sociocultural Studies*, Routledge, London & New York.

Sanches, D., (2014), Shadow Banking and the Crisis of 2007-08. Business Review, Q2, pp. 7–14. http://philadelphiafed.org/research-and-data/publications/business-review/2014/q2/brQ214_shadow_banking.pdf, accessed May 2015.

Santosus, M., (1998), Business management, *CIO Enterprises Magazine*, 15 April, www.cio.com/archive/enterprise/041598_qanda.html?printversion=yes, accessed February 2006.

Sargent, W.E., (1944), *Teach Yourself Psychology*, English Universities Press Ltd, London.

Sargeson, S., (2002), *Collective Goods; Collective Futures in Asia*, Routledge, London.

Sawyer, R.K., (1998), The Interdisciplinary Study of Creativity in Performance, *Creativity Research Journal*, 11(1): 11–19.

Scarbrough, H., (1996), Blackboxes, Hostages and Prisoners, *Organization Studies*, 16: 991–1020.

Scaruffi, P., (2009), *The Worst Genocides of the 20th and 21st Centuries*, www.scaruffi.com/politics/dictat.html, accessed June 2015.

Schartz, S.J., Luychx, K., & Vignie, V.L., (2011), *Handbook of Identity Theory and Research: Volume 1 Structures and Processes*, Springer, New York.

Schein, E.H., (1985), *Organizational Culture and Leadership*, Jossey-Bass, San Francisco, CA.

(1992), *Organizational Culture and Leadership* (2nd edn.), Jossey-Bass, San Francisco.

(1996), Kurt Lewin's Change Theory in the Field and in the Classroom: Notes Toward a Model of Managed Learning, *Systems Practice*, 9(1): 27–47.

(1985). *Organizational Culture and Leadership*, San Francisco, CA: Jossey-Bass.

Scherer, A.G., (1998), Pluralism and Incommensurability in Strategic Management and Organization Theory: A Problem in Search of a Solution, *Organization*, 5: 147–168.

Schlevogt, K.A., (2000), Strategies, Structures and Processes for Managing Uncertainty and Complexity: Worldwide Learning from the Chinese Organizational Model of Private Enterprises. In Rahim, M.A., Golembiewski, R.T., & Mackenzie, K.D., (Eds), *Current Topics in Management*, Vol. 5, (pp. 305–328), JAI Press, Stamford, CT.

Schmitt, D.P., (2005), Sociosexuality from Argentina to Zimbabwe: A 48-Nation Study of Sex, Culture, and Strategies of Human Mating, *Behavioural and Brain Sciences*, 28: 247–275.

Schmitt, D.P., Allik, J., McCrae, R.R., & Benet-Martinez, V., (2007), The Geographic Distribution of Big Five Personality Traits: Patterns and Profiles of Human Self-Description across 56 Nations, *Journal of Cross-Cultural Psychology*, 38(2): 173–212.

Schneider, S.C., (1988), National vs. Corporate Culture: Implications for Human Resource Management, *Human Resource Management*, 27(2): 231–246. See http://onlinelibrary.wiley.com/doi/10.1002/hrm.3930270207/abstract, accessed February 2014.

Schoenfeld, A.H., (1986), What's all the Fuss about Metacognition? In Schoenfefeld, A.H., (Ed.), *Cognitive Science and Mathematical Education*, (pp. 189–215), Hillside, NJ.

Schonfeld, I.S., (1986), The Genevan and Cattell-Horn Conceptions of Intelligence Compared: The Early Implementation of Numerical Solution Aids, *Developmental Psychology*, 22, 204–212.

Schuler R.S., (2001), HR Issues in International Joint Ventures and Alliances. In Storey, J., (Ed.), *Human Resource Management: A critical text* (2nd edn., pp. 314–336), Thomson Learning, London.

Schultz, M., Hatch, M.J., & Larsen, M.H., (Eds), (2000), *The Expressive Organization*, Oxford University Press, Oxford.

Schumpeter, J.A. (1911), Theorie der wirtschaftlichen Entwicklung. Leipzig: Duncker & Humblot. Also see 2003. "The Theory of Economic Development": 61–116. In Backhaus, J., (Ed.), *J. A. Schumpeter*, Kluwer, Boston, translated by U. Backhaus.

Schutz, A., (1967), *Phenomenology of the Social World*, Heinemann Educational Books, London.

Schutz, A., & Luckmann, T., (1974), *The Structures of the Lifeworld*, Heinemann, London.

Schwalbe, M. L., & Schwalbe, M. L., (1991), The Autogenesis of the Self, *Journal for the Theory of Social Behaviour*, 21(3): 269–295.

Schwaninger, M., (2001), Intelligent Organizations: An Integrative Framework, *Systems Research and Behavioural Science*, 18: 137–158.

Schwarz, E., (1994) (April), A Metamodel to Interpret the Emergence, Evolution and Functioning of Viable Natural Systems. Presented at the European Meeting on Cybernetics and Systems Research, Vienna, and in Trappl, R., (Ed.), 1994, *Cybernetics and Systems '94* (pp. 1579–1586), World Scientific, Singapore.

(1994) (September), *A Trandisciplinary Model for the Emergence, Self-Organization and Evolution of Viable Systems*. Presented at the International Information,

Systems Architecture and Technology, Technical University of Wroclaw, Szklaska Poreba, Poland.
- (1996), Personal communication.
- (1997), Summary of The Main Features of a Holistic Metamodel To Interpret The Emergence, The Evolution And The Functioning of Viable Self-Organizing Systems, www.autogenesis.ch/Res1997.html, accessed January 2009.
- (1997), Towards a Holistic Cybernetics: From Science through Epistemology to Being, *Cybernetics and Human Knowing*, 4(1): 17–50.
- (1998), Seven Steps in the General Evolution of Systems: An Application to the Levels of Existence by C. W. Graves Systems, *Journal of Transdisciplinary Systems Science*, 3(1), Wroclaw, Poland 1998.
- (2001), Anticipating Systems: An Application to the Possible Futures of Contemporary Society, Invited paper at CAYS'2001, Fifth International Conference on Computing Anticipatory Systems, Liege, Belgium, August 13–18.
- (2003), Is Consciousness Reality or Illusion? A Non-Dualist Interpretation of Consciousness, Computing Anticipatory Systems: CASYS'03 - Sixth International Conference, Liege (Belgium), 11–16 August.

Schwartz, S.H., (1990), Individualism-Collectivism. Critique and Proposed Refinements, *Journal of Cross-Cultural Psychology, June 1990* 21(2): 139–157.
- (1994), Beyond Individualism/Collectivism: New Dimensions of Values. In Kim, U., Triandis, H.C., Kagitcibasi, C., Choi S.C., & Yoon, G., (Eds), *Individualism and Collectivism: Theory Application and Methods*, Sage, Newbury Park, CA.
- (1994a), Are there Universal Aspects in the Structure and Contents of Human Values? *Journal of Social Issues*, 50(4): 19–45. Available at http://dev.crs.org.pl:4444/rid=1K6GFZBH9-255VHHF-GZ/Schwartz%201994%20-%20Are%20there%20universal%20aspects%20in%20the%20content%20of%20human%20values.pdf, accessed February 2014.
- (1999), A Theory of Cultural Values and Some Implications for Work, *Applied Psychology: An International Review*, 48(1): 23–47.
- (2004), Mapping and Interpreting Cultural Differences around the World. In Vinken, H., Soeters, J., & Ester, P., (Eds), *Comparing Cultures, Dimensions of Culture in a Comparative Perspective* (pp. 43–73), Brill, Leiden, The Netherlands.
- (2008), *Cultural Value Orientations: Nature and Implications of National Differences*, State University – Higher School of Economics Press, Moscow.
- (2009), Values: Cultural and Individual. Chapter to appear in S.M. Breugelmans, A. Chasiotis, & F.J.R. van de Vijver (Eds), Fundamental questions in cross-cultural psychology (forthcoming).

Schwartz, S.H., & Bardi, A., (2001), Value Hierarchies across Culture: Taking a Similarities Perspective, *Journal of Cross-Cultural Psychology*, 32: 268–290.
- (2004). Mapping and Interpreting Cultural Differences Around the World, Contained in Vinken, H., Soeters, J., & Ester, P. (Eds): *Comparing Cultures, Dimensions of Culture in a Comparative Perspective*, Brill, Leiden, The Netherlands, pp. 43–73.

Scott Murray, T.Y., Clermont, M., & Binkley, M., (2005), Measuring Adult Literacy and Life Skills: New Frameworks for Assessment, International Adult Literacy Survey by Candian Ministry of Industry, Catalogue no. 89-552-MIE, no. 13, http://dsp-psd.pwgsc.gc.ca/Collection/CS89-552-13E.pdf. June 2015.

Scott, J., & Marshall, G., (Eds), (1998), *A Dictionary of Sociology*, Oxford University Press, Oxford.

Seed, A., & Tomasello, M., (2010), Primate Cognition, *Topics in Cognitive Science*, 2 (3): 407–419. http://onlinelibrary.wiley.com/doi/10.1111/j.1756–8765.2010.01099.x/full, accessed May 2014.

Seidl, D., (2003), Organizational Interactions in Luhmann's Theory of Social Systems, Munich Business Research No. 2003–9, www.zfog.bwl.uni-muenchen.de/files/mitarbeiter/paper2004_2.pdf.

— (2004), Luhmann's theory of autopoietic social systems. Ludwig-Maximilians-Universität München-Munich School of Management. www.zfog.bwl.uni-muenchen.de/files/mitarbeiter/paper2004_2.pdf, accessed January 2014. Also, reformulated as: Seidl, D., & Schoeneborn, D., (2010), Niklas Luhmann's Autopoietic Theory of Organizations: Contributions, Limitations, and Future Prospects, Institute of Organization and Administrative Science working paper no. 5, University of Zurich.

Shani, A.B., & Basuray, M.T., (1988), Organization Development and Comparative Management Action Research as an Interpretive Framework, *Leadership & Organization Development Journal*, 9(2): 3–10.

Shanon, B., (1993), *The Representational and the Presentational: An Essay on Cognition and the Study of Mind*, Harvester-Wheatsheaf, London.

Shannon, C.E., & Weaver, W., (1964), *The Mathematical Theory of Communication*, University of Illinois Press, Urbana.

Shapiro, I., (2005), What New CBO Data Indicate about Long-Term Income Distribution Trends, US Center on Budget and Policy Priorities, 7 March 2005.

Sharot, T., & Phelps, E.A., (2004), How Arousal Modulates Memory: Disentangling the Effects of Attention and Retention, *Cognitive, Affective, & BehaviouralNeuroscience*, 4(3): 294–306.

Sharpley, D., (2006), Key Steps Contributing to Employee Engagement & High Performance, Annual conference of the British Psychological Society, Glasgow. Also see Finding the Star Performers: An Alternative to Trait-Based Explanations of Work Behaviour, at http://space.businessballs.com/wilkobilko/resources/Prism%20for%20Star%20Performers.doc, accessed August 2008.

Shaw, S., & Meier, J., (1994), Second-Generation' MNCs in China, *China Business Review*, 10–15. September-October.

Shen. L.Y., Wu, G.W.C., & Ng, C.S.K., (2001), Risk Assessment for Construction Joint Ventures in China, *Journal of Construction Engineering and Management*, 127(1, January/ February) 76–81.

Shenkar, O., Luo, Y., & Yeheskel, O., (2008), From "Distance" To "Friction": Substituting Metaphors and Redirecting Intercultural Research, *Academy of Management Review*, 33: 905–923.

Sherman, H.J., & Schultz, R., (1998), *Open Boundaries: Creating Business Innovation Through Complexity*, Perseus Books, Reading, MA.

Sheth, J.N., & Sisodia, R.S., (2002), Competitive Markets and the Rule of Three, *Ivey Business Journal*, http://iveybusinessjournal.com/publication/competitive-markets-and -the-rule-of-three/, accessed May 2014.

Shoham, Y., Powers, R., & Grenager, T., (2006), If Multi-Agent Learning Is the Answer, What Is the Question? Based on a paper presented at American

Association for Artificial Intelligence, Fall Symposium in 2004, http://robotics.stanford.edu/~shoham/www%20papers/LearningInMAS.pdf, accessed September 2009.

Shotwell, J.M., Wolf, D., & Gardner, H., (1980), Styles of Achievement in Early Symbol Use. In Brandes, F., (Ed.), *Language, Thought, and Culture* (pp. 175, 199), Academic Press, NY.

Shover, N., & Bryant, K.M., (1993), Theoretical Explanations of Corporate Crime. In Blankenship, Michael B., (Ed.), *Understanding Corporate Criminality*, Garland Publishing, New York.

Shulruf, B., Hattie, J., & Dixon, R., (2011), Intertwinement of Individualist and Collectivist Attributes and Response Sets, *Journal of Social, Evolutionary, and Cultural Psychology*, 5(1): 51–65.

Shute, V.J., Hansen, E.G., Underwood, J.S., & Razzouk, R., (2011), A Review of the Relationship between Parental Involvement and Secondary School Students' Academic Achievement, Education Research International, Volume 2011, Article ID 915326, 10 pages, www.hindawi.com/journals/edri/2011/915326/. June 2015.

Sicking, M., (2011), *Die häufigsten Gründe für eine Insolvenz. Nicht Wirtschaftskrisen, sondern Managementfehler sind das größte Problem*. Published on Heise Online 05.04.11. www.heise.de/resale/artikel/Die-haeufigsten-Gruende-fuer-eine-Insolvenz-1204279.html. Last accessed 21 June 2015, 16:16.

Siegel, Jordan I., Licht, Amir N., & Schwartz, Shalom H., (2012), Egalitarianism, Cultural Distance, and FDI: A New Approach (June 6, 2012). Organization Science, Forthcoming. Available at SSRN: http://ssrn.com/abstract=957306 or http://dx.doi.org/10.2139/ssrn.957306SSRN or http://papers.ssrn.com/sol3/papers.cfm?abstract_id=957306. June 2015.

Simon, L., & Davies, G., (1996), A Contextual Approach to Management Learning: The Hungarian Case, *Organization Studies*, 17(2): 269–289.

Sloman, A., (1984), The Structure of the Space of Possible Minds. In Torrance, S. (Ed.), *The Mind in the Machine* (pp. 35–42), Ellis Harwood, Chichester, UK, see www.cs.bham.ac.uk/research/projects/cogaff/sloman-aaai-consciousness.pdf, accessed September 2009.

Sloman, A., & Chrisley, R., (2003), Virtual Machines and Consciousness, *Journal of Consciousness Studies*, 10(4–5): 113–172.

Smith, A.M.J., (2011), Exploring the Farm Enterprise through a Business Life Cycle, paper presented at the 9th Rural Entrepreneurship Conference, 3rd – 24th June, 2011, Nottingham Business School, UK.

Smith, P., (2002), Culture's Consequences: Something Old and Something New, *Human Relations*, 55(1): 119–135.

Smith, P.B., Dugan, S., & Trompenaars, F., (1996), National Culture and the Values of Organizational Employees: A Dimensional Analysis across 43 Nations, *Journal of Cross-Cultural Psychology*, 27(2): 231–264.

Smith, W.K., & Lewis, M.W., (2011), Toward a Theory of Paradox: A Dynamic Equilibrium Model of Organizing, *Academy of Management Review*, 36: 381–403.

Sneeringer, S., & Key, N., (2011), Effects of Size-Based Environmental Regulations: Evidence of Regulatory Avoidance, *American Journal of Agricultural Economics*, 93(4), 1189–1211.

Snyder, L.J., (2001), William Whewell, The Stanford Encyclopedia of Philosophy, Zalta, E.N., (Ed.), http://plato.stanford.edu/archives/spr2001/entries/whewell/, accessed 2002.

Sonesson, G., (2000), The life of signs in society and out of it: Critique of the communication critique, www.arthist.lu.se/kultsem/sonesson/life_of_signs1.html, accessed February 2003. Originally available in Torop, P., Lotman, M., & Kull, K., (Eds), 1999, Trudy po znakyvym sistemam/Sign System Studies 27:.88,127 (with summaries in Russian and Estonian). Tartu, Estonia.

(2008), Prolegomena to a General Theory of Icopicity. In Willems, K., & De Cuypere, L., (Eds), *Naturalness and Iconicity in Language* (pp. 7–47), John Benjamins Publishing Company.

Sørnes, J.O., Stephens, K.K., Sætre, A.S., & Browning, L.D., (2004). The Reflexivity between ICTs and Business Culture: Applying Hofstede's Theory to Compare Norway and the United States, *Informing Science Journal*, 7, originally presented in 2003 at the Informing Science and IT Education Conference in Pori, Finland http://2003.insite.nu.

Sorokin, P.A., (1937–1942), *Social and Cultural Dynamics* (in 4 volumes), Amer. Book. Co., NY.

(1962), *Social and Cultural Dynamics*, in 4 volumes, Bedminster Press, New York, Originally published in 1937–1942 by the Amer, Book, Co., NY.

Soros, G., (2008), *The New Paradigm for Financial Markets: The Credit Crisis of 2008 and What It Means*, Perseus Books, New York.

Spear, A.D., (2006), Ontology for the Twenty First Century: An Introduction with Recommendations, Paper presented at the Institute for Philosophical Studies, April 11, Green Bay, Wisconsin.

Spearman, C., (1904), General Intelligence, Objectively Determined and Measured, *American Journal of Psychology*, 15: 201–293.

Speece, M., (2001), Asian Management Style: An Introduction, *Journal of Managerial Psychology*, 16(2): 86–96.

Spence, A.M., (1975), The Economics of Internal Organization: An Introduction, *Bell Journal of Economics*, 6, 163–172.

Spencer-Oatey, H., (2000), *Culturally Speaking: Managing Rapport through Talk across Cultures*, Continuum, London.

Stacey, R., (1993), *Managing Chaos*, Kogan Page Ltd, London.

Staver, J.R., (1995), Scientific Research and Oncoming Vehicles: Can Radical Constructivist Embrace One and Dodge the Other? *Journal of Research in Science Teaching*, 32(10): 1125–1128.

Staw, B.M., (1991), Dressing Up Like an Organization: When Psychological Theories can Explain Organizational Action, *Journal of Management*, 17(4): 805–819.

Sterelny, K., (2004), Externalism, Epistemic Artefacts, and the Extended Mind. In Schantz, R., (Ed.), *The Externalist Challenge: New Studies on Cognition and Intentionality*, de Gruyter, Berlin & New York.

Sternberg, R.J., (1985), *Beyond IQ: A Triarchic Theory of Intelligence*, Cambridge University Press, Cambridge.

(1996), *Cognitive Psychology*, Harcourt Brace College Publishers, New York.

Stevens, L., & Rodin, I., (2001), *Psychiatry: An Illustrated Colour Text*, Churchill Livingstone, Edinburgh.

Stewart, I., (1989), *Does God Play Dice? The Mathematics of Chaos*, Blackwell, Oxford.

Stiglitz, J., (2012), This Week, Joseph Stiglitz: Merkel Needs a Change in Attitude to Save Euro, www.theweek.co.uk/eurozone/eurozone-crisis/47713/joseph-stiglitz-merkel-needs-change-attitude-save-euro. June 2015.

Stone. W.R., & Heany, D.F., (1984), Dealing with a Corporate Identity Crisis, *Long Range Planning*, 17(1): 10–18.

Stonehouse, G.H., & Pemberton, J.D., (1999), Learning and Knowledge Management in the Intelligent Organization, *Participation & Empowerment: An International Journal*, 7(5): 131–144.

Strang, D., & Meyer, J.W., (1993), Institutional Conditions for Diffusion, *Theory and Society*, 22(4): 487–511.

Strelau, J., (2002), *Temperament: A Psychological Perspective*, Kluwer, New York, NY.

Stubbart, C., & Smalley, R., (1999), The Deceptive Allure of Stage Models of Strategic Processes, *Journal of Management Inquiry*, 8(3): 273–286.

Suddaby, R., & Huy, Q.N., (2009), (April), Theory Development: Where are the New Theories of Organization? Academy of Management Review Special Topic Forum, http://apps.aomonline.org/Calls/cfp/paper_info.asp?user_lname=&user_id=&cfp_id=458. June 2015.

Suddaby, R., Hardy, C., & Huy, Q.N., (2008), Theory Development: Where are the New Theories of Organization, *The Academy of Management Review*, 33(2): 569–570.

Sullivan, E.L., (2000), An Examination of Identity in the Professional Context of Social Work, Leading to the Introduction of a Systemic Model of Identity. Doctoral Thesis, Royal Holloway University of London.

Sundarasaradula, D., & Hasan, H., (2004), A Unified Open Systems Model for Explaining Organizational Change, Conference paper presented at the Information Systems Foundations: Constructing and Criticising Workshop at The Australian National University, 16–17 July, from http://epress.anu.edu.au/info_systems/mobile_devices/ch11.html, accessed November 2011

Sunshine B, & Wang, Y.H., (2003), Qi, Rui Dan and Self-Excitation, *Journal of World Science*, 1: 197–212, Article No. 20030107, www.nobelac.com/science/jws/jws200301/Web/paperforJWS/new333qipaperjws.pdf, accessed June 2005.

Sutcliffe-Braithwaite, F., (2013), Margaret Thatcher, individualism and the welfare state, History & Policy, www.historyandpolicy.org/opinion-articles/articles/margaret-thatcher-individualism-and-the-welfare-state, accessed May 2015.

Symons, G.L., (2002), Constructing a Culture of Access in the Federal Public Service, Report 10, Government of Canada's Access to Information Review Task Force, www.Atirtf-Geai.Gc.Ca/Paper-Culture1-E.Html, accessed April 2010.

Taber, K.S., (2006), Beyond Constructivism: The Progressive Research Programme into Learning Science, *Studies in Science Education*, 42(1): 125–184.

Tam, K.O., (2008), Emerging Best Governance Practices in Commercial Financial Institutions: Corporate Governance in Chinese Banks, Executive Roundtable and Professional Placements Conference, Melbourne, Australia, 2–10 October.

Tamis-LeMonda, C.S., Yoshikawa, H., Niwa, K., & Niwa, E.Y., (2007), Parents' Goals for Children: The Dynamic Coexistence of Individualism and Collectivism in Cultures and Individuals, *Social Development*, 17(1): 183–209.

Tangen, K.I., (2009), Ecclesial Identification Beyond Transactional Individualism? PhD Thesis MF, The Norwegian School of Theology.

Tao, J., (2015), China's Hunt for Tigers and Flies Is Taking a Toll on Business, *Financial Times*, May 7, www.ft.com/cms/s/0/b2cb7c7a-f25c-11e4-b914-00144feab7de.html.

Taylor, J.R., (2000), Is There a "Canadian" Approach to the Study of Organizational Communication? *Canadian Journal of Communication*, 25(1): 69–86.

Teather, D., (2002), Andersen falls deeper into Enron crisis, *The Guardian*, Jan 18, UK, www.guardian.co.uk/business/2002/jan/18/corporatefraud.enron, accessed January 2013.

Tecuci, G., (1998), *Building Intelligent Agents: An Apprenticeship Multistrategy Learning Theory, Methodology, Tool and Case Studies*, Academic Press, London.

Tepeci, M. (1999), Increasing Brand Loyalty in the Hospitality Industry, *International Journal of Contemporary Hospitality Management*, 11(5): 223–229.

Tesfatsion, L., (2003), Agent-Based Computational Economics, Iowa State University Economics Working Paper #1.

Tesfatsion, L., & Judd, K.L., (2006), *Handbooks in Economics: Vol. 2, Agent-Based Computational Economics*, Elsevier, London.

Thamas, D.C., & Inkson, K., (2009), *Cultural Intelligence: Living and Working Globally*, Berrett-Koehler Publishers, Inc., San Francisco.

Thatcher, M., (1980), Speech to Conservative Party Conference ('the lady's not for turning'), Margaret Thatcher Foundation, October 10, www.margaretthatcher.org/document/104431. June 2012.

(1987), Interview for *Woman's Own* ("no such thing as society"), September 23, Margaret Thatcher Foundation, www.margaretthatcher.org/document/106689, accessed May 2015.

(1987a), Epitaph for the Eighties? "There Is No Such Thing as Society", *The Sunday Times*, http://.com/social/thatcher-society.htm.

The Loch Journal, (2011), Jürgen Habermas's Communicative Reason: Triumphs and Limitations, October 17, https://ldmac5.wordpress.com/2011/10/17/jurgen-habermas%E2%80%99s-communicative-reason-triumphs-and-limitations/.

Theiner, G., Allen, C., & Goldstone, R.L., (2010), Recognizing Group Cognition, *Cognitive Systems Research*, 11: 378–395.

Thompson, M., Grendstad, G., & Selle, P., (1999), *Cultural Theory as Political Science*, Routledge, London, New York.

Toennies, F., (1957), *Community and Society* (trans. Charles P. Loomis), Book I. Michigan State University Press, East Lansing, MI.

Tofler, A., (1980), *The Third Wave*, Bantam Book published in association with William Morrow & Co., Inc.

Tomkins, S.S., (1979), Script theory. In Howe Jr., H.E., & Dienstbier, R.A., (Eds), *Nebraska Symposium on Motivation* (Vol. 26, pp. 201–236), University of Nebraska Press, Lincoln.

Tran, V., (1998), The Role of The Emotional Climate in Learning Organizations, *The Learning Organization*, 5(2): 99–103. Transparency International, 2006, Corruption

Perceptions Index, www.transparency.org/publications/gcr/download_gcr#15. June 2015.

Transparency International, (2007), Global Corruption Report 2007, www.ti-bangladesh.org/GCR-07-Judiciary-Highlights1.pdf. June 2015.

Triandis, H.C., (1988), Collectivism and Development. In Sinha, D., & H. S. R. Kao, H.S.R., (Eds), *Social Values and Development: Asian Perspectives* (pp. 285–303), Sage Publications, Inc., Thousand Oaks, CA.

(1989), The Self and Social Behaviour in Differing Cultural Contexts, *Psychological Review*, 96(3): 506–520.

2006, Cultural Intelligence in Organizations, Group & Organization Management, 31(Feb,1)20,26.

Triandis, H.C., Leung, K.,Villareal, M. J., & Clack, F. L., (1985),. Allocentric versus Idiocentric Tendencies: Convergent and Discriminant Validation. *Journal of Research in Personality*, 19: 395–415.

(1994), Theoretical and Methodological Approaches to the Study of Collectivism and Individualism. In Kim, U., Triandis, H.C., Kâgitçibasi, Ç., Choi S.-C., & Yoon, G., (Eds), *Individualism and Collectivism: Theory, Method, and Applications*, Sage Publications, Thousand Oaks, CA.

(1995), *Individualism and Collectivism*, Westview Press, Boulder, Colorado.

(1999), Theoretical Concepts of use to Practioners. In Brislin, R., (Ed.), *Cross-Cultural Aplied Psychology* (pp. 34–55), Sage, Newberry Park, CA.

(2003), Some Hypotheses on the Psychology of Terrorism, *Cross-Cultural Psychology Bulletin*, 37(3): 33–40.

Triandis, H.C., Bontempo, R., Villareal, M., Asai, M., & Lucca, N., (1988), Individualism and Collectivism: Cross-Cultural Perspectives on Self-Ingroup Relationships, *Journal of Personality and Social Psychology*, 54: 328–338.

Triandis, H.C., Leung, K., Villareal, M.J., & Clack, F.I., (1985), Allocentric versus Idiocentric Tendencies: Convergent and Discriminant Validation, *Journal of Research in Personality*, 19(4): 395–415.

Triandis, H.C., Suh, E.M., (2002), Cultural Influences on Personality, *Annual Review of Psychology*, 53:133–60. Also see https://psy-web.psy.ed.ac.uk/people/awei/Lecture%20notes/triandis%20ann%20rev%20psychol%202002.pdf, accessed January 2007.

Triandis, H.C., & Suh, E.M., (2002), Cultural Influences on Personality, *Annual Review of Psychology*, 53: 133–160. Also see https://psy-web.psy.ed.ac.uk/people/awei/Lecture%20notes/triandis%20ann%20rev%20psychol%202002.pdf, accessed January 2007.

Triantis. A., & Pintelas, P., (2006), An Architecture for Developing Multi-Agent Educational Applications for the Web. In Alkhalifa, E.M., (Ed.), *Cognitively Informed Systems: Utilizing Practical Approaches to Enrich Information Presentation and Transfer* (pp. 235–259), Idea Group Inc. London, UK.

Trompenaars, F., (1997), *Riding the Waves of Culture: Understanding Diversity in Global Business*, McGraw-Hill, New York.

Trosby, D., (2001), *Economics and Culture*, Cambridge University Press.

Tsai, K.S., (2002), *Back-Alley Banking: Private Entrepreneurs in China*, Cornell University Press, Ithaca, NY.

Tsai, Y.J., Chen, Y.P., Lin, C.L., & Hung, J.H., (2014), The Effect of Banking System Reform on Investment–Cash Flow Sensitivity: Evidence from China, *Journal of Banking & Finance*, 46(2014): 166–176.

Tu, Y.C., Chou, M.J., & Lee, H.C., (2013), Parent-Child Shared Reading Meets Information Technology: Revealing Links between Parenting and Children's Character Development, *Journal of Applied Sciences*, 13(7): 1029–1036.

Tuckman, B.W., (1965), Developmental Sequence in Small Groups, *Psychological Bulletin*, 63: 384–399. The article was reprinted in Group Facilitation: A Research and Applications Journal – Number 3, Spring 2001. Available at http://dennislearningcenter.osu.edu/references/GROUP%20DEV%20ARTICLE.doc, accessed January 14, 2005.

Tung, R.L., (1995), International Organizational Behaviour. In Luthans, F., (Ed.) *Virtual O,B, Electronic Database* (pp. 487–518), McGraw-Hill Inc., New York.

Turchin, V., & Joslyn, C., (1999), The Metasystem Transition, http://pespmc1.vub.ac.be/MST.html, accessed 2003.

Turner, J.R. (1999), *The Handbook of Project-Based Management* (2nd edn.), McGraw Hill, London.

Tushman, (1977), A Political Approach to Organizations: A Review and Rationale, *Academy of Management Review*, 2: 206–216.

Twigger-Ross, C.L., Bonaiuto, M., & Breakwell, G., (2003), Identity Theories and Environmental Psychology. In Bonnes, M., Lee, T., & Bonaiuto, M., (Eds), *Psychological Theories for Environmental Issues* (pp. 203–233), Ashgate Publishing Limited, Aldershot.

Tybout, A.M., (1995), The Value of Theory in Consumer Research. In Kardes, F.R., & Sujan, M., (Eds), *Advances in Consumer Research*, Association of Consumer Research, Provo, UT.

Tymieniecka, A.T., (2001), The Early History of the World Phenomenology Institute, www.phenomenology.org/article.html, accessed 2002.

Ulrich, W., (1977), The Design of Problem-Solving Systems, *Management Science*, 23, 1099–1108.

(1983), *Critical Heuristics of Social Planning: A New Approach to Practical Philosophy*, Haupt, Berne.

(2005), *A Brief Introduction to Critical Systems Heuristics (CSH)*, ECOSENSUS Publications, knowledge Media Institute (KMI), The Open University, Milton Keynes, UK.

Ulrich, W., & Reynolds, M., (2010), Critical Systems Heuristics. In Reynolds, M., & Holiwell, S., (Eds), *Systems Approaches to Managing Change: A Practical Guide* (pp. 243–292), Springer, New York.

Vancouver, J.B., (1996), Living Systems Theory as a Paradigm for Organizational Behaviour: Understanding Humans, Organizations, and Social Processes, *Behavioural Science*, 41(3, July): 165–204.

Van der Leeuw, S.E., (1981), Information Flows, Flow Structures and the Explanation of Change in Human Institutions. In *Archaeological Approaches to the Study of Complexity*, Universiteit van Amsterdam.

Van de Vliert, E., & Janssen, O., (2002), 'Better Than' Performance Motives as Roots of Satisfaction across More and Less Developed Countries, *Journal of Cross-Cultural Psychology*, 33(4): 380–397.

Van de Vijver, G., (1999), Psychic Closure: A Prerequisite for the Recognition of the Sign-Function? *Semiotica*, 127(1–4): 613–616.

Van Egeren, L.F., (2009), A Cybernetic Model of Global Personality Traits, *Personal Social Psychology Review*, 13(2): 92–108.

Van Gigch, J.P., (1987), *Decision Making about Decision Making: Metamodels and Metasystems*, Abacus, Tunbridge Wells, Kent, UK.

Van Knippenbern, D., Kooij-de Bode, H.J.M., & Van Ginkel, W.P., (2010), The Interactive Effects of Mood and Trait Negative Affect in Group Decision Making, *Organization Science*, 21(3): 731–744.

Van Lommel, P., Van Wees, R., Meyers, V., & Elfferich, I., (2001), *Near Death Experience in Survivors of Cardiac Arrest: A Prospective Study in the Netherlands*, THE LANCET, Vol. 358, December 15, 2039–45. For an abstract see www.ncbi.nlm.nih.gov/entrez/query.fcgi?cmd= Retrieve&db=PubMed&list_uids=11755611&dopt=Abstract, and a review www. nderf.org/Lancet%20von%20Lommel%20Review.htm accessed 2002.

Van Nispen, F.K., (2007), The Art and Craft of Budgeting: Fiscal Policy in the Eurozone, *Current Politics and Economics of Europe*, 18(2): 275–305, www.researchgate.net/publication/254804490_The_Art_and_Craft_of_Budgeting_Fiscal_Policy_in_the_Euroz one. June 2015.

Van Staden, C.W., & Fulford, K.W.M., (2004), Changes in Semantic Uses of First Person Pronouns as Possible Linguistic Markers of Recovery in Psychotherapy, *Australian and New Zealand Journal of Psychiatry*, 38(4): 226–232.

Varela, F.J., (1979), *Principles of Biological Autonomy*, Elsevier, NY.

Vaughan, D., (1983), *Controlling Unlawful Organizational Behaviour: Social Structure and Corporate Misconduct*, University of Chicago Press, Chicago.

Vaughan, L., & Finch, G., (2012) (July 19), Interest Rates from Sweden to South Korea under Scrutiny, Bloomburg Business Week, www.businessweek.com/news/2012-07-19/interest-rates-from-sweden-to-south-korea-under-fresh-scrutiny. June 2015.

Veblen, T., (1898), *Why Is Economics Not an Evolutionary Science?* reprinted in The Place of Science in Modern Civilization (New York, 1919).

Veenhoven, R., (1999), Quality-of-Life in Individualistic Society: A Comparison of 43 Nations in the Early 1990's, *Social Indicators Research*, 48: 157–186.

Verenikina, I., & Gould, E., (1998), Cultural-Historical Psychology and Activity Theory. In Hasan, H., Gould, E., & Hyland P., (Eds), *Information Systems and Activity Theory: Tools in Context* (pp. 7–18), University of Wollongong Press, Wollongong.

Verma, A., (1999), Cultural Roots of Police Corruption in India, *Policing: An International Journal of Police Strategies & Management*, 22(3): 264–279.

Veron, N., (2011), The European Debt and Financial Crisis: Origins, Option, Congressional Testimony Submitted to the US Senate Committee on Banking, Housing, and Urban Affairs: Subcommittee on Security and International Trade and Finance, September 22. See www.piie.com/publications/testimony/testimony.cfm?ResearchID=1928.

Vickers., G, (1965), *The Art of Judgement*, Chapman and Hall, London (Reprinted 1983, Harper and Row, London).

Viskovatoff, A., (1999), Foundations of Niklas Luhmann's Theory of Social Systems, *Philosophy of the Social Sciences*, 29(4): 481–515.

Visser, E. J., & Boshma, R., (2002), *Clusters and Networks as Learning Devices for Individual Firms*, Utrecht University.

Vitalari, N.P., (1981), An Investigation into the Problem Solving Behaviour of Systems Analysists. Doctoral thesis, University of Minnesota, Minneapolis.

Vitalari, N.P., & Dickinson, G.W., (1983), Problem Solving for Effective Systems Analysis: An Exploration, *Communications of the ACM*, 26(11), Nov: 948–956.

Volkery, C., (2012), Too Poor for Stimulus? Europe Eyes Shift from Austerity to Growth, May 10, Spiegal International, www.spiegel.de/international/europe/eu-considers-proposals-to-boost-growth-a-832379.html. June 2015.

Von Bertalanffy, L., (1949), The Concepts of Systems in Physics and Biology, *Bulletin of the British Society for the History of Science*, 1: 44–45.

(1950), An Outline of General Systems Theory, *British Journal for the Philosophy of Science*, 1: 139–164.

Von Glasersfeld, E., (1982), An Interpretation of Piaget's Constructivism, *Revue internationale de philosophie*, 36(4): 612–635.

(1984), "An introduction to radical constructivism", In Watzlawick, P. (Ed.), The Invented Reality, W.W. Norton and Company, New York, NY, pp. 17–40.

(1998), Why Constructivism must be Radical. In Larochelle, M., Bednarz, N., & Garrison J., (Eds), *Constructivism and Education* (pp. 23–28), Cambridge University Press, Cambridge.

Von Neumann, J., & Morgenstern, O., (1947), *The Theory of Games and Economic Behaviour*, (2nd edn.) Princeton University Press, Princeton.

Voros, J., & Schermerhorn, J., (1993), Institutional Roles in Higher Education for Business and Management in Hungary, *Management Education and Development*, 24(1): 70–82.

Vygotsky, L.S., (1978), *Mind and Society: The Development of Higher Psychological Process*, Harvard University Press, Cambridge, MA.

(1987), *The Collected Works of L. S. Vygotsky, Volume 1: Problems of General Psychology*. Rieber, R.W., & Carton, A.S., (Eds), Plenum Press, New York.

(1994), *The Vygotsky reader, Van Der Veer, R., & Valsiner, J., (Eds)*, Blackwell, Oxford.

Wade, M., & Hulland, J., (2004), The Resource-Based View and Information Systems Research: Review, Extension, and Suggestions for Future Research, *MIS Quarterly*, 28(1): 107–142.

Wallis, S.E., & Wright, B., (2015), *Strategic Knowledge Mapping: The Co-Creation of Useful Knowledge*. Paper presented at the Association for Business Simulation and Experiential Learning (ABSEL) 42nd annual conference, Las Vegas, CA.

Wang, A., (2007), The Effects of Varied Instructional Aids and Field Dependence-Independence on Learners' Structural Knowledge in a Hypermedia Environment, Doctoral Thesis presented to Department of Educational Studies, College of Education of Ohio University, USA.

Wang, J., Wang G.G., Ruona W.E.A., & Rojewski, J.W., (2005), Confucian Values and the Implications for International HRD, *Human Resource Development International*, 8(3): 311–326.

Waterfield, B., (2015), Greece must Bow to Austerity or go Bust, says EU, *Daily Telegraph*, 26 January, www.telegraph.co.uk/news/worldnews/europe/greece/11368634/Greece-must-bow-to-austerity-or-go-bust-says-EU.html. June 2015.

Watson, G., (1969), Resistance to Change. In Bennis, W.G., Benne, K.F., & Chin, R., (Eds), *The Planning of Change*, Holt, Reinhart, Winston, New York.
Weber, Michel, (2003), Personal Communication.
Weed, L., (2002), Kant's Noumenon and Sunyata, *Asian Philosophy*, 12(2): 77–95.
Wei, S.J., (2001), Corruption and Globalization, The Brookings Institute, paper no. 79, April, www.brookings.edu/~/media/research/files/papers/2001/corruption-wei/pb79.html, accessed May 2016.
Weibull, J.W., (1995), *Evolutionary Game Theory*, MIT Press.
Weick, K.E., (1969) *The Social Psychology of Organizing*, Addison-Wesley, Reading.
(1989), Theory Construction as Discipline Imagination, *Academy of Management Review*, 14(4): 516–531.
(1995) *Sensemaking in Organizations*, Sage, Thousand Oaks, CA.
Weick, K.E., & Roberts, K.H., (1993), Collective Mind in Organizations: Heedful Interrelating Onflight Decks, *Administrative Science Quarterly*, 38(3): 357–382.
Weiland, I.H., & Legg, D.R., (1964), Formal Speech Characteristics as a Diagnostic Aid in Childhood Psychosis, *American Journal of Orthopsychiatry*, 34(1): 91–94.
Weinberg, G.M., (1975), *An Introduction to General Systems Thinking*, Wiley, New York.
Weinstein, E.A., (1969), The Development of Interpersonal Competence. In Goslin, D.A., (Ed.), *Hand-Book of Socialization Theory and Research*, Rand McNally, Chicago.
Welborn, J.W., (2002), Review of *Back-Alley Banking: Private Entrepreneurs in China*, Cornell University Press, Ithaca, NY, by Tsai, K.S., Cato Journal, pp. 398–401.
Welch, I., (2000), Herding among Security Analysts, *Journal of Financial Economics*, 58(2000): 369–396.
Welzel, C., Inglehart, R., & Klingemann, H.-D., (2003), The Theory of Human Development, *European Journal of Political Research*, 42(2): 341–380.
Wertsch, J.V., (Ed.), (1979), *The Concept of Activity in Soviet Psychology*, M.E. Sharpe, Armonk, NY.
Whewell, W., (1860), *On the Philosophy of Discovery: Chapters Historical and Critical*, Parker & Son, London.
White, D.R., Tambayong, L., and Kejžar, N., (2008), Oscillatory Dynamics of City-Size Distributions in World Historical Systems. Chapter 9, In Modelski, G., Devezas, T., & Thompson, W., (Eds), *Globalization as Evolutionary Process: Modeling, Simulating, and Forecasting Global Change* (pp. 190–225), Routledge, London. See www.imbs.uci.edu/files/imbs/docs/technical/2007/MBS07_03.pdf, accessed May 2013.
Whitehead, A.N., & Russell, B., (1910), *Principia Mathematica*, Cambridge University Press, Cambridge.
Whittington, R., (1993), *What Is Strategy – and Does It Matter?* Routledge, London.
Wicks, D., (2001), Institutionalized Mindsets of Invulnerability: Differentiated Institutional Field and the Antecendents of Organizational Crisis, *Organization Studies*, 22(4): 659–692.
Wiig, K.M., (1993), *Knowledge Management Foundations: Thinking about Thinking-How People and Organizations Create, Represent, and Use Knowledge*, Schema Press, Arlington, TX.

Wilber, K., (2004), On the Nature of a Post-Metaphysical Spirituality: Response to Habermas and Weis, taken from endnotes to his book published in 2000, Integral Psychology: Consciousness, Spirit, Psychology, Therapy, Shambhala, Boston & London (also see http://wilber.shambhala.com/html/misc/habermas/appendix1.cfm/). June 2015.

Wilhelm, R., (1950), *The I Ching or Book of Changes*, Princeton University Press, Princeton.

Williams, A., Dobson, P., & Walters, M., (1993), *Organizational Culture: New Organizational Approaches*, IPM, London.

Williams, B., & Imam, I., (2006), Systems Concepts in Evaluation: An Expert Anthology, American Evaluation Association, http://preval.org/files/Kellogg%20enfoque%20sistematico%20en%20evaluacion.pdf. June 2015.

Williams, S.L., (1992), Perceived Self-Efficacy and Phobic Disability. In Schwarzer, R., (Ed.), *Self-Efficacy: Thought Control of Action* (pp. 149–176), Hemisphere, Washington, DC.

Williamson, D., (2002), Foreward from a Critique of Hofstede's Model of National Culture, *Human Relations*, 55(11): 1373–1395.

Wilson, E.O., (1998), *Consilience: The Unity of Knowledge*, Knopf, New York.

Wilson, R., (2005), Collective Memory, Group Minds, and the Extended Mind Thesis, *Cognitive Processes*, 6(4): 227–236.

Wolff, E. N., Zacharias, A., & Masterson, T., (2009), *Postwar Trends in Economic Well-Being in the United States, 1959–2004*, The Levy Economics Institute, February 2009. www.levy.org/pubs/lmw_feb_09.pdf, accessed May 2014.

Wollheim, R., (1999), *On The Emotions*, Yale University Press.

Wong, C.S., Law, K.S., & Huang, G.H., (2008), On the Importance of Conducting Construct-Level Analysis for Multidimensional Constructs in Theory Development and Testing, *Journal of Management*, 34: 744.

World Bank, (2015), Data: Greece, http://data.worldbank.org/country/Greece.

World Report, (2012), China, Human Rights Watch, www.hrw.org/world-report-2012/world-report-2012-china. June 2015.

Wu, S.Y., & Rubin, D.L., (2000), Evaluating the Impact of Collectivism and Individualism on Argumentative Writing by Chinese and North American College Students, Research in the Teaching of English, 35(2, November):148–178, National Council of Teachers of English, www.jstor.org/stable/40171513.

Xie, K., (2001), The Challenge and Countermeasure: Research of Internet Banking Brought by China's Entry to WTO, *Journal of Financial Research*, 5: 82–90.

Yaghoubi, N.,M., Moloudi, J., & Haghi, A., (2010), Relationship of Organizational Culture and Organizational Intelligence in Public Organization, *Business Management Quarterly Review*, 1(1): 1–8.

Yan, Z., (2006), *A New Methodology of Measuring Corporate Life-Cycle Stages*, *Working paper*, Brandeis University, MA, USA.

Yang, H.H., Yu, J.C., & Yang, H.J., (2009), Towards an Understanding of Reusable Knowledge Reuse in an Online Environment, in Mastorakis, N., Proceedings of the European Computing Conference, Volumen 2, Madenov V., Kontargyri, V., pp. 243, 259, Springer.

Ybema, S., (1996). A Duck-Billed Platypus in the Theory and Analysis of Organizations: Combinations of Consensus and Dissensus. In Koot, W., Sabelis, I., & Ybema, S., (Eds), *Contradictions in Context* (pp. 39–61), Vrije Universiteit, Amsterdam.

Yeh, R.S., (1989), On Hofstede's Treatment of Chinese and Japanese Values, *Asia-Pacific Journal of Management*, 6(1): 149–160.
Yin, R.K., (1989), *Case Study Research, Design and Methods*, Sage Publications, Newbury Park/ London/ New Delhi.
Yolles, M.I., (1996) (October), Critical Systems Thinking, Paradigms, and the Modelling Space, *Systems Practice*, 9(6): 549–570.
  (1999), *Management Systems: A Viable Approach*, Financial Times Pitman, London.
  (2000), From Viable Systems to Surfing the Organization, *Journal of Applied Systems*, 1(1): 127–142.
  (2001), Viable Boundary Critique, *Journal of Operational Research Society*, 51 (January): 10–12.
  (2003), The System-Metasystem Dichotomy, *Kybernetes*, in process.
  (2004), Implications for Beer's Ontological System/Metasystem Dichotomy, *Kybernetes*, 33(3): 726, 764.
  (2006), *Organizations a Complex Systems: An Introduction to Knowledge Cybernetics*, Information Age Publishing, Inc., Greenwich, CT, USA.
  (2007), The Dynamics of Narrative and Antenarrative and Their Relation to Story, *Journal of Organizational Change Management*, 20(1): 74–94
  (2007b), Exploring Cultures through Knowledge Cybernetics, *Journal of Cross-Cultural Competence and Management (JCCM)*, 5: 19–74.
  (2007a), Modelling Pathologies in Social Collectives, *European Journal of International Management*, 1(1/2): 81–103.
  (2009), Understanding the Dynamics of European Politics, European Integration online Papers (EIoP), Vol. 13, Art. 27, http://eiop.or.at/eiop/texte/2009-027a.htm.
  (2009a), A Social Psychological basis of Corruption and Sociopathology, *Journal of Organizational Change Management*, 22(6): 691–731.
  (2009b), Migrating Personality Theories Part 1: Creating Agentic Trait Psychology? *Kybernetes*, 38(6): 897–924.
  (2010), Exploring Complex Sociocultural Situations through Soft Operational Research. *Pesqui. Oper.*, 30(2): 345–370.
Yolles, M.I., & Dubois, D., (2001), Anticipatory Viable Systems, *International Journal of Computing Anticipatory Systems*, 9: 3–20.
Yolles, M.I., & Fink, G., (2009), Migrating Personality Theories Part 2: Towards a Theory of the Balanced Personality? *Kybernetes*, 38(9): 1461–1490.
  (2011), Narratives, Paradigms, and Change, in Boje (ed), Storytelling and the Future of Organizations, Taylor Francis, Abingdon, UK.
  (2012), Understanding the Relationship between Policy and Economics, in process.
  (2012a), Personality, Pathology and Sagiv-Schwartz Mindscapes, in process.
  (2013), An Introduction to Mindset Theory: Part 1: The Fundamentals, Submitted to PSPR.
  (2013a), Exploring the Common Roots of Culture, Politics and Economics, *Business Systems Review*, 2(2): 1–57.
  (2014), Sustainability of Sustainability. Business Systems Review. Volume 3 – Issue 2, 2014. Special Issue – Selected papers of the 2nd B.S.Lab International Symposium. www.business-systems-review.org/Yolles_&_Fink(2014) .Sustainability.of.Sustainability.htm.
  (2014a), Personality, Pathology and Mindsets: Part 1 – Agency, Personality and Mindscapes, *Kybernetes*, 43(1): 92–112.

(2014b), Personality, Pathology and Mindsets: Part 2 – Cultural Traits and Enantiomers, *Kybernetes*, 43(1): 113–134.

(2014c), Personality, Pathology and Mindsets: Part 3 – Pathologies and Corruption, *Kybernetes*, 43(1): 135–143.

Yolles, M.I., Fink, G., & Dauber, D., (2011a), Organizations as Emergent Normative Personalities: Part 1: the concepts, *Kybernetes*, 40(5/6) 635–669.

(2011b), Understanding Normative Personality, *Cybernetics and Systems: An International Journal*, 42(6): 447–480.

(2015a), A General Theory of Generic Modelling and Paradigm Shifts: Part 1 – the Fundamentals, *Kybernetes*, 44(2): 283–298.

(2015b), A General Theory of Generic Modelling and Paradigm Shifts: Part 2 – Cybernetic Orders, *Kybernetes*, 44(2): 299–310.

(2015c), A General Theory of Generic Modelling and Paradigm Shifts: Part 3 – the Extension, *Kybernetes*, 44(2): 311–328.

Yolles, Gerhard Fink, B., & Frieden, Roy, (2012), Organizations as Emergent Normative Personalities: Part 2, Predicting the Unpredictable, *Kybernetes*, 41(7): 1014–1049.

Yolles, M.I., Fink, G., Iles, P., & Sawagvudcharee, O., (2013), Generating Corporate Life Cycles from the Paradigm Life Cycle, *Journal of Organizational Change Management*, in process.

Yolles, M.I., Frieden, R., & Kemp, G., (2008), Toward a Formal Theory of Sociocultures: A Yin-Yang Information-Based Theory of Social Change, *Kybernetes*, 37(7): 850–909.

Yolles, M.I., & Guo, K., (2003), Paradigmatic Metamorphosis and Organizational Development, *Sys. Res.*, 20: 177–199.

Yolles, M.I., & Iles, P., (2006), Understanding Public-Private Alliances through Knowledge Cybernetics: Ethical Frameworks and Trust, *Systems Research and Behavioural Science*, in process.

Yolles M.I., & Iles, P., (2006), The Knowledge Cybernetics of Culture: The Case of China, *International Journal of Knowledge and Systems Sciences*, 3(4): 8–17.

Yolles, M.I., & Sawagvudcharee, O., (2010), Understanding Corporate Paradigm Change, IACCM Conference, 22–25 June, University of Central Lancashire, Preston, UK.

Yoon, K.I., (2010), Political Culture of Individualism and Collectivism, Doctoral dissertation in Political Science, University of Michigan.

You, Jong-sung, (2005), A Comparative Case Study of Corruption in South Korea, Relative to Taiwan and the Philippines:Focusing on the Role of Land Reform and Industrial Policy, Chapter IV of a PhD thesis at Harvard University, http://ksghome.harvard.edu/~youjong/Ch%204%20Corruption%20in%20Korea.doc. June 2015.

(2005a), Embedded Autonomy or Crony Capitalism?: Explaining Corruption in South Korea, Relative to Taiwan and the Philippines, Focusing on the Role of Land Reform and Industrial Policy, Annual Meeting of the American Political Science Association, Washington, DC, September 1–4.

Young, H., (2013), *One of Us: The Life of Margaret Thatcher*, Pan Macmillan.

Young, H.P., (2009), Innovation Diffusion in Heterogeneous Populations: Contagion, Social Influence, and Social Learning, *The American Economic Review*, 1899–1924.

Yueh, L., (2010), Thirty Years of Legal and Economic Reform in China: Growth, Institutions, and Laws, *Journal of Chinese Economic and Business Studies*, 8(2, May): 117–132.

Zack, M.H., (1999), Developing a Knowledge Strategy, *California Management Review*, 41(3): 125–145, http://web.cba.neu.edu/~mzack/articles/kstrat/kstrat.htm, accessed February 2006.

Zalta, E.N., (1999), Principia Metaphysica, http://mally.stanford.edu/principia.pdf, accessed July 2010.

(2004), The Theory of Abstract Objects, http://mally.stanford.edu/theory.html, accessed July 2010.

Zaltman, G., & Duncan, R., (1977), *Strategies for Planned Change*, Wiley, New York.

Zekos, G.I., (2004), Ethics versus Corruption in Globalization, *Journal of Management Development*, 23(7): 631–647.

Zetterberg, H.L., (1997), The Study of Values. In Swedberg, R., & Uddhammar, E., (Eds), *Sociological Endeavor* (pp. 191–219), Selected Writings, City University Press, Stockholm. Also see www.zetterberg.org/Lectures/l920821.htm, accessed June 2004.

Zhang, H., Shu, C., Jiang, X., & Malter, A. J., (2010), Managing Knowledge for Innovation: The Role of Cooperation, Competition, and Alliance Nationality, *Journal of International Marketing*, 18(4): 74–94.

Zhang, W.-R., (2009), YinYang Bipolar Relativity – A Unifying Theory of Nature, Agents, and Life Science, Proceeding of The International Joint Conference on Bioinformatics, Systems Biology and Intelligent Computing, pp. 377–383.

(2011), YinYang Bipolar Relativity: A Unifying Theory of Nature, Agents and Causality with Applications in Quantum Computing, Cognitive Informatics and Life Sciences, IGI Global.

Index

abuse, 168, 213, 369
accountability, 361, 362, 365–7
achievement, 98, 102, 109, 110, 126, 130, 131, 149, 163, 167, 169, 273, 290, 319, 325
action, xv, 4, 21, 43, 86, 139, 174, 218, 239, 265, 306, 348
action-directed, 31, 121
action orientation, 30, 175, 296
action oriented processes, 104, 320
action systems, 266–8, 270, 271, 283
actor, 11, 24, 38, 54, 72, 73, 76, 77, 152, 156, 219, 236, 266, 267, 276, 277, 280–5, 287, 298–300, 312, 314, 338
actor-network-theory, 236
acts in space, 280
acts in time, 280
adaptation, 8, 24–6, 28, 30, 31, 43, 51, 66, 68, 79, 91, 97, 103, 117, 119, 123, 133, 141, 150, 154, 171, 175, 176, 186, 188, 244–5, 256, 267, 271, 279, 284n.5, 293, 295, 313–15, 317, 319–21
adaptive, xiv, 54, 55, 118, 121, 174, 189, 221, 230, 241, 262, 311, 313, 315
adaptive learning, 25
adjustment, 26, 30, 32, 45, 56, 71, 97, 105, 108, 109, 127, 129, 131, 154, 164, 244, 249, 305, 321, 322, 368
affect, xv, xvi, 7–8, 10, 21, 24, 25, 29, 36, 37, 39, 42, 64, 69, 72, 77, 83, 84, 91, 92, 94, 97, 99, 109, 111–12, 130–2, 141, 142, 153, 156, 160, 161, 165, 166, 174, 177, 179–80, 182, 186, 189, 208, 216, 245, 267–9, 300, 302, 317, 322, 349, 354, 357, 359, 366
affective, 24, 25, 36, 37, 39, 42, 69, 83, 94, 156, 174, 177, 179–80, 182, 186, 189, 267–9, 302
affective autonomy, 156, 161
agencies, xiii, 2, 21, 41, 83, 111, 138, 174, 205, 231, 265, 303, 333
agency behaviour, xv, 32, 41, 43, 83, 88, 91, 174, 178, 316

agency capital, 2
agency culture, xv, 22, 37, 49, 108, 131, 134, 149, 223, 224
agency identity, 29, 92
agency intelligence, 14, 28, 126, 187
agency learning, 56, 65, 74
agency operative system, 32, 36, 37, 40, 64, 65, 100, 134, 189, 190, 194–5, 288, 320, 350, 353
agency pathologies, 75–6, 84, 353
agency theory, xiv, xv, xvi, 14, 15, 17, 18, 21, 22, 24, 25, 31, 33, 35, 61, 66, 94–104, 114, 126, 133, 137, 139, 141, 142, 144, 149–59, 175, 177, 240, 265, 275, 286–8, 294, 295, 298, 299, 301–4, 311, 315, 331, 368
agency traits, xv, 31, 32, 94–104, 138–73
agency types, 15, 138–73
aggression, 79, 198
agnosticism, 34–5
alliance, xiii, 16, 17, 24, 45, 170, 205–62, 341–2
allocentric collectives, 158, 166, 167
alter ego, 274
ambient culture, 103, 245, 249, 250, 252, 256, 262, 282
analytical intelligence, 123
Anschlussfahigkeit, 132
antenarrative, 232, 236, 243
anticipation, xiii, xv, xvi, 15, 18, 24, 40, 67, 68, 71–2, 74, 87, 96, 97, 101, 118, 122, 142, 149, 175, 195–7, 239, 278, 290, 303, 305, 308–10, 312, 313, 315–17, 320, 321, 331, 332
apperception, 87, 174, 191, 197, 201, 202
artefact, 224, 282
atrophy, 257
attention, 107, 112, 115, 126, 134, 138, 150, 171, 193, 208, 224, 238, 282, 294, 302, 305, 328, 353, 357
attitudes, 6, 23, 29, 34–8, 53, 64, 65, 67, 73, 89, 90, 92–4, 101, 103, 106–9, 112, 114–16,

Index

127, 129, 131, 134, 135, 139, 143, 153, 160, 165, 169, 179–80, 186, 190, 196, 200, 210, 214, 217, 219n.2, 223, 224, 231, 239, 244, 247, 249, 250, 283, 286, 289, 294, 295, 300, 311, 316, 350, 351, 354, 358–60
authoritarian, 248, 250, 294, 354, 358, 369
authority, 5, 152, 154, 157, 161, 162, 198, 209, 254, 258, 327, 334, 335, 340, 349, 352, 365
autogenesis, xvi, 28, 33, 34, 37, 62, 64, 75–6, 82, 94, 108, 127, 128, 187, 302, 318
autogenetesis, 183, 184, 187
autogenetic figurative intelligence, 64, 180
autogenetic function, 318
autonomy, 22, 34, 43, 60, 62, 71, 97, 102, 135, 149, 151, 153, 156, 161, 164, 165, 174, 208, 241, 276, 279n.2, 292, 334, 335
autopoiesis, xvi, 28, 31–4, 39–41, 43, 62–4, 70, 75, 76, 81, 82, 94, 104, 108, 127, 128, 132, 178, 187, 241, 271, 273, 299, 302, 318, 357
autopoietic, 32, 33, 36, 62, 64, 77, 132, 177–8, 180, 194, 241, 271, 276, 296–9, 318, 320
autopoietic function, 318
autopoietic operative intelligence, 34, 62, 63, 75, 81, 94, 104, 177–81, 184, 241
autopoietic systems, 33, 276, 296, 299

behavioural intelligence, 188, 190, 318, 320, 350, 351
behaviouralism, 289, 290
behaviour, xiii, 1, 21, 41, 83, 111, 138, 174, 213, 241, 266, 303, 337
behavioural style, 91
behavioural theory, 140, 313
being, xvi, 4, 6–8, 13, 21, 35, 39, 40, 43, 44, 49, 51–3, 62, 64, 67, 69, 79–86, 93, 103, 104, 108, 112, 114, 118–19, 123, 124, 132, 137–9, 143, 150, 154, 156, 157, 160, 162, 163, 167, 169, 174, 177, 178, 180, 189, 192, 196, 198, 209, 212, 213, 222, 225, 237, 238, 242–5, 252, 255, 256, 259, 267, 269, 271–3, 279, 280, 282, 285, 289, 290, 297, 304, 309, 310, 314–16, 319, 320, 327, 330, 332–6, 340, 341, 344, 348, 351–4, 356, 359, 361, 363, 369, 370
belief, 2, 8, 14, 23, 27–30, 33, 37–9, 49, 50, 61, 64, 73, 88–95, 101, 102, 104, 106, 112, 113, 115, 116, 125, 126, 128–30, 137, 138, 140, 145, 158, 165–7, 170, 175, 188, 191, 198, 200–2, 212, 217, 219, 219n.2, 225, 231, 233, 239, 241, 243, 253, 256, 259, 269, 277, 286, 288, 290, 294, 295, 304, 311, 315, 316, 329, 338, 347, 350–2, 358–9, 361

bi-polar enantiomer, 143, 149, 156
bounded, 9, 12, 16, 71n.1, 107, 142, 151, 153, 156, 177, 186, 187, 193, 196, 225, 235, 270, 309, 311, 317, 334, 355
bounded rationality, 21, 309, 311–13
bureaucracy, 159, 250, 320, 328, 358, 359, 365
bureaucratic, 99, 144, 154, 212, 257

cacophony, 232, 243
capabilities, 25, 34, 44–5, 47–50, 55–7, 65–6, 68, 74, 84, 109, 110, 114–16, 122, 125, 127, 130, 131, 141, 143, 188, 208, 214–16, 224, 230, 231, 235, 244, 250, 262, 287, 293, 302, 312–15, 319, 320, 322, 331, 346
capacity, xiii, xiv, 9, 13, 14, 16, 17, 21–4, 27, 29, 32–4, 42, 43, 45, 48, 54, 56, 60, 61, 66–8, 72, 75, 76, 80, 84, 85, 88, 91–5, 97, 99, 101, 104–7, 109, 110, 113, 118, 119, 124, 126–31, 140, 143, 154, 168, 171, 176–9, 186, 189, 205, 207, 211, 214, 221, 224, 232, 239, 241, 246, 249, 255, 260, 267, 269–71, 296, 300, 305, 308, 310, 314–17, 319, 321, 348, 349, 351, 354–6, 360, 361, 364
centrifugal, 188
centripetal, 284
change, xiii, 1, 24, 41, 84, 111, 139, 175, 205, 231, 266, 305, 334
change process, 1, 16, 231, 252, 255, 270
chaos, 15, 57, 61, 166, 171, 192–3, 230, 231, 240, 272
child pathologies, 221
child socialization process, 169
Chinese, xiii, xvi, 16–18, 211, 212, 252, 256, 333–47, 349, 350, 352, 362, 366, 368, 370
climate of fear, 248
climate of security, 249
closure, 145, 175, 200, 225, 241, 249, 310
cognition, xiii–xvi, 21, 22, 34, 43, 55, 72, 83, 87, 95, 96, 107, 115, 138, 139, 179, 241, 267–8, 272, 279, 288, 289, 318
cognitive, xiii, 10, 21, 41, 83, 112, 138, 174, 216, 231, 267, 304, 351
cognitive purposes, 29, 93, 153, 216–18, 220, 228–30
cognitive schemas, 36–8, 64, 65, 67, 92, 93, 126–7, 131, 177, 179, 186, 193, 197, 351
cognitive system, xv, 28, 29, 36–8, 64–9, 73, 80, 90, 92, 101, 105, 108, 131, 133, 134, 178, 179, 181, 186, 196, 197, 351
cognitive trait, 32, 100, 142, 147
coherent social collectives, 83

436　Index

collaboration, 119, 132, 146, 170, 171, 210, 222, 227, 247, 249, 272, 347
collective, xiii, 2, 22, 42, 83, 111, 138, 175, 219, 236, 272, 305, 343
collective agency, 14, 85, 86, 95, 110, 125, 130, 132, 138, 142, 317, 355–6
collective creativity, 24, 25
collective 'emergent intelligence', 113
collective individualism, 163, 168, 170, 171, 305, 328, 329
collective intelligence, 113, 132
collective mind, 83–6, 88, 89, 111, 128, 316
collective socio-pathology, 355
collectivism, 2–4, 15, 142, 159–72, 198–201, 303–5, 308, 317, 328, 329, 331–2, 352–3, 368, 369
combination, 1, 30, 76, 77, 93, 110, 131, 143, 150, 160, 267, 317, 325, 346, 355, 369
communication, xiv, 9, 22, 53, 88, 116, 152, 175, 207, 236, 265, 306, 360
competitive, 2, 15, 43–56, 58, 60, 61, 65, 72, 99, 102, 121, 141, 167, 213, 228, 232, 285, 293, 313, 337, 341
complexity, xv, 6, 11, 13–17, 22, 24, 31–2, 43, 53–9, 61, 62, 72, 112, 120, 166, 176, 177, 186–8, 217, 231, 236, 238, 239, 241, 247, 261, 262, 280, 292, 296, 315, 318, 319, 331, 342, 349, 353, 367
complexity theory, 54, 112, 238
configuration, 14, 25–6, 49, 67, 155, 158, 161, 167, 247–8
configuration approach, 13, 18, 26–31, 33
conscious, 34, 37–9, 74, 83, 86, 87, 103, 115, 116, 139, 147, 176
consciousness, 16, 17, 22, 36–40, 68, 111, 113–14, 117, 166, 174–202, 205, 218, 241, 249, 276–7, 282, 296, 297, 301, 317
conservative individualism, 162–3
constraint, 1, 43, 45, 50, 55, 67, 71, 72, 76–8, 81, 88, 93, 96, 97, 99, 116–18, 126, 134–6, 149, 153, 196, 198, 201, 224, 226, 235, 236, 241, 250, 262, 300, 304, 305, 309, 310, 319, 325, 334, 342, 343, 348, 367
continuity, 39, 53, 105, 128, 169, 171
continuous improvement, 15, 51–3
control, xiv, 2, 21, 45, 83, 111, 139, 177, 214, 247, 278, 316, 334
control system, 186, 216, 257
core competence, 49, 53
corporate, xiii, xvi, 1, 4, 14–17, 23, 24, 38, 48, 49, 51, 53, 54, 61, 76–82, 89, 103, 122, 133, 170, 171, 200, 212, 219, 221, 245, 247–52, 254–8, 298–300, 317, 341, 342, 347, 354, 358, 364, 366, 369

corporate knowledge, 51, 53
corporate social responsibility (CSR), 15, 17, 61, 76–82
correct economic thinking, 306
corruption, 4, 5, 17, 294, 333–70
creative, 4, 25, 53, 139, 175, 188, 193, 250, 270, 345, 362
creative learning, 25
creativity, 24, 25, 156, 161, 247
crime, 24, 333, 365
crisis, 1, 2, 4–15, 61, 171, 196, 199, 200, 210, 233–6, 239, 243, 246–50, 252, 257, 259, 261, 262, 303, 304, 306, 326–33, 345–7, 361, 362, 368, 369
critical realism, 237
critical thinking, 68
CUDOS, 235
cultural, xiii, 3, 21, 55, 83, 111, 140, 174, 205, 231, 265, 303, 335
cultural agency, xv, 15, 17, 21–40, 62, 66, 69, 72, 81, 83, 114, 125–8, 134, 136, 137, 151, 174, 177, 178, 180, 183, 189, 190, 195, 205, 249, 265, 288, 294, 295, 301–2, 304, 349, 358
cultural agency theory, 17, 22, 33, 114, 126, 137, 265, 295, 301–2, 304
cultural figurative intelligence, 25, 106, 129, 175, 187, 188, 224
cultural instability, 76, 150, 245, 250, 293, 295, 352, 353, 361, 362, 368, 369
cultural intelligence, 24, 25, 106, 114, 124, 129, 134, 175, 186–8, 196, 224, 245, 318, 320, 351
cultural intelligence by Earley and Ang, 24, 124, 129, 175, 188, 224
culture, xiii, 4, 22, 43, 83, 115, 150, 175, 210, 231, 266, 303, 337
cybernetics, xiv, xvi, 9–10, 12, 14, 17, 22, 29–34, 36, 37, 54, 55, 59, 66, 91, 92, 111, 112, 114, 115, 117, 121, 122, 129, 132, 155, 176, 178, 238, 269, 273, 275, 303, 315, 318, 321, 331, 360
cycle of change, 241, 242, 255, 259, 308

decentralization, 247, 334–6, 341, 365, 368
decision, xv, 14, 28, 29, 37, 63, 65, 66, 68–71, 73, 81, 83, 89, 90, 93, 94, 96, 98, 103, 108, 118, 127, 133, 135, 138, 139, 143–5, 148, 151, 153, 159, 172, 174, 176–8, 180, 190, 196, 197, 202, 207, 216, 218, 219, 223, 234, 250, 253, 257, 289–91, 293, 295, 300, 301, 303, 309, 313, 316, 325, 331, 338, 350–2, 358
decision making structure, 69, 81, 180, 352
deconstraint, 145, 148

Index

deeper level of consciousness, 202
defining agency, 185
defining socio-cultural agency, 177
demise, 4, 9, 17–18, 208, 231, 247, 250, 258, 346
deregulation, 2, 4, 326, 340, 343
deterministic, 102, 197, 240, 248, 313
deviation-amplifying, 99, 149
deviation-counteracting, 99
dialectic interaction, 193, 355
dichotomy, 143, 234, 369
disorganization, 242, 243, 256
distorting the data, 248–9
distorting the system, 248
domain, 9, 25, 28–31, 36–8, 55, 62–4, 66, 69, 70, 73–5, 77, 81–3, 90, 93, 94, 110, 115, 126, 127, 130, 138, 147, 207, 210–11, 217, 218, 220, 222–4, 230, 233, 235, 240–1, 243, 262, 276, 284, 286, 287, 317–20, 349, 353, 356, 357
dominant epistemology, 232–4, 246
dominant paradigm, 16, 88, 189, 219, 231, 234, 246, 262, 361
double-loop learning, 26, 27, 55, 56
dramatism, 158, 167
dramatist, 152, 155, 167, 171, 328
dramatizing political right, 168
durable collective agency, 317
durable personality traits, 142, 317
dysfunction, 23–4, 28, 85, 101, 108, 110, 111, 131, 132, 153, 225, 327, 351

economic, 21, 48, 125, 150, 199, 206, 257, 289, 303, 333
economic despotism, 352
economic individualism, 163, 368
economic intelligence, 320, 322, 323
economic pressure, 367
effective, xvi, 2, 40, 44, 48, 49, 53–7, 60, 67, 68, 80, 99, 111, 119, 121, 123–6, 141, 144, 150, 152, 167, 179, 187, 188, 190, 211, 224, 228, 232, 246, 265, 285, 293, 295, 300, 304, 306, 320, 321, 343, 354, 364
effectiveness, 48, 58, 81, 95, 106, 121–3, 130, 132, 188, 222, 278, 320, 347, 360, 367
efficacy, 14, 15, 89, 91, 94, 95, 97–9, 101, 104–10, 125–32, 141, 153, 154, 179, 188, 190, 295, 314, 319, 321, 322, 325, 350, 351, 368
efficiency, 80, 106, 130, 132, 222, 314, 320, 342, 367
egalitarianism, 149, 152, 154, 155, 157, 162, 198, 199
ego, 37–9, 76, 86, 88, 274, 275, 283

elaborating knowledge, 150
elaboration information, 68, 69, 81, 82, 182
embeddedness, 97, 102, 151, 153, 156, 161, 162
emergent causation, 176
emotional climate, 248, 249
emotional intelligence, 127, 130, 141, 319, 322
emotional-motivational system, 141
emotions, xv, 22, 34, 38–40, 69, 83, 87, 88, 94, 95, 126, 127, 130, 138, 141, 142, 147, 179, 182, 190, 199, 249, 283, 289, 299, 302, 317, 319, 322
empathy, 87, 88
enantiomers, 138, 139, 142–60, 321, 325, 329
enhanced definition of intelligence, 319
environment, 21, 41, 84, 111, 138, 174, 205, 231, 270, 313, 333
epistemic base, 29, 92, 120
epistemic mapping, 82, 160
espoused values, 28, 30, 108, 110, 131
ethical norms, 366
ethics, 4–7, 24, 37, 68, 69, 78, 80, 81, 89, 93, 96–100, 102, 104, 106, 107, 109, 115, 125, 128–30, 145, 147, 149, 153, 164, 178, 180, 190, 220, 222, 223, 244, 245, 257, 261, 288, 289, 294, 295, 316, 350, 351, 356, 358–62, 366, 368
ethics-ideology coupling, 361
ethnocentricity, 175, 214
European Union, 2, 17, 199, 200, 202, 217, 303, 326, 328, 330
evolution, 43, 62, 135, 180, 238, 241, 243, 244, 246, 250, 271, 273, 277, 285, 286, 341
evolutionary economics, 3, 313–15, 332
evolution-revolution, 246
execution information, 18, 69, 82, 181
executor knowledge, 73, 150, 338
existential domain, 28, 36, 37, 66, 69, 74, 75, 77, 81, 82, 115, 127, 217, 218, 223, 356, 357
expectations, xv, 1, 12, 17, 22, 60, 71, 72, 94, 101, 125, 139, 152, 157, 198, 200, 202, 216, 217, 250, 261, 267, 275–8, 307, 310, 311, 320
explicit knowledge, 30, 49, 53, 54, 66, 74, 94, 135
external environment, 21, 27, 44, 45, 59, 69, 98, 126, 139, 154, 180, 205, 218, 221, 315, 319, 321, 354
externalization, 26, 27, 30, 93
extraversion, 155
extreme collectivism, 199, 352
extreme individualism, 172, 173, 199, 352
extreme political positioning, 173

extrinsic, 52, 53, 61, 114, 115, 119–21, 125, 134, 189
extrovert, 143, 144, 245

fatalistic, 199
feed-back, 10, 16, 26, 30, 31, 36, 57, 71n.1, 77, 87, 94, 99, 104, 105, 111–12, 135, 137, 175, 177, 179, 181–6, 190, 194, 198, 202, 244, 250, 258, 282, 287, 291, 292, 294, 302, 314, 319, 320
feed-forward, 26, 30, 31, 36, 175, 183, 320
feeling, 40, 69, 85, 87, 108, 109, 111, 124, 127, 130, 131, 141, 143, 145, 147, 151, 153, 155, 156, 201, 212, 227, 244, 268, 273, 289, 295, 322
figurative base, 29, 93, 94, 105, 106, 118, 234, 239–40
figurative emotional intelligence, 127, 130
figurative intelligence, 25, 28–30, 34, 64, 65, 94, 105–6, 108, 109, 118–20, 126–9, 135, 175, 178–80, 183, 186–8, 197, 202, 224, 239, 240, 249, 250, 302, 318, 351, 355
figurative pathology, 104
figurative schemas, 29, 36–8, 64–6, 68–71, 76, 77, 82, 93, 118, 125, 127, 131, 137, 155, 179, 186, 301, 351
figurative system, 28, 29, 37–9, 41–3, 62, 65, 66, 68, 71, 80–2, 93, 98, 108–10, 127, 131, 135, 181, 189, 195, 197, 286, 319
figurative trait, 147, 323, 324
finance, 99, 252–4, 307, 325, 327, 339–44
financial crisis, 1, 5, 196, 304, 306, 327, 329, 345
first order cybernetics, 32, 178
Fisher information theory, 316
Five Factor Model, 96, 140, 232, 234
formative traits, 31, 40, 95
fragmentation, 9, 22, 141, 166, 232, 236
fraud, 4, 6, 23, 250, 327, 346–7, 362
functionalism, 272, 276, 280
functional-structural theory, 272

general intelligence, 113, 122, 319
General Theory of Action, 266–8, 272, 301
generative, 42, 102, 114, 115, 135, 136, 148, 161
generative reformer, 159, 328
generic, 9, 13, 16, 22, 25, 27–8, 34, 36, 37, 55, 57, 58, 61, 65, 99, 110, 111, 115, 126, 127, 132, 140, 174–81, 183, 184, 186–91, 194–6, 201, 205, 249, 270, 314, 317, 319
global economic crisis, 326
goal, xvi, 2, 26, 41, 86, 117, 141, 178, 216, 231, 267, 319, 352
grand theories, 237

Greece, 196, 199–202
grid and group, 198
growth, xiii, xvi, 3, 18, 61, 78, 119, 168, 171, 199–201, 206, 245–8, 250, 256, 257, 303, 307, 308, 310, 312, 315, 327, 329, 330, 336, 339–41, 343, 345–9, 363–6, 368, 370
guanxi, 346, 369
Guatemala, 265, 296–8

harmony, 57, 98, 102, 111, 133, 149, 151, 153, 157, 161, 232, 269, 281, 287, 322–5, 366, 369
herding, 111
heterogenistic, 101, 102, 156, 157
hierarchical, 66, 101, 102, 149, 152, 154, 157, 161, 176, 195, 209, 247, 318, 328, 354, 358
hierarchical bureaucrat, 159, 161
hierarchy, 13, 16, 22, 34, 66, 97, 99, 149, 152, 154–5, 157, 161–2, 174, 176, 178, 183, 186, 189, 194–5, 199, 247, 249, 318, 332, 334, 369
higher order system, 176, 195, 297, 318
homeostatic, 101, 102
homogenistic, 101, 156, 157, 161
horizon of meanings, 11, 33, 223, 235, 283, 318
human activity system, 159, 189, 231, 239, 241, 245, 262, 310–12, 315, 331

idealistic culture, 168
ideational, 103, 150, 151, 155, 156, 161, 168, 245, 246, 290, 308, 317, 328, 330, 332
ideational culture, 150, 155, 168, 245, 317, 330
identification, 13, 60, 66, 67, 69, 82, 87, 117, 124, 140, 150, 183, 361
identification information, 67, 82
identity, 22, 23, 25, 29, 34, 36, 37, 57, 64, 65, 68, 71, 92, 105, 128, 155, 159, 165, 170, 171, 201, 208, 271, 272, 287
identity loss, 256
identity theory, 23
ideological, 4, 5, 29, 43, 68, 69, 81, 89, 93, 98, 106, 109, 128, 129, 145, 153, 163, 222, 231, 232, 235, 245, 298, 304, 316, 356, 359, 361, 362
ideological dogmatism, 232
ideology, 29, 62, 65, 81, 93, 101, 112, 115, 118, 125, 145, 153, 220, 222, 231, 232, 244, 289, 300, 334, 356, 358–62, 368
idiosyncratic knowledge, 34, 186
ignorance, 250
image, 29, 37, 71, 75, 77, 83, 85–8, 94, 98, 153, 161, 209, 221, 250, 257, 345, 354–7, 359, 361

Index

immanence, 3, 142, 246, 248
immanent change, 16, 84, 103, 120, 169, 170, 245, 246
immanent dynamics, xiv, xv, 21, 103, 246, 248, 255
imperative, 16, 65, 68, 69, 80, 93, 94, 97, 98, 101, 104, 107–10, 123, 127, 130, 131, 138, 153, 154, 179, 186, 189, 219, 231, 232, 235, 255, 294, 302, 322, 336, 337, 353, 363, 364
implementation, 57, 137, 205, 215, 224, 250, 258, 300, 305, 310, 316, 320, 361, 364
imposed causation, 43, 88, 97, 99, 176, 283
improving the system, 249
incommensurability, 13, 112, 113, 189, 191–3, 220, 223, 230, 232, 233
incompleteness theorem, 193
increase order, 241
independent, 8, 14, 42, 54, 55, 76, 77, 86, 89, 102, 111, 116, 122, 123, 144, 155, 156, 159, 161, 164, 165, 171, 224, 237, 240, 241, 252, 259, 267–9, 309, 328, 341, 358, 367
independent prince, 159, 161, 328
individual, 2, 24, 45, 83, 111, 138, 183, 214, 232, 266, 303, 343
individualism, 2–4, 15, 142, 159–72, 198–201, 303–5, 308, 317, 328, 329, 331, 332, 352, 353, 368, 369
individualist, 1, 101, 155, 158, 161, 162, 164–71, 196, 197, 200, 201, 304, 308, 328, 329, 331, 351, 369
individual pathologies, 84
inductive methodology, 245
inefficacy, 98, 104, 109, 130, 153, 322
inefficient, 250, 257, 340, 341
inequality, 157, 161, 365
inference, 48, 67, 80, 117, 195, 202, 255, 258, 311
information, xv, 8, 28, 48, 87, 112, 141, 177, 226, 239, 273, 309, 337
information migration, 10, 274
innovation, 22, 24, 52, 53, 56, 62, 171, 206, 229, 247, 249, 257, 325, 345
instability, xiv, 17, 58, 76, 150, 186, 214, 244, 245, 250, 293, 294, 332, 333, 348, 352, 353, 361, 362, 368, 369
institutional decline, 294
institutions, 1, 12, 23, 31, 159, 162–4, 170, 171, 200, 207–9, 214, 221, 225, 228, 244, 257, 265–7, 271, 287–94, 304, 305, 312, 314, 319, 326, 329, 333–5, 341–5, 347, 364, 368
instrumental agency, 15, 33, 36, 41–3, 48, 64, 71, 177–9, 183, 186, 194, 195, 353
instrumental systems, 43

integration, 55–8, 60, 62, 64, 65, 68, 69, 74, 82, 86, 119, 146, 161, 207, 236, 244, 259, 261, 268–70, 284 n.5, 287, 341
integrity, 171, 306
intellectual, 9, 48, 49, 122, 132, 156, 161–3, 232, 235, 306, 310
intellectual autonomy, 156, 161
intellectual imperialism, 310
intellectual orthodoxy, 9, 232
intelligence, 14, 24, 62, 92, 111, 141, 175, 224, 234, 267, 318, 351
intelligence at large, 188, 319
intelligence by Haeckel and Nolan, 120
intelligence in cultural agency, 125
intelligence limitation, 104, 109, 127
intelligent organization, 74, 114, 120–3, 286
intention, xv, xvi, 10, 21, 22, 29, 34, 69, 71, 82, 86, 91, 92, 99, 101, 106, 113, 124, 130, 150, 153, 172, 201, 220, 259, 268, 269, 274–7, 291, 310, 348, 360, 368
interactive, 3, 13, 17, 21, 26, 30, 31, 40, 42, 53, 101, 102, 106, 114, 121, 132, 139, 163, 179, 218, 222, 241, 287, 288, 300, 302, 318, 321, 331, 332, 357, 362, 368, xv
interdependence, 165, 208, 267
interdisciplinary, 9, 111, 291
interest, 2, 23, 41, 83, 111, 138, 174, 205, 231, 268, 304, 333
internalization, 16, 17, 26, 30, 34, 87, 93, 99, 145, 149, 174–6, 180, 183, 191–202, 249, 266, 276, 301, 319
intrinsic dynamics, 119, 120
intrinsic knowledge development, 53
introversion, 155
introvert, 143, 144, 155, 245
intuition, 133, 143, 146, 147, 236
invented meanings, 193
investment, 1, 2, 47, 50, 53, 199, 207, 247, 250, 254, 293, 303, 308, 322, 323, 323 n.2, 324, 326, 327, 337, 339, 340, 342, 344–8, 368

joint alliance, xiii, 16, 17, 24, 170, 205–30, 341, 342
joint ventures, 205, 207, 210, 211, 217, 221, 230, 339
judgement, 7, 34, 98, 125, 143, 153, 236, 244, 245, 277, 294, 351, 359–61
judging, 143–5, 147

Keynesian economics, 308
knowledge cybernetics, 22, 66, 315
knowledge more than, 9, 22, 42, 83, 112, 138, 175, 205, 265, 309, 337
knowledge organization, 74

440 Index

language, xvi, 105, 116, 118, 125, 128, 166, 183, 207, 210, 217, 220, 224, 239, 277, 279 n.3, 280, 281, 299
lateral, 30, 31, 64, 66, 82, 85, 94, 272, 353–4, 356–61, 368
leadership, 60, 80, 133, 136, 226, 227, 247–50, 253, 257, 306, 328, 332, 354, 358, 367
learning agency, 74
learning loops, 179, 183, 187
learning organization, 74
learning theory, 22, 31, 89, 113, 170, 176, 179, 185, 187, 210, 225, 314
legitimacy, 16, 27, 164, 191, 257, 359–63, 365, 368
legitimizing environment, 27, 31
lensing, 238
life cycle, 16, 246–52, 255–8, 262
lifeworld, 10–12, 14, 66, 191, 266, 269–72, 279–84, 286–8, 295
living system, xv, xvi, 10, 12–14, 22, 26, 31–40, 43, 48, 65, 66, 71, 132, 137, 174, 175, 177, 179, 186, 188, 189, 191, 194, 195, 265, 270–3, 289, 298, 301, 302, 313, 315, 317–19, 331
living systems theory, xv, xvi, 31–3, 265
local agency paradigm, 191
local worldviews, 10, 269
loyal, 162, 250
Lucas critique, 303, 304, 309, 310, 317, 331, 352

macroeconomics, 1, 2, 4, 17, 304, 305, 308–16, 320–6, 331, 332
madman, 172
management cybernetics, 32, 33, 54, 112, 114, 178, 238
management style, 215, 216, 257
manifestation, 39, 65, 68, 70, 74, 76, 94, 95, 104, 106, 109, 110, 113–17, 122, 127, 129, 131, 188, 189, 197, 219, 220, 224, 293, 294, 319, 322, 331, 358
manipulation, 5, 6, 118, 196, 239, 327, 359
many-views, 149
marginalized, 306, 322
market assessment, 250
market based view, 44–6, 57, 99
market oriented strategy, 44
Maruyama mindscape theory, 94–104, 160, 161
Marxism, 290, 291, 334
mass communication, 279
mastery, 98, 151, 153, 157, 161, 162, 322, 323, 325
mastery oriented, 153, 162
maturity, 171, 247, 250, 308, 343

meaning, 22, 43, 85, 111, 141, 176, 205, 231, 267, 303, 336
mental, 10, 38–40, 67, 73, 83, 85, 86, 88, 89, 94, 105, 113–15, 125, 128, 134, 138, 139, 142–5, 147, 179, 189, 211, 239, 273, 277, 301, 317, 338, 355
mental disposition, 38–40, 67, 73, 86, 115, 134, 142, 179, 317
mental models, 40, 94, 145, 211
mental state, 38–40, 73, 86, 147
mercantile agency theory, 311
merit-based system, 212
meritocratic bureaucracy, 365
meso-economics, 314
message sinks, 280
message sources, 270, 280
message transfer, 270, 278
meta-framework, xiv, xv, 9, 111, 112, 238
metaphors, xiv, 23, 25, 62, 84, 119, 141, 142, 206, 210, 220, 234, 235, 355
meta-system, 109, 127, 131
meta-theory, 9, 13, 14, 22, 111–13, 174, 237, 238
meta-triangulation, 238
method, 33, 96, 103, 119, 150, 226, 233, 234, 237, 243, 248, 290, 312, 366
methodological individualism, 162, 163, 304–5, 329
methodological institutionalism, 162, 163, 304–5, 329
microeconomics, 1, 4, 309, 312, 314, 320
mind, 4, 16, 22, 27, 35, 37, 38, 40, 83–9, 91, 105, 114, 118, 128, 138, 142, 160, 193, 217, 239, 246, 262, 270, 273, 276, 277, 316, 328, 329, 332
mindedness, 145, 147, 148, 156, 161
mindscape, 17, 18, 94–104, 140, 141, 147, 148, 159–61, 172, 303, 304, 325–32
mindscape theory, 17, 96, 101, 147, 148, 159, 160, 303, 304, 326, 331, 332
mindscape types, 140, 160
mindsets, 326, 328
missionaries, 209
modelling, xvi, 9, 12, 13, 16–18, 23, 26, 33, 41, 59, 64, 65, 85, 91, 96, 125, 127, 141, 145, 175–7, 187–91, 194, 209, 217, 232, 235, 265, 290, 301, 303, 308–12, 316, 318, 320, 332, 368
modernization, 294
monetary policy, 310
mono-ocularity, 149
moral crusades, 209
moral equals, 152, 154, 157, 161
moral judgements, 359
moral justification, 285

Index

moral orientations, 220–1
more of the same, 242, 243, 256
morphing, 255–7
morphogenesis, 43, 62, 233, 241–3, 256
morphogenic, 69, 101, 102, 117, 244
motivation, 12, 21, 27, 64, 76, 92, 95, 105, 109, 126, 128, 131, 132, 137, 139, 141, 143, 147, 178, 182, 183, 206, 214, 230, 262, 317, 354
multiple intelligences, 15, 113, 137
Mundell–Fleming model, 308
Myers-Briggs Type Inventory (MBTI), 96, 104, 139, 140, 143–9, 234
myth, 29, 71, 72, 92, 117, 134, 285, 294, 351

narratives, 140, 145, 152, 167, 232, 235, 236, 240, 243, 289, 325, 330
national culture, 215, 251, 255
national security, 161, 297
nconscious, 37–40, 75–7, 86, 139, 146, 147
negotiation, 17, 152, 154, 157, 171, 195–202, 210, 221, 298
neoclassical economics, 310
neoDarwinian, 285
neo-institutionalism, 290
neurotic organizations, 85, 111
new institutionalism, 290, 291
noncompliance, 24
non-equilibrium conditions, 247
non-equilibrium systems, 312
non-normative, 269
non-rational argument, 285
normal, 69, 96, 101, 115, 137, 149, 156, 234, 239, 240, 243, 246, 250, 254–6, 262, 311, 318, 320, 352, 355
normal mode, 233, 242, 244, 245, 262
normal science, 233, 235–7, 239–41, 244–6, 262
normative, xvi, 2, 10, 14, 15, 24, 29, 30, 67, 69, 76, 77, 83–6, 88, 89, 92, 93, 99, 106, 111, 113, 116, 118, 129, 134, 141, 145, 147, 154, 155, 165, 168, 189, 191, 239, 240, 246, 252, 269, 282, 287, 289, 314–16, 355, 359, 361, 362
normative agency, 29, 94, 104, 106, 128
normative belief system, 116
normative epistemology, 234, 242, 245, 246
normative mind, 83, 85
normative personality, 15, 24, 25, 31, 32, 88–92, 94, 95, 100, 101, 103, 106–8, 110, 128–32, 142, 150, 155, 162, 189, 195, 224, 289, 303, 315–17, 320, 331, 352
normative symbolic structure, 219n.1
normative validity, 283

norms, xiii, xiv, xv, 3, 4, 23–6, 37, 76, 88, 89, 112, 115, 124, 125, 146, 163, 169, 179, 196, 207, 217, 224, 235, 239, 244, 249, 250, 267–9, 280, 283, 284, 284n.5, 285, 287–9, 294, 295, 299, 316, 332, 339, 352, 353, 360, 361, 366, 368
noumenal domain, 28, 36, 37, 55, 83, 90, 127, 218, 220, 222, 240, 284, 286
object, 29, 66, 68, 84, 86–8, 93, 107, 115–17, 134, 135, 138, 146, 150, 152, 155, 167, 171, 180, 193, 194, 282, 285, 286, 328, 354–7, 359
object free, 115–17, 134
object free intelligence, 116
objective, 33, 38, 48, 65, 154, 193, 208, 215, 216, 227, 228, 237, 265–8, 285, 299, 309, 311, 312, 326, 347
objectivism, 147
objectivity, 84, 102, 107, 193, 290, 354
object of attention, 107, 138, 150, 171, 193, 282, 328, 357
obligation, 152, 154, 157, 267, 268, 342
observed system, 178
observing system, 178
one-view, 11, 149
ontological, xv, 2, 8, 12–14, 25, 27, 28, 41, 58, 61, 64, 66, 75–7, 85, 92, 106, 108, 126, 131, 165, 171, 176, 183, 195, 222, 276, 277, 304, 322, 329, 353
ontology, 8, 12, 61–2, 85, 273
open, 2, 9, 35, 124, 139, 145, 227–9, 240, 250, 270, 276, 300, 310, 311, 318, 335–7, 339, 367
openness, 175, 214, 249, 300, 310, 335, 367
open system, 139, 240, 270, 311
operations, 2, 5, 26–8, 30, 31, 37, 51, 55, 57–60, 62, 63, 65, 72, 73, 79, 80, 86, 87, 90, 97–9, 115–17, 123, 126, 153, 154, 157, 161, 177, 190, 205, 222, 224, 225, 229, 231, 241, 270, 272–4, 276, 284, 297, 298, 302, 319, 333, 340, 348, 353–5, 358–60, 367
operative couple, 99, 108, 109, 127, 155, 158–9
operative emotional intelligence, 127
operative intelligence, 28–30, 34, 62, 63, 65, 75, 81, 90, 94, 97, 100, 104–6, 108, 110, 118, 119, 126–8, 130, 131, 135, 136, 154, 177–81, 183–7, 190, 194, 197, 198, 202, 223, 234, 239–41, 249–51, 288, 294, 302, 318–20, 328, 350, 351, 355
operative (self-producing) intelligence, 319
operative intention, 69–71, 76
operative lifeworld, 286

operative orientation, 90, 97, 100, 104, 129, 153–5, 190, 320, 350
operative pathology, 104
operative schemas, 37, 38, 65, 69–72, 81, 82, 90, 93, 100, 127, 131, 181, 182, 185, 350, 351
operative system, 27–8, 30–2, 36–43, 62–6, 68–73, 75, 76, 81, 90, 93, 97, 100, 104, 108, 109, 127, 131, 134, 136, 155, 177–82, 184, 185, 189, 190, 194–5, 197, 198, 202, 218, 223, 224, 251, 271, 288, 297, 299, 301, 320, 321, 328, 349, 350, 353, 356
operative trait, 100, 147, 148, 162
opinion, 2, 27, 144, 183, 306, 311
opportunity, xvi, 2, 24, 25, 44, 47, 49, 56, 57, 60, 97–9, 119, 148, 153, 214, 227, 244–5, 261, 269, 299, 312, 325, 340, 351, 360–5, 367, 368, 370
opportunity-legitimacy coupling, 361
optimal choice, 310
organic system, 133, 134
organism, 241, 247, 266, 271, 284 n.5
organizational chaos, 231, 240
organizational character, 141
organizational culture, 14, 23, 26, 27, 30, 99, 125, 126, 170, 249, 320
organizational culture theory, 125, 126
organizational dysfunction, 327
organizational intelligence, 119–26, 133
organizational pathology, 23
organizational personality, 23, 24
organizational structure, 9, 30, 37, 43, 93, 159, 165, 170, 191, 261, 365
organizational theory, 7, 18, 23, 24, 26, 85, 126, 232, 236
organizational vision, 122
organization goals, 257
organization of action, 267
organizations, 22, 43, 85, 111, 141, 176, 205, 231, 267, 303, 336
organization theory, 9, 13, 23, 26, 119, 125, 176, 235, 246, 261, 262, 314
organize, 54, 72, 147, 193, 240, 276, 319, 355
orthodoxy, 9, 219, 232
outdated strategies, 249, 250
outputs, xiii, 7, 35, 49, 60, 71, 240, 257, 291, 292, 294, 309, 314, 322, 323
overt actions, 318, 351
overt-covert, 139

paradigmatic death, 233, 243
paradigmatic narrative, 232, 236
paradigm bracketing, 238
paradigm change, 16, 233, 306
paradigm incommensurability, 13, 112, 113, 191, 192, 230
paradigms, 9, 13, 16, 18, 22, 32, 33, 36, 48–55, 58, 61, 88, 105, 111, 112, 116, 122, 126, 128, 170, 172, 178, 183, 187–9, 191–3, 217, 219, 230–46, 258, 265, 306–8, 316, 329, 330, 361
paradigm shift, 172, 183, 187, 188, 240, 245, 258, 329
paradox, 50, 192, 193, 234, 298
parent, 1, 7, 16, 169, 170, 208, 211, 213–17, 220–6, 228–30
parent-child metaphor, 220
parochial interests, 171, 172, 328
parochialism, 330
parsimony, 112, 238
participative, 10, 21, 91, 135, 145, 156, 211, 234, 272, 293, 295, 348
pathological, 71, 110, 160, 199, 202, 249, 346, 352, 358, 362, 363, 365
pathologies, 12–14, 17, 23, 24, 29, 54, 55, 61, 71, 76, 82, 84, 89, 104, 108–10, 122, 128, 131, 132, 138, 177–9, 181, 183, 190, 191, 197, 201, 221, 301, 320, 321, 327, 351, 353–60, 362, 364, 368
pathology, 75–7, 104, 110, 128, 172, 268, 301, 350, 354, 355, 362
pathology type, 77, 355, 360
paths, 56, 75, 78, 243, 248, 318, 368
pattern, 4, 8, 11, 24, 29, 37, 39, 40, 43, 48, 62, 64, 67, 72, 82, 83, 86, 87, 91, 92, 101, 102, 105, 106, 110, 120, 128, 129, 133, 139, 140, 142, 144, 146, 152, 155, 158, 160, 161, 167, 220, 231, 232, 240, 247, 250, 262, 266, 267, 270, 272, 281, 282, 284 n.5, 288, 294, 302, 341
patterning, 101, 152, 155, 168, 171, 329
patternism, 158, 167
patterns of behaviour, xiii, xiv, 15, 17, 18, 24–6, 29–31, 72, 76, 77, 89, 91, 93, 96, 99, 101, 132, 140, 143, 153, 175, 189, 223, 230, 291, 316, 317, 331, 332
patterns of beliefs, 29, 92, 358
patterns of knowledge, 40, 72, 105, 118, 128, 132, 133, 148, 207, 219, 240–2, 358
patterns of meaning, 11, 281, 288
perceived, 7, 17, 31, 39, 43, 49, 85, 88, 94, 101, 103, 110, 130–2, 140, 143, 150, 163, 171, 193, 197, 217, 228, 261, 270, 287, 295, 311, 312, 314, 326, 328, 334, 342, 370
perception, 8, 16, 39, 87, 91, 96, 101, 105, 114, 115, 118, 128, 130, 134–6, 143, 147, 162, 163, 174, 198, 239, 258–61, 279, 305, 306, 309, 348, 355

performance, xiv, xvi, 7, 16, 25–7, 30, 31, 44, 45, 47, 53, 55, 60, 61, 68, 77, 79, 80, 86, 91, 92, 94, 99, 104, 106, 109–11, 121, 123, 126, 129–33, 138, 142, 143, 150, 208, 209, 212, 215, 216, 221, 228, 248, 249, 252, 260, 267, 312, 314, 317, 319, 320, 322, 335, 342, 356, 366, 368
personal intelligence, 116, 117, 134
personality, 12, 22, 62, 83, 114, 138, 174, 224, 232, 265, 303
personality cognitive structure, 83
personality creation, 180
personality differences, 138, 139
personality evaluation, 138
personality evolution, 62
personality indicators, 114, 138, 140
personality orientations, 97, 108, 131, 154, 197, 355
personality preferences, 108, 109, 131
personality styles, 95, 317
personality system, 27, 35, 37, 84, 92, 150, 265, 267, 284 n.5
personality theory, 140–2, 169, 232, 302, 317
personality traits, 83, 89, 94, 95, 100, 103, 104, 139, 142, 144, 148–50, 317
personality type, 91, 95, 101, 106, 107, 129, 130, 142, 143, 150–2, 172, 316, 317
personal narratives, 140
personal political salience, 144
personal rewards, 257
personal trust, 208
perspective, 2, 21, 57, 84, 111, 144, 174, 206, 232
perspectivism, 88
phenomenal domain, 28, 30, 36, 37, 81, 82, 127, 217, 218, 220, 222, 224, 240
phenomenal system, 43
planning, 55, 57, 60, 65, 71, 96, 102, 122, 125, 133, 313
plural agency, xiii, xiv, 15, 16, 22, 25, 37, 67, 83–6, 88, 90, 129, 174, 184, 231, 269, 270, 353–5, 359, 361, 364, 365
plural collective actor, 87, 219, 236
plural culture, 196, 197, 201
plural economic system, 306
pluralistic, 98, 112, 145, 147, 148, 151, 153, 157, 175, 238, 359
plurality of paradigms, 193, 232, 236, 310
plural personality, 25
policy, 1, 55, 143, 198, 209, 234, 291, 303
political change, 271
political culture, 4, 150, 159, 211, 249, 289, 291, 294, 295, 328, 351–3, 358, 359, 361, 362, 368
political cycle, 315

political decay, 294
political despotism, 352
political development, 289, 293–5
political favoritism, 212
political ideology, 118, 359
political individualism, 198, 200
political left, 2, 168
political legitimacy, 359
political myths, 294, 351
political operative system, 350
political power, 148, 308, 330, 352
political regime, 2, 168, 295, 308, 317
political right, 2, 167, 168, 369
political science, 18, 234, 279
political system, 290–2, 294, 306, 335, 352, 360, 361, 367
political views of agency, 265
politicization, 365
politico-economic agency, 349, 350, 353, 362
poly-ocularity, 149
positive emotional climate, 249
positive-sum, 102
post-academic science, 235, 236
post-behaviouralism, 284 n.5
postcolonial analyses, 236
Post-Marxism, 291
postmodernism, 234
post-neoclassical, 311
post-normal, 234, 236, 237, 239–41, 244–6, 262, 318
post-normal science, 234, 236, 237, 239–41, 246, 262
Postpositivism, 310
post-sensate, 328, 332
post-structuralist, 166
poverty, 322, 325, 362, 365, 367, 369
power, 3, 23, 44, 85, 111, 138, 144, 178, 208, 242, 282, 306, 334
power trait, 97–9, 105, 106, 130, 149
practical intelligence, 133
practices, 1, 5–7, 14, 17, 18, 24, 78, 79, 114, 115, 122, 132, 134, 135, 169, 211–15, 221, 228, 250, 294, 303, 327, 336, 347–9, 351, 360–2, 365, 368–70
pragmatic base, 30, 93
pragmatics, 8, 18, 29, 30, 35, 93, 94, 105, 110, 112, 114, 119, 121, 138, 156, 161, 235, 239, 240, 243, 244, 278, 334
precedence, 158, 166, 167, 247
preconscious, 37–40, 86, 107, 114, 129, 142, 317
preferences, 6, 29, 58, 93, 107–10, 127, 129, 131, 132, 138–40, 142–4, 146, 151, 153, 156, 209, 308, 310, 312, 317, 320, 349, 364

pre-living system, 33, 177
prescription, 327
primary knowledge, 52, 53
prince, 144, 159, 161, 328
principle of emergence, 318
principle of immanent change, 84, 103, 169
principles, xiv, 2, 7, 9, 10, 12, 18, 25, 33, 62, 64, 65, 67, 78 n.3, 81, 83, 84, 91, 98, 102, 103, 105, 112–14, 120, 128, 133, 140, 142, 153, 163–5, 169, 171, 172, 177, 178, 180, 189, 206, 207, 233, 235, 238, 240, 241, 245, 253, 289, 310, 312, 318, 320, 331, 334, 345, 352, 361, 366
proactive, 21, 91, 121
problem, 1, 23, 42, 85, 111, 138, 174, 208, 233, 265, 309, 336
procedural trust, 214
process intelligence, xvi, 28–30, 92, 94, 125–32, 137, 224, 239, 289, 321, 325
production, 47, 55, 60, 66, 72, 98, 105, 110, 115, 133, 177, 180, 241, 270, 272, 276, 309, 322–5, 339
products, 1, 44–6, 49, 53, 56–8, 60, 61, 78, 79, 104, 115, 132, 133, 210, 229, 257, 260, 294, 297, 313, 322–4, 343, 344, 347, 348
properties, xv, xvi, 2, 22, 28, 34–6, 40, 55, 62, 66, 74, 84, 86, 95, 96, 103, 105, 119, 122, 129, 143, 163, 165, 167, 174, 176, 189, 218, 230, 233, 237, 239, 267, 346, 354, 355
property, 25, 138, 235, 272, 274, 297, 340, 341, 344, 346, 347, 354
propositions, xv, 8, 9, 13, 22, 29, 34, 35, 45, 53, 65, 84, 87, 92, 107, 108, 112, 113, 131, 138–40, 189, 191–3, 217, 219 n.2, 221, 231, 235, 238, 240, 243, 278, 284, 285, 290, 301–3, 309, 310, 313, 316, 355, 364, 366
psychic, 12, 37–9, 177, 273, 275, 296–9, 301, 302
psychological, 3, 23, 37, 75, 76, 83–5, 89, 94, 99, 107, 111, 113–15, 125, 135, 137, 139–41, 165, 171, 183, 262, 273, 278, 289, 290, 295, 321, 326
psychological models of intelligence, 113
psychology, 10, 22, 23, 26, 39, 40, 67, 83–8, 115, 141, 144, 150, 165, 210, 275, 279
psychology of the collective, 10, 141
psychosis, 172, 173, 352
psycho-social dynamics, 138
psycho-social framework, 142, 316
public sector, 210
punishment, 347
purpose, xv, 2, 9–11, 22, 29, 32, 34, 52, 54, 60, 80, 82, 86, 92, 93, 116, 120–2, 124, 132, 147, 153, 159, 165, 175, 189, 191, 192, 197, 205, 216–22, 228–31, 240, 269, 270, 275, 280, 281, 284 n.5, 286, 297, 308, 324, 354, 356, 364, 367
purposeful, 11, 29, 93, 189, 205, 218–21, 230, 269, 280, 367
purposeful adaptable organization, 218
purpose of national security, 297

random, 101, 102, 139, 143, 240, 271, 310, 311
rational, 1, 3, 14, 21, 34, 35, 45, 58, 68, 69, 72, 73, 75, 80, 81, 86, 89, 111, 117, 118, 122, 138, 143, 145, 158, 160, 165, 167, 179, 217, 220, 225, 231, 234, 250, 258, 267, 273, 281, 282, 285–7, 293, 299, 300, 307, 309–13, 326, 330, 356, 358, 361
rational determinism, 310
rational expectations, 1, 307, 310, 311
reactions, 28, 44, 72, 90, 104, 123, 126, 127, 139, 143, 155, 174, 321
realism, 237
realist paradigms, 239
real world situation, 219
recursion, 65, 189, 191, 194, 195
recursively embedded systems, 318
re-definition, 257
reduction of complexity, 296
reference, 7, 10, 18, 33, 75, 77, 84, 107, 111–13, 117, 118, 133, 147, 164, 168, 170, 199, 205, 211, 218, 230, 260, 270, 273, 275, 276, 282, 285, 286, 288, 294, 297, 357
reform, 144, 159, 161, 212, 213, 305, 306, 326–8, 334, 335, 339–43, 349, 352, 367, 368
regime, 2, 150, 168, 198, 292, 295, 307–9, 315, 317, 367
regularities, 272, 290, 347
regulation, 10, 29, 43, 55, 57, 60, 64, 67, 68, 73, 78, 93, 97–9, 101, 111, 145, 149, 154, 228, 241, 250, 269, 284, 337, 341, 343, 344, 347, 349, 361–5, 367, 369
regulatory environment, 337
relational collectivism, 162, 163, 166
relational logic, 220
relational patterning, 155, 158, 161, 167, 168, 171, 329
relativism, 234, 237, 245
reliable, 68, 250
reproductive, 87, 197, 296
reputation, 15, 56, 74, 257
requisite variety, 41–3, 55, 81, 241, 284, 364
resource based, 43–4, 46–8, 55, 57, 61, 99, 206, 207, 225, 228, 313

Index

responsibility, 1, 15, 17, 60, 61, 76–82, 152, 154, 156, 157, 161, 169–71, 212, 213, 228, 300, 304, 326, 334
responsible business, 77
restore, 99, 326, 335
restrictive hierarchical structures, 354, 358
restructuring, 205, 209, 215–17, 221, 227, 229, 257, 303
revolution, 233, 234, 236, 245, 246, 262, 271, 291, 333, 335–7
revolutionary, 144, 159, 161, 234, 246, 290, 328
rewards, 29, 93, 147, 215, 235, 244, 257
rigid hierarchical decisions, 247
risk-proneness, 248
rivalry, 44–6
role-obligations, 152, 154

Sagiv-Schwartz mindsets, 326
satisfaction, 103, 126, 134, 150, 151, 244, 319
schema, 27, 29, 36–8, 40, 41, 55, 62, 64–72, 77, 80–2, 87, 88, 92, 93, 95, 96, 108, 109, 112, 114, 117–20, 125–9, 131, 133, 135, 137, 141, 143, 144, 155, 174, 175, 177–9, 186, 193, 196, 197, 201, 202, 217, 222, 224, 232, 235, 266, 289, 301, 351, 353, 360, 362, 368
scientific revolutions, 234, 262
Search of Excellence, 60
secondary knowledge, 52, 53
secondary socialization, 99, 149
second order cybernetics, xvi, 32, 33, 178
second order generic hierarchy, 183, 194
second order judgement, 34
second order observation, 297
self, xiii, 29, 35, 68, 88, 89, 94, 105, 112, 115, 116, 128, 149, 156, 171, 172, 238, 274n.1, 275, 282, 301, 316
self-assertion, 157, 161
self-awareness, 22, 34, 68, 114, 117, 137, 245
self-control, 4, 24, 95
self-create, xvi, 318
self-defining network, 184
self-evident, 192
self-goals, 197, 202
self-identity, 71, 166, 170
self-indulged, 303
self-interest, 21, 149, 311
self-motivation, 141
self-negotiation, 35
self-observation, 272
self-observing viewers, 224
self-organization, 14, 22, 30, 32, 34, 35, 43, 69, 71, 72, 93, 97, 120, 141, 155, 241, 262, 286, 320

self-organize, 21, 41, 54, 60, 62, 91, 240, 319
self-process, 105, 117, 128, 137, 241
self-production, 43, 64, 127, 241
self-reference, 22, 29, 34, 71, 72, 92, 132, 150, 155, 159, 241, 272, 298
self-referencing, 68, 80
self-referral loop, 114
self-reflection, 22, 32, 34, 35, 72, 300
self-regulation, 21, 35, 57, 71n.1, 72, 98, 99, 119, 153
self-reinforcing cycle, 50
self-relational ethics, 98, 100, 102, 104, 106, 107, 129, 130
self-repair, 35
self-reproduction, 272, 320
self-reproductive systems, 296
self-schema, 29, 65, 81, 87, 141, 144, 147, 178, 179, 197, 202, 286, 289, 294, 352
self-system, 21, 126
self-verifying, 34
semantic, xiii, xiv, 11, 12, 58, 82, 104, 108, 109, 112, 115, 126, 186, 236, 238, 249, 250, 266, 275–9, 281, 285–8, 297, 350, 353
semantic goods, 28, 66, 67, 74, 92, 126, 127
semantic harmony, 232
semantic migration, 191
semantic transposability, 67, 80
semiosis, 279, 280
semiotics, 17, 112, 238, 265, 278, 279, 285
sender, 222, 279
senior executive, 80, 221, 347
sensate, 150, 156, 161, 168, 245, 246, 290, 308, 317, 328
sensate culture, 155, 168, 171, 245, 246, 317, 328, 330
sensate orientation, 101, 332
sense, 10, 16, 35, 53, 89, 98, 103, 114, 125, 150, 165, 186, 193, 211, 219, 231, 234, 239, 245, 262, 266, 267, 271, 290, 297, 310, 316, 318, 365
sensing, 143, 146, 147
shared belief, 88, 89, 129, 170, 239, 316
shared commitments, 233
shared fate, 123
shared meaning, 120, 220
shared understanding, 219, 299, 300
shared values, 170, 233
sign, 17, 58, 268, 276–80, 326
sign concept, 276
simplifying, 237
simultaneity, 119, 193
single paradigm, 22
situation, xv, 4, 7, 9, 11–14, 17, 25, 27, 29, 42, 53, 57, 61, 64, 65, 67–9, 71, 75, 80, 85–7,

92, 93, 95, 98, 99, 107, 119, 122–5, 139, 140, 145, 152, 153, 155, 165, 169–72, 174–7, 188, 192, 199–202, 212, 222, 224, 227, 229, 231, 234, 235, 237, 240, 241, 245, 250, 258, 261, 262, 267, 268, 272, 281–4, 288, 289, 294, 298–300, 304, 306, 309–11, 313, 315, 317, 326–31, 333, 346, 356, 358, 360, 364
social, 2, 21, 42, 83, 111, 138, 178, 205, 232, 265, 303, 333
social action, 106, 130, 265–7, 272, 280, 301, 355, 361
social and cognitive psychology, 279
social behaviour, 14, 36, 83, 106, 111, 129, 267, 280, 287
social coherence, 272, 322, 325, 332
social contexts, 10, 14, 27, 37, 85, 92, 111, 124, 189, 211, 278, 279
social environment, 6, 25, 27, 79, 84, 92, 97–9, 104, 105, 114, 124, 129, 137, 141, 144, 149, 151, 153–5, 157, 159, 166, 188, 189, 195, 232, 281, 287, 288, 318, 320, 354, 365
social good, 78
social harmony, 149
social institution, 170, 271, 287
social integration, 268–70, 287
social intelligence, 105, 123, 124, 129, 132, 134, 188, 295
socialist individualism, 163, 167
socialization, 30, 50, 94, 97, 99, 149, 155, 169, 267, 270, 287, 358
socialization theory, 266
social knowledge, 186
social living systems, 22, 271
social mass, 292
social need, 91, 130, 280
social orientation, 95, 97, 101, 104, 149, 154, 155, 159, 320, 351
social personality, 96, 141
social problems, 314, 315
social psychological models of intelligence, 113
social psychology, 10, 22, 83–5, 150, 210
social reformer, 161
social responsibility, 15, 17, 76–82, 169
social revolutionary, 159, 328
social roles, 226, 267
social rules, 276
social science paradigm shift, 183
social system, 12, 13, 16, 25, 33, 35, 105, 129, 130, 154, 163, 248, 266, 267, 271–8, 284n.5, 288, 291, 296–9, 301, 308, 312, 314, 315
social trait, 145, 159, 162

social world, 12, 14, 123, 164, 166, 285, 299, 301
society, xiv, 3, 4, 12, 16, 78, 79, 102, 144, 155, 161, 162, 165, 166, 168, 171, 188, 198n.1, 199, 254, 258, 266–73, 280, 282, 284n.5, 287, 288, 291, 292, 294, 297, 303, 304, 307, 308, 314, 319, 321, 325, 328–30, 332–70
socio-cognitive theory, 22, 26, 27, 34, 91, 94, 141, 232, 233
socio-cultural dynamics, 4, 170, 245, 304, 308, 332
socio-cultural environment, 244
sociological, xvi, 10, 12, 18, 36, 96, 265–302
sociological political theory, 265
sociology, 26, 279, 284n.5, 290, 291, 314
sociopathic, 98, 154, 172, 326, 327, 354, 355, 358, 362
socio-pathology, 355
socio-political, 16, 18, 24, 25, 43, 196, 226, 249, 304, 317, 331, 352
socio-psychological, 302, 314
solidarity, 151, 153, 156, 161, 267, 287
speech-acts, 280, 286, 301
stability, xiii, xiv, 1, 42, 53, 55, 80, 142, 175, 179, 186, 196, 202, 245, 246, 249, 252, 255–7, 267, 291, 293–5, 298, 317, 328, 343, 346, 348, 352, 353
stable patterns, 91, 96, 101, 102, 143, 144, 267, 291
stable periods, 168
stages of evolution, 246
state bureaucracy, 250
statements, 14, 78, 176, 279, 282, 299, 304, 329, 346
state of traits, 103, 140
static intelligence, 119
stimulation, 135, 171, 205, 304, 327, 329, 330
story, 221, 232, 233, 235, 236, 243, 259, 262, 326, 332, 359
strategic, xiv, xv, 3, 4, 7, 13, 15, 17, 18, 29, 34–6, 41, 43–51, 54, 55, 57–9, 61, 62, 64–9, 74, 76, 79–81, 92, 93, 99, 109, 110, 114, 121, 122, 126, 128, 133, 175, 178, 179, 188, 196, 197, 202, 205, 207, 208, 212, 213, 218, 220–2, 224, 228, 230, 260, 270, 272, 281, 289, 294, 295, 300, 308, 313–15, 319, 321, 326, 331, 332, 351, 353, 354, 356, 368
strategic agency, xv, 15, 17, 35, 36, 41–82, 126, 134, 137, 174, 195, 218, 349, 351, 360
strategic agency operative intelligence, 130
strategic cognitive system, 68, 351

Index

strategic economic agency, 151–2, 159, 162, 303, 315, 319
strategic figurative system, 319
strategic gap, 51
strategic groups, 111
strategic interests, 208
strategic knowledge, 51
strategic knowledge intensifying organization, 74
strategic model of intervention, 218
strategic motivations, 230, 354
strategic part, 29, 93
strategic schemas, 40, 128, 217, 222, 224, 351, 368
strategic system, 37, 41, 71, 271, 349, 353
strategic vision, 74, 123
strategy, 12, 13, 15, 26, 29–31, 43–5, 47–51, 55–7, 65, 68, 69, 77–81, 93, 97, 122, 124, 132–7, 197, 201, 212, 215, 236, 238, 250, 253, 255, 259, 296, 308, 310, 314, 325, 326, 335, 368
strong anticipation, 278, 313, 315–17, 320
strong hierarchy, 97
structural, xv, 6, 8, 12, 14, 27, 28, 30, 33, 45, 55, 56, 60, 64, 65, 71, 72, 74, 76, 93, 108, 114, 131, 148, 164, 209, 213, 244, 270, 287, 305, 343, 349, 352, 358, 369
structural coupling, 12, 64, 94, 188, 222, 224, 273–5, 278, 297, 318, 320, 356, 358
structural criticality, 243
structural expectation, 278
structure, 2, 24, 41, 83, 111, 140, 174, 208, 235, 267, 312, 335
structuring, 51, 69, 80, 88, 120, 267
sub-agent, xiv, 25, 86, 99, 154, 174, 196, 197, 269, 349
subconscious, 37–40, 75–7
subjectification, 355
subjectification-objectification, 147
subjectifying, 145, 147
subjectify the object, 355
subjective, 7, 11, 39, 79, 94, 102, 145, 147, 193, 237, 265, 268, 269, 277, 278, 281, 283, 285, 287, 309, 355
subjective association, 355
subjective assumptions, 266
subjective feeling, 87
subjective knowledge, 193, 355
subjective world, 285
subjectivist epistemology, 275
subjectivity, 40, 87, 88, 193, 279, 359
subjects, 16, 57, 84, 87, 95, 104, 107, 118, 120, 146, 147, 166, 169, 186, 191, 193, 194, 227, 235, 240, 255, 262, 266, 280, 281, 284, 290, 294, 295, 301, 321, 335, 341, 344, 349, 351, 354, 355, 357, 359, 364, 368
subnational, 334
sub-prime meltdown, 326
substitutes, 44, 45, 86, 155
sub-structure, xv, 22, 34, 40, 143, 144, 174, 176–90, 290, 301
sub-system, 12, 25, 37, 55, 139, 273, 277, 284, 284n.5, 297, 318
success of yesterday, 61
summarize, 14, 67, 68, 101, 108, 139, 147, 150, 155, 215, 257, 274, 296, 348, 366
super, 144
superstructure, xv, 22, 34, 39, 40, 104, 144, 174, 176, 177, 188–91, 301, 349
supervision, 343, 365
suppliers, 44, 45, 79, 222
support, xiv, 2, 3, 5, 9, 18, 41, 43, 45, 55, 78n.3, 89, 105, 107, 112, 116, 128, 132, 133, 140, 164, 168, 170, 187–9, 193, 199, 200, 207–9, 214, 215, 217, 222, 226–9, 233–5, 237, 247, 253, 254, 278, 291, 292, 294–6, 300, 307, 324, 327, 333, 335, 341, 343, 344, 347, 348, 352, 358, 359, 362, 364, 367, 368
suprametasystem, 207, 219, 220, 223, 230
suprasystem, 11, 121, 123, 207, 218–20, 230, 281
survival, xiv, 30, 42, 93, 221, 257, 328, 330
sustainable, 43, 45, 47–53, 56, 77, 78, 121, 168, 210, 303, 325
swings, 248
symbolic behaviour, 155
symbolic form, 277
symmetry, 152, 158, 167
synergy, 23, 33, 57, 62, 307
syntactic level of analysis, 277
syntax, 276, 278
system, 1, 21, 41, 84, 111, 139, 174, 206, 231, 265, 306, 333
system hierarchy, 176
systemic emergence, 163
systemic hierarchy, 195, 249, 318
systemic structural coupling, 222, 224
systemic structures, 10, 111
system integration, 269
system of activity, 266
system of truths, 192
systems of administration, 359
systems of communication, 272, 297
systems-theoretical concepts, 266, 270

tacit knowledge, 11, 49–54, 134, 211, 355
tactics, 196–8, 202, 297, 366
task environment, 27, 99, 138, 319, 321

448 Index

tax, 154, 199–201, 250, 310, 322–5, 323n.2, 337, 367
taxation, 154, 200, 250, 340, 367, 370
technical intelligence, 123
technical interest, 129, 130
technical interest power, 97–100, 102, 104–7, 130
technology, 4, 22, 54, 56, 57, 206, 207, 211, 213, 222, 229, 259, 307-10, 313, 315, 335, 337, 366
temperament, 138, 141, 142, 144, 145, 147, 148, 267, 289
temperament theory, 139–41
tension increase, 243
tensions, 164, 188, 193, 243, 256, 258, 259, 266, 307, 308
terrorism, 365
theatre metaphor, 84, 355
thematic reality, 235
theories of instability, 294
theorists, 12, 23, 24, 54, 138–40, 239, 276
theory cleavage, 266, 268, 269, 301
theory construction, 9, 236, 266, 268
theory of attention, 112, 238
theory of cognitive development, 315
theory of communicative action, 12, 280, 281, 284
theory of individual differences, 94
theory of knowledge and communication, 315
theory of learning, 33, 113, 277
theory of meaning, 9, 111, 112, 238, 276
theory of normative personality, 91, 315
theory of pathology, 268
theory of personality assessment, 140, 233, 234
theory of 'possible selves', 105, 128
theory of psychological types, 321
thinking, 35, 36, 54, 68, 83, 84, 95, 109, 117, 119, 122, 131, 132, 141, 143, 145, 147, 179, 220, 234, 244, 255, 273, 284n.5, 306, 308, 319, 330, 359
third order generic agency model, 189
third order generic hierarchy, 183
time, xiv, 1, 32, 50, 56, 57, 60, 67, 103, 120, 122, 169, 186, 188, 200, 208, 216, 220, 229, 240, 252, 253, 258, 272, 277, 279, 280, 283, 292, 296, 306–9, 314, 318, 319, 327, 334, 353, 360, 365–7
totalitarian, 237
traditional, xiv, 3, 9, 15, 43, 44, 54, 78, 138, 151, 153, 156, 161, 176, 236, 255, 284n.5, 289, 294, 343, 344
trait, 15, 24, 83, 128, 139, 189, 232, 316, 351
trait based agency, 303, 331
trait theory, 91, 94–104, 141, 160, 317, 321

transaction, 7, 45, 58, 98, 126, 149, 206, 339, 347, 348, 363
transactional, 98, 99, 102, 130, 146, 147, 149, 156, 166, 167, 176, 347
transactional collectivism, 166, 168
transactional dramatism, 167, 168, 171, 328
transactional individualism, 162, 163, 166
transactionalism, 166, 167
transformation, 56, 65, 67, 87, 98, 99, 105, 115, 118, 128, 149, 180, 194, 197, 202, 206, 208, 233–6, 239, 240, 242–6, 257, 262, 280, 318, 330, 337, 363
transformational, 102, 118, 146, 230, 235, 239, 242, 365
transformational personality, 147
transformational science, 235
transformation scripts, 99, 149
transformative, 234, 237, 239
transitive, 30, 66, 82, 85, 94, 176, 178, 179, 237, 288, 301, 351, 353–8, 360, 368
transparency, 160, 212, 250, 300, 347, 367, 369, 370
Transparency International, 365, 370
transposable, 114, 115, 134, 135
traps of dependence, 210
traps of local convenience, 210
trials, 240, 314
tribulations, 240
trifurcation, 243, 255, 258
tripartite partnership, 252
triple generic learning-loop, 183
triple-loop learning, 183, 184
trust, 3, 29, 52, 53, 60, 92, 132, 134, 208, 214–16, 221, 227, 249, 274n.1, 296, 306, 339, 341, 344, 346–8
truth, 29, 38, 92, 102, 138, 192, 193, 231, 233, 235, 246, 283, 285, 299, 300
type preferences, 317

unaccountability, 365
unanticipated, 42, 221
uncertainty, xiv, 10, 18, 21, 68, 82, 175, 197, 232, 234, 236, 237, 240, 241, 243, 245, 250, 262, 311, 317
unconsciousness, 38, 86
undecidability, 174–7, 179, 183, 186, 187, 194
underlying assumptions, 29, 30, 92
understanding, xiii, xiv, xvi, 7, 10, 11, 18, 34, 35, 44, 49, 61, 65, 67, 68, 72, 74, 87, 88, 106–8, 116, 119, 120, 123, 124, 130, 131, 134, 138, 141, 157, 161, 172, 174, 179, 180, 205, 206, 208, 210, 219, 220, 223, 225, 227, 232, 235–9, 266, 267, 270, 271, 274, 275, 277, 278, 279n.3, 280–3, 286,

Index 287, 296, 297, 299, 300, 302, 303, 305, 319, 320, 331, 343, 349–66
unequal distribution of power, 152, 154, 157
unity, 157, 161, 236, 318, 353
universalism, 235
unstable, xiii, 4, 11, 168, 225, 236, 245, 246, 248, 250, 270, 353
utility maximization, 309
utterance, 11, 274, 275, 277, 283

value creating, 48, 65, 196, 197, 201
value maximization, 366
value minimization, 366
values, xiii, xiv, 3, 6, 12, 23, 29, 30, 33, 37, 39, 57, 64, 78n.3, 89, 91–4, 96–9, 101, 102, 106, 108, 112, 113, 115, 116, 124, 125, 127, 129, 131, 132, 139, 140, 142–54, 156, 157, 160, 161, 163–5, 170–2, 175, 183, 188, 189, 192, 196, 197, 201, 215, 217, 219n.2, 225, 233, 234, 236, 239, 244, 245, 249, 250, 254, 255, 262, 267–9, 283–8, 290, 294, 300, 316, 317, 320, 321, 352, 353, 359–61, 368
values in dispute, 234
value universe, 162
variations of economic policy, 321
variety, 10, 14, 26, 41–3, 54, 55, 58, 61, 64, 68, 75, 80, 81, 110, 113–15, 125, 137, 226, 231, 237, 241, 247, 248, 250, 255, 262, 277, 284, 289, 301, 315, 316, 333, 343, 344, 364
viability, xv, 22, 32–5, 42, 43, 54, 60, 61, 71, 77, 80, 111, 121, 123, 145, 174, 175, 189, 194, 231, 234, 249, 262, 269, 272, 284, 337, 348, 360, 364, 365
viable, xiii, xiv, 42, 55, 60, 62, 133, 189, 213–17, 224, 240, 288, 318, 342, 358

viable human activity system, 239, 241, 262
viable living system, 31–40, 65, 194
viable paradigms, 240–2
viable system, 32, 33, 35, 36, 42, 54–9, 61, 71n.2, 178, 189, 226, 229, 230, 235, 241
viable systems theory (VST), 55, 217, 230
virtual, 36, 117, 135, 199, 282, 287, 356
virtual construction, 220, 223
virtual paradigm, 188, 217, 219, 236, 237
virtual suprametasytem, 219
voluntary-involuntary, 139
VST. *See* viable systems theory (VST)
vulnerability, 109, 257
Vygotsky School, 113, 180, 186

wage, 60, 250, 307, 322–5
wants, 80, 107, 129, 162, 201, 244, 283, 325, 331, 346, 352, 355
weak anticipation, 313
weak institutions, 364
Weltanschauung, 217
Western economic crisis, 171, 199, 333, 346
will to power, 97
will to serve, 97, 99
win-lose, 196, 201
win-win, 196, 201
withdrawal-and-return, 198
worldview, 10, 11, 52–3, 117, 134, 217–20, 222–5, 230, 269, 270, 275, 281, 283, 286, 337, 338
wrong images of the future, 250

Yin Yang bipolar activity, 103

zero-sum, 102, 196